Lecture Notes in Computer Science 11854

More information about this series at http://www.springer.com/series/7412

Chilwoo Lee · Zhixun Su ·
Akihiro Sugimoto (Eds.)

Image and
Video Technology

9th Pacific-Rim Symposium, PSIVT 2019
Sydney, NSW, Australia, November 18–22, 2019
Proceedings

 Springer

Editors
Chilwoo Lee
Chonnam National University
Gwangju, Korea (Republic of)

Zhixun Su
Dalian University of Technology
Dalian, China

Akihiro Sugimoto
National Institute of Informatics
Tokyo, Japan

ISSN 0302-9743   ISSN 1611-3349 (electronic)
Lecture Notes in Computer Science
ISBN 978-3-030-34878-6   ISBN 978-3-030-34879-3 (eBook)
https://doi.org/10.1007/978-3-030-34879-3

LNCS Sublibrary: SL6 – Image Processing, Computer Vision, Pattern Recognition, and Graphics

This Springer imprint is published by the registered company Springer Nature Switzerland AG
The registered company address is: Gewerbestrasse 11, 6330 Cham, Switzerland

Preface

We welcome you to the 9th Pacific-Rim Symposium on Image and Video Technology (PSIVT 2019). PSIVT is a premier level biennial series of symposiums that aim at providing a forum for researchers and practitioners who are involved in or contribute to theoretical advances or practical implementations for image and video technology. Following the editions held at Hsinchu, Taiwan (2006), Santiago, Chile (2007), Tokyo, Japan (2009), Gwangju, South Korea (2011), Singapore (2010), Guanajuato, Mexico (2013), Auckland, New Zealand (2015), and Wuhan, China (2017), this year, PSIVT was held in Sydney, Australia, during November 18–22, 2019.

The main conference comprised 11 major subject areas that span the field of image and video technology, namely, imaging and graphics hardware and visualization, image/video coding and transmission, image/video processing and analysis, image/video retrieval and scene understanding, applications of image and video technology, biomedical image processing and analysis, biometrics and image forensics, computational photography and arts, computer and robot vision, pattern recognition, and video surveillance. To heighten interest and participation, PSIVT also included workshops, demonstrations, and three invited talks by established researchers (Lei Wang from the University of Wollongong, Thomas Bräunl from the University of Western Australia, and Yalin Zheng from The University of Liverpool) in addition to the traditional technical presentations.

For the technical program of PSIVT 2019, a total of 55 paper submissions underwent the full review process. Each of these submissions were evaluated in a double-blind manner by a minimum of three reviewers. The review assessments were determined by the program chairs based on the suggestions from the 17 area chairs. To improve the quality of each review, the number of papers assigned to each reviewer was limited to two. Final decisions were jointly made by the area chairs, with some adjustments by the program chairs in an effort to balance the quality of papers among the subject areas and to emphasize novelty. Rejected papers with significant discrepancies in review evaluations received consolidation reports that explained the decision.

At the end, there were 14 papers accepted for oral presentation and 17 for poster presentation. The review process was highly selective, yielding an acceptance rate of less than 56.3%. Because of the limited size of the symposium and the inevitable variability in the review process, we regret that some worthy papers have likely been excluded. However, we believe that a strong set of papers was identified, and an excellent program was assembled. Among the presented papers, the Best Paper Award and the Best Student Paper Awards were selected and announced during PSIVT 2019.

We like to acknowledge a number of people for their invaluable help in putting this symposium together. Many thanks to the Organizing Committee for their excellent logistical management, the area chairs for their rigorous evaluation of papers, the reviewers for their considerable time and effort, and the authors for their outstanding contributions.

We hope that you found the symposium enjoyable, enlightening, and thought provoking. We hope you had a very memorable PSIVT.

November 2019

Chilwoo Lee
Zhixun Su
Akihiro Sugimoto

Organization

General Chairs

Manoranjan Paul   Charles Sturt University, Australia
Weisi Lin   Nanyang Technological University, Singapore
Junbin Gao   University of Sydney, Australia

Program Chairs

Chilwoo Lee   Chonnam National University, South Korea
Zhixun Su   Dalian University of Technology, China
Akihiro Sugimoto   National Institute of Informatics, Japan

Area Chairs

Weidong Cai   University of Sydney, Australia
Kanghyun Jo   Ulsan University, South Korea
Chang-Su Kim   Korea University, South Korea
Shang-Hong Lai   National Tsing Hua University, Taiwan
Risheng Liu   Dalian University of Technology, China
Brendan McCane   University of Otago, New Zealand
Shohei Nobuhara   Kyoto University, Japan
Jinshan Pan   Nanjing University of Science and Technology, China
Xi Peng   Sichuan University, China
Antonio Robles-Kelly   Deakin University, Australia
Jun Sato   Nagoya Institute of Technology, Japan
Terence Sim   National University of Singapore, Singapore
Robby Tan   Yale-NUS College, Singapore
Diego Thomas   Kyushu University, Japan
Ryo Yonetani   OMRON SINICX Corporation, Japan
Shaodi You   Data61-CSIRO, Australia
Wangmeng Zuo   Harbin Institute of Technology, China

General Workshop Chairs

Mark Pickering   University of New South Wales, Australia
Yanyan Xu   MIT, USA
Anwaar Ulhaq   Charles Sturt University, Australia
D. M. Motiur Rahaman   Charles Sturt University, Australia

Tutorial Chairs

Subrata Chakraborty	University of Technology Sydney, Australia
Ferdous Sohel	Murdoch University, Australia

Demo/Exhibition Chairs

Lihong Zheng	Charles Sturt University, Australia
Fay Huang	National Ilan University, Taiwan

Proceeding Chairs

Ashfaqur Rahman	CSIRO, Australia
Joel Dabrowski	CSIRO, Australia

Publicity Chairs

Ashad Kabir	Charles Sturt University, Australia
Jun Zhou	Griffith University, Australia
Ulrich Engelke	CSIRO, Australia
Eduardo Destefanis	TU Cordoba, Argentina
Paul Rosin	Cardiff University, UK
Han Wang	NTU, Singapore
Young Woon Woo	Dong-Eui University, South Korea

Sponsor Chairs

Reji Mathew	University of New South Wales, Australia
Zhiyong Wang	University of Sydney, Australia

Web Chairs

Domingo Mery	Pontificia Universidad Catolica, Chile
Sourabhi Debnath	Charles Sturt University, Australia
Junjie Cao	Dalian University of Technology, China

Local Arrangement Chairs

Jeffrey Gosper	Charles Sturt University, Australia
Chandana Withana	Charles Sturt University, Australia
Abeer Alsadoon	Charles Sturt University, Australia
Michael Antolovich	Charles Sturt University, Australia
Tanmoy Debnath	Charles Sturt University, Australia
Paul Forbes	Charles Sturt University, Australia
Rodney Wallace	Charles Sturt University, Australia

Steering Committee

Kap Luk Chan	Yau Lee Holdings Limited, Singapore
Yo-Sung Ho	Gwangju Institute of Science and Technology, South Korea
Reinhard Klette	Auckland University of Technology, New Zealand
Wen-Nung Lie	National Chung Cheng University, Taiwan
Domingo Mery	Pontificia Universidad Catolica, Chile
Manoranjan Paul	Charles Sturt University, Australia
Mariano Rivera	Centro de Investigacion en Matematicas, Mexico
Akihiro Sugimoto	National Institute of Informatics, Japan
Xinguo Yu	Central China Normal University, China

Program Committee

Hanno Ackermann
Ryoma Bise
Anko Boerner
Chao-Ho Chen
Li Chen
Shyi-Chyi Cheng
Wei-Ta Chu
Patrice Delmas
Feng Ding
Veena Dodballapur
Ryo Furukawa
Trevor Gee
Minglun Gong
Yuanbiao Gou
Atsushi Hashimoto
Hideaki Hayashi
Jean-Bernard Hayet
Hidekata Hontani
Zhenyu Huang
Go Irie
Takafumi Iwaguchi
Yoshio Iwai
Xiaoyi Jiang
Kang-Hyun Jo
Yusuke Kameda
Li-Wei Kang
Mohan Kankanhalli
Hirokatsu Kataoka
Rei Kawakami
Kazuhiko Kawamoto

Yukiko Kenmochi
Tariq Khan
Chang-Su Kim
Itaru Kitahara
Reinhard Klette
Ajay Kumar
Laksono Kurnianggoro
Rushi Lan
Trung-Nghia Le
Boyun Li
Xiaoming Li
Feng Li
Mu Li
Jun Li
Wen-Nung Lie
Guo-Shiang Lin
Dongnan Liu
Kaiyue Lu
Yasushi Makihara
Elisa Martinez-Marroquin
Tetsu Matsukawa
Nasir Memon
Domingo Mery
Tsubasa Minematsu
Ikuhisa Mitsugami
Shoko Miyauchi
Yoshihiko Mochizuki
Yasuhiro Mukaigawa
Hajime Nagahara
Yuta Nakashima

Karthik Nandakumar

Takeshi Oishi

Takayuki Okatani

Yuko Ozasa

Dongwei Ren

Benjamin Renoust

Ashraf Uddin Russo

Ryusuke Sagawa

Fumihiko Sakaue

Imari Sato

Shin'ichi Satoh

Ajmal Shahbaz

Aashish Sharma

Hidehiko Shishido

Yang Song

Zhixun Su

Kyoko Sudo

Jian Sun

Keita Takahashi

Toru Tamaki

Kewei Tang

YingLi Tian

Kar-Ann Toh

Hideaki Uchiyama

Norimichi Ukita

Xuan Thuy Vo

Jinqiao Wang

Qilong Wang

Brendon Woodford

Xiaohe Wu

Chunlin Wu

Yong Xia

Zhaoyi Yan

Keiji Yanai

Jie Yang

Wenhan Yang

Chia-Hung Yeh

Wong Yongkang

Xinguo Yu

Xin Yu

Chao Zhang

Fang-Lue Zhang

Fan Zhang

Kai Zhang

Liangli Zhen

Tao Zhou

Jianlong Zhou

Wengang Zhou

Ju Jia Zou

Contents

A Fused Pattern Recognition Model to Detect Glaucoma Using Retinal Nerve Fiber Layer Thickness Measurements

Mohammad Norouzifard[1]($\boxtimes$), Ali Nemati[2], Anmar Abdul-Rahman[3],
Hamid GholamHosseini[1], and Reinhard Klette[1]

[1] Department of Electrical and Electronic Engineering,
School of Engineering, Computer, and Mathematical Sciences,
Auckland University of Technology (AUT), Auckland, New Zealand
mnorouzi@aut.ac.nz

[2] School of Engineering and Technology, University of Washington, Tacoma, USA

[3] Department of Ophthalmology, Counties Manukau DHB, Auckland, New Zealand

Abstract. It is estimated that approximately 1.3 billion people live with some form of vision impairment. Glaucomatous optic neuropathy is listed as the fourth major cause of vision impairment by the WHO. In 2015, an estimated 3 million people were blind due to this disease.

Structural and functional methods are utilized to detect and monitor glaucomatous damage. The relationship between these detection measures is complex and differs between individuals, especially in early glaucoma.

In this study, we aim at evaluating the relationship between retinal nerve fibre layer (RNFL) thickness and glaucoma patients. Thus, we develop a fused pattern recognition model to detect healthy vs. glaucoma patients. We also achieved an F1 score of 0.82 and accuracy of 82% using 5-fold cross-validation on a data set of 107 RNFL data from healthy eyes and 68 RNFL data from eyes with glaucoma; 25% of data have been selected randomly for testing.

The proposed fused model is based on a stack of supervised classifiers combined by an ensemble learning method to achieve a robust and generalised model for glaucoma detection in the early stages. Additionally, we implemented an unsupervised model based on K-means clustering with 80% accuracy for glaucoma screening. In this research, we have followed two purposes; first, to assist the ophthalmologists in their daily Patient examination to confirm their diagnosis, thereby increasing the accuracy of diagnosis. The second usage is glaucoma screening by optometrists in order to perform more eye tests and better glaucoma diagnosis.

Therefore, our experimental tests illustrate that having only one data set still allows us to obtain highly accurate results by applying both supervised and unsupervised models. In future, the developed model will be retested on more substantial and diverse data sets.

Keywords: Glaucoma detection · RNFL · Machine learning · Pattern recognition · Unsupervised classifier · Hybrid classifier · Ensemble learning

© Springer Nature Switzerland AG 2019
C. Lee et al. (Eds.): PSIVT 2019, LNCS 11854, pp. 1–12, 2019.
https://doi.org/10.1007/978-3-030-34879-3_1

1   Introduction

Globally, it is estimated that approximately 1.3 billion people live with some form of vision impairment. Glaucomatous optic neuropathy is listed as the fourth major cause of vision impairment by the WHO [18]; in 2015, an estimated 3 million people were blind due to this disease [16]. In New Zealand, glaucoma is responsible for seven percent (1,192 patients) of cases of bilateral blindness, ranking the third most common reported etiology [17].

Structural and functional methods are utilized to detect and monitor glaucomatous damage. The relationship between these detection measures is complex and differs between individuals, especially in early glaucoma [8]. Cross-sectional studies, comparing the visual field with optic disc appearance, have established that there is a relationship between structural aspects of the optic nerve head and functional areas of the visual field [5,6].

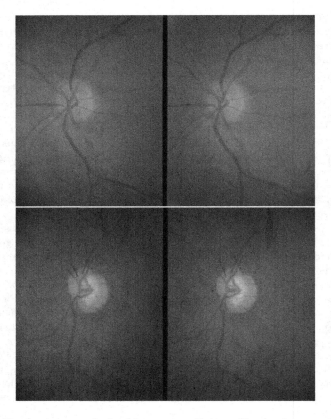

Fig. 1. *Top*: Fundus images of a healthy person. *Bottom*: Fundus images of a glaucoma patient. These two images belong to our non-public data set

However, although some longitudinal studies have demonstrated structural change before functional change [14], other studies have shown the opposite [4]. These findings demonstrate objective detection of early structural change depends upon the variability of the tests involved, in addition to the criterion that is used to determine that structural change has occurred.

Due to the irreversible nature of the pathological changes early diagnosis is imperative in order to preserve functional vision [8]. While glaucomatous structural damage can be assessed subjectively by clinically examining the *optic nerve head* (ONH) and *peripapillary retinal nerve fibre layer* (RNFL), the introduction of ocular imaging modalities into clinical management has allowed for supplemental objective and quantitative evaluation of ocular structure [1]. See Fig. 1 for examples of fundus images showing the ONH.

We used a fused pattern recognition model where results of multiple supervised models are combined to develop a hybrid model [9]; this was used to evaluate RNFL thickness in healthy eyes and those of patients with glaucoma. As a result, we classify towards diagnosing glaucomatous eyes and healthy eyes and develop a proposed hybrid model to detect glaucoma accurately with two properties, robustness and generalization.

In this study, we used one hundred and seventy-five eyes of 87 (42 female and 45 male) healthy and glaucoma patients. We propose an ensemble machine learning approach for healthy and glaucoma patients by applying and comparing supervised and unsupervised models.

The remainder of this article is structured as follows: Sect. 2 introduces materials used from a dedicated (non-public) database and performed statistical analysis that will be used in this research. In Sect. 3, we inform about our approach and details of the used unsupervised and supervised hybrid model. Results of this fused pattern recognition algorithm are briefly explained in Sect. 4, and we evaluate the proposed model through an expert ophthalmologist and evaluation measures. Section 5 concludes.

2 Materials and Data Analysis

In this section, we will explain about the collected data set and show the complexity of data in two different classes based on the $Z - score$ [11] and PCA to compare across RNFL measures. There are 175 RNFL in the database which has a non-homogeneous distribution of healthy class versus glaucoma class cases.

2.1 Data Set

In our RNFL data set, there are 175 RNFL data of 87 (42 female and 45 male) healthy and glaucoma patients, including a few patients with glaucoma without cupping. Some patients also have two RNFL data which were collected at different dates. 39% RNFL data are from patients with glaucoma and the rest of the data belongs to healthy eyes.

Table 1. Demographic characteristics of study participants (L: left, R: right, G: glaucoma, H: healthy).

	Healthy	Glaucoma	L eye	R eye	L eye G	L eye H	R eye G	R eye H	Gender
Male	62%	38%	50%	50%	34%	76%	38%	62%	52%
Female	60%	40%	49%	51%	44%	66%	35%	75%	48%

Also, we show the participants' data demographic distribution in Table 1. There are three age ranges in our non-public data set which 37 data belong to 8–60 years old patients, 87 data are of age 61–80, and the remaining 51 data belong to the patients over 80 years old. Thus, our database indicates that the majority of people ranges by age in 60–80 years old. The data set has a healthy and a glaucoma patients classes defined by a binary classification (healthy or glaucoma label) which was annotated by an ophthalmologist. Furthermore, we can see in Table 1 that there are 52% male and 48% female patients. This data set illustrates that we have approximately a balance in male and female patients.

There are 1,024 attributes for each eye, indicating the thickness of the retina at points in the circle to the centre of the optic nerve and within a radius of 6 micrometre. Also, data distribution is shown in Figs. 2 and 3. Adhering to the tenets of the Declaration of Helsinki the study was considered minimally observational. Therefore, it did not require ethics approval as indicated by recommendations from the New Zealand Health and Disability Ethics Committee.

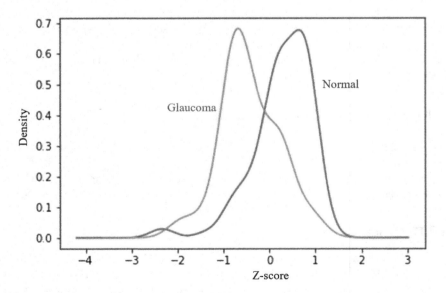

Fig. 2. RNFL distribution of healthy versus glaucoma patients with mean Z-score for each patient.

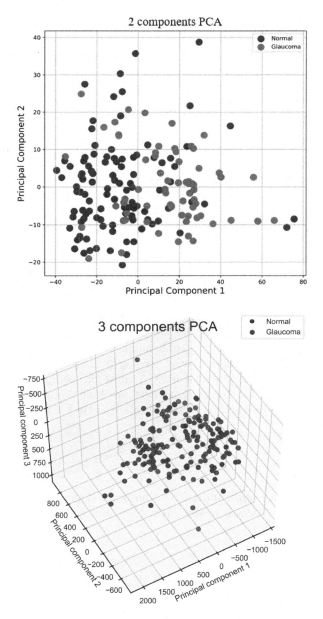

Fig. 3. Complexity of data distribution based on 2– and 3–PCA components.

2.2 Statistical Data Analysis

In this study, we calculated the *Z-score* (see Eq. (1)) for all 1,024 features of each value in the normalized data set; then the mean of each record was determined.

Also, we applied a *kernel density estimation* (KDE) function to generate the probability density function for density estimation to present the data distribution for each class. Afterwards, we used the Gaussian kernels for visualising the distribution of those high-dimensional data [12].

The Z-score is the distance of the standard deviation away from the mean, and it is calculated by

$$z = \frac{\mathbf{x} - \mu}{\sigma} \tag{1}$$

where $\mathbf{x}$ represents the data point (RNFL value for each feature) from the data set, μ is the mean, and σ is the standard deviation.

For a data point, a Z-score helps to point out how "unusual or usual" a data point is compared to other values. Also, the Z-scores have a normal distribution curve where the mean is zero and the variance is equal to 1, so the Z-scores do not follow the normal distribution unless the original data follow the normal distribution.

Figure 2 shows an RNFL standard normal probability distribution of healthy versus glaucoma patients. There is a significant overlap among healthy and glaucoma RNFL thickness data. Therefore, we proposed a hybrid classifier to detect glaucoma accurately.

Besides, the number of variables to analyse the data is 1,024. Thus, to reduce the dimensionality of each of them, we use *principal component analysis* (PCA) [3]. The overlapping section is the challenging area to classify eyes into two groups based on global RNFL thickness; see Fig. 3.

Also, the first three components of PCA show the complexity of the data. Figure 3 on the bottom illustrates that there are high complexity in our data set that we are not able to classify the data correctly by using a plane in 3-dimensional space.

3   Methods

In Fig. 4, we sketch our overall approach for automated glaucoma diagnosis based on a fused pattern recognition model with RNFL data.

3.1   Overview

The schematic diagram is a mind map of the proposed model that represents the main components of the process. RNFL data are entered as input numeric values. Then, data cleaning is performed on input data as a pre-processing step. Data cleaning has been done on missing values that includes dropping missing features and filling in not available values with any number comes directly after it in the same row. Afterwards, data is fed into the fused pattern recognition model. There are two stages on the proposed model, unsupervised and hybrid supervised phases. The hybrid model was trained on 75% of the data. Meanwhile, all data are used for clustering by using a K-means model.

The proposed hybrid system works with an ensemble model that includes top-ten classifiers with high 5-fold cross-validation accuracy and 5-fold cross-validation F1 score. All results of applied models in one particular ensemble are amalgamated to acquire hard votes for all models together. Even though we have high accuracy in an individual model, we apply the ensemble model to be more robust and generalised in case of our relatively small data set. Appropriately, the proposed ensemble model accomplishes the integrated output with high accuracy and F1 score by applying 5-fold cross-validation. The top-ten selected classifiers for our ensemble model are listed in Table 3 on next section which we modified elements to get a better result.

We also determine the hyper-parameters of the classifiers with nested loops defined by the upper and lower bound of the elements to get the highest performance. We are combining results of classifiers to generate a hybrid model that could improve robustness and a generalisation of the final model as main advantage of this research. Finally, the test data set was entered into the tuned hybrid classifiers to detect healthy and glaucoma eyes. Even though the size of the testing set is not very large, we used 5-fold cross-validation on hole data to detect the top-ten classifier that can affect effectively to have high accuracy on our data set.

Also, we used all of our labelled data set to evaluate the performance of our tuned unsupervised model, and the results on K-means model compare with labels that show us the 80% accuracy with our tuned unsupervised model.

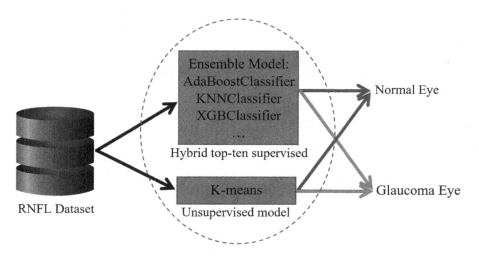

Fig. 4. Overall approach based on the proposed fused pattern recognition model.

3.2 Proposed Hybrid Supervised Model

RNFL thickness measurements from 107 healthy eyes and 68 eyes with glaucoma were acquired with Spectralis OCT. We developed twenty six independent machine learning classifiers including the top-10 listed in Table 3.

We integrated the result of those well-tuned 26 classifiers into an ensemble learning model to generate a "more informed" decision. We used a total of 1,024 RNFL measurements as input for the machine learning classifiers. We used 5-fold cross-validation to find out top-ten models and test the models and examined the accuracy and the F1 score of the hybrid model and of each independent classifier to have a robust and generalized model.

We selected the top-10 most discriminating classifiers based on the best 5-fold cross-validation F1 score and accuracy measures. The hybrid model was generated by ensemble models of top-10 classifiers which are mentioned based on accuracy of 5-fold cross-validation: AdaBoost, GridSearchcv (cv; cross-validation), XGBoost, RandomForest, NuSVC, KNN, RidgeClassifier, SVM_svc, ExtraTrees and SVC. This defines our stack of top-10 classifiers to achieve an accurate model.

3.3 Proposed Unsupervised Model

We proposed an unsupervised model based on a tuned K-means classifier for screening. This model was trained based on two clusters and without any random state. At the end, the predicted labels were compared with the real labels that annotated by an ophthalmologist, and we obtained 80% performance based on the unsupervised tuned model. It shows that the proposed model can be used for screening to aid ophthalmologists. Also, the unsupervised model can be used by optometrists for screening participants and refer suspected glaucoma cases to do more medical examinations and check by an ophthalmologist accurately.

3.4 Validation of Our Study

We divided the data into 75% for training and 25% for testing for validation of our hybrid model, where the test set was not to be used during the training. The evaluation has been done based on the test set. In addition, K-fold cross-validation will be conducted to tune the parameters using the training data.

Multiple measures were used for performance evaluation of the proposed model such as accuracy (AC), specificity (SP), sensitivity (SE), and F1 score (F1) which are defined as follows:

$$AC = \frac{TP + TN}{TP + TN + FP + FN} \tag{2}$$

$$SE = \frac{TP}{TP + FN} \tag{3}$$

$$SP = \frac{TN}{TN + FP} \tag{4}$$

$$F1 = \frac{2TP}{2TP + FP + FN} \tag{5}$$

where these definitions involve numbers of true positives (TP), true negatives (TN), false positives (FP), and false negatives (FN). TP stands for the results that are correlated to "true" in our predicted output and "true" for the actual output. TN stands for the results that are correlated to "false" in our predicted output and "false" for the actual output. FP stands for the results that correlated to "true" in our predicted output and "false" for the actual output. FN stands for the results that correlated to "false" in our predicted output and "true" for the actual output. F1 score represents the harmonic mean of precision and recall as in Eq. 5. The value of F1-score is ranged from zero to one, and high values of F1-score specify high classification performance [13,15].

Table 2. Results of our hybrid model based on 1,024 feature for 175 patients.

F1_5cv	Acc_5cv	F1	Acc	Recall	Precision
0.82	81.7	0.82	81.8	0.82	0.82

Table 3. Results of the proposed hybrid model based on top-ten of 26 classifiers.

No	Models	All data		Test data set							
	Proposed top-ten models	F1_5cv	Acc_5cv	F1	Acc	Recall	Precision	TN	FP	FN	TP
1	AdaBoostClassifier_robust	0.82	82.3	0.77	77.3	0.77	0.77	19	4	6	15
2	GridSearchCV	0.82	81.7	0.82	81.8	0.82	0.82	20	20	3	5
3	XGBClassifier_robust	0.82	81.8	0.77	77.3	0.77	0.77	19	4	6	15
4	RandomForestClassifier_robust	0.82	81.7	0.75	75.0	0.75	0.76	20	3	8	13
5	NuSVC	0.82	81.2	0.82	81.8	0.82	0.82	1	20	3	5
6	KNeighborsClassifier_robust	0.82	81.2	0.80	79.6	0.80	0.80	20	3	6	15
7	RidgeClassifier_robust	0.81	81.1	0.82	81.8	0.82	0.83	21	2	6	15
8	svm_svc_robust	0.81	81.1	0.82	81.8	0.82	0.82	20	3	5	16
9	ExtraTreesClassifier_robust	0.81	81.2	0.75	75.0	0.75	0.76	20	3	8	13
10	SVC	0.82	80.6	0.75	75.0	0.75	0.76	1	20	3	8
11	RidgeClassifiercv_robust	0.80	80.6	0.77	77.3	0.77	0.79	21	2	8	13
12	LogisticRegression	0.78	78.3	0.72	72.7	0.73	0.74	1	20	3	9
13	GaussianNB_robust	0.77	77.2	0.73	72.7	0.73	0.73	18	5	7	14
14	NearestCentroid__robust	0.77	76.5	0.77	77.3	0.77	0.77	18	5	5	16
15	MLPClassifier	0.76	76.5	0.77	77.3	0.77	0.78	20	3	7	14
16	LinearSVC	0.75	74.9	0.68	68.2	0.68	0.68	17	6	8	13
17	OneVsRestClassifier	0.74	74.9	0.77	77.3	0.77	0.77	19	4	6	15
18	Perceptron	0.73	74.8	0.70	70.5	0.71	0.71	15	8	5	16
19	PassiveAggressiveClassifier	0.73	73.1	0.65	65.9	0.66	0.67	19	4	11	10
20	GradientBoostingClassifier	0.72	72.6	0.72	72.7	0.73	0.73	1	19	4	8
21	SGDClassifier	0.72	73.6	0.53	61.4	0.61	0.78	23	0	17	4
22	BaggingClassifier	0.71	70.9	0.65	65.9	0.66	0.66	18	5	10	11
23	DecisionTreeClassifier	0.68	68.2	0.63	63.6	0.64	0.64	1	18	5	11
24	LinearDiscriminantAnalysis	0.63	62.9	0.64	63.6	0.64	0.64	1	16	7	9
25	QuadraticDiscriminantAnalysis	0.49	50.3	0.38	45.5	0.46	0.39	1	18	5	19
26	BernoulliNB	0.43	53.2	0.40	52.3	0.52	0.51	22	1	20	1

4   Results

We used different evaluation measures [10] to show the probability that a patient has glaucoma or not. We obtained the results (shown in Table 2) by our proposed robust model.

Sensitivity or recall was 82% for detecting glaucoma eyes correctly. Also, the F1 score for 5-fold cross-validation was 0.82 for detecting top-ten classifiers to obtain healthy versus glaucoma eyes successfully, and the F1 score is usually more indicative than accuracy.

All results of the top-ten selected classifiers for our ensemble model are listed in Table 3.

We also used the top-10 classifiers for testing of 25% unseen data with different evaluation measures. The confusion matrix (see Fig. 5) shows the performance of the proposed model.

Based on the results of our proposed fused pattern recognition model, we demonstrate that our model can work on a variety of new data from the same device with 80% accuracy. We also obtained 80% accuracy with the unsupervised model what is quite promising because ophthalmologists usually can classify 80% of patients based on one modality data.

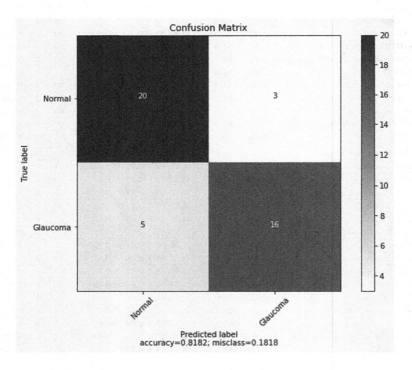

Fig. 5. Confusion matrix based on proposed hybrid model on testing data.

5   Conclusions

In this paper, we propose a method based on a stack of supervised classifiers and an unsupervised model. We did some data cleaning prior to analysis to obtain a better performance. Our results are approved by an ophthalmologist.

The performance of our model is 82% and this documents two features, robustness and generalisation which points to usefulness for screening. The proposed model is ready to be re-tested on large and diverse data sets and can assist the ophthalmologists in their daily examination tasks to confirm their diagnosis, thereby increasing the accuracy of diagnosis.

This study also shows that the proposed ensemble model and K-means performs well for real-time implementation of a classifier for healthy and glaucoma eyes. It is also suitable for development of medical devices based on IoT (*internet-of-things*) and remote monitoring via a web interface. Finally, the contributions of this paper can be summarised as follows:

- Classification of healthy versus glaucoma patients through RNFL data with 1024 feature points with 0.82 of F1 score.
- Visualization of our complex data with Z-score metric in both glaucoma and healthy classes.
- Robustness and generalizability improvement through results combination of traditional classifiers to generate the hybrid.

There are not any public RNFL data set. There are also some related research on private and not large data sets [2, 7, 9] and available high accuracy results on those research because of less complexity of data, but we get promising result based on small, complex and high dimensional data with ensemble technique. Moreover, the accuracy of our result is not quite high, but it can generally detect over 80% of ophthalmologist's diagnosis. Additionally, in other studies [2, 7, 9] were used different data features and complexity that was why no comparison results with other state-of-the-art algorithms are given. For future, we will use time series and multimodal retina data to prognosis of glaucoma disease, and will do retest our proposed model on the new data set with the same data structure.

References

1. Bussel, I.I., Wollstein, G., Schuman, J.S.: OCT for glaucoma diagnosis, screening and detection of glaucoma progression. Br. J. Ophthalmol. **98**(Suppl. 2), ii15–ii19 (2014)
2. Christopher, M., et al.: Retinal nerve fiber layer features identified by unsupervised machine learning on optical coherence tomography scans predict glaucoma progression. Invest. Ophthalmol. Vis. Sci. **59**(7), 2748–2756 (2018)
3. Gour, N., Khanna, P.: Automated glaucoma detection using GIST and pyramid histogram of oriented gradients (PHOG) descriptors. Pattern Recogn. Lett. (2019)
4. Heijl, A., Leske, M.C., Bengtsson, B., Hyman, L., Bengtsson, B., Hussein, M., Early Manifest Glaucoma Trial Group: Reduction of intraocular pressure and glaucoma progression: results from the Early Manifest Glaucoma Trial. Arch Ophthalmol. **120**, 1268–1279 (2002)

5. Johnson, C.A., Cioffi, G.A., Liebmann, J.R., Sample, P.A., Zangwill, L.M., Weinreb, R.N.: The relationship between structural and functional alterations in glaucoma: a review. Semin. Ophthalmol. **15**, 221–233 (2000)
6. Kass, M.A., Heuer, D.K., Higginbotham, E.J., et al.: The Ocular Hypertension Treatment Study: a randomized trial determines that topical ocular hypotensive medication delays or prevents the onset of primary open-angle glaucoma. Arch Ophthalmol. **120**, 701–713 (2002)
7. Lee, J., Kim, Y., Kim, J.H., Park, K.H.: Screening glaucoma with red-free fundus photography using deep learning classifier and polar transformation. J. Glaucoma **28**(3), 258–264 (2019)
8. Lucy, K.A., Wollstein, G.: Structural and functional evaluations for the early detection of glaucoma. Exp. Rev. Ophthalmol. **11**(5), 367–376 (2016)
9. Norouzifard, M., Nemati, A., Klette, R., GholamHosseini, H., Nouri-Mahdavi, K., Yousefi, S.: A hybrid machine learning model to detect glaucoma using retinal nerve fiber layer thickness measurements. Invest. Ophthalmol. Vis. Sci. **60**(9), 3924 (2019)
10. Palacio-Niño, J.O.: Evaluation metrics for unsupervised learning algorithms. arXiv preprint. arXiv:1905.05667 (2019)
11. Patel, N.B., Sullivan-Mee, M., Harwerth, R.S.: The relationship between retinal nerve fiber layer thickness and optic nerve head neuroretinal rim tissue in glaucoma. Invest. Ophthalmol. Vis. Sci. **55**(10), 6802–6816 (2014)
12. Silverman, B.W.: Density Estimation for Statistics and Data Analysis. Routledge, Boca Raton (2018)
13. Sokolova, M., Japkowicz, N., Szpakowicz, S.: Beyond accuracy, F-score and ROC: a family of discriminant measures for performance evaluation. In: Sattar, A., Kang, B. (eds.) AI 2006. LNCS (LNAI), vol. 4304, pp. 1015–1021. Springer, Heidelberg (2006). https://doi.org/10.1007/11941439_114
14. Sommer, A., Katz, J., Quigley, H.A., et al.: Clinically detectable nerve fiber atrophy precedes the onset of glaucomatous field loss. Archive Ophthalmol. **109**, 77–83 (1991)
15. Tharwat, A.: Classification assessment methods. Appl. Comput. Inf. (2018)

Websites

16. Glaucoma in 2015 (2015). www.iapb.org/knowledge/what-is-avoidable-blindness/glaucoma/
17. New Zealand: Latest stats at a glance (2015). www.blindfoundation.org.nz
18. World Health Organization (2018). www.who.int/news-room/fact-sheets/detail/blindness-and-visual-impairment. Accessed 22 July 2019

A Robust Face Recognition System for One Sample Problem

Mahendra Singh Meena[1], Priti Singh[2], Ajay Rana[3], Domingo Mery[4], and Mukesh Prasad[1(✉)]

[1] School of Computer Science, FEIT, University of Technology Sydney, Ultimo, Sydney, Australia
mahendra737@gmail.com, mukesh.nctu@gmail.com
[2] Amity University Haryana, Gurgaon, Haryana, India
psingh@ggn.amity.edu
[3] Amity University Utter Pradesh, Noida, Utter Pradesh, India
ajay_rana@amity.edu
[4] Department of Computer Science, University of Chile, Santiago, Chile
domingo.mery@uc.cl

Abstract. Most of the practical applications have limited number of image samples of individuals for face verification and recognition process such as passport, driving licenses, photo ID etc. So use of computer system becomes challenging task, when image samples available per person for training and testing of system are limited. We are proposing a robust face recognition system based on Tetrolet, Local Directional Pattern (LDP) and Cat Swam Optimization (CSO) to solve this problem. Initially, the input image is pre-processed to extract region of interest using filtering method. This image is then given to the proposed descriptor, namely Tetrolet-LDP to extract the features of the image. The features are subjected to classification using the proposed classification module, called Cat Swarm Optimization based 2-Dimensional Hidden Markov Model (CSO-based 2DHMM) in which the CSO trains the 2D-HMM. The performance is analyzed using the metrics, such as accuracy, False Rejection Rate (FRR), & False Acceptance Rate (FAR) and the system achieves high accuracy of 99.65%, and less FRR and FAR of 0.0033 and 0.003 for training percentage variation and 99.65%, 0.0035 and 0.004 for k-Fold Validation.

Keywords: Face recognition · Tetrolet · Local Directional Pattern (LDP) · Cat Swarm Optimization (CSO) · 2-Dimensional Hidden Markov Model (2DHMM) · k-fold validation · Training percentage

1 Introduction

The face of human performs as an essential biometrics because of the characteristics, such as high social acceptability, accessibility, and the nature of non-intrusiveness [1] and having various applications, such as security, surveillance,

© Springer Nature Switzerland AG 2019
C. Lee et al. (Eds.): PSIVT 2019, LNCS 11854, pp. 13–26, 2019.
https://doi.org/10.1007/978-3-030-34879-3_2

commerce, forensics, and entertainment [2]. The human face recognition is desirable for the applications, where the biometrics of retinal scans, finger prints, and the iris images are not available due to non-interactive environment [3]. Though, 2D face recognition is gaining interest since last few years, but still remains challenging due to the presence of various factors, such as scale differences, pose, facial expressions, illumination, intensity, k-fold validation, training percentage variation and makeup. In addition, at the time of acquisition, the 2D images are subjected to affine transformation that increases the complexity in the recognition of the 2D images [4].

The face recognition process undergoes three basic steps. The first step is the acquisition of the face, which holds the region of face detection and the localization. The facial data extraction is the second step, where the geometric and the appearance related features are extracted and finally the recognition of face. Features of face can be identified in a local and global manner as per requirements & applications [1,4]. The algorithms for the existing face recognition system are of two classes, such as holistic-based and the local feature based algorithms [2]. The common examples of the holistic algorithms are the extended Gaussian images [5], spherical harmonic features [6]; Iterated Closest Point (ICP) based surface matching algorithms [3], and the canonical forms [7]. The main drawback of the holistic algorithms is the need for the exact normalizations of the 2D faces, and the more sensitiveness in case of the facial occlusions and the expressions [1,8]. Guo et al. [9] designed the local feature-based shape matching algorithm, which was capable of providing the global similarity information among the faces using the face recognition process. In addition, this method was capable to perform robust even in the presence of the local features, but failed in the detection of nose tip with enough accuracy.

The variation in the facial expression, availability of training and testing sample images are considered as the some of the problems in the face recognition process, due to these problems performance of recognition process degrades. Most of the recognition methods that perform very well with multiple sample problem (MSP) and fails completely if few training and testing sample are used [10]. In most of the real life problems only few sample are available for training. National identification databases such as national ID card, passport or student ID card all have few samples and should contain enough biometric information of individuals to be used in recognition purposes. In literature there are number of methods available to project the training set and converting it into MSP. Few such methods are one dimension space [11], using noise model to synthesize new face [12] and geometric views of the sample image [13]. Drawbacks of these methods are increase in computational & storage costs and at the same time projected samples have very high correlation and will not fulfill the purpose [14].

k-fold validation is a statistical approach to estimate effectiveness of testing model. It's preferred by majority of researches due to simplicity in understanding & implementation and good results in estimating effectiveness of testing method, which generally have very low bias and less optimistic estimate compared to other approaches such as a simple train/test split. It is basically a resampling method which evaluated effectiveness of validation models on limited data sample. It uses single parameter k which represents the number of groups in the data is to be split into. k-fold validation is an important method in testing of face recognition techniques on unseen data. Method can estimate how a model will perform when it is subjected data not used in training of model. The process of validation starts with shuffling dataset randomly, then dataset is split into k unique groups. One of groups is taken as test dataset and other group as training datasets. Evaluation of test set can be done by fitting a model on the training set. After careful repetition, evaluation scores can be summarized by taking mean of all scores. Each member of data sample is assigned to an individual group and stays in the group during the entire procedure. That results in each sample to be used as testing set once and for training $k - 1$ times [15]. In this approach dataset is divided into k groups or folds of approximately same size. One set is used as validation set and method is fit on rest of the $k - 1$ folds.

The choice of k values must be careful done as if the value of k is chosen small then this may result in misrepresentation of performance of method such as high variance or high bias. If chosen value of k high the difference between size of training and testing becomes very small and as this difference decreases the bias of techniques becomes smaller. So there is always a trade-off associated between bias and variance. There is no set formal rule for choosing the value of k but there are three tactics. The reason behind using HMMs is its ability to classify faces into meaningful regions which can be converted to probabilistic characteristics. So the concentrating of specific facial features can results in person identification. Texture methods are widely applied for face recognition. As we know that, LBP and Gabor pattern played a major role in face recognition. After that, LDP proved that it is very effective for invariant facial recognition due to stability of gradients compared to gray value in the presence of noise and non-monochromatic illumination change. This is the reason that we considered LDP for feature extraction. Performance of Tetrolet transform very good in recovering shape of edges and directional details. Also, it was very effective in image fusion. For optimizing the HMM structure, genetic algorithm (GA) was applied initial days. GA is the popular and old technique for optimization. As its faces the local search issue in finding the optimal structure. In order to overcome these issues in structure optimization, we are using Cat Swarm Optimization (CSO); which proved to be efficient and effective in searching.

In this paper we are introducing an automatic face recognition method based on Tetrolet LDP along with 2D HMM and optimized by CSO for face recognition, which is very effective for intrapersonal variation, variation in training percentage and variation in k-fold validation.

2   Methodology

An automatic face recognition method using the concept of the modified Hidden Markov Model has been introduced. The three basic steps involved in the automatic face recognition are pre-processing, feature extraction, and face recognition. At first, the image from the input database is fed to the pre-processing module, where pre-processing is carried out using the filtering method. The pre-processed image is then allowed to the feature extraction process using Tetrolet-Local Directional Pattern (Tetrolet-LDP). The proposed Tetrolet-LDP is obtained with the combination of the Local Directional Pattern (LDP) [16] and Tetrolet transform [17] that engage in extracting the features. These facial features are used in the recognition of the face with the proposed classification model, which is obtained from the modification of the 2-Dimensional Hidden Markov Model (2D-HMM) and the Cat Swarm Optimization (CSO) [18]. The CSO trains the 2D-HMM, and the performance of the method is analyzed through inputting the intrapersonal variations, variation in training percentage and k-fold validation. Block diagram of proposed face recognition system is shown in Fig. 1.

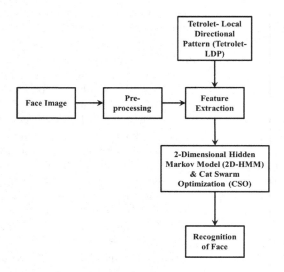

Fig. 1. Block diagram of the proposed face recognition

2.1   Pre-processing of the Input Facial Image

The image from the input database is subjected to preprocessing using the filtering method in order to remove the background of the input sample image J. For filtering we use skin segmentation to get only facial region in the image. Following three face databases are taken for experimentation of proposed system:

- Grimaces [19] face database has 20 images per individual for 18 individuals using a fixed camera, with image resolution 180×200 pixels and contains male and female subjects. Background of images is kept plain. Database has small head scale variation and considerable variation in head turn, tilt & slant. Database also includes major variation in expressions of subject. From the point of view of testing a face recognition system Grimaces face database is small but effective as there are a lot of intrapersonal variations.

- Faces95 [19] face database has 1440 images of 72 individuals subjects using a fixed camera. Subject moves one step forward towards the camera, to introduce head variation between images and lighting changes on face. Database contains 20 images per subject and has male and female subjects. Image resolution for all the images is 180×200 pixels. Background of image is red and variation is caused by shadow of moving subject.
- The CVL face database [20] considers the features that are obtained from 114 persons with 7 images of each person. The resolutions of the images of the persons are 640×480 pixels in the jpeg format, which are shoot using the Sony Digital Mavica in the presence of uniform illumination, projection screen at the background and with no flash. The persons selected are around 18 years of old and around 90% of them are male.

2.2   Feature Extraction Using the Proposed Feature Descriptor

The feature extraction process is carried out with the Tetrolet LDP. The proposed descriptor enables the analysis through inputting the intrapersonal variations, intensity variations, illumination variations, and training data variations. Figure 2 depicts the process of feature extraction with the use of the proposed Tetrolet - LDP feature descriptor.

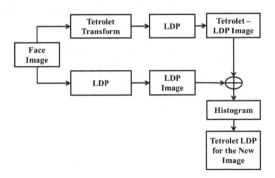

Fig. 2. Feature extraction using Tetrolet LDP

Step 1: Extraction of LDP Image: As shown in Fig. 2 preprocessed image goes through LDP and binary image J_1 is obtained as the output of this step.

Step 2: Extraction of Tetrolet LDP Image: On the other hand, the preprocessed face image is given to tetrolet transform for obtaining the Tetrolet-LDP image. The binary image J_2 is obtained as the output of this step Fig. 3(c).

Step 3: Development of Histogram Features: Image J_1 and J_2 are EX-ORed to obtain the Tetrolet LDP image, J_n from which the histogram features are extracted. These histogram features are fed as the input to the 2D-HMM, which is then trained using the Cat Swam Optimization in order to perform the task of face recognition Fig. 3(d).

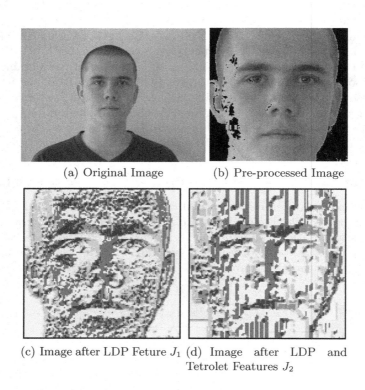

(a) Original Image   (b) Pre-processed Image

(c) Image after LDP Feture J_1 (d) Image after LDP and Tetrolet Features J_2

Fig. 3. Feature extraction steps

2.3   Face Recognition Using 2D-Hiden Markov Model (2DHMM)

The face image that is needed to be classified is partitioned into various blocks in the 2D-HMM model, and the feature vectors are obtained as the block statistics. The image is then classified based on the feature vectors, which are assumed to be produced using the Markov model that changes its state from one block to the other. During classification, the classifier finds the classes of optimal combination for large number of blocks at the same time.

2D-HMM structure can be obtained by linking 1D left to right HMMs to form vertical super-state as shown in Fig. 4. Transitions are allowing in horizontal states of super-state and vertical transitions occur among different super-states. A mathematical definition of parameters of 2D-HMM is as follows:

- N is the number of super-states in the vertical direction
- $A = \{a_{kj} : 1 \leq k, j \leq N\}$ is the super-state transition probability matrix
- $\Pi = \{\pi_j : 1 \leq j \leq N\}$ is the initial super-state probability distribution
- $\Lambda = \{\lambda^j : 1 \leq j \leq N\}$ is the set of left-right 1D HMMs in each super-state. Each λ^j is specified by the standard 1D HMM parameter
  - N^j is the number of states
  - $A^j = \{a^j_{kj} : 1 \leq k, i \leq N^j\}$ is the state transition matrix
  - $B^j = \{b^j_i(.) : 1 \leq i \leq N^j\}$ is the output probability function
  - $\Pi^j = \{\pi^j_i : 1 \leq i \leq N^j\}$ is the initial state probability distribution

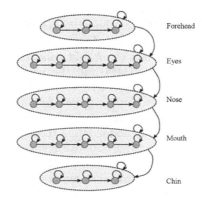

Fig. 4. Structure of a 2D-HMM

2.4 Optimal Tuning of the 2D-HMM Parameters

The transition probability of the 2D-HMM are tuned optimally using the CSO to perform the task of face recognition with increased accuracy and effectiveness. The size of the 2D-HMM parameters decides the size of the solution. The CSO algorithm is the one among the recent Swarm Intelligence (SI)-based optimization algorithms developed on the basis of the characteristics of the cats. The cat takes maximum time to rest, but provides more concern and sharpness on the objects that moves in their surroundings. This sharp characteristic of the cats motivates them in catching their prey with the conservation of very less time. The CSO is developed based on two modes, namely "seeking mode" depending on the resting time of cats, and the "tracing mode" depending on the chasing time of the cats.

3   Results

We have compared the results of existing methods of face recognition such as, Local Binary Pattern based Hidden Markov Models (HMM & LBP) [21], Local

Directional Pattern based Hidden Markov Models (HMM & LDP) [16], and 2-dimension Hidden Markov Models (2DHMM) [22] with our proposed method. The performance is analyzed using three metrics, such as Accuracy, FRR, and FAR. Training percentage is varied from 0.4 to 0.8 and value of k varied form 6 to 10 for k-fold validation variation. Experiments are performed using three face databases namely Grimaces, Faces95 and CVL. To prove the superiority of proposed method we have compiled the results of existing methods on CVL database and compared with our proposed method. We have also compared the results of proposed method for different databases.

Comparative results of existing techniques and proposed method in terms of accuracy are shown in Fig. 5(a) with respect to variation in training percentage, when the training percentage is 0.4, the accuracy of the methods, such as HMM & LBP, HMM & LDP, 2DHMM and the proposed method is 0.6861, 0.7402, 0.7554, and 0.9965, respectively; whereas, Fig. 5(b) shows the accuracy in terms of k-fold validation variation. When the k-fold validation is 7, the accuracy of HMM & LBP, HMM & LDP, 2DHMM and the proposed method is 0.7166, 0.7199, 0.7316, and 0.9965, respectively. Proposed method is performing better in terms of accuracy compared to existing methods not only for variation in training percentage but also for variation in k-fold validation.

Comparative results of proposed and existing technique in terms of FRR are shown in Fig. 6. Figure 6(a) shows the FRR with respect to variation in training percentage. When the training percentage is 0.4, the FRR of HMM & LBP, HMM & LDP, 2DHMM and the proposed method is 0.3139, 0.2598, 0.2446, and 0.003509, respectively, whereas Fig. 6(b) shows the FRR in terms of k-fold validation variation. When the k-fold validation is 7, the FRR of HMM & LBP, HMM & LDP, 2DHMM and the proposed method is 0.2834, 0.2801, 0.2684, and 0.003509, respectively. Performance of proposed method based on FRR is much better when variation in training percentage and k-fold validation are considered.

The comparative results based on FAR are shown in Fig. 7. Figure 7(a) shows the FAR with respect to variation in training percentage. When the illumination variation is 0.4, the FAR of the methods, such as HMM & LBP, HMM & LDP, 2DHMM and the proposed method is 0.0066, 0.0058, 0.0045, and 0.0041, respectively. Similarly, Fig. 7(b) shows the FAR in terms of k-fold validation variation. When the intensity variation is 7, the FAR of the methods, such as HMM & LBP, HMM & LDP, 2DHMM and the proposed method is 0.0074, 0.0065, 0.0045, and 0.0041, respectively. Simulation results show that proposed method is better the existing methods.

4   Discussion

Table 1 shows the comparative results of simulation of proposed method and existing methods of face recognition in terms of Accuracy, FRR, and FAR under training percentage variation. The accuracy of the methods, such as HMM & LBP, HMM & LDP, 2DHMM and the proposed method is 84%, 87%, 90%, and 99.65%, respectively. The FRR of the methods, namely HMM & LBP, HMM &

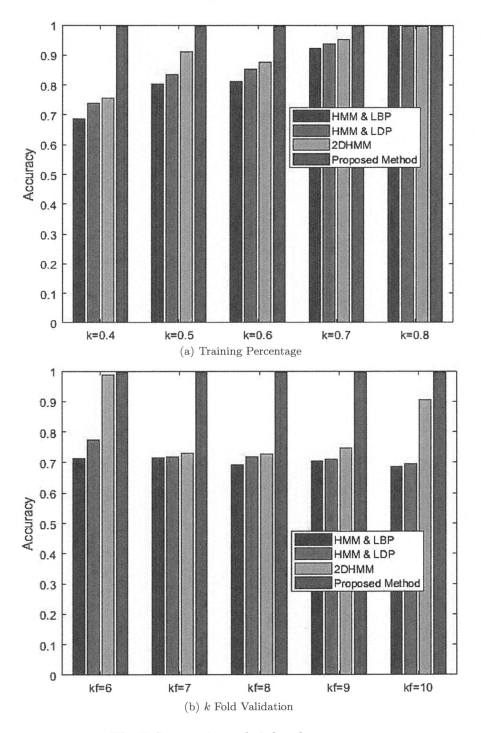

(a) Training Percentage

(b) k Fold Validation

Fig. 5. Comparative analysis based on accuracy

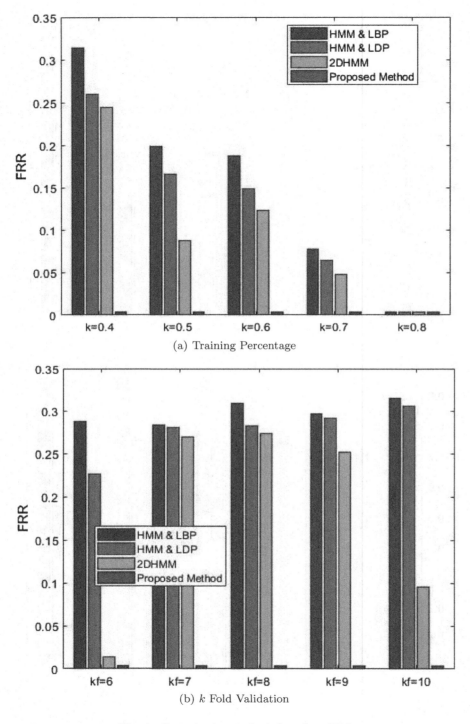

(a) Training Percentage

(b) k Fold Validation

Fig. 6. Comparative analysis based on FRR

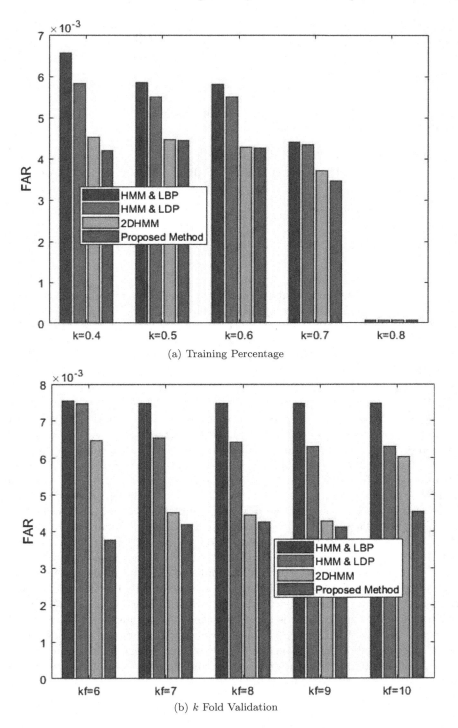

(a) Training Percentage

(b) k Fold Validation

Fig. 7. Comparative analysis based on FAR

LDP, 2DHMM and the proposed method is 0.156, 0.1283, 0.1012, and 0.0035, respectively. Similarly, the FAR of the methods, such as HMM & LBP, HMM & LDP, 2DHMM and the proposed method is 0.0045, 0.0043, 0.0034, and 0.003, respectively.

Table 1. Comparison of proposed and existing methods of face recognition under variation in training percentage and k-fold validation

Methods	Training % variation			k-fold validation		
	Accuracy	FRR	FAR	Accuracy	FRR	FAR
HMM & LBP [21]	84%	0.1560	0.0045	70%	0.2981	0.0074
HMM & LDP [16]	87%	0.1283	0.0043	72%	0.277	0.0066
2D HMM [22]	90%	0.1012	0.0034	82%	0.1804	0.0051
Proposed Method	**99.65%**	**0.0035**	**0.003**	**99.65%**	**0.0035**	**0.004**

Table 1 shows the comparative results of simulation of proposed method and existing methods of face recognition in terms of Accuracy, FRR, and FAR under k-fold validation variation. The accuracy of the methods, such as HMM & LBP, HMM & LDP, 2DHMM and the proposed method is 70%, 72%, 82%, and 99.65%, respectively. The FRR of the methods, namely HMM & LBP, HMM & LDP, 2DHMM and the proposed method is 0.2981, 0.277, 0.1804, and 0.0035, respectively. Similarly, the FAR of the methods, such as HMM & LBP, HMM & LDP, 2DHMM and the proposed method is 0.0074, 0.0066, 0.0051, and 0.004, respectively. Table 2 shows the comparative results of simulation of proposed method for Grimaces, faces95 and CVL face databases in terms of Accuracy, FRR, and FAR under variation in training percentage. The accuracy of the proposed method is 98%, 98%, and 99.65%, respectively. The FRR of the proposed method is 0.0235, 0.0225, and 0.0035, respectively. Similarly, the FAR of the methods, the proposed method is 0.0225, 0.0063, and 0.003, respectively.

Table 2 shows the comparative results of simulation of proposed method for Grimaces, faces95 and CVL face databases in terms of Accuracy, FRR, and FAR under k-fold validation variation. The accuracy of the proposed method is 95%, 98%, and 99.65%, respectively. The FRR of the proposed method is 0.0471, 0.0225, and 0.0035, respectively. Similarly, the FAR of the methods, the proposed method is 0.0227, 0.0055, and 0.004, respectively. Results form Table 2 shows that proposed method performs very well for different face databases.

Thus, from the analysis, it is clear that the proposed method produces high accuracy, and less FRR and FAR measures, which shows the effectiveness of the proposed method in face recognition. Proposed method can be utilized in the area of criminal identification, forensic and finding missing persons where number of samples available for training is limited.

Table 2. Comparison of proposed method over various databases under variation in training percentage and k-fold validation

Database	Training % variation			k-fold validation		
	Accuracy	FRR	FAR	Accuracy	FRR	FAR
Grimace [19]	98%	0.0235	0.0225	95%	0.0471	0.0227
Faces95 [19]	98%	0.0225	0.0063	98%	0.0225	0.0055
CVL [20]	99.65%	0.0035	0.003	99.65%	0.0035	0.004

5 Conclusion

The accurate face recognition is performed using the Tetrolet - Local Directional Pattern (Tetrolet - LDP) and CSO. The proposed method achieves high accuracy, and less FRR and FAR of 99.65%, 0.0033 and 0.003 respectively for training percentage variation and 99.65%, 0.0035 and 0.004 respectively for k-Fold Validation, which shows the superiority of the proposed method in recognizing the face in an effective manner under limitation of availability samples for training and testing. The system was tested on three databases and results shows consistent performance over the various databases. Implementation and computation cost are the major advantages of the proposed system over recent methods like deep learning.

References

1. Mian, A., Bennamoun, M., Owens, R.: Key-point detection and local feature matching for textured 3D face recognition. Int. J. Comput. Vision **79**(1), 112 (2008)
2. Bennamoun, M., Guo, Y., Sohel, F.: Feature selection for 2D and 3D face recognition. In: Encyclopedia of Electrical and Electronics Engineering, p. 154. Wiley (2015)
3. Mian, A., Bennamoun, M., Owens, R.: An efficient multimodal 2D–3D hybrid approach to automatic face recognition. IEEE Trans. Pattern Anal. Mach. Intell. **29**(11), 1927–1943 (2007)
4. Berretti, S., Werghi, N., del Bimbo, A., Pala, P.: Selecting stable key-points and local descriptors for person identification using 3D face scans. Vis. Comput. **30**(11), 1275–1292 (2014)
5. Wong, H.S., Cheung, K., Ip, H.: 3D head model classification by evolutionary optimization of the extended Gaussian Image representation. Pattern Recogn. **37**(12), 2307–2322 (2004)
6. Liu, P., Wang, Y., Huang, D., Zhang, Z., Chen, L.: Learning the spherical harmonic features for 3-D face recognition. IEEE Trans. Image Process. **22**(3), 914–925 (2013)
7. Bronstein, A.M., Bronstein, M.M., Kimmel, R.: Expression invariant representations of faces. IEEE Trans. Image Process. **16**(1), 188–197 (2007)
8. Zaman, F.K., Shafie, A.A., Mustafah, Y.M.: Robust face recognition against expressions and partial occlusions. Int. J. Autom. Comput. **13**(4), 319–337 (2016)

9. Guo, Y., Lei, Y., Liu, L., Wang, Y., Bennamoune, M., Sohel, F.: EI3D: expression-invariant 3D face recognition based on feature and shape matching. Pattern Recogn. Lett. **83**, 403–412 (2016)
10. Zhao, W., Chellappa, R., Philips, P.J., Rosenfeld, A.: Face recognition: a literature survey. ACM Comput. Surv. **35**(4), 399–458 (2003)
11. Wu, J., Zhou, Z.H.: Face recognition with one training image per person. Pattern Recogn. Lett. **23**(2), 1711–1719 (2001)
12. Jung, H.C., Hwang, B.W., Lee, S.W.: Authenticating corrupted face image based on noise model. In: Proceedings of the 6th IEEE International Conference on Automatic Face and Gesture Recognition, vol. 272 (2004)
13. De la Torre, F., Gross, R., Baker, S., Kumar, V.: Representational oriented component analysis (ROCA) for face recognition with one sample image per training class. In: Proceedings of IEEE Conference on Computer Vision and Pattern Recognition, vol. 2, pp. 266–273 (2005)
14. Martinez, A.M.: Recognizing imprecisely localized, partially occluded, and expression variant faces from a single sample per class. IEEE Trans. Pattern Anal. Mach. Intell. **25**(6), 748–763 (2002)
15. A Gentle Introduction to k-fold Cross-Validation. https://machinelearningmastery.com/k-fold-cross-validation/. Accessed 16 April 2019
16. Jabid, T., Hasanul, K.Md., Chae, O.: Local Directional Pattern (LDP) for face recognition. In: Proceedings of the Digest of Technical Papers International Conference on Consumer Electronics (ICCE), pp. 329–330 (2010)
17. Krommweh, J.: Tetrolet transform: a new adaptive Haar wavelet algorithm for sparse image representation. J. Vis. Commun. Image Represent. **21**(4), 364–374 (2010)
18. Chu, S.-C., Tsai, P., Pan, J.-S.: Cat swarm optimization. In: Yang, Q., Webb, G. (eds.) PRICAI 2006. LNCS (LNAI), vol. 4099, pp. 854–858. Springer, Heidelberg (2006). https://doi.org/10.1007/978-3-540-36668-3_94
19. Collection of Facial Images. https://cswww.essex.ac.uk/mv/allfaces/. Accessed 12 Apr 2019
20. CVL face database. http://www.lrv.fri.unilj.si/facedb.html. Accessed 27 Aug 2018
21. Chihaoui, M., Bellil, W., Elkefi, A., Amar, C.B.: Face recognition using HMM-LBP. In: Abraham, A., Han, S.Y., Al-Sharhan, S.A., Liu, H. (eds.) Hybrid Intelligent Systems. AISC, vol. 420, pp. 249–258. Springer, Cham (2016). https://doi.org/10.1007/978-3-319-27221-4_21
22. Bevilacqua, V., Cariello, L., Carro, G., Daleno, D., Mastronardi, G.: A face recognition system based on Pseudo 2D HMM applied to neural network coefficients. Soft Comput. **12**(7), 615–621 (2008)

Analysis of Motion Patterns in Video Streams for Automatic Health Monitoring in Koi Ponds

Christian Hümmer[1]($\boxtimes$), Dominik Rueß[1]🄳, Jochen Rueß[1], Niklas Deckers[1],
Arndt Christian Hofmann[2], Sven M. Bergmann[2], and Ralf Reulke[1]

[1] Institut für Informatik, Humboldt-Universität zu Berlin,
Unter den Linden 6, 10117 Berlin, Germany
{hummerch,reulke}@hu-berlin.de
[2] Friedrich-Loeffler-Institut, Südufer 10, 17493 Greifswald - Insel Riems, Germany
sven.bergmann@fli.de

Abstract. We present a motion analysis framework for anomaly detection in the context of health monitoring in carp and koi ponds. We study recent advances in computer vision and deep learning for an automated motion assessment based on video streams and propose a specifically designed image acquisition system.

It turned out that the accurate detection and recognition of individual fish objects remains a difficult topic for scenarios with dense homogeneous groups and frequently occurring occlusions. We thus tackled this challenging field of aquatic scene understanding by applying deep state-of-the-art architectures from the areas of object detection, semantic segmentation and instance segmentation as a first step for further extraction of motion information. We used dense optical flow as an estimation of collective fish movements and restricted the motion extraction according to the resulting masks from the previous image segmentation step.

We introduce a heatmap visualization as an intermediate representation of the spatio-temporal distribution of fish locations. We derived several metrics to quantify changes in motion patterns and apparent location hotspots as indicators of anomalous behavior. Based on this representation, we were able to identify different classes of behavior like feeding times, shoaling or night's rest as well as anomalous group behavior like mobbing or hiding in an experimental setup.

Keywords: Object detection · Deep image segmentation · Optical flow · Fish health monitoring · Heatmap · Motion analysis

1 Introduction

The fish farming industry relies on ways of assessing the health status of fish to ensure appropriate habitat conditions and realize early warning systems in

© Springer Nature Switzerland AG 2019
C. Lee et al. (Eds.): PSIVT 2019, LNCS 11854, pp. 27–40, 2019.
https://doi.org/10.1007/978-3-030-34879-3_3

order to control and automatically detect spreading diseases. Physiological stress, physical injury and environmental stress are the primary contributing factors of outbreaks of infectious fish diseases and mortality in aquaculture [17, 25]. Comprehensive studies on applications of machine vision systems in aquaculture showed that continuous monitoring and quantifying behavioral response of fish are potential methods of assessing stress, diseases and water pollution, with activity and motion analysis quantifying the behavior parameters automatically [22]. In addition to its advantages of continuous surveillance and automatic evaluation methods, the use of computer vision systems provides the possibility of non-intrusive health monitoring, eliminating possible behavioral changes caused by the presence of humans outside of the aquarium.

We therefore aimed for developing an approach towards the automated health monitoring of densely crowded carp and koi based on computer vision and deep neural networks. According to the behavioral response of fish, shifts in the movement patterns as well as an assessment of the spatio-temporal distribution were used as indicators for anomalous events. To evaluate our algorithms in an experimental setup, we used recorded long-term monitoring of different aquariums with healthy populations of koi and common carp (Cyprinus carpio). As there are no present diseases, we focused on finding regularities in the motion patterns and extracting different types of anomalies like feeding activity, hiding or mobbing in terms of deviations from those regularities. The presented anomaly detection framework is able to deal with challenges arising from the severe conditions of aquatic environments with dense homogeneous fish swarms, frequently occurring occlusions, non-rigid body deformations and abrupt motion changes.

This paper provides an overview of related research and presents our specifically designed image acquisition system, followed by applied fish detection methods. We used those results for motion estimation in densely crowded scenes and describe derived measures for behavioral regularity extraction and anomaly detection. We then conclude and discuss the achieved results.

2   Related Work

Object detection and recognition build the first step in a vision based monitoring system. In cases with small background movements, classical methods like feature based classification or background subtraction [24, 32] are widely used to detect fish objects in video frames. With their recent success in computer vision, deep neural networks have lately been applied to the task of fish detection as well. Sung et al. [26] used a convolutional neural network based on the YOLO network [18] for the task of fish detection in underwater videos and showed superior results compared to non-deep methods. In Li et al. [11] fish detection and species recognition was performed by using the two stage region based convolutional neural networks RCNN [3] and Fast-RCNN [2], which showed superior results compared to a HOG-based model.

Many approaches for motion analysis in fish videos try to extract motion information by tracking fish individuals. Terayama et al. [29] proposed an appearance model with an adapted template matching step for multiple fish tracking.

An extension of this approach tackled the problem of frequently occurring occlusions with a deformable parameterized appearance model representing the fish bodies [27]. A recent approached for underwater fish tracking based on appearance models extended the kernelized correlation filter tracking method [7] by an adaptive multi-appearance model [10]. A solution for the specific case of koi tracking with its challenges like shadows, speckling and abrupt motion changes was presented in Jiang et al. [8], where they used a particle filter with an extended matching function.

The problem of motion estimation in fish scenes with homogeneous swarms in high density regions can also be tackled without tracking by estimating the speed distribution of collective motions with dense optical flow from video streams [28]. Yu et al. [31] proposed a tracking-free anomaly detection method for zebra fish schools based on statistical methods for motion feature extraction. They used sparse optical flow to calculate joint histograms and joint probability distributions of turning angles and velocities and applied outlier detection to find anomalous group behavior. Comprehensive surveys, studying the use of computer vision technologies in aquaculture and fish behavioral analysis, can be found in Saberioon et al. [22], Zion [33] and Niu et al. [15] respectively.

Tracking based approaches however suffer from their dependency on tracking accuracy, which remains a challenging task in computer vision, especially in aquatic environments with highly crowded scenes and frequent occurring occlusions as in fish school monitoring.

3   Experimental Setup

We performed fish observation on long-term video recordings of koi and common carp for an automatic health monitoring. A specialized image acquisition system was used to overcome the limitations in aquatic environments.

3.1   Fish Observation

We used two different datasets to evaluate our proposed methods on long-term real-world observations. The first dataset consists of continuous front-view recordings of an aquarium containing ten common carp, obtained by an external camera setup. The second dataset consists of a longer period of continuous top-view recordings of an aquarium with 37 koi, acquired by a specialized underwater image acquisition system, as described in Sect. 3.2. Both datasets do not contain any known diseases or predefined anomalies, especially no animals were harmed or intoxicated during the observation. However, there is a small subset of annotated video samples from the common carp dataset, manually labeled as being normal or anomalous[1]. The koi dataset provides additional monitored parameters like water temperature and feeding times. Its continuous long-term

---

[1] The recording of the fish video dataset, as well as the manual fish observations, were done by co-author Arndt Christian Hofmann as part of the data acquisition process for his unpublished PhD thesis at Friedrich-Loeffler-Institut.

recordings of one and a half months contain a temperature shift from 8 °C to 20 °C in the time from May 14th to May 26th.

3.2 Image Acquisition

Image acquisition constitutes a crucial step in the development of computer vision based monitoring systems, especially in the context of aquatic environments. In general, limiting factors like object distance, aperture, viewing angle, lens or focal length affect the resulting image quality as well as the detectable image area, which plays an important role in the scope of further behavioral analyses. Aquatic environments are further affected by disturbing effects like flow and turbidity of water or external reflections and pollutions on the water surface, especially in the use case of unconstrained outdoor ponds. In order to minimize the aforementioned external influences, we propose a specialized underwater image acquisition system. To overcome the shortcomings of shorter object distances, the system consists of a 360° fish-eye PoE camera. We extended the camera by a plexiglass dome hemisphere with a diameter of 300 mm to enlarge the distance between the camera lens and the surrounding water, fish objects and water flows. Sample images are shown in Figs. 1 and 4.

4   Scene Analysis with Deep Neural Networks

Image classification and scene understanding as well as object detection and localization constitute the first step in the image processing pipeline of many visual tasks. With object detection, identifying, classifying and localizing multiple instances of distinct objects in the image, the resulting bounding boxes only provide coarse positional information. In contrary, semantic segmentation results in segmentation masks with pixel-wise classifications into given object classes. While leading to a scene understanding on pixel level, it discards information about individual objects. Combining both, instance segmentation identifies distinct instances of different classes on a per pixel basis. We used recent advances in deep State-of-the-Art architectures from the aforementioned areas to achieve highly robust and accurate fish segmentations with a focus on whole fish groups rather than individuals. To cope with the generalizability to potentially unknown camera and aquarium geometries, we performed the scene analysis steps on the raw image data without any preceding calibration or distortion correction steps.

4.1 Object Detection

In contrary to the family of two-stage object detection networks, which depend on the generation of region proposals in the first step [2,3,21], the one-shot models like Single Shot MultiBox Detector [14] or You Only Look Once [18] directly predict bounding box coordinates and class probabilities from the input image in a single feed-forward pass. We chose to apply the end-to-end trainable YOLOv3 [20] network for the task of fish detection, providing a good trade-off between accuracy and detection speed, allowing for accurate real-time detections in video streams. The basic idea of YOLO [18] is to apply a single network to the entire input image, reframing object detection as a single regression problem. The improved version YOLOv2 [19] gained higher accuracies by extensions like adding batch normalization in the convolutional layers, introducing anchor boxes, removing the fully connected layers for bounding box predictions and using a custom darknet architecture. The latest version [20] introduced minor changes like bounding box predictions across three different scales, similar to the idea of feature pyramid networks [12].

We finetuned the pre-trained network with an additional dataset, containing a variety of data samples from carp and koi video frames in different viewing angles. Including this additional training procedure, we were able to accurately extract bounding boxes in our experimental setup under severe conditions of highly crowded scenes and frequent occlusions. Detections from the YOLO network were used for tracking-by-detection experiments and the generation of coarse heatmap variants.

4.2   Semantic Segmentation

While the proposed model for object detection resulted in accurate bounding box predictions for individual fish objects, we strived for a dense per-pixel prediction of fish locations. This pixel-wise classification does not distinguish between individuals, but allows for a subsequent extraction of fine-grained swarm information. As classical background modelling approaches lack the ability to deal with ongoing background movements like strong water streams and objects moving outside of the aquarium, we decided for a motion-free foreground extraction with a deep neural network architecture. We applied a variant of the Global Convolutional Network [16] for the task of semantic segmentation, which outputs a binary segmentation mask, separating the classes fish and background on pixel-level. Semantic segmentation networks generally have to deal with the contradictory tasks of transformation-invariant classification as well as the transformation-sensitive localization. GCN aims for tackling both challenges simultaneously. The architecture is fully-convolutional without any fully-connected or global pooling layers to retain the localization information. It uses separable large filters in the network architecture. Peng et al. [16] found that those large kernels play an important role for simultaneous classification and localization. The latter is improved by an additional boundary refinement block. A FCN-like [23] structure is used as the basic segmentation framework with a pretrained ResNet [6] as feature extraction network, whose multi-scale feature maps are used to generate class-specific semantic score maps with the global convolutional network structures.

We fine-tuned the segmentation model with a manually annotated carp and koi dataset, containing pixel-wise binary segmentation masks for the classes background and fish. The predicted masks from the retrained network were used for the steps of optical flow refinement and heatmap generation.

4.3   Instance Segmentation

To extend the ideas of individual object analysis based on object detection and fine-grained collective analysis based on semantic segmentation, we applied the *Mask-RCNN* [5] network for the task of pixel level instance segmentation. Mask-RCNN is based on the region-based convolutional neural network approach, which generally performs object classification and bounding box regression on computed CNN features from previously extracted regions of interest [2,3,21]. An added mask extraction branch predicts an object mask for each instance in parallel with the former bounding box recognition.

We used a Mask-RCNN model pre-trained on the large-scale COCO dataset [13] for scene understanding. As an extension, we extracted and annotated additional frames from both carp and koi video streams with individual pixel-wise object masks for fine-tuning the model. We used the retrained model for an accurate extraction of individual segmentation masks and refinement steps.

5   Motion Analysis

The analysis of motion patterns plays an important role in the assessment of fish behavior, welfare, stress response or environmental changes. Experiments with recent tracking approaches, based on appearance [7] or Kalman filter [1], using bounding box detections from the object detection step, performed weakly on our crowded fish datasets. We therefore present a tracking-free approach for motion assessment in crowded fish swarms, including a compact visualization as well as quantitative measures, to avoid the inaccuracies in individual tracking.

5.1   Visual Assessment

As the continuous tracking of individuals remains a challenging task in the setting of highly dense crowds, we present the heatmap visualization as a global representation of the spatio-temporal distribution of fish locations in the observed tank. In contrary to the individual evaluation, it represents an effective group-based approach for estimating region-specific fish location probabilities over time. The heatmap therefore offers a compact representation of fish activity and location hot spots over observed time windows of variable length t. Derived measures like shape features, compactness or homogeneity of that spatio-temporal distribution can be used for further analyses.

The introduced heatmap representation provides a distinctive visualization of typical behavior patterns like shoaling, hiding or agitation caused by either feeding times or mobbing, allowing for the visual detection of unexpected activities over multiple scales in the temporal domain. We obtained it by accumulating the binary masks of detected fish locations over time to obtain a pixel-wise 2d location histogram over an observation period, as shown in Fig. 1.

Fig. 1. Heatmap generation. The input sequence of length t (left) is fed into the semantic segmentation network, which outputs one binary mask for each input frame (middle). The resulting binary sequence is summed up along the temporal dimension and normalized to visualize the spatio-temporal fish location distribution of the input time window (right).

5.2 Motion Estimation

We approximated the projection of the actual real world 3D motion onto the 2D image plane by applying dense optical flow computation, estimating apparent motion of brightness patterns between consecutive frames in the 2d image plane. The resulting vector field consists of one displacement vector $v = [u, v]^T$ for each pixel in the image space with vertical and horizontal displacement components. While optical flow estimation constitutes a well studied field in computer vision, many approaches suffer from inaccurate results handling large displacements and homogeneous texture regions.

However, the optical monitoring of carp and koi has to be able to deal with rapidly changing movement patterns and high velocities resulting in large displacements between the video frames. We therefore applied a specific optical flow approach called *Deepflow* [30]. With its robustness to large displacements and its ability to handle repetitive textures and non-rigid deformations, this method provided useful benefits for the optical flow estimation in this challenging underwater scenario.

5.3 Objective Motion Analysis

The heatmap provides a compact visual representation of fish locations over time windows of variable length t, as described in Sect. 5.1. We further aimed for quantitative measures to assess significant properties of this spatio-temporal distribution and the optical flow results.

Heatmap Features. The measures for motion evaluation derived from the heatmap representation include the heatmap entropy:

$$H(X) = - \sum_i^{width} \sum_j^{height} p(x_i, y_j) \log_2 p(x_i, y_j). \tag{1}$$

The two-dimensional random variable (X,Y) represents possible fish locations in the image space. The heatmap with relative frequencies constitutes the probability distribution p(X,Y), which is normalized, such that it's probabilities sum up to one. As entropy only considers information content of the spatio-temporal distribution and the compactness of the current heatmap representation, it discards any structural information and spatial context. We thus further derived statistical measures from texture analysis, considering the spatial relationships of heatmap entries. We used the classical approach of creating a gray-level co-occurrence matrix to extract those textural features [4]. The co-occurrence matrix is created by treating the heatmap of a time window of length t as a single channel image with an offset $o = (\Delta u, \Delta v)$, with the pixel-wise frequencies representing its intensity values, resulting in a distribution of co-occurring frequencies. For a given offset, the obtained $t \times t$ co-occurrence matrix $C(u, v)$ is defined as:

$$C_{\Delta u, \Delta v}(i, j) = \sum_{u=1}^{n} \sum_{v=1}^{m} \begin{cases} 1, & \text{if } H(u, v) = i \text{ and } H(u + \Delta u, v + \Delta v) = j \\ 0, & \text{otherwise} \end{cases}, \quad (2)$$

with frequency values i, j, observed window length t and the image coordinates u, v in the extracted heatmap H. Based on that, we extract different texture features, with each co-occurrence matrix being normalized to have a sum of 1 before the computation. The energy or uniformity is defined as

$$energy = \sqrt{\sum_{i,j=0}^{levels-1} C_{i,j}^2}, \quad (3)$$

being the square root of the angular second moment. The measure of contrast weights the matrix entries by their squared frequency difference, implicitly weighting them by their distance to the matrix diagonal:

$$contrast = \sum_{i,j=0}^{levels-1} C_{i,j}(i - j)^2. \quad (4)$$

Similarly, the *dissimilarity* feature weights the matrix elements by the absolute value of the frequency difference. In contrast, *homogeneity* as a measurement of closeness of the matrix elements to its diagonal weights the matrix elements by the inverse of their frequency difference.

Optical Flow. The quantitative motion evaluation of the optical flow estimation was based on the restricted pixel areas derived from the scene analysis step. It was assessed either individually on top of instance segmentation or collectively on top of semantic segmentation. By restricting the optical flow evaluation to the detected fish pixels from the segmentation step, we minimized the influence of non-related object movements in the motion assessment. We used the mean magnitudes of frame pairs over time as a global swarm activity measure to extract changes in long-term motion behavior.

6   Experimental Results

As described in Sect. 3, we used the two datasets with long-term video recordings of koi and common carp for an evaluation of the proposed methods. The subset of the carp dataset with labelled short-time anomalies was used to evaluate the features derived from the heatmap visualization. As the labels of this annotated subset are only represented by a binary variable indicating normal (0) or anomalous (1) behavior, we measure the relationship between the labels and the extracted heatmap features by calculating the point biserial correlation coefficient r_{pb}:

$$r_{pb} = \frac{M_1 - M_0}{s_n} \sqrt{\frac{N_1, N_0}{N(N-1)}}. \tag{5}$$

Here, M_1, M_0 are the mean values of the feature variable for all data points in the anomalous group and the normal group respectively and s_n the standard deviation for all observations of the feature variable. N_1, N_0 are the number of observations being labeled as anomaly or normal behavior and N is the total number of observations Eq. (5).

Table 1. Point biserial correlation coefficient for different heatmap features. The features are extracted from heatmaps computed over time windows of varying length. The GLCM based texture features are extracted for different pixel offsets, affecting distance and angle of the neighborhood of co-occurring frequencies.

	Energy	Homogeneity	Contrast	Dissimilarity	Entropy
Window size $= 120$					
$(\Delta u, \Delta v) = (1, 0)$	−0.82	−0.13	−0.87	−0.66	
$(\Delta u, \Delta v) = (0, 1)$	−0.82	−0.12	−0.92	−0.61	
$(\Delta u, \Delta v) = (5, 0)$	−0.83	−0.47	−0.89	−0.76	
$(\Delta u, \Delta v) = (0, 5)$	−0.83	−0.58	−0.92	−0.75	0.76
Window size $= 360$					
$(\Delta u, \Delta v) = (1, 0)$	−0.85	−0.57	−0.65	−0.28	
$(\Delta u, \Delta v) = (0, 1)$	−0.85	−0.66	−0.77	−0.20	
$(\Delta u, \Delta v) = (5, 0)$	−0.85	−0.75	−0.75	−0.52	
$(\Delta u, \Delta v) = (0, 5)$	−0.85	−0.77	−0.77	−0.57	0.77

Since the co-occurrence matrix represents the histogram of co-occurring frequency values at a given offset over the heatmap, we computed the features for different neighbourhood relationships. We focused on horizontal and vertical offset for the direct neighbours as well as a five pixel offset. We chose the co-occurrence matrix to be symmetric, thus $C(i, j) = C(j, i)$. The entropy computation was not affected by the aforementioned variations. We chose to perform feature extraction from heatmaps computed over time windows of varying length, such that the features can reflect behavior-induced changes on multiple scales in the temporal domain. To focus on rapid changes in the spatio-temporal distribution and with the training set mostly containing samples of short-time anomalies, we set the window lengths to 120 frames (10 s) and 360 frames (30 s). The resulting correlation coefficients show that some heatmap based features reflect anomalous changes in the spatio-temporal swarm distribution. While homogeneity and dissimilarity only correlate with the assigned labels for specific offset combinations, the contrast feature shows high negative correlations for short window sizes, but also tends to vary with changing offset parameters. In contrary, the energy feature represents a robust indicator over different offset constellations and window sizes, being highly and negatively correlated with the assigned video annotations. The entropy feature also seems to reflect a relationship with the assigned labels for both window sizes but is not affected by the changed parameters. As the results on the test set suggest the potential applicability of the energy and entropy feature for anomaly detection, their correlation has to be validated on bigger datasets with long-term anomalies for future work.

Although there are no labelled anomalies for the koi dataset, it provided high quality video streams from our specialized image acquisition system in combination with additional monitored parameters like water temperature and feeding times. We assessed the general long-term motion activity by computing the proposed restricted mean magnitude of optical flow vectors between frame pairs as a measure for collective fish swarm motion. For each day, the feature was computed for one frame pair per second and the resulting signal was filtered to receive a time series on a daily basis.

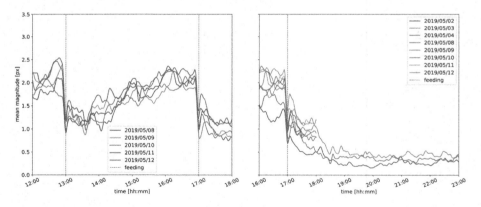

Fig. 2. Analysis of motion regularities over multiple subsequent days. Daily repeated patterns evolve around the feeding times, especially in the low temperature period (left). The main activity can be seen during day time with a strong decrease towards the late evening (right).

Different conclusions can be drawn from the plotted daily activity measures in Figs. 2 and 3. Firstly, it reveals regularities in daily motion patterns evolving around the feeding times, especially in the observed low temperature period. The activity is almost linearly increasing towards the feeding times, followed by low-activity regions afterwards. Secondly, the highest activity can be seen during day time, lowering towards the evening hours with a period of minimum activity in the late evening hours. We could only observe this at a small subset of days with illumination during night time, after which the lights were turned off each night. Thirdly, there is a clear change in the global motion behavior after the temperature change. The general activity level rises while there is an increasing variance between the daily motion patterns of consecutive frames. Those three basic observations confirm the subjective assessment of motion regularities from manual observations made by veterinarians of the FLI.

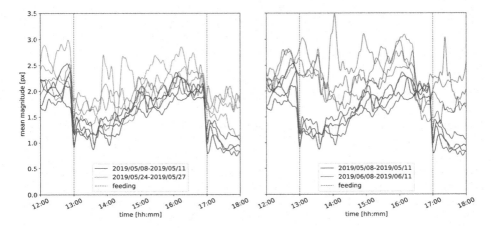

Fig. 3. Comparison of the global swarm activity measure over periods of four subsequent days before (green) and after (red) the temperature rise. The period just before the temperature change is compared to a period during the change (left) and a few weeks after the change (right). Both diagrams show that the measure indicates a change in the motion behavior. (Color figure online)

Apart from regularity extraction, the proposed swarm activity measure was also used to find unknown anomalies in unlabeled long-term recordings. We were able to reveal several anomalous scenes and accurately locate them in the raw video data by examining strong signal peaks and unusual signal sequences. We applied a simple moving average Z-score model as baseline anomaly detector to find those anomalous signal changes. Therefore both regularity extraction and anomaly detection can be performed in a semi-automated manner by using automatically detected anomalies or comparing signals of successive days, easing the time consuming manual assessment of long-term video observations. Anomalous scenes included events like mobbing, hiding, long-term shoaling during unusual time slots or missing detections caused by the camera pointing outside of the aquarium. An example of anomalous video sequences revealed by detected changes in the activity measure is shown in Fig. 4.

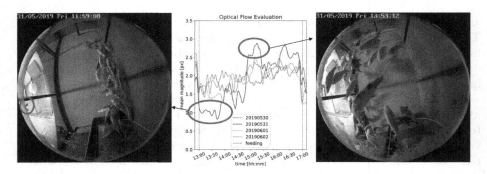

Fig. 4. Detected anomalous changes in the swarm activity measure. Compared to other days, the signal indicates a lower collective activity after feeding (middle) due to the koi hiding in the aquarium because of a veterinarian being present in front of it (left). There is a strong increase in the activity level after the veterinarian left the room (right). Note: The internal camera time is shifted by one hour ($t_c = t - 1\,\text{h}$).

7   Conclusion and Future Work

In this work we successfully obtained accurate fish locations and pixel-wise segmentation masks in the challenging area of crowded scenes with frequent occlusions by leveraging recent advances in deep neural networks. We derived expressive features from the spatio-temporal fish distribution and an optical flow based collective swarm motion estimation. We used optical flow features to successfully extract motion regularities from long-term observations and detect anomalous behavior in terms of unexpected motion patterns. We evaluated the impact of different texture features derived from the heatmap on a small annotated subset of our video data with labeled anomalies. By analyzing our proposed motion feature over unlabeled long-term recordings, we were able to locate unknown anomalies in the video streams and find differences in motion patterns. The results can be used by fish owners to locate and find anomalies in long-term observations as deviations from regular behavior in a semi-automated manner. As the proposed unsupervised method does not rely on predefined normality models or labeled anomalies, it showed its general applicability by revealing unknown anomalous behavior in long-term recordings without any annotations.

Object detection and segmentation are crucial preprocessing steps for the subsequent methods for motion assessment and anomaly detection, as they ensure the analysis being dependent on fish movements only, minimizing the influence of external factors. Our future work will therefore include the extension of the fish specific training data sets for retraining the proposed deep neural networks in order to avoid overfitting and ensure the generalizability of our models. Concerning the time consuming manual labeling work, we will extend our training set by the publicly available large-scale dataset Open Images [9], which contains thousands of labeled fish images, including individual segmentation masks in their newest release. Another focus of our future work will be set on further analysis of the proposed features for motion assessment. The analysis will include their applicability to other large-scale datasets, feature combination for a unified multivariate time series evaluation, as well as more complex detection methods for a robust and fully-automated anomaly detection framework.

References

1. Bewley, A., Ge, Z., Ott, L., Ramos, F., Upcroft, B.: Simple online, realtime tracking. In: IEEE International Conference on Image Processing, pp. 3464–3468 (2016)
2. Girshick, R.: Fast R-CNN. In: IEEE International Conference on Computer Vision, pp. 1440–1448 (2015)
3. Girshick, R., Donahue, J., Darrell, T., Malik, J.: Rich feature hierarchies for accurate object detection, semantic segmentation. In: IEEE Conference on Computer Vision, Pattern Recognition, pp. 580–587 (2014)
4. Haralick, R.M., Shanmugam, K., Dinstein, I.: Textural features for image classification. IEEE Trans. Syst. Man Cybern. SMC **3**(6), 610–621 (1973)
5. He, K., Gkioxari, G., Dollar, P., Girshick, R.: Mask R-CNN. In: IEEE International Conference on Computer Vision, pp. 2980–2988 (2017)
6. He, X., Zhang, X., Ren, S., Sun, J.: Deep residual learning for image recognition. In: IEEE Conference on Computer Vision, Pattern Recognition, pp. 770–778 (2016)
7. Henriques, J.F., Caseiro, R., Martins, P., Batista, J.: High-speed tracking with kernelized correlation filters. IEEE Trans. Pattern Anal. Mach. Intell. **37**(3), 583–596 (2015)
8. Jiang, Y., Fang, J., Li, Z., Yue, J., Wang, Z., Li, D.: Automatic tracking of swimming koi using a particle filter with a center-surrounding cue. Mathe. Comput. Model. **58**(3), 859–867 (2013)
9. Kuznetsova, A., et al.: The open images dataset V4: unified image classification, object detection, and visual relationship detection at scale. arXiv:1811.00982 (2018)
10. Li, X., Wei, Z., Huang, L., Nie, J., Zhang, W., Wang, L.: Real-time underwater fish tracking based on adaptive multi-appearance model. In: 25th IEEE International Conference on Image Processing, pp. 2710–2714 (2018)
11. Li, X., Shang, M., Qin, H., Chen, L.: Fast accurate fish detection, recognition of underwater images with Fast R-CNN. In: OCEANS 2015 MTS, pp. 1–5. IEEE, Washington (2015)
12. Lin, T.Y., Dollar, P., Girshick, R., He, K., Hariharan, B., Belongie, S.: Feature pyramid networks for object detection. In: IEEE Conference on Computer Vision, Pattern Recognition, pp. 936–944 (2017)
13. Lin, T.-Y., et al.: Microsoft COCO: common objects in context. In: Fleet, D., Pajdla, T., Schiele, B., Tuytelaars, T. (eds.) ECCV 2014. LNCS, vol. 8693, pp. 740–755. Springer, Cham (2014). https://doi.org/10.1007/978-3-319-10602-1_48
14. Liu, W., et al.: SSD: single shot MultiBox detector. In: Leibe, B., Matas, J., Sebe, N., Welling, M. (eds.) ECCV 2016. LNCS, vol. 9905, pp. 21–37. Springer, Cham (2016). https://doi.org/10.1007/978-3-319-46448-0_2
15. Niu, B., Li, G., Peng, F., Wu, J., Zhang, L., Li, Z.: Survey of fish behavior analysis by computer vision. J. Aquac. Res. Dev. **9**(5) (2018)
16. Peng, C., Zhang, X., Yu, G., Luo, G., Sun, J.: Large kernel matters - improve semantic segmentation by global convolutional network. In: IEEE Conference on Computer Vision, Pattern Recognition, pp. 1743–1751 (2017)

17. Raman, R., Prakash, C., Marappan, M., Pawar, N.A.: Environmental stress mediated diseases of fish: an overview. Adv. Fish Res. **5**, 141–158 (2013)
18. Redmon, J., Divvala, S., Girshick, R., Farhadi, A.: You only look once: unified, real-time object detection. In: IEEE Conference on Computer Vision, Pattern Recognition, pp. 779–788 (2016)
19. Redmon, J., Farhadi, A.: YOLO9000: better, faster, stronger. In: IEEE Conference on Computer Vision, Pattern Recognition, pp. 6517–6525 (2017)
20. Redmon, J., Farhadi, A.: YOLOv3: an incremental improvement. arXiv:1804.02767 (2018)
21. Ren, S., He, K., Girshick, R., Sun, J.: Faster R-CNN: towards real-time object detection with region proposal networks. IEEE Trans. Pattern Anal. Mach. Intell. **39**(6), 1137–1149 (2017)
22. Saberioon, M., Gholizadeh, A., Cisar, P., Pautsina, A., Urban, J.: Application of machine vision systems in aquaculture with emphasis on fish: state-of-the-art, key issues. Rev. Aquac. **9**(4), 369–387 (2017)
23. Shelhamer, E., Long, J., Darrell, T.: Fully convolutional networks for semantic segmentation. In: IEEE Conference on Computer Vision, Pattern Recognition, pp. 3431–3440 (2015)
24. Shevchenko, V., Eerola, T., Kaarna, A.: Fish detection from low visibility underwater videos. In: 24th International Conference on Pattern Recognition, pp. 1971–1976 (2018)
25. Snieszko, S.F.: The effects of environmental stress on outbreaks of infectious diseases of fishes. J. Fish Biol. **6**(2), 197–208 (1974)
26. Sung, M., Yu, S., Girdhar, Y.: Vision based real-time fish detection using convolutional neural network. In: OCEANS 2017, Aberdeen, pp. 1–6 (2017)
27. Terayama, K., Habe, H., Sakagami, M.: Multiple fish tracking with an NACA airfoil model for collective behavior analysis. IPSJ Trans. Comput. Vis. Appl. **8**(1), 1–7 (2016)
28. Terayama, K., Hioki, H., Sakagami, M.: A measurement method for speed distribution of collective motion with optical flow, its application to estimation of rotation curve. In: IEEE International Symposium on Multimedia, pp. 32–39 (2014)
29. Terayama, K., Hongo, K., Habe, H., Sakagami, M.: Appearance-based multiple fish tracking for collective motion analysis. In: 3rd IAPR Asian Conference on Pattern Recognition, pp. 361–365 (2015)
30. Weinzaepfel, P., Revaud, J., Harchaoui, Z., Schmid, C.: DeepFlow: large displacement optical flow with deep matching. In: IEEE International Conference on Computer Vision, pp. 1385–1392 (2013)
31. Yu, X., Hou, X., Lu, H., Yu, X., Fan, L., Liu, Y.: Anomaly detection of fish school behavior based on features statistical, optical flow methods. Trans. Chin. Soc. Agric. Eng. **30**(2), 162–168 (2014)
32. Zhao, X., Yan, S., Gao, Q.: An algorithm for tracking multiple fish based on biological water quality monitoring. IEEE Access **7**, 15018–15026 (2019)
33. Zion, B.: The use of computer vision technologies in aquaculture - a review. Comput. Electron. Agric. **88**, 125–132 (2012)

Attention-Guided Model for Robust Face Detection System

Laksono Kurnianggoro[(⊠)] and Kang-Hyun Jo[(⊠)]

Graduate School of Electrical Engineering, University of Ulsan, Ulsan, South Korea
laksono@islab.ulsan.ac.kr, acejo@ulsan.ac.kr

Abstract. Face detection is a basic computer vision task which is required by various higher level applications including surveillance, authentication, and security system. To satisfy the demand on a high quality face detection method, this paper proposes a robust system based on deep learning model which utilize an attention-based training mechanism. This strategy enables the model to not only predicting the bounding boxes of faces but also outputs a heatmap that corresponds to the existence of faces on a given input image. The proposed method was trained on the most popular face detection dataset and the results show that it produces comparable performance to the existing state of the arts methods.

Keywords: Face detection · Deep learning · Machine learning · Neural network

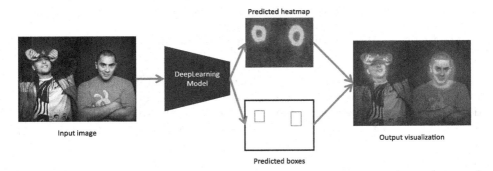

Fig. 1. Overview of the proposed method. A deep learning model is designed to predict heatmap of faces as well as their corresponding bounding boxes. Best viewed in color or monitor. (Color figure online)

1 Introduction

The research in face detection has been evolved rapidly since the boosted cascade method introduced by Viola-Jones [15]. Despite of its simplicity and real-time

C. Lee et al. (Eds.): PSIVT 2019, LNCS 11854, pp. 41–51, 2019.
https://doi.org/10.1007/978-3-030-34879-3_4

applicability, this method suffers from lack robustness on realistic scene under various conditions as reported in the WIDER face detection benchmark [18].

Deep learning has been shaping the modern computer vision algorithms, including face detection system. It is adopted in most of the recent face detector methods as recorded in the Wider benchmark [18]. This kind of method allows the system to learn the useful features for detecting face by itself, unlike the traditional face detectors which requires manual feature engineering [9,15,17]. As the results, deep learning based methods achieve better performance by a big margin compared to the feature engineering based methods with the availability of dataset that has large amount of sample in it [1,5,10,18–20].

In the deep learning based face detection methods, architecture design and training strategy play important roles in the performance improvement. In term of model design, the two stages object detection models [3,13] and single shot detectors [7,11,12] are influencing the architecture design. Meanwhile, other training strategy are including data augmentation method [5,19], multi-task learning [4,16], anchoring strategy [2,20], and context-aware training [5,14].

The work in this paper aims to utilize the merit of multi-task learning strategy which is expected to helps the training step. Specifically, attention mechanism is integrated in the model as illustrated in Fig. 1. Given an input image, the deep learning model is trained to predict the bounding boxes of faces as well as the attention map which corresponds to the existence of faces in the image. This kind of strategy make this paper provides the following contributions:

- This paper demonstrated the effect of multi-task learning which able to boost the model performance.
- Extensive evaluation has been conducted in the widely used face detection benchmark and the result shows that the proposed method deliver comparable results against other state of the arts methods.
- The predicted attention map makes the model more interpretable for human observer.

The remaining of this paper is organized as follow. Firstly, several related works on face detection are summarized. The Proposed method is explained in details followed by experiments and discussion in Sects. 3 and 4. Finally, conclusion is provided to summarize the contents of this paper.

2   Related Works

Single shot detector (SSD) [7] is one of the popular deep learning model in face detection. Research in [19] extends the SSD network for detecting faces from natural images. There are several challenges in face detection such as diversity of face scales, large amount of negative regions in the image, and small sized objects. These problems are alleviated in [19] by several strategies encapsulated as S^3FD method. Detection of different face scales are commonly performed in several network layers. In S^3FD, detection is started at layer with stride 4 (quarter of input size) to allows the network predict small faces. This is contrast with common SSD model which start the detection in layer with stride 8. In SSD-like model, the detection result is largely affected by anchor shape and features summarizing its corresponding receptive field. To ensure that the anchors matched with its corresponding receptive fields [8], the sizing is designed to match its effective receptive field. Lastly, the big amount of negative regions which causes classification imbalance is tackled using the max-out background class prediction which is basically designing the classifier to have several background predictors which is then summarized by their maximum confidence to be compared with the face score.

Following the success of S^{3}FD, the research in [5] extends the single shot detector in several aspects. Firstly, the feature pyramid network (FPN) model [6] is incorporated to allow the model extracts richer features from the input image. With the existence of FPN, each prediction layer is affected by low level feature which is comes from the lower level layer and the richer feature which come from the deeper layer. Therefore, two kind of predictions loss are utilized in the training stages, from the lower level (first shot) and the deeper layers (second shot) which allows the model to produce better performance compared to the single shot model.

3   Attention-Guided Face Detector

In this section, the detailed explanation about the proposed method is covered. Firstly, the architecture design of the deep learning model is presented. The model is designed to be able predict not only the bounding box of faces but also the attention map that emphasize the region that have high probability to contains a face. Furthermore, the dataset need to be augmented in order to train the proposed model. Ground-truth of attention map for each sample in the dataset is required to train the model. Thus the soft attention mask generation will be explained in this section.

3.1   System Architecture

The detector system in this work is designed based on single stage detector model with feature pyramid network to allow extraction of rich features for the higher resolution of detection layer which is depicted in Fig. 2. There are 6 layers of detector where each of them works for different scales of face. The prediction start at layer with stride 4 which corresponds to the quarter size of the input image. Since the feature in this layer is not rich enough, it will be enhanced by feature enhancement module (FEM) as in [5] which combines the high level feature from the pyramid layers and low level information from the current layer. As the result, prediction of face and non-face will be derived by rich features which is expected to give better representation of the face or background region. This kind of strategy is applied in all of the detection layers to encourage the utilization of both low and high level feature representation.

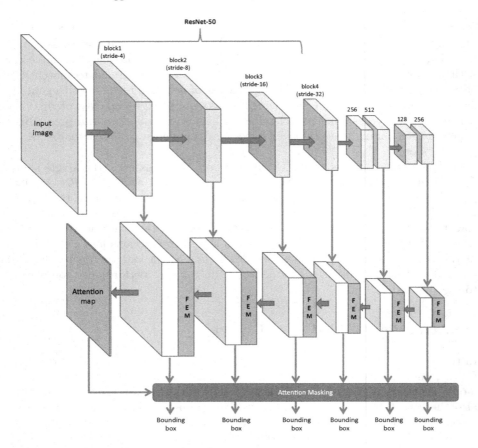

Fig. 2. Overview of the proposed method. A deep learning model is designed to predict heatmap of faces and the face bounding boxes at multiple scales.

The attention map is predicted by an extra convolution after the feature enhancement module which correspond to the finest detection region (i.e. stride 4 layer). This map is incorporated with a purpose to help the training process and making the network to focus on region that has high probability to contains a face. Optionally, it can be used to perform feature masking in each detection layer before the prediction of bounding box offset as shown in Fig. 2.

In order to train the proposed model, a common detection loss which consist of classification loss and localization loss is utilized as formulated in (1). The classification loss (L_{cls}) is cross-entropy loss between predicted logits and the classification ground-truth while the L_{loc} is Huber loss between predicted bounding box offset to its corresponding ground-truth as in SSD [7]. Classification loss is calculated for all of the anchors while localization loss is only calculated for the positive anchors.

$$L_d = \frac{1}{N_{cls}} \sum_m^{N_{cls}} L_{cls}\left(c_i, \tilde{c}_i\right) + \frac{1}{N_{loc}} \sum_m^{N_{loc}} L_{loc}\left(o_i, \tilde{o}_i\right) \tag{1}$$

Meanwhile for the attention loss, the mean of squared difference between ground-truth A and predicted mask $\tilde{A}$ is utilized as shown in (2). In this case W and H are the width and height of the attention map, respectively.

$$L_a = \frac{1}{WH} \sum_i^H \sum_j^W \left(A_{i,j} - \tilde{A}_{i,j}\right)^2 \tag{2}$$

To fully train the model, multi-task loss utilized by combining the detection loss and attention prediction loss. As in [5], two kinds of detection loss is calculated for both first shot (from top stream in Fig. 2) ad second shot (from 2nd stream in Fig. 2). The final loss value is formalized as (3) where L_d^i is the detection loss for the ith-shot of bounding box prediction.

$$L_{total} = L_d^{p1} + L_d^{p2} + L_a \tag{3}$$

Fig. 3. Example of the data augmentation result.

3.2 Soft Attention Mask and Data Augmentation

To provide the ground-truth for training, an attention mask is derived from the provided bounding boxes that are available in the dataset for each image sample. The mask is designed as multivariate Gaussian distributed values where the maximum is located in the center of a given face bounding box. It is formulated as (4) where σ_1 and σ_2 are set as half value of face bounding box width and height, respectively. Therefore, for each position at row r and column c in the ground-truth attention mask, the value is determined by exponentially decayed distance between this location and the center of bounding box (b_y, b_x) with standard deviation σ_1 and σ_2.

$$A_{r,c} = e^{-\frac{1}{2\sigma_1\sigma_2}(r-b_y)(c-b_x)} \tag{4}$$

The proposed method was trained using dataset augmentation similar to [5,7]. Specifically, from a given image, one face is randomly selected and then a square region around it is sampled at random location to ensure the selected face is inside the cropped region while the size is set to make the face area falls within ratio nearby [16, 32, 64, 128, 256, 512]/640 compared to the cropped region. Furthermore, random padding is also employed to make sure that the cropped region has square size and generate samples with small faces in it.

Several data augmentation results are shown in Fig. 3. On the left-most image, the sample was generated with padding resulting an augmented image with small faces on it. On the second image, some faces are not fully contained in the crop region because they are not selected as the main sample, the ground-truth corresponds to these kinds of faces will be retained only if the original center of bounding box is included in the crop region. In all of the image, attention mask are shown highlighting the face region and its nearby. The attention is designed in this way to ensure that region nearby faces are also contributing to the detection result.

4   Experiments and Results

To evaluate the proposed method, WIDER dataset [18] is used to train the model. Augmentation and generation of attention mask ground-truth is performed as specified in Sect. 3.2. The model was trained with batch size set to 32 during 150k iteration using the gradient descent optimizer (momentum = 0.9) and L_2 weight regularization scaled to 5e-4. The learning rate is set as 1e-3 and dropped by factor of 0.1 at 80k, 100k and 120k of training steps.

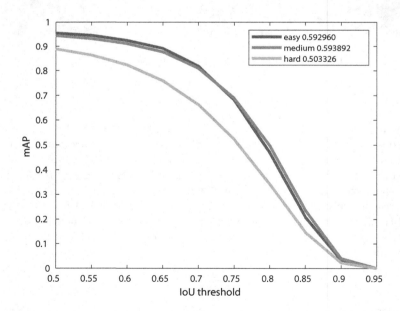

Fig. 4. Performance of the proposed method under different IoU threshold.

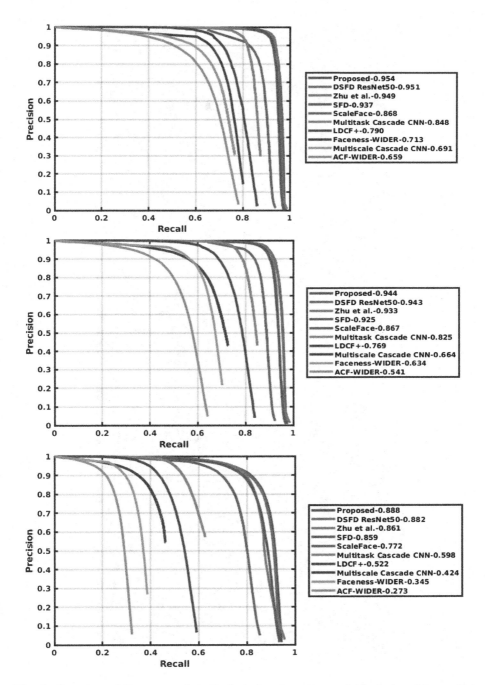

Fig. 5. Overview of the proposed method. A deep learning model is designed to predict heatmap of faces as well as their corresponding bounding boxes.

Fig. 6. Examples of the successful detection result using the proposed method. Best viewed in color or monitor. (Color figure online)

Table 1. Mean of Average Precision (mAP) of the Proposed Model at IoU 0.5.

Method	Evaluation set		
	Easy	Medium	Hard
DSFD-ResNet50 [5]	95	94.1	88.4
DSFD-ResNet50 own impl.	94.9	94.1	87.4
Proposed - Guided	95.7	**94.6**	87.9
Proposed - Guided w/ pyramid scaling	95.4	94.4	**88.9**
Proposed - Masked	**95.8**	94.6	87.9
Proposed - Masked w/ pyramid scaling	95.4	94.4	88.8

In this study, the ResNet50 is utilized as backbone network to make it comparable with the experiments in [5]. To preserve the fairness of performance comparison, DSFD-ResNet50 model is re-implemented as the baseline for this experiment. As shown in Table 1, the performance between our implementation is similar to the original result in [5]. It should be noted that we did not test our own DSFD-ResNet50 implementation using the pyramid scaling test as utilized in [5]. Therefore, there is 1% of performance gap on the hard evaluation set.

As summarized in Table 1, 2 types of the proposed model are examined. The first variation is guided model where the attention mask is only utilized in the training step as an extra regularizer. For the second type, the attention mask is used to perform masking on the extracted features before the prediction is performed. According to the experiments, both of the variations deliver similar results. Test using pyramid scaling scheme as in [5] was also performed on both types of the proposed model. This scaling strategy is basically performing the detection at various scales of input image and then combines the results using non-maximum suppression (NMS) to remove any detection where the intersection over union (IoU) score is more then 0.3. In the pyramid scaling scheme the image is tested at 0.25, 1, 1.25, 1.75, and 2.25 of original size where in our standard test the scale is started from 0.5 doubled in several steps until the GPU is approximately full. Additionally, test on the flipped image is also performed on both type of test.

As shown in the Table 1 the pyramid scaling strategy is able to boost the mAP score on the hard evaluation set but unfortunately it is lowering down the score in both easy and medium set. However, the overall results are still better compared to the baseline. This is showing the proof that our proposed method is useful to boost the performance of the baseline which is not utilizing attention mechanism in either training or inference phase.

The quality of the proposed method is also examined under various IoU thresholds from 0.5 until 0.95 with interval 0.05. As shown in Fig. 4 the proposed method deliver almost stable performance until IoU of 0.6. The performance is then dropped rapidly starting from IoU 0.7. The authors argue that this effect could be highly related to the NMS strategy used to filter out the detection result which may remove true positive detected faces.

Performance evaluations against the state of the arts method is also presented in the Fig. 5. It is summarize the comparison of various methods in the easy, medium, and hard validation set from top to bottom respectively. As reflected in all of the evaluation set, the proposed method delivers competitive results compared to the other state of the arts methods. It should be noted that the deep learning based models are outperforming the feature-engineering based method such as ACF by large margin as shown clearly in the Fig. 5.

Several examples of qualitative results are presented in Fig. 6. The predicted attention map produce acceptable results as designed to emphasize the regions nearby faces. Often, it also highlight incomplete face region such as the one on top-right side of the first image and same goes in the second image.

5   Conclusions

This paper presented study of face detection model with attention mechanism. The utilization of attention model is not only helping the network to generate a better feature representation for the detection phase but also useful to visualize the prediction of the model. This proposed method deliver competitive results compared to other existing state of the arts methods as reflected by the experiment result which were conducted on the largest face detection benchmark. The author believe that the performance of the model could be improved using a more complex backbone network which will be examined in the future work.

Acknowledgment. This research was supported by the MSIT (Ministry of Science and ICT), Korea, under the ICT Consilience Creative program (IITP-2019-2016-0-00318) supervised by the IITP (Institute for Information & communications Technology Planning & Evaluation).

References

1. Cai, Z., Fan, Q., Feris, R.S., Vasconcelos, N.: A unified multi-scale deep convolutional neural network for fast object detection. In: Leibe, B., Matas, J., Sebe, N., Welling, M. (eds.) ECCV 2016. LNCS, vol. 9908, pp. 354–370. Springer, Cham (2016). https://doi.org/10.1007/978-3-319-46493-0_22
2. Chi, C., Zhang, S., Xing, J., Lei, Z., Li, S.Z., Zou, X.: Selective refinement network for high performance face detection. In: Association for the Advancement of Artificial Intelligence (AAAI) (2019)
3. Dai, J., Li, Y., He, K., Sun, J.: R-FCN: object detection via region-based fully convolutional networks. In: Advances in Neural Information Processing Systems, pp. 379–387 (2016)
4. Deng, J., Guo, J., Zhou, Y., Yu, J., Kotsia, I., Zafeiriou, S.: RetinaFace: single-stage dense face localisation in the wild. arXiv preprint arXiv:1905.00641 (2019)
5. Li, J., et al.: DSFD: dual shot face detector. In: Proceedings of the IEEE Conference on Computer Vision and Pattern Recognition (2019)
6. Lin, T.Y., Dollár, P., Girshick, R., He, K., Hariharan, B., Belongie, S.: Feature pyramid networks for object detection. In: Proceedings of the IEEE Conference on Computer Vision and Pattern Recognition, pp. 2117–2125 (2017)

7. Liu, W., et al.: SSD: single shot multibox detector. In: Leibe, B., Matas, J., Sebe, N., Welling, M. (eds.) ECCV 2016. LNCS, vol. 9905, pp. 21–37. Springer, Cham (2016). https://doi.org/10.1007/978-3-319-46448-0_2

8. Luo, W., Li, Y., Urtasun, R., Zemel, R.: Understanding the effective receptive field in deep convolutional neural networks. In: Advances in Neural Information Processing Systems, pp. 4898–4906 (2016)

9. Mathias, M., Benenson, R., Pedersoli, M., Van Gool, L.: Face detection without bells and whistles. In: Fleet, D., Pajdla, T., Schiele, B., Tuytelaars, T. (eds.) ECCV 2014. LNCS, vol. 8692, pp. 720–735. Springer, Cham (2014). https://doi.org/10.1007/978-3-319-10593-2_47

10. Najibi, M., Samangouei, P., Chellappa, R., Davis, L.S.: SSH: single stage headless face detector. In: Proceedings of the IEEE International Conference on Computer Vision, pp. 4875–4884 (2017)

11. Redmon, J., Divvala, S., Girshick, R., Farhadi, A.: You only look once: unified, real-time object detection. In: Proceedings of the IEEE Conference on Computer Vision and Pattern Recognition, pp. 779–788 (2016)

12. Redmon, J., Farhadi, A.: Yolo9000: better, faster, stronger. In: Proceedings of the IEEE Conference on Computer Vision and Pattern Recognition, pp. 7263–7271 (2017)

13. Ren, S., He, K., Girshick, R., Sun, J.: Faster R-CNN: towards real-time object detection with region proposal networks. In: Advances in Neural Information Processing Systems, pp. 91–99 (2015)

14. Tang, X., Du, D.K., He, Z., Liu, J.: PyramidBox: a context-assisted single shot face detector. In: Ferrari, V., Hebert, M., Sminchisescu, C., Weiss, Y. (eds.) ECCV 2018. LNCS, vol. 11213, pp. 812–828. Springer, Cham (2018). https://doi.org/10.1007/978-3-030-01240-3_49

15. Viola, P., Jones, M., et al.: Rapid object detection using a boosted cascade of simple features. In: CVPR, vol. 1, no. 1, pp. 511–518 (2001)

16. Wang, J., Yuan, Y., Yu, G.: Face attention network: an effective face detector for the occluded faces. arXiv preprint arXiv:1711.07246 (2017)

17. Yang, B., Yan, J., Lei, Z., Li, S.Z.: Aggregate channel features for multi-view face detection. In: IEEE International Joint Conference on Biometrics, pp. 1–8. IEEE (2014)

18. Yang, S., Luo, P., Loy, C.C., Tang, X.: Wider face: a face detection benchmark. In: IEEE Conference on Computer Vision and Pattern Recognition (CVPR) (2016)

19. Zhang, S., Zhu, X., Lei, Z., Shi, H., Wang, X., Li, S.Z.: S3FD: single shot scale-invariant face detector. In: Proceedings of the IEEE International Conference on Computer Vision, pp. 192–201 (2017)

20. Zhu, C., Tao, R., Luu, K., Savvides, M.: Seeing small faces from robust anchor's perspective. In: Proceedings of the IEEE Conference on Computer Vision and Pattern Recognition, pp. 5127–5136 (2018)

BackNet: An Enhanced Backbone Network for Accurate Detection of Objects with Large Scale Variations

Md Tahmid Hossain[✉], Shyh Wei Teng, and Guojun Lu

School of Science, Engineering and Information Technology,
Federation University, Churchill, VIC 3842, Australia
{mt.hossain,shyh.wei.teng,guojun.lu}@federation.edu.au

Abstract. Deep Convolutional Neural Networks (CNNs) have induced significant progress in the field of computer vision including object detection and classification. Two-stage detectors like Faster RCNN and its variants are found to be more accurate compared to its one-stage counterparts. Faster RCNN combines an ImageNet pretrained backbone network (e.g VGG16) and a Region Proposal Network (RPN) for object detection. Although Faster RCNN performs well on medium and large scale objects, detecting smaller ones with high accuracy while maintaining stable performance on larger objects still remains a challenging task. In this work, we focus on designing a robust backbone network for Faster RCNN that is capable of detecting objects with large variations in scale. Considering the difficulties posed by small objects, our aim is to design a backbone network that allows signals extracted from small objects to be propagated right through to the deepest layers of the network. This being our motivation, we propose a robust network: BackNet, which can be integrated as a backbone into any two-stage detector. We evaluate the performance of BackNet-Faster RCNN on MS COCO dataset and show that the proposed method outperforms five contemporary methods.

1 Introduction

Object detection has long been a fundamental task in the field of computer vision. With the emergence of self-driving cars, intelligent surveillance systems, autonomous traffic monitoring, and other smart applications, the demand for an accurate detection system is on the rise. Handcrafted features like SIFT [1,30], SURF [25], HOG [29] and Deformable Part models [26–28] have long been used as traditional object detectors. The momentum has shifted towards CNN based detectors since the success of AlexNet [11] and other deep networks [10,12–14] in a variety of tasks. State-of-the-art detectors employ pretrained classification network as the detector backbone. Although classification networks have achieved superhuman level performance in a number of competitions, object detection still remains to be a much more difficult problem to solve [9,15,36]. There is a difference between the two tasks and a detector's requirement from

© Springer Nature Switzerland AG 2019
C. Lee et al. (Eds.): PSIVT 2019, LNCS 11854, pp. 52–64, 2019.
https://doi.org/10.1007/978-3-030-34879-3_5

Fig. 1. Proposed BackNet-based Faster RCNN is capable of detecting objects with large variations in scale within the same image.

the backbone network is different from that of a classification network [15]. One distinct dissimilarity between the two tasks is that classification datasets contain one prominent object per image, whereas multiple-class objects with large scale variations may appear within the same image in detection. An image with high resolution may contain extremely small objects which adds to the complexity. Faster RCNN uses an ImageNet pretrained classification network as the backbone. The last layer feature maps of the backbone network act as the input to the RPN. The spatial dimension of an input image is iteratively reduced in the intermediate convolution and pooling layers of a classification network. These layers are particularly helpful for keeping memory requirement low and according to recent studies [17,18], pooling also helps in ensuring the network's invariance to the small translation of the input. As a side effect of downsampling the original image, signals from small objects fades away in the intermediate layers and the deeper layer feature maps cannot retain enough information for these small objects. Consequently, detectors using such classification networks as the backbone struggle with small objects in the images.

One simple solution is to maintain high-resolution feature maps by avoiding several pooling/downsampling steps [15]. However, the loss of translation invariance has adverse effects on the detector's overall accuracy [17,18]. Another solution is to incorporate shallower layer features with the deeper ones [5,6,20]. However, the shallow layer features lack in semantic meaning resulting in a weak set of feature maps when combined with the semantically strong deeper ones. In this work, we propose a novel backbone network that we call BackNet for Faster RCNN. We argue that it is extremely difficult for RPN to generate accurate object proposals for small objects if the feature maps fed to the RPN do not contain enough signals from those small objects. BackNet is based on the VGG16 network [14] with an additional subnetwork that maintains high-resolution feature maps up to the last layer. The final layer output of the VGG16 network is upsampled and merged with the corresponding subnetwork output to form a robust set of feature maps. These strong feature maps act as the RPN input and boost the overall detector performance (Fig. 1).

The remaining sections of this paper are organized as follows: Sect. 2 discusses the related works. In Sect. 3, we introduce the proposed backbone network BackNet and the design rationales. In Sect. 4, we discuss the training and test dataset and provide a performance comparison of existing works with our proposed approach. Section 5 concludes this paper.

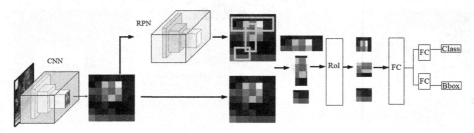

Fig. 2. An overview of the Faster RCNN detector [35]. The final layer feature maps from the backbone (ImageNet pretrained CNN) are fed to the RPN and it generates a set of object proposals (red rectangles). The Region of Interest (RoI) pooling layer pools and warps the features into a predefined fixed size compatible with the backbone network. These features ultimately traverse through the fully connected layers and a class label and a bounding box are predicted as the detector output. (Color figure online)

2   Related Works

Object detection is one of the most widely explored tasks in the field of computer vision. Two-stage detectors, like RCNN [33], Fast RCNN [4], and Faster RCNN [35] (Fig. 2), as well as one-stage detectors, like YOLO [31,32,34], and SSD [22], have made giant strides in recent years. While YOLO is regarded as the fastest in terms of inference time, Faster RCNN has been proved to be more accurate, especially while detecting small objects. Hence in this work, we focus on Faster RCNN and its variants.

Girshick et al. [33] first proposed RCNN which is a Region-based CNN for object detection. Rather than brute force cropping of image segments and feeding it to a trained deep classifier, RCNN makes use of an external object proposal method (Selective Search [24]) to create about 2,000 RoIs (Region of Interest) for each image. Since the input spatial dimension of a trained CNN classifier is fixed, the regions provided by Selective Search are warped into a fixed size and then fed to a CNN. RCNN is extremely slow in training and inference time as each of the region proposals is processed by a CNN separately. It means the feature extraction process is repeated 2,000 times for a single image. Instead of repetitive feature extraction from scratch, Girshick et al. later proposed Fast RCNN [4] that computes the convolution layers once per image and RoI pooling is done on the last layer feature maps, based on the regions proposed by Selective Search.

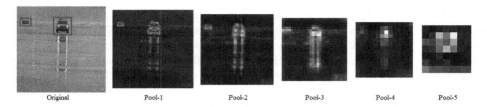

| Original | Pool-1 | Pool-2 | Pool-3 | Pool-4 | Pool-5 |

Fig. 3. Feature maps are extracted after each of the five pooling layers in VGG16. The original image contains three instances of vehicle-one relatively large in the front and two smaller in the back (inside red box). It is intriguing to see that the large vehicle's activation signal can be found even in the deepest layer (Pool-5). However, activations from the small vehicles fade away with increasing depth. Pool-4 has very few weak activations and Pool-5 retains even lesser (almost nothing) information. Feature maps are enlarged from their original size for better visibility. Successive spatial dimension reductions from left to right is for illustration only-exact downsampling factor in VGG16 is 2. (Color figure online)

RCNN and Fast RCNN rely on a slow external object proposal method which becomes the detector bottleneck. To further speed up the detection process and improve the overall accuracy, Ren et al. presented Faster RCNN [35], where a Region Proposal Network (RPN) replaces Selective Search as the object proposal generator in Fast RCNN. An overall work-flow of the Faster RCNN detector is depicted in Fig. 2. RPN shares the convolution layers with a traditional ImageNet pretrained backbone for computational efficiency. It takes the last layer feature maps from the backbone as input and outputs a set of object proposals. A predefined set of anchors are slid over the original image to check against the ground truth bounding boxes. This is to generate the object proposals and discard the backgrounds. Based on the proposals, the RoI pooling layer pools with a fixed size from the same feature maps and feeds the features to the fully connected layer. Finally, the class label and bounding box are predicted.

Although detecting medium and large objects is relatively easier, it is the smaller ones which appear to be extremely challenging for the detectors. Various techniques can be found in the literature striving to alleviate this particular problem. Multi-scale feature pyramid representation is exploited to detect objects across varied scales [5,6,20]. Lin et al. proposed Feature Pyramid Network (FPN) [20] that works on top of Faster RCNN and makes use of the inherent pyramid representation of the CNN features. The feed forward backbone network reduces the input spatial size at different stages. For each training image, the last layer low-resolution feature maps are upsampled and merged laterally with the previous layer feature map. This backward upsampling and merging process is repeated until the first convolution layer to form a feature pyramid. Finally, RPN exploits the pyramidal features to attain accurate object proposals. One major drawback of FPN is that the shallower layer features are not semantically strong and combining them with the deeper ones can degrade the overall detection performance.

Li et al. [15] subscribed to the idea of keeping large feature maps intact. However, this is done by avoiding pooling and dimension reduction layers which are pivotal for the detector's translation invariance capability. Fattal et al. [2] aimed to find the most informative and important feature maps for detecting small objects by frequency spectrum analysis (small objects have high frequency). Gao et al. [3] showed that in addition to the original three predefined anchors (9 in total) used in Faster RCNN, two additional smaller anchor boxes with sizes 32^2 and 64^2 improve the overall accuracy for tiny vehicles. Yang et al. [7] made use of scale-dependent pooling in order to accurately detect objects of all sizes. VGG16-based Faster RCNN is employed and the height of the RPN object proposals are used to choose the layer for RoI pooling. Shorter object proposals make use of shallower layers for pooling and larger ones use deeper layers for pooling. This can be attributed to the fact that small object's information or activation is highly unlikely to reach the deeper layers due to spatial dimension reduction. A cascaded rejection classifier is used to eliminate negative proposals for better performance. Bell et al. [8] followed a different approach and conducts RoI pooling from several layers at a time. Since smaller objects are harder to detect, adding contextual information to tiny objects via multi-layer pooling may improve the detector's performance. The pooled features are concatenated and 1×1 convolution is used to reduce the feature map depth. The semantic gap in the meaning of shallow layer features is a concern here as well. Cai et al. [23] combined several sub-networks in the backbone of a Faster RCNN detector. Since relatively shallower layers retain the information of small objects, multiple output layers from the subnetworks are used as the RPN input. Maintaining several additional subnetworks heavily adds to the memory complexity. Wang et al. [38] proposed a new expansion layer that helps the RoI pooling layer to extract background context along with the small object; surrounding area of the object is used as a cue for accurate detection. Although it might work well in some cases, inconsistent and ambiguous background context can deteriorate the performance of these detectors. Singh et al. [36] conducted a study on multi-scale image pyramid training. In this scheme, the detector is trained with images of different resolutions for each training sample. For example, a training image sample of size 224×224 is transformed to the following resolutions: $224 \times 224, 448 \times 448, 896 \times 896$ and 1200×1200. Pyramid representation of the input imagery ensures the variety of object scale while testing. Singh et al. argue that while it does add variety, it also introduces domain shift effect since large objects become too large in high-resolution version of the original image and small objects become too small in low-resolution ones. Their proposed solution module ensures that RPN does not generate object proposals beyond a predefined limit to avoid the domain shift effect.

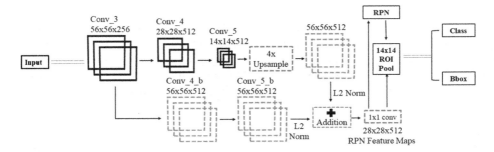

Fig. 4. VGG16 is used as the base of our backbone network. BackNet is identical to VGG16 up to stage 3 (Conv_3) hence not shown here. Dashed green boxes represent the additional operation introduced in BackNet. Solid boxes are the original components of a Faster RCNN network. Newly introduced subnetwork originating from Conv_3 maintains the same spatial resolution of 56×56 whereas the main network goes through multiple subsampling layers resulting in 14×14 feature maps. These Conv_5 feature maps go through a 4x upsampling layer and are merged with Conv_5_b feature maps. The merged feature map's spatial dimension is reduced to half and fed forward to the RPN. RPN yields object proposals and RoI pooling extracts feature from RPN input feature maps. Pooled features are warped to a fixed size (14×14) as it proceeds further inside the network. (Color figure online)

3   BackNet: Proposed Backbone Network

In this section, we first explain the impact of an effective backbone CNN in Faster RCNN architecture and in the subsequent section, the detailed architecture of BackNet and the design rationales are discussed.

3.1   Backbone Network

Starting from RCNN, it has taken a number of iterations to reach the upgraded variant Faster RCNN. Despite the evolutionary steps, the use of an ImageNet pretrained backbone network has been a constant. It highlights the important role a strong backbone network plays in the detection setup. Region Proposal Network (RPN) takes the last layer feature maps produced by the backbone as input. RPN then processes this input within its own network and outputs a set of object proposals. If RPN is not supplied with strong feature maps containing ample signals from both small and large objects, it becomes extremely difficult for it to produce accurate object proposals. ImageNet classification networks are explicitly designed for optimum classification performance. Spatial dimension reduction through pooling and longer stride convolution are common characteristics for these networks. Unlike classification tasks where one prominent object is present per image, object detectors need to identify multiple object instances in the same image. The variety of object shape and scale adds to the complexity and the challenges here are far greater than classification. To design an effective backbone network, a couple of factors should be considered.

1. Dimension reduction layers of a backbone network are important for translation invariance and efficient memory utilization, but the loss of activation signals from small objects is a critical drawback for any detector.
2. A number of contemporary research works build feature pyramids by combining deep layer information with shallower ones. Even so, the semantic meaning of the shallower features is weak and combining these layers with deeper ones may not yield expected results.

3.2 BackNet Architecture

We consider VGG16 as the base of our backbone network with the introduction of an additional subnetwork originating from Conv_3 (Fig. 4). VGG16 generates a series of features at several stages (downsampled with a factor of 2 at each stage and layers producing feature maps of the same size are considered to be in the same network stage). VGG16 has five such stages where the original input of 224×224 is reduced to 14×14. We refer these five stages as Conv_1, Conv_2, Conv_3, Conv_4, and Conv_5.

We observed from our experimental studies that most of the small objects' ($\approx 30 \times 30$ pixels) signals starts getting attenuated beyond Conv_3 stage (see Fig. 3 for a visual interpretation). Therefore, a subnetwork originating from Conv_3 is introduced that computes the convolution layers with the same configuration as the corresponding VGG16 layers (Fig. 4). However, this subnetwork does not downsample the feature maps and maintains the same resolution throughout the rest of the network. On the other hand, Conv_3 feature maps in the VGG16 network are downsampled twice resulting in 14×14 feature maps in the Conv_5 stage. Adding Conv_5 feature maps with the output (Conv_5_b) of the subnetwork will form one set of merged features that contain activation signals from both small and large objects. Conv_5 feature maps are upsampled by a factor of 4 to match the spatial dimension of Conv_5_b before element-wise addition. Feature maps are upsampled using the two-dimensional cubic convolution interpolation function [19]. When (x, y) is a point in the rectangular subdivision $[x_j, x_{j+1}] \times [y_k, y_{k+1}]$, the two-dimensional cubic convolution interpolation function is expressed using Eq. 1.

$$g(x,y) = \sum_{l=-1}^{2} \sum_{m=-1}^{2} c_{j+l,k+m} u\left(\frac{x - x_{j+l}}{h_x}\right) u\left(\frac{y - y_{k+m}}{h_y}\right) \tag{1}$$

where u is the one dimesional interpolation kernel and h_x, and h_y, are the x and y coordinate sampling increments. $C_{j,k}$'s are derived using Taylor's Expansion.

Both outputs from Conv_5 (upsampled) and Conv_5_b (subnetwork) are L2 Normalized before merging. Merged feature maps then undergo $1 \times 1 \times 512$ convolution with stride 2 resulting in $28 \times 28 \times 512$ feature maps; these act as the input to the RPN. We employ 14×14 RoI pooling rather than original 7×7 with a view to incorporating sufficient object features. The pooled features are propagated through to the regular Faster RCNN layers for a class label and a bounding box.

4 Performance Evaluation

In this section, we evaluate the performance of BackNet with five contemporary detectors based on a benchmark dataset. Table 1 compares different configurations of our proposed BackNet while Tables 2 and 3 illustrate how the BackNet-based Faster RCNN detector fares against other detectors for detecting objects with large scale difference. Table 2 focuses on the Precision and Table 3 focuses on the Recall values on the MS COCO dataset.

4.1 Dataset

We train and test our proposed method on MS COCO [21] dataset. It consists of 123,000 images which belong to a total of 80 object classes. We follow the standard split of 118,000/5,000 for training/validation. We use the standard metric of mean Average Precision (mAP) at Intersection over Union $IoU = .50 : .05 : .95$. Average Precision is also calculated for small (AP_S), medium (AP_M) and large (AP_L) objects separately with the specified IoU. According to MS COCO definition, objects with spatial dimension less than 32×32 are small, objects ranging from 32×32 to 96×96 are medium and objects with spatial dimension greater than 96×96 are considered large. Average Recall (AR) is computed at 1, 10 and 100 detections per image denoted by AR_1, AR_{10} and AR_{100} respectively.

4.2 Experimental Setup

We use the ImageNet pretrained novel BackNet as the detector backbone. We follow the pragmatic four-step detector training scheme adopted in Faster RCNN [35]. First, the RPN is trained and it is allowed to output a maximum of 2,000 object proposals per image. Among these 2,000, 256 regions are randomly chosen to form a minibatch and calculate the loss. RPN weights are initialized from a zero-mean Gaussian distribution with standard deviation of 0.01. In the second step, BackNet-based Fast RCNN network is trained using the RPN output (object proposals) from Step 1. In the third step, BackNet and RPN are trained together and the shared convolution layers along with the RPN layers are fine-tuned. In the last step, only the unique Fast RCNN layers are fine-tuned while the shared layer weights are frozen. Initial learning rate used for all four steps is 0.0001. Stochastic Gradient Descent (SGD) is used with a momentum value set to 0.9 and a weight decay of 0.0005 with adaptive dropout [37]. Minibatch size of one and a maximum of 40 epochs are used for each of the training stages mentioned above.

Table 1. Performance comparison among different configurations for the proposed BackNet. The detector performs best when the newly introduced subnetwork originates from Conv_3. Best Precision and Recall values are presented in Bold.

MS COCO											
Conv_3 (56 × 56)	Conv_4 (28 × 28)	2x Upsample	4x Upsample	Batch norm	mAP	AP_S	AP_M	AP_L	AR_S	AR_M	AR_L
✓			✓		38.15	22.58	42.11	49.76	34.16	62.05	71.49
✓			✓	✓	**38.55**	**22.88**	**42.46**	50.31	**34.95**	**62.30**	72.85
	✓	✓		✓	37.45	19.90	41.77	**50.68**	30.01	59.26	**73.96**
	✓	✓			37.15	19.60	41.45	50.40	29.62	58.85	73.56

Table 2. Proposed BackNet based Faster RCNN improves Precision on small objects while maintaining stable performance on medium and large objects. Best Precision values are presented in Bold.

MS COCO				
Method	Mean Average Precision (mAP)	AP_S	AP_M	AP_L
Faster RCNN [35]	24.20	7.20	26.40	36.90
Faster RCNN + RS [16]	29.50	11.90	32.70	41.80
Faster RCNN + FPN [20]	35.80	17.50	38.70	47.80
ION [8]	30.70	11.82	32.78	44.80
DetNet [15]	38.20	22.05	42.10	**50.45**
BackNet-Faster RCNN (Ours)	**38.55**	**22.88**	**42.46**	50.31

Table 3. Proposed BackNet based Faster RCNN improves Recall on small objects while maintaining stable performance on medium and large objects. Best Recall values are presented in Bold.

MS COCO						
Method	AR_1	AR_{10}	AR_{100}	AR_S	AR_M	AR_L
Faster RCNN [35]	23.80	34.10	34.70	11.50	38.90	54.40
Faster RCNN + RS [16]	27.30	40.00	40.90	17.90	45.50	58.60
Faster RCNN + FPN [20]	30.90	46.30	47.90	26.40	52.40	63.00
ION [8]	27.70	42.80	45.40	23.00	50.08	63.02
DetNet [15]	32.00	58.33	49.35	28.80	52.10	67.15
BackNet-Faster RCNN (Ours)	**32.40**	**59.64**	**56.70**	**34.95**	**62.30**	**72.85**

4.3 Quantitative Results Analysis

We have experimented with different configurations of the proposed BackNet components. Table 1 provides a summary of the detectors overall performance on the MS COCO dataset. As stated earlier, VGG16 is used as the base network with upsampled last layer features. A new subnetwork is introduced which maintains the same feature map spatial dimension from its stage of origin. When the subnetwork originates from Conv_3 stage (56 × 56), the detector performs the best both in terms of Precision and Recall; it scores an mAP of 38.55 and

AR of 56.70. Note that this particular network configuration outperforms others on small object dataset with AP_S 22.88% and AR_S 34.95%. On the contrary, the subnetwork originating from Conv_4 stage improves the detector's performance on large objects (28×28), but both Precision and Recall drop on small objects. The reason can be explained by observing the lower resolution feature maps in Conv_4 (28×28) compared to Conv_3 (56×56). Some of the small object activations are lost when Conv_3 features are downsampled by a factor of 2 in the main branch and the Conv_4 origin subnetwork is also deprived of these activations. Consequently, the detector's performance does not degrade on large objects but its performance does degrade for smaller ones. Using Batch Normalization before adding the upsampled and subnetwork feature maps are found to increase detector Precision (mAP) and Recall (AR) for both configurations.

Tables 2 and 3 compare the performance of the proposed and five contemporary object detectors in terms of Precision and Recall respectively. Average Recall is calculated at 1, 10 and 100 detections per image denoted by AR_1, AR_{10} and AR_{100} respectively. AR_{100} is the mean Recall and mAP is the mean Precision across all object shapes available in the dataset. BackNet-based faster RCNN achieves the highest mAP of 38.55% while securing an Average Precision of 22.88% on small objects (second best DetNet 22.05%). Although DetNet produces the maximum AP for large objects (50.45%), our proposed method is comparable (50.31%). Since BackNet is capable of retaining both small and large object information in the final layer feature maps, the Average Recall for BackNet-Faster RCNN is also better than other detectors on all three different sizes of objects.

5   Conclusions

Compared to the methods applied in the relevant literature to deal with the challenge posed by objects of small scale, our approach is theoretically straight forward and yields better results. The motif behind deploying the proposed BackNet subnetwork is to prevent the signals of small object from dying down across a number of down-sampling layers within a CNN. While the subnetwork takes care of the small objects, the regular objects cascade through the Conventional VGG16 layers and the merging layer still ensure a robust set of features inclusive of objects with all possible shape and size. Although VGG16 is used as the base of the proposed method, BackNet can be incorporated with other traditional pretrained networks as well which further strengthens our contribution.

Acknowledgement. This work has been Funded by Federation University Australia research grants.

References

1. Teng, S.W., Hossain, M.T., Lu, G.: Multimodal image registration technique based on improved local feature descriptors. J. Electron. Imaging **24**(1), 013013 (2015)
2. Fattal, A.-K., Karg, M., Scharfenberger, C., Adamy, J.: Distant vehicle detection: how well can region proposal networks cope with tiny objects at low resolution? In: Leal-Taixé, L., Roth, S. (eds.) ECCV 2018. LNCS, vol. 11129, pp. 289–304. Springer, Cham (2019). https://doi.org/10.1007/978-3-030-11009-3_17
3. Gao, Y., et al.: Scale optimization for full-image-CNN vehicle detection. Paper presented at the 2017 IEEE Intelligent Vehicles Symposium (IV) (2017)
4. Girshick, R. Fast R-CNN. Paper presented at the proceedings of the IEEE international conference on computer vision (2015)
5. Yang, W., Li, S., Ouyang, W., Li, H., Wang, X. Learning feature pyramids for human pose estimation. Paper presented at the proceedings of the IEEE international conference on computer vision (2017)
6. Zhou, P., Ni, B., Geng, C., Hu, J., Xu, Y. Scale-transferrable object detection. Paper presented at the proceedings of the IEEE conference on computer vision and pattern recognition (2018)
7. Yang, F., Choi, W., Lin, Y. Exploit all the layers: fast and accurate CNN object detector with scale dependent pooling and cascaded rejection classifiers. Paper presented at the proceedings of the IEEE conference on computer vision and pattern recognition (2016)
8. Bell, S., Lawrence Zitnick, C., Bala, K., Girshick, R.: Inside-outside net: Detecting objects in context with skip pooling and recurrent neural networks. Paper presented at the proceedings of the IEEE conference on computer vision and pattern recognition (2016)
9. Hu, P., Ramanan, D.: Finding tiny faces. Paper presented at the proceedings of the IEEE conference on computer vision and pattern recognition (2017)
10. He, K., Zhang, X., Ren, S., Sun, J.: Deep residual learning for image recognition. In: Proceedings of the IEEE Conference on Computer Vision and Pattern Recognition, pp. 770–778 (2016)
11. Krizhevsky, A., Sutskever, I., Hinton, G.E.: Imagenet classification with deep convolutional neural networks. In: Advances in Neural Information Processing Systems, pp. 1097–1105 (2012)
12. Zeiler, M.D., Fergus, R.: Visualizing and understanding convolutional networks. In: Fleet, D., Pajdla, T., Schiele, B., Tuytelaars, T. (eds.) ECCV 2014. LNCS, vol. 8689, pp. 818–833. Springer, Cham (2014). https://doi.org/10.1007/978-3-319-10590-1_53
13. Szegedy, C., et al.: Going deeper with convolutions. In: Proceedings of the IEEE Conference on Computer Vision and Pattern Recognition, pp. 1–9 (2015)
14. Simonyan, K., Zisserman, A.: Very deep convolutional networks for large-scale image recognition. arXiv preprint arXiv:1409.1556 (2014)
15. Li, Z., Peng, C., Yu, G., Zhang, X., Deng, Y., Sun, J.: Detnet: a backbone network for object detection. arXiv preprint arXiv:1804.06215 (2018)
16. Chen, X., Gupta, A.: An implementation of faster RCNN with study for region sampling. arXiv preprint arXiv:1702.02138 (2017)
17. Scherer, D., Müller, A., Behnke, S.: Evaluation of pooling operations in convolutional architectures for object recognition. In: Diamantaras, K., Duch, W., Iliadis, L.S. (eds.) ICANN 2010. LNCS, vol. 6354, pp. 92–101. Springer, Heidelberg (2010). https://doi.org/10.1007/978-3-642-15825-4_10

18. Goodfellow, I., Bengio, Y., Courville, A.: Deep Learning. MIT Press, Cambridge (2016)
19. Keys, R.: Cubic convolution interpolation for digital image processing. IEEE Trans. Acoust. Speech Signal Process. **29**(6), 1153–1160 (1981)
20. Lin, T.Y., Dollár, P., Girshick, R., He, K., Hariharan, B., Belongie, S.: Feature pyramid networks for object detection. In: Proceedings of the IEEE Conference on Computer Vision and Pattern Recognition, pp. 2117–2125 (2017)
21. Lin, T.-Y., et al.: Microsoft COCO: common objects in context. In: Fleet, D., Pajdla, T., Schiele, B., Tuytelaars, T. (eds.) ECCV 2014. LNCS, vol. 8693, pp. 740–755. Springer, Cham (2014). https://doi.org/10.1007/978-3-319-10602-1_48
22. Liu, W., et al.: SSD: single shot MultiBox detector. In: Leibe, B., Matas, J., Sebe, N., Welling, M. (eds.) ECCV 2016. LNCS, vol. 9905, pp. 21–37. Springer, Cham (2016). https://doi.org/10.1007/978-3-319-46448-0_2
23. Cai, Z., Fan, Q., Feris, R.S., Vasconcelos, N.: A unified multi-scale deep convolutional neural network for fast object detection. In: Leibe, B., Matas, J., Sebe, N., Welling, M. (eds.) ECCV 2016. LNCS, vol. 9908, pp. 354–370. Springer, Cham (2016). https://doi.org/10.1007/978-3-319-46493-0_22
24. Uijlings, J.R., Van De Sande, K.E., Gevers, T., Smeulders, A.W.: Selective search for object recognition. Int. J. Comput. Vision **104**(2), 154–171 (2013)
25. Bay, H., Tuytelaars, T., Van Gool, L.: SURF: speeded up robust features. In: Leonardis, A., Bischof, H., Pinz, A. (eds.) ECCV 2006. LNCS, vol. 3951, pp. 404–417. Springer, Heidelberg (2006). https://doi.org/10.1007/11744023_32
26. Girshick, R.B., Felzenszwalb, P.F., McAllester, D.: Discriminatively trained deformable part models, release 5 (2012)
27. Zhang, N., Farrell, R., Iandola, F., Darrell, T.: Deformable part descriptors for fine-grained recognition and attribute prediction. In: Proceedings of the IEEE International Conference on Computer Vision, pp. 729–736 (2013)
28. Azizpour, H., Laptev, I.: Object detection using strongly-supervised deformable part models. In: Fitzgibbon, A., Lazebnik, S., Perona, P., Sato, Y., Schmid, C. (eds.) ECCV 2012. LNCS, vol. 7572, pp. 836–849. Springer, Heidelberg (2012). https://doi.org/10.1007/978-3-642-33718-5_60
29. Dalal, N., Triggs, B.: Histograms of oriented gradients for human detection. In: IEEE Conf. CVPR, vol. 2, pp. 886–893, June 2005
30. Lowe, D.G.: Distinctive image features from scale-invariant keypoints. Int. J. Comput. Vision **60**(2), 91–110 (2004)
31. Redmon, J., Farhadi, A.: YOLO9000: better, faster, stronger. In: Proceedings of the IEEE Conference on Computer Vision and Pattern Recognition, pp. 7263–7271 (2017)
32. Redmon, J., Divvala, S., Girshick, R., Farhadi, A.: You only look once: unified, real-time object detection. In: Proceedings of the IEEE Conference on Computer Vision and Pattern Recognition, pp. 779–788 (2016)
33. Girshick, R., Donahue, J., Darrell, T., Malik, J.: Region-based convolutional networks for accurate object detection and segmentation. IEEE Trans. Pattern Anal. Mach. Intell. **38**(1), 142–158 (2015)
34. Redmon, J., Farhadi, A.: Yolov3: an incremental improvement. arXiv preprint arXiv:1804.02767 (2018)
35. Ren, S., He, K., Girshick, R., Sun, J.: Faster r-cnn: towards real-time object detection with region proposal networks. In: Advances in Neural Information Processing Systems, pp. 91–99 (2015)

36. Singh, B., Davis, L.S.: An analysis of scale invariance in object detection snip. In: Proceedings of the IEEE Conference on Computer Vision and Pattern Recognition, pp. 3578–3587 (2018)
37. Hossain, M.T., Teng, S.W., Zhang, D., Lim, S., Lu, G.: Distortion robust image classification using deep convolutional neural network with discrete cosine transform. In: 2019 IEEE International Conference on Image Processing (ICIP), pp. 659–663 (2019)
38. Wang, W., Wu, B., Lv, J., Dai, P.: Regular and Small Target Detection. Paper presented at the international conference on multimedia modeling (2019)

Body Detection in Spectator Crowd Images Using Partial Heads

Yasir Jan$^{(\boxtimes)}$(iD), Ferdous Sohel(iD), Mohd Fairuz Shiratuddin(iD), and Kok Wai Wong(iD)

Murdoch University, Perth, Australia
{Y.Jan,F.Sohel,F.Shiratuddin,K.Wong}@murdoch.edu.au
https://www.murdoch.edu.au

Abstract. In spectator crowd images, the high number of people, small size and occlusion of body parts, make the body detection task challenging. Due to the similarity in facial features of different people, the variance in head features is less compared to the variation in the body features. Similarly, the visibility of the head in a crowd is more, compared to the visibility of the body. Therefore, the detection of only the head is more successful than the detection of the full body. We show that there exists a relation between head size and location, and the body size and location in the image. Therefore, head size and location can be leveraged to detect full bodies. This paper suggests that due to lack of visibility, more variance in body features, and lack of available training data of occluded bodies, full bodies should not be detected directly in occluded scenes. The proposed strategy is to detect full bodies using information extracted from head detection. Additionally, body detection technique should not be affected by the level of occlusion. Therefore, we propose to use only color matching for body detection. It does not require any explicit training data like CNN based body detection. To evaluate the effectiveness of this strategy, experiments are performed using the S-HOCK spectator crowd dataset. Using partial ground truth head information as the input, full bodies in a dense crowd is detected. Experimental results show that our technique using only head detection and color matching can detect occluded full bodies in a spectator crowd successfully.

Keywords: Spectator crowd · Body detection · Color matching

1 Introduction

Body detection is useful for image understanding applications including surveillance [19], group behavior modeling [26], semantic context extraction [10], and crowd disaster prevention [19]. Body detection techniques can follow a top-down or bottom-up approach [12,13]. In top-down approaches the full bodies are detected from the images, without detecting individual parts of the body. These

© Springer Nature Switzerland AG 2019
C. Lee et al. (Eds.): PSIVT 2019, LNCS 11854, pp. 65–77, 2019.
https://doi.org/10.1007/978-3-030-34879-3_6

approaches do not perform well when there are overlapping bodies since occlusion prevents detecting full body altogether [14,22]. Therefore, in images of dense crowd, which have occluding bodies, the top-down approaches are less applicable. In the bottom-up approaches the individual body parts are first located and then are grouped together to form the full body. Bottom-up approaches face the issues of joint pairing and high computational complexity [2,8,15]. With an increasing number of people in the image, the number of potential joint pairs increases exponentially. The possibility of incorrect joint pairing is also high due to a large number of people in a dense crowd. Furthermore, the issue of occluding body parts further reduces body detection [2,27]. Bottom-up approach can be effective, if the effects of multiple joint pairing and occlusion are reduced.

Spectator crowd in a stadium is an example of a dense crowd [21]. As shown in Fig. 1, people are usually seated in a specific arrangement, relative to a camera. The images taken from the front view of the crowd have spectators with revealed heads and of limited variation in dimensions. However, the bodies of spectators at the back of the scene are occluded behind the spectators in front of them [1,21]. Thus, there is a variation in the visible body parts. The stadium crowd remains seated most of the time and has a low level of body movement, unlike other crowd scenes such as pedestrians [21,27]. Therefore, techniques relying on body movement information, such as pedestrian detection, are not suitable for detecting people in spectator crowd videos. The videos need to be analyzed frame by frame. Therefore, an image-based detection technique is required which does not require movement information, and can also handle issues such as, an increased number of people/parts, body occlusions and low image resolutions.

Image-based head and body detection are challenging because of the low resolution [2,27] of the body parts. The low resolution reduces the availability of detailed facial and body features in the images. Therefore, we need to rely on techniques which detect body parts without visibility of detailed shapes. Similarly, color matching techniques are based on individual pixel intensities. Pixels belonging to a range of similar intensity can be grouped into a single form, regardless of any shape, or partial visibility. Thus, if color matching is used on the pixels of partially visible body parts, then small visible parts can be grouped into a single object with partial occlusion. Shape detection-based techniques may lack this robustness feature. However, in a dense crowd image, the large number of potential matching pixels, can be computationally extensive. This issue can be resolved by using a spatial reference for grouping pixels. Hierarchical structure of joints in human skeleton convey important information for action recognition [24]. But all joints are not easily detected due to occlusion. Since, existing techniques have achieved high accuracy in head detection [1,7,9,16]. Therefore, head positions can be used as a reference for grouping pixels around it into a single body. Taking all the issues into account, instead of relying on the detection of possible visible/non-visible body parts/joints, we can leverage the detected head information and use color matching for detecting body pixels.

Overall, this paper proposes that body detection in spectator crowd images, should rely on detection of the most visible part i.e. head. The detected head information should be leveraged to detect full bodies, using color matching of surrounding pixels. To evaluate the effectiveness of this technique, we use partial ground truth head information, and detect body bounding boxes.

Fig. 1. A spectator crowd image from the S-HOCK dataset [21].

The rest of the paper is organized as follows. Section 2 discusses the existing work related to body detection. Section 3 discusses the proposed methodology. Section 4 discusses the S-HOCK dataset used for experimentation. Section 5 explains the experimental protocol and in Sect. 6 the results are shown. Section 7 concludes the paper.

2   Related Work

Body detections are dealt like object detections, using image features like HOG [3] and HASC [20]. The S-HOCK dataset performs experiments for body detection using various baselines. SVM is applied on HOG and HASC features for body detection. Other than these basic features ACF [6], DPM [4] and CUBD [5] techniques are also used for body detection. Previously, occlusion issue in body detection is overcome by using multiple weak part detectors [25]. These techniques perform classification based on the feature set to detect body parts. The head, torso and lower body are separately identified. Some of them locate individual limbs as well. However, detecting only the head is relatively simpler than the rest of the body, because of high visibility and less variability of the head features compared to the body features.

Deep learning-based techniques consider head and body detection as a type of object detection task [16–18]. Some work also performs pedestrian detection as an object detection [25, 27]. Techniques for full object detection are not suitable for part body detection in crowd scenes, because of few reasons. The lack of available training data of varying situations of occlusion limits the training of networks. Smaller sized objects, i.e. body parts and heads in an image with a large number of people are also hard to detect using state of the art object detection techniques. Existing networks used for object detection are usually pretrained on the ImageNet data. Because ImageNet images have large object dimensions [7], these networks cannot successfully locate and identify objects of small dimensions [7, 11]. The issue of small dimensions is handled in various ways. For detecting tiny faces, image upscaling [7] is used, so that the face becomes large enough to be detected by these networks. Instead of upscaling, "super-resolved" CNN features [11] can be used to detect small faces. It convolves small object CNN features and makes them similar to large object CNN features. Thus, existing networks are not trained for smaller objects, or a range of sizes. In a crowd scene if the heads and body parts vary over a wide range, then the network has to be trained for each size. Such a technique would require training data for each scale size, and training for each size is also a computationally intensive task. Existing face detection techniques have achieved high accuracy in challenges like occlusion, small size and a wide range of variability. However, for the body detection task, these issues are still challenging.

The issue of occlusion is handled by other approaches [23, 25, 27]. These techniques [14, 22, 28] use part-based models to handle occlusion, therefore, train and detect visible body parts. Ideally, to handle a wide range of occlusion, a network has to be trained for all possibilities of variation in occlusion, and all possibilities of orientation of the body parts. In crowd images, the range of variance is wide, due to the high number of different possibilities, and it becomes hard to get training data for each possibility. Thus, ideal body detection technique should be independent of the available data, for varying occlusion level and orientation of each body part.

3 Methodology

The study evaluates the effectiveness of detecting body through color matching, using head information as input. We do not implement head detection ourselves but rely on preexisting head information. For evaluation, the proposed technique takes the crowd image and the partial ground truth head locations as inputs.

The relationship between head dimensions and body dimensions is very important to make any assumption for this technique. Since our target is spectator crowd scene, therefore it allows us to select some specific parameters for such a controlled environment. Figures 2a and b, show the relationship between the widths and heights of the heads and the full bodies of the people in the dataset [21]. The images in the dataset have some constraints. The images of the spectators are taken from the front, thus restricting the viewing angle of the scene. This restricts all the people to have the same full body size i.e. with less variation. But the overlapping of bodies causes the spectators to have varying visible body sizes. It can be observed that the width and height of the head are within a narrow range, but the width and height of the body varies a lot. The relatively high variance in body height is due to the high variance in occlusion, showing that the people in the dataset have occluded bodies in a wide range. Another important information lies in the relative position of the head and the body. We consider the body joints to be always present below the head, and not the other way around. This allows us to select a probable body region lying below the head.

Existing head detection techniques may detect partial heads with 50% or more overlapping head region. We may approximate a square full head region by extending the head dimensions around the detected area. There is a possibility that the extended full head location may not match the ground truth full head. Since, in our proposed methodology the body search region is larger than the head region, thus, if the head location mismatches, it will still lie within the search space. For evaluation purposes, we select 50% overlapping ground truth partial head bounding box values. We then approximate the full head dimension by extending into a square region and use it as input for evaluation.

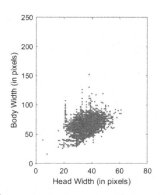
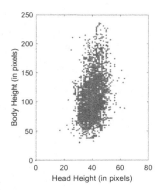

(a) Head width vs Full Body width.   (b) Head height vs Full Body height.

Fig. 2. Relation between the head and full body dimensions, in S-HOCK dataset.

Figure 3 shows all the steps involved in estimating the bounding box from the crowd scene image. The details of the steps are discussed below. Pixels which can be grouped together with their neighborhood pixels, based on their color similarity, form a shape of an object. Other lonely pixels which are different from its surrounding pixels can be noise pixels. The lonely pixels which are part of an object but are encompassed by the other group of similar pixels can also

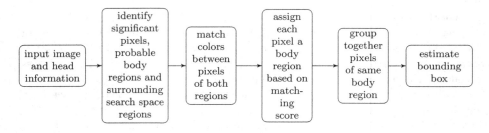

Fig. 3. Steps of the proposed technique.

be ignored, because only the grouped pixels may form the shape of the object without utilizing the lonely pixels. Such lonely pixels, whether noise or no-noise, can be considered insignificant for identifying an object. Therefore, the first step is to remove all the pixels which do not play any significant role in body identification. Based on Eq. (1), each pixel is compared with its neighboring pixels, and the difference image $D(x, y, c)$ is calculated, where x and y are the image pixel location on both image axes, and c is the color channel.

$$D(x, y, c) = a_1 sqrt(\sum_{i=-n}^{n} \sum_{j=-n}^{n} (I(x, y, c) - I(x + i, y + j, c))^2)) \qquad (1)$$

Each pixel is compared with its 9×9 neighborhood pixels ($n = 4$). The neighborhood of 9×9 is selected to achieve similarity with HOG feature cell size, i.e. 8×8, in the dataset benchmark. Parameter $a_1 = 1/80$, to compute the average of the difference of intensities across neighborhood of 9×9.

The pixels which have the cumulative difference across all channels ($\sum_{c=1}^{3} D$) less than a tolerance value t_1 are more similar to their neighbors and therefore considered as the significant pixels. The significant body pixels image $S(x, y)$ is calculated by Eq. (2).

$$S(x, y) = \sum_{c=1}^{3} D(x, y, c) < t_1 \qquad (2)$$

Value of t_1 is selected based on the acceptable color difference of neighborhood. 10% of the color range i.e. 255/10 across each channel is considered a similar color. Therefore, for a pixel $I(x, y)$ a neighborhood of 9×9 will have $S(x, y)$ approximately 8.5 (rounded to 10). Hence, we select $t_1 = 10$. For calculations, parameters a_1 and t_1 from Eqs. 1 and 2 respectively, can be merged to form a single parameter. But we present them separately to explain the reason behind their selected value.

After calculating the significant pixels, the head region pixels are also removed to avoid excessive calculation and color matching. Figure 4 shows the significant pixels with both head pixels and noise pixels removed. Since the

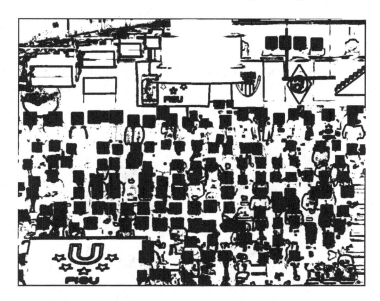

Fig. 4. Significant pixels in a scene (white pixels).

approximate head location is already known, we leverage this information for selecting a probable body region. The probable body region is the group of significant pixels below the head region, as shown in Fig. 5, and can be considered as the center of a full body. The bounding box values of the probable body region are calculated from the head bounding box values using (3) and (4).

$$ProbBody[xmin, xmax] = Head[xmin, xmax] \qquad (3)$$

$$ProbBody[ymin, ymax] = Head[ymin, ymax] + headheight \qquad (4)$$

Probable body region pixels are color matched with the significant pixels. Since the crowd images have a large number of people, therefore it is not practical to search for matching pixels across the whole image for a particular head. The search space for each head h needs to be limited. We select the search space as a square region ($s_d \times s_d$) around the body region center. Each significant pixel within the square region, excluding the head pixels, is matched with the pixels within the probable body region. Matching is calculated by the following two steps.

First, the search space significant pixels of head h is matched with the body region pixels of that head. Difference Q_h of each pixel is calculated using (5). $Q_h(x, y, i, h)$ shows how much each pixel at location (x, y) in search space is different than the rest of the pixels within the probable body region $h_x \times h_y$. A smaller value means the pixels will be less different, i.e. more matching.

$$Q_h(x,y,i,j) = 1/q \times \sum_{c=1}^{3}(P(x,y) - P(x_i,y_j,c))^2 \qquad (5)$$

where $i = 1, ...h_x$, $j = 1, ...h_y$, and q is equal to $3 \times (255/10)^2$. Here, 3 represents the number of channels, and 255 is the difference between the maximum and minimum color channel values.

Fig. 5. Red, Green, and Blue regions represent the ground truth head bounding box, the probable body region and ground truth body bounding box respectively. (Color figure online)

Second, to differentiate between more matching pixels and less matching pixels, the proportion of difference is calculated using (6). The pixels which have difference Q less than a tolerance value $t_2 = 0.1$ (10% color difference is allowed) are counted and compared to the number of total pixels. $M_h(x,y)$ gives the matching score of pixel (x,y) with the head h. The higher value means more matching score.

$$M_h(x,y) = 1/(h_x \times h_y) \times \sum_{i=1}^{h_x}\sum_{j=1}^{h_y}(Q(x,y,i,j) < t_2) \qquad (6)$$

Steps of calculation of pixel matching are repeated for all heads and their respective probable body centers, using Eqs. (5) and (6).

The distance of the pixel from the head center $(Hcenter_x, Hcenter_y)$ and probable body center $(PBcenter_x, PBcenter_y)$ plays an important role in the selection of that pixel as being a part of the body. Eqs. (7) and (8) are used to calculate the proportionate distance of pixel at location (x,y) from the head center and probable body center.

$$F_h(x,y) = 1/f \times (abs(x - Hcenter_x) + abs(y - Hcenter_y)) \qquad (7)$$

where f = Width of head × Height of head, and

$$G_h(x,y) = 1/g \times (abs(x - PBcenter_x) + abs(y - PBcenter_y)) \qquad (8)$$

where g = Width of Probable Body Region × Height of Probable Body Region.

Then the overall relationship $R(x,y,h)$ between each pixel at location (x,y) in the search space and the head h is calculated, using (9).

$$R(x,y,h) = a_2 \times M_h(x,y)/(F_h(x,y) \times G_h(x,y)) \qquad (9)$$

a_2 assigns the probability of a pixel becoming part of the body, based on its position relevant to the head. a_2 is selected as 0.05 for all pixels above the head. Otherwise, 1, to give the least importance to the pixels above the head. Parameters f, g and a_2 and Eqs. (7), (8) and (9) can be merged together for simplifying the calculation, but they have been identified separately, to discuss steps in detail.

Each pixel is assigned to a head with which it has maximum relation. $H(x,y)$ lists the head index h with maximum relation R at each pixel location (x,y).

$$H(x,y) = \operatorname*{argmax}_{h} R(x,y,h) \qquad (10)$$

Figure 6 shows the final body pixels selected from all the significant pixels. Each of these pixels is assigned to a head, based on the value of Eq. (10). Once each pixel is assigned a head, then the pixels belonging to the same head are grouped together. The locations of all grouped pixels are used to calculate the bounding box limits of the body.

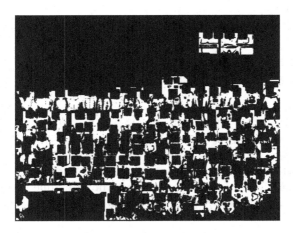

Fig. 6. Selected body pixels from all the significant pixels.

4   Dataset

The Spectator Hockey (S-HOCK) dataset [21] is used for the analysis of this technique. To the best of our knowledge, it is the only publicly available dataset for spectator crowd. The dataset consists of videos of 15 different matches with 5 different camera angles. Each video is of 31-s duration made up of 930 frames. Each frame has a resolution of 1280 × 1024 pixels, with around 150 people per frame. A sample frame is shown in Fig. 1. The 930 frames from a single camera view of each match video (930 × 15) have been annotated with head and body bounding box values. Out of the 15 videos, 2 are provided for training, 2 for validation and 11 for testing.

5   Experiments

Experiments are performed on image frames extracted from testing videos of the S-HOCK dataset. There is too much redundancy in 930 frames per 31-s duration. Therefore, out of 930 frames from each of the 11 testing videos, only 1 out of 10 frames are extracted, so making it a total of 1023(93 × 11) frames. The total number of annotated heads in these frames is 155081, so on average there are 151 people per frame.

The value of s_d, i.e. search space region dimension, is chosen based on the dataset body height. It is estimated that the height of only body region, i.e. excluding the head, is around 90 pixels. Therefore, experiments were performed for two different values of the s_d i.e. 81 × 81 and 101 × 101. This dimension is almost double the size of the head dimension. This shows that even if there is a slight mismatch in detected head location and the ground truth, the results will not be affected much.

6   Results

Accurately detected body bounding boxes which have an intersection over union (IoU) overlap with the ground truth of more than 0.5 are considered accurate. Results of the accurately detected number of people in each of the 1023 testing frame are shown in Fig. 7. Comparing with the ground truth people count, it shows that a high percentage of people are accurately detected in each frame. Detecting heads is not the focus of this paper, therefore the proposed technique cannot be directly compared with the existing full body detection techniques with no prior information. Instead we compare the technique with grid prior i.e. the seating arrangement of the spectator crowd, based results. Since the spectator crowd [21] seats in a specific grid arrangement, the benchmark experiment utilizes the seating arrangement grid information as an input. Since we initiate with ground truth heads, there are no false positives and precision is 1 for our technique. Table 1 shows the benchmark results compared with our detection scores, without precision values. The results show that our recall and f1 score is higher than the grid prior based body detection. High scores show that color matching technique can be used successfully for locating bodies in crowd scenes. Once the pixels are grouped into a body, then shape-based object detection techniques may be further applied for improving the detection.

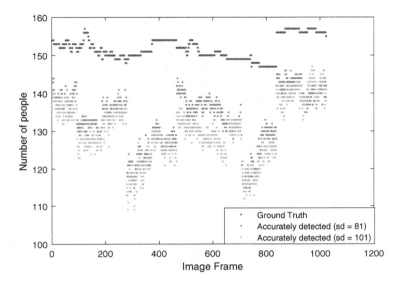

Fig. 7. Accurately detected bodies using different values of s_d, compared with the actual count of people per frame.

Table 1. Comparison of results

Method	Recall	f1 score
With grid prior [21]		
HOG + SVM [3]	0.709	0.684
HASC + SVM [20]	0.685	0.469
ACF [6]	0.649	0.580
DPM [4]	0.618	0.502
CUBD [5]	0.553	0.581
With head information		
Ours ($s_d = 81$)	0.877	0.935
Ours ($s_d = 101$)	0.856	0.922

7   Conclusion

Spectator crowd is a special type of crowd which has a high number of people, with less movement. The body movement-based head and body detection techniques are not practical for such a crowd. The spectator crowd images may have low resolution and occluded bodies. Techniques for detecting bodies in the spectator crowd should be robust to low resolutions and varying occlusion. The heads in crowd scenes are relatively more visible than the occluded body parts, therefore the head detection is relatively easier than the body detection. Leveraging the high head detection accuracy of existing techniques, we propose a robust technique for full-body detection under severe occlusion. The proposed technique does not rely on body parts detection, however, it uses color matching for body pixels. The pixels which are more similar to their neighborhood are grouped into a full body. This technique detects occluded bodies, irrelevant to the level of occlusion and resolution.

References

1. Alyammahi, S., Bhaskar, H., Ruta, D., Al-Mualla, M.: People detection and articulated pose estimation framework for crowded scenes. Knowl.-Based Syst. **131**, 83–104 (2017)
2. Cao, Z., Simon, T., Wei, S., Sheikh, Y.: Realtime multi-person 2D pose estimation using part affinity fields. In: 2017 IEEE Conference on Computer Vision and Pattern Recognition (CVPR), pp. 1302–1310, July 2017
3. Dalal, N., Triggs, B.: Histograms of oriented gradients for human detection. In: 2005 IEEE Computer Society Conference on Computer Vision and Pattern Recognition (CVPR 2005), vol. 1, pp. 886–893, June 2005
4. Dollár, P., Appel, R., Belongie, S., Perona, P.: Fast feature pyramids for object detection. IEEE Trans. Pattern Anal. Mach. Intell. **36**(8), 1532–1545 (2014)
5. Eichner, M., Marin-Jimenez, M., Zisserman, A., Ferrari, V.: 2D articulated human pose estimation and retrieval in (almost) unconstrained still images. Int. J. Comput. Vis. **99**(2), 190–214 (2012)
6. Felzenszwalb, P.F., Girshick, R.B., McAllester, D., Ramanan, D.: Object detection with discriminatively trained part-based models. IEEE Trans. Pattern Anal. Mach. Intell. **32**(9), 1627–1645 (2010)
7. Hu, P., Ramanan, D.: Finding tiny faces. In: 2017 IEEE Conference on Computer Vision and Pattern Recognition (CVPR), pp. 1522–1530, July 2017
8. Insafutdinov, E., Pishchulin, L., Andres, B., Andriluka, M., Schiele, B.: Deepercut: A deeper, stronger, and faster multi-person pose estimation model. CoRR abs/1605.03170 (2016)
9. Jan, Y., Sohel, F., Shiratuddin, M.F., Wong, K.W.: WNet: joint multiple head detection and head pose estimation from a spectator crowd image. In: Carneiro, G., You, S. (eds.) ACCV 2018. LNCS, vol. 11367, pp. 484–493. Springer, Cham (2019). https://doi.org/10.1007/978-3-030-21074-8_38
10. Lee, M.W., Cohen, I.: A model-based approach for estimating human 3D poses in static images. IEEE Trans. Pattern Anal. Mach. Intell. **28**(6), 905–916 (2006)
11. Li, J., Liang, X., Wei, Y., Xu, T., Feng, J., Yan, S.: Perceptual generative adversarial networks for small object detection. In: 2017 IEEE Conference on Computer Vision and Pattern Recognition (CVPR), pp. 1951–1959, July 2017
12. Li, M., Zhou, Z., Li, J., Liu, X.: Bottom-up pose estimation of multiple person with bounding box constraint. CoRR abs/1807.09972 (2018)
13. Li, S., Fang, Z., Song, W.F., Hao, A.M., Qin, H.: Bidirectional optimization coupled lightweight networks for efficient and robust multi-person 2D pose estimation. J. Comput. Sci. Technol. **34**(3), 522–536 (2019)

14. Ouyang, W., Wang, X.: A discriminative deep model for pedestrian detection with occlusion handling. In: 2012 IEEE Conference on Computer Vision and Pattern Recognition, pp. 3258–3265, June 2012
15. Pishchulin, L., et al.: Deepcut: joint subset partition and labeling for multi person pose estimation. In: 2016 IEEE Conference on Computer Vision and Pattern Recognition (CVPR), pp. 4929–4937, June 2016
16. Ranjan, R., Patel, V.M., Chellappa, R.: Hyperface: a deep multi-task learning framework for face detection, landmark localization, pose estimation, and gender recognition. IEEE Trans. Pattern Anal. Mach. Intell. **41**, 1–1 (2018)
17. Ranjan, R., Sankaranarayanan, S., Castillo, C.D., Chellappa, R.: An all-in-one convolutional neural network for face analysis. In: 2017 12th IEEE International Conference on Automatic Face Gesture Recognition (FG 2017), pp. 17–24, May 2017
18. Ren, S., He, K., Girshick, R., Sun, J.: Faster R-CNN: Towards real-time object detection with region proposal networks. IEEE Trans. Pattern Anal. Mach. Intell. **39**(6), 1137–1149 (2017)
19. Rodriguez, M., Laptev, I., Sivic, J., Audibert, J.: Density-aware person detection and tracking in crowds. In: 2011 International Conference on Computer Vision, pp. 2423–2430, November 2011
20. San, M., Crocco, M., Cristani, M., Martelli, S., Murino, V.: Heterogeneous auto-similarities of characteristics (HASC): exploiting relational information for classification. In: 2013 IEEE International Conference on Computer Vision, pp. 809–816, December 2013
21. Setti, F., et al.: The s-hock dataset: a new benchmark for spectator crowd analysis. Comput. Vis. Image Underst. **159**(Supplement C), 47–58 (2017)
22. Tian, Y., Luo, P., Wang, X., Tang, X.: Deep learning strong parts for pedestrian detection. In: 2015 IEEE International Conference on Computer Vision (ICCV), pp. 1904–1912, December 2015
23. Wang, X., Xiao, T., Jiang, Y., Shao, S., Sun, J., Shen, C.: Repulsion loss: Detecting pedestrians in a crowd. CoRR abs/1711.07752 (2017)
24. Wen, Y.H., Gao, L., Fu, H., Zhang, F.L., Xia, S.: Graph CNNs with motif and variable temporal block for skeleton-based action recognition. In: Proceedings of the AAAI Conference on Artificial Intelligence (2019)
25. Wu, B., Nevatia, R.: Detection and tracking of multiple, partially occluded humans by bayesian combination of edgelet based part detectors. Int. J. Comput. Vis. **75**(2), 247–266 (2007)
26. Zhan, B., Monekosso, D.N., Remagnino, P., Velastin, S.A., Xu, L.Q.: Crowd analysis: a survey. Mach. Vis. Appl. **19**(5), 345–357 (2008)
27. Zhang, S., Wen, L., Bian, X., Lei, Z., Li, S.Z.: Occlusion-aware R-CNN: detecting pedestrians in a crowd. In: Ferrari, V., Hebert, M., Sminchisescu, C., Weiss, Y. (eds.) ECCV 2018. LNCS, vol. 11207, pp. 657–674. Springer, Cham (2018). https://doi.org/10.1007/978-3-030-01219-9_39
28. Zhou, C., Yuan, J.: Learning to integrate occlusion-specific detectors for heavily occluded pedestrian detection. In: Lai, S.-H., Lepetit, V., Nishino, K., Sato, Y. (eds.) ACCV 2016. LNCS, vol. 10112, pp. 305–320. Springer, Cham (2017). https://doi.org/10.1007/978-3-319-54184-6_19

Deep Learning for Breast Region and Pectoral Muscle Segmentation in Digital Mammography

Kaier Wang$^{(\boxtimes)}$, Nabeel Khan, Ariane Chan, Jonathan Dunne,
and Ralph Highnam

Volpara Health Technologies Ltd, Wellington, New Zealand
{kyle.wang,nabeel.khan,ariane.chan,jonathan.dunne,
ralph.highnam}@volparasolutions.com

Abstract. The accurate segmentation of a mammogram into different anatomical regions, such as breast or pectoral muscle, is a critical step in automated breast image analysis. This paper evaluates the performance of u-net deep learning architecture on segmenting breast area and pectoral muscle from digital mammograms and digital breast tomosynthesis. To minimise the image variations due to vendor and modality specifications, Volpara^{TM} algorithm was used to normalise the raw image to a unity representation that is independent of imaging conditions. Four factors and their interactions were investigated for their effects on the performance of u-net segmentation: image normalisation; zero and extrapolated padding techniques for image size standarisation; different contrast between breast and background; and image resolution. By training u-net on 2,000 normalised images, we obtained median dice-similarity coefficients of 0.8879 and 0.9919, respectively for pectoral and breast segmentations from 825 testing images. The model training speed was boosted by using down sampled images without compromising segmentation accuracy. Using normalised breast images by Volpara^{TM} algorithm, u-net was able to perform robust segmentation of breast area and pectoral muscle.

Keywords: Mammography · Pectoral segmentation · Breast segmentation · U-Net · Volpara

1 Introduction

Digital mammography (DM) is a medical imaging technique that uses low-dose x-rays to generate two-dimensional (2D) images of the internal breast structure, for breast cancer screening and diagnosis. Digital breast tomosynthesis (DBT) is a recent advancement in mammography, whereby a series of low-dose x-ray projections are captured at varying angles and reconstructed to generate three-dimensional (3D) images of the breast. In breast cancer screening, both the 2D and 3D images are heavily processed by proprietary algorithms to facilitate

© Springer Nature Switzerland AG 2019
C. Lee et al. (Eds.): PSIVT 2019, LNCS 11854, pp. 78–91, 2019.
https://doi.org/10.1007/978-3-030-34879-3_7

radiologists' visualization of breast tissues and structures in their search for abnormalities. Automated breast image analysis is a rapidly evolving field that can augment the work of radiologists, with technologies that can, for example, detect and characterize breast lesions or quantify breast tissue composition. In current work, the central slice is used for analysis, because the central slice is similar to a conventional 2D mammogram and is being used for automated diagnosis [2, 6].

Screening DM or DBT often involves obtaining two views of each breast, i.e. a craniocaudal (CC) and mediolateral oblique (MLO) of each breast side. Although the pectoral muscle is visible in approximately a third of CC views [3], the pectoral muscle should be visible in all standard MLO views, and it is the MLO view that is the focus of this work. Accurate breast image analysis requires the pectoral muscle to be reliably segmented from the rest of the breast tissue. However, this is a challenging task, not only because pectoral muscle and the fibroglandular (dense) tissue in the breast have similar x-ray attenuation properties (i.e. they have a homogeneous pixel intensity), but also due to the different post-processing algorithms used by each x-ray vendor, artefacts, and low contrast along the skin-air interface. Furthermore, depending on a woman's individual anatomy and breast positioning differences, the pectoral muscle can have quite varied appearances (e.g. covex/straight/concave shapes, and differences in widths, angles, the proportion of the breast that the pectoral muscle occupies, and textures). Regardless, removal of both background and pectoral muscle during pre-processing steps is critical and allows for a cleaner exposure of dense tissue for automated quantification of breast density and lesion detection.

Segmentation of the outer breast region is mainly affected by noisy backgrounds (in heterogeneous pixel value distribution) i.e. artefacts (e.g. presence of medical labels, non-target body parts, and compression paddles). Furthermore, the discernibility of breast anatomy and fibroglandular structures can be significantly reduced at the low x-ray doses used in both DM and DBT [23], due to the low contrast at the skin-air interface, which increases the possibility of over-segmentation to the breast tissue at key anatomical landmarks in the breast such as the nipple and the inframammary fold area (IMF). It is worth mentioning that the Mammographic Image Analysis Society (MIAS) database [25] has been widely used in the breast imaging studies. The images in MIAS database are digitized film mammograms and were down-sampled to 200 microns. Nowadays digital imaging technologies predominate breast screening, so it is more feasible to develop algorithms capable of processing the Raw mammographic image directly streamed from the x-ray modality (i.e. before any image processing applied by the x-ray manufacturers).

For pectoral segmentation, the classical Hough transform is often utilised to approximate the pectoral muscle edge as a straight line. The straight line is then converted to a smooth curve, which represents the pectoral boundary [11, 15, 28]. Other commonly used conventional methods include thresholding [15, 18], active contour [30, 31], edge enhancement [7, 13]. These methods generally work well when the pectoral muscle is fully visible and well separated from other breast tissue. In one study, Chen *et al.* [5] incorporated *region growing* for pectoral muscle segmentation. Region growing examines neighboring pixels of initial points (referred as seed points) in an iterative fashion and determines whether the pixel neighbors should be added to the region. The breast boundary was first extracted using histogram thresholding and then refined using contours to segment the breast region from the background. The seed point was selected along the pectoral muscle and the breast tissue boundary followed by region growing to segment the pectoral. The authors performed a qualitative analysis and reported an acceptable segmentation in 93.5% out of 240 mammograms for pectoral muscle separation. In another similar work, Raba *et al.* [18] performed breast orientation followed by region growing to segment the pectoral muscle, resulting in a 86% 'good' extraction out of 320 mammograms. The proposed methods are promising, but Raba *et al.* claim an over–segmentation issue when the contrast between the muscle and the dense tissue is fuzzy.

One work proposed combining a few metrics, such as position or intensity for pectoral segmentation [16]. The proposed method models the probability of a pixel to belong to background, breast, or pectoral muscle based on its position, intensity, and texture information. The authors reported a dice similarity coefficient (DSC) of 0.83 on 149 images for pectoral muscle segmentation. This approach also suffers, when the pectoral muscle starts overlapping with the breast tissue.

In the past few years, deep convolutional neural networks (CNNs) have demonstrated tremendous success in the medical imaging field [29], including in lesion detection and diagnosis [26]. A number of studies have shown the potential of CNNs in mammography. Petersen *et al.* [17] and Kallenberg *et al.* [10] presented a pixel-wise classifier for breast mass segmentation. Ribli *et al.* [19] developed a CNN that outperforms manual classification of malignant or benign lesions on a mammogram. Further, CNNs have shown superior performance in classifying breast density categories for cancer risk prediction in recent studies [1,12,14].

Among various CNN architectures, u-net is designed especially for medical image segmentations [22] and has demonstrated its utility via its successful implementation in segmenting neuron structures, or tracking microscopic time series of living cells [21]. In a subsequent work by Rodriguez-Ruiz *et al.*, they trained u-net over 136 breast tomosynthesis images for breast area and pectoral muscle segmentations [20]. The trained u-net achieved a DSC greater than 0.97 between model prediction and ground truth on 161 breast images. The study was limited to two manufacturers (Hologic and Siemens) and did not investigate the impact of any pre-processing technique, such as resolution. The pre-processing can influence the robustness of a deep learning model [27].

Our study further expands on the work by Rodriguez-Ruiz *et al.* with two additional contributions as outlined below:

1. An examination of the robustness of u-net in a larger dataset of DM and DBT images (over 2,000 images) from a range of different x-ray vendors.
2. An investigation of the effects of several imaging factors on u-net performance:

- image normalisation
- zero and extrapolated image paddings
- contrast between target object and background
- image resolution

To our knowledge, it is the first study to evaluate the effects of these image factors on the performance of u-net for breast area and pectoral segmentation. Since u-net follows the CNN framework, our discoveries may be applicable to other CNNs.

2   Method

2.1   Data

The breast is mainly composed of fatty and fibroglandular tissues. The fibroglandular tissue appears brighter on mammograms because it attenuates x-rays to a greater extent than fatty tissue. The American College of Radiology has developed a BI-RADS (Breast Imaging-Reporting and Data System, 5th Edition) to give an indication of the breast composition [24]. There are four categories; BI-RADS A (The breasts are almost entirely fatty), BI-RADS B (There are scattered areas of fibroglandular density), BI-RADS C (The breasts are heterogeneously dense, which may obscure small masses), and BI-RADS D (The breasts are extremely dense, which lowers the sensitivity of mammography). Pectoral segmentation becomes challenging, particularly for BI-RADS C–D categories, because the pectoral muscle often overlaps with the breast tissue.

In this work 2,825 Raw MLO images (2,671 DM and 154 DBT) were obtained. Our dataset had a distribution of at least 15% MLO images in each BI-RADS category. 2,000 images were randomly selected for training and the remaining 825 were used for testing. The modality and manufacturer distributions of the data are summarised in Tables 1 and 2. Each image had a corresponding ground truth mask indicating the regions of breast area and pectoral muscle. The masks were created by overlaying a segmentation line (generated by the Volpara^{TM} algorithm [9], Volpara Health Technologies, Ltd., Wellington, New Zealand) onto a processed image (i.e. the raw image transformed to increase the contrast within the breast and enhance the breast edge). The segmentation lines were then confirmed for accuracy by a reviewer who had been trained by imaging scientist specialising in mammography. Where the reviewer disagreed with the segmentation, the pectoral muscle was outlined manually and the pixel co-ordinates recorded.

Table 1. Summary of image modalities

Training		Testing	
DM	DBT	DM	DBT
1888	112	783	42

Table 2. Summary of imaging system manufacturers

System	Training	Tesing	System	Training	Testing
FujiAres	3	1	MediFuture	3	1
FujiAspire	0	4	MediFutureSoul	5	2
FujiCR	195	95	Metaltronica	9	2
GE	1133	460	PlanmedNuance	5	2
GEPristina	2	0	Sectra	14	11
GEPristinaTomo	42	9	SectraMDM15	10	7
GETomo	3	3	SiemensInspiration	391	155
Hologic	110	36	SiemensNovation	7	7
HologicTomo	66	27	SiemensTomo	1	3
ImsGiotto	1	0			

2.2 Data Pre-processing

Data pre-processing is an important step in any learning procedure [8]. In some cases, the pre-processing corrects the image deficiencies such as noise and arte-facts. In other cases, the pre-processing alters the image presentation (such as rescaling, or cropping) for optimised training [27]. The data pre-processing techniques used in our study are discussed below.

Image Normalisation. Although DM and DBT images are fundamentally radiation attenuation maps, the Display images (i.e. the images used for radiologist interpretation) vary significantly across different modalities and manufacturers since there is an inconsistency not only in the processing algorithms applied to the Raw images, the image acquisition (e.g. lower dose per projection on DBT) factors also lead to differences in the raw and display images. For example, Figs. 1(a) and (b) show different modality presentations for the same breast (i.e. DM versus DBT images). Varying image contrast is also demonstrated in Figs. 2(a) and (b), where the same breast has been imaged on different manufacturer x-ray systems.

We used the Volpara^{TM} algorithm [9] to normalise the Raw image to a dense tissue map, where the pixel value represents the dense tissue thickness. Normalisation mitigates some of the issues that can arise when using processed display images from varying manufacturers, for applications such as CNN training datasets. Examples of images normalised using the Volpara^{TM} algorithm are shown in Figs. 1(c) and (d) and Figs. 2(c) and (d).

Padding. Most CNNs require the input images to share the same size and aspect ratio [1,27]. The size of DM and DBT images depends on the imaging detector, which is variable across different units. Usually images are padded or cropped to achieve a uniform size and aspect ratio. Padding is often preferable to cropping, since cropping may remove important tissue information at the image edge. In this study, we compared two padding techniques: (1) zero and (2) extrapolated paddings. Figure 3(**a**) shows a breast image being zero padded to its right-hand side to match the width of other images in the dataset. Zero padding simply adds zero-value pixels and leads to a stark distinction between the actual image background and the padding. Figure 3(**b**) shows extrapolated padding of the image background, whereby the padding was resized from a portion of the background and further Gaussian filtered to blend into the original image.

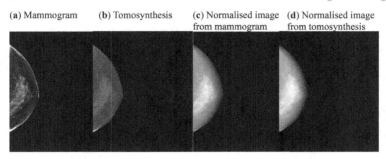

Fig. 1. The presentations of (**a**) mammogram and (**b**) tomosyhthesis for the same breast. Their respective Volapra normalisations in (**c**) and (**d**) show better consistency.

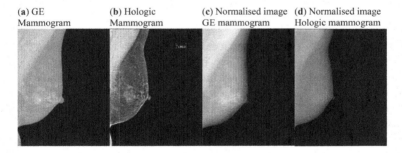

Fig. 2. The presentations of (**a**) GE and (**b**) Hologic mammograms for the same breast. The Volpara normalisation removed manufacturer-specific imaging conditions, yielding almost identical breast representation shown in (**c**) and (**d**).

Contrast. The breast image has two monochrome representations: (1) a negative image, where the breast area intensity is lower than the background intensity (see Fig. 4(**a**)); and (2) a positive image, where the breast area intensity is greater than the background intensity (see Fig. 4(**b**)).

Scaling. Down-scaling is another critical step in the pre-processing of training images. In our study, the breast area and pectoral muscle are relatively large objects compared to image size. Thus, it is feasible to use an abstracted image by reducing the image resolution for faster training. We applied two down-scaling settings, 0.5 and 0.25, to the DM and DBT images.

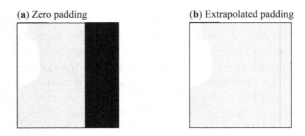

(a) Zero padding   **(b)** Extrapolated padding

Fig. 3. Demonstration of (**a**) zero and (**b**) extrapolated paddings. The image contrast was adjusted for better visualisation of the background and padding effects.

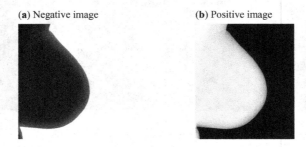

(a) Negative image   **(b)** Positive image

Fig. 4. Same breast image in its (**a**) negative and (**b**) positive representations.

Image Pre-processing Combinations. In summary, we applied the four main pre-processing factors described above in various combinations (as detailed in Table 3) and investigated their impact on u-net performance. Normalised images were those processed by Volpara^{TM} algorithm, then padded to the same size. For a comparative analysis, we also experimented with non-normalised (Raw) images. Considering the 4 different imaging factors, there are a total of 16 different comparison experiments that can be performed. Our prior investigation discovered that the image type and monochrome are the primary factors on u-net performance. So we only showed a subset of experiment results here for simplicity.

Table 3. Summary of image pre-processing

Setting	Image type	Monochrome	Padding	Down-scaling
1	Normalised image	Positive	Extrapolated	0.50
2	Normalised image	Positive	Zero	0.50
3	Normalised image	Negative	Extrapolated	0.50
4	Normalised image	Negative	Zero	0.50
5	Normalised image	Negative	Zero	0.25
6	Raw image	Negative	Zero	0.50
7	Raw image	Positive	Zero	0.50

2.3   U-Net Architecture

The winning challengers of the ISBI (IEEE International Symposium on Biomedical Imaging) 2015 challenge, to segment dental x-ray images and microscopic time series of living cells, demonstrated the potential of u-net for successful biomedical image segmentation [21]. As seen in Fig. 5, the coupled contracting and expansive paths allow a combination of high-resolution features and output, assembling a more precise pixel label localisation, as compared to CNNs with contracting paths only.

The highlights of u-net are its adaptability to image deformation and its capability to separate touching objects of the same class. The latter is especially useful in the pectoral muscle segmentation since pectoral muscle and fibroglandular tissue appear adjacent or overlapping on DM or DBT and have similar intensity.

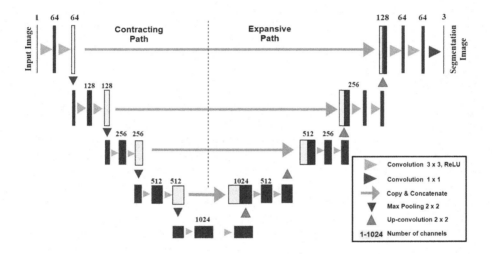

Fig. 5. Diagram of u-net architecture.

All 2,825 MLO images were pre-processed using the settings illustrated in Table 3, yielding seven independent datasets. In each dataset, the images were split into training and testing categories as described in Table 2, such that the training and testing images across different datasets were comparable. U-net was then trained on each of the seven datasets.

2.4   Analysis

The performance of the u-net was evaluated in terms of the breast area and pectoral muscle segmentation accuracy on the testing data. In this study, we used a dice similarity coefficient (DSC, see Eq. (1)) to measure how close the u-net prediction of the segmentations were to the ground truth. In Eq. (1), $Obj^{u\text{-net}}$ and Obj^{Truth} are the u-net prediction and ground truth of an object of interest in the image, respectively. The DSC can also be expressed in terms of true positives (TP), false positives (FP) and false negatives (FN) as in Eq. (2).

$$DSC = \frac{2|Obj^{u\text{-net}} \cap Obj^{Truth}|}{|Obj^{u\text{-net}}| + |Obj^{Truth}|} \tag{1}$$

$$DSC = 2 * TP/(2 * TP + FP + FN) \tag{2}$$

The DSC score ranges between 0 and 1 where 1 indicates a perfect pixel-wise match between prediction and ground truth.

ANOVA was applied to the DSCs to test the null hypothesis that the DSC mean of each setting is the same versus the alternative hypothesis that at least one DSC mean is different from others. The same ANOVA procedure was applied to both pectoral and breast segmentation DSCs. Subsequently, a Tukey pairwise comparison test was performed to find the setting that resulted in the leading u-net performance.

3   Results

The u-net performance on each segmentation task are illustrated as DSC box-plots in Fig. 6, and median DSC scores are shown in Table 4. For pectoral segmentation, settings 3, 4, and 5 gave the highest DSC median scores; however, setting 3 had the lowest DSC median score on the breast area segmentation and completely failed in locating the breast (i.e. u-net labelled the entire image as breast). Settings 1, 2, 4, 5, and 7 had comparably high DSC median scores for the breast area segmentation task. Setting 6 performed poorly at segmenting the pectoral muscle, with u-net labelling the entire image as pectoral.

ANOVA returned p-values less than 0.05 for both pectoral and breast area segmentation, supporting the alternative hypothesis that at least one DSC mean is different from the others. Figure 7 illustrates the Tukey results from 21 (i.e. 7 choose 2) pairwise comparison of DSC means. For either segmentation task, the settings are arranged in ascending order with respect to their DSC mean. The Tukey results show that settings 4 and 5 have the highest DSC means, and their means are not significantly different from each other at a 5% experiment-wise significance level. In other words, the u-net trained by either setting 4 or 5 would result in a similar performance. Recalling the pre-processing settings in Table 3, both settings 4 and 5 correspond to normalised image, negative monochrome (breast area intensity smaller than background intensity) and zero paddings, while the only difference is their down-scaling factors. Hence, it would be optimal to choose setting 5, because lower resolution images impose less pressure on memory and provide faster training speed.

Table 4. Summary of DSC statistics (medians and interquartile range) for u-net segmentation with different pre-processing settings specified in Table 3. The Setting Code column describes each setting, i.e. Norm = normalized; Raw = Raw (non-normalized); Pos = monochrome positive; Neg = monochrome negative; Zero = zero padding; Ex = extrapolated padding; 0.5 = 0.5 scaling; 0.25 = 0.25 scaling.

Setting	Setting code	Pectoral		Breast	
		DSC Median	DSC IQR	DSC Median	DSC IQR
1	NormPosEx0.5	0.5508	0.2010	0.9951	0.0124
2	NormPosZero0.5	0.6186	0.2057	0.9945	0.0194
3	NormNegEx0.5	0.8737	0.1390	0.3513	0.1503
4	NormNegZero0.5	0.8893	0.1315	0.9967	0.0046
5	NormNegZero0.25	0.8879	0.1361	0.9919	0.0072
6	RawNegZero0.5	0.1926	0.1263	0.6089	0.1976
7	RawPosZero0.5	0.7197	0.2043	0.9861	0.0247

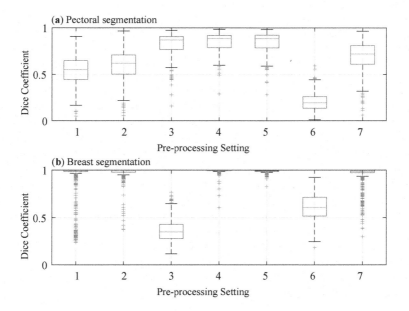

Fig. 6. Boxplots of DSCs for (a) pectoral and (b) breast segmentations across different pre-processing settings defined in Table 3.

From Fig. 7, we can see that settings 6 and 7 (Raw images) fall behind settings 4 and 5 (normalised images) in both segmentation tasks, which highlights the advantage of the normalised image over the Raw image in training. The effect of monochrome can be determined by comparing settings 1 (normalised/positive/extrapolated/0.5) versus 3 (normalised/negative/extrapolated

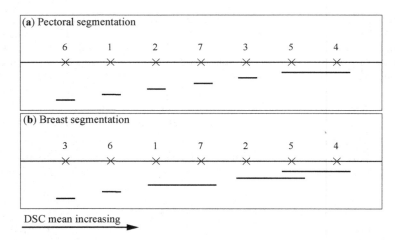

Fig. 7. Tukey underlining diagram for pair-wise DSC comparisons between different pre-processing settings for (**a**) pectoral and (**b**) breast segmentations. The mean DSCs from settings with a common underline do not differ significantly at the 5% level. The settings are placed according to their mean DSC scores in an ascending order from left to right.

/0.5) and settings 2 (normalised/positive/ zero/0.5) versus 4 (normalised/ negative/ zero/0.5). For pectoral segmentation, settings 3 and 4 are significantly better than settings 1 and 2, indicating the need for negative monochrome. For breast area segmentation, setting 4 is significantly better than setting 2 (as noted earlier, setting 3 failed completely in segmenting the breast). As a result, u-net training would benefit from using negative images.

Lastly, by allowing image normalisation the padding effect is examined by comparing settings 1 versus 2 for positive monochrome, and settings 3 versus 4 for negative monochrome. From the Tukey analysis, it is clear that setting 4 of zero padding yields the highest DSC score.

Therefore, the most optimal pre-processing setting in this study include image normalisation, negative monochrome, zero padding and a rather small down-scaling factor 0.25 (i.e. 1 mm per pixel). Some examples of u-net segmentation with the chosen setting are shown in Fig. 8.

(a) Examples of pectoral DSC > 0.90

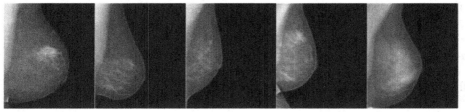

(b) Examples of pectoral DSC < 0.80

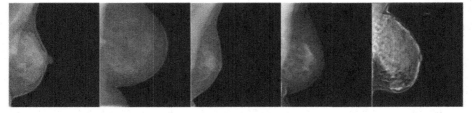

Fig. 8. Exmples of u-net segmentations for pectoral (in green) and breast (in red) using pre-processing setting 5 (explained in Table 3). The top row shows five examples of pectoral DSC > 0.90, and bottom row shows another five examples of pectoral DSC < 0.80. (Color figure online)

4   Conclusion and Discussions

In this study, we investigated the effects of different image pre-processing techniques on the performance of u-net for segmenting pectoral muscle and breast area from DM and DBT images from a range of manufacturers. We used raw rather than display images in this study. Because the display images are highly variable between modalities and manufacturers. They are synthetic alteration of the raw images, so it may not be possible to further normalise the display image. The results demonstrated that the u-net performance was improved by training with normalised, negative monochrome images that have been padded with zeros to standardise their size. Further, we found the training of u-net is robust to low resolution images, which can facilitate optimisation of the training speed and memory usage. Being trained on 2,000 images with the optimal setting, out of 825 testing images the u-net achieved a median DSC of 0.8879 in pectoral segmentation and 0.9919 in breast segmentation.

Meanwhile, we noticed two segmentation failures. U-net failed in segmenting the pectoral after being trained with negative raw images with zero padding; it also failed in segmenting breast after being trained with negative normalised images with extrapolated padding. We argue that the negative raw image has poor contrast between the pectoral muscle and dense tissue, which may make it more challenging for u-net to extract valid descriptive features of the pectoral muscle. The Volpara^{TM} normalisation creates an anatomical map describing the actual tissue thickness independent of imaging conditions. Using this technique, the contrast between breast tissue and pectoral muscle is naturally enhanced. Hence, u-net trained on normalised images is able to locate the pectoral muscle better than when trained on Raw images. However, the extrapolated padding may increase the complexity of the background, which probably explains the failed breast segmentation. In future work, we will systematically investigate these failures, and we will compare the classification performance of u-net with other popular CNNs such as deepLab [4].

References

1. Ahn, C.K., Heo, C., Jin, H., Kim, J.H.: A novel deep learning-based approach to high accuracy breast density estimation in digital mammography. In: Armato, S.G., Petrick, N.A. (eds.) Medical Imaging 2017: Computer-Aided Diagnosis (2017)
2. Ariaratnam, N.S., Little, S.T., Whitley, M.A., Ferguson, K.: Digital breast tomosynthesis vacuum assisted biopsy for tomosynthesis-detected sonographically occult lesions. Clin. Imaging **47**, 4–8 (2018)
3. Camilus, K.S., Govindan, V.K., Sathidevi, P.S.: Computer-aided identification of the pectoral muscle in digitized mammograms. J. Digit. Imaging **23**(5), 562–580 (2009)
4. Chen, L.-C., Zhu, Y., Papandreou, G., Schroff, F., Adam, H.: Encoder-decoder with atrous separable convolution for semantic image segmentation. In: Ferrari, V., Hebert, M., Sminchisescu, C., Weiss, Y. (eds.) ECCV 2018. LNCS, vol. 11211, pp. 833–851. Springer, Cham (2018). https://doi.org/10.1007/978-3-030-01234-2_49
5. Chen, Z., Zwiggelaar, R.: Segmentation of the breast region with pectoral muscle removal in mammograms (2010)
6. Ekpo, E.U., McEntee, M.F.: Measurement of breast density with digital breast tomosynthesis—a systematic review. Br. J. Radiol. **87**(1043), 20140460 (2014)
7. Ferrari, R., Rangayyan, R., Desautels, J., Borges, R., Frere, A.: Automatic identification of the pectoral muscle in mammograms. IEEE Trans. Med. Imaging **23**(2), 232–245 (2004)
8. García, S., Luengo, J., Herrera, F.: Data Preprocessing in Data Mining, vol. 72. Springer, Cham (2015). https://doi.org/10.1007/978-3-319-10247-4
9. Highnam, R., Brady, M.: Mammographic Image Analysis. Computational Imaging and Vision. Springer, Netherlands (1999). https://doi.org/10.1007/978-94-011-4613-5
10. Kallenberg, M., et al.: Unsupervised deep learning applied to breast density segmentation and mammographic risk scoring. IEEE Trans. Med. Imaging **35**(5), 1322–1331 (2016)
11. Kwok, S., Chandrasekhar, R., Attikiouzel, Y.: Automatic pectoral muscle segmentation on mammograms by straight line estimation and cliff detection. In: The Seventh Australian and New Zealand Intelligent Information Systems Conference (2001)
12. Li, S., et al.: Computer-aided assessment of breast density: comparison of supervised deep learning and feature-based statistical learning. Phys. Med. Biol. **63**(2), 025005 (2018)
13. Liu, L., Liu, Q., Lu, W.: Pectoral muscle detection in mammograms using local statistical features. J. Digit. Imaging **27**(5), 633–641 (2014)

14. Mohamed, A.A., Berg, W.A., Peng, H., Luo, Y., Jankowitz, R.C., Wu, S.: A deep learning method for classifying mammographic breast density categories. Med. Phys. **45**(1), 314–321 (2017)
15. Mustra, M., Grgic, M.: Robust automatic breast and pectoral muscle segmentation from scanned mammograms. Sig. Process. **93**(10), 2817–2827 (2013)
16. Oliver, A., Llado, X., Torrent, A., Marti, J.: One-shot segmentation of breast, pectoral muscle, and background in digitised mammograms. In: IEEE International Conference on Image Processing (2014)
17. Petersen, K., Chernoff, K., Nielsen, M., Ng, A.: Breast density scoring with multiscale denoising autoencoders. In: MICCAI Workshop on Sparsity Techniques in Medical Imaging (2012)
18. Raba, D., Oliver, A., Martí, J., Peracaula, M., Espunya, J.: Breast segmentation with pectoral muscle suppression on digital mammograms. In: Marques, J.S., Pérez de la Blanca, N., Pina, P. (eds.) IbPRIA 2005. LNCS, vol. 3523, pp. 471–478. Springer, Heidelberg (2005). https://doi.org/10.1007/11492542_58
19. Ribli, D., Horváth, A., Unger, Z., Pollner, P., Csabai, I.: Detecting and classifying lesions in mammograms with deep learning. Sci. Rep. **8**(1), 4165 (2018)
20. Rodriguez-Ruiz, A., et al.: Pectoral muscle segmentation in breast tomosynthesis with deep learning. In: Mori, K., Petrick, N. (eds.) Medical Imaging 2018: Computer-Aided Diagnosis (2018)
21. Ronneberger, O.: U-net: Convolutional networks for biomedical image segmentation. https://lmb.informatik.uni-freiburg.de/people/ronneber/u-net/. Accessed 05 Jul 2019
22. Ronneberger, O., Fischer, P., Brox, T.: U-Net: convolutional networks for biomedical image segmentation. In: Navab, N., Hornegger, J., Wells, W.M., Frangi, A.F. (eds.) MICCAI 2015. LNCS, vol. 9351, pp. 234–241. Springer, Cham (2015). https://doi.org/10.1007/978-3-319-24574-4_28
23. Smith, A.P., Niklason, L., Ren, B., Wu, T., Ruth, C., Jing, Z.: Lesion visibility in low dose tomosynthesis. In: Astley, S.M., Brady, M., Rose, C., Zwiggelaar, R. (eds.) IWDM 2006. LNCS, vol. 4046, pp. 160–166. Springer, Heidelberg (2006). https://doi.org/10.1007/11783237_23
24. Spak, D., Plaxco, J., Santiago, L., Dryden, M., Dogan, B.: BI-RADs fifth edition: a summary of changes. Diagn. Intervent. Imaging **98**(3), 179–190 (2017)
25. Suckling, J.H., et al.: Mammographic image analysis society (MIAS) database v1.21 (2015)
26. Suzuki, K.: Overview of deep learning in medical imaging. Radiol. Phys. Technol. **10**(3), 257–273 (2017)
27. Tabik, S., Peralta, D., Herrera-Poyatos, A., Herrera, F.: A snapshot of image preprocessing for convolutional neural networks: case study of MNIST. Int. J. Comput. Intell. Syst. **10**(1), 555 (2017)
28. Tzikopoulos, S.D., Mavroforakis, M.E., Georgiou, H.V., Dimitropoulos, N., Theodoridis, S.: A fully automated scheme for mammographic segmentation and classification based on breast density and asymmetry. Comput. Methods Programs Biomed. **102**(1), 47–63 (2011)
29. Voulodimos, A., Doulamis, N., Doulamis, A., Protopapadakis, E.: Deep learning for computer vision: a brief review. Comput. Intell. Neurosci. **2018**, 1–13 (2018)
30. Williams, D.J., Shah, M.: A fast algorithm for active contours and curvature estimation. CVGIP: Image Underst. **55**(1), 14–26 (1992)
31. Wirth, M., Stapinski, A.: Segmentation of the breast region in mammograms using snakes. In: IEEE First Canadian Conference on Computer and Robot Vision (2004)

Detection of Age and Defect of Grapevine Leaves Using Hyper Spectral Imaging

Tanmoy Debnath, Sourabhi Debnath, and Manoranjan Paul$^{(\boxtimes)}$

Charles Sturt University, Bathurst, Australia
{tdebnath, sdebnath, mpaul}@csu.edu.au

Abstract. This paper demonstrates the potential of using hyperspectral imaging for detecting age and defects of grapevine leaves. For age detection studies a number of grapevine healthy leaves and for defect detection analysis 9 different defective leaves have been selected. Hyperspectral images of these leaves covered spectral wavelengths from 380 nm to 1000 nm. A number of features from the brightness in ultra violet (UV), visible (VIS) and near infrared (NIR) regions were derived to obtain the correlation of age and defect. From the experimental studies it has been observed that the mean brightness in terms of original reflection in visible range has correlation with different ages of grapevine leaves. Moreover, the position of mean 1st derivative brightness peak in VIS region, variation index of brightness and rate of change of brightness i.e., mean 1st derivative brightness at NIR provide a good indication about the age of the leaves. For defect detection whole area and selective areas containing the defects on the leaves have been experimentally analysed to determine which option provides better defect detection. Variation index of brightness was also employed as a guide to obtain information to distinguish healthy and unhealthy leaves using hyperspectral imaging. The experimental results demonstrated that hyperspectral imaging has excellent potential as a non-destructive as well as a non-contact method to detect age and defects of grapevine leaves.

Keywords: Hyperspectral imaging · Grapevine leaves · Age detection · Defect

1 Introduction

Grapes are one of the most widely grown berries in the world due to their nutrition values and importance in the multibillion dollar wine industry thereby related to thousands of jobs worldwide and hence are an active area of research [1]. Grapevine leaves are source of biomolecules which have an influence on the quality and quantity of grapes. Photosynthetic performance of grapevine leaves is an important process for producing fruits both qualitatively and quantitatively [2]. The photosynthesis depends on the intensity of light, temperature as well as chlorophyll, carotenoids and other accessory molecules such as nitrogen, and protein [3–5]. The contents of chlorophyll as well as other molecules change during the life cycle of leaves. In the early stage of development contents of chlorophyll, nitrogen and protein are high in leaves, but after a period when leaves enter senescence phase, they gradually lose chlorophyll and protein. On the other hand, health of leaves also affect photosynthetic process as cellular

© Springer Nature Switzerland AG 2019
C. Lee et al. (Eds.): PSIVT 2019, LNCS 11854, pp. 92–105, 2019.
https://doi.org/10.1007/978-3-030-34879-3_8

structures of unhealthy leaves undergo changes thereby influencing grapes production [6–8]. Therefore, it is believed that an experimental study which is in the context of determining age and analysing various defects in grapevine leaves would be important and interesting to improve the general understanding in this research area.

Over the ages, researchers in Computer Science and other disciplines have utilized various image based (including but not limited to hyperspectral image methods) experimental and analytical techniques for performing investigations with different fruits and vegetables. Diseases for pomegranate, betel vine and fungal diseases in plants were detected using image processing [9–11], image segmentation and soft computing techniques were applied for detection of plant leaf diseases and effect of leaf age and psyllid damage of Eucalyptus saligna foliage [12, 13]. Additionally, head blight contamination in wheat kernels was detected by using multivariate imaging Fusarium [14]. Detection of multi-tomato leaf diseases (late blight, target and bacterial spots) in different stages by using a spectral-based sensor was also reported [15]. Early blight and late blight diseases on tomato leaves, Fusarium head blight in wheat kernels, early detection of tomato spotted wilt virus and stress were detected using hyperspectral imaging [16–19]. Hyperspectral imaging with high spectral and spatial resolutions is one of the most widely used techniques for studies in disease/defect detection in leaves. It collects both spatial and spectral information simultaneously from an object in a non-destructive and non-contact way between ultra violet (UV) and infrared (IR) regions. As a result, its high spectral resolution provides an extensive volume of information in recognizing, classifying and measuring objects [20–22]. But very few research papers are available at present that demonstrate the analysis of grapevine leaves utilizing hyperspectral imaging. This work presents an extensive experimental study to detect age and defect of grapevine leaves with the aid of hyperspectral imaging. The primary contributions of this manuscript are:

- to predict age of grapevine leaves through experimental study of both adaxial and abaxial leaf surfaces with the aid of hyperspectral imaging;
- to determine effective wavelength region for age detection;
- to obtain information for distinguishing unhealthy leaves from healthy leaves;
- to determine optimum wavelength region for defect detection;
- to introduce a new metric called the variation index that indicates the deviation of a leaf's brightness compared to a benchmark leaf which was employed for both age and defect detection studies.

This report is organized as follows: Sect. 2 details the experimental setup, Sect. 3 describes the experimental results and related in depth discussions and Sect. 4 presents the conclusion of this work.

2 Experimental Setup

A number of healthy and unhealthy grapevine leaves as presented in Fig. 1(b) were collected from a vineyard located in central west NSW, Australia. They were scanned by us to generate hyperspectral data cubes on the same day of procurement by utilizing Resonon's benchtop hyperspectral imaging system available in our research laboratory.

The hyperspectral imaging system is shown in Fig. 1(a) and is comprised of a Pika XC2 high-precision hyperspectral camera, linear translation stage, mounting tower, lighting assembly, and software control system known as SpectrononPro. The imaging spectrometers are line-scan imagers, which means they collect data one line at a time. The Pika XC2 hyperspectral camera is Resonon's highest precision Visible and Near-Infrared imager covering the 380–1000 nm spectral range.

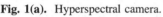

Fig. 1(a). Hyperspectral camera.

Fig. 1(b). Samples of grapevine leaves according to age including the benchmark leaf.

To assemble a complete two dimensional image, multiple lines are scanned as the object is translated. The multiple line-images are then assembled line by line to form a complete image. Two-dimensional images are constructed by translating the sample relative to the camera. This is typically accomplished by placing the sample leaves on a linear translation stage. For camera settings the frame rate and integration time were selected as 62.04244 Hz (default) and 244.01 ms respectively. The dark current has been acquired in absence of a light source. After collecting multiple dark frames *SpectrononPro* then uses these measurements to subtract the dark current noise from the measurements. Measuring absolute reflectance of an object requires calibration to account for illumination effects. To implement this a white reflectance reference was placed on the stage under light for a scan of the reference material. The collected data is then scaled in reflectance to the reference material, including flat-fielding to compensate for any spatial variations in lighting. Once the imager is calibrated for both dark current and reflectance reference, the imager will remain calibrated until the references are removed by the user. The speed unit and scanning speed were selected to be linear and 0.07938 cm/s (lowest). All samples were scanned for 10000 lines. The above-mentioned setting parameters were selected by trial and error method to obtain optimum resolution and quality of the hyperspectral images of the experimental samples. Each scan of a leaf generated a hyperspectral image file with *.bil* extension with approximate size of 700 MB–900 MB which were later processed by the SpectrononPro software.

For age detection studies the experiments were conducted on a number of grapevine leaves according to ascending order of their age i.e. the youngest to the oldest leaf of a vine. All leaves in this group were healthy by appearance. For the defect detection the experiment was done on 9 defective leaves. For both age and defect detection analysis the images of both up (i.e. adaxial) and down sides (i.e. abaxial) of the sample leaves were analysed.

3   Results and Discussions

Sections 3.1 and 3.2 present experimental results and discussions related to age detection and defect detection respectively. Spectra for each leaf were taken for 380 nm to 1000 nm.

3.1   Age Detection

Figure 1(b) displays samples of grapevine leaves including benchmark leaf used for the age detection studies. In this experiment both adaxial and abaxial grapevine leaves in the wavelength between 379 nm and 1000 nm have been studied. In the visible range of spectra, a characteristic high brightness peak within the green wavelength range has been obtained. This is because in the visible wavelength range the curve shape is governed by absorption effect from chlorophyll and other leaf pigments. It absorbs blue and red wavelengths more strongly than green. As a result it reflects higher amount of green compared to blue and red and hence the characteristic high brightness [23, 24]. From the experimental study it has been found that the brightness of the adaxial leaves is higher than those of abaxial leaves. At ∼551.6 nm wavelength the brightness difference between spectra of adaxial leaves are higher compared to those of abaxial leaves. This could be because grapevine is a C3 plant [2, 25] and for C3 plants the adaxial leaves contain several times higher concentration of chloroplasts and photosynthetic pigments i.e. chlorophylls and carotenoids than abaxial leaves [23]. Therefore adaxial leaves reflect higher amount of green light compared to abaxial leaves [26].

Figure 2 corroborates that at NIR wavelength range the brightness of adaxial leaves is higher than that of visible wavelength range. This is because a plant leaf has low reflectance in the visible spectral region due to strong absorption by chlorophylls and carotenoids. On the other hand, a relatively high reflectance in the near-infrared is observed because of internal leaf scattering and no absorption [24, 27]. From the experimental study it has been found that the brightness of the adaxial and abaxial leaves are almost same in the NIR region. Therefore, apart from the difference in intensity there is no significant observed difference between the characteristics of brightness spectra of adaxial and abaxial leaves. Hence, in this manuscript graphs obtained from the spectra of adaxial leaves have only been presented for the age detection studies. Although mean brightness spectra from UV to NIR range provide characteristics curves the indication of age of leaves is not significantly observed.

Although mean brightness spectra from UV to NIR range provide characteristics' curves the indication of age of leaves is not significantly observed. Therefore, for further age detection study the brightness of other leaves were compared with respect to the brightness of benchmark leaf at 554.3 nm. This wavelength was selected as a reference wavelength because it has been found from the spectral analysis that between UV and NIR ranges the brightness difference is higher for the consecutive leave according to their age at ∼554.3 nm. On the other hand, the benchmark leaf has been selected as a reference leaf because by visual inspection this leaf (see Fig. 1(b)) could be considered as a matured and healthy leaf. From Fig. 2 it has been found that the ratio of brightness of first few young leaves increases and after that it decreases with the increasing age of leaves at 554.3 nm. The phenomenon of increasing brightness ratio for the first few young leaves could be due to the relatively lower chlorophyll content in the younger leaves than the comparatively either matured or older leaves [13]. Hence absorption of green wavelength for the leaf is comparatively higher than the rest of leaves. Therefore, this youngest leaf has lower reflectance as well as lower brightness compared to first few younger leaves. As leaves get older the amount of chlorophyll increases therefore brightness is enhanced. From Fig. 2 it can be seen that few young leaves have slightly lower brightness ratio than those of first few younger leaves. As leaves transit from young state to matured state the brightness ratio decreases sharply and for matured to oldest leaves transition the brightness ratio decreases gradually. From literature study it has been found that expanding leaves combine high greenness with low photosynthetic rate as well as the decrease in photosynthetic capacity is caused by effects such as leaf aging [28, 29]. Therefore decreasing brightness ratio could be because of the low photosynthetic rate of leaves due to the ageing effect.

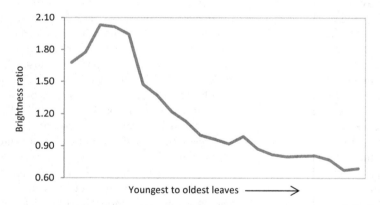

Fig. 2. Ratio of brightness intensity of all adaxial leaves with benchmark leaf at 554.3 nm.

To further study the age detection, mean 1st derivatives brightness data have been analysed. From the mean 1st derivative spectral analysis, longer wavelength shifts of the 1st derivatives brightness peaks according to age with respect to wavelength has been observed. These shifts of brightness peaks are clearly demonstrated in Fig. 3 where it can be found that there is a correlation between these shifts and age of the leaves. For the ease of explanation leaves are presented here according to the ascending order of age. As the leaves get older the brightness peaks shift to the higher wavelength between 470 nm and 550 nm. Similar to adaxial leaves, mean 1st derivatives brightness peak shift for abaxial leaves have also been observed. There is no significant shift based on age of leaves is observed for abaxial leaves compared to adaxial leaves (see Fig. 3).

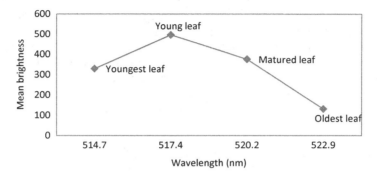

Fig. 3. Maximum brightness peak as a function of wavelength in the 470 to 550 nm range.

To clearly understand the effect of age of leaves in the red and near infrared region (675 nm–775 nm) the mean 1st derivative brightness data have been considered. Figure 4 represents the mean 1st derivatives brightness of a number of grapevine adaxial leaves between 675 nm and 775 nm. From Fig. 4 it could be stated that the brightness peak started gradually broadening when leaves transit from matured to old phase. This broadening could be due to the ageing effect of leaves. As leaves proceed towards maturity the mean rate of change of brightness becomes slower. As in Fig. 3, shifts of mean 1st derivatives brightness peak between 675 nm and 775 nm could be observed, but there is no significant shift based on age of leaves for this wavelength range. Similarly mean 1st derivatives' brightness peak broadening in this wavelength for abaxial leaves could be noticed.

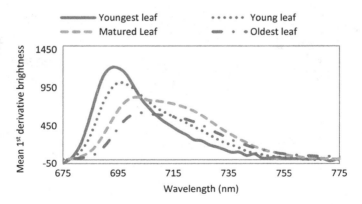

Fig. 4. Mean 1st derivative of brightness of adaxial leaves in the 675 to 775 nm range.

From the standard deviation of brightness, a variation index (v_i) has been defined:

$$v_i = \frac{(\sigma_{\text{benchmark leaf}} - \sigma_i) \times 100}{\sigma_{\text{benchmark leaf}}} \%$$

(1)

where v_i is the variation index of ith leaf, $\sigma_{\text{benchmark leaf}}$ and σ_i are the standard deviations of benchmark leaf and i^{th} leaf respectively. This index represents how much the brightness of a leaf deviates from that of a matured leaf. Figure 5 demonstrates that there is a correlation between age of leaves and v_i in both UV and NIR regions. It can be observed that v_i follows a specific trend according to the age of leaves in both UV and NIR regions. As the leaves continue to age, v_i starts increasing in the UV region but demonstrates the opposite characteristics in the NIR region.

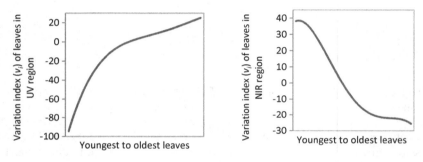

Fig. 5. Variation index (v_i) of youngest to oldest leaves at different spectrum regions for determination of age of leaves.

3.2 Defect Detection

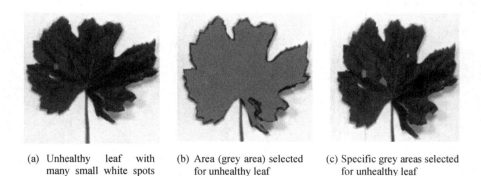

(a) Unhealthy leaf with many small white spots and few small brown spots.

(b) Area (grey area) selected for unhealthy leaf

(c) Specific grey areas selected for unhealthy leaf

Fig. 6. Unhealthy leaf with white spots and few brown spots and its selected areas for data cube accusation. (Color figure online)

For the defect detection studies the data cubes have been obtained by selecting both whole area and as well as selective areas of leaves using Lasso tool of SpectrononPro software. Both whole and selective areas have been studied to obtain an optimum selection method for distinguishing healthy and unhealthy leaves. The following paragraphs detail the experimental results and analysis for the 9 defective leaves in terms of mean brightness and mean 1st derivatives brightness vs wavelength. The characteristics of these leaves were also compared with a healthy leaf from the age detection group i.e. the benchmark leaf. This was selected as it appeared to be a matured leaf. As seen in Fig. 6(a), this particular unhealthy leaf contains white spots along with few brown spots. Figure 6(b and c) represent examples of the whole area and selective areas.

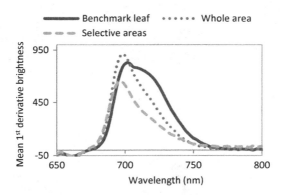

Fig. 7. Demonstration of mean 1st derivatives of brightness of healthy (benchmark leaf) and unhealthy (whole and selective areas) leaves to differentiate healthy and unhealthy leaves.

Figure 7 demonstrates that mean 1st derivative brightness in the NIR wavelength range is higher for unhealthy leaf of whole area case compared to benchmark leaf. Narrowing of brightness curves for unhealthy leaf is also observed for whole area case compared to benchmark leaf. A whole area case shorter wavelength shift of mean 1st derivative brightness peak is also observed for unhealthy leaf compared to benchmark leaf. From the literature study it has been found that reflectance in NIR is insensitive to change in chlorophyll content but sensitive to internal leaf structure, water content, structural compound and changing of internal mesophyll structure [30, 31]. Therefore, the deviation of mean 1st derivative brightness curves of unhealthy leaf with respect to benchmark leaf could be due to the difference in internal leaf structures of unhealthy and healthy leaves. From Fig. 7 it can be observed that though selective areas case exhibits similar features as whole area the magnitude of mean 1st derivatives brightness is lower compared to whole area case. For selective areas case areas have been selected based on the visible spots or defective areas. Therefore characteristic feature of only visibly defective areas have been obtained. On the other hand, for whole area case whole area of a leaf has been selected regardless of visible defects. As a result the features of both visible and nonvisible defective areas have been acquired with the aid of hyperspectral imaging in the NIR region. Therefore whole area case probes significant features compared to selective areas' case.

Sample of unhealthy leaves with visible defects are presented in Fig. 8. For most of the unhealthy leaves similar features to Fig. 7 such as narrowing and shorter wavelength shift of the curves have also been observed. It has been found that a sharp transition from low to high reflectance usually occurs in the wavelengths between the

Unhealthy leaf with brown areas and many small brown spots

Unhealthy leaf with several big brown spots

Unhealthy leaf with few brown spots

Unhealthy leaf with some brownish areas

Unhealthy leaf with few brown spots and some holes surrounded with brown regions

Unhealthy leaf with brown and yellowish regions

Unhealthy leaf with many large brown regions

Unhealthy leaf with few brownish areas and holes surrounded by brownish areas

Fig. 8. Sample of unhealthy leaves with visible defects. (Color figure online)

visible and the NIR regions, and this transition usually shifts to shorter wavelengths in diseased crops [32]. The wavelength where this transition occurs can be observed in the 1st derivative brightness curves. Hence, this deviation of 1st derivative brightness curve shapes of leaves with respect to benchmark leaf could be due to the brown spots of the leaf. Mean 1st derivative brightness curves were able to significantly distinguish the healthy and most (though not all) unhealthy leaves in the NIR region. Therefore, mean spectral ratios analysis has been employed.

Mean Spectral Ratios

To highlight the difference between healthy and unhealthy leaves, the mean brightness spectra for the unhealthy leaves were each divided by the mean brightness spectrum of the representative healthy leaf *i.e.* benchmark leaf for both whole and selective areas of unhealthy leaves.

Unhealthy leaf with many small white and few brown spots and unhealthy leaf with few brown spots exhibit almost similar ratio curve trends from $\sim$400 nm to 1000 nm as per Fig. 9(a). In this wavelength range the brightness ratio is higher for unhealthy leaf with few brown spots than that of unhealthy leaf with many small white and few brown spots. From Fig. 9(b) it can be surmised that unhealthy leaf with several big brown spots and unhealthy leaf with brownish regions have almost similar ratio curves. The brightness ratio of unhealthy leaf with several big brown spots is greater than unhealthy leaf with brownish regions between the wavelength range $\sim$491 nm and $\sim$825 nm. After 825 nm the brightness ratio is higher for unhealthy leaf with brownish regions than unhealthy leaf with several big brown spots. Figure 9(c) presents that unhealthy leaf with brown spots and holes and unhealthy leaf with brownish regions and holes have similar shaped ratio curves. The brightness ratio of unhealthy leaf with brownish regions and holes is greater than unhealthy leaf with brown spots and holes between the wavelength range $\sim$400 nm and 1000 nm. Figure 9(d) demonstrates that for whole area cases unhealthy leaves with brown and yellowish regions and unhealthy leaf with many large brown regions have similar ratio curves with higher ratio value for unhealthy leaf with many large brown regions between $\sim$570 nm to 1000 nm compared to unhealthy leaves with brown and yellowish regions. Between $\sim$400 nm and $\sim$570 nm the ratio value is greater for unhealthy leaves with brown and yellowish regions than that of unhealthy leaf with many large brown regions. On the other hand for unhealthy leaf with brown regions and many small brown spots the ratio curve is similar shaped to unhealthy leaves with brown and yellowish regions and unhealthy leaf with many large brown regions between $\sim$603 nm and 1000 nm. From $\sim$400 nm to $\sim$603 nm the unhealthy leaf with brown regions and many small brown spots ratio curve is different to unhealthy leaves with brown and yellowish regions and unhealthy leaf with many large brown regions as well as curves of other unhealthy leaves.

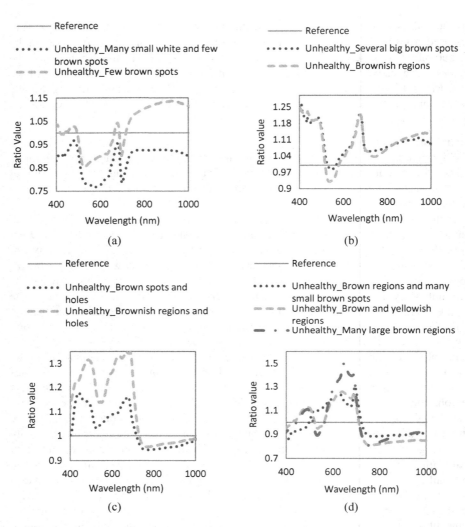

Fig. 9. Mean spectral ratios of different unhealthy leaves (whole area) to benchmark leaf. (Color figure online)

Variation Index

To obtain a correlation between healthy and unhealthy leaves, variation index v_i index has also been applied by using Eq. (1). Figure 10 demonstrates that at NIR region healthy leaves have v_i index closer to benchmark leaf, i.e. unhealthy leaves have higher value of v_i index compared to healthy leaves. No such pattern has been observed for unhealthy and healthy leaves in the UV region.

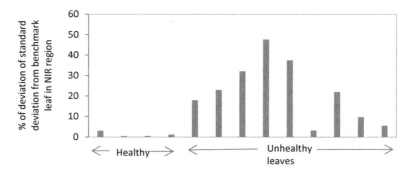

Fig. 10. Variation index (v_i) of healthy and unhealthy leaves in NIR region for distinguishing healthy and unhealthy leaves.

4 Conclusion

In this paper detection of age and defects of grapevine leaves with the aid of hyper-spectral imaging in the range between 400 nm and 1000 nm were demonstrated. For age detection leaves aged very young to old have been studied. From the analysis it was found that the magnitude of mean brightness of leaves has strong correlation with aging. This variation was found to be more prominent at ~ 554.3 nm. Mean 1st derivative brightness study demonstrated that mean 1st derivatives brightness peaks in visible wavelengths shifted to the longer wavelengths as the leaves age. Mean 1st derivatives brightness curves in the range between ~ 675 nm and ~ 775 nm revealed that the rate of change of mean brightness decrease with gradual aging of leaves. Variation index, a new metric introduced in this manuscript, also indicated to be correlated with age of leaves.

For defect detection both whole area and selective areas containing defects on the leaves were investigated. From these studies it was found that mean 1st derivatives brightness in the NIR region disclosed distinguishable curves for both whole area and selective areas' leaves compared to a healthy leaf. But the variation of curve shapes were more significant for whole areas' leaves compared to selective areas' leaves. On the other hand ratio analysis study established that more distinguishable curves could be obtained from the whole leaves' study. Experimental results suggest that variation index could be employed to detect defective leaves. Future in depth analysis could indicate more specifically age and defect detection of grapevine leaves as well as to identify or classify the differences between various defects as well as defective leaves.

References

1. ABC News Australia. https://www.abc.net.au/news/rural/2019-01-22/aussie-wine-exports-grow-by-10-per-cent/10737050. Accessed 20 July 2019
2. Liakopoulos, G., Nikolopoulos, D., Karabourniotis, G.: The first step from light to wine: photosynthetic performance and photoprotection of grapevine (Vitis vinifera L.) leaves. Funct. Plant Sci. Biotechnol. **1**(1), 112–119 (2007)

3. Mirás-Avalos, J.M., Buesa, I., Llacer, E., Jiménez-Bello, M.A., Risco, D., Castel, J.R., et al.: Water versus source-sink relationships in a semiarid tempranillo vineyard: vine performance and fruit composition. Am. J. Enol. Viticulture **68**(1), 11–22 (2017)

4. Greer, D., Weedon, M.: Modelling photosynthetic responses to temperature of grapevine (Vitis vinifera cv. Semillon) leaves on vines grown in a hot climate. Plant Cell Environ. **35** (6), 1050–1064 (2011)

5. Knoll, L., Redl, H.: Gas exchange of field-grown vitis vinifera l. cv. zweigelt leaves in relation to leaf age and position along the stem. Int. J. Vine Wine Sci. **46**(4), 281–295 (2012)

6. Martinelli, F., Scalenghe, R., Davino, S., Panno, S., Scuderi, G., Ruisi, P.: Advanced methods of plant disease detection. a review. Agron. Sustain. Dev. **35**(1), 1–25 (2015)

7. Mahlein, A.K.: Plant disease detection by imaging sensors – parallels and specific demands for precision agriculture and plant phenotyping. Plant Dis. **100**(2), 241–251 (2016)

8. Junges, A.H., Lampugnani, C.S., Almança, M.A.K.: Detection of grapevine leaf stripe disease symptoms by hyperspectral sensor. Phytopathologia Mediterr. **57**(3), 399–406 (2018)

9. Bhange, M., Hingoliwala, H.A.: Smart farming: pomegranate disease detection using image processing. Procedia Comput. Sci. **58**, 280–288 (2015). In: James, A.P., Al-Jumeily, D., Thampi, S.M. (eds.) Second International Symposium on Computer Vision and the Internet (VisionNet 2015) 2015. ScienceDirect

10. Dey, A.K., Sharma, M., Meshram, M.R.: Image processing based leaf rot disease, detection of betel vine (Piper BetleL.). Procedia Comput. Sci. **85**, 748–754 (2016). In: Ibrahim, S.A., Mohammad, S., Khader, S.A. (eds.) International Conference on Computational Modelling and Security (CMS 2016) 2016. ScienceDirect

11. Pujari, D.J., Yakkundimath, R., Byadgi, A.: Image processing based detection of fungal diseases in plants. Procedia Comput. Sci. **46**, 1802–1808 (2015). In: Samuel, P. (ed.) Proceedings of the International Conference on Information and Communication Technologies (ICICT 2014) ScienceDirect

12. Singh, V., Misra, A.K.: Detection of plant leaf diseases using image segmentation and soft computing techniques. Inf. Process. Agric. **4**(1), 41–49 (2017)

13. Stone, C., Chisholm, L., McDonald, S.: Effect of leaf age and psyllid damage on the spectral reflectance properties of eucalyptus saligna foliage. Aust. J. Bot. **53**(1), 45–54 (2005)

14. Jaillais, B., Roumet, P., Pinson-Gadais, L., Bertrand, D.: Detection of fusarium head blight contamination in wheat kernels by multivariate imaging. Food Control **54**, 250–258 (2015)

15. Lu, J., Ehsani, R., Shi, Y., De Castro, A., Wang, S.: Detection of multi-tomato leaf diseases (late blight, target and bacterial spots) in different stages by using a spectral-based sensor. Sci. Rep. **8**, 1–11 (2018). Article 2793

16. Xie, C., Shao, Y., Li, X., He, Y.: Detection of early blight and late blight diseases on tomato leaves using hyperspectral imaging. Sci. Rep. **5**, 1–11 (2015). Article 16564

17. Barbedo, J.G.A., Tibola, S.C., Fernandes, J.M.C.: Detecting fusarium head blight in wheat kernels using hyperspectral imaging. Biosyst. Eng. **131**, 65–76 (2015)

18. Wang, D., et al.: Early Detection of tomato spotted wilt virus by hyperspectral imaging and outlier removal auxiliary classifier generative adversarial nets (OR-AC-GAN). Sci. Rep. **9**, 1–14 (2019). Article 4377

19. Lowe, A., Harrison, N., French, A.: Hyperspectral image analysis techniques for the detection and classification of the early onset of plant disease and stress. Plant Methods **13** (1), 80–92 (2017)

20. Kishore, M., Kulkarni, S.B.: Hyperspectral imaging technique for plant leaf identification. 2015 International Conference on Emerging Research in Electronics. Computer Science and Technology (ICERECT), pp. 209–213. IEEE, Mandya (2016)

21. Ariana, D.P., Lu, R.: Hyperspectral waveband selection for internal defect detection of pickling cucumbers and whole pickles. Comput. Electron. Agric. **74**(1), 137–144 (2010)
22. Rice University USA. https://www.sciencedaily.com/releases/2019/05/190520125750.htm. Accessed 21 July 2019
23. Lagorio, M.G., Cordon, G.B., Iriel, A.: Reviewing the relevance of fluorescence in biological systems. Photochem. Photobiol. Sci. **14**(9), 1538–1559 (2015)
24. Kume, A.: Importance of the green color, absorption gradient, and spectral absorption of chloroplasts for the radiative energy balance of leaves. J. Plant. Res. **130**(3), 501–514 (2017)
25. Sawicki, M., et al.: Leaf vs. inflorescence: differences in photosynthetic activity of grapevine. Photosynthetica **55**(1), 58–68 (2017)
26. Terashima, I., Fujita, T., Inoue, T., Chow, W.S., Oguchi, R.: Green light drives leaf photosynthesis more efficiently than red light in strong white light: revisiting the enigmatic question of why leaves are green. Plant Cell Physiol. **50**(4), 684–697 (2009)
27. Merzlyak, M.N., Chivkunova, O.B., Melø, T.B., Naqvi, K.R.: Does a leaf absorb radiation in the near infrared (780–900 nm) region? a new approach to quantifying optical reflection, absorption and transmission of leaves. Photosynth. Res. **72**(3), 263–270 (2002)
28. Dillena, S.Y., Beeck, M.O., Hufkens, K., Buonanduci, M., Phillips, N.G.: Seasonal patterns of foliar reflectance in relation to photosynthetic capacity and color index in two co-occurring tree species, quercus rubra and betula papyrifera. Agric. For. Meteorol. **160**, 60–68 (2012)
29. Bielczynski, L.W., Łącki, M.K., Hoefnagels, I., Gambin, A., Croce, R.: Leaf and plant age affects photosynthetic performance and photoprotective capacity. Plant Physiol. **175**(4), 1634–1648 (2017)
30. Liu, L., Huang, W., Pu, R., Wang, J.: Detection of internal leaf structure deterioration using a new spectral ratio index in the near-infrared shoulder region. J. Integr. Agric. **13**(4), 760–769 (2014)
31. Neuwirthová, E., Lhotáková, Z., Albrechtová, J.: The effect of leaf stacking on leaf reflectance and vegetation indices measured by contact probe during the season. Sensors **17**(6), 1202–1224 (2017)
32. Gazala, I.F., et al.: Spectral reflectance pattern in soybean for assessing yellow mosaic disease. Indian J. Virol. **24**(2), 242–249 (2013)

Discrete Cosine Basis Oriented Homogeneous Motion Discovery for 360-Degree Video Coding

Ashek Ahmmed[1,2] and Manoranjan Paul[1(✉)]

[1] School of Computing and Mathematics, Charles Sturt University,
Bathurst, Australia
{aahmmed,mpaul}@csu.edu.au
[2] Asia Pacific International College, Chippendale, Australia

Abstract. Motion modeling plays a central role in video compression. This role is even more critical in 360-degree video sequences given the associated enormous amount of data that need be stored and communicated. While the translational motion model employed by modern video coding standards, such as HEVC, is sufficient in most cases, using higher order models is beneficial; for this reason, the upcoming video coding standard, VVC, employs a 4-parameter affine model. Discrete cosine basis has the ability to efficiently model complex motion fields. In this work, we employ discrete cosine basis to model the underlying motion field in 360-degree video frames. In particular, we discover discrete cosine basis oriented homogeneous motion regions over the current frame. Then employ these estimated motion models, guided by their associated applicability regions, to form a prediction for the target frame. Experimental results show a delta bit rate of 5.13% can be achieved on 360-degree test sequences, over conventional HEVC, if this predicted frame is used as an additional reference frame.

Keywords: 360-degree · Discrete cosine · HEVC

1 Introduction

To provide immersive experience for users, video is captured with 360-degree view of the world on a sphere and the users are allowed to dynamically control the viewing direction. This mimics the head movement of a viewer in the real world. For storage, transmission and efficient access to target regions of the 360-degree video, captured data is projected onto planes where the projection formats could be equirectangular, cubemap, octahedron, icosaherdon, etc. Due to the increased field of view, 360-degree video represents a significantly larger volume of data than traditional 2D rectilinear video, and hence there is requirement of efficient compression algorithms to facilitate applications adopting 360-degree video.

Conventional video compression standards are pixel and frame centric. Motion modeling is a core component in these standards; the higher coding efficiency obtained with each newer video coding standard can mainly be

© Springer Nature Switzerland AG 2019
C. Lee et al. (Eds.): PSIVT 2019, LNCS 11854, pp. 106–115, 2019.
https://doi.org/10.1007/978-3-030-34879-3_9

attributed to the employment of better motion modeling. Modern video codecs like H.264/AVC [1] and HEVC [2] use a block-based translational motion model. With this model, neighbouring pixels are grouped together into square or rectangular blocks to form an artificial partitioning of the current frame i.e. the frame being predicted. Motion modeling then involves performing a search in the set of already coded frames (i.e. reference frames), for an identically shaped block that closely resembles the target block.

Employing higher order motion models can improve coding gain, but this comes with increased computational complexity, which is needed to estimate the motion parameters of such models. The emerging video coding standard, known as versatile video coding (VVC), has adopted a 4-parameter affine motion model [3]; experimental results show that this can reduce the required bit rate by 1% compared to HEVC [4]. For 360-degree video sequences, the projection employed to map the spherical surface onto a panoramic frame introduces warping distortions. Furthermore, these warping distortions are not homogeneous across the frame e.g. in the equirectangular projection, polar areas are over-sampled. All these results in a complex motion field cannot be accurately described by a translational or affine motion model.

In [5], a rotational motion model is proposed for 360-degree video coding that captured object motion on the sphere. The model employs a radial motion search pattern that does not depend on a block's location over the sphere. Another direction of work deals with extending the block-based translational motion model for omnidirectional video sequences, with the motion model could account for the spherical geometry of the imaging system [6].

In [7], a bi-directional affine motion model is employed to encode rectilinear video sequences. Homogeneous motion groups are formed, over the current frame, by classifying blocks to one of the two available affine motion models. Conformance to the motion description provided by the affine models is used as the classification criterion. This approach yielded a savings of bit rate around 2% over the HM reference codec for HEVC [8] when 1080p video sequences are used. As for 4K video sequences, the gain in bit rate increased to around 4% with HM being the reference coder [9].

The discrete cosine basis has the ability to efficiently model complex motion fields by providing a smooth and sparse representation. In [10], the discrete cosine basis is employed to capture motion in fisheye video sequences; a bit rate saving of up to 6.54% over HM is reported. The basic discrete cosine basis, employed in [10], is used to perform motion compensation in highly textured video sequences. Experimental results reported an average bit rate saving of 4.5% over HM reference [11]. Recently, the discrete cosine basis oriented motion model has been applied to model the underlying motion in 360-degree video sequences [12]. An initial investigation involving such a model oriented prediction scheme resulted a bit rate savings of around 2% over conventional HEVC.

Leveraging on the promising results shown by: *(i)* homogeneous motion discovery oriented prediction paradigm being able to provide motion coherence and *(ii)* discrete cosine basis oriented motion model that can compensate for complex motion vector field; in this paper, we propose to discover homogeneous motion regions over the current frame of 360-degree video sequence. Here, the motion description is provided by discrete cosine vectors rather than affine vectors. In particular, two high-order motion models and their associated applicability regions (domains) are discovered over the target frame and then employed the estimated models and domains to generate an additional reference frame within HEVC. This new reference frame then can be used along with conventional reference frame(s) offered by HEVC to take rate-distortion optimized prediction unit decision during the encoding process of target frame.

The rest of this paper is organized as follows. Section 2 gives an overview of the discrete cosine basis. Section 3 details our prediction policy together. Experimental results are presented in Sect. 4, and Sect. 5 states our conclusions.

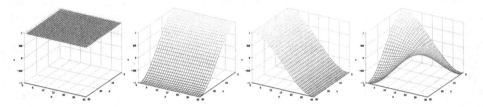

Fig. 1. The two-dimensional cosine vectors used in this work to represent motion; from left to right, the plots are for $\mathbf{u} = (0,0)$, $(1,0)$, $(0,1)$, and $(1,1)$.

2   The Discrete Cosine Basis for Motion

A two-dimensional vector $\phi_{\mathbf{u}}$ in the 2D discrete separable cosine basis can be characterized by $\mathbf{u} = (u_1, u_2)$, where $u_1 \in \{0, 1, \ldots\}$ and $u_2 \in \{0, 1, \ldots\}$ represent, respectively, the horizontal and vertical frequencies of this vector. This vector is evaluated, at location $\mathbf{x} = (x_1, x_2)$ of the frame under consideration, using

$$\phi_{\mathbf{u}}(\mathbf{x}) = \cos\left(\frac{(2x_1 + 1)\pi u_1}{2W}\right) \cdot \cos\left(\frac{(2x_2 + 1)\pi u_2}{2H}\right) \tag{1}$$

where W and H are the width and height of the frame, respectively. Then, the motion vector $\mathbf{v} = (v_1, v_2)$ at location $\mathbf{x}$ is obtained from

$$v_1(\mathbf{x}) = \sum_{\mathbf{u} \in \mathbf{U}} m_{1,k} \phi_{\mathbf{u}}(\mathbf{x}) \tag{2}$$

$$v_2(\mathbf{x}) = \sum_{\mathbf{u} \in \mathbf{U}} m_{2,k} \phi_{\mathbf{u}}(\mathbf{x}) \tag{3}$$

where $\{m_{1,k}, m_{2,k}\}_k$ are the parameters of the model. In this work, we choose $U = \{(0,0), (1,0), (0,1), (1,1)\}$ and $k = 2 \cdot u_1 + u_2$; thus, $k \in \{0, 1, 2, 3\}$ and the model has 8 parameters.

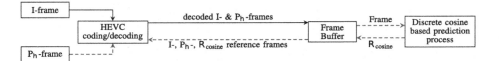

Fig. 2. Block diagram of the coding/decoding framework that uses the discrete cosines based motion model compensated prediction as a reference frame, along with the usual temporal reference(s), for the P-frames. This additional reference frame is generated by discovering homogeneous motion regions over the current P-frame.

Figure 1 shows the cosine vectors used in this work. The parameters $\{m_{1,k}, m_{2,k}\}_{k=0}^{3}$ are estimated using gradient-based image registration techniques [13,14]. The advantage of using a cosine basis is that the parameters associated with higher-order models can be estimated without altering the gradient-descent algorithm [14]. Thus, motion modeling using a discrete cosine basis can describe more complex motion than can be described with an affine model while they are more tractable to estimate than higher order polynomial models.

3 Prediction Using the Proposed Motion Model

In this work, the terms intra-coded frames (I-frames) and inter-coded or predicted frames (P-frames) are used in their conventional meaning; i.e., they have the same interpretation as that used in MPEG-2 and the following video coding standards.

Figure 2 shows a simplified block diagram of the proposed coding/decoding architecture. The first frame of a 360-degree video sequence is coded/decoded, as an I-frame, conventionally with HEVC. This coded frame is then propagated to a discrete cosines basis oriented motion model compensation process, that generates a reference frame (R_{cosine}) for the target P-frame. The P-frame coding/decoding then takes place using HEVC, where along with the usual temporal reference frame, the R_{cosine} reference frame can also be used.

Further details of the coding/decoding architecture are provided in the following subsections. In Sect. 3.1, the formation procedure of the R_{cosine} reference frame is described. Section 3.2 gives an insight into how R_{cosine} is used in conjunction with the usual temporal reference to predict the current frame.

3.1 Discrete Cosines Basis Oriented Prediction Generation

This step begins by estimating the discrete cosines based motion model parameters between the reference frame R and the current P-frame, C using standard gradient-based image registration technique [13,14]. The domain, $f_1^{(R \to C)}$, used to estimate the associated 8-parameter motion model is the entire C frame, where $f_1^{(R \to C)}$ is a binary image, of same resolution as C, with all intensity values equal to 1. The resultant motion model is denoted by $M_1^{(R \to C)}$ herein.

(a) *Balboa* sequence

(b) *Broadway* sequence

(c) *KiteFlite* sequence

Fig. 3. The discrete cosines based motion model, $\widetilde{M}_1^{(R \to C)}$ performed poorly in blocks with white boundary pixels i.e. these blocks have high mean absolute error (MAE) values. The example scenario is for predicting frame 100 using coded frame 99 of each 4K (3840 × 2160) sequence [15]. Used block size is 240 × 240 pixels. Together these blocks form the domain $f_2^{(R \to C)}$.

The fractional part of the estimated motion parameters are quantized to the accuracy of 1/64-th of a pixel and then encoded using the Exponential-Golomb coding technique [16]. This quantized motion model, $\widetilde{M}_1^{(R \to C)}$ is employed to warp R for generating a discrete cosines based motion compensated prediction, $\widehat{C}_1^{R \to C}$ of C.

$$\widehat{C}_1^{R \to C} = \widetilde{M}_1^{(R \to C)}(R) \tag{4}$$

Next, an error analysis is carried out over the prediction error associated to the prediction $\widehat{C}_1^{R \to C}$. Prediction error blocks having the mean-absolute-error (MAE) greater than the block-wise mean MAE of this error image are identified. In this way, blocks with high MAE values are determined and then used to form another domain, $f_2^{(R \to C)}$. An example of this domain is shown in Fig. 3. Then the domain $f_2^{(R \to C)}$ is fed into the discrete cosine based motion model estimation process involving R and C, for generating a second motion model, namely $\widetilde{M}_2^{(R \to C)}$. The reference frame R is warped by this newly estimated and quantized affine motion model to generate another prediction of C, specifically $\widehat{C}_2^{R \to C}$.

$$\widehat{C}_2^{R \to C} = \widetilde{M}_2^{(R \to C)}(R) \tag{5}$$

Now with the help of the domain $f_2^{(R \to C)}$, the predictions $\widehat{C}_1^{R \to C}$ and $\widehat{C}_2^{R \to C}$ are fused into a single prediction of C, from the reference frame R, in the following way:

$$R_{cosine} = f_2^{(R \to C)} \cdot \widehat{C}_2^{R \to C} + \left(1 - f_2^{(R \to C)}\right) \cdot \widehat{C}_1^{R \to C} \tag{6}$$

To generate the predicted frame R_{cosine} at the decoder, the discrete cosine based motion parameters $\widetilde{M}_1^{(R \to C)}$ and $\widetilde{M}_2^{(R \to C)}$ are communicated from the encoder. That means in total $2 \times 8 = 16$ parameters, each with 1/64-th of a pixel accuracy are necessary to yield the R_{cosine} frame at the decoder.

3.2 Discrete Cosine Based Motion Compensated Prediction as a Reference Frame

In addition to the normal temporal reference frames for the P-frames, the homogeneous motion oriented prediction, R_{cosine} is used as a reference frame similarly to inter-layer reference frame in the multiview extension of HEVC [17].

Table 1. The Bjøntegaard delta gains obtained for the 360-degree test sequences over standalone HEVC when the discrete cosine-based reference R_{cosine} is employed.

Sequence	Delta-rate	Delta-PSNR
Balboa	−5.07%	+0.18 dB
Broadway	−5.13%	+0.19 dB
KiteFlite	−3.24%	+0.10 dB

The employed approach enables the encoder to make a rate-distortion optimized decision on prediction unit basis to determine which of the available reference to use. Additionally, it provides the flexibility of a discrete cosine based motion model compensated prediction that can be locally adapted with conventional motion vectors and motion-compensated prediction from the R_{cosine} reference frame. Finally, the generation of R_{cosine} reference frames can be implemented as an inter-layer process into a multi-layer HEVC encoder/decoder architecture meaning that existing multi-layer HEVC implementations can be re-used and no block-level changes to the HEVC encoding/decoding processes are needed.

4   Experimental Analysis

The rate-distortion performance of the proposed coder is investigated on 3 different 4K resolution 360-degree video sequences [15]: *Balboa*, *Broadway*, and *Kite-Flite* sequence. The equirectangular projection (ERP) format is used for experimentation. The initial 120 frames of each 4K (3840×2160) sequence are coded by the HM 16.10 reference software [8] for HEVC. The HM encoder is configured using the low delay P- GOP structure i.e. IPPP...P as per the common test conditions [18]. Four different quantization parameter values (QP = 22, 27, 32, 37) are used. For each P-frame, the available I- or P-frame is used to estimate the parameters of the two discrete cosine-based motion models $\widetilde{M}_1^{(R \to C)}$ and $\widetilde{M}_2^{(R \to C)}$ respectively. The fractional part of these parameters is limited to 1/64, and they are coded using the Exponential Golomb coding technique [16].

To use the R_{cosine} frames as additional reference frames with the usual references offered by HEVC, all the R_{cosine} frames are grouped together and supplied to the SHM 12.4 reference encoder [19] for the scalable extension of HEVC, as a base layer, with inter-layer non-zero motion estimation enabled. The additional reference frame is inserted as a reference frame into LIST0. In the enhancement layer, original video sequence is used to perform quality scalability for P-frames only, using the same QP values. Therefore, the average PSNR for a test sequence, in the case where the R_{cosine} frames are used as additional references, is calculated using the PSNR of the I- frame from the HM encoder and the PSNR of P-frames from the SHM encoder. To generate the overall bit rate, the code lengths for these frames are summed up, together with the code lengths of the per-frame parameters of the two discrete cosine-based motion models $\widetilde{M}_1^{(R \to C)}$ and $\widetilde{M}_2^{(R \to C)}$ respectively. Table 1 tabulates the Bjøntegaard Deltas [20] for all 360-degree test sequences under consideration.

The employed hybrid prediction paradigm generates a bit rate saving for all test sequences. The maximum gain is obtained in the *Broadway* sequence; with the *Balboa* sequence came in a close second. The discrete cosine-based motion model managed to capture their underlying motion fields reasonably well compared to the *KiteFlite* sequence. Figure 4 shows a rate-distortion curve for the *Broadway* sequence.

The considered approach for coding 360-degree video sequences has a higher computational cost than standalone HEVC, because of the additional reference

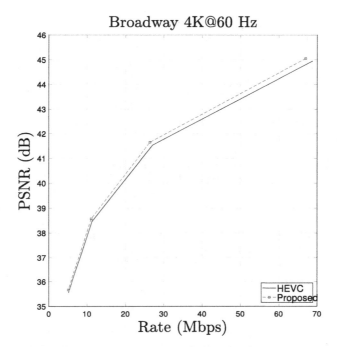

Fig. 4. Rate-distortion curve for the *Broadway* sequence. A bit rate savings of up to 5.13% is achieved over standalone HEVC reference.

frames and their associated estimation cost. The encoder complexity grows if more discrete cosine-based motion models are employed per frame, while the increase in the decoder's complexity is only minimal with that increase.

5   Conclusion

In this paper, we proposed to find homogeneous motion regions, equipped with discrete cosines basis oriented motion model, over the current P-frame in 360-degree video sequences. The estimated motion models and their domains are used to form a prediction of the target frame. Experimental results show a reduction in bit rate of up to 5.13% over standalone HEVC, if that predicted frame is employed as an additional reference frame.

References

1. Wiegand, T., Sullivan, G., Bjøntegaard, G., Luthra, A.: Overview of the H.264/AVC video coding standard. IEEE Trans. Circuits Syst. Video Technol. **13**(7), 560–576 (2003)

2. Sullivan, G.J., Ohm, J.R., Han, W.J., Wiegand, T.: Overview of the high efficiency video coding (HEVC) standard. IEEE Trans. Circuits Syst. Video Technol. **12**(22), 1649–1668 (2012)
3. Zhang, K., Chen, Y., Zhang, L., Chien, W., Karczewicz, M.: An improved framework of affine motion compensation in video coding. IEEE Trans. Image Process. **28**(3), 1456–1469 (2019). https://doi.org/10.1109/TIP.2018.2877355
4. Sidaty, N., Hamidouche, W., Deforges, O., Philippe, P.: Compression efficiency of the emerging video coding tools. In: 2017 IEEE International Conference on Image Processing (ICIP), pp. 2996–3000, September 2017. https://doi.org/10.1109/ICIP. 2017.8296832
5. Vishwanath, B., Nanjundaswamy, T., Rose, K.: Rotational motion model for temporal prediction in 360 video coding. In: 2017 IEEE 19th International Workshop on Multimedia Signal Processing (MMSP), pp. 1–6, October 2017. https://doi. org/10.1109/MMSP.2017.8122231
6. De Simone, F., Frossard, P., Birkbeck, N., Adsumilli, B.: Deformable block-based motion estimation in omnidirectional image sequences. In: 2017 IEEE 19th International Workshop on Multimedia Signal Processing (MMSP), pp. 1–6, October 2017. https://doi.org/10.1109/MMSP.2017.8122254
7. Ahmmed, A., Taubman, D., Naman, A.T., Pickering, M.: Homogeneous motion discovery oriented reference frame for high efficiency video coding. In: 2016 Picture Coding Symposium (PCS), pp. 1–5, December 2016. https://doi.org/10.1109/PCS. 2016.7906335
8. HM Reference Software for HEVC. https://hevc.hhi.fraunhofer.de/
9. Ahmmed, A., Naman, A.T., Taubman, D.: Enhanced homogeneous motion discovery oriented prediction for key intermediate frames. In: 2018 Picture Coding Symposium (PCS), pp. 238–242, June 2018. https://doi.org/10.1109/PCS.2018. 8456251
10. Ahmmed, A., Hannuksela, M.M., Gabbouj, M.: Fisheye video coding using elastic motion compensated reference frames. In: 2016 IEEE International Conference on Image Processing (ICIP), pp. 2027–2031, September 2016
11. Ahmmed, A., Naman, A., Pickering, M.: Leveraging the discrete cosine basis for better motion modelling in highly textured video sequences. In: 2019 IEEE International Conference on Image Processing (ICIP), pp. 3542–3546, September 2019. https://doi.org/10.1109/ICIP.2019.8803718
12. Ahmmed, A., Paul, M.: Discrete cosine basis oriented motion modeling for fisheye and 360 degree video coding. In: IEEE International Workshop on Multimedia Signal Processing, September 2019
13. Baker, S., Matthews, I.: Lucas-kanade 20 years on: a unifying framework. Int. J. Comput. Vis. **56**(3), 221–255 (2004)
14. Muhit, A.A., Pickering, M.R., Frater, M.R., Arnold, J.F.: Video coding using elastic motion model and larger blocks. IEEE Trans. Circuits Syst. Video Technol. **20**(5), 661–672 (2010). https://doi.org/10.1109/TCSVT.2010.2045804
15. Asbun, E., He, Y., He, Y., Ye, Y.: Interdigital test sequences for virtual reality video coding in joint video exploration team (JVET) 4th meeting. In: Document JVET-D0039. Chengdu, China (2016)
16. Richardson, I.E.: The H.264 Advanced Video Compression Standard, 2nd edn. Wiley, Chichester (2010)
17. Hannuksela, M.M., Yan, Y., Huang, X., Li, H.: Overview of the multiview high efficiency video coding (MV-HEVC) standard. In: IEEE International Conference on Image Processing, pp. 2154–2158, September 2015

18. Bossen, F.: Common test conditions and software reference configurations. In: Document JCTVC-H1100, JCT-VC. San Jose, CA, February 2012
19. SHM Reference Software for SHVC. https://hevc.hhi.fraunhofer.de/shvc
20. Bjøntegaard, G.: VCEG-M33: Calculation of Average PSNR Differences between RD curves. Video Coding Experts Group (VCEG), April 2001

Double Channel 3D Convolutional Neural Network for Exam Scene Classification of Invigilation Videos

Wu Song[✉] and Xinguo Yu

National Engineering Research Center for E-Learning,
Central China Normal University, Wuhan 430079, China
songwu@mails.ccnu.edu.cn

Abstract. This paper presents a double channel 3D convolution neural network to classify the exam scenes of invigilation videos. The first channel is based on the C3D convolution neural network, which is the status-of-arts method of the video scene classification. The structure of this channel is redesigned for classifying the exam-room scenes of invigilation videos. Another channel is based on the two-stream convolution neural network using the optical flow graph sequence as its input. This channel uses the data from the optical flow of video to improve the performance of the video scene classification. The formed double channel 3D convolution neural network has appropriate size of convolution kernel and pooling kernel design. Experiments show that the proposed neural network can classify the exam-room scenes of invigilation videos faster and more accurately than the existing methods.

Keywords: Exam invigilation video · Video scene classification · Convolutional neural network

1 Introduction

The problem of the exam scene classification of invigilation videos is a core function of automatic invigilation system, which is a kind of video scene classification [1, 2]. In recent years deep learning has significantly improve the performance of video scene classification [3]. With the development of convolutional neural network, more and more related works for complex human-object or human-human interaction [4–6] and abnormal phenomena of human group activities were proposed [7–9], which proved that the neural network classification method can effectively improve various video scene classification in terms of speed and accuracy. Deep learning method mainly studies the video domain from two aspects: the number of input channels and the dimension of convolution kernel. Simonyan et al. [10] proposed two-stream convolution neural network, where spatial and temporal information were extracted separately, and video spatial-temporal information was reproduced by fully training data.

This study is funded by the General Program of the National Natural Science Foundation of China (No: 61977029).

C. Lee et al. (Eds.): PSIVT 2019, LNCS 11854, pp. 116–127, 2019.
https://doi.org/10.1007/978-3-030-34879-3_10

Feichtenhofer et al. [11] studied the fusion of spatial information flow and temporal information flow on the basis of two-stream convolution neural network. This method greatly reduced the number of parameters and achieved higher accuracy of classification. Zhu et al. [12] proposed Hidden two-stream convolution neural network. Wang et al. [13] proposed a two-stream cyclic neural network method to study human skeleton behavior, and established a time-space relationship model. In addition, Ji et al. [14] proposed a 3D convolution neural network model for video behavior recognition. This method can synchronously extract and fuse the spatial and temporal features of video, which retains the motion information between adjacent frames. Tran et al. [15] proposed a general 3D convolution neural network C3D, which can be applied to behavior recognition, scene recognition and video similarity analysis. Qiu et al. [16] proposed a deep neural network based on Pseudo-3D convolution trained by large dataset, which can reduce the amount of computation and parameters and improve the computational performance. However, all of these researches do not study the classification of video scene in exam invigilation video, which pays attention to the group movement trend and has difficulties in taking both nearly static motion for a empty exam-room and a middle-level examination scene and intense motion for the examine leaving scene into account together. Therefore, in this paper, a double channel 3D convolution neural network model is proposed, where spatial-temporal features are extracted and fused from the original image frame sequence and optical flow graph sequence to improve the recognition ability of the neural network for motion features. This method can classify the scene more quickly and accurately.

This paper is organized as follows. Section 2 proposes a double channel 3D convolutional neural network model (D3DCNN), which is used to classify video scene for exam invigilation video (flow chart is shown in Fig. 1). Section 3 introduces some experimental settings and makes experimental comparison between D3DCNN model and other neural networks on EMV-1 test dataset, which proves our network has better performance. Section 4 is the conclusion and the future prospect.

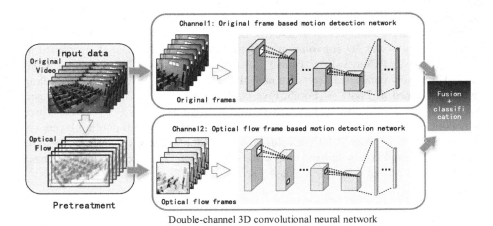

Double-channel 3D convolutional neural network

Fig. 1. Flow chart of classifying the exam scenes of invigilation videos.

2 Problem Definition and Problem Solving Model

2.1 Problem Definition

According to the movement patterns at different exam stages in exam rooms, this paper defines the following five scene categories of invigilation videos:

(1) Empty exam-room: no staff and no activities in exam-room;
(2) Preparing and closing: there are no candidates in the exam-room. Only the invigilator does the examination work before and after the examination in the exam-room, such as opening the sealed examination papers before the examination, collecting the examination papers table by table after the examination, summarizing the examination papers and sealing the bags;
(3) Entering the exam-room: candidates appear one after another from the entrance of the exam-room, enter the location of each area of the exam-room and sit down;
(4) Leaving the exam-room: at the end of the examination, candidates stand up and rush to the exit of the exam-room from all areas of the exam-room and disappear from the monitoring;
(5) Exam ongoing: the candidate answers in his own position. The invigilator distributes the examination papers table by table, walks around, stops and sits down.

This paper is to develop an algorithm for classifying the video scene segments into the defined five kinds of events of the exam-room invigilation videos in the coming several sections.

2.2 Double Channel 3D Convolutional Neural Network Model (D3DCNN)

In this section it is presented a double channel 3D Convolutional Neural Network Model (D3DCNN) and its network structure is illustrated in Fig. 2. In order to simplify the network structure and improve training efficiency, channel C1 emphasizes spatial flow information and channel C2 emphasizes temporal flow information.

The structure parameters of D3DCNN network are given in Table 1. Eight convolution layers of the 3D convolution network structure in C1 channel are named as Conv1_1\Conv2_1\Conv3_1 $\sim$ Conv3_2\Conv4_1 $\sim$ Conv4_2\Conv5_1 $\sim$ Conv5_2. Three fully connected layers are named as FC0 $\sim$ FC2. Five maximum pooling layers are named as Pool1 $\sim$ Pool5. Five convolution layers of 3D convolution network structure in C2 channel are named as Conv1\Conv2\Conv3 $\sim$ Conv5. Three fully connected layers are named as FC0 $\sim$ FC2. Three maximum pooling layers are named as Pool1 $\sim$ Pool3. All convolution layers adopt 3D convolution kernel. The convolution kernel size is uniform to k $\times$ k$\times$ 3(k $\in$ {3, 5, 7}). The convolution kernel size of the pool layer is k $\times$ 2 $\times$ 2(k $\in$ {1, 2}).

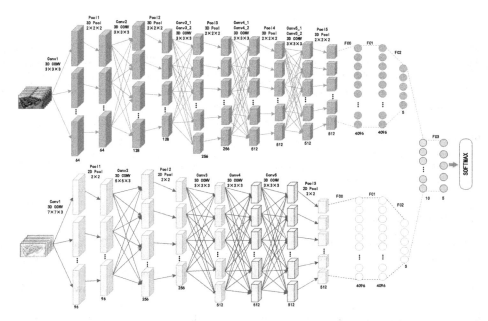

Fig. 2. Double channel 3D convolutional neural network model.

Table 1. D3DCNN network structure parameters

C1 channel				C2 channel			
Layer	Convolution kernel size	Number	Step	Layer	Convolution kernel size	Number	Step
Conv1_1	$3 \times 3 \times 3$	64	$1 \times 1 \times 1$	Conv1	$7 \times 7 \times 3$	96	$1 \times 1 \times 1$
Pool1	$2 \times 2 \times 2$	1	$1 \times 2 \times 2$	Pool1	2×2	1	2×2
Conv2_1	$3 \times 3 \times 3$	128	$1 \times 1 \times 1$	Conv2	$5 \times 5 \times 3$	256	$1 \times 1 \times 1$
Pool 2	$2 \times 2 \times 2$	1	$2 \times 2 \times 2$	Pool2	2×2	1	2×2
Conv3_1	$3 \times 3 \times 3$	256	$1 \times 1 \times 1$	Conv3	$3 \times 3 \times 3$	512	$1 \times 1 \times 1$
Conv3_2	$3 \times 3 \times 3$	256	$1 \times 1 \times 1$	Conv4	$3 \times 3 \times 3$	512	$1 \times 1 \times 1$
Pool 3	$2 \times 2 \times 2$	1	$2 \times 2 \times 2$	Conv5	$3 \times 3 \times 3$	512	$1 \times 1 \times 1$
Conv4_1	$3 \times 3 \times 3$	512	$1 \times 1 \times 1$	Pool3	2×2	1	2×2
Conv4_2	$3 \times 3 \times 3$	512	$1 \times 1 \times 1$	FC0	–	4096	–
Pool 4	$2 \times 2 \times 2$	1	$2 \times 2 \times 2$	FC1	–	4096	–
Conv5_1	$3 \times 3 \times 3$	512	$1 \times 1 \times 1$	FC2	–	5	–
Conv5_2	$3 \times 3 \times 3$	512	$1 \times 1 \times 1$				
Pool5	$2 \times 2 \times 2$	1	$2 \times 2 \times 2$				
FC0	–	4096	–				
FC1	–	4096	–				
FC2	–	5	–				
Layer FC3 5							

2.3 Improvement on C3D Model (C1 Channel)

The C1 channel in our network improves the C3D model on the basis of the original data, so as to get the channel with emphasis on spatial flow. In our method, a $3 \times 3 \times 3$ 3D convolution kernel is adopted in 8 convolution layers, which can fully extract the space-time information of exam-room. Compared with larger scale convolution kernel, such as 5×5, 7×7, etc., the performance of our convolution kernel is more stable, which can efficiently extract spatial information from each sub-area of the exam-room and avoid information omission caused by over-abstraction of local information. In addition, the pooling kernel of $2 \times 2 \times 2$ are used in the five pooling layers of the model to preserve the spatial flow information and avoid excessive consumption in the temporal dimension.

2.4 Improvement on Two-Stream Network Model (C2 Channel)

Based on the improvement of the two-stream network model, C2 channel with emphasis on time flow is obtained. In our method, C2 channel expands the 2D convolution neural network part to 3D and add a convolution kernel of size 3 to the time dimension, so as to extract the temporal and spatial features of optical flow sequence efficiently. The first two layers of C2 adopt 3D convolution kernel of 7×7 and 5×5 in spatial dimension, which can accelerate the information abstraction of spatial dimension, avoid excessive consumption on spatial scale, and enhance the sensitivity of network to local information changes on time axis. In addition, the pooling layer of C2 channel retains two-dimensional pooling kernel, which can avoid the reduction of information in the time dimension, so as to retain the information in the time dimension fully.

2.5 Double Channel Spatial-Temporal Feature Fusion Algorithms

Through the above two sections, we get the output D_3 from the final pooling layer, which is a three-dimensional feature graph. In order to further abstract the output of D_3 through the full connection layer, it is necessary to "flatten" it in 3D space (space X, space Y and time Z) and a new one-dimensional eigenvector is formed by linear stitching. The by inputting this one-dimensional eigenvector into the full connection layer, the final high-level features of the channel can be calculated, and then the subsequent fusion can be carried out through the connection operation. The algorithm is shown in Table 2.

The two N1-dimensional feature vectors extracted from the image sequence by single channel C1 and C2 are as follows:

$$\begin{cases} T_1 = F_{C1}(v_i) = \left(x_1^{C1}, x_2^{C1}, \ldots, x_{N_1}^{C1}\right) \\ T_2 = F_{C2}(v_i) = \left(x_1^{C2}, x_2^{C2}, \ldots, x_{N_1}^{C2}\right) \end{cases} \tag{1}$$

Table 2. Double channel spatial-temporal feature fusion algorithms

Algorithms: Feature Fusion Algorithms
Input: Output feature maps M1 and M2 of final pooling layer C1-D3 and C2-D3 in channel C1 and C2, weight matrix W1, W2, W3 offset vectors b1, B2 and B3 of full connection layer C1-FC0, C1-FC0 and FC1.
Output: Fusion of eigenvectors $F(v_i)$.
1:     Flattening Two Feature Matrices M_1, M_2, obtaining K_i=reshape(M_i).($i=1,2$)
2:     Calculated by Full Connection Layer V_i=$K_i W_i$+b_i.
3:     V_i is activated by SigmoidT_i=Sigm (V_i).
4:     Combining two vectors T_1, T_2, obtaining T=concat (T_1, T_2).
5:     The final eigenvector is obtained by calculating the full connection layer and activating the Sigmoid. X=Sigm (TW_3+b_3).
6:     **Return X**

By connecting the output vectors of two channels, the fusion features of $2 \times N1$ dimension can be obtained as follows:

$$T = \mathrm{F}(v_i) = \left(x_1^{C1}, x_2^{C1}, \ldots, x_{N_1}^{C1}, x_1^{C2}, x_2^{C2}, \ldots, x_{N_1}^{C2}\right)_{v_i} \tag{2}$$

where $N_1 = 512$. And $F_{C1}(\cdot)$ and $F_{C2}(\cdot)$ are the feature extraction operations of input image sequences for channel C1 and C2 respectively.

We can continue to abstract and reduce dimensionality through two full connection layers to further fuse the temporal and spatial features extracted from the two channels. The number of neurons with two full junction layers is N2 and N3, respectively. The N3 dimension feature vector X is obtained as follows:

$$X = (x_1, x_2, \ldots, x_{N_3})_{v_i} \tag{3}$$

where N3 is the number of sample categories.

D3DCNN adopts the Softmax function $\varphi(x) = e^x / \sum e^x$ as its classifier. The output of Softmax layer is the final output of D3DCNN which is called as $Y(\cdot)$. Then the network output is expressed as follows:

$$\begin{cases} Y(v_i) = (y_1, y_2, \ldots, y_{N_3}) \\ y_j = \varphi(x_j) = \frac{e^{x_j}}{\sum e^{x_j}} \end{cases} \tag{4}$$

where y_j is the probability that the current image sequence v_i which belongs to class j. Therefore, the correct category of v_i is the ordinal number of the largest element in $(y_1, y_2, \ldots, y_{N_3})$.

The training process of D3DCNN is realized by stochastic gradient descent method to minimize the loss function. The loss function of D3DCNN is the sum of cross-entropy loss and regularization term. The loss function is as follows:

$$loss = -\sum y_j' \log(y_j) + \frac{\lambda}{2} \|W_i\|^2 \qquad (5)$$

Where the first term is the cross-entropy loss function, the second term is the L2 regular term of the network weight, and the second term λ is the coefficient of the regular term. The loss function is determined by the product of the attenuation coefficient of the weight.

3   Experiment and Analysis

3.1   Experimental Dataset and Experimental Settings

In this study, a 5-fold cross-validation scheme was adopted and carried out on graphics CARDS with two NVIDA GeForce GTX1080, Inter®core™i7-6700KCPU@ 4.00 GHz and RAM: 32.0 GB, with Python2.7, anaconda3 (Python3.5 included), caffe, TensorFlow, etc. The experiment in this paper is mainly completed by TensorFlow.

The data used in this paper is from real invigilation video of standardized exam-room. The data consists of 14 h and is chosen from 10 different examination venues. The original resolution is 1920 × 1080 and frame rate is 24FPS and MP4 format. In this paper, sliding sampling is carried out with 6 frames in effective fragments and 32 frames are adopted in per sample in the aspect of sample fragment acquisition.

We adjusted the image size of each frame of the sample fragment to 144 × 82, where D3DCNN can achieve the best balance between lower time consumption and classification accuracy. Define each sample fragment size for l × h × w × c, where l is the number of frame segments, c is the number of frame image channels and h and w are the height and width of sample segment frames. Therefore, the sample fragment size in this paper was 144 × 82 × 3 × 32. In this paper, 3260 sample fragments were adopted. According to the semantics of manual annotation, we obtained the classification and annotation of scene simultaneously. The number of sample fragments in various examination venues is shown in Table 3. Because of the 5-fold cross-validation scheme, the number of training sample fragments and test sample fragments was 4 to 1 in each category. The sample fragment set used in this paper was marked as EMV-1 dataset (Examination Monitoring video).

Table 3.   The number of sample fragments in various examination venues

Type	Label	Number of image sequences	Training dataset	Test dataset
1	Empty exam-room	516	413	103
2	Preparing and closing	826	661	165
3	Entering the exam-room	778	622	156
4	Leaving the exam-room	543	434	109
5	Exam ongoing	597	478	119
Total		3260	2608	652

In this paper, the Stochastic Gradient Descent (SGD) method was applied to train the D3DCNN model. The initial learning rate was set to 0.001 and the learning attenuation rate was set to 0.99. Batch size for reading EMV-1 dataset in training was set to 32, which means the five-dimensional tensor of $32 \times 144 \times 82 \times 3 \times 32$ was read every time in the training. At the same time, the labels of each sample fragment were read and used for training in the form of 32×1 tensor. A round of epoch required 82 iterations, and the maximum number of iterations was set as 82000. During the training, the model was retained every 1000 iterations.

3.2   Optical Flow Experiment of Video Dataset in Exam-Room

The channel C2 of D3DCNN model adopted pre-processed optical flow graph as data input. In this paper, the dense optical flow method was applied in the specific problem of exam invigilation video based on two following aspects: First, it is not necessary to calculate the optical flow graph frame by frame, but only one frame per $\lceil 0.5 * FPS \rceil$ frame. Second, it does not care about the precise motion of the specific object but mainly considers the overall movement trend of the exam-room. Figure 3(a) is an example of an optical flow graph extracting from two exam-room images with $\lceil 0.5 * FPS \rceil$ frames apart. Figure 3(b) is an example of the optical flow graph sequence (candidates leave the exam-room) of the input double channel 3D convolution neural network.

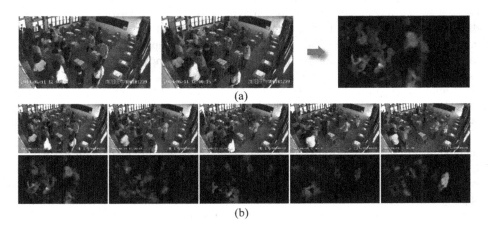

(a)

(b)

Fig. 3. Optical flow graph of exam invigilation video. (a) An optical flow graph extracting from two exam-room images. (b) A sample of optical flow graph sequence of exam invigilation video.

3.3   Analysis of Experimental Results of EMV-1 Dataset

In this section, experimental analysis and comparison of D3DCNN model and single channel C1 and C2 neural networks on EMV-1 test dataset proved the validity of the double channel 3D convolution network and proved the superiority of D3DCNN model by comparing with many frontier methods.

Figure 4 shows confusion matrix diagrams of C1 channel model, C2 channel model and D3DCNN model for classification of five types of exam-room video scene respectively, where Y-axis is the real category of sample fragments and X-axis is the predicted sample category of sample fragments.

From the comparative analysis of Fig. 4(a) and (b), it can be seen that the classification accuracy of C1 channel model is higher than that of C2 channel model for Category 2 (preparation and closing) scenarios. The reason is that the C2 channel model uses optical flow graphs sequence to extract features, and the recognition of type 2 is mainly realized by learning the action features of the invigilators. When the action amplitude of the invigilators does not change significantly, it is easy to confuse with other sample categories which also have weak action changes. However, the classification accuracy of C1 channel model for Category 3 (candidates enter the exam-room) and Category 4 (candidates leave the exam-room) is lower than that of C2 channel model. That is because the C1 channel model is classified by the original frame image samples, and the two types of sample sequences present complex and confusing personnel distribution. The lack of distinguishing ability of the C1 channel model leads to confusion between the two types. In these two kinds of video scenarios, the direction and trend of candidates' movement have obvious trend in the optical flow graph, and C2 channel model makes full use of this to improve the recognition accuracy of these two kinds of sample fragments.

Generally, the C1 channel model has better discriminant ability to classify samples with the distribution of personnel and the movement of only a few people and the C2 channel model has a good ability to distinguish the types of personnel distribution disorder or mass movement. D3DCNN compensates the C1 and C2 channel models, combines their advantages, and effectively fuses image spatial content and action information. The classification accuracy of all kinds of samples is improved to more than 0.88, and the overall accuracy is up to 0.92 (shown in Fig. 4(c)).

Table 4 compares the classification accuracy of several frontier methods and D3DCNN on the dataset EVM-1. The traditional BoW method combined with the BoW model has a general performance. The accuracy of the BoW method based on HOG, HOF and MoSIFT features is only about 55%. Compared with traditional method, the accuracy of most deep learning methods can reach more than 80%, such as C3D, C1 and C2 channel models.

Under the same input data, the classification accuracy of C3D model is 87.48% slightly lower than that of C1 channel model 88.03%, which proves that the single channel network model designed in this paper is better. The C2 channel model applies the same model structure to the optical flow map data and obtains 86.74% classification results. D3DCNN model further uses double channel network models to learn the features of different source data and fuses the temporal and spatial features of C1 and C2 channel models, which can improve the classification accuracy to the highest 92.27%.

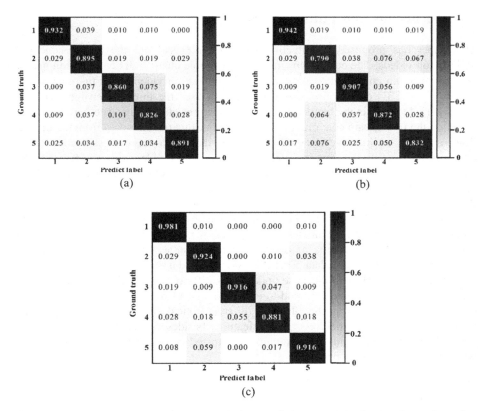

Fig. 4. Comparison of the classification confusion matrix between D3DCNN and two channels. (a) Classification confusion matrix of C1 channel model. (b) Classification confusion matrix of C2 channel model. (c) D3DCNN classification confusion matrix.

Table 4. Comparison of classification accuracy on the EMV-1

SN	Methods	Accuracy in %
1	HOG + BoW	54.29
2	HOF + BoW	55.36
3	MoSIFT + BoW	54.91
4	MoSIFT + KDE + Sparse Coding	58.13
5	C3D	87.48
6	C1	88.03
7	C2	86.74
8	D3DCNN	92.27

4   Conclusions and Future Work

This paper has proposed an effective method for classifying the exam scenes of invigilation videos. The core of this method is a double channel 3D convolution neural network that can classify the exam scenes of invigilation videos. The first channel is based on the C3D convolution neural network. It uses the three-dimensional convolution kernel to extract the temporal and spatial features effectively. Another channel is based on the two-stream convolution neural network that uses the data from the optical flow of videos to improve the performance of the video scene classification. Two channels are fused to the synergy effect on classifying the video scenes. After training with a large number of samples, the model can achieve an efficient classification of the exam-room's global motion state. Experiments on the EMV-1 dataset of exam invigilation video demonstrate the superiority of the model.

Although the end-to-end training method can be realized on the double channel 3D convolution neural network model in this paper, it needs to be prepared in advance since the optical flow graphs of one of the data sources needs to be obtained by computing the source video data. Therefore, this method has not yet formed a complete end-to-end system. How to integrate optical flow information acquisition into network model and realize the complete end-to-end training and reasoning is one of the key points of future researches. The effects of different optical flow methods on the model results, the effects of different types of features besides optical flow data as input sources on the model results, and the more optimized network model structure design will be the next research priorities.

References

1. Adil, M., Simon, R., Khatri, S.K.: Automated invigilation system for detection of suspicious activities during examination. In: IEEE Amity International Conference on Artificial Intelligence (AICAI) (2019)
2. Cote, M., Jean, F., Albu, A.B., Capson, D.W.: Video summarization for remote invigilation of online exams. In: IEEE Winter Conference on Applications of Computer Vision (WACV), pp. 1–9 (2016)
3. Andrej, K., George, T., Sanketh, S., et al.: Large-scale video classification with convolutional neural networks. In: IEEE Conference on Computer Vision and Pattern Recognition (CVPR), pp. 1725–1732 (2014)
4. Park, E., Han, X., Berg, T.L., et al.: Combining multiple sources of knowledge in deep CNNS for action recognition. In: IEEE Winter Conference on Applications of Computer Vision (WACV), pp. 1–8 (2016)
5. Wang, L., Qiao, Y., Tang, X.: Action recognition with trajectory-pooled deep-convolutional descriptors. In: IEEE Conference on Computer Vision and Pattern Recognition, pp. 4305–4314 (2015)
6. Wang, H., Kläser, A., Schmid, C., et al.: Action recognition by dense trajectories. In: IEEE Conference on Computer Vision and Pattern Recognition (CVPR), pp. 3169–3176 (2011)
7. Shao, J., Chen, C.L., Kang, K., et al.: Slicing convolutional neural network for crowd video understanding. In: IEEE Conference on Computer Vision and Pattern Recognition, pp. 5620–5628 (2016)

8. Shao, J, Loy C.C., Wang, X.: Scene-independent group profiling in crowd. In: IEEE Conference on Computer Vision and Pattern Recognition, pp. 2227–2234 (2014)
9. Zhang, J., Zheng, Y., Qi, D.: Deep spatio-temporal residual networks for citywide crowd flows prediction. In: Proceedings of the Thirty-First AAAI Conference on Artificial Intelligence, pp. 1655–1661 (2016)
10. Simonyan, K., Zisserman, A.: Two-stream convolutional networks for action recognition in videos. In: Advances in Neural Information Processing Systems, Montreal, Canada, pp. 568–576 (2014)
11. Feichtenhofer, C., Pinz, A., Zisserman, A.: Convolutional two-stream network fusion for video action recognition. In: IEEE Conference on Computer Vision and Pattern Recognition, pp. 1933–1941 (2016)
12. Zhu, Y., Lan, Z., Newsam, S., et al.: Hidden two-stream convolutional networks for action recognition. arXiv preprint arXiv:1704.00389 (2017)
13. Wang, H, Wang, L.: Modeling temporal dynamics and spatial configurations of actions using two-stream recurrent neural networks. In: CVPR, pp. 499–508 (2017)
14. Ji, S., Xu, W., Yang, M., et al.: 3D convolutional neural networks for human action recognition. IEEE Trans. Pattern Anal. Mach. Intell. 35(1), 221–231 (2013)
15. Tran, D., Bourdev, L., Fergus, R., et al.: Learning spatiotemporal features with 3D convolutional networks. In: IEEE International Conference on Computer Vision, pp. 4489–4497 (2015)
16. Qiu, Z., Yao, T., Mei, T.: Learning spatio-temporal representation with pseudo-3D residual networks. In: IEEE International Conference on Computer Vision (ICCV), pp. 5534–5542 (2017)

Efficient Self-embedding Data Hiding for Image Integrity Verification with Pixel-Wise Recovery Capability

Faranak Tohidi[1,2,3], Manoranjan Paul[3(✉)],
Mohammad Reza Hooshmandasl[1,2], Tanmoy Debnath[3],
and Hojjat Jamshidi[4]

[1] The Laboratory of Quantum Information Processing,
Yazd University, Yazd, Iran
ftohidi@stu.yazd.ac.ir, hooshmandasl@yazd.ac.ir
[2] Department of Computer Science, Yazd University, Yazd, Iran
[3] School of Computing and Mathematics, Charles Sturt University,
Bathurst, Australia
{mpaul, tdebnath}@csu.edu.au
[4] Tehran University, Tehran, Iran
jamshidh@ut.ac.ir

Abstract. Due to the powerful image editing tools, image integrity protection is becoming important, for instance, in a court of law, news reports, insurance claims or telemedicine. Digital image watermarking is a technique for detecting, localizing and recovering of tampered image but capability and accuracy of performance by the existing methods are still issues especially when tampering rate is relatively high. This paper proposes a novel blind fragile watermarking mechanism for effective image authentication and recovery. In the proposed scheme, not only the probability of detection and localization of tampering is increased because of embedding appropriate authentication code in the proper position but also there is an efficient post-processing of recovery in a way that any pixel has treated differently leading to higher quality of recovered image. Furthermore, embedding more fragile authentication code with a smaller number of bits can help to provide a second opportunity for content recovery while the quality of watermarked image is preserved. Thus, better results have been achieved in terms of accuracy of detection and the quality of recovered image after higher tampering rate compared with some of the state-of-the-art schemes.

Keywords: Watermarking · Tamper detection · Image recovery · Image security · Image authentication

1 Introduction

Modifying, transmitting and exchanging digital content have become more convenient and frequent due to the advancements in modern communication technologies and the availability of numerous image processing tools. It may result in challenges when truthfulness of digitized information contained in the images is important and can lead

© Springer Nature Switzerland AG 2019
C. Lee et al. (Eds.): PSIVT 2019, LNCS 11854, pp. 128–141, 2019.
https://doi.org/10.1007/978-3-030-34879-3_11

to problems in application areas like medical imaging, forensic documents, news reports etc. During transmission such sensitive contents may be intentionally or unintentionally manipulated leading to undesired consequences. Therefore, it is really a significant problem to confirm the integrity of received images as well as the original ownership authentication. For this reason, digital image integrity verification has become a popular and crucial research subject [1–5].

Image integrity verification can be implemented by digital signatures or digital watermarking. The digital signature method includes extracting the feature information of digital images and saving it as independent authentication information. A digital image can be verified if the authentication information is determined. However, a digital signature cannot distinguish where exactly tampering has happened. Whereas, a digital watermarking is able to not only detect, but also identify the location of tampering. "Digital Watermarking" is a method in which additional information is embedded into a digital signal with the purpose of authentication or verifying its integrity. This method has important applications in copyright protection, detection of fraud and document forgery, authentication of imagery and combatting fake news. Invisible watermark could be a company logo, a literary message indicating the ownership of the image, some features of the original image, and even a full copy of the compressed original image itself. Watermark data can be extracted for various purposes, including content integrity verification or ownership authentication [1–6].

According to applications, watermark techniques, can be categorized as fragile watermarking, semi-fragile watermarking and robust watermarking. Fragile watermarking can be easily altered or damaged by any modification. Since it is sensitive to any kind of modifications, it can be used for verifying the integrity of the received images. Semi-fragile watermarking scheme is able to resist some malicious attacks while it is sensitive to some other forms of tampering and can be used for multiple purposes. Robust watermarking can be used to ownership authentication or copyright protection. Watermarking for tamper detection and recovery has received much attention recently. Fragile image watermarking has been studied for content authentication and integrity verification. In recent studies, more self-embedding fragile watermarking schemes have been developed to recover the contents of the detected, tampered regions using the intact information. In this type of schemes watermark data are usually basic features related to the original image [7–9].

Although there are variety of schemes that are able to recover the tampered image, there is no general model for the integrity verification and content recovery due to the trade-off between the recovered image quality and tampering rate. The performance of tamper detection, localization and recovery schemes are usually given in terms of accuracy of detection, localization and quality of recovered image in different recovery conditions. Recovery condition can be tampering rate or the amount of modifications. In most fragile image watermarking least significant bit (LSB) embedding method generally has been used because it is simple and has high capacity of data hiding with good quality [5]. Some methods [5, 7] have used more than 2 LSBs of image's pixels for data embedding while the others [6, 10, 11] only used 2 LSBs or even less. Obviously using less LSBs for embedding watermark data can result in better quality of watermarked image. However, there is more limitation for embedding data.

Shehab et al. [6] proposed a new fragile watermarking scheme for image authentication and self-recovery for medical applications. In their method an image is divided to blocks. Blocks are non-overlapping with the same size of 4 × 4 then for every block *singular value decomposi*tion (SVD) is used to obtain block authentication bits and the self-recovery information is calculated with the help of the average values of every four pixels inside the block. Block authentication and self-recovery bits are inserted into the two least significant bits (LSBs) of the image pixels of the other block for authentication and providing a way to detect different attacked area of the watermarked image and recover the original image after tampering. Arnold transformation is also used to determine the insertion of both authentication and self-recovery bits. This method can achieve reasonable quality of recovered image but the validity of localization of tampering cannot be trusted exactly. This problem occurs because of embedding both authentication and recovery bits in the same block. Here a lack of capability is noticed in realizing that which block is tampered with, whether the block contained authentication bits or the source block; thus, there would be an increase in False Positive Rate (FPR). Moreover, methods which use average pixels values same as [6] has the problem of mosaic appearance for recovered blocks. Hsu and Tu [7] used smoothness to distinguish the types of image blocks, and employ different watermark embedding, tamper detection, and recovery strategies for different block types to enhance hiding efficiency, authentication, and recovery effects. They proposed further processing for recovered blocks to eliminate mosaic appearance after being recovered. In their method although the problem of mosaic appearance was solved, the quality of recovered image after post-processing has decreased.

Kim et al. [10] proposed a self-embedding fragile watermarking scheme to restoration of a tampered image. An absolute moment block truncation coding was used to compress the original image. Then, compressed version of the original image was embedded using the LSB and 2LSB for the pixels of the cover image. In their scheme, at receiver side, a compressed version of the original image is reconstructed by using extracted watermarked data and compared with compressed version of received image in order to detect tampering. In their method, due to lacking separated authentication and recovery bits, the probability of error could be high. In many self-embedding block-wise schemes, the recovery bits related to a particular block are often hidden into the other block of the image. Sometimes, this recovery method could be unsuccessful as a result of tampering the block contained the recovery bits. This is called tampering coincidence problem [5].

To solve the problem, in some papers, redundant information of the recovery codes has been embedded into the original image. However, embedding redundant data needs more embedding bits resulting in greater distortion. Therefore, the quality of watermarked image has decreased due to more embedding data. *Optimal iterative block truncation coding* (OIBTC) has been proposed by Qin et al. [11], which can acquire better visual quality of decoded images than *Block Truncation Coding* (BTC). They used OIBTC in order to generate reference bits with high efficiency for content recovery. Their method can achieve good performance of tampering recovery. They applied two sizes of blocks and obtained different results for each size (4 × 4 and 8 × 8). As a result of higher compression rate and having greater redundancy of recovery data, the largest restorable tampering rates are higher for block sizes of 8 × 8.

But the quality of recovered image is better for block size of 4 × 4 when tampering rate is low due to the fact that watermarked data can have more detailed recovery bits for each block. Although, the quality of the recovered image after higher tampering rate can be improved for the block size of 8 × 8 because of embedding redundant information, the localization accuracy will be also reduced due to using a large block size. It is obvious that more watermark data can be embedded into a large block size, but it delivers a poor accuracy for tamper localization [6, 12].

In the proposed method, authentication code is more compressed but with greater sensitivity to any modification. Instead, the second chance for block recovery can be embedded inside the watermarked image. Furthermore, pixels in the recovered blocks are differently treated concerning to their positions. Therefore, the proposed method will be capable to recover more tampered block with higher quality. The experimental results demonstrate that this method is truly efficient, especially when the tampered area is relatively large.

The contributions of the paper are:

- Introduction of more fragile and compressed authentication code with higher probability of detecting tampering.
- Introduce embedding the second recovery data for better recovery while the quality of the watermarked image is preserved.
- Introduction of effective pixel-wise mechanism after content recovery to eliminate mosaic visual.

2 Proposed Method

The image is divided into 4 × 4 blocks then authentication code and reference code are computed for each block separately. Do to the fact that, the smaller block size can provide more accurate tamper localization [12], the block size of 4 × 4 has been selected in this proposed method. However, choosing smaller block size such as 2 × 2 is not possible because there is more limitation on the capacity of data hiding. Unlike the [6] method the location of authentication code for each block is different from its recovery code to achieve greater accuracy. Authentication data will be embedded in each block itself and recovery data will be embedded into the other block. Recovery data can be achieved firstly with the help of average pixels values of the blocks then authentication code for each block will be made with reference to calculated watermark data of the block and their parity bits. To ensure the security and providing better recovery ability, the recovery data related to each block transform in the other block in a way that it can only be reversed back by the previous unique and secret key. For this reason, Arnold transformation is used to find destination block for embedding recovery codes such a way that watermarked data can be distributed into an image's blocks [6, 12]. A digital image which is divided into non-overlapping blocks can be considered as a two unit function $f(x, y)$. It is a mapping function which changes a source block (x, y) to a destination block (x', y') using (1).

$$\begin{bmatrix} x' \\ y' \end{bmatrix} = \begin{bmatrix} 1 & a \\ b & ab+1 \end{bmatrix} \begin{bmatrix} x \\ y \end{bmatrix} mod\, N \tag{1}$$

Parameter of "N" is the total number of blocks in an image. Parameters "a" and "b" can be used as the secret keys.

2.1   Generating and Embedding Watermarked Data

Self-recovery information consists of two parts, the first and the second recovery code. The embedding locations of block recovery codes are different and should be calculated with secret keys to have greater protection. It helps with hiding the neighboring block recovery data at a distant location in order to prevent an attacker from more tampering and provide better self-recovery.

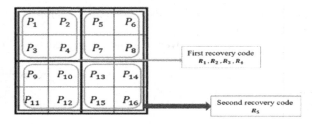

Fig. 1. The first and second recovery codes

To reduce the amount of watermark data and increase the quality of watermarked image, the watermark recovery data are divided into two kinds of recovery codes. The first recovery code can be used more frequently therefore it is more complete and deliver better quality. The first recovery data for every 4 × 4 block includes four average values related to four 2 × 2 blocks which are inside this block. The average value of the 4 × 4 block is considered as its second recovery data which is more compressed and will be used in case of damaging the first one. The number of 5 bits is assigned for every average value as its 5 Most Significant Bits (MSBs). There are five average values which should be embedded in every block such a way that one of them (R_5 in Fig. 1) is the second recovery code and it belongs to one block of the image and the other four codes (R_1, R_2, R_3, R_4 in Fig. 1) are altogether as the first recovery code and they belong to another block of the image (see Figs. 1 and 2).

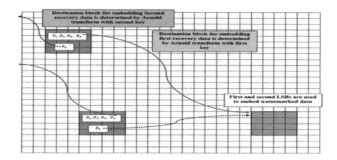

Fig. 2. Finding destination block for embedding recovery codes

In order to generate reference bits of recovery codes, mean values and their 5 MSB can be calculated by the following formulas (2, 3, 4, and 5).

$$R_x = \frac{1}{4} \sum\nolimits_{i=1}^{4} P_{i+4(x-1)} \quad x = 1, 2, 3, 4 \tag{2}$$

$$R_{x,t} = floor[round(R_x)/2^t] mod\, 2, \ t = 0, 1, \ldots, 4 \tag{3}$$

$$R_5 = \frac{1}{16} \sum\nolimits_{i=1}^{16} P_i \tag{4}$$

$$R_{5,t} = floor[round(R_5)/2^t] mod\, 2, \ t = 0, 1, \ldots, 4 \tag{5}$$

Where P_i (1 = 1, 2... 16) are pixels inside the block and R_i (1 = 1, 2... 5) are related mean values. The function floor (.) returns the nearest integer towards minus infinity of the input, the function round (.) returns the nearest integer of the input, R_i (1 = 1, 2... 5) denote the recovery codes of the block (see Fig. 1), and t (t = 0, 1... 4) denote the 5 MSB bits of the mean values. After embedding all reference codes in their related destination block, authentication code of each block should be calculated according to its embedded data. Thus, the parity bit for any of the five average values should be calculated and added to them. In order to achieve more accuracy and decrease FNR, the other two parity checks should be done on the first and second LSBs of destination block to ensure that the probability of detecting tampering can be high enough. Therefore, the number of bits for authentication code is 7. In order not to degrade the quality of the image noticeably, the two LSBs of the pixels in every block are used to embed watermarked data. The 7 bits of all LSBs in every block are reserved for authentication bits. There are 5 average values which are needed to embed as recovery code and each average value has 5 bits separately in every block. An extra bit is added to every average value as parity bit to check whether data has been tampered or not. These bits are included authentication code. In the Fig. 3 $R_{x,i}$ are the recovery codes and p_y are authentication codes which are embedded in 2 LSBs of destination block. As it mentioned before, authentication code for every block should be computed according its embedded recovery data then embedded into the block itself.

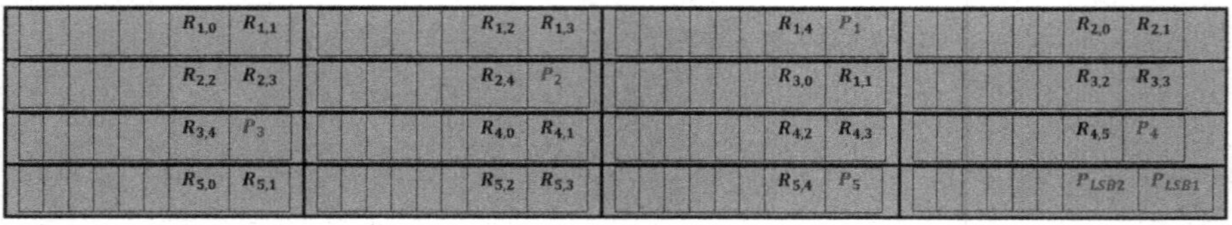

$R_{1,0}$	$R_{1,1}$	$R_{1,2}$	$R_{1,3}$	$R_{1,4}$	P_1	$R_{2,0}$	$R_{2,1}$
$R_{2,2}$	$R_{2,3}$	$R_{2,4}$	P_2	$R_{3,0}$	$R_{1,1}$	$R_{3,2}$	$R_{3,3}$
$R_{3,4}$	P_3	$R_{4,0}$	$R_{4,1}$	$R_{4,2}$	$R_{4,3}$	$R_{4,5}$	P_4
$R_{5,0}$	$R_{5,1}$	$R_{5,2}$	$R_{5,3}$	$R_{5,4}$	P_5	P_{LSB2}	P_{LSB1}

Fig. 3. Embedding authentication and recovery codes in first and second LSB of a block

Since there are seven times of checking parity, the probability of not to detect tampering is very low and can be calculated by binomial distribution formula. When the number of bit errors becomes even a single parity bit fails to detect, therefore the probability of undetected error is calculated by taking into account the number of combinations that even bits are in error by (6).

$$Pr(undetected) = \binom{n}{x} p^x q^{n-x} \tag{6}$$

Here "n" is the number of bits and "x" is the number of errors which are even. "p" is the probability of changing or error for one bit and "q" is the probability of not changing for one bit. When parity checks are done on the amounts of averages, the number of bits is 5. As a result, the probability of error can be calculated by (7).

$$Pr(undetected)_{n=5} = \binom{5}{2}\left(\frac{1}{2}\right)^2\left(\frac{1}{2}\right)^3 + \binom{5}{4}\left(\frac{1}{2}\right)^4\left(\frac{1}{2}\right)^1 < \frac{1}{2} \tag{7}$$

When parity check are done on LSBs, the number of bits is 15. Consequently, the probability of error can be calculated by (8).

$$Pr(undetected)_{n=15} = \binom{15}{2}\left(\frac{1}{2}\right)^2\left(\frac{1}{2}\right)^{13} + \binom{15}{4}\left(\frac{1}{2}\right)^4\left(\frac{1}{2}\right)^{11} + \binom{15}{6}\left(\frac{1}{2}\right)^6\left(\frac{1}{2}\right)^9$$
$$+ \binom{15}{8}\left(\frac{1}{2}\right)^8\left(\frac{1}{2}\right)^7 + \binom{15}{10}\left(\frac{1}{2}\right)^{10}\left(\frac{1}{2}\right)^5 + \binom{15}{12}\left(\frac{1}{2}\right)^{12}\left(\frac{1}{2}\right)^3 + \binom{15}{14}\left(\frac{1}{2}\right)^{14}\left(\frac{1}{2}\right)^1 \cong \frac{1}{2} \tag{8}$$

As a result of 7 times checking parity, the probability of not detecting of tampering (FNR) can be far less than $\left(\frac{1}{2}\right)^7$.

2.2 Tamper Detection and Localization

An image should be divided to 4×4 blocks to detect tampering. The watermark data should be extracted from the two LSBs of pixel values of every block. Then five average values will be separated and parity bit for any of them should be calculated and compared with the related extracted parity bit to distinguish whether the image block is tampered with or not. If parity for all average values are valid the other two parity checks should be done on the first and second LSBs as well. If the data extracted are not same compared with the parity bits it indicates that block has been tampered with and recovery is necessary.

2.3   Recovery of Tampered Blocks

In case of detecting tampering in a block, its recovery data which have been embedded in the other areas of the image should be extracted to reconstruct its modified data. The addresses of the recovery codes can be calculated by the inverse of Arnold transformation with the two secret keys that have been used during embedding procedure. Our priority is the first recovery data since it has more quality. For this reason, another authentication test is done to ensure that the block contained the first recovery data is still undamaged. If the first recovery code related to tampered block is valid this recovery data will be used to recover the block. Otherwise if the second recovery code is available and intact it can be used as well. If both recovery codes of a block have been damaged, the average value of all its available intact adjacent blocks can be considered as its mean value.

When above recovery steps are done the 5 Most Significant Bits (MSBs) of all pixels related to the tampered blocks could be recovered. The recovered blocks may have mosaic appearance since the same average values have been used for some pixels similarly. In order to solve this problem further processing can be done for every pixels of the recovered blocks. Every pixel of the recovered blocks should be processed in a different way according to their position in the block in order to avoid substituting same values for all of them and achieving better quality. The quality of the block can be improved with the assist of its neighbors. This is because every pixel can be affected by its four neighbors as it can be clearly seen from the Fig. 4. Any pixels of the 2×2 block which is recovered by the mean of the block is affected two times by its own block mean and one time by its two neighbor blocks mean as well. Therefore, the process after recovery can be done by (9).

$$Px_i = [2 \times R_x + MB_1 + MB_2/4], \; i = 1, 2, \ldots, 4, \; x = 1, 2, \ldots, 4 \qquad (9)$$

Where "i" defines the number of pixels in the 2×2 block, "x" defines the number of the block, MB_1 and MB_2 are its neighbour blocks mean values.

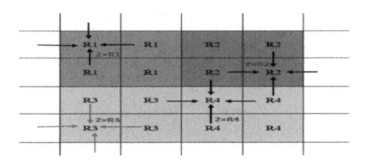

Fig. 4. Post-processing for pixels individually

In the method [7] this point is not paid attention. Instead they used the corner neighbors which do not have much influence on the mentioned pixels. For this reason, the quality of recovered block has decreased in their method. After using above formula, the 6 MSBs of all block pixels are recovered. Figure 5 illustrates detection and recovery of tampered blocks in the image.

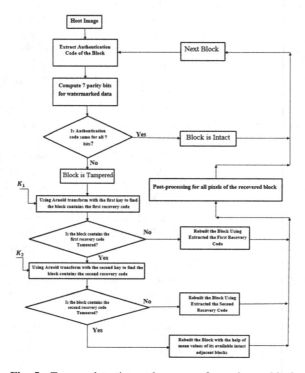

Fig. 5. Tamper detection and recovery for an image block

2.4   Recovery of Tampered Image

The image can be reconstructed by integrating the undamaged blocks and the recovered blocks. In order to decrease the distortion between original image and recovered image caused by first and second LSBs, further processes should be consulted with. Since distortion for two bits is calculated by (10), the binary value of 10 can be best value for first and second LSBs to minimize the amount of distortion.

$$D = \sum_{i=0}^{i=3} (L_i - x)^2 \tag{10}$$

Where "D" defines alteration by two LSBs, L_i is the real amount of two LSBs and can be 0, 1 and 2 to 3 as a decimal value. It can be simply calculated that the amount of 2 (10 in binary form) is the best value to minimize the distortion.

3   Experimental Results

Some standard images have been utilized to demonstrate the effectiveness of proposed method. Performance analysis of the proposed method has been done on the quality of watermarked images and recovered image with standard quality measurements Peak Signal-to-Noise Ratio (PSNR)) in same conditions or similar tampering rates. The comparison between the results of the proposed method and [6] and [7] are listed in Table 1, when tampering rates (t) were 30%.

Table 1. Comparison the results of proposed method with [6] and [7] in terms of PSNR for different standard images when tampering rate is 30%

Standard images	[6]	[7]	Proposed method
Lena	35.2832	33.6408	36.2505
Barbara	26.8452	24.8220	26.2362
Mandril	34.3247	32.0925	34.7858
Woman-Darkhair	43.1291	42.0440	45.4568
Woman-Blonde	33.4915	32.2753	33.9269
Living Room	31.3660	29.5539	31.6878
pepper	35.3788	34.1731	36.7211
Lake	32.9030	31.4760	33.9225
JetPlane	37.2206	35.4477	38.6208
CameraMan	37.5171	34.4148	37.4082
House	44.4450	43.2550	49.7387
Pirot	33.6052	31.9483	33.9626

As it can clearly be seen from the table all our results are better except for Barbara image because of having mosaic shape in this image itself. It is obvious that our method has even better results than [6] and [7] in higher tampering rate (between 30%–50%) as a result of having second chance of recovery. The quality of watermarked image in proposed method and [6] for all images are more than 43 dB thanks to embedding watermark data in only two LSBs. But the quality of watermarked image in [7] is less and (around 40.9) due to an increased use of LSBs to embed data hiding for each pixel in average. Our method is able to detect, localize and recover tampered image when tampering rate is less than 50% with acceptable quality. This capability can prove the high proficiency and capability of our method. The Fig. 6 shows the results of tampering localization and recovery by the proposed method after copy paste attack.

The Fig. 7 shows recovered image by the proposed method and the method of [6] and [7] in similar conditions after cropping attack. The other images are also prepared including two medical 512 × 512 images of Liver and Brain since the proposed method can work on medical images as well. The Fig. 8 shows recovered image after tampering by the proposed method and the scheme of [6]. To show the superior performance of this method, the picture of Liver has been selected to show the details in a way that can be seen by eyes more clearly. As it can be clearly seen in the Fig. 9 the quality of recovered area in the image in proposed method is better than that of [6] as a result of eliminating mosaic visual in our method.

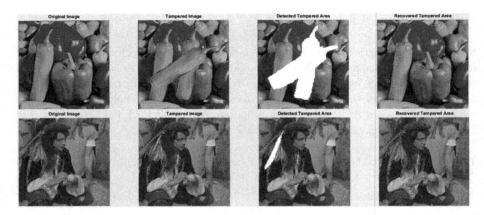

Fig. 6. (Results of copy and paste attack by proposed method) Original image – Tampered image – Detected Tampered Area – Recovered image by proposed method

Fig. 7. (Results of Cropping attack) Tamper image t = 30% - Recovered image by [6] - Recovered image by Proposed method - Recovered image by [7]

The experimental results show the proposed scheme has better performance in terms of tamper detection accuracy in compared with latest methods as can be seen in Table 2. The authentication code in our method is more sensitive to any kind of modification. The probability of detecting tampering for each block is far higher than the trace of SVD which is used in [6] as authentication code. Although SVD has

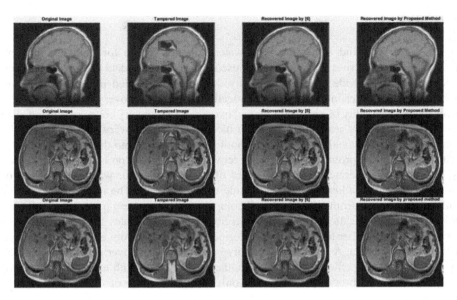

Fig. 8. Original image - Tamper image - Recovered image by [6] - Recovered image by Proposed method

Fig. 9. Recovered tampered area by [6] - Recovered tampered area by proposed method after eliminating mosaic visual

characteristic of robustness, it is not helpful in this type of application. Furthermore, since each block has its own authentication code and recovery code belonged to the other block, the possibility of happening *False Positive Rate* (FPR) will decrease. The rate of error of FPR in the scheme of [6] is more because the destination block includes both the authentication and the recovery codes. Thus, if the destination block is tampered, an error will happen in detecting where the image is tampered exactly. The improvement can be clearly seen in Table 2 when the proposed scheme has been compared with the scheme of [6] and [7] in terms of authentication error rates.

Table 2. Comparison the results in average in terms of FRN and FPR

Paper	FNR	FPR
[6]	0.41	0.013
[7]	0.0008	0.0044
Proposed scheme	<0.0078	0.0003

4 Conclusion

In this paper, a blind self-embedding watermarking scheme for tamper detection, localization and recovery has been proposed using a novel data hiding embedding mechanism. To provide additional security the image is divided into the blocks and watermarked data are included as authentication code and recovery code. In order to achieve greater quality of recovered image, two types of recovery code are utilized. The average mean values are applied for each block to create recovery codes. Any of the recovery codes belonged to each block should be embedded into the other blocks at a distant location for providing better self-recovery. Authentication code for each block is 7 bits and is generated through 7 times of parity checks for watermarked data of every block and should be embedded inside the block itself. The receiver can extract authentication code from each block and compare with its content parity checks for the purpose of authentication. If the data are not same, it indicates that tampering has occurred. Then another test would be performed to prevent it from extracting tampered data as recovery data. A second opportunity is provided to recover the tampered block by embedding more efficient and fragile authentication code with a smaller number of bits. Therefore, the proposed method not only has high quality of watermarked image but also is able recover tampered image in higher tampering rate. Moreover, further processes have been done in order to increase the quality of recovered image and elimination of the mosaic visual. Experimental results show this method can achieve superior performance in terms of authentication and recovering of the image.

References

1. Liu, X.-L., Lin, C.-C., Yuan, S.-M.: Blind dual watermarking for color images' authentication and copyright protection. IEEE Trans. Circ. Syst. Video Technol. **28**(5), 1047–1055 (2018)
2. Wang, N., Cheng, X., Li, Z., Chen, Y.: Dual watermarking algorithm based on singular value decomposition and compressive sensing. In: IEEE 17th International Conference on Communication Technology (ICCT), pp. 1763–1767 (2017)
3. Qin, C., Ji, P., Zhang, X., Dong, J., Wang, J.: Fragile image watermarking with pixel-wise recovery based on overlapping embedding strategy. Sig. Process. **138**, 280–293 (2017)
4. Dole, V.S., Patil, N.N.: Self-embedding fragile watermarking for image tampering detection and image recovery using self recovery blocks. In: IEEE International Conference on Computing Communication Control and Automation, (ICCUBEA) (2015)
5. Sing, D., Sing, S.K.: Effective self-embedding watermarking scheme for image tampered detection and localization with recovery capability. J. Vis. Commun. Image Represent. **38**, 775–789 (2016)
6. Shehab, M., et al.: Secure and robust fragile watermarking scheme for medical images. IEEE Access **6**, 10269–10278 (2018)
7. Hsu, C.-S., Tu, S.-F.: Image tamper detection and recovery using adaptive embedding rules. Measurement **88**, 287–296 (2016)
8. Haghighi, B.B., Taherinia, A.H.: TRLH: fragile and blind dual watermarking for image tamper detection and self-recovery based on lifting wavelet transform and half toning technique. J. Vis. Commun. Image Represent. **50**, 49–64 (2018)

9. Tai, W.L., Liao, Z.J.: Image self-recovery with watermark self-embedding. In: IEEE International Conference on Signal Processing, Signal Processing: Image Communication, vol. 65, pp. 11–25, July 2018

10. Kim, C., Shin, D., Yang, C.-N.: Self-embedding fragile watermarking scheme to restoration of a tampered image using AMBTC. Pers. Ubiquit. Comput. **22**(1), 11–22 (2018)

11. Qin, C., Ji, P., Chang, C.-C., Dong, J., Sun, X.: Non-uniform watermark sharing based on optimal iterative BTC for image tampering recovery. IEEE Multimedia **25**, 36–48 (2018)

12. Rakhmawati, L., Wirawan, W., Suwadi, S.: A recent survey of self-embedding fragile watermarking scheme for image authentication with recovery capability. EURASIP J. Image Video Process. **2019**, 1–22 (2019)

Enhanced Transfer Learning with ImageNet Trained Classification Layer

Tasfia Shermin[1]([✉]), Shyh Wei Teng[1], Manzur Murshed[1], Guojun Lu[1], Ferdous Sohel[2], and Manoranjan Paul[3]

[1] School of Science, Engineering and Information Technology, Federation University, Churchill, Australia
`{t.shermin,shyh.wei.teng,manzur.murshed,guojun.lu}@federation.edu.au`
[2] Murdoch University, Perth, Australia
`F.Sohel@murdoch.edu.au`
[3] Charles Sturt University, Albury-Wodonga, Australia
`mpaul@csu.edu.au`

Abstract. Parameter fine tuning is a transfer learning approach whereby learned parameters from pre-trained source network are transferred to the target network followed by fine-tuning. Prior research has shown that this approach is capable of improving task performance. However, the impact of the ImageNet pre-trained classification layer in parameter fine-tuning is mostly unexplored in the literature. In this paper, we propose a fine-tuning approach with the pre-trained classification layer. We employ layer-wise fine-tuning to determine which layers should be frozen for optimal performance. Our empirical analysis demonstrates that the proposed fine-tuning performs better than traditional fine-tuning. This finding indicates that the pre-trained classification layer holds less category-specific or more global information than believed earlier. Thus, we hypothesize that the presence of this layer is crucial for growing network depth to adapt better to a new task. Our study manifests that careful normalization and scaling are essential for creating harmony between the pre-trained and new layers for target domain adaptation. We evaluate the proposed depth augmented networks for fine-tuning on several challenging benchmark datasets and show that they can achieve higher classification accuracy than contemporary transfer learning approaches.

Keywords: CNNs · Parameter fine-tuning · Depth augmentation

1 Introduction

Convolutional neural networks [1–4] require a huge amount of labelled training data to yield optimal performance. Luckily, training CNNs on a large and diverse dataset (e.g. ImageNet) has been shown to enable the knowledge transfer across a wide range of tasks [5]. Parameter fine-tuning is one of the best performing transfer learning approaches used by the deep learning community. Parameter fine-tuning

© Springer Nature Switzerland AG 2019
C. Lee et al. (Eds.): PSIVT 2019, LNCS 11854, pp. 142–155, 2019.
https://doi.org/10.1007/978-3-030-34879-3_12

assists transferring learned knowledge to accomplish the target task with limited labelled data and increases the performance of the target model over random initialization [6]. The sequence of traditional parameter fine-tuning is to replace the classification layer of a CNN, pre-trained on a large and diverse dataset (e.g. ImageNet), with a randomly initialized new classification layer as per the target task. Then the new model undergoes forward-backward propagation to tune gradient descent on the target set. This transfer learning approach is exploited successfully by a number of contemporary transfer learning research [7–10].

Fig. 1. The t-SNE visualization of extracted features from the pre-trained classification layer. Dark pink colour represents ImageNet features, and other colours represent features from eight different target sets. (Color figure online)

The intuition behind so far not using the pre-trained classification layer while fine-tuning is that this layer holds category-specific features [6] that may not generalize well to target sets. However, our research manifests that even the classification layers of CNNs pre-trained on ImageNet have of overlapping or neighbouring high-level features with the target sets of images of natural and artificial objects, since ImageNet consists of a massive amount of labelled images of natural and human-made objects. Figure 1 shows the t-SNE [29] visualization of the relative distribution of extracted features from the classification layer of pre-trained AlexNet for widely used eight transfer learning target datasets (Sect. 3.1) and ImageNet (source). The t-SNE algorithm tries to minimize the divergence between two distribution by preserving the close or related clusters of high dimension in converted low dimension: one distribution is that measures pair-wise similarity in higher dimensional input data (in our case thousand dimensional features of source-target datasets) and the other distribution that measures pair-wise similarity in lower dimension (in our case two-dimensional space for visualization). We have used t-SNE for visualizing the relation or closeness between source and target features. The high intermingling or neighbouring between source and target feature distribution manifests that the classification layer of ImageNet pre-trained CNN may well assist the target network to adapt to the target domain via parameter fine-tuning. Also, by jointly adapting pre-trained classification and other representation layers for the target task, we could essentially bridge the domain shift underlying both the marginal distribution and the conditional distribution, which is pivotal for enhancing transfer learning [11]. Thus, we argue that the pre-trained classification layer is important for transfer learning and propose to include this layer in the fine-tuning procedure. In this work, we evaluate all fine-tuning approaches with our layer-wise fine-tuning scheme to observe fine-tuning from which layer produces optimal performance.

A significant number of works have experimented with incremental and lifelong learning [12–14]. For developmental transfer learning, in consistent with the traditional fine-tuning sequence, Wang et al. [15] and Oquab et al. [9] have discarded the pre-trained classification layer and appended new layers after the penultimate fully-connected (FC) layer of AlexNet. However, inspired by our empirical analysis of the transferability of the pre-trained classification layer (Sect. 3.2), we argue that the presence of the pre-trained classification layer is vital to increasing the network depth for transfer learning. Thus, we propose to consider this layer as the last FC layer and to append new layers beyond it for developmental transfer learning.

During fine-tuning, our proposed depth augmented networks might struggle from internal covariate shift of activations across pre-trained and new layers. Thus, to establish harmony between the learning of new and pre-trained layers, and to reduce sensitivity to random initialization, we introduce a normalization scheme to the network. We experiment with L_2-norm normalization [15] and batch normalization [16] to search for the best performing normalization scheme for the proposed depth augmented networks.

The main contributions of the paper are as follows:

- We propose to include the pre-trained classification layer in fine-tuning and find that the transfer learning performance with the pre-trained classification layer is higher than the traditional fine-tuning approach without it.
- We investigate which layers should be frozen during fine-tuning for optimal performance.
- For developmental transfer learning, we propose to augment new layers beyond the pre-trained classification layer to adapt better to target task. We also investigate the best fit normalization scheme for our proposed depth augmented networks.

The rest of the paper is organized as follows. Our proposed approaches are presented in Sect. 2. Section 3 presents the setup and analysis of our experimentation. Section 4 summarizes the contributions of this paper.

2   Methodology

We introduce the architectural and notational details of the proposed and traditional fine-tuning, the proposed depth augmented networks, and the layer-wise fine-tuning scheme in this section. Let us assume χ_N be a CNN pre-trained with a large dataset (e.g. ImageNet) having N layers $L_1, ..., L_N$, including the classification layer.

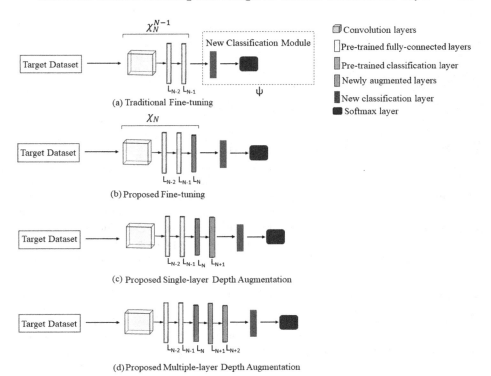

Fig. 2. Block diagram of the (a) traditional fine-tuning, (b) proposed fine-tuning and (c)–(d) depth augmented networks for fine-tuning, illustrating architectures of fine-tuning TLN $[\chi_N^\kappa]_\nu^\psi$, $[\chi_N]_\nu^\psi$, $[\chi_N]_\nu^{1+\psi}$, and $[\chi_N]_\nu^{2+\psi}$, respectively.

2.1 Traditional and Proposed Fine-Tuning

Let χ_N^κ denote the sub-network comprising the first κ layers of χ_N, $1 \leq \kappa < N$. Let $[\chi_N^\kappa + \psi]_\nu \equiv [\chi_N^\kappa]_\nu^\psi$ denote a transfer-learning network (TLN) from the first κ, $1 \leq \kappa < N$, layers of the pre-trained CNN χ_N, with parameter fine-tuning from layer L_ν onwards, $1 \leq \nu \leq \kappa$, where ψ is a classification module for new classes, which is a FC classification layer C followed by a Softmax layer. Figure 2(a) illustrates the block diagram of a TLN ($[\chi_N^{N-1}]_\nu^\psi$) which follows traditional fine-tuning sequence where the pre-trained classification layer L_N is discarded before fine-tuning. On the contrary, we include the pre-trained classification layer L_N in the proposed fine-tuning approach, as shown in Fig. 2(b). Our proposed fine-tuning TLN which comprises of all the layers of χ_N, is denoted as $[\chi_N]_\nu^\psi$, with parameter fine-tuning from layer L_ν onwards.

2.2 Proposed Depth Augmented Networks for Fine-Tuning

We increase the depth capacity of the network by constructing new FC layers comprising $S \in \{512, 1024, 2048, 4096\}$ neurons on top of the classification layer

L_N as shown in Fig. 2(c) and (d). Let $[\chi_N + L_{N+1} + ... + L_{N+\tau} + \psi]_\nu \equiv [\chi_N]_\nu^{\tau+\psi}$ denote a depth augmented TLN from the pre-trained CNN χ_N augmented with τ, $\tau \geq 0$, additional FC layers $L_{N+1}, ..., L_{N+\tau}$, with parameter fine-tuning from layer L_ν onwards, $1 \leq \nu \leq N + \tau$, where ψ is the new classification module, which has a FC classification layer C with a Softmax layer. Appended layers are treated as adaptation layers to compensate for the different image statistics of the source and target sets. Moreover, they allow for suitable compositions of pre-existing parameters and avoid unwanted modifications to the parameters of pre-trained layers for their adaptation to the new task.

To maintain learning pace, we propose to include a normalization scheme in proposed depth augmented networks. We explore both L_2-norm normalization and batch normalization. For the first normalization approach, consistent with [15], we apply L_2-norm normalization to the input activations of new layers. In case of batch normalization, we standardize the mean and variance of the input activations of new layers for stabilizing the learning process. Finally, we employ the learnable scaling parameter to scale the normalized activations.

2.3   Layer-Wise Fine-Tuning Scheme

We evaluate all the approaches discussed above (Sects. 2.1 and 2.2) using a two-step layer-wise fine-tuning scheme. At the first step, we initialize the transferred layers with pre-trained parameters and new layers randomly. In the second step, we start fine-tuning from the last transferred layer and freeze other layers. These two steps are repeated K times with different setups (K is the number of transferred layers), i.e. each time we unfreeze one more penultimate layer. For instance, in the second setup, we start fine-tuning from the penultimate transferred layer onwards. It is worth mentioning that the fine-tuning setups are mutually exclusive and parameters of all the different setups are initialized according to Step 1. We record transfer learning performance for each of these fine-tuning setups to determine which setup yields optimal performance.

3   Performance Study and Analysis

This section describes the datasets used in our experiments, the implementation details, and our evaluation outcomes for proposed approaches.

3.1   Datasets and Implementation Details

We assembled eight different fine-grained and coarse target datasets, as stated in Table 1. Fine-grained datasets used in this work are 102 Flowers [17] with 102 categories, CUB 200-2011 [18] with 200 types of birds, Stanford Dogs [19] with 120 classes and Oxford Pets [20] with 37 classes. The Coarse or mixed semantic datasets are Caltech-256 [21] with 256 categories, Pascal VOC-07 [22] having 20 different classes, MIT-67 scenes [23] with 67 classes of indoor scenes and SUN-397 scenes [24] with 397 categories. We have used ImageNet as the source dataset.

Table 1. Selected datasets for target task.

Type	Name	Images	Categories
Fine grained	102 Flowers	8189	102
	CUB 200-2011	11788	200
	Stanford Dogs	20580	120
	Oxford Pets	7400	37
Coarse	Caltech-256	30607	256
	Pascal VOC-07	9963	20
	MIT-67 scenes	15620	67
	SUN-397 scenes	108754	397

We have used AlexNet [1] and VGG-16 [2] pre-trained on ImageNet as source networks. Networks with two different depths, i.e. AlexNet, and VGG-16 are used to observe whether proposed parameter fine-tuning has consistent performance across different architectures. For pre-processing the training dataset, input images are first randomly cropped, horizontally flipped, and then normalized. A split of 75% of target dataset is used for training, and the remaining 25% for testing. We execute 2000 iterations with a batch size of 100 and momentum 0.9 for fine-tuning. A global learning rate of 0.005 is used with a piece-wise scheduler which lowers down the learning rate by 10 times less than the previous one at every 10 epochs. We have used 10 times higher learning rate in the newly appended layers of proposed depth augmented networks.

3.2 Evaluation and Analysis of Proposed Fine-Tuning

To investigate the impact of pre-trained classification layer in parameter fine-tuning and to compare the performance of proposed fine-tuning with traditional fine-tuning, we utilize our layer-wise fine-tuning scheme (Sect. 2.3). Figure 3 presents the results of two coarse (Caltech-256 and Pascal VOC-07) and two fine-grained datasets (CUB 200-2011, 102 Flowers). Traditional fine-tuning setup (dotted lines) lags far behind the proposed fine-tuning (dashed lines) consistently for almost all fine-tuning setups. This finding substantiates that fine-tuning pre-trained classification layer along with other transferred layers assist better transfer learning. Note that other datasets also perform similarly.

3.3 Layers to Be Frozen for Optimal Performance

Proposed and traditional fine-tuning performance seems to increase when we continue to unfreeze and fine-tune more pre-trained layers according to different layer-wise fine-tuning setups (Sect. 2.3), as shown in Fig. 3(a) and (b). However, we observe a significant drop in performance when we tune initial convolutional layers, more specifically, convolutional layer 1 and 2 for AlexNet, and convolution block 1 and 2 for VGG-16. The intuition is that fine-tuning these generic layers

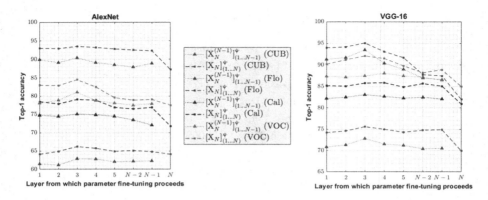

Fig. 3. Both graphs present the performance of proposed fine-tuning with the pre-trained classification layer (dashed lines), and traditional fine-tuning (dotted lines) for CUB 200-2011, 102 Flowers, Caltech-256 and Pascal VOC-07 datasets. (a) Here, the *x-axis* represents 8 layers of the AlexNet as $1, 2, ..., N - 2, N - 1, N$ and shows the layer from which fine-tuning proceeds while earlier layers are frozen (e.g. $N - 2$ denotes fine-tuning of layer L_{N-2} to L_N and other layers are frozen). (b) Here, the *x-axis* shows 16 layers (5 convolution blocks and 3 FC layers) of the VGG-16 as $1, 2, ..., N - 2, N - 1, N$. For both networks, proposed fine-tuning significantly outperforms traditional fine-tuning for all datasets.

might introduce noisy or unwanted modifications of parameters. That is, updating parameters would force the network to learn highly generic features of target set which are already learned from source set. The fine-tuning procedure has far fewer data and iterations than training from scratch, which might not let a vast number of pre-trained parameters of initial convolutional layers find another such equilibrium to interact with next convolutional layer in the same pace. Figure 3(a) portrays that fine-tuning from the third convolution layer onwards of AlexNet yields the highest accuracy. Figure 3(b) manifests that VGG-16 holds a similar trend for the third convolution block, which gives another perception that the first two convolution blocks of VGG-16 may contain highly generic or low-level features.

3.4   Performance Analysis of Proposed Depth Augmented Networks

We append a new FC layer on top of the pre-trained classification layer, employ normalization scheme to the augmented network, and perform layer-wise fine-tuning. We discuss details about our normalization scheme later in this section. Our results shown in solid lines of Fig. 4(a) and (b) present our best performing augmented networks with 2048 neurons and signify that parameter fine-tuning with increased network capacity paves the way to learn better. Our proposed single-layer depth augmented network performed better than fine-tuning with the pre-trained classification layer. This observation verifies the effectiveness of increasing model capacity beyond the pre-trained classification layer when

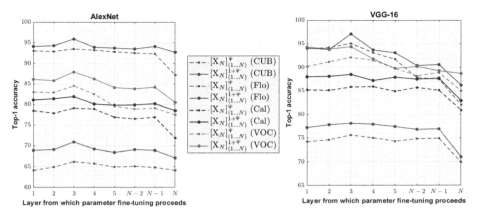

Fig. 4. These accuracy graphs present the performance of proposed fine-tuning with the pre-trained classification layer (dashed lines), and proposed single-layer depth augmented network (solid lines) for CUB 200-2011, 102 Flowers, Caltech-256 and Pascal VOC-07 datasets. (a) Here, the *x-axis* represents 8 layers of the AlexNet as $1, 2, ..., N - 2, N - 1, N$ and shows the layer from which fine-tuning proceeds while earlier layers are frozen (e.g. $N - 2$ denotes fine-tuning of layer L_{N-2} to L_N and other layers are frozen). (b) Here, the *x-axis* shows 16 layers (5 convolution blocks and 3 FC layers) of the VGG-16 as $1, 2, ..., N - 2, N - 1, N$. Single-layer depth augmented networks further boost performance over proposed fine-tuning for all datasets.

adapting it to both fine-grained and coarse novel classification task. Considering the best layer-wise fine-tuning performance, CUB and 102 Flowers seem to achieve more gain than the other two.

A detailed analysis of our investigation with single-layer depth augmented networks having different combinations of neurons, such as 512, 1024, 2048, and 4096, is shown in Table 2. Our empirical results indicate that the increase in performance is proportional to the increase in the magnitude of the new layer; however, for 4096 neurons, it diminishes marginally. In proposed depth augmentation approach, the bridge between new and pre-trained layers is the layer consisting only 1000 neurons; it might suffer from an overabundance of parameters while propagating information through to four times larger neural layer. Single-layer depth augmentation with 2048 neurons happens to yield best performance. It is worth mentioning that our augmented networks also perform similarly for other datasets.

Comparison with Contemporary Transfer Learning Works. To further prove the robustness of proposed single-layer depth augmented networks, we summarize the performance comparison with different existing transfer learning approaches from literature in Tables 3 and 4. The best outcomes among various combinations of our single-layer depth augmented AlexNet and VGG-16 evaluated by our layer-wise fine-tuning scheme are shown. For other approaches, the performance gap between our implementation and that reported by [5, 15, 25–28]

Table 2. Diagnostic performance analysis of our depth augmented networks. Here, S denotes the number of neurons in newly appended FC layer L_{N+1}. Fine-tuning from layer $N - 5$ (i.e. third convolution layer/ block) yields best performance for almost all combinations.

Network	Dataset	S	$[\chi_N]_N^{(1+\psi)}$	$[\chi_N]_{N-1}^{(1+\psi)}$	$[\chi_N]_{N-2}^{(1+\psi)}$	$[\chi_N]_{N-5}^{(1+\psi)}$	All
AlexNet	CUB 200-2011	512	65.2	66.5	66.9	67.8	67.2
		1024	66.2	67.5	68.9	69.9	68.4
		2048	66.3	68.7	69.0	**70.9**	69.2
		4096	66.7	68.1	67.1	68.1	66.8
	Caltech-256	512	75.5	78.2	78.6	79.5	79.1
		1024	75.9	78.3	78.9	80.9	80.3
		2048	75.2	77.9	78.5	**81.9**	81.1
		4096	75.0	78.1	78.3	81.0	80.9
VGG-16	CUB 200-2011	512	76.4	76.8	77.1	77.9	77.6
		1024	76.8	77.1	77.5	77.6	77.9
		2048	76.7	77.6	77.9	**78.1**	77.1
		4096	75.9	77.7	77.0	77.5	77.4
	Caltech-256	512	85.5	86.1	87.7	87.9	87.1
		1024	85.9	86.3	86.9	87.8	87.5
		2048	85.5	87.8	88.0	88.4	88.1
		4096	85.3	88.1	89.5	**88.5**	88.1

Table 3. Performance comparison of proposed single-layer depth augmented fine-tuned AlexNet network with contemporary fine-tuning approaches.

Approach	CUB 200-2011	102 flowers	Stanford dogs	Oxford pets	Caltech-256	VOC07	MIT-67	SUN-397
Normal_FT_CNN	62.3	88.9	63.8	80.0	72.1	77.9	61.2	53.9
CNN-SVM [5]	53.3	74.7	66.8	79.6	72.3	75.3	58.4	55.9
CNNAug-SVM [5]	61.8	86.8	66.6	79.9	74.8	76.8	69.0	56.2
LSVM [25]	61.4	87.1	65.0	77.6	69.7	75.2	66.7	55.8
MsML+ [25]	66.6	89.4	69.5	81.1	68.4	74.8	59.8	52.1
CombinedAlexNet [26]	63.3	83.3	64.5	76.9	69.2	77.1	58.8	54.2
WA-CNN [15]	69.0	92.8	66.9	82.4	79.5	83.4	66.3	58.3
Grow-conv [27]	66.1	91.4	67.2	82.1	78.3	77.0	70.1	50.2
Proposed network	**70.9**	**95.9**	68.7	**84.5**	81.9	**87.9**	69.9	**62.6**

is due to different target sets, train-test splits, network architectures, and iterations. Note that we have used similar hyper-parameters, iterations, and train-test splits for all approaches in Tables 3 and 4 to maintain a fair comparison. Consistent superior outcomes validate that the presence of the pre-trained classification layer in increasing model capacity for parameter fine-tuning is effective for adjusting the network to a wide range of target tasks.

Table 4. Performance comparison of proposed single-layer depth augmented fine-tuned VGG-16 network with contemporary fine-tuning approaches.

Approach	CUB 200-2011	102 flowers	Stanford dogs	Oxford pets	Caltech-256	VOC07	MIT-67	SUN-397
Normal_FT_CNN	70.5	85.6	68.2	85.2	83.9	86.5	66.5	61.8
CNN-SVM [5]	66.5	81.5	66.7	86.4	79.9	82.4	60.4	56.6
Muldip-Net [28]	71.5	81.9	65.0	86.1	80.9	87.5	68.9	63.5
Grow-conv [27]	72.5	88.7	75.1	89.1	86.1	89.1	72.1	67.5
DA-CNN [15]	76.1	93.3	72.8	88.4	84.9	91.4	73.1	67.2
Proposed network	**78.1**	**97.1**	**76.1**	**90.6**	**88.5**	**94.4**	**76.8**	**69.8**

Table 5. Performance comparison between single-layer and multiple-layer depth augmented networks. Only the highest performing combination is presented here. Multiple-layer depth augmented networks for other datasets also yield consistent performance.

Network	Dataset	Configuration	Accuracy (%)
AlexNet	CUB 200-2011	$[\chi_N]_{N-5}^{1+\psi}$	70.9
		$[\chi_N]_{N-5}^{2+\psi}$	**72.1**
	102 Flowers	$[\chi_N]_{N-5}^{1+\psi}$	95.9
		$[\chi_N]_{N-5}^{2+\psi}$	**97.2**
	Caltech-256	$[\chi_N]_{N-5}^{1+\psi}$	81.9
		$[\chi_N]_{N-5}^{2+\psi}$	**82.8**
	VOC-07	$[\chi_N]_{N-5}^{1+\psi}$	87.9
		$[\chi_N]_{N-5}^{2+\psi}$	**88.8**
VGG-16	CUB 200-2011	$[\chi_N]_{N-5}^{1+\psi}$	78.1
		$[\chi_N]_{N-5}^{2+\psi}$	**78.9**
	102 Flowers	$[\chi_N]_{N-5}^{1+\psi}$	97.1
		$[\chi_N]_{N-5}^{2+\psi}$	**98.2**
	Caltech-256	$[\chi_N]_{N-5}^{1+\psi}$	88.5
		$[\chi_N]_{N-5}^{2+\psi}$	**89.4**
	VOC-07	$[\chi_N]_{N-5}^{1+\psi}$	94.4
		$[\chi_N]_{N-5}^{2+\psi}$	**95.9**

Comparison of Single and Multiple-layer Depth Augmentation. Augmenting two new layers beyond pre-trained classification layer is observed to be the cut-off point as performance starts to diminish after that. Table 5 shows the results of the best combination (i.e. $L_{N+1} = 2048$ and $L_{N+2} = 1024$) of two-layer and single-layer depth augmentation. Appending two new layers after the pre-trained classification layer facilitate network marginally over single-layer augmentation by increasing representational capacity. It is proven once again that the pre-trained classification layer holds prominent high-level features which are capable of propagating learned knowledge to multiple newly appended layers. This also manifests increasing network incrementally by augmenting depth is a stable parameterization for improving performance.

Table 6. Performance comparison between single-layer depth augmented networks with L_2-norm and batch-norm normalization scheme.

Network	Dataset	Norm	Accuracy (%)				
			$[\chi_N]_N^{(1+\psi)}$	$[\chi_N]_{N-1}^{(1+\psi)}$	$[\chi_N]_{N-2}^{(1+\psi)}$	$[\chi_N]_{N-5}^{(1+\psi)}$	All
AlexNet	CUB 200-2011	Standardization	66.2	67.5	68.9	**69.9**	68.4
		L_2	62.1	64.2	64.3	**64.5**	63.5
VGG-16	CUB 200-2011	Standardization	76.7	77.6	77.9	**78.1**	78.5
		L_2	71.5	72.1	73.1	**73.2**	72.7

Best Fit Normalization Scheme. After exploring two types of normalization, we observe that standardization [16] assisted better learning for proposed single and multiple-layer depth augmented networks. We represent the results of diagnostic experiments with $S = 1024$ and standardization in Table 6. Results of the single-layer depth augmented AlexNet trained on CUB 200-2011 dataset show that the improvement of our depth augmented network is around 2% compared to traditional fine-tuning for L_2-norm normalization, and more than 6% otherwise. A similar significant boost in performance is also noticed in other datasets, which are not stated in this paper for limited space. Increase in task performance states that standardization reduces the chances of the pre-trained activations to dominate the randomly initialized ones.

3.5   Average Performance Gain

Tables 7 and 8 show that in average both coarse and fine-grained target datasets leverage the presence of the pre-trained classification layer in proposed fine-tuning and depth augmentation. However, coarse datasets manifest slightly more significant performance gain than fine-grained ones. This suggests that this layer possesses general information to transfer to a wide range of datasets. Results show that both the networks gain significant improvement for single-layer augmentation while for two-layer, the increase is marginal. Moreover, less deep backbone network seems to be more benefited from depth augmentation.

Table 7. Performance gain of proposed fine-tuning $[\chi_N]_{N-5}^{\psi}$ from traditional fine-tuning $[\chi_N^{N-1}]_{N-5}^{\psi}$, single-layer depth augmented networks $[\chi_N]_{N-5}^{1+\psi}$ from proposed fine-tuning, and double-layer $[\chi_N]_{N-5}^{2+\psi}$ from single-layer depth augmented networks respectively for fine-grained datasets, where parameter fine-tuning proceeds from layer L_{N-5}.

	CUB 200-2011		102 Flowers		Stan. dogs		Oxf. pets		Avg.	
	AlexNet	VGG-16	AlexNet	VGG-16	AlexNet	VGG-16	AlexNet	VGG-16	AlexNet	VGG-16
$[\chi_N]_{N-5}^{\psi}$	3.3	2.8	3.1	1.6	1.4	1.6	4.2	2.0	**3.0**	**2.0**
$[\chi_N]_{N-5}^{1+\psi}$	4.7	2.5	2.0	2.9	1.8	3.7	2.1	3.7	**2.7**	**3.2**
$[\chi_N]_{N-5}^{2+\psi}$	1.2	0.8	1.3	1.1	0.4	1.2	1.0	0.9	**1.0**	**1.0**

Table 8. Performance gain of proposed fine-tuning $[\chi_N]_{N-5}^{\psi}$ from traditional fine-tuning $[\chi_N^{N-1}]_{N-5}^{\psi}$, single-layer depth augmented networks $[\chi_N]_{N-5}^{1+\psi}$ from proposed fine-tuning, and double-layer $[\chi_N]_{N-5}^{2+\psi}$ from single-layer depth augmented networks respectively for coarse datasets, where parameter fine-tuning proceeds from layer L_{N-5}.

	Caltech-256		VOC-07		MIT-67		SUN-397		Avg.	
	AlexNet	VGG-16	AlexNet	VGG-16	AlexNet	VGG-16	AlexNet	VGG-16	AlexNet	VGG-16
$[\chi_N]_{N-5}^{\psi}$	4.0	2.7	3.4	4.6	5.1	6.5	6.7	4.5	**4.8**	**4.6**
$[\chi_N]_{N-5}^{1+\psi}$	2.8	2.7	3.4	2.3	3.6	3.8	2.0	3.5	**3.0**	**3.1**
$[\chi_N]_{N-5}^{2+\psi}$	0.9	0.9	0.9	1.5	1.4	1.1	1.7	1.3	**1.2**	**1.2**

4 Conclusion

In this paper, we demonstrate that the ImageNet and widely used transfer learning target sets have neighbouring high-level features, therefore, adapting the pre-trained classification layer which catches high-level features would help fine-tuning. We propose a novel fine-tuning approach with the pre-trained classification layer. We empirically establish that proposed fine-tuning approach outperforms traditional fine-tuning for all selected target datasets. Also, we notice on average, the coarse target datasets with ImageNet achieve more performance gain than fine-grained ones. For evaluating traditional and proposed fine-tuning approaches, we use our layer-wise fine-tuning scheme. Our layer-wise fine-tuning scheme manifests that freezing initial convolutional layers yield optimal fine-tuning performance for all target datasets.

Being inspired by developmental transfer learning and impact of the pre-trained classification layer in fine-tuning, we augment new layers beyond the pre-trained classification layer for a better adaptation of the target task. Moreover, to tune pre-trained and new parameters at a steady speed and to encourage better learning, we normalize and scale input activations of augmented layers. Assessment of the proposed depth augmented networks on eight different datasets show that they outperform existing transfer learning approaches. Our empirical study has provided practitioners strong justification to utilize the ImageNet pre-trained classification layer for fine-tuning and depth augmentation beyond it for adapting the network to target tasks.

References

1. Krizhevsky, A., Sutskever, I., Hinton, G.: ImageNet classification with deep convolutional neural networks. In: Advances in Neural Information Processing Systems, pp. 1097–1105 (2012)
2. Simonyan, K., Zisserman, A.: Very deep convolutional networks for large-scale image recognition. arXiv preprint arXiv:1409.1556 (2014)
3. He, K., Zhang, X., Ren, S., Sun, J.: Deep residual learning for image recognition. In: Proceedings of the IEEE Conference on Computer Vision and Pattern Recognition, pp. 770–778 (2016)

4. Szegedy, C., et al.: Going deeper with convolutions. In: Proceedings of the IEEE Conference on Computer Vision and Pattern Recognition, pp. 1–9 (2015)
5. Sharif Razavian, A., Azizpour, H., Sullivan, J., Carlsson, S.: CNN features off-the-shelf: an astounding baseline for recognition. In: Proceedings of the IEEE Conference on Computer Vision and Pattern Recognition Workshops, pp. 806–813 (2014)
6. Yosinski, J., Clune, J., Bengio, Y., Lipson, H.: How transferable are features in deep neural networks? In: Advances in Neural Information Processing Systems, pp. 3320–3328 (2014)
7. Hariharan, B., Arbeláez, P., Girshick, R., Malik, J.: Hypercolumns for object segmentation and fine-grained localization. In: Proceedings of the IEEE Conference on Computer Vision and Pattern Recognition, pp. 447–456 (2015)
8. Yang, S., Ramanan, D.: Multi-scale recognition with DAG-CNNs. In: Proceedings of the IEEE International Conference on Computer Vision, pp. 1215–1223 (2015)
9. Oquab, M., Bottou, L., Laptev, I., Sivic, J.: Learning and transferring mid-level image representations using convolutional neural networks. In: Proceedings of the IEEE Conference on Computer Vision and Pattern Recognition, pp. 1717–1724 (2014)
10. Sermanet, P., Eigen, D., Zhang, X., Mathieu, M., Fergus, R., LeCun, Y.: OverFeat: integrated recognition, localization and detection using convolutional networks. arXiv preprint arXiv:1312.6229 (2013)
11. Zhang, K., Schölkopf, B., Muandet, K., Wang, Z.: Domain adaptation under target and conditional shift. In: International Conference on Machine Learning, pp. 819–827 (2013)
12. Sigaud, O., Droniou, A.: Towards deep developmental learning. IEEE Trans. Cogn. Dev. Syst. **8**, 99–114 (2016)
13. Tessler, C., Givony, S., Zahavy, T., Mankowitz Daniel J., Mannor, S.: A deep hierarchical approach to lifelong learning in minecraft. In: Thirty-First AAAI Conference on Artificial Intelligence (2017)
14. Pickett, M., Al-Rfou, R., Shao, L., Tar, C.: A growing long-term episodic & semantic memory. arXiv preprint arXiv:1610.06402 (2016)
15. Wang, Y., Ramanan, D., Hebert, M.: Growing a brain: fine-tuning by increasing model capacity. In: Proceedings of the IEEE Conference on Computer Vision and Pattern Recognition, pp. 2471–2480 (2017)
16. Ioffe, S., Szegedy, C.: Batch normalization: accelerating deep network training by reducing internal covariate shift. In: Proceedings of the 32nd International Conference on International Conference on Machine Learning, vol. 37 (2015)
17. Nilsback, M., Zisserman, A.: Automated flower classification over a large number of classes. In: Sixth Indian Conference on Computer Vision, Graphics & Image Processing, pp. 722–729 (2008)
18. Wah, C., Branson, S., Welinder, P., Perona, P., Belongie, S.: The caltech-ucsd birds-200-2011 dataset. California Institute of Technology (2011)
19. Aditya K., Nityananda J., Bangpeng Y., Li F.: Novel dataset for fine-grained image categorization. In: First Workshop on Fine-Grained Visual Categorization, IEEE Conference on Computer Vision and Pattern Recognition (2011)
20. Parkhi, O. M., Vedaldi, A., Zisserman, A., Jawahar, C. V.: Cats and dogs. In: IEEE Conference on Computer Vision and Pattern Recognition (2012)
21. Griffin, G., Holub, A., Perona, P.: Caltech-256 object category dataset. California Institute of Technology (2007)
22. Everingham, M., Van Gool, L., Williams, C. K. I., Winn, J., Zisserman, A.: The PASCAL Visual Object Classes Challenge 2007 (VOC 2007) Results (2007)

23. Quattoni, A., Torralba, A.: Recognizing indoor scenes. IEEE Conference on Computer Vision and Pattern Recognition, pp. 413–420 (2009)
24. Xiao, J., Hays, J., Ehinger, K., Oliva, A., Torralba, A.: SUN database: large-scale scene recognition from abbey to zoo. In: IEEE Computer Society Conference on Computer Vision and Pattern Recognition, pp. 3485–3492 (2010)
25. Qian, Q., Jin, R., Zhu, S., Lin, Y.: Fine-grained visual categorization via multi-stage metric learning. In: Proceedings of the IEEE Conference on Computer Vision and Pattern Recognition, pp. 3716–3724 (2015)
26. Joulin, A., van der Maaten, L., Jabri, A., Vasilache, N.: Learning visual features from large weakly supervised data. In: Leibe, B., Matas, J., Sebe, N., Welling, M. (eds.) ECCV 2016. LNCS, vol. 9911, pp. 67–84. Springer, Cham (2016). https://doi.org/10.1007/978-3-319-46478-7_5
27. Azizpour, H., Sharif Razavian, Ali., Sullivan, J., Maki, A., Carlsson, S.: From generic to specific deep representations for visual recognition. In: Proceedings of the IEEE Conference on Computer Vision and Pattern Recognition Workshops, pp. 36–45 (2015)
28. Tamaazousti, Y., Le Borgne, H., Hudelot, C., El Amine Seddik, M., Tamaazousti, M.: Learning more universal representations for transfer-learning. arXiv preprint arXiv:1712.09708 (2017)
29. Maaten, L., Hinton, G.: Visualizing data using t-SNE. J. Mach. Learn. Res. **9**, 2579–2605 (2008)

Equine Welfare Assessment: Horse Motion Evaluation and Comparison to Manual Pain Measurements

Dominik Rueß[1]([✉]) [iD], Jochen Rueß[1], Christian Hümmer[1], Niklas Deckers[1],
Vitaliy Migal[1], Kathrin Kienapfel[2], Anne Wieckert[3], Dirk Barnewitz[4],
and Ralf Reulke[1]

[1] Humboldt-Universität zu Berlin, Institut für Informatik, 10099 Berlin, Germany
{ruess,reulke}@informatik.hu-berlin.de
[2] Ruhr-Universität Bochum, 44801 Bochum, Germany
Kathrin.Kienapfel@ruhr-uni-bochum.de
[3] Tierärztliche Klinik für Pferde, 17109 Demmin, Germany
[4] Tierärztliche Klinik der fzmb GmbH, 99947 Bad Langensalza, Germany
DBarnewitz@fzmb.de
http://www.tierklinik-demmin.de/

Abstract. Pain estimation for horses is a tedious task since they are flight animals and tend to suppress pain specific behaviour. We obtained continuous video data of horse in different levels of pain, to evaluate their behaviour – while they were undergoing routine castration. During the whole time we regularly and manually evaluated the horses' pain.

To quantify the horses' motions, we automatically extracted horse masks from which we derive their orientation and position. We then performed a motion feature selection based on the different types of manual pain measurements. This is thus a first time comparison of long term manual and automatically derived equine pain evaluation.

A result is the decreased motion entropy of horses in pain and a tendency of staying in a place for longer periods of time. This was reflected with large observation time windows and features related to this behaviour – features which measure the entropy, for instance, or the change quantiles. It also turned out horses behave differently when humans are nearby, thus this method gives an unbiased view on the pain behaviour, especially motion under pain conditions.

These results can decrease the workload in veterinary clinics and provides means of remotely displaying potential discomfort of horses.

Keywords: Image processing · Signal processing · Equine welfare monitoring · Time series · Pain estimation

1 Introduction

Horses are flight animals. Flight animals tend to suppress discomfort by trying to visually fit into the rest of the group as much as possible. This makes it very

© Springer Nature Switzerland AG 2019
C. Lee et al. (Eds.): PSIVT 2019, LNCS 11854, pp. 156–169, 2019.
https://doi.org/10.1007/978-3-030-34879-3_13

difficult to tell the well-being of horses. In fact, this can be very dangerous, since for instance, the occurrence of a colic is one of the most dreaded ones, due to its high prevalence and since it may lead to death even within a few hours, if not discovered early and treated properly.

By looking at horses carefully enough, however, veterinarians are able to conclude how much horses actually suffer. For one, the facial expression changes subtly, which can be evaluated by muscle tension, ear positions, mouth muscle tension, nostril strain and more features. This "Horse Grimace Scale" (HGS) is evaluated in a questionnaire which is described in Costa et al. [5]. Secondly, there are short and long-term effects on physiological parameters such as pulse, blood pressure and heart rate variability (HRV). Lastly, experienced veterinarians and animal attendants are able to tell the level of discomfort by looking at the (lack of) full-body movement of the horses.

All of these methods require experienced staff to regularly look after horses whose conditions are dangerous, which quite time-consuming. In this article we describe methods to evaluate the well-being of horses by automated video analysis – see Fig. 1 for an example input frame. A major goal of this evaluation was to derive motion features for remote supervisors to decide if these features have changed in a way that advises manual evaluation. We describe the steps taken to distinguish a horse's normal motion behaviour from its discomfort condition. Thus, this is the first time to extensively extract and correlate horses' movement from video data and correlate it with manually measured pain.

Fig. 1. A sample frame of a horse in a box with the camera viewing from above.

We provide an overview of related research, after which we explain our developed image processing and feature extraction routines, including the hardware setup. Then we describe how we manually evaluated the horse welfare. Finally we compare measurements and image processing results and discuss how this can be improved and developed into an even more autonomous monitoring system.

2   Related Work

There are few works specifically dealing with automated video assessment of animals or even horses. In the next two sections we will refer to relevant computer vision and veterinarian research.

2.1 Image Processing

The recent years have seen some increase in automated animal welfare research. Livestock surveillance was one of the early applications. In Shao and Xin [15] thermal comfort of pigs was classified using computer vision techniques, already using implicit behaviour classification. Costa et al. [4] used proprietary group tracking software to extract behaviour differences of piglets induced by different barn climate conditions. A recent PhD thesis of Nasirahmadi [10] provides insights into pig and cattle monitoring by computer vision methods. It lists methods of animal instance segmentation and 3D tracking (e.g. by time of flight cameras) and 2D image acquisition techniques, some of which use thermal infrared. Also, methods of classification movement into feeding, drinking, lying, locomotion, aggressive and reproductive behaviours are suggested. The segmentation of livestock can be done using learning approaches as in Nilson et al. [11], where the location of pigs is of interest. Other sensors are interesting, too, for instance in Pezzuolo et al. [12], different types of low cost 3D body measurements were studied for livestock buildings. Matthews et al. [8] provide a survey about manual and automated measurements in livestock surveillance. For pigs, they exemplify the activity budget approach, were different classes of activity can be observed. Based on the daily activity budgets, deviation from normal behaviour can be detected to assess pig welfare.

Deep neuronal networks have become interesting due to their massive success in other fields. Guzhva et al. [6] have implemented a tracking algorithm for cow detection and motion extraction, based on convolutional networks.

From other computer vision fields, especially segmentation networks are interesting for this article, which can segment object classes in an image on a per pixel basis. The deeplab (v3) of Chen et al. [3] is a fast and highly accurate such DNN. It optimizes the classification result with a conditional random field for optimized masks in terms of holes or fringes.

Apart from this, there's also a lot of proprietary software to track animals in laboratories, such as insects, rats and mice.

2.2 Horse Physiology and Pain Estimation

Correct recognition and evaluation of pain is crucial for correct diagnosis and treatment of horses. A definition of pain by the International Association for the Study of Pain (IASP) is "An unpleasant sensory and emotional experience associated with actual or potential tissue damage, or described in terms of such damage", see Merskey [9]. However, horses cannot communicate what level of pain they experience, they actually try to hide their discomfort from potential predators. Individuals may express pain substantially different, Wagner [16].

There are different parameters to measure pain. Physiological parameters are heart and breathing rate, rectal temperature, blood pressure etc. Some parameters are more reliable than others, for instance breathing and heart rate can hint for pain, Price et al. [13] and have at most short-term effects but can still be used in composite assessment surveys (CPS), Bussieres et al. and van Loon et al. [2,7]. Blood pressure and HRV give a fair indication to pain, Von Borell et al. and Bussieres et al. [1,2].

Important parameters are behavioral parameters, some of which are lameness, restlessness, head-lowering, teeth-grinding, flaring of nostrils, sweating, rigid posture, head-turning as in Wagner [16].

Pain scales can describe the pain for certain types of symptoms, for instance laminitis, synovitis. Pain can be evaluated fairly symptom independently and reproducible by using surveys which result in scales. One of these generic and frequently used scales is the HGS, Costa et al. [5]. It is a questionnaire of 6 questions, each of which can be answered with values of 0, 1 or 2, resulting in a maximum value of 12. These questions look for ear position, orbital tightening, tension above eye area, the tension of chewing muscles, mouth and nostril strain. We used a CPS of Bussières et al. and van Loon et al. [2,7]. It assesses facial expression, behaviour and the physiological parameters heart and breathing frequency, borborygmus and body temperature.

3   Veterinary Horse Welfare Evaluation

3.1   Experiment Layout

We performed the horse welfare evaluation by means of a routine castration at the stud farm Meura, which was performed at the request of the owners. We had a test group of 15 two-year-old stallions, stalled one week before castration. The castration was conducted in April 2018. We measured the horse welfare before surgery, during and after, at least once a day – twice, close to surgery. See also Sect. 3.2.

The measurements included general clinical examination (respiratory frequency, heart rate, temperature) and blood pressure measurement via High Definition Oscillometry. A group of 7 animals was resettled one day after castration into an open barn, the second group of 8 animals remained in the boxes, the latter were of most interest for this article. We noticed the second group had to deal with much stronger wound swelling and they showed less motion than the animals in the open barn. One day after surgery, the animals showed a reduced general condition and mildly increased temperature due to the castration. In the following days, the animals recovered from the surgical pain. From day 4 post OP, the wound swelling began to increase, which in turn resulted in a renewed rise in temperature and pain behaviour. From day 7 post OP on, the wound swelling gradually decreased and the animals felt more comfortable. This problem could not be observed as strongly in the open barn because, since these horses moved much more and thereby reduced their wound swelling. Also, it turned out that horses behave differently, when a doctor or generally a person is present.

3.2   Manual Measurement Description

The manual measurements of interest are: HGS, a more general questionnaire including physiological and behavioral parameters – a CPS of Bussieres et al.

and van Loon et al. [2,7], mean arterial pressure (MAP) and a basic computation of the HRV. We represent the HRV as standard deviation of the heart beat duration, i.e. the duration between R-peaks. Since the duration of the measurements was short ($\approx$ 30–60s), this is only an indication of the true HRV standard deviation at the time of the measurement.

Other measurement types were heart rate and systolic and diastolic pressure. However these have turned out not to be as relevant for this article, i.e. did not correlate as strongly to other measurements. The pulse and blood pressure measurements (and thus, HRV, too) were performed at least three times consecutively, to reduce measurement noise. These measurements were still very sparse, from a signal processing perspective. Obviously, extrapolation can only guess what has happened in between, so we fixed all comparisons to a window around the times of measurements. Refer to Fig. 3 for an measurement example.

These different, manually acquired measurements do not perfectly relate, see also Sect. 5.1. However, we consider all these measurements as our "ground truth" for the further evaluation of the movement pattern. This ground truth is not perfect, i.e. comes with a lot of noise, however since we had different ground truth signals, we hoped all together give a hint to the true horse stress and pain level.

4   Extraction and Evaluation of Horse Motion Parameters

4.1   Experiment and Hardware Setup

For data recording we used a digital video recording system. We installed four cameras for each stable box, for different perspectives, where we mounted one of these cameras as a top view camera. For this particular evaluation we only used the top view, which ensures least perspective distortion of the motion. The Full-HD video data of 12 frames per second is collected and saved as hourly H264-AVI files. For the time of the castration we collected 10TB of video data. Figure 1 shows a sample input image of a video stream from the ceiling camera.

4.2   Mask Generation for Horse Candidate Extraction

Mask generation cannot work well in different settings with classic background estimation (BGE). The application of BGE is limited to certain environments and many manually set parameters. Also our environment showed lots of interfering factors like flying dust, insects/birds in front of the camera, cleaning staff, animal attendants and veterinarians. Lastly horses tend to stand still for long periods of time, every now and then – especially sick horses – and thus BGE is not a good method in the first place.

Thus, to extract horse masks, we collected 2500 images of horses, mainly viewed from above. The horses were of different breed and size, with different posture and with varying background scenes. We created the segmentation masks manually, such that we could apply a deep neuronal network approach for semantic segmentation. The semantic segmentation is for achieving pixel-based object classification and a reasonable grouping of pixels into connected objects. The latter is usually performed after DNN classification of the pixels, e.g. with conditional random fields. We chose the deeplab v3, Chen et al. [3], which has a high detection quality and a fast run-time. The masks were extracted for 4 frames per second of the original video data.

We had to deal with false positives and only partly correct segmentations, i.e. missing body parts. To select the most likely mask contour representing the horse, we computed parameters: The total number of contours, the deviation of the expected horse's shape describing ellipse, the distance of the center to the previous description and the deviation of the expected horse area in pixels. These are all only hints but can be turned into a pseudo-probability of values of $]0, 1]$, by normalizing given a and roughly expected properties b with:

$$p = \frac{1}{1 + s \cdot (a - b)^2},$$
(1)

where s is some kind of shape factor of the curve. We chose the contour with the highest product of all these pseudo-probabilities as the horse contour.

4.3   Extracting Horse Orientation and Viewing Direction

A horse can move its neck and look around without moving its torso and limps, which allows for discrimination of looking and standing direction. By the same argument, the dock of the horse is the most visually stable position. In Reulke et al. [14] a horse mask and a best fit ellipse were extracted. However, this approach is very sensitive to any body-part movement, especially the rather long neck: Viewed from above, it may appear short, when the horse is feeding, or long, when it is leaning or looking forward. Also it may turn its neck left and right, which in turn changes the ellipse's orientation. The ellipse would generally change its shape, center and orientation, even though the horse was standing in the same position.

To overcome this type of problem, we introduced a new method which aims to detect the dock of the horse and its standing direction. Since the mask extraction of Sect. 4.2 reliably produces few holes and fringes we decided to perform topological skeletonization. The resulting skeleton can be traced with trace segments obtained by skeleton intersections. We merged these segments to horse longitudinal axis candidates, with the requirement of low angle change at the contact points. The longest such axis is considered the visual longitudinal axis. Since the horses' caudal ends (towards tail) are visually almost always wider than the cranial ones (towards head), the horse standing orientation can be extracted, too.

This approach can be sensitive to a range of scenarios: missing body parts (i.e. low camera field of view), unexpected postures, segmentation issues, etc. However, it turns out the whole process is quite stable, also due to the fact of the horses staying in a controlled environment of a stable or a veterinary hospital.

Again we computed a pseudo-probability of the orientation correctness, which we extracted by comparing the widths of the caudal and cranial ends.

4.4 Tracking and Motion Parameters

We individually filtered the position and the horse orientation with Kalman's filter. The updates have a weight given by the product of pseudo-probabilities of Sects. 4.2 and 4.3. The influence of a measure on the Kalman Filter update process can be controlled by the process co-variance noise setting. This procedure is illustrated in Fig. 2.

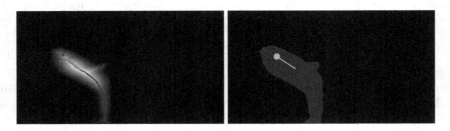

Fig. 2. The algorithm extracts a horse mask and determines the position and orientation by utilizing a thinning algorithm, the right hand side depicts a result after filtering.

We turned the result, a 2D positional image space vector and an orientation angle, into a vector by stacking both outputs. The angle was weighed such that the absolute values of the mean changes of both inputs is similar. The length of this vector results in a 1D time series, which we call *horse activity time series*.

As the Sects. 2.2 and 3 have stated, there might be a correlation of horses' motion and its stress or pain. The more pain horses experience, the less or even more they tend to move, based on different types of pain.

To find suitable types of features, which describe the measurements from Sect. 3.2 as best as possible by extracting an selecting from multiple time series features. In Python there's a package called *tsfresh*, which does exactly that, extracting hundreds of features.

We were interested in shorter evaluation times, thus we tested possible shifting window lengths of 10 min, 1 h, a half and a full day.

We wanted to find the best fitting features in terms of weighted Pearson's correlation coefficient. The weights represented the time distance to the next measurement, since these were sparse. The weights were 1 when simultaneous to a measurement date or 0 when the time difference is more than 5 h – everything in between has linearly interpolated weights.

5   Results

5.1   Interpretation of the Measurements

In this section we provide an overview and a brief interpretation of the measurements. A more comprehensive veterinary medical interpretation will follow in a separate publication.

The pairwise correlation of the different measurements shows the difficulty of horse welfare or pain assessment. The two manual horse scales are influenced by human experience, day-to-day bias and subjective interpretation of the questionnaires (Table 1).

Table 1. The Spearman Rank correlation coefficients for the different measurements of all horses. The actual comparisons of the different signals (measurements) are individual-based and this table represents the overall sum of all individuals. The individual distributions are not properly known, that's why we chose the Spearman Rank correlation over Pearson's Correlation coefficient. HRV is the standard deviation of the heart rate variability and MAP is short for *mean arterial pressure*. Refer to the text for a discussion of the values.

	CPS [2, 7]	HRV	Heart rate	Sys. pressure	MAP	Dias. pressure
HGS [5]	0.34	−0.10	0.06	0.10	0.10	0.09
CPS [2,7]		−0.09	0.21	0.08	0.15	0.18
HRV			−0.01	−0.09	−0.16	−0.16
Heart rate				−0.07	0.03	0.05
Systolic pressure					0.87	0.76
MAP						0.94

The heart rate seems to be influenced least by the stress or pain, but the second scale incorporates this measure, thus the higher correlation. Blood pressure has a very slight correlation to the measured scales, as expected from Sect. 2.2.

The standard deviation of the heart beat durations is slightly negatively correlated to all other measurements, as expected, too. A stressed mammal would have much more evenly distributed heart beat durations than in a relaxed state and this is reflected here in the negative correlation. The exemplary measurements of one horse are depicted in Fig. 3.

5.2   Interpreting Horses' Motion in Relation to Stress or Pain

One major result of the experiment was that horses tend to be more present or visibly express less pain, when humans, especially veterinarians or animal

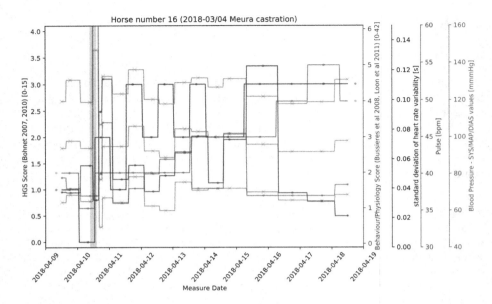

Fig. 3. Example manual measurement data of horse 16, which did not show many complications until the end of the measurement period where the pain seems to increase (wound swelling). The yellow blood pressure values are systolic, mean arterial pressure (MAP) and diastolic pressure. (The orange bar marks the event of the castration). (Color figure online)

attendants are nearby. For instance, stallions were not known to lick the post-surgical swellings, but in our videos we observed exactly this behaviour.

The second important confirmation is the coupling of stress or pain to motion – *motion* here includes moving the head and change of location or posture. Horses in castration tended to move less, the more pain they had evaluated on the two pain scales. This is the result which we explain in more details in this section.

We tried to derive features which most closely relate to the two different scales and measurements described above.

Using multiple measurements might stabilize the sparsity of measurements and due to the different nature and low pair-wise correlation it might result in a selection of robust features for pain or stress.

As similarity measure we used the weighted Pearson Coefficient. Our weight for each feature point x_i is defined by

$$w_i = \max\left(0, \frac{m - \delta t}{m}\right), \tag{2}$$

where m is the maximum temporal distance (5 h) to the next respective measurement and δt the respective time difference.

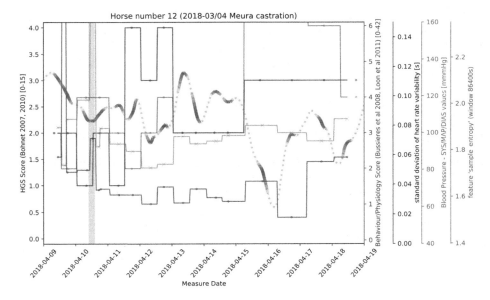

Fig. 4. Sample Entropy of the motion of horse 12, which was the horse exhibiting most pain by the behavioral/physiological scale, in the wound swelling stage. The *sample entropy* is a measure for the signal complexity and roughly inversely correlates with the pain measurements. The feature is plotted with dots in times where no correlation was measured (i.e. the weights were zero). Time window was 24 h.

Best Features Evaluation: For the time window of 10min none of the extracted features reflected the measurements, the absolute correlation values of the best features were significantly less than 0.1 for all of the selected measurements.

A good feature will relate well to all measurements y_i, we combined this by a *quality* term q:

$$q := |\text{corr}(x, y_1, w) \cdots \text{corr}(x, y_n, w)|, \tag{3}$$

which means optimizing the geometric mean of all correlations. This weighs individual correlations independently of possible preferences towards single measurement types.

In Table 2 we provide an overview of the feature selection result. Similar features with the same name but different parameters are omitted for readability, hence the table contains a list of groups of features which correlate well with the given measurements.

A first glance reveals: The larger the windows, the better the selected features tend to describe the horse stress or pain. This may be due to larger windows being able to capture repeating effects, especially diurnal effects.

The second result is the existence of features which fairly well correlate to all the different types of measurements – this had been an open question prior

Table 2. A list of the five best features groups (in terms of q) for different sliding window sizes and their correlations to the measurements. We picked the best feature of a parameter group. Also refer to the library *tsfresh* for more details.

Feature name (x-values)	$y_1 = $ HGS [5]	$y_2 = $ CPS [2,7]	HRV	MAP	$1000 \cdot q$
Window of 3600 s (1 h)					
Approx. entropy ($m = 2, r = 0.9$)	−0.07	−0.15	0.09	−0.11	0.011
Change quant. (mean, abs., [0.4, 0.8])	−0.13	−0.13	0.05	−0.08	0.007
Mean abs change	−0.09	−0.12	0.06	−0.11	0.007
Longest strike below mean	0.08	0.09	−0.07	0.12	0.005
Quantile ($q = 0.1$)	0.18	0.04	0.07	−0.08	0.004
Window of 43200 s (12 h)					
Sample entropy	−0.17	−0.32	0.24	−0.06	0.081
Count below mean	0.27	0.30	−0.07	0.07	0.042
Median	−0.15	−0.19	0.15	−0.08	0.034
Quantile ($q = 0.4$)	−0.14	−0.17	0.18	−0.08	0.034
Approx. entropy ($m = 2, r = 0.5$)	−0.17	−0.22	0.24	−0.03	0.028
Window of 86400 s (24 h)					
Change quant. (variance, [0.6, 0.8])	0.18	0.29	−0.22	0.13	0.145
Longest strike below mean	0.24	0.39	−0.13	0.12	0.141
Approx. entropy ($m = 2, r = 0.3$)	−0.20	−0.25	0.31	−0.08	0.123
Ar coefficient (coeff 0, $k = 10$)	−0.25	−0.17	0.21	−0.11	0.101
Sample entropy	−0.16	−0.23	0.30	−0.06	0.072

to the experiments. This, too, means that the pain of horses seems to correlate to the exhibition of motion, which is a veterinary medical confirmation.

The features correlating well all tend to somehow describe the lack of motion when the horses are in pain. The less pain a horse experiences, the more it will move unpredictably, see the different kinds of entropy features. And the less it will have long periods of idleness, see also the features which counts or compares strikes above or below mean. Interestingly, the feature *median*, which is a median of the motion itself (speed), seems to capture the pain rather well, too, for the 12 h window.

In Figs. 4 and 5 we plotted some of the features and results for two of the horses. Horse 9 did not show much pain, Fig. 5, however it was still affected by the surgery and its after-effect. This is visible in the selected feature *count below mean* and others, too. Horse 12, Fig. 4, did show quite some wound swelling complications, with high fever, a couple of days after surgery. This can be seen in all of the features, here we displayed the *sample entropy*.

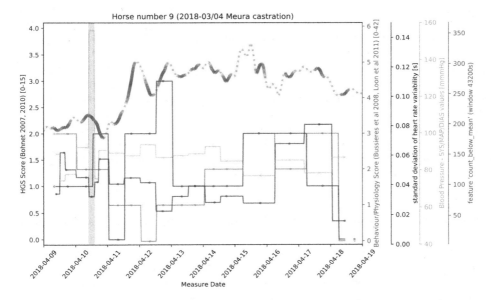

Fig. 5. Another interesting feature is the *count below mean* value of a signal. Here it is display for a horse which was behaving rather normal, after surgery. However, pain scales give a hint of slight stress after surgery, including the swelling, for roughly 6 days – which is capture well with this feature. Time window was 12 h.

6   Summary and Discussion

We showed how deep image segmentation, image and signal processing can be used to assess the welfare of single horses in a box. We extracted the horses' motion by segmenting the horse body using the *deeplab* neuronal network, followed by a smoothed position and orientation extraction. The horses' pain or stress was measured manually, by different means, up to three times a day. We could use this as a clue to the real ground truth. These measurements mutually did not correlate strongly. This may have different effects, due to different physiological processes and delays. However, we used many of these measurements to select robust motion time-series features which correlate well to all of this selection of measurements.

We evaluated the correlation only close to the measurements, since in the meantime we simply cannot tell the pain level. The resulting features fit the different measurements well. Features which correlate best to all measurements were usually entropy types and other kinds of restlessness measures, but at this point in time we can not suggest a bullet-proof selection of features – this has to be evaluated on a large and varied database of horse video recordings.

A veterinary medical result of this evaluation is the reflection of pain in the motion of horses. The more pain this breed of horses underwent in a castration, the less it moved, generally and the longer the periods and proportion of predictable motion (especially standing still). This may be different for other breeds and for other types of pain, especially for colic pain, where horses constantly tend to try to find a good position with little pain. Note, the motion of horses may reflect excitement, pain, stress or other influences, however here we were able to show a tendency of motion changes being related to stress and pain.

The result can be used to monitor horses semi-automatedly, where veterinarians can estimate deviations from normal behaviour and look after the respective horses if the behaviour deviates too much. This video based monitoring also has the advantage that horses will not disguise their pain behaviour from nearby staff. A fully automated evaluation will need a lot more data from many more horses, especially almost constant measurements from different kinds of sensors (e.g. EKG).

For the first time we were able to evaluate and compare manual equine welfare assessment with automatically extracted, continuous motion features – for a long period of time and under the controlled circumstances of a castration.

In our future work we will address the possible instability of the position and orientation extraction – which could possibly extracted more robustly by deep interest point detectors. It might be better to keep two dimensions in the data: speed and orientation – this inherently carries more information than the reduction to vector lengths. This would imply multivariate time-series evaluation. Also we can now optimize the camera requirements, especially for visibility of the horses. Up until now we also only worked with constellations where only one horse is allowed in a box. However, some of the mares had their foals with them. Since different measurements may have different delays to occurring pain, dynamic time warping based correlation could improve and stabilize the results here.

References

1. von Borell, E., et al.: Heart rate variability as a measure of autonomic regulation of cardiac activity for assessing stress and welfare in farm animals - a review. Physiol. Behav. **92**(3), 293–316 (2007)
2. Bussières, G., et al.: Development of a composite orthopaedic pain scale in horses. Res. Vet. Sci. **85**(2), 294–306 (2008)
3. Chen, L.C., Papandreou, G., Schroff, F., Adam, H.: Rethinking Atrous Convolution for Semantic Image Segmentation. arXiv (2017)
4. Costa, A., Ismayilova, G., Borgonovo, F., Viazzi, S., Berckmans, D., Guarino, M.: Image-processing technique to measure pig activity in response to climatic variation in a pig barn. Anim. Prod. Sci. **54**(8), 1075–1083 (2014)
5. Dalla Costa, E., Minero, M., Lebelt, D., Stucke, D., Canali, E., Leach, M.C.: Development of the Horse Grimace Scale (HGS) as a pain assessment tool in horses undergoing routine castration. PLoS ONE **9**(3), e92281 (2014)
6. Guzhva, O., Ardö, H., Nilsson, M., Herlin, A., Tufvesson, L.: Now you see me: convolutional neural network based tracker for dairy cows. Front. Robot. AI **5**, 107 (2018)
7. van Loon, J.P., Back, W., Hellebrekers, L.J., van Weeren, P.R.: Application of a composite pain scale to objectively monitor horses with somatic and visceral pain under hospital conditions. J. Equine Vet. Sci. **30**(11), 641–649 (2010)

8. Matthews, S.G., Miller, A.L., Clapp, J., Plötz, T., Kyriazakis, I.: Early detection of health and welfare compromises through automated detection of behavioural changes in pigs. Vet. J. **217**, 43–51 (2016)

9. Merskey, H.: Pain terms: a list with definitions and notes on usage. Recommended IASP Subcommittee on Taxonomy. Pain **6**(3), 249 (1979)

10. Nasirahmadi, A.: Development of automated computer vision systems for investigation of livestock behaviours (2017)

11. Nilsson, M., Herlin, A.H., Ardö, H., Guzhva, O., Åström, K., Bergsten, C.: Development of automatic surveillance of animal behaviour and welfare using image analysis and machine learned segmentation technique. Animal **9**(11), 1859–1865 (2015)

12. Pezzuolo, A., Guarino, M., Sartori, L., González, L.A., Marinello, F.: On-barn pig weight estimation based on body measurements by a Kinect v1 depth camera. Comput. Electron. Agric. **148**, 29–36 (2018)

13. Price, J., Catriona, S., Welsh, E.M., Waran, N.K.: Preliminary evaluation of a behaviour-based system for assessment of post-operative pain in horses following arthroscopic surgery. Veterinary Anaesth. Analg. **30**(3), 124–137 (2003)

14. Reulke, R., Rueß, D., Deckers, N., Barnewitz, D., Wieckert, A., Kienapfel, K: Analysis of motion patterns for pain estimation of horses. In: 15th IEEE International Conference on Advanced Video and Signal Based Surveillance, pp. 1–6 (2018)

15. Shao, B., Xin, H.: A real-time computer vision assessment and control of thermal comfort for group-housed pigs. Comput. Electron. Agric. **62**(1), 15–21 (2008)

16. Wagner, A.E.: Effects of stress on pain in horses and incorporating pain scales for equine practice. Vet. Clin. Equine Pract. **26**(3), 481–492 (2010)

Exposure Correction and Local Enhancement for Backlit Image Restoration

Sobhan Kanti Dhara$^{(\boxtimes)}$ and Debashis Sen

Department of Electronics and Electrical Communication Engineering,
Indian Institute of Technology Kharagpur, Kharagpur, India
`dhara.sk@gmail.com`, `dsen.eece.iitkgp@gmail.com`

Abstract. Backlighting is a poor illumination condition where the primary light source illuminates a part of the scene from behind. While the part of the scene (often termed as backlit) suffers from low lighting condition, rest of the scene is either well-exposed or over-exposed. We aims to restore such images through enhancement using exposure correction. We generate pseudo images based on the relation of exposure with aperture and shutter speed in a camera. Human visual system (HVS)-sensitive and spatial frequency-aware multi-scale fusion is carried out for exposure correction to produce a globally enhanced image from the input and the pseudo images. Following this, we locally enhance the globally enhanced image to incorporate the information of frequently appearing intensity differences in a spatial neighborhood. Experimental results show that our technique outperforms other relevant approaches subjectively. Quantitative evaluation in terms of DE, EME, PixDist, LOE, AMBE measures shows the superiority of our technique over the other techniques. Our technique is faster than the approaches compared here while generating enhanced and naturalness preserved outputs.

Keywords: Backlit image · Exposure · Enhancement · Fusion

1 Introduction

When a camera captures a scene, the visibility of the areas/objects in the acquired image depends on the amount of light reflected back to the camera, from the areas/objects in the scene. While an object in the scene in front of the camera is illuminated by the light source from behind, the object often suffers from under-exposure. Such a lighting condition is commonly known as backlighting and the generated image is known as a backlit image [18]. In such images, when a part of the scene suffers from poor illumination due to backlighting, the rest of the scene (we refer as non-backlit) is either well-exposed or over-exposed. Such an abrupt variation in exposure of the same scene creates a problem in the capturing, which is usually beyond photographers limit or camera's exposure and aperture setting [18]. Ill-capturing due to such a lighting condition creates a

C. Lee et al. (Eds.): PSIVT 2019, LNCS 11854, pp. 170–183, 2019.
https://doi.org/10.1007/978-3-030-34879-3_14

serious degradation with simultaneous presence of under-exposed, well-exposed and over-exposed areas in the captured image. Thus, the acquired image often suffers from poor visual quality. The conventional image contrast enhance ment techniques fail to restore such images due to the presence of the extreme variation in the intensities [18]. On the other hand, such poorly illuminated images affect the performance of high level machine vision applications like detection and recognition [24].

In general, image enhancement techniques can be classified into two types, global and local. Among the global enhancement techniques, a basic approach is histogram equalization (HE) [8], where the histogram of input image is stretched using cumulative distribution function. But such stretching fails to restore the backlit images generating undesired artifacts [18]. Histogram modification before stretching helps to minimize such artifacts but it limits the amount of enhancement [2, 10].

Global enhancement techniques do not include local neighbourhood information and therefore does not consider local contextual information. To include such contexts, a technique is proposed in [4] which generates 2D histogram for local enhancement. Such local information is also exploited through layered difference representation (LD) in [12]. Although, the technique is efficient in enhancing local details and produce satisfactory outputs in generic low contrast images, it does not enhance backlit images properly.

A backlit image is a low light image generated due to a special kind of ill-illumination condition where only a part of the object in an image suffers from low-lighting [17]. The authors in [6] proposed a technique which exploits the presence of interactions among the luminance levels and performs well for low-light images. Low-light image can be enhanced in a better way through retinex based approaches [7, 20]. In [20], the authors proposed a retinex based approach for low-light image enhancement where reflectance and the illumination map are estimated through optimization and then, illumination map is gamma-corrected to generate enhanced image. But it suffers from artifacts in the output. To remove noise from the low light images, the authors in [14] proposed a retinex based approach for low-light image enhancement where reflectance, illumination, and noise map estimated through optimization and then, illumination is gamma-corrected to generate enhanced image. But such technique produce artifacts in dark region especially images with limited or low noise.

Coventiontional contrast enhancement or low light image enhancement techniques usually not able to restore the illumination problem in backlit images. Thus, backlit images require a specified modeling to handle the underlying special ill-illumination problem [18]. The authors in [18] have specifically designed a learning-based algorithm for backlit image restoration. The algorithm first segments backlit objects from the non-backlit and then applies two different tone mapping functions for backlit image restoration. But, the effectiveness of the algorithm highly depends on the segmentation output, and a misclassification between backlit and non-backlit may generate undesired variations of illumination in the output.

Fig. 1. Backlit Image Enhancement: The first row presents the input backlit images and second row presents the corresponding enhanced outputs using our technique.

This paper adopts the relation of aperture and shutter speed with exposure, to generate exposure varied representations of the input image. We then generate weights based on exposedness and gradient energy of the images, and carry out multi-scale image fusion for input image exposure correction. Such approach globally enhances the input image. Then, a local enhancement considering the context around image pixel is performed. The results show that our approach is good at enhancing the backlit images while preserving the naturalness (See Fig. 1). The contributions of the paper are as follows:

- A technique which generates pseudo multi-exposure images exploiting the relation of aperture and shutter speed with camera exposure.
- HVS-sensitive spatial frequency aware global enhancement and neighborhood intensity difference boosting local enhancement for backlit image restoration.
- Substantially faster than other algorithms while producing state-of-the-art results.

Rest of the paper is organized as follows. Section 2 elaborates the motivation and details of the proposed technique. Section 3 presents the quantitative and subjective evaluation. Finally, Sect. 4 concludes the technique.

2   Proposed Approach

2.1   Motivation

Whenever humans view a scene, both global processing and local processing act together. As a part of it, they perceive a scene by adjusting the exposure of the pupil based on the ambient light centered around the field of view. Such a processing allows a viewer to adapt to different parts of the same scene to achieve better details and perception. Due to the limitations of sensor and device technology, a camera can capture only one of the possible representations of the real world scene that we perceive. The incapability of achieving the said adaptation makes the images captured by a camera vulnerable to wrong exposure in certain areas. A captured image can be considered as an image

- based on a single exposure yielding only one representation of many possible representations.
- vulnerable to under/over exposure both locally or globally due to the non-adaptability.

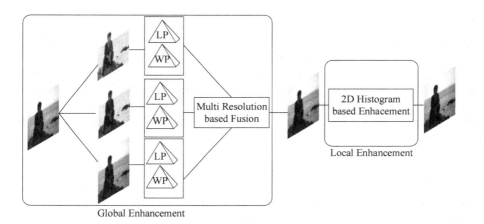

Global Enhancement

Fig. 2. A schematic diagram of our proposed technique which generates better exposed pseudo images to blend through multi-scale image fusion for exposure correction based global enhancement. Laplacian pyramid (LP) contains the bandpass versions of the images and weight pyramid (WP) contains the weights corresponding to each bandpass versions of the images. The image is then locally enhanced incorporating local context through 2D histogram.

Due to the said limitations, if an image is captured such that it has underexposed regions due to backlighting, it can be enhanced to reveal the details by generating different representations of the image which form a bracketed sequence of low dynamic range (LDR) images. The LDR images upon fusion generate a high dynamic range image (HDR) [25]. Though, HDR image contains extensive information, a common standard display device cannot visualize the content. On the other hand, if we restrict to generate an output image of the same dynamic range while capturing the useful information from the bracketed captured LDR images, the output image can provide visual aesthetic quality like HDR [19]. Moreover, such a technique neither requires to compute inter HDR images nor the generated output requires a special device to display. In such a case, the user needs a set of appropriate bracketed images suited to capture the information of the whole dynamic range of the scene. Such a sequence often suffers from motion artifacts (due to subject and camera motions) and misalignment. Moreover, such a technique cannot be used for the restoration of already captured images. Therefore, we will be required to virtually generate bracketed images based on the relation between exposure with aperture and shutter speed. The multiple images generated with these multiple lightness maps carry different but relevant information of the actual scene. A suitable exposure fusion [16,19] technique is required to fuse the images to generate one enhanced image with all the relevant information of the images. Such exposure fusion should include local details enhancement [29]. A schematic diagram of our proposed technique is shown in Fig. 2.

2.2   Pseudo Image Generation

In images, the lightness is directly related to the amount of ambient light leading to visual sensation. So, it can be claimed that the lightness component in images is primarily affected by under/over exposed conditions due to the lightness condition. In a camera, changing in photometric exposure value (PEV) allows varying amount of light to enter into the lens, which reflects in the lightness map (L) of the captured image [11,23,30]. The change in the values of lightness map due to the PEV [23,30] is defined as follows

$$PEV \propto \frac{t}{N^2} \tag{1}$$

where, t is the exposure time that quantifies the shutter speed. The amount of light that enters the lens is proportionately related to exposure time. N which represents f-number is defined as follows

$$N = \frac{f}{D} \tag{2}$$

where, f is the focal length and D is the diameter of the lens. Therefore, two different pairs of exposure time and f-number, can be related as,

$$\frac{PEV_1}{PEV_2} = \frac{t_1 N_2{}^2}{t_2 N_1{}^2} \tag{3}$$

Let us consider the f-stop exposure sequence [11]. In such a sequence a particular exposure value allows twice the amount of light with respect to its successor f-stop and allows only half the light compared to its predecessor [11]. Similarly, in the case of exposure time, the consecutive values in the exposure time scale allow the doubling or halving of the amount of light [23,30]. Based on the above statements and expressions (1–3), we consider that the lightness component L is related to PEV as follows

$$L = K \times 2^{PEV} \tag{4}$$

where K is a constant, and PEV can be a value from natural number. Two lightness maps L_1 and L_2 based on two PEVs, PEV_1 and PEV_2 are related as:

$$\frac{L_1}{L_2} = 2^{PEV_1 - PEV_2} \tag{5}$$

To capture structure aware lightness map (L), we consider the brightest channel which gives the maximum intensity across the color channels [6]. We consider level $N/2$ as the best exposed level and the levels $N/4 - 3N/4$ as the well exposed levels for a k-bit image having $N = 2^k$ levels in the map. Therefore, our algorithm will generate a set of images with consecutive exposure values higher than the actual image by applying (6) until the mean value of the lightness map is less than $3N/4$.

$$L_{HE}(i,j) = \begin{cases} L(i,j) \times 2^{PEV}, if\ L(i,j) \times 2^{PEV} < N \\ N \qquad\ , if\ L(i,j) \times 2^{PEV} \geq N \end{cases} \tag{6}$$

Note that the generated images with higher exposure value usually contain more artifacts like blocking and halo artifacts. Therefore, we restrict our method to generate a maximum of two virtual lightness maps (with $PEV = 1$ and 2). The generated lightness maps represent highly exposed lightness map with higher exposure values than the input.

Note that computationally very less-intensive hardware-friendly process in (6) generates L_{HE} which has a linear relationship with the input lightness map. Such a process preserves the underlying structural information, which is basically represented by the reflectance component (R) [6] in an image.

2.3 Weight Computation for Fusion

The psuedo images along with the input image are to be fused to generate a well-exposed image with backlit region having sufficient visibility. Here, we consider pixel level fusion [15] where our enhanced output will be a weighted sum of the images to be fused using a multi-scale fusion approach [16,19]. The weights are to be determined according to the value of the pixel in consideration. As mentioned already, the backlight image suffers from under-exposure in the backlit part and well or over exposed in non backlit part. So, technique should properly enhance the under exposed pixels, preserve the well exposed pixels, and limit the exposedness in the over exposed pixels. Moreover, the output should preserve the high frequency details for pleasant output. Therefore, we compute weights based on exposedness and gradient value.

The images are first normalized to [0, 1], where 0 is considered as darkest possible and 1 is the brightest possible pixel. In such a case, the best exposed pixel is 0.5 which is exactly the middle of the darkest and brightest pixel possible in the defined range. In the contribution to weight value from exposedness, pixel value having intensity 0.5 will be assigned maximum weight. Any deviation from 0.5 will be penalized (lesser weight). For such a weighting strategy, we consider the Gaussian function, which is the function usually adopted [19].

$$W_E{}^c(i,j) = \exp\left\{ -\frac{I^c(i,j) - 0.5}{2 \times (0.3)^2} \right\}; c = \{R, G, B\} \tag{7}$$

Combining the three channels, we have $W_E = W_E^R \times W_E^G \times W_E^B$. To capture the details of the image, different approaches propose different contrast measures

[19]. HVS is sensitive to spatial frequency [21]. So, image enhancement in terms of contrast should include spatial frequency [22]. In the contribution to weight value from contrast, we therefore, compute gradient energy which is directly related to spatial frequency. To minimize the effect of noise, we consider Sobel (Sobel vertical and Sobel horizontal) [8] for gradient computation. The weight based on the gradient energy is given by

$$W_G = \sum_{(i,j)\in\Omega} I_x(i,j)^2 + I_y(i,j)^2 \tag{8}$$

I_x is obtained by convolving the image with the vertical Sobel operator and I_y with horizontal Sobel operator.

The weights W_E and W_G are combined and normalized. The final weight for n^{th} image at pixel (i,j) is defined as

$$W_n(i,j) = \frac{W_{E,n}(i,j) \times W_{G,n}(i,j)}{\sum W_{E,n}(i,j) \times W_{G,n}(i,j)} \tag{9}$$

2.4 Multi-scale Image Fusion

The multiple images generated with these multiple lightness maps carry different but relevant information of the actual scene. A straight-forward image fusion strategy is the weighted average of the inputs. But such an operation results in output with artifacts, especially in the area of the image with details. Thus a suitable image fusion technique is required to fuse the images to generate a single well-exposed enhanced image with all the relevant information present in the output. HVS is sensitive to spatial frequency [21]. So, image enhancement in terms of contrast should include spatial frequency [22]. In [22], the authors have defined contrast based on spatial frequency in terms of bandpass filtered version of the image. Therefore, we consider spatial frequency sensitive pyramidal structure for processing the images.

In [22], the authors have defined contrast in terms of band pass filtered version of image. A pyramidal structure is considered for processing input image with band pass filter for 'perceived contrast' analysis. This multi-scale pyramidal structure based processing is a well accepted approach for image enhancement [9,27]. This motivates us to consider the spatial frequency aware pyramidal structure for suitable fusion of the images generated. Among different variant of multi-scale decomposition based image fusion, Laplacian pyramid [3] is most suitable for our case because Laplacian pyramid allows to access directly a set of quasi-bandpass version of original input image. Such elements in Laplacian pyramid allow simultaneous space-frequency localization. This is one of the most important feature which will help us to process based on 'perceived contrast' analysis for image enhancement. Moreover, generation for Laplacian pyramid needs very simple hardware friendly computations which are not only local but also can be processed in parallel in pipeline hardware architecture. Thus, this kind of system can give real time [3] performance. This motivates us to consider the spatial frequency aware Laplacian pyramid for suitable fusion of the images generated. Our approach is similar to Laplacian pyramid based image fusion [3,19] where fusion is carried out in each scale as a weighted average operation. However, computed weight $W_n(i,j)$ for n^{th} image is determined based on the exposedness and gradient energy at the scale of the input image. So, for fusion through Laplacian pyramid, we generate weights for n^{th} image at scale l, as follows

$$W_{l,n}(i,j) = \sum_p \sum_q G(p,q)W_l(2i+p,2j+q) \tag{10}$$

where G is Gaussian mask used as a low pass filter to generate the weights at different scales. Let us denote a bandpass version of higher resolution n^{th} input image of scale l in Laplacian pyramid as $LA\{I\}_{i,j,n}$. The fusion operation is a weighted average of the bandpass images in a particular scale.

$$LA\{I\}^l_{i,j} = \sum_{n=1}^{N} W^S_{l,n}(i,j)LA\{I\}^l_{i,j,n} \tag{11}$$

Expansion and addition [19] of all the band pass versions of Laplacian pyramid $LA\{I\}^l_{i,j}$ will generate the output image I_o, which in our case is the enhanced well-exposed image.

2.5   2D Histogram Based Local Enhancement

The above globally enhanced image may suffer from a loss in a local neighborhood [24]. Thus a suitable local enhancement is required.

HVS is more perceptive towards intensity difference rather than intensity in a spatial neighborhood [12]. A desired transformation $p = [p(0), p(1), ..., p(N-1)]$ for a k-bit image with $N = 2^k - 1$ should map intensity values m and $m + n$ to $p(m)$ and $p(m+n)$ such that the frequently appearing intensity difference in a spatial neighborhood is boosted up in the final output. To generate such a transformation, the authors in [12] have proposed a layered representation of 2D histogram h such that the index $h(m, m+n)$ represents the count of the occurrence of intensity levels $m+n$ and m in a spatial neighborhood. Overstretching due to the presence of large values in h is tackled using logarithmic function for attenuation. The attenuated 2D histogram for layer n in the layered representation is $h^n_m = \log(h(m, m+n) + h(m+n, m))$ [12]. For the layer n in the layered representation $d^n_m = p_{m+n} - p_m$ for $0 \le m \le N-1-n$ should be related to h^n_m such that $d^n_m = \kappa_n \times h^n_m$ for $0 \le m \le N-1-n$ where κ_n is a normalizing factor. Under such a condition, constrained optimization in [12] generates the desired transformation p, which is used here on the fused output to boost up frequently occurring intensity pairs in a local context for image enhancement.

3   Experimental Result

To determine the efficiency of our algorithm, we compare it with the state-of-the-art low-light image enhancement LLVORM [20] and SRL [14] and state-of-the-art backlit image restoration (LRB) [18]. The 38 test images from the backlit

(a) Original Input Image   (b) Original (Cropped)

(c) LLVORM   (d) LLVORM (Cropped)

(e) SRL   (f) SRL (Cropped)

(g) LRB   (h) LRB (Cropped)

(i) Proposed   (j) Proposed (Cropped)

Fig. 3. Subjective analysis of a backlit image having very low-light condition for backlit object. Left column and right column show the entire image and its cropped version respectively for comparative evaluation.

(a) Original Input Image   (b) Original (Cropped)

(c) LLVORM   (d) LLVORM (Cropped)

(e) SRL   (f) SRL (Cropped)

(g) LRB   (h) LRB (Cropped)

(i) Proposed   (j) Proposed (Cropped)

Fig. 4. Subjective analysis of a backlit image having medium low-light condition for backlit object. Left column and right column show the entire image and its cropped version respectively for comparative evaluation.

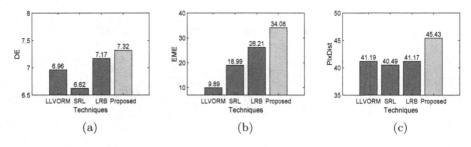

Fig. 5. Average Results in terms of (a) LOE (b) AMBE (c) Time

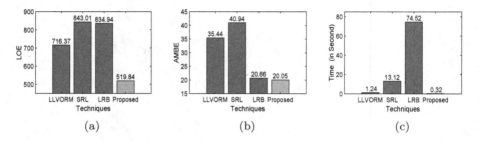

Fig. 6. Average Results in terms of (a) LOE (b) AMBE (c) Time

image database shared by [18] are used for the evaluation. We have generated the results on an Intel i5-4590 CPU 3.30 GHz machine with 16 GB RAM.

In Figs. 3 and 4, we present the subjective evaluation of two standard images and their cropped versions for detailed analysis. It can be observed that LLVORM is not able to enhance the images sufficiently. The results of LLVORM suffer from certain undesired artifacts. SRL produces better results, but it also produce artifacts. In terms of visibility of backlit part of the images, LRB and our proposed technique are better which are specifically proposed for backlit image restoration. But LRB suffers from washed out effect (as marked in the head part of Fig. 3(h)), artifacts at the edges (as marked in hand part of Fig. 3(h)). Moreover, LRB can generate undesired output due to the misclassification of backlit from non-backlit. Figure 4(h) shows such an example where the background between left hand and the tree is treated as backlit part and the dress (backlit) and background (non-backlit) adopt to the same tone. The same can be observed for the right hand (marked area) where the edge of the right hand gets the tone of the nearest background.

For the quantitative evaluation, we consider discrete entropy (DE) [26], measure of enhancement (EME) [1], and PixDist [5] to quantify the degree of enhancement in the output. DE is a measure of information present in the image. Higher is the value of DE, higher is the variability in image [12]. EME [1] and PixDist [5] are two widely used measures of enhancement. Higher is the value better is the enhancement for EME and PixDist. While enhancing image,

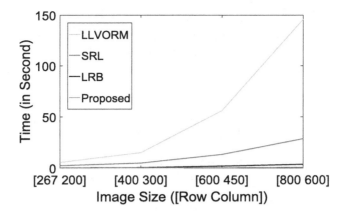

Fig. 7. Time vs image size

the lightness order should be maintained for naturalness preservation [13]. LOE which measures lightness order error is a measure of naturalness [28]. Lower is the value better is the quality of an image. AMBE measures the absolute change between mean gray value of input and output image. Lower is value better is the mean brightness preservation. We also consider the execution time for evaluation. Figure 5 and 6 present the average values of DE, EME, PixDist, LOE, AMBE, and execution time of all the images from the dataset. The green color in the Figs. 5 and 6 indicates the best results. It is clear that in terms of all the measures, our algorithm outperforms the rest. Note that the average time required for our algorithm is 0.36 s, which is substantially lower than others.

We finally show the Time vs Image Size analysis in Fig. 7. We can see that our techniques outperforms the rest of the techniques on the increase in time with respect to the increase in image size. On the other hand, as the image size increases, the competing backlit image enhancement algorithm LRB requires substantially higher time.

From the above discussion, it is evident that our technique performs better than others, subjectively and quantitatively. The presence of noise generated by our technique is limited. But, the technique may generate comparatively noisy output from an input backlit image having extremely low-lighting condition with the presence of considerable noise. Handling such issues can be a future scope of improvement.

4 Conclusion

This paper presents an approach for backlit image restoration through HVS-sensitive multi-scale fusion of multiple pseudo exposed images along with the input. We generate pseudo images exploiting the relation of exposure with aperture and shutter speed. The fused image is locally enhanced by boosting the intensity difference in a spatial neighborhood to generate the output. The proposed technique is found to be faster. Moreover, the technique enhances the backlit images sufficiently while preserving the naturalness.

References

1. Agaian, S.S., Silver, B., Panetta, K.A.: Transform coefficient histogram-based image enhancement algorithms using contrast entropy. IEEE Trans. Image Process. 16(3), 741–758 (2007)
2. Arici, T., Dikbas, S., Altunbasak, Y.: A histogram modification framework and its application for image contrast enhancement. IEEE Trans. Image Process. 18(9), 1921–1935 (2009)
3. Burt, P.J., Adelson, E.H.: The Laplacian pyramid as a compact image code. IEEE Trans. Commun. 31, 532–540 (1983)
4. Celik, T., Tjahjadi, T.: Contextual and variational contrast enhancement. IEEE Trans. Image Process. 20(12), 3431–3441 (2011)
5. Chen, Z., Abidi, B.R., Page, D.L., Abidi, M.A.: Gray-level grouping (GLG): an automatic method for optimized image contrast enhancement-Part I: the basic method. IEEE Trans. Image Process. 15(8), 2290–2302 (2006)
6. Dhara, S.K., Sen, D.: Low light image enhancement using Grover's algorithm on superposed luminance levels. In: 2018 25th IEEE International Conference on Image Processing (ICIP), pp. 1113–1117. IEEE (2018)
7. Gao, Y., Hu, H.M., Li, B., Guo, Q.: Naturalness preserved nonuniform illumination estimation for image enhancement based on retinex. IEEE Trans. Multimedia 20(2), 335–344 (2018)
8. Gonzalez, R.C., Woods, R.E.: Digital Image Processing. Prentice Hall, Upper Saddle River (2002)
9. Jobson, D.J., Rahman, Z.u., Woodell, G.A.: A multiscale retinex for bridging the gap between color images and the human observation of scenes. IEEE Trans. Image Process. 6(7), 965–976 (1997)
10. Kim, T., Paik, J.: Adaptive contrast enhancement using gain-controllable clipped histogram equalization. IEEE Trans. Consum. Electron. 54(4), 1803–1810 (2008)
11. Lee, C.H., Chen, L.H., Wang, W.K.: Image contrast enhancement using classified virtual exposure image fusion. IEEE Trans. Consum. Electron. 58(4), 1253–1261 (2012)
12. Lee, C., Lee, C., Kim, C.S.: Contrast enhancement based on layered difference representation of 2D histograms. IEEE Trans. Image Process. 22(12), 5372–5384 (2013)
13. Li, B., Wang, S., Geng, Y.: Image enhancement based on retinex and lightness decomposition. In: 18th IEEE International Conference on Image Processing, pp. 3417–3420. IEEE (2011)
14. Li, M., Liu, J., Yang, W., Sun, X., Guo, Z.: Structure-revealing low-light image enhancement via robust retinex model. IEEE Trans. Image Process. 27(6), 2828–2841 (2018)
15. Li, S., Kang, X., Fang, L., Hu, J., Yin, H.: Pixel-level image fusion: a survey of the state of the art. Inf. Fus. 33, 100–112 (2017)
16. Li, Z., Wei, Z., Wen, C., Zheng, J.: Detail-enhanced multi-scale exposure fusion. IEEE Trans. Image Process. 26(3), 1243–1252 (2017)

17. Li, Z., Cheng, K., Wu, X.: Soft binary segmentation-based backlit image enhancement. In: 2015 IEEE 17th International Workshop on Multimedia Signal Processing (MMSP), pp. 1–5. IEEE (2015)
18. Li, Z., Wu, X.: Learning-based restoration of backlit images. IEEE Trans. Image Process. **27**(2), 976–986 (2018)
19. Mertens, T., Kautz, J., Van Reeth, F.: Exposure fusion: a simple and practical alternative to high dynamic range photography. In: Computer Graphics Forum, vol. 28, pp. 161–171. Wiley Online Library (2009)
20. Park, S., Yu, S., Moon, B., Ko, S., Paik, J.: Low light image enhancement using variational optimization based retinex model. IEEE Trans. Consum. Electron. **63**(2), 178–184 (2017)
21. Párraga, C.A., Troscianko, T., Tolhurst, D.J.: The human visual system is optimised for processing the spatial information in natural visual images. Curr. Biol. **10**(1), 35–38 (2000)
22. Peli, E.: Contrast in complex images. J. Opt. Soc. Am. A **7**(10), 2032–2040 (1990)
23. Ray, S.F.: Applied Photographic Optics: Imaging Systems for Photography. Focal Press London, Film and Video (1988)
24. Ren, W., et al.: Low-light image enhancement via a deep hybrid network. IEEE Trans. Image Process. (2019)
25. Sen, P., Kalantari, N.K., Yaesoubi, M., Darabi, S., Goldman, D.B., Shechtman, E.: Robust patch-based HDR reconstruction of dynamic scenes. ACM Trans. Graph. **31**(6), 203–1 (2012)
26. Shannon, C.E.: A mathematical theory of communication. Bell Syst. Tech. J. **27**(3), 379–423 (1948)
27. Velde, K.V.: Multi-scale color image enhancement. In: Proceedings 1999 International Conference on Image Processing (Cat. 99CH36348), vol. 3, pp. 584–587. IEEE (1999)
28. Wang, S., Zheng, J., Hu, H.M., Li, B.: Naturalness preserved enhancement algorithm for non-uniform illumination images. IEEE Trans. Image Process. **22**(9), 3538–3548 (2013)
29. Wang, T.H., et al.: Pseudo-multiple-exposure-based tone fusion with local region adjustment. IEEE Trans. Multimedia **17**(4), 470–484 (2015)
30. Ward, P., Jacobson, R., Ray, S., Attridge, G.G., Axford, N.: The Manual of Photography: Photographic and Digital Imaging. Taylor & Francis (2000)

Grapevine Nutritional Disorder Detection Using Image Processing

D. M. Motiur Rahaman[1]([✉]), Tintu Baby[1], Alex Oczkowski[1],
Manoranjan Paul[1,2], Lihong Zheng[1,3], Leigh M. Schmidtke[1],
Bruno P. Holzapfel[1,4], Rob R. Walker[1,5], and Suzy Y. Rogiers[1,4]

[1] National Wine and Grape Industry Centre, Charles Sturt University,
Wagga Wagga, NSW, Australia
{drahaman,tbaby,aoczkowski,mpaul,lzheng,lschmidtke,
bholzapfel,srogiers}@csu.edu.au
[2] School of Computing and Mathematics, Charles Sturt University,
Bathurst, NSW, Australia
[3] School of Computing and Mathematics, Charles Sturt University,
Wagga Wagga, NSW, Australia
[4] NSW Department of Primary Industries, Wagga Wagga, NSW, Australia
[5] Commonwealth Scientific and Industrial Research Organisation,
Adelaide, SA, Australia
Rob.Walker@csiro.au

Abstract. Vine nutrition is a key element of vineyard management. Nutrient disorders affect vine growth, crop yield, berry composition, and wine quality. Each vineyard may have a unique combination of soil type, vine age, canopy architecture, cultivar and rootstock. Therefore nutritional requirements vary between vineyards and even locations within a vineyard. Nutritional disorders can be detected visually on leaves, fruits, stems or roots. The advancement of image processing and machine learning has made it feasible to develop rapid tools to assess vine nutritional disorders using these symptoms. This paper presents our proposed method of using a smartphone app to capture and analyse images of vine leaves for identifying nutritional disorders of grapevines rapidly and conveniently. Nutrient deficiency/toxicity symptoms were created in hydroponically grown grapevines of both red and white varieties. RGB (red, green, and blue) images of old and young leaves were taken weekly to track the progression of symptoms. A benchmarked dataset was developed through a laboratory based nutrient analysis of the petioles. A wide range of features (e.g., texture, smoothness, contrast and shape) were selected for the following customised machine learning techniques. Our proposed algorithm was developed to identify specific deficiency and toxicity symptoms through training and testing process. The support vector machine has achieved a 98.99% average accuracy in the testing.

Keywords: Nutrition · Features · Grapevines · Viticulture · Support vector machine · Deficiency

© Springer Nature Switzerland AG 2019
C. Lee et al. (Eds.): PSIVT 2019, LNCS 11854, pp. 184–196, 2019.
https://doi.org/10.1007/978-3-030-34879-3_15

1 Introduction

The efficiency of an agricultural system is directly related to the timely and optimal management of pests and diseases, and precise management of irrigation and fertilizers. Pests, diseases and nutritional problems significantly affect the quality and yield of crops. Thus, early identification of symptoms for pests, disease and nutritional disorders is crucial in any agricultural practice to ensure productivity and profitability. Symptoms of nutritional disorders or infections are visual signs to variations in the normal physiological and metabolic functions of the plant [1, 2]. Usually, the symptoms are apparent in leaves, fruits, stems or roots. As a result, the correct identification of specific plant symptoms can be a useful diagnostic tool for the assessment of diseases and nutritional disorders in plants [3, 4].

In addition to water, oxygen and carbon dioxide, plants require at least 14 nutrients to maintain their physiological functions. Six mineral elements which are required in relatively greater amounts are called macronutrients: nitrogen (N), potassium (K), phosphorus (P), magnesium (Mg) calcium (Ca), and sulphur (S). The other elements, which are required in smaller amounts are called micronutrients: zinc (Zn), iron (Fe), copper (Cu), boron (B), manganese (Mn), chlorine (Cl), molybdenum (Mo), and nickel (Ni) [5, 6]. Deficiency and toxicity in any one of these mineral elements negatively impact plant health and productivity and may cause the development of visual symptoms. The usual diagnostic techniques for nutritional disorders are based on crop growth responses, leaf symptoms and soil and plant tissue analysis [7, 8]. General nutrient deficiency symptoms include reduced growth, yellowing, purple or red discoloration, interveinal chlorosis or necrosis. Nutrient toxicity can also cause abnormal growth patterns, leaf discolouration, chlorosis and necrotic patches. Many nutrients when in excess, may interfere with the uptake of other nutrients and can potentially cause deficiency symptoms [9]. Hence, an accurate diagnosis of nutrient disorders is essential for successful fertilizer management.

The assessment of nutritional disorders in the field is a very labor intensive process requiring tissue diagnostics by qualified laboratories [10]. Researchers have applied new technologies to improve the efficiency and accuracy of the identification of plant disorders and diseases. Hyperspectral imaging has resulted in vegetation indices for indirect monitoring of plant disorders [11]. However, specific disorders cannot be identified. A new spectral index was developed to identify three distinct pathogens in winter wheat disease [12]. Using the RELIEFF algorithm, the most and least appropriate wavelengths for various illnesses were collected. The classification accuracies of these new indices were 86.5%, 85.2%, 91.6% and 93.5% respectively for healthy and leaves infected with powdery mildew, yellow rust or aphids.

Image processing techniques were used for disease identification and fruit grading [10, 13]. Applying an artificial neural network for disease detection, two distinct databases were employed, one for the purpose of training and the other for testing. Back propagation was used for the weight adjustment of the training databases. Three feature vectors were considered i.e., texture, colour, and morphology [13]. They found that the morphological characteristics yielded better results compared to the other two features.

Chili plant leaf images were recorded and processed to determine their health status [14]. Pre-processing was performed using filtering, edge detection and morphological operations. MATLAB software was applied to extract features, however, the segmentation of the leaf from the background is an important preliminary step. The technique proposed in [15] compared the threshold of both the Otsu and clustering algorithms to analyse infected leaves [4]. The authors found that the value of the extracted features was smaller for the k-means clustering algorithm and more precise than any other technique. In this technique, the green pixels were recognised after implementing k-means clustering methods and the variable threshold value was determined by using the Otsu algorithm to make a final decision regarding leaf health status. The technique of color co-occurrence was used for feature extraction. The *spatial gray-level dependence matrices* (SGDM) was used to compute the texture statistics and the features were calculated using the *gray-level co-occurrence matrix* (GLCM) [16].

Zhang et al. developed a *field programmable gate arrays* (FPGA) and a *digital signal processor* (DSP) based system to monitor and control plant diseases [17]. The FPGA was used for collecting field crop images or videos for monitoring and diagnosing. A rice disease detection technique using a pattern recognition method is elaborated in [18]. At first, the authors selected the *region of interest* (ROI) manually, then they used a model incorporating *hue, saturation,* and *intensity* (HIS) to segment the image. Later, a boundary and spot detection was performed to define the infected portion of the leaf.

All the above-mentioned techniques are used to identify plant nutrient deficiency and toxicity symptoms, but they are not specific to the viticulture. In viticulture, there are several kinds of plant disorders including physiological and nutrient disorders (e.g., nitrogen deficiency), pathological diseases (e.g., powdery mildew) and pests (e.g., blister mite) as shown in Fig. 1. It should be mentioned here that we have developed the benchmarked dataset through nutrient analysis of petioles with matching symptom severity. Each disorder contains a different kind of symptom, and to cover all symptoms we carefully chose a wide range of innovative features (i.e., 10 features) and customised machine learning technique to identify specific deficiency and toxicity symptoms. Moreover, we have devolved a prototype of a smartphone app to capture and analyse images of vine leaves quickly and conveniently for assessing nutritional disorders of grapevines with minimal cost.

The rest of this paper is organised as follows: Sect. 2 describes the proposed vine nutritional disorders detection approach, Sect. 3 presents experimental results. Finally, the conclusions are given in Sect. 4.

2 Proposed Grapevine Nutritional Disorder Detection Technique

Here we outline the image analysis and smartphone App development process of vine leaves to assess nutritional disorders of grapevines rapidly and conveniently with minimal cost. This process consists of three steps: (i) development of nutrient deficiency/toxicity symptoms, (ii) machine learning and image analysis and (iii) app development.

Fig. 1. Grapevine leaves: (a), (b), (c) and (d) are the upper surface of the leaves whereas (e), (f), (g) and (h) are the corresponding lower surface of the Chardonnay grapevine leaves.

2.1   Development of Nutrient Deficiency/Toxicity Symptoms

In order to develop an image processing algorithm for the identification of nutrient deficiency/toxicity symptoms in grapevines, an image database with various symptoms were developed. Nutrient deficiency/toxicity symptoms were created in potted grapevines grown in a washed sand medium, for Shiraz (a red variety) and Chardonnay (a white variety) (Fig. 2). Modified Hoagland's nutrient solutions, with high or low levels of specific elements, were used as treatments to create the symptoms. The

Fig. 2. Potted vines are grown in washed sand with specific nutrient formulations.

experimental design was a completely randomised block design with eight replicate plants for each treatment. RGB (red, green, and blue) images of old and young leaves were taken weekly to track the progression of symptoms. Chemical nutrient analysis of the leaf petioles was matched with symptom development.

2.2 Machine Learning and Image Analysis

The basic steps leading to symptom detection and classification though image processing is shown in Fig. 3. RGB images of healthy and symptomatic leaves were captured for training and testing purposes. In most cases, a specific portion of the leaf was affected. Therefore, the ROI for the nutritional disorder was cropped and processed for feature extraction. In order to distinguish the different nutritional disorders, a comprehensive set of image features (e.g., contrast, correlation, energy, homogeneity, mean, standard deviation, entropy, root means square (RMS), kurtosis and skewness) have been selected and fed into the customised machine learning (i.e., support vector machine (SVM)) techniques; intelligent algorithms were created to identify specific deficiency and toxicity symptoms. Two critical steps i.e., (a) feature extraction and (b) classification are further described below.

(a) Feature Extraction
Haralick introduced the most popular two step feature extracting technique i.e., (i) computing *co-occurrence matrix* (CM) and (ii) calculating the texture feature based on the CM. This technique is useful in a wide range of image analysis applications [19]. In image processing, the *gray-level co-occurrence matrix* (GLCM) characterises the texture of an image by calculating how often pairs of pixels with specific values and in

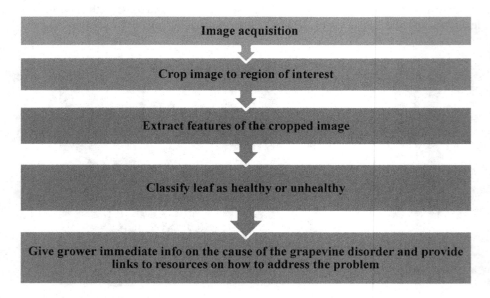

Fig. 3. Basic steps for grapevine diseases detection.

a specified spatial relationship occur in an image. In the transformation from the image space into the co-occurrence matrix space, the neighbouring pixels in one or some of the eight (e.g., 0°, 45°, 90°, 135°, 0°, −45°, −90°, and −135°) directions can be used. It contains information about the positions of the pixels having similar gray level values. In general, each element (i, j) in the GLCM specifies the number of times that the pixel with a value i occurred horizontally adjacent to a pixel with value j.

Figure 4 outlines a computation that has been applied in the manner where the element $(1, 1)$ in the GLCM contains the value 1 because there is only one instance in the image where two horizontally adjacent pixels have the values 1 and 1. Element $(1, 2)$ in the GLCM contains the value 2 because there are two instances in the image where two, horizontally adjacent pixels have the values 1 and 2 [19, 20]. In the second step, we calculate four features (i.e., contrast, correlation, energy and homogeneity) based on the GLCM.

Following is the summary of selected image features.

(i)   **Contrast**
    The contrast is a measure of the intensity of a pixel and its neighbour over the image. In the visual perception of the real world, contrast is determined by the difference in the colour and brightness of the object and other objects within the same field of view. The intensity contrast between a pixel and its neighbor over the whole image in the range of $0 \leq \text{contrast} \leq (\text{size}(\text{GLCM}, 1) - 1)^2$. For a constant image, the value of contrast is 0. Contrast can be calculated using Eq. (1)

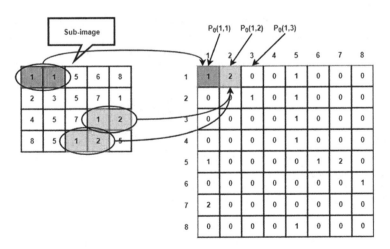

Fig. 4. Creation of GLCM from the image [20].

$$\text{Contrast} = \sum_{i,j} |i - j|^2 p(i,j). \tag{1}$$

where i and j are the gray level values in the image and p is the relative frequency matrix of the texture.

(ii) **Correlation**

Correlation shows a statistical measure of how correlated a pixel is to its neighbor over the whole image. Correlation is 1 or −1 for a perfectly positively or negatively correlated image. Correlation is not defined for a constant image. Correlation can be calculated using Eq. (2)

$$\text{Correlation} = \sum_{i,j} \frac{(i - \mu_i)(j - \mu_j)p(i,j)}{\sigma_i \sigma_j}. \tag{2}$$

where μ_i and μ_j represents the mean and σ_i and σ_j represents the standard deviation of the rows and columns.

(iii) **Energy**

Energy (E) can be defined as the measure of the extent of pixel pair repetitions and is repented by the sum of squared elements in the GLCM (i.e., Eq. (3)). When pixels are very similar, the energy value will be large. Energy is 1 for a constant image.

$$E = \sum_{i,j} p(i,j)^2 \tag{3}$$

(iv) **Homogeneity**

Homogeneity represents the closeness of the distribution of elements in the GLCM to the GLCM diagonal and is defined by Eq. (4). The maximum and minimum value of the homogeneity is 0 to 1. Homogeneity is 1 for a diagonal GLCM.

$$\text{Homogeneity} = \sum_{i,j} \frac{p(i,j)}{1 + |i - j|} \tag{4}$$

(v) **Entropy**

Entropy is the measure of randomness that is used to characterize the texture of the input image. Its value will be maximum when all the elements of the co-occurrence matrix are the same. It is defined as in Eq. (5) as follows

$$\text{Entropy} = \sum_{i,j} p(i,j)(-log_2(p(i,j))) \tag{5}$$

(vi) **Mean**

Suppose, z to be a random variable denoting image gray levels and I(zi) be the corresponding histogram, where i = 1, 2, 3.... The mean gives the average gray level of each region and it is defined by Eq. (6)

$$m = \sum_i z_i I(z_i) \tag{6}$$

(vii) **Standard Deviation**

Standard deviation expresses by how much the members of a group differ from the mean value for the group and is defined by Eq. (7). A low standard deviation indicates that the data points tend to be close to the mean, while a high standard deviation indicates that the data points are spread out over a wider range of values.

$$\text{Standard Deviation} = \sqrt{\sum_i (z_i - m)^2 I(z_i)} \tag{7}$$

(viii) **Skewness**

Skewness is a measure of the asymmetry of the gray levels around the sample mean and defined as Eq. (8). If skewness is negative, the data are spread out more to the left of the mean than to the right. If skewness is positive, the data are spread out more to the right.

$$\text{Skewness} = \sum_i (z_i - m)^3 I(z_i) \tag{8}$$

(ix) **Kurtosis**

In digital image processing kurtosis values are interpreted in combination with noise and resolution measurement. High kurtosis values should go hand in hand with low noise and low resolution.

$$\text{Kurtosis} = \sum_i (z_i - m)^4 I(z_i) \tag{9}$$

(x) **Root Mean Square (RMS)**

The RMS value of each row or column of the input, along vectors of a specified dimension of the input, or of the entire input. The RMS value of the jth column of a $M \times N$ input matrix I is given by Eq. (10) as follows

$$RMS = \frac{\sqrt{\sum_{i=1}^{M} |I(i,j)|^2}}{M} \tag{10}$$

(b) Classification

After extraction, the features were given as input of the SVM for training purpose as shown in Fig. 5. Then, for the testing purpose, features were extracted from the testing images and given as input of the SVM. The multiclass SVM is built up by various two-class SVMs to solve the problem, either by using one-versus-all or one-versus-one. The winning class is then determined by the highest output function or the maximum votes respectively. This helps the multiclass SVM to perform effectively to predict a healthy or unhealthy leaf.

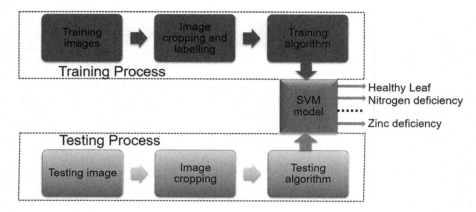

Fig. 5. Classification algorithm.

2.3 App Development

We have developed an Android Mobile Application to demonstrate these disease recognition algorithms. Figure 6 shows the features of the proposed App. The Application is developed at Android version 9.0 and requires a minimum Android version of 4.0.3. It uses an open-source software library - OpenCV to implement our proposed machine learning algorithms.

The application is designed to have the following functionalities:

- Acquire/label leaf images for analysis
- Provide information about relevant leaf/vine diseases
- Analyse a leaf region with an SVM algorithm to detect whether the leaf has a disorder or no

3 Experimental Results

To evaluate the performances of the proposed technique, we extracted features from 40 images for training purposes. Then, we tested evaluation metrics (e.g., precision, recall and F1-measure) of the proposed technique on 145 images to evaluate their overall performances. It should be mentioned here that both the training and testing images are captured within the same environment (e.g., illumination, temperature). The definition of precision, recall and F1-measure can be defined by the Eqs. (11)–(13) [21].

$$Precision = \frac{T_p}{T_p + F_p}. \tag{11}$$

$$Recall = \frac{T_p}{T_p + F_n}. \tag{12}$$

$$F1 - measure = 2 \times \frac{Precision \times Recall}{Precision + Recall}.$$ (13)

where *Tp*, *Fp* and *Fn* are the number of images correctly identified by the proposed technique and the laboratory experiment, the number of images correctly identified by the proposed technique but not by the laboratory experiment, the number of images correctly identified by the laboratory experiment but not by the proposed technique respectively. However, either precision or recall alone cannot provide a good indication of a perfect measurement [21, 22]. For example, a technique can offer better precision but poor recall or vice versa. To be an effective and robust method, it must achieve both higher precision and recall. To represent this measure, the F1-measure is defined as combining precision, recall, and represented by Eq. (13). A high value for both the precision and recall indicate that the F1-measure is also very high. Thus, a method with a high F1-measure value confirms a better technique to classify a leaf as healthy or unhealthy. Table 1 shows the precision is 100% for both the healthy and unhealthy

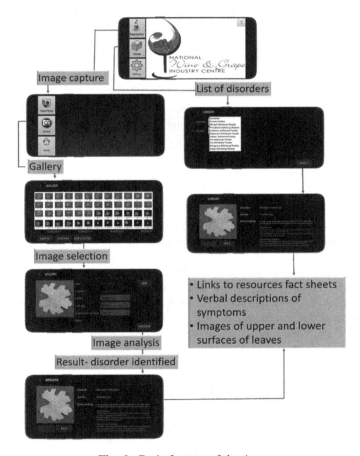

Fig. 6. Basic features of the App.

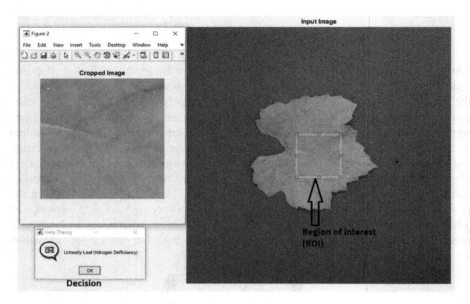

Fig. 7. Visual output.

Table 1. Precision, recall, and F1-measure for the proposed technique

	Chardonnay		Shiraz		Average F1-measure (%)
	Healthy	Unhealthy	Healthy	Unhealthy	
Precision (%)	100	100	100	100	98.99
Recall (%)	100	95.02	100	97.06	
F1-measure (%)	100	97.44	100	98.51	

leaves whereas the recall was 100% and 96.04% for the healthy and unhealthy leaves respectively. Similarly, the F1-measure for healthy and unhealthy leaves are 100% and 97.98% respectively. The average F1-measure is 98.99% which represents the overall performance of the proposed technique. An example is shown in Fig. 7. This leaf appears visually healthy, however, a laboratory test confirmed that it has nitrogen deficiency (i.e., unhealthy). Our proposed technique was thus able to detect it correctly and outperformed the human assessment.

4 Conclusion

Successful crop cultivation is highly dependent on the ability to accurately detect and classify a grapevine disease and this can be done using image processing. This article has elaborated feature extraction and classification methods of leaf symptoms. The SVM technique was highly effective at correctly identifying and classifying the disorder. We have thus been able to create a prototype for the first version of the mobile app. The experimental results show that image analysis and the machine learning approach can be applied to the identification of nutritional disorders.

References

1. Agrios, G.N.: Plant Pathology. Elsevier Academic Press, Amsterdam (2005)
2. Taiz, L., Zeiger, E.: Plant Physiology, vol. 4, pp. 67–86. Sinauer Associates, Sunderland (2006). https://doi.org/10.1109/icacea.2015.7194375
3. Bock, C.H., Parker, P.E., Cook, A.Z., Gottwald, T.R.: Characteristics of the perception of different severity measures of citrus canker and the relationships between the various symptom types. Plant Dis. **92**, 927–939 (2008). https://doi.org/10.1094/pdis-92-6-0927
4. Kaur, S., Pandey, S., Goel, S.: Plants disease identification and classification through leaf images: a survey. Arch. Comput. Methods Eng. **26**, 507–530 (2019). https://doi.org/10.1007/s11831-018-9255-6
5. Brady, N.C., Weil, R.R.: Instructor's manual with test item file to accompany The Nature and Properties of Soils, Fourteenth Edition (2008)
6. Fageria, N.K.: Maximizing Crop Yields. Marcel Dekker, New York (1992). https://doi.org/10.1109/CIS2018.2018.00044
7. Fageria, N.K., Filho, M.P.B., Moreira, A., Guimarães, C.M.: Foliar fertilization of crop plants. J. Plant Nutr. **32**, 1044–1064 (2009). https://doi.org/10.1080/01904160902872826
8. Landon, J.R.: A Handbook for Soil Survey and Agricultural Land Evaluation in the Tropics and Subtropics. Taylor & Francis, London (2014)
9. Nagabhushan, T.N., Aradhya, V.N.M., Jagadeesh, P., Shukla, S., Chaydevi, M.L. (eds.): CCIP 2017. CCIS, vol. 801. Springer, Singapore (2018). https://doi.org/10.1007/978-981-10-9059-2
10. Bhange, M., Hingoliwala, H.A.: Smart farming: pomegranate disease detection using image processing. Procedia Comput. Sci. **58**, 280–288 (2015). https://doi.org/10.1016/j.procs.2015.08.022
11. Shi, Y., Huang, W., Luo, J., Huang, L., Zhou, X.: Detection and discrimination of pests and diseases in winter wheat based on spectral indices and kernel discriminant analysis. Comput. Electron. Agric. **141**, 171–180 (2017). https://doi.org/10.1016/j.compag.2017.07.019
12. Huang, W., et al.: New optimized spectral indices for identifying and monitoring winter wheat diseases. IEEE J. Sel. Top Appl. Earth Obs. Remote Sens. **7**, 2516–2524 (2014). https://doi.org/10.1109/JSTARS.2013.2294961
13. Jhuria, M., Kumar, A., Borse, R.: Image processing for smart farming: detection of disease and fruit grading. In: IEEE 2nd International Conference on Image Information Process, ICIIP 2013, pp. 521–526. IEEE (2013). https://doi.org/10.1109/ICIIP.2013.6707647
14. Husin, Z., Bin Md Shakaff, A.Y., Bin Abdul Aziz, A.H., Bin Mohamed Farook, R.B.S.: Feasibility study on plant chili disease detection using image processing techniques. In: Proceedings of the 3rd International Conference on Intelligent Systems Modelling and Simulation, ISMS 2012, pp. 291–296 (2012) https://doi.org/10.1109/ISMS.2012.33
15. Badnakhe, M.R.: Infected leaf analysis and comparison by Otsu threshold and k-means clustering. Int. J. Adv. Res. Comput. Sci. Softw. Eng. **2**, 449–452 (2012)
16. Al Hiary, H., Bani Ahmad, S., Reyalat, M., Braik, M., ALRahamneh, Z.: Fast and accurate detection and classification of plant diseases. Int. J. Comput. Appl. **17**, 31–38 (2011)

17. Zhang, C., Wang, X., Li, X.: Design of monitoring and control plant disease system based on DSP&FPGA. In: 2nd International Conference on Networks Security, Wireless Communications and Trusted Computing, NSWCTC 2010, vol. 2, pp. 479–482 (2010). https://doi.org/10.1109/NSWCTC.2010.246

18. Phadikar, S., Sil, J.: Rice disease identification using pattern recognition techniques. In: Proceedings of the 11th International Conference on Computer and Information Technology, ICCIT 2008, pp. 420–423 (2008). https://doi.org/10.1109/ICCITECHN.2008.4803079

19. Kiaee, N., Hashemizadeh, E., Zarrinpanjeh, N.: Using GLCM features in Haar wavelet transformed space for moving object classification. IET Intell. Transp. Syst. 13, 1148–1153 (2019). https://doi.org/10.1049/iet-its.2018.5192

20. Sun, W., Zeng, N., He, Y.: Morphological Arrhythmia automated diagnosis method using gray-level co-occurrence matrix enhanced convolutional neural network. IEEE Access 7, 67123–67129 (2019). https://doi.org/10.1109/ACCESS.2019.2918361

21. Shoumy, N.J., Ang, L.-M., Motiur Rahaman, D.M.: Multimodal big data affective analytics. In: Seng, K.P., Ang, L.-M., Liew, A.W.-C., Gao, J. (eds.) Multimodal Analytics for Next-Generation Big Data Technologies and Applications, pp. 45–71. Springer, Cham (2019). https://doi.org/10.1007/978-3-319-97598-6_3

22. Paul, M., Musfequs Salehin, M.: Spatial and motion saliency prediction method using eye tracker data for video summarization. IEEE Trans. Circ. Syst. Video Technol. 29, 1856–1867 (2019). https://doi.org/10.1109/TCSVT.2018.2844780

Hierarchical Colour Image Segmentation by Leveraging RGB Channels Independently

Sheikh Tania[✉], Manzur Murshed, Shyh Wei Teng, and Gour Karmakar

Federation University Australia, Gippsland Campus,
Churchill, Victoria 3842, Australia
{ttania,manzur.murshed,shyh.wei.teng,gour.karmakar}@federation.edu.au

Abstract. In this paper, we introduce a hierarchical colour image segmentation based on cuboid partitioning using simple statistical features of the pixel intensities in the RGB channels. Estimating the difference between any two colours is a challenging task. As most of the colour models are not perceptually uniform, investigation of an alternative strategy is highly demanding. To address this issue, for our proposed technique, we present a new concept for colour distance measure based on the inconsistency of pixel intensities of an image which is more compliant to human perception. Constructing a reliable set of superpixels from an image is fundamental for further merging. As cuboid partitioning is a superior candidate to produce superpixels, we use the agglomerative merging to yield the final segmentation results exploiting the outcome of our proposed cuboid partitioning. The proposed cuboid segmentation based algorithm significantly outperforms not only the quadtree-based segmentation but also existing state-of-the-art segmentation algorithms in terms of quality of segmentation for the benchmark datasets used in image segmentation.

Keywords: Cuboid segmentation · Agglomerative merging · Colour image segmentation

1 Introduction

Image segmentation is a significant pre-processing step for most image processing techniques such as object recognition, object-based image classification, and content-based image retrieval. These computer vision techniques are being used in many cutting edge applications, including the latest medical imaging, traffic control system, remote sensing, and video surveillance.

There are mainly two different approaches to image segmentation [2]: (i) edge detection-based and (ii) region-based segmentation. Edge detection aims to detect edges between different group of pixels and does not guarantee to detect the closed object contours. Region-based segmentation divides an image into disjoint regions. Image derivative was the basic concept of early edge detection

© Springer Nature Switzerland AG 2019
C. Lee et al. (Eds.): PSIVT 2019, LNCS 11854, pp. 197–210, 2019.
https://doi.org/10.1007/978-3-030-34879-3_16

algorithms [5]. Recently, gPb-OWT-UCM [2] put forth a contour detector and combined it with a hierarchical image segmentation. Again, there exists a wide spectrum of region based techniques, including normalized cut [24], mean shift [7], random walk [11], region grow [30], graph-based [9], watershed [32], fuzzy c-means clustering [17], JSEG [8], and hierarchical segmentation [18,27,33].

Even with the overabundance of segmentation techniques, there are demands for new techniques because all the methods could not be suitable for all types of applications. For example, segmentation techniques for medical imaging cannot be applied to natural images. A recent work [21] proposes an unconventional way of segmentation, where the output of the algorithm comes in the form of cuboids. The motivation for the task is to facilitate efficient and effective content-based image retrieval and video coding. In this era of multimedia, most video contents are transmitted and also stored in the compressed form, thus the post-processing (e.g., video object recognition [12], action recognition [6], and video summarization [3]) needs to decompress them. Embedding relevant coding metadata can facilitate the post-processing exempting the decompression. The only available data are in the form of rectangular blocks in the compression format. The arbitrarily shaped partitions of video segmentation techniques are not appropriate to serve the purpose. The rectangular-shaped output of cuboid segmentation can serve it best.

Cuboid segmentation [21] uses simple statistical features (e.g., mean and variance), derived from the distribution of pixel values. The main idea is to use a greedy heuristic to recursively split a rectangular image into two rectangular halves with an optimal split-line, orthogonal to one of the axes so that the value of the distance metric is maximized. The recursion is terminated when the distance is below a threshold or when the targeting granularity is reached. Cuboid segmentation has some outstanding benefits. It is very simple to implement and preserves spatial relationships among neighbours. The complexity is bounded to linear form by utilizing the integral imaging approach [29] to generate the colour moments. Again, the cuboid segmentation is very fast as the depth of recursion is bounded logarithmically. Moreover, it can also take advantages of matrix processing and the specialized hardware e.g., the graphics processing unit. Again, the hierarchical approach is amenable to parallel processing. Lastly, the output of segmentation (i.e., the boundary of cuboid segments) can be stored using only the four corner points of each cuboid.

The cuboid segmentation can easily be confused with the quadtree (QT) decomposition [26] as both of them produce segments of rectangular shape. QT decomposition is widely used for coding purposes. The main idea is to segment the image into homogeneous and heterogeneous parts to allocate fewer bits to homogeneous regions and more bits to those regions that contain additional detail and sharper features. Although both the algorithms partition an image recursively, they differ from each other greatly. First of all, the original quadtree decomposition requires images not only with equal height and width but also the value of height and width must be of the power of two but cuboid segmentation does not care about the image size. Again, the QT decomposition divides the image into four equal-sized blocks in each iteration until a specified homogeneity criterion is achieved. In contrast, the cuboid segmentation does not use any arbitrary division. Rather it uses the local optimum distance to divide the image into two regions based on a specific feature space (e.g., colour, texture, or both).

However, the very first cuboid segmentation algorithm suffers from over-segmentation of regions with a similar colour. This is because it quantizes the HCL colour model into a fixed number of colours in cubic spaces and uses the Euclidean distance measure in that cubic space. In CSeg'18 [28], the HCL colour space and quantization is ignored and l_∞-norm is used while selecting the optimal split s^* among all possible splits. This means for each possible split, a dominant RGB channel was selected for which the distance between the halves in that channel is the maximum of all three channels. As an image (or sub-image thereafter) is static while considering the optimal split, the distance-dependent dominant channel selection leads to inconsistency in the decision process as different channels may become dominant for different splits of the same image. Again, in the CSeg'18, contrast measure has been used to determine whether a cuboid needs to be partitioned further. The contrast value used in CSeg'18 can be influenced by the local contrast, which limits the efficacy of accurate decision making for cuboid partitioning.

In this paper, the first shortcoming of CSeg'18 has been overcome in two stages. A dominant channel is selected first among the three RGB channels where the variance is the maximum. Then the best split based on the maximum distance between the cuboid halves is chosen in that dominant channel. The variance represents the variation among the pixels of a cuboid more accurately. Hence, the variation of contrasts within a cuboid indicates the use of variance in decision making for partitioning will improve the performance of segmentation. Therefore, we use the variance of any cuboid instead of its contrast to decide further partitioning of it, thus addressing the second shortcoming of CSeg'18.

We use the statistical property of the pixel values to find out the maximum contrast between the foreground and the background of an image to eventually perform the cuboid segmentation algorithm to distinguish regions. Besides, we include the variance as a threshold to determine the homogeneity of image regions. Because of perceptually distinctive differences in the contrast between foreground and background objects and the more intuitive distance value, the proposed cuboid segmentation algorithm can detect and separate the background and foreground objects more accurately.

The idea of superpixels is being used in many segmentation techniques [15, 16, 22, 33] as they are more convenient to compute region-based image features by reducing the number of image primitives significantly. Although the output of cuboid segmentation is a set of cuboids, these cuboids can admittedly be considered as superpixels. Among the existing superpixel segmentation techniques, Turbopixels [14] and SLIC [1] have linear time complexity with the ability to control the number of segments. However, in both the algorithms the initial seeds evolve over a smaller spatial extent resulting in a collection superpixels of almost similar size. On the contrary, cuboid segmentation enforces strong spatial relationships among neighbouring pixels and the homogeneity criteria used to terminate the split process results in a combination of cuboids of homogeneous image regions with different sizes.

In this paper, we use cuboids as superpixels and then exploit the hierarchical agglomerative merging approach to group them into meaningful regions describing objects in an image. By controlling the number of cuboids, the complexity of further merging process is also bounded to linear form that ensures the linear complexity of total segmentation process. Comprehensive experiments are performed using four standard measurements for quantitative evaluation namely the Probabilistic Rand Index (PRI) [31], Global Consistency Error (GCE) [19], Variation of Information (VoI) [20] and Boundary Displacement Error (BDE) [10] on benchmark datasets (BSDS500 [19] and MSRC [25]). These are widely used to evaluate segmentation performance. In comparing the results, we have implemented the same merging algorithm using the output of CSeg'18 and quadtree. The experimental results exhibit better performance for the CSeg'19 based approach than both the CSeg'18 based and quadtree-based approaches. In addition, the proposed approach gains in the evaluation criteria against some state-of-the-art techniques.

The rest of the paper is organized as follows. Section 2 depicts the theory behind our proposed technique and the proposed algorithm. The performance studies are presented in Sect. 3. Section 4 provides the conclusion.

2   Proposed Technique

In this section, we present our partitioning technique that uses simple statistical features of pixel intensities to partition an image into a collection of cuboids. Next, we describe the hierarchical merging process of the cuboids to form meaningful image regions.

2.1   Cuboid Segmentation

Variance and Its Impact on Pixel Data: Variance is a measurement that depicts the dispersion of a dataset relative to its mean, or expected value. For a dataset $x_1, x_2, ..., x_N$ with mean $\overline{x}$, the variance σ^2 can be denoted as

$$\sigma^2 = \frac{1}{N} \sum_{i=1}^{N} (x_i - \overline{x})^2. \tag{1}$$

A low variance indicates that the data points tend to be close to the mean, while a high variance indicates that the data points are spread out over a wider range of values. We used this insight to select the dominating channel in each iteration of our proposed algorithm. As RGB colour space ($0 \leq R, G, B \leq 255$) is orthogonal in nature, the dominating channel among R, G or B is the one that has more pixel values far from their mean. As natural images may contain different objects of different colours, the dominant channel for the different parts

Fig. 1. In clockwise order from top-left: original image, channel R, channel B, and channel G. While the image and Cuboid 1 (top) have the dominant B channel, Cuboid 2 (bottom) has dominant R channel.

of an image might not be the same (Fig. 1). Therefore, in each iteration, we first select the dominant channel and then perform the cuboid segmentation only on that channel. As a consequence, the more we separate different objects or parts of an image, the dominating channel turns more explicit. As RGB colour space is not perceptually uniform, the difference of the centroid (RGB mean) between any two distinct part of the image is not perceptually consistent. Since each channel of the RGB colour model is more intuitive separately than the whole colour model, the distance of the centroid in a single channel will be more perceptually consistent. This paves the way of manipulating the distance of their mean colour in a single channel which conforms with human perception closely.

Proposed Algorithm: Let $I_{X,Y} = (R_{X,Y}^I, G_{X,Y}^I, B_{X,Y}^I)$ denote an RGB image of size $X \times Y = n$. If $\sigma_{\max}^2(I_{X,Y})$ defines the maximum variance among the three colour channels, the dominating colour channel, Ch of an image can be defined as

$$Ch = \begin{cases} R, & \text{if } \sigma_{\max}^2(I_{X,Y}) = \sigma^2(R_{X,Y}^I); \\ G, & \text{else if } \sigma_{\max}^2(I_{X,Y}) = \sigma^2(G_{X,Y}^I); \\ B, & \text{otherwise.} \end{cases} \qquad (2)$$

If $\mu_I^{R,G,B}$ is the first order raw RGB colour moment of image I, then the colour-contrast distance between two images I and J can be estimated as,

$$D_{I,J}^* = |\mu_I^{Ch} - \mu_J^{Ch}|. \tag{3}$$

To determine the homogeneity property of regions we use a threshold called variance threshold, V_{X,Y,n_s} and the variance of a region is the average of the variances in each R, G and B channel

$$\sigma^2(I_{X,Y}) = \frac{1}{3}\left(\sigma^2(R_{X,Y}^I) + \sigma^2(G_{X,Y}^I) + \sigma^2(B_{X,Y}^I)\right). \tag{4}$$

Image I can be split into two sub-cuboids I_i^1 and I_i^2 of sizes $i \times Y$ and $(X - i) \times Y$ pixels respectively, using a vertical line $x = i + 0.5$ in $X - 1$ ways with $i \in 1, 2, ..., X - 1$. Similarly, it can be split into two sub-cuboids I_{X-1+j}^1 and I_{X-1+j}^2 of sizes $X \times j$ and $X \times (Y - j)$ pixels respectively, using a horizontal line $y = j + 0.5$ in $Y - 1$ ways with $j \in 1, 2, ..., Y - 1$.

For a user-defined number of cuboid, n_s, a split is considered valid only if the variance of the cuboid meets the variance threshold and the area of the cuboid meets the area threshold

$$v(s|I_{X,Y}) = XY \geq A \wedge \sigma^2(I_{X,Y}) \geq V_{X,Y,n_s}. \tag{5}$$

The colour contrast distance of the half-cuboids is the objective function

$$f(s|I_{X,Y}) = D_{I_s^1, I_s^2}^*. \tag{6}$$

Then the greedy optimization heuristic to find the best split of I from the possible $X + Y - 2$ ways as

$$\max_{1 \leq s \leq X+Y-2} f(s|I_{X,Y}) \atop \text{subject to } v(s|I_{X,Y}). \tag{7}$$

A hierarchical partitioning algorithm may be designed by recursively splitting the two half-cuboids using the optimal split s^*. The algorithm terminates when all possible ways of splitting are found to be obsolete that means if one or both of the variance threshold and area threshold is not satisfied. The algorithm is now formally presented below as Algorithm 1.

2.2   Merging

The output of the previous stage is a full binary tree where the original image represents the root and the segmented cuboids represent the leaf nodes. In this stage, we perform merging of the leaf cuboids using hierarchical agglomerative clustering of Ward's minimum variance method [13] where the criterion for choosing the pair of clusters to merge at each step is based on the optimal value of an objective function. Ward's minimum variance criterion minimizes the total

Algorithm 1. CSeg'19 $(I_{X,Y})$

$d_{\max} = 0$;
$s^* = 0$;
for $s = 1, 2, ..., X + Y - 2$ **do**
    if $v(s|I_{X,Y,n_s}) \wedge f(s|I_{X,Y}) > d_{\max}$ **then**
        $d_{\max} = f(s|I_{X,Y})$;
        $s^* = s$;
    end if
end for
if $d_{\max} > 0$ **then**
    CSeg'19$(I_{s^*}^1)$
    CSeg'19$(I_{s^*}^2)$
end if

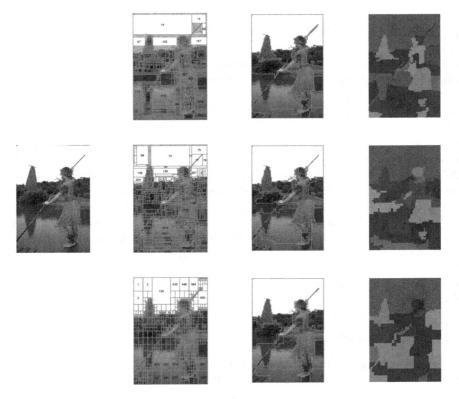

Fig. 2. Visual comparison of CSeg'19 (top), CSeg'18 (middle) and quadtree (bottom) based segmentation outcome.

within-cluster variance. The merging is accomplished in two steps. In the first step, we merge the pair of sibling leaf nodes that contribute minimum impact in the division process of their parent node.

Let C_1 be an internal node of size n_1 and $C_{1.1}$ and $C_{1.2}$ be two child nodes of it with size $n_{1.1}$ and $n_{1.2}$. If σ_1^2, $\sigma_{1.1}^2$ and $\sigma_{1.2}^2$ be the variance of the parent (i.e. the variance if they are merged) and two leaf nodes correspondingly, the within cluster variance of the C_1 and C_2 can be defined as,

$$\sigma_{C_{12}}^2 = n_1 \sigma_1^2 - (n_{1.1} \sigma_{1.1}^2 + n_{1.2} \sigma_{1.2}^2). \tag{8}$$

If $C \in C_1, C_2, ..., C_N$ be the set of internal cuboids having two leaf nodes as children, then in each iteration the internal cuboid having minimum value of impact factor will be considered to be merged. In the next step, we consider merging of those pair of nodes that are a neighbour of each other using the same criteria. The first step of merging eliminates some trivial splitting while the second step emphasizes merging of the image regions partitioned into two different subtrees as well as into the same subtree.

3   Results and Discussion

In this section, we present both the quantitative and the visual results of our proposed technique and compare them with others.

3.1   Evaluation Metric and Dataset

In our experiment, we use four quantitative metrics widely used in evaluating performance of image segmentation techniques, namely PRI [31], GCE [19], VoI [20] and BDE [10]. We conducted our experiments using the two widely used benchmark image datasets: Berkeley Segmentation Data Set 500 (BSDS500) [19] and Microsoft Research Cambridge (MSRC) dataset [25]. The BSDB500 dataset contains 500 natural images with 300 train, and 200 test images and each image has multiple ground truths. The MSRC dataset comprises 591 natural images of 21 object classes. Among the 21 classes, we used 7 classes having 203 images. To compare our proposed technique, we have implemented another algorithm by exploiting the output of quadtree decomposition and then using the same hierarchical merging algorithm we used in our technique.

3.2   Performance Evaluation

To preserve the size of images, we implemented the quadtree algorithm depending on the aspect ratio of images. For both techniques, we used the same value of area threshold $A = 4$ for all the images. The value of the variance threshold varies according to the contrast of an image. As an image is divided into two blocks in cuboid segmentation, while it is divided into four blocks in quadtree decomposition, we set the variance threshold in such a way that in the split step, the number of cuboids, n_s remain at least 2000 in both the techniques. It is evident that if the number of cuboids is higher in merging phase, the more accurate segmentation results are expected to have in the final segmentation output. We set the number of cuboids, n_s to be equal for both QT and Cseg'19 to ensure none of them is penalized. According to the resolution of images, we set $n_s = 1000$ for BSDS500 and $n_s = 550$ for MSRC dataset, which ensures the complexity of the whole process to be linear. We also implement the merging algorithm using the output of CSeg'18 on both of the datasets.

Table 1. Performance comparison of CSeg'19, CSeg'18 and quadtree (QT) based segmentation for BSDS500 and MSRC dataset

	BSDS500				MSRC			
	PRI↑	VoI↓	GCE↓	BDE↓	PRI↑	VoI↓	GCE↓	BDE↓
CSeg'19	**0.813**	**1.785**	**0.089**	**11.135**	**0.804**	**1.188**	**0.116**	**9.121**
CSeg'18	0.808	1.817	0.097	11.470	0.787	1.195	0.121	9.125
QT	0.809	1.836	0.098	11.224	0.799	1.196	0.122	9.413

Table 2. Performance comparison of the proposed technique with state-of-the-art methods for BSDS500 dataset using 300 training images used in the reported result

	BSDS500			
	PRI↑	VoI↓	GCE↓	BDE↓
NCut [24]	0.79	1.84	-	-
SWA [23]	0.80	**1.75**	-	-
ICM [27] (only colour)	0.79	1.79	-	-
CSeg'19	**0.82**	**1.75**	**0.09**	**11.34**

As both techniques yield hierarchical region trees, there can be many possible segmentation outcomes. Selecting a single outcome from them involves personal choice because every person has their perception of segmentation. We select the criteria OIS (Optimum Image Scale) [2] where the optimum number of segments or regions, n_r is selected by an oracle on a per-image basis. The quantitative evaluation of both techniques is shown in Table 1. The CSeg'19 based technique outperforms both the CSeg'18 based and quadtree based techniques for all the metrics for both BSDS500 and MSRC datasets.

In Table 2, we also compare the results of our proposed cuboid based technique with those of several state-of-the-art techniques reported in their papers where 300 training images of BSDS500 data set were used.

Fig. 3. (Top to Bottom) Segmentation result of CSeg'19 based hierarchical image segmentation for $n_r = 2, 4, 6,$ and 8.

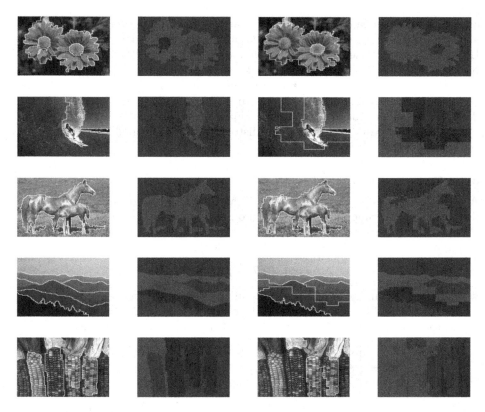

Fig. 4. Visual comparison of CSeg'19 based (left 2 columns) and quadtree based (right 2 columns) hierarchical segmentation techniques (top to bottom) $n_r = 4$, 4, 2, 5, and 5. First and third column present segment boundaries, and the second and fourth column present corresponding region maps.

Among those, Iterative Contraction and Merging (ICM) [27] is another hierarchical image segmentation algorithm. In that work, they provided their performance evaluation over a different combination of colour, size, texture, border, and spatial intertwining factors. As our proposed technique uses only the colour feature, we compare our performance with their performance that is based on colour. All the benchmark scores rather than the ICM are collected from [2] where they choose only PRI and VoI as evaluation metric and reported values are presented by two digits followed by the decimal point. Our proposed CSeg'19 based technique performs better for both PRI and VoI than all other techniques.

Figure 2 imparts the qualitative performance of CSeg'19, CSeg'18, and QT based segmentation outcomes for $n_r = 20$. The outcome of CSeg'19 indicates larger cuboids for large homogeneous regions (sky and lake water) and smaller cuboids at curved region boundaries. In contrast, QT decomposition produces relatively smaller blocks for both large and small homogenous regions. As a consequence, we can observe some visually prominent regions like the stick and the hula skirt in CSeg'19 based method than the quadtree based method. Besides, CSeg'18 based approach cannot distinguish the hand and the upper portion of the stick properly. Figure 3 exemplifies the hierarchical segmentation showing the different number of image regions. We can see that the image contents become more explicit as the number of segment increases. Again Fig. 4 illustrates some output of both the techniques for the same number of segments. Quadtree based results present more distortions than CSeg'19 based results in separating the regions.

3.3 Complexity Analysis

According to master theorem of divide and conquer recurrences [4], if $T(n)$ denotes the total time for the algorithm on an input of size n, and $f(n)$ denotes the amount of time taken at the top level of the recurrence then the time can be expressed by a recurrence relation of the form

$$T(n) = aT(\frac{n}{b}) + f(n) \tag{9}$$

where a is the number of subproblems in the recursion and b is the factor by which the subproblem size is reduced in each recursive call. By comparing the asymptotic behaviour of $f(n)$ with $n^{log_b a}$, there are three possible cases,

$$T(n) = \begin{cases} \Theta(n^{\log_b a}), & \text{if } f(n) = O(n^{\log_b a}); \\ \Theta(n^{\log_b n} \log^{k+1} n), & \text{if } \Theta(n^{\log_b a} \log^k n), k \geq 0; \\ \Theta(f(n)), & \text{if } f(n) = \Omega(n^{\log_b a}). \end{cases} \tag{10}$$

As CSeg'19 recursively divides an image $I_{X,Y}$ of $n = X \times Y$ pixels at the optimal split into two cuboids, we may assume $a = 2$. For the sake of simplicity, we may also assume $b = 2$, as each cuboid will have roughly $O(n/2)$ pixels, and $f(n) = O(\sqrt{n}) = \Omega(n^{\log_b a})$, as the optimal split is selected from $X + Y - 2$ possible splits, and $X = O(\sqrt{n})$ and $Y = O(\sqrt{n})$. Hence, by (10), $T(n) = \Theta(n)$.

In the merge step, the complexity of hierarchical clustering is $O(N^2)$ for input of size N. We used the number of cuboids in the merging step in such a way that $N = O(\sqrt{n})$. Thus the overall complexity of the proposed algorithm is $\Theta(n) + O(\sqrt{n}^2) = O(n)$, i.e., the complexity order of CSeg'19 is *linear*.

4 Conclusion

In this paper, we have introduced an innovative cuboid partitioning method to split an image into homogeneous regions. By using the initial cuboids, we have gradually merged adjacent regions into greater ones and finally formed a hierarchical tree. In each step of merging, we have adopted the minimum variance criteria to detect the most similar region pairs among all the neighbouring region pairs. We have used the colour feature only. The computational complexity of our proposed segmentation technique is linear. Results of quantitative evaluation admit the performance of the proposed technique is superior over the existing state-of-the-art methods, including quadtree based segmentation technique.

References

1. Achanta, R., Shaji, A., Smith, K., Lucchi, A., Fua, P., Süsstrunk, S.: Slic superpixels compared to state-of-the-art superpixel methods. IEEE Trans. Pattern Anal. Mach. Intell. **34**(11), 2274–2282 (2012)
2. Arbelaez, P., Maire, M., Fowlkes, C., Malik, J.: Contour detection and hierarchical image segmentation. IEEE Trans. Pattern Anal. Mach. Intell. **33**(5), 898–916 (2011)
3. Bagheri, S., Zheng, J.Y., Sinha, S.: Temporal mapping of surveillance video for indexing and summarization. Comput. Vis. Image Underst. **144**, 237–257 (2016). http://www.sciencedirect.com/science/article/pii/S1077314215002581. Individual and Group Activities in Video Event Analysis
4. Bentley, J.L., Haken, D., Saxe, J.B.: A general method for solving divide-and-conquer recurrences. SIGACT News **12**(3), 36–44 (1980). https://doi.org/10.1145/1008861.1008865
5. Canny, J.: A computational approach to edge detection. IEEE Trans. Pattern Anal. Mach. Intell. **PAMI-8**(6), 679–698 (1986)
6. Chen, C., Shao, Y., Bi, X.: Detection of anomalous crowd behavior based on the acceleration feature. IEEE Sens. J. **15**(12), 7252–7261 (2015)
7. Comaniciu, D., Meer, P.: Mean shift: a robust approach toward feature space analysis. IEEE Trans. Pattern Anal. Mach. Intell. **24**(5), 603–619 (2002)
8. Deng, Y., Manjunath, B.S.: Unsupervised segmentation of color-texture regions in images and video. IEEE Trans. Pattern Anal. Mach. Intell. **23**(8), 800–810 (2001)
9. Felzenszwalb, P.F., Huttenlocher, D.P.: Efficient graph-based image segmentation. Int. J. Comput. Vis. **59**(2), 167–181 (2004). https://doi.org/10.1023/B:VISI.0000022288.19776.77
10. Freixenet, J., Muñoz, X., Raba, D., Martí J., Cufí, X.: Yet another survey on image segmentation: region and boundary information integration. In: 7th European Conference on Computer Vision (2002)
11. Grady, L.: Random walks for image segmentation. IEEE Trans. Pattern Anal. Mach. Intell. **28**(11), 1768–1783 (2006)
12. Huang, K., Tan, T.: Vs-star: a visual interpretation system for visual surveillance. Pattern Recognit. Lett. **31**(14), 2265–2285 (2010). http://www.sciencedirect.com/science/article/pii/S0167865510001868
13. Ward Jr., J.H.: Hierarchical grouping to optimize an objective function. J. Am. Stat. Assoc. **58**(301), 236–244 (1963). https://www.tandfonline.com/doi/abs/10.1080/01621459.1963.10500845
14. Levinshtein, A., Stere, A., Kutulakos, K.N., Fleet, D.J., Dickinson, S.J., Siddiqi, K.: Turbopixels: fast superpixels using geometric flows. IEEE Trans. Pattern Anal. Mach. Intell. **31**(12), 2290–2297 (2009)
15. Li, S., Wu, D.O.: Modularity-based image segmentation. IEEE Trans. Circ. Syst. Video Technol. **25**(4), 570–581 (2015)
16. Linares, O.A.C., Botelho, G.M., Rodrigues, F.A., Neto, J.B.: Segmentation of large images based on super-pixels and community detection in graphs. IET Image Proc. **11**(12), 1219–1228 (2017)
17. Liu, G., Zhang, Y., Wang, A.: Incorporating adaptive local information into fuzzy clustering for image segmentation. IEEE Trans. Image Process. **24**(11), 3990–4000 (2015)
18. Liu, T., Seyedhosseini, M., Tasdizen, T.: Image segmentation using hierarchical merge tree. IEEE Trans. Image Process. **25**(10), 4596–4607 (2016)

19. Martin, D., Fowlkes, C., Tal, D., Malik, J.: A database of human segmented natural images and its application to evaluating segmentation algorithms and measuring ecological statistics. In: Proceedings of the 8th International Conference on Computer Vision, vol. 2, pp. 416–423, July 2001

20. Meilă, M.: Comparing clusterings by the variation of information. In: Schölkopf, B., Warmuth, M.K. (eds.) COLT-Kernel 2003. LNCS (LNAI), vol. 2777, pp. 173–187. Springer, Heidelberg (2003). https://doi.org/10.1007/978-3-540-45167-9_14

21. Murshed, M., Teng, S.W., Lu, G.: Cuboid segmentation for effective image retrieval. In: 2017 International Conference on Digital Image Computing: Techniques and Applications (DICTA), pp. 1–8, November 2017

22. Ren, X., Malik, J.: Learning a classification model for segmentation. In: Proceedings Ninth IEEE International Conference on Computer Vision, vol. 1, pp. 10–17, October 2003

23. Sharon, E., Galun, M., Sharon, D., Basri, R., Brandt, A.: Hierarchy and adaptivity in segmenting visual scenes. Nature **442**(7104), 810–813 (2006). https://doi.org/10.1038/nature04977

24. Shi, J., Malik, J.: Normalized cuts and image segmentation. IEEE Trans. Pattern Anal. Mach. Intell. **22**(8), 888–905 (2000)

25. Shotton, J., Winn, J., Rother, C., Criminisi, A.: *TextonBoost*: joint appearance, shape and context modeling for multi-class object recognition and segmentation. In: Leonardis, A., Bischof, H., Pinz, A. (eds.) ECCV 2006. LNCS, vol. 3951, pp. 1–15. Springer, Heidelberg (2006). https://doi.org/10.1007/11744023_1

26. Horowitz, S.L., Pavlidis, T.: Picture segmentation by a tree traversal algorithm. J. ACM **23**(2), 368–388 (1976)

27. Syu, J., Wang, S., Wang, L.: Hierarchical image segmentation based on iterative contraction and merging. IEEE Trans. Image Process. **26**(5), 2246–2260 (2017)

28. Tania, S., Murshed, M., Teng, S.W., Karmakar, G.: Cuboid colour image segmentation using intuitive distance measure. In: 2018 International Conference on Image and Vision Computing New Zealand (IVCNZ), pp. 1–6, November 2018

29. Tapia, E.: A note on the computation of high-dimensional integral images. Pattern Recogn. Lett. **32**(2), 197–201 (2011). https://doi.org/10.1016/j.patrec.2010.10.007

30. Ugarriza, L.G., Saber, E., Vantaram, S.R., Amuso, V., Shaw, M., Bhaskar, R.: Automatic image segmentation by dynamic region growth and multiresolution merging. IEEE Trans. Image Process. **18**(10), 2275–2288 (2009)

31. Unnikrishnan, R., Pantofaru, C., Hebert, M.: Toward objective evaluation of image segmentation algorithms. IEEE Trans. Pattern Anal. Mach. Intell. **29**(6), 929–944 (2007)

32. Vincent, L., Soille, P.: Watersheds in digital spaces: an efficient algorithm based on immersion simulations. IEEE Trans. Pattern Anal. Mach. Intell. **13**(6), 583–598 (1991)

33. Wang, X., Tang, Y., Masnou, S., Chen, L.: A global/local affinity graph for image segmentation. IEEE Trans. Image Process. **24**(4), 1399–1411 (2015)

High-Resolution Realistic Image Synthesis from Text Using Iterative Generative Adversarial Network

Anwar Ullah[1], Xinguo Yu[1(✉)], Abdul Majid[1], Hafiz Ur Rahman[2], and M. Farhan Mughal[3]

[1] National Engineering Research Center for E-Learning,
Central China Normal University, Wuhan, China
anwar.ccnu@gmail.com, xgyu@mail.ccnu.edu.cn, majid20205020@gmail.com
[2] School of Computer Science, Guangzhou University,
Guangzhou 510006, China
hafiz_rahman@e.gzhu.edu.cn
[3] Tianjin University of Finance and Economics, Tianjin, China
farhan.mughal0786@qq.com

Abstract. Synthesizing high-resolution realistic images from text description using one iteration Generative Adversarial Network (GAN) is difficult without using any additional techniques because mostly the blurry artifacts and mode collapse problems are occurring. To reduce these problems, this paper proposes an Iterative Generative Adversarial Network (iGAN) which takes three iterations to synthesize high-resolution realistic image from their text description. In the 1st iteration, GAN synthesizes a low-resolution 64×64 pixels basic shape and basic color image from the text description with less mode collapse and blurry artifacts problems. In the 2nd iteration, GAN takes the result of the 1st iteration and text description again and synthesizes a better resolution 128×128 pixels better shape and well color image with very less mode collapse and blurry artifacts problems. In the last iteration, GAN takes the result of the 2nd iteration and text description as well and synthesizes a high-resolution 256×256 well shape and clear image with almost no mode collapse and blurry artifacts problems. Our proposed iGAN shows a significant performance on CUB birds and Oxford-102 flowers datasets. Moreover, iGAN improves the inception score and human rank as compare to the other state-of-the-art methods.

Keywords: Generative Adversarial Network (GAN) · Iterative GAN · Text-to-image synthesis · CUB dataset · Oxford-102 dataset · Inception score · Human rank

This study is funded by the General Program of the National Natural Science Foundation of China (No: 61977029).

© Springer Nature Switzerland AG 2019
C. Lee et al. (Eds.): PSIVT 2019, LNCS 11854, pp. 211–224, 2019.
https://doi.org/10.1007/978-3-030-34879-3_17

1   Introduction and Related Work

Synthesizing high-resolution realistic images from text description is an active research problem owing to this way can produce the wanted images at a very low cost. The problem of synthesizing high-resolution realistic images from text description can be shortened as the text-to-image synthesis, which can be considered as the reverse problem of caption generation for the images. In this way, this research problem links two research topics of Natural language Processing (NLP) and Computer Vision (CV). This technology of the text-to-image synthesis has a huge demand for applications such as removing unlike objects in your photographs, producing new images, editing images, generating or synthesizing videos, generating sketch, and generating or synthesizing speech and many more. One iteration Generative Adversarial Network (GAN) is the status-of-arts method to synthesize images from text. However this method is difficult in synthesizing high quality images without using any additional techniques to solve the issues of the blurry artifact and mode collapse.

In 2014, Goodfellow et al. [1] proposed a method called Generative Adversarial Network (GAN) that showed an excellent result in many applications such as images, sketches, and video synthesis or generation, later it is also used for text to image, sketch, videos, etc, synthesis as well. Generative Adversarial Network (GAN), showed a tremendous result because it deals the physical applications, but still a lot of work need to improve.

Scott et al. [2] proposed a method called GAN-INT-CLS, that was the first attempt to synthesize images from the text description using GAN. They convert the input text into a text embedding vector (φ_t) using a recurrent network. Conditioned on the φ_t, the Generator (G) maps a noise vector (z) to synthesized image. The Discriminator (D) is also conditioned on text embedding vector (φ_t) and it is designed to evaluate whether the input image is real or fake. By using these techniques, GAN-INT-CLS synthesised or generate images from a text description which is closer to the actual images. GAN-INT-CLS showed a very good result in birds (CUB [3]), flowers (Oxford-102 [4]), and multi-categories (MS-COCO [5]) datasets.

After successful attempt in text to image synthesis many methods are proposed in the literature. GAN-INT-CLS fails to capture the localization constraints of the objects in the images. To solve this problem Reed et al. [6] proposed another model called Generative Adversarial What-Where Network (GAWWNs), which considers location constraint in addition to the text description. GAWWN learn to perform content-controllable and location-controllable that what content to draw in which location. GAWWN accurately generate compelling 128 × 128 pixel images. GAWWN works only on images with single objects, its works very good on the CUB, while the synthetic or generated images using MPII Human Pose (MHP) [7] dataset are blur. In 2017 Zhang et al. [8] proposed a two iterations GAN model called Stack Generative Adversarial Network (StackGANs). StackGAN has the ability to generate realistic high-resolution 256 × 256 pixels image from the given text description. The Stage-I GAN produce 64 × 64 pixels low-resolution image with a basic shape and basic color of the object from a given text description, while Stage-II GAN takes the generated low-resolution 64×64 image of the Stage-I GAN and text description again and synthesis 256×256 pixels a high-resolution image. It is the first work to generate high-resolution (256×256) image from a text description. The author's also proposed conditioning data augmentation techniques as well. Recently an improved version of StackGAN, StackGAN++ [9] proposed with multiple Generator (G) and Discriminator (D) instead of two, to synthesis more high-resolution images from text descriptions with a tree like structure to synthesis low, better, and high-resolution images from the text.

Similarly Xu et al. [10] proposed AttnGAN model, which further extend the architecture of StackGAN++ [9] by using attention mechanism over text description and an image. AttnGAN allows attention driven, multi iterations refinement for a fine-grained T2I generation or synthesis. They generate a high-resolution (256×256) image with attention from a text description in multiple iterations. It shows a very good result in CUB and COCO datasets.

Dash et al. [11] proposed Text Auxiliary Classifier Generative Adversarial Network (TAC-GAN), which built upon Auxiliary Classifier Generative Adversarial network (AC-GAN) [12], but they use text description condition instead of class label condition for generated images. Similarly they used Oxford-102 dataset and Skip-Thought vector to generate text embedding (φ_t) from the image captions. The generated images of TAC-GAN are not only high discriminable, but are also diverse. This method shows the slightly better result from others.

Recently, in 2018 some methods are proposed that can synthesis more high-resolution images from the previous proposed methods. Zhang et al. [13] proposed a new method called HDGAN, which can generate high-resolution photographic images and performs significantly better than existing state of the arts on three (CUB, Oxford-102, and MS-COCO) public datasets. Similarly, Yuan and Peng [14] proposed another new network for synthesizing high-resolution images from a text descriptions called Symmetrical Distillation Networks (SDN) [14], which addressed the problem of heterogeneous and homogeneous gaps in the text-to-image synthesis task.

Cha et al. [15] aim to extend the state of the art for GAN-based text-to-image synthesis by improving the perceptual quality of the generated images. They build a DCGAN and train it with contextual and perceptual loss terms by conditioning on the input text. The proposed method synthesis or generate realistic images which match with text descriptions. The main contribution of the authors is the inclusion of additional perceptual loss in training the generator. The proposed method achieved a very good result in the image synthesis from text description. Some more famous methods are proposed recently like MirroGAN [16] which address a lot of complex text-to-image problems by some more novel approaches. MirrorGAN addressed semantic consistency between the text description and visual content problems.

Synthesizing high-resolution images from just a text description using one iteration GAN is hard because just simply increasing the up-sampling blocks to synthesise a high-resolution image normally the blurry artifact and mode collapse problems occur in the results. In this paper, we proposed three iterations method namely iGAN to synthesis high-resolution images out off mode collapse and blurry artifacts problems. The significant contributions of this paper are; (1) we proposed a novel Iterative Generative Adversarial Network (iGAN), which has the ability to synthesized high-resolution images from their related text description. (2) Iterative GAN solves the text-to-image synthesis mode collapse problem. (3) Iterative GAN also solved the text-to-image synthesis blurry artifacts problem. (4) Iterative GAN contains three iterations, every iteration is able to synthesize different resolution (64×64, 128×128, and 256×256) pixel image. More details are discussed in below section.

2   Proposed Method

The proposed Iterative Generative Adversarial Network (iGAN) is presented in this section, which contains three iterations. The iGAN addresses some of the current text-to-image (T2I) research problems. Instead of directly generating high-resolution images from text description (one iteration), we simply divide it into three iterations to generate high-resolution images, reduce synthesizing time, and provide more facilities to synthesis different resolution images whenever we need that. More details of iGAN are given in below sections.

2.1   Common Techniques

The following techniques are often used and hence they are presented here first. These techniques are: conditional Generative Adversarial Network (cGAN) [17], Char-CNN-RNN (Text encoder) [18], and Conditioning Augmentation (CA) [8].

Conditional Generative Adversarial Network (CGAN). CGAN [17] is used to extend the GAN into a conditional model. Some extra information "c" is given to the Generator (G) and the Discriminator (D) in cGAN. This extra information could be text, class labels, or a sketch etc. In our model the extra information (c) is text description. Conditional Generative Adversarial Network (cGAN) provide some additional control on which kind of data is being generated, while the original GAN doesn't have such control. In that reason cGAN is popular for synthesis or generation of images, video, speech, text, image editing and other applications.

$$\min_{G} \max_{D} V(D, G) = E_{x \sim p_{data}}[log D(x|y)] + E_{z \sim p_z}[log(1 - D(G(z|y)))].$$

The above formulation allow the Generator (G) to synthesis or produce image conditioned on variable "c" means from text description. The complete proof of this formula is given in [17].

Char-CNN-RNN (Text Encoder). Computer or machine doesn't understand words, characters and other things, but it can represent the words or characters in term of something it does "understand", that's actually the text embedding (φ_t). Text description or words must be converted to a vector before using it in any model. However, in natural language processing (NLP) systems usually treat words as distinct atomic symbols, and therefore "dog" may be represented as "Id143" and "cat" as "Id537". This encoding is just arbitrary, it's didn't provide any useful information to the system regarding the relationship which may exist between the individual. Text-to-image synthesis model is very difficult to train because of two reasons: (1) Convert the text to a vectors which capture the important features. (2) After that use those vectors representations to synthesis images using generative models like GAN. To convert sentence into vectors a lot of methods are introduced but Char-CNN-RNN shown a very good result in text embedding. According to many researchers Char-CNN-RNN is the superior, because it's trained using image and text jointly. In this method authors collected a large and high quality dataset of fine-grained visual descriptions. After that evaluated many deep neural text encoders like RNN, that text encoder trained from the beginning from the scratch. That's why we used Char-CNN-RNN for our work.

Conditioning Augmentation (CA). Most of the text-to-image synthesis or generated models get the text description and encode it by using encoder in the result get text embedding (φ_t). The text embedding (φ_t) is a non-linear transformation to generate the dependent latent variable with respect to the independent variable of the generator (G). Moreover, the latent-space for the φ_t is very high-dimensional, which is greater than 100 dimension. That's why, if we have less number of data it normally causes break or discontinuity in the latent data manifold, so for the generator (G) it is not desirable. This is some kind of big problem because of this mostly blurry artifacts and mode collapse problems occurs, to reduce this problem Zhang et al. [8] introduced a new technique namely Conditioning Augmentation (CA) which produce additional conditioning variable $\hat{c}$. Due to the contradiction with the fixed or static conditioning text variable "c", determined the latent variable $\hat{c}$ from an independent or autonomous Gaussian Distribution $\mathcal{N}(\mu(\varphi_t), \Sigma(\varphi_t))$, here mean (average) denoted by $\mu(\varphi_t)$ and principle diagonal co-variance matrix is denoted by $\Sigma(\varphi_t)$. This suggested conditioning amplification provide better results and more training pairs which give as small as possible number of text and images pairs, and thus motivate robustness to share minimal perturbations with the conditioning assorted. To improve the smoothness of the conditioning asserted and to avoid overfitting, in the meantime, the below equation is for the better result of the G during training,

$$D_{KL}(\mathcal{N}(\mu(\varphi_t), \Sigma(\varphi_t))||\mathcal{N}(O, 1)).$$

This equation is called Kullback-Leibler (KL) divergence between the two parameters Standard Gaussian distribution (Conditioning Gaussian distribution), respectively. The randomness which is introduced or presented in the CA means Conditioning Augmentation is more favourable to convert the modelling text to image translation, because it gives different result of poses and appearance corresponding to the same sentence. Simply, It's a novel technique for smoothness in the condition manifold. To make the condition manifold smooth and reliable, we also used CA to increase enhancement and performance of the method. The structure of CA is given in Fig. 1.

2.2 The 1st Iteration Details

As we discussed that iGAN contains three iterations. The 1st iteration GAN generating a low-resolution 64×64 basic shape images. First, we get text description of the CUB and Oxford-102 datasets and used Char-CNN-RNN text encoder to make text embedding (φ_t) from the given description for the birds and flowers. After that to capture the meaning of text embedding (φ_t) with variations the Gaussian conditioning variable (extra variable) $\hat{c}$ for (φ_t) are sampled from $\mathcal{N}(\mu_0(\varphi_t), \Sigma_0(\varphi_t))$. Noise or random variable (z) and conditioned on $\hat{c}_0$, 1st iteration GAN trains the generator (G_0) and the discriminator (D_0) by alternatively minimizing H_{G_0} in the below first equation and maximizing H_{D_0} in the below second equation.

$$H_{G_0} = \mathbb{E}_{z \sim p_z, t \sim P_{data}}[log(1 - D_0(G_0(z, \hat{c}_0), \varphi_t)] + \eta D_{KL}(\mathcal{N}(\mu_0(\varphi_t), \Sigma_0(\varphi_t)) || \mathcal{N}(0, I))$$

$$H_{D_0} = \mathbb{E}_{(I_0, t) \sim p_{data}}[log D_0(I_0, \varphi_t)] + \mathbb{E}_{z \sim p_z, t \sim p_{data}}[log(1 - D_0(G_0(z, \hat{c}_0), \varphi_t))]$$

In the above equations p_{data} represent the true data distribution (real dataset), p_z represent Gaussian distribution, where z represent a noise vector which is randomly sampled of p_z. I_0 and t represent real image and text description respectively, which are taken from the true distribution (p_{data}). We set the η by 1 for the whole experiments which is the regularization parameter.

In the structure diagram of iGAN (Fig. 1), we can see that (φ_t) is passed to the Conditional Augmentation (CA) and after that concatenate $\hat{c}_0$ with a N_z dimensional noise vector and passed it to the up-sampled blocks of the generator to synthesis (64×64) low-resolution image. Another side, the text embedding (φ_t) is first compressed into a specific dimensions N_d by passing it into a fully-connected layer and after that spatially pretend it into a form $M_d \times M_d \times N_d$ tensor for the discriminator D_0. In the mean time the synthesized or generated image is fed over down-sampling blocks upto it's spatial dimension $M_d \times M_d$. Onward, concatenate the image filter with the text tensor along with the channel dimension. Moreover, to mutually receive the features beyond the text description and image, the appearing tensor (value) is in addition give to a 1×1 Convolutional Layer. At the last, a fully connected layer with only one node is used to generate the decision score.

2.3   The 2nd Iteration Details

We generate a low-resolution image in our 1st iteration, but some of the features of the image and text description as well are omitted, which affect the result. To reduce these problems and synthesis high-resolution image we trained the 2nd iteration GAN, which is built upon on 1st iteration result. In 2nd iteration, GAN took the result of the 1st iteration and generate a better-resolution 128×128 pixels image with more detail shape and efficiency.

1st iteration GAN and 2nd iteration GAN are sharing the same text embedding (φ_t). Gaussian conditioning variable $\hat{c}_0$ was used in 1st iteration, while $\hat{c}_1$ are used in 2nd iteration, but to generate particular means (μ) as well as standard deviations (σ) rather than 1st iteration GAN the Conditioning Augmentation (CA) have disparate fully connected layers in 2nd iteration. Because of that reason 2nd iteration GAN learns more useful features and information of the image and text description which are omitted or ignored by 1st iteration GAN. Looks the below equations, on the low-resolution result $s_0 = G_0(z, \hat{c}_0)$ of the 1st iteration and Gaussian conditioning variable $\hat{c}_1$ the 2nd iteration generator (G_1) and the discriminator (D_1) are trained alternatively by minimizing H_{G_1} in first equation and maximizing H_{D_1} in the second equation.

$$H_{G_1} = \mathbb{E}_{s_0 \sim pG_0, t \sim P_{data}}[log(1 - D_1(G_1(s_0, \hat{c}_1), \varphi_t)] + \eta D_{KL}(\mathcal{N}(\mu_1(\varphi_t), \Sigma_1(\varphi_t))||\mathcal{N}(0, I))$$

$$H_{D_1} = \mathbb{E}_{(I_1, t) \sim p_{data}}[log D_1(I_1, \varphi_t)] + \mathbb{E}_{s_0 \sim pG_0, t \sim p_{data}}[log(1 - D_1(G_1(s_0, \hat{c}_1), \varphi_t))]$$

We can see that these equations are different or distinct from the initial GAN equation, the only difference is that the (z) means random noise didn't use in these equations in this 2nd iteration, because the randomness which we need has already well-preserved by s_0 in 1st iteration. The other variables are represent the same data.

The 2nd iteration structure (in Fig. 1) is little different from the 1st iteration. We used the same text embedding (φ_t) of 1st iteration to generate the N_g dimensional text conditioning vector $\hat{c}_1$. After that $\hat{c}_1$ is spatially replicated to a $M_g \times M_g \times N_g$ form tensor. In the meantime the generated 1st iteration result 64×64 pixels image is fed into several down-sampling blocks of the generator upto its spatial dimension $M_g \times M_g$. Similarly the $\hat{c}_1$ is sampled from the Gaussian distribution but this time the CA have different fully connected layers then 1st iteration. Onward concatenate the text features and encoded the dawn-sampled image along the channel dimension. After that the encoded image features joined with the text features and fed into several residual blocks [20]. Residual blocks are specially designed to learn multi-modal representation across text and image features. At the last we applied several up-sampling blocks or layers to synthesis a better resolution 128×128 pixels image. The 2nd iteration generated or synthesized image is more realistic and clear then the 1st iteration with almost no mode collapse and blurry artifact problems.

On the other side the structure of the discriminator is similar with 1st iteration GAN but this time one extra down-sampling block are used because the size of the image is greater then the 1st iteration GAN generated image.

2.4   The 3rd Iteration Details

In the last iteration of iGAN, we synthesis a good shape, clear, and high-resolution 256×256 pixels images from the given text description. The 3rd iteration is developed with the help of the result of 2nd iteration. In the 3rd iteration, GAN took the synthesized 128×128 pixels image of the 2nd iteration GAN and generate a high-resolution 256×256 pixels image.

The 1st, 2nd, and the 3rd iteration GANs are sharing the same text embedding (φ_t). The Gaussian conditioning variable $\hat{c}_0$, $\hat{c}_1$, and $\hat{c}$ are used in 1st iteration GAN, 2nd iteration GAN, and 3rd iteration GAN respectively, but in every iteration the CA has distinct and separate fully connected layers to generate different or distinct means (μ) as well as different standard deviations (σ) through that reason 2nd iteration GAN learns more useful information and features of the image and text description which are ignored or omitted by 1st iteration GAN, and 3rd iteration learn more useful features of text and image which are ignored by 2nd iteration GAN. In the below equations, on the better resolution result $s_1 = G_0(s_0, \hat{c}_1)$ of the 2nd iteration and Gaussian conditioning variable $\hat{c}$ the 3rd iteration Generator and the Discriminator are trained alternatively by minimizing H_G in the first equation and maximizing H_D in the second equation.

$$H_G = \mathbb{E}_{s_1 \sim pG_1, t \sim P_{data}}[log(1 - D(G(s_1, \hat{c}), \varphi_t)] + \eta D_{KL}(\mathcal{N}(\mu(\varphi_t), \Sigma(\varphi_t))||\mathcal{N}(0, I))$$

$$H_D = \mathbb{E}_{(I,t) \sim p_{data}}[logD(I, \varphi_t)] + \mathbb{E}_{s_1 \sim pG_1, t \sim p_{data}}[log(1 - D(G(s_1, \hat{c}), \varphi_t))]$$

Similarly these equations also don't have random noise (z) because the randomness has already well-preserved by s_0 means in 1st iteration, through that reason these equations are different from the original GAN equation.

The 3rd iteration GAN architecture (in Fig. 1) have some changes, those changes can differentiate it from 1st iteration and 2nd iteration GANs. In 3rd iteration same steps of the 2nd iteration are applied but the generated image of the 2nd iteration GAN, which is 128×128 pixels is fed into several down-sampling blocks of the generator upto its spatial dimension $M_g \times M_g$. As well as the $\hat{c}$ is sampled from the Gaussian distribution but again the CA has different fully connected layers. After that concatenate the text features and down-sampled image along the channel dimension. Similar like 2nd iteration the encoded picture features are joined with the text description features and give it into several residual blocks. Moreover, applied several up-sampling blocks or layers to generate or synthesis a very high-resolution 256×256 pixels image. 3rd iteration GAN synthesized image is more realistic, clear, and excellent with no mode collapse and blurry artifact problems. The discriminator structure is almost same with 2nd iteration, but 3rd iteration discriminator have one more extra down-sampling block because of the greater size of generated image.

3   Experiments

In this section, we evaluate our proposed iGAN method, we compare the results of iGAN with other state-of-the-art methods by generated images, inception

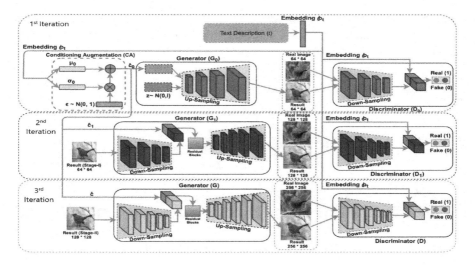

Fig. 1. Overall structure of our proposed Iterative GAN, including 3rd iteration GAN.

score [19] and human rank method. We compared iGAN results with 4 famous methods namely; GAN-INT-CLS, GAWWN, StackGAN, and TAC-GAN. More details are given below.

3.1 Datasets

We used the CUB [3] birds dataset, which contains 200 different birds categories with $(11, 788)$ test and training images with also annotations, bounding boxes, rough segmentation, and attributes. Moreover, we also used Oxford-102 [4] flower dataset which contains $8, 189$ training and test images of 102 different categories of flowers with image segmentation, image label, Chi^2 distance, and data split as well. For both datasets 10 description are provided by S. Reed for each image.

3.2 Results of iGAN All Iterations

In this section we show the result of all iterations of the Iterative Generative Adversarial Network (iGAN). In below figures the first row express the low-resolution images which are synthesised by 1st iteration GAN. The second row shows the synthesised pictures of the 2nd iteration GAN, while the last row express the synthesised pictures of the 3rd iteration GAN from the given text description. The result is look full realistic, we can not distinguished it with the real pictures. The first row pictures are low-resolution 64×64 pixel. The second row pictures are better-resolution 128×128 Pixels, while the third row pictures are high-resolution 256×256 pixels, which are synthesised by 1st, 2nd, and 3rd iteration GANs respectively from the given text description. We used CUB birds and Oxford-102 flowers datasets. Figure 2 shows the result of iGAN using CUB birds dataset, while Fig. 3 shows the result of iGAN using Oxford-102 flowers dataset.

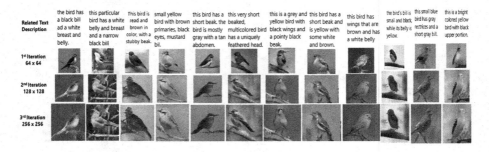

Fig. 2. Results of iGAN using CUB birds dataset.

Fig. 3. Results of iGAN using Oxford-102 flowers dataset.

3.3   Comparisons

It is hard to compare and evaluate the result of generative models like GAN, but still there are some techniques from which we can compare and evaluate them such as; by generated images, by inception score, and by human rank. we compared our introduced iGAN method with other researchers proposed methods in details. We compared our method through the generated images, a new comparison technique namely "Inception Score" [19], and by "human rank". We compared our model with GAN-INT-CLS, StackGAN, and GAWWN methods. Additionally, we compared the iGAN result with the TAC-GAN and StackGAN using Oxford-102 flowers dataset especially.

Comparison by Generated Images. Our novel proposed iGAN model synthesised high-resolution realistic images from text description using CUB birds and Oxford-102 flowers datasets. We compared our iGAN methods with other very famous proposed methods, especially with StackGAN, GAWWN, and GAN-INT-CLS, and TAC-GAN methods. The synthesised pictures which are generated by other state-of-the-art models and our novel introduced iGAN model are given in Fig. 4. If we see the images which are synthesised by GAN-INT-CLS using CUB birds dataset. It's just reflect the basic color and general shape of the birds and include mode collapse and blurry artifacts problems, as well as not much realistic and high-resolution. In the GAWWN authors used additional conditioning variable which is location constraints to synthesised better resolution images. Its generates a better resolution images using CUB dataset but still it's not very high-resolution and realistic like generated images of our iGAN. StackGAN contains on two iterations, first iteration generates a low-resolution images, while second iteration generate high-resolution (256×256) images from text description using CUB birds dataset, Oxford-102 flowers dataset, and MS COCO dataset multi-categories dataset. The generated images is looks realistic and high-resolution, but in the other side it still need some improvement. In that reason, we proposed a novel Iterative Generative Adversarial Network (iGAN), which contains on three iterations. 1st iteration GAN synthesis a low-resolution image with little mode collapse and blurry artifacts problems. 2nd iteration GAN generates a better-resolution realistic images with very less mode collapse and blurry artifacts problems. The last iteration generate a very high-resolution 256×256 images with almost no mode collapse and blurry artifacts problems. It looks completely realistic and it is high-resolution. Our generated pictures is shown better result then StackGAN, GAN-INT-CLS, GAWWN, and other proposed methods. The comparison result in shown is Fig. 4.

Onward, We compared our novel proposed iGAN method with StackGAN, GAN-INT-CLS, especially with TAC-GAN as well using Oxford-102 dataset.

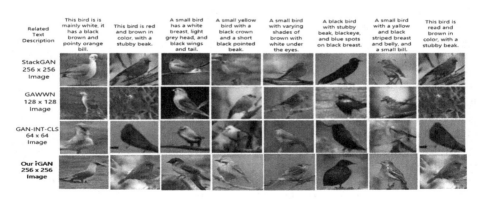

Fig. 4. The comparison of our iGAN and other state-of-the-art methods (StackGAN, GAWWN, and GAN-INT-CLS).

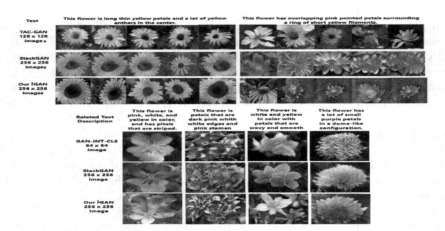

Fig. 5. The comparison of our iGAN and other state-of-the-art methods.

TAC-GAN achieved a better result in synthesising images and inception score, the generated images and inception score are can seen below. Out iGAN shown a tremendous result using Oxford-102 flowers dataset as well. The comparison results are shown in Fig. 5.

Comparison by Inception Score and Human Rank. In this section we discussed the numerical assessment approach "Inception Score [19]" method for quantitative evaluation. It is not easy to judge the performance of Generative Adversarial Network (GAN) and other generative models, so we divert our attention towards the numerical approach.

$$I = exp(E_x D_{KL}(p(y|x)||p(y))).$$

Where x is denoted by the one produced sample, and y is labelled as predicted parameter of the inception model. The main reason to introduce this metric was to generate or synthesis a meaningful images, with showing of a great deal of variety in a model. Therefore, the KL divergence should be large in between the conditional probability distance $p(y|x)$ and the probability marginal distribution $p(y)$. We adjust the fine-grained datasets, Caltech birds as well as Oxford-102 flowers, precisely "sp" as to bring the highest level of performance in the Inception model. On the basis of [19], we evaluated the measure on a large number of samples, with each model randomly selecting more than 20K samples. The drawback of this model is that, we can not determine weather the generated or synthesised images are in well conditioned or not, according to the given descriptions. Although the Inception score has shown a good comparison with human perception of sample visual quality [19] and a human assessment is also conduct by us. For each class of CUB birds and Oxford-102 flowers test sets, we randomly select 30 text descriptions, 3 images are generated by each model with respect to each sentence. We choose 25 users except the authors, by taking the same text

Table 1. The "Inception Score" and "Human rank" of StackGAN, GAWWN, GAN-INT-CLS, TAC-GAN and our iGAN on Oxford-102 flowers and CUB birds Datasets.

Method name	Dataset	Inception score	Human rank
StackGAN	CUB	$3.70 \pm .04$	$1.37 \pm .02$
	Oxford-102	$3.20 \pm .01$	$1.13 \pm .03$
GAWWN	CUB	$3.62 \pm .07$	$1.99 \pm .04$
GAN-INT-CLS	CUB	$2.88 \pm .04$	$2.81 \pm .03$
	Oxford-102	$2.66 \pm .03$	$1.87 \pm .03$
TAC-GAN	Oxford-102	$3.45 \pm .05$	$1.08 \pm .03$
Our iGAN	CUB	$4.12 \pm .04$	$1.10 \pm .03$
	Oxford-102	$3.41 \pm .03$	$1.03 \pm .03$

descriptions and asked to rank the results by different methods. To evaluate all compared methods, the average ranks by human users are calculated. We can see in Table 1 that our proposed iGAN method archive a tremendous result in both inception score and human rank as well. In Table 1, first column show the method name, the second column express the dataset. third column deals with inception score, while the last column expressed the human rank.

4   Conclusions

This paper has presented an iterative Generative Adversarial Network (iGAN), which can synthesize a high-resolution (256×256) images from text descriptions through three iterations. In 1st iteration GAN generate low-resolution 64×64 image from the text description. In 2nd iteration GAN takes the result of 1st iteration and text description again and synthesising a better high-resolution 128×128 image. In 3rd iteration GAN takes the result of 2nd iteration and text description as well and synthesising a high-resolution 256×256 image. Our proposed method iGAN shows a very good inception score in CUB birds and Oxford-102 flowers datasets.

References

1. Goodfellow, I.J., et al.: Generative adversarial nets. In: 27th International Conference on Neural Information Processing Systems, Montreal, Canada, pp. 2672–2680 (2014)
2. Reed, S., Akata, Z., Yan, X., Logeswaran, L., Schiele, B., Lee, H.: Generative adversarial text-to-image synthesis. In: ICML (2016)
3. Welinder, P., et al.: Caltech-UCSD Birds 200. California Institute of Technology, CNS-TR-2010-001 (2010)
4. Nilsback, M.-E., Zisserman, A.: Automated flower classification over a large number of classes. In: Proceedings of the Indian Conference on Computer Vision, Graphics and Image Processing (2008)

5. Lin, T.-Y., et al.: Microsoft coco (Common objects in context). In: European Conference on Computer Vision (2014)
6. Reed, S., Akata, Z., Mohan, S., Tenka, S., Schiele, B., Lee, H.: Learning What and Where to Draw. arXiv:1610.02454v1 [cs.CV] (2016)
7. Andriluka, M., Pishchulin, L., Gehler, P., Schiele, B.: 2D human pose estimation: new benchmark and state of the art analysis. In: Proceedings of the IEEE Conference on Computer Vision and Pattern Recognition 2014, pp. 3686–3693 (2014)
8. Huang, X., Li, Y., Poursaeed, O., Hopcroft, J., Belongie, S.: Stacked generative adversarial networks. In: CVPR (2017)
9. Zhang, H., et al.: StackGAN++: realistic image synthesis with stacked generative adversarial networks. arXiv:1710.10916 (2017)
10. Xu, T., et al.: AttnGAN: Fine-Grained Text to Image Generation with Attentional Generative Adversarial Networks. arXiv: 1711.10485v1 [cs.CV] (2017)
11. Dash, A., Gamboa, J., Ahmed, S., Liwicki, M., Afzal, M.Z.: TAC-GAN: Text Conditioned Auxiliary Classifier Generative Adversarial Network. arXiv:1703.06412v2 [cs.CV] (2017)
12. Odena, A., Olah, C., Shlens, J.: Conditional Image Synthesis with Auxiliary Classifier GANs. arXiv:1610.09585v4 [stat.ML] (2017)
13. Zhang, Z., Xie, Y., Yang, L.: Photographic Text-to-Image Synthesis with a Hierarchically-nested Adversarial Network. arXiv:1802.09178v2 [cs.CV] (2018)
14. Yuan, M., Peng, Y.: Text-to-image Synthesis via Symmetrical Distillation Networks. arXiv:1808.06801v1 [cs.CV] (2018)
15. Cha, M., Gwon, Y., Kung, H.T.: Adversarial nets with perceptual losses for text-to-image synthesis. arXiv:1708.09321v1 [cs.CV] (2017)
16. Qiao, T., Zhang, J., Xu, D., Tao, D.: MirrorGAN: Learning Text-to-image Generation by Redescription. arXiv:1903.05854v1 [cs.CL], 14 March 2019
17. Mirza, M., Osindero, S.: Conditional generative adversarial nets. arXiv preprint arXiv: 1411.1784 (2014)
18. Reed, S., Akata, Z., Schiele, B., Lee, H.: Learning deep representations of fine-grained visual descriptions. In: IEEE Computer Vision and Pattern Recognition (2016)
19. Salimans, T., Goodfellow, I.J., Zaremba, W., Cheung, V., Radford, A., Chen, X.: Improved techniques for training GANs. In: NIPS (2016)
20. He, K., Zhang, X., Ren, S., Sun, J.: Deep residual learning for image recognition. In: CVPR (2016)

Human Shape Reconstruction with Loose Clothes from Partially Observed Data by Pose Specific Deformation

Akihiko Sayo[1]([✉]), Hayato Onizuka[1], Diego Thomas[1], Yuta Nakashima[2], Hiroshi Kawasaki[1], and Katsushi Ikeuchi[3]

[1] Kyushu University, Fukuoka, Japan
{a.sayo.004,h.onizuka.392}@s.kyushu-u.ac.jp
{thomas,kawasaki}@ait.kyushu-u.ac.jp
[2] Osaka University, Suita, Japan
n-yuta@ids.osaka-u.ac.jp
[3] Microsoft Corp, Redmond, USA
katsuike@microsoft.com

Abstract. Reconstructing the entire body of moving human in a computer is important for various applications, such as tele-presence, virtual try-on, etc. For the purpose, realistic representation of loose clothes or non-rigid body deformation is a challenging and important task. Recent approaches for full-body reconstruction use a statistical shape model, which is built upon accurate full-body scans of people in skin-tight clothes. Such a model can be fitted to a point cloud of a person wearing loose clothes, however, it cannot represent the detailed shape of loose clothes, such as wrinkles and/or folds. In this paper, we propose a method that reconstructs 3D model of full-body human with loose clothes by reproducing the deformations as displacements from the skin-tight body mesh. We take advantage of a statistical shape model as base shape of full-body human mesh, and then, obtain displacements from the base mesh by non-rigid registration. To efficiently represent such displacements, we use lower dimensional embeddings of the deformations. This enables us to regress the coefficients corresponding to the small number of bases. We also propose a method to reconstruct shape only from a single 3D scanner, which is realized by shape fitting to only visible meshes as well as intra-frame shape interpolation. Our experiments with both unknown scene and partial body scans confirm the reconstruction ability of our proposed method.

Keywords: Non-rigid registration · Eigen-deformation · Neural network · Human shape reconstruction

1 Introduction

A full-body human shape reconstruction with realistic clothes deformations is important for various applications, such as tele-presence, virtual try-on, etc. in

© Springer Nature Switzerland AG 2019
C. Lee et al. (Eds.): PSIVT 2019, LNCS 11854, pp. 225–239, 2019.
https://doi.org/10.1007/978-3-030-34879-3_18

order to achieve immersive feelings and realistic sensations. Unlike skin-tight clothes, loose clothes can be deformed dynamically, and thus, it is an open problem to capture and represent them. There are two main approaches to solve this problem: non-prior and prior based methods. Non-prior methods can reconstruct any shape and the resolution of the reconstructed model varies depending on the resolution of the camera [6,14,21,25,26]. Some recent approaches [6,14] fused non-rigid deforming surfaces into a volumetric model by using a single-RGBD camera and could achieve real-time reconstruction. These approaches can reconstruct any shape as they are not specified to a human body. Therefore, they cannot also describe deformations of clothes efficiently that are caused by human motion and pose. Although recent approaches can reconstruct humans who wear any type of clothes [25,26], they may generate holes, wrong connections in the meshes, unwanted shapes at unobserved regions.

On the other hand, prior based methods can reconstruct full-body human with a consistent mesh without any hole. Recently, statistical shape models [1,2,4,11] are often used as full-body human priors. Statistical shape models can represent pose-dependent deformations, such as bending arms or deformed muscles, with only a few shapes and pose parameters. There are some methods that can reconstruct full-body 3D human shape only from a single image using a statistical shape model [3,8,15,17,20,23]. One severe drawback of these methods is that the model can only be used with people wearing skin-tight clothes; however, in real situation, people rarely wear such clothes.

Although statistical shape models have several limitations as mentioned above, their ability on shape representation by shape and pose parameters is still promising. In this paper, we propose a non-rigid full-body human shape reconstruction from point clouds measurements, even when the person is wearing loose clothes and captured from a single viewpoint. To this end, we use a statistical shape model as a base for full-body human modeling and regress the displacements between the base mesh and the clothed mesh by training a neural network. This allows us to take advantage of the efficient representation of the model and represent the clothed human mesh in lower-dimension. Similar to our work, Yang *et al.* [24] regresses coefficients corresponding to eigenvectors which are obtained through PCA of the displacements and reconstruct full-body human with the same resolution as the target mesh. However, they assume that the target mesh is consistent through the process, whereas such limitation does not exist in our method. Kimura *et al.* [9] also regress the coefficients corresponding to eigenvectors obtained by PCA of target displacements. In contrast, we not only regress the coefficients but also train eigenvectors as weight of the last layer of a neural network which is used as a regressor. The main contributions of this paper are summarized as follows:

1. Eigenvectors and coefficients are obtained by training a neural network to achieve accurate full-body reconstruction with using a lower dimensional space compared with previous method.

2. Direct regression of displacement values by neural network is proposed to enable reconstruction of full-body human shape even if parts of the body were not observed for training data.

2   Related Work

The 3D reconstruction problem is extremely challenging for the case of non-rigid objects/scenes because it requires a non-rigid 3D registration.

In the case of human body, deeper prior knowledge has been used. For example, Malleson et al. [12] proposed a method that assumes that each body part is rigid. A human body is then described as a combination of these body parts under this assumption, and a voxel carving-based approach is used for reconstructing each body part with texture. Due to the rigidity assumption, however, this method sometimes suffers from discontinuity at body part joints.

Another interesting approach is to use a statistical human body shape model, such as SCAPE [1] or SMPL [11]. A statistical shape model for the human body is usually trained with many full-body measurements of different body shapes and poses, and these variations are parameterized in a low dimensional space. Therefore, aligning the human body model to a depth measurement is much easier. Bogo et al. presented a high-quality method for full-body reconstruction upon a statistical shape model [2] from a single RGB-D camera. Recently, several methods perform full-body reconstruction from a single RGB image [3,8,17,20].

One major criticism on such methods is their insensitivity to deformations that are not described by the statistical shape model. In most cases, the full-body measurements used for training the model are in skin-tight clothes. Thus, such methods are usually tested with skin-tight clothes.

Recently, several methods have used statistical shape models to reconstruct not only the human body but also the clothes [5,7,9,18,24,26]. Pons-moll et al. [18] proposed to use 4D scan data of human with clothes as input and fit a model. By segmenting the body part and clothes part, they can retarget the clothes to a novel model. Yu et al. [26] used SMPL model as a semantic and real non-rigid human motion prior. They pre-defined an on-body node graph on the SMPL model and a method ran similar to DynamicFusion [14], which means that the outer surface is parameterized by such nodes and the deformations of the surface can be represented by a rigid transformation of the nodes. They also define the points far from the SMPL body as far-body nodes. This enables their method to be robust against noise. Nevertheless, their results are still noisy and cannot describe pose-dependent clothes deformations. Joo et al. [7] presented the Adam model in their work. Adam model can represent not only the body pose and shape but also facial expressions, finger motion, head and clothes. The reconstruction results are impressive but their model is too smooth to represent clothes deformations and thus cannot represent the deformations depending on the human pose. Habermann et al. [5] proposed a model-based full-body reconstruction method via a low cost single RGB camera. They built subject and cloth specific models in a pre-process and reconstruct full-body 3D model using pose

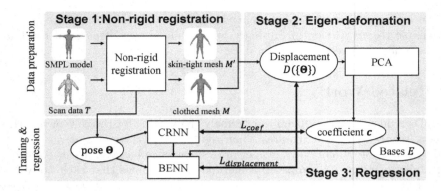

Fig. 1. Overview of our system. We first calculate the displacements between human shape with clothes and a template model. Then, these displacements are represented by small number of bases and coefficients. The displacements and coefficients are estimated by regressing the human pose parameters.

optimization and non-rigid deformation. Their results are attractive but due to the final non-rigid deformation method, clothes deformations of their model are not realistic.

The methods proposed by Kimura et al. [9] and Yang et al. [24] are similar to our work. Both of them represent clothes deformations as displacements from the skin-tight model, which is reconstructed from shape and pose parameter of statistical shape model. They both represent such deformations in lower-dimensional space and deal with the deformations of the clothes caused by the pose of the person wearing it. Based on this assumption they regress the coefficients corresponding to the eigenvector of lower-dimensional space. Although Yang et al. [24] assume that the input data has topologically consistent mesh, Kimura et al. [9] does not. This means that their method can be applied to any point cloud data. However, Kimura et al. [9] only estimate the coefficients, that is, they cannot estimate if the input data is partially observed.

In our proposed method, deformations that cannot be described by a statistical shape model are obtained by fitting a 3D mesh to a depth measurement. The deformations in each triangle in the mesh are then embedded in a space parameterized by body part rotations, which we call eigen-deformations, assuming that the deformations are dependent only on them. For the back side of the measurements, we regress the deformations based on the eigen-deformation. Note that our registration process is modular: we introduce our own implementation, but Bogo et al. [2], for example, can be used instead.

3   Method

3.1   Overview

The deformations of clothes are in general due to the specific pose of the person wearing them. Therefore, our proposed method regresses displacements between loose and skin-tight clothes from the pose. Figure 1 shows an overview of our proposed method. In the data preparation, which consists of non-rigid registration (Sect. 3.2) and eigen-deformation (Sect. 3.3), we use a sequence of point cloud data T as input, the input sequence can contain data about either the full body or only a part of it and obtain full-body human meshes with skin-tight and loose clothes (M' and M) as output. In the regression stage (Sect. 3.4), we input a human pose and regress displacements D. We describe how to train a neural network to regress the displacements with partially observed data in Sect. 3.5.

We use a statistical shape model to represent the full-body human mesh and deform it to represent loose clothes. Specifically, we use the SMPL model [11] as our base model, which is parameterized with the body shape parameter $\boldsymbol{\beta}$ and body pose parameter $\boldsymbol{\theta}$.

First, we fit the SMPL model to the scanned point cloud data frame by frame. This is done step by step. Through this stage, we obtain skin-tight mesh M', which has the optimized joint angles $\boldsymbol{\theta}$ and body shape $\boldsymbol{\beta}$ of the SMPL model, and clothed mesh M, which represents clothes deformations. Second, we calculate displacements D between M and M' and perform PCA on it to obtain bases of the displacements and the coefficients corresponding to the bases. Third, we train two types of neural network (NN): a coefficient regression neural network (called CRNN) and a bases estimation neural network (called BENN). CRNN is a network that regresses the coefficients corresponding to the bases obtained in the previous stage. BENN is a network that has the bases of the displacements as a part of weight parameters and directly regresses displacements $D(\{\boldsymbol{\Theta}\})$. When the training data is partially occluded, we use a visibility map to ignore the occluded parts.

To summarize these notations, the mesh $\bar{M}$ obtained by regression is represented as:

$$\bar{M} = M'(\boldsymbol{\beta}, \boldsymbol{\theta}) + D(\{\boldsymbol{\Theta}\}), \tag{1}$$

Our goal is to regress unobserved pose-dependent clothes deformations from the pose of the human body.

3.2   Non-rigid Registration of the SMPL Model

First, Our system fits the SMPL model [11] to the input sequence of point clouds, each of which is a human body scan. This facilitates compression (and efficient representation) of human bodies with loose clothes, because the SMPL model gives us an efficient parametrization of the human body by body shape parameters $\boldsymbol{\beta}$ and joint angles $\boldsymbol{\theta}$.

First, our algorithm fits the SMPL model to the target point cloud T in the input sequence in the coarsest level, which means optimizing only the SMPL pose and shape parameters. The following energy function is minimized over body shape parameters $\boldsymbol{\beta}$ and joint angles $\boldsymbol{\theta}$.

$$E(\boldsymbol{\beta}, \boldsymbol{\theta}) = \sum_{i \in C_{\mathrm{anc}}} \|x'_i(\boldsymbol{\beta}, \boldsymbol{\theta}) - y_i\|^2$$
$$+ P(\boldsymbol{\theta}) + R(\boldsymbol{\theta}) + S(\boldsymbol{\beta}) + Q(\boldsymbol{\beta}, \boldsymbol{\theta}) \tag{2}$$

where $x_i'(\beta, \theta)$ and y_i are the i-th vertex in $M'(\beta, \Theta)$ and its corresponding point in T. P is a pose prior built as logarithm of as sum of mixture of Gaussians, which keeps θ in probable pose space. R is the penalties for unusual joint angles, S for large β values that correspond to implausible shapes, Q for inter-penetration of body parts. More details on these penalty terms can be found in [3].

Second, the skin-tight 3D mesh M' is inflated to roughly minimize the distance between the mesh of M' and the target cloud points T according to their silhouette points. The silhouette points are identified in 2D reprojected images. When using a single camera, we project both M' and T to the image plane of the camera to find the silhouette points. This step introduces more flexibility in vertex positions so that M can be closer to T, which makes the finest step's fitting more stable.

In this step, we restrict the possible displacement of the i-th vertex in M to

$$x_i(\beta, \theta, \{n, l\}) = x_i'(\beta, \theta) + n_i l_i, \tag{3}$$

for all i, where $x_i \in M$, $x_i' \in M'$, n_i is the direction of the movement on M' at x', and l_i is the amplitude of the displacement. Here, Kimura $et\ al.$ [9] allowed each vertex to move only in their normal direction, while we allow for more freedom in the displacement direction. This new formulation prevents each mesh to interpenetrate ($e.g.$ around the crotch when a person stand). The energy function to be minimized according to the silhouette correspondences C_{sil} during the fitting process is:

$$E(\{n, l\}) = \sum_{i,j \in C_{sil}} \|x_i - y_j\|^2 + \lambda_l \sum_{i,j \in A_{ver}} (l_i - l_j)^2$$
$$+ \lambda_{normal} \sum_{i,j \in A_{face}} |N_i^{face} - N_j^{face}|$$
$$+ \lambda_{rot} \sum |n_i - n_i'| + \lambda_{laplacian} \sum |x_i - \frac{1}{z_i} \sum_{j \in \mathcal{N}_i} x_j|, \tag{4}$$

where A_{ver} and A_{face} are adjacency of vertices and faces of the SMPL model respectively. N_i^{face} is the normal of the i-th face. n_i' is the normal vectors of the i-th vertex of M'. $\mathcal{N}_i$ is the set of adjacent indices of the i-th vertex and z_i is the number of the adjacent vertices around the i-th vertex. λ_l, λ_{normal}, λ_{rot}, and $\lambda_{laplacian}$ are weights to control the contributions of the associated terms. The second term is a regularizer to keep the displacement of the adjacent vertices similar. The third term regularizes the direction of the adjacent mesh normals to avoid too flat surfaces. The fourth term keeps the vertex direction of the movement as rigid as possible. The last term is the Laplacian mesh regularizer inspired from [13, 19], which enforces smoothness.

At the finest step, we use all vertices and points instead of the silhouettes to make correspondences. Also, the displacements are not restricted by (Eq. (3)), $i.e.$,

$$x_i(\beta, \theta, \{d\}) = x_i'(\beta, \theta) + d_i. \tag{5}$$

With these modifications, the energy function to be minimized is:

$$E(\{d\}) = \sum_{i \in C_{\text{all}}} \|x_i - y_i\|^2 + \lambda_{normal} \sum_{i,j \in A_{face}} |N_i^{face} - N_j^{face}|$$

$$+ \lambda_{laplacian} \sum |x_i - \frac{1}{d_i} \sum_{j \in \mathcal{N}_i} x_j|, \tag{6}$$

where C_{all} are the correspondences between M and T. In this step, the nearest neighbors from T to M are updated in an iterative manner. At the final iteration, if the target point cloud T is a full-body human data, we identify correspondences not only from T to M but also from M to T. This allows us to fill gaps, which sometimes occur around the armpit and the crotch. Owing to the Laplacian regularizer term, vertices in the SMPL model which do not have any correspondence also move by being dragged by the other vertices.

After this non-rigid registration step, we obtain the body shape parameters β, the joint angles θ, and a fully-registered 3D mesh M for each point cloud in the input sequence. The hands and feet in M may be collapsed because hands' configuration can be different (the SMPL model assumes that the hands are open) and the scanned person may wear shoes (the SMPL model assumes no shoes). We consider that the appearance of the resulting 3D mesh is important, so we do not reconstruct the hands and feet through this non-rigid registration.

3.3 Sparse Representation of Human Shape Deformation

The deformations of clothes (*e.g.* clothing wrinkles and folds) are difficult to be reconstructed using only statistical shape models and pose parameters. We employ the eigen-deformation method [9] to deal with such deformations. We reason that the deformations can be represented by displacements from the skin-tight model to the model with loose clothes and that the displacements can be compressed to a low dimensional space.

If the angles of joints are the same but the orientation of the human body is different, the values of the displacements will change. Therefore, we perform the eigen-deformation method for each body part independently in each body part local coordinate system. We compute the displacement vector d_{lk} of the k-th vertex of the l-th body part in mesh M', which is represented by $d_{lk} = H_l(x_{lk} - x'_{lk})$, where x_{lk} and x'_{lk} are the k-th vertices in the l-th body parts in M and M'. As mentioned above, every vertex is transformed to the local coordinates of each body part using each rigid transformation matrix H_l. On each body part, we concatenate these displacement vectors to make the column vector $d_l^\top = (d_{l1}^\top \ d_{l2}^\top \ \ldots)$. We perform these calculations to each frame and then aggregate these displacement vectors over all frames to obtain the matrix $D \in \mathbb{R}^{(3 \times K_l) \times F}$. K_l is the number of vertices that belong to l-th body part. F is the number of frames used to perform PCA calculation. With the eigen-deformation, we obtain bases (eigenvectors) $E_l \in \mathbb{R}^{(3 \times K_l) \times L}$ and coefficients $c_l \in \mathbb{R}^L$ for each body part respectively. L is the number of bases. So, the displacements in the low dimensional space is represented by

$$\tilde{d}_{lk} = E_l c_l + \overline{d_l}, \tag{7}$$

that is, a linear combination. This means that if we can regress the low dimensional coefficients, unobserved deformations can be estimated.

When reconstructing $\bar{M}$, we firstly recover M' from β and θ, and then recover $\tilde{d}_{lk}$ using a small number of eigen vectors. Finally $H_l^{-1}\tilde{d}_{lk}$ is calculated for each vertex of each body part and added to M'.

3.4   Shape Deformation Bases and Coefficients Estimation by Neural Network

We train two types of neural networks to estimate the detailed shape of the clothed human from a given pose of the SMPL model: a coefficient regressor network (called CRNN) [9], and a bases estimation network (called BENN). BENN is composed of the CRNN with an additional output layer. In the layer, the bases and the means calculated in the previous section are used as weight and bias parameters and updated in training. This allows the network to output more accurate displacements to regress the displacements directly.

We train one CRNN for each body part using the coefficients obtained from the eigen-deformation of the displacement vectors as training data and the poses Θ, which consist of the combination of the SMPL pose parameters θ and the angle between each body part and the gravity as input. We reason that the displacements of the vertices of a body part are affected not only by the motion of adjacent body parts, but also by the motion of non adjacent body parts that affect the deformation of the clothes. For example, when a person raises his arms, deformations occur not only on the shoulders but also on the torso of the clothes he wears. Therefore, for each body part we use the pose of multiple joints as input for both the CRNN and the BENN. For each body part, the CRNN is composed of four fully connected layers. As mentioned above, at any time, the body pose is represented using a set of quaternions, which is calculated from θ and an angle formed by the vertically downward $\Theta \in \mathbb{R}^{5 \times G}$, where G is the number of joints that used for each body part. Once the CRNN is trained, we obtain the coefficients $\tilde{c} \in \mathbb{R}^L$ for any body pose Θ.

For each body part we also train a BENN, whose weights and bias are initialized with those of the trained CRNN. The bases E and mean shape $\overline{d}$ obtained at the end of the eigen-deformation stage are used as the initial weights and bias of the additional output layer. The inputs of the BENN are the same as those of the CRNN. The output of the BENN are the displacements $\tilde{d} \in \mathbb{R}^{(3 \times K_l)}$ of all vertices that belong to the body part. The bases are determined by the output of the BENN and the means of all bases are equal to the bias of the BENN (Fig. 2). Finally, the displacement values are computed as:

$$\tilde{d}(\Theta) = W\tilde{c}(\Theta) + b, \tag{8}$$

where W is in $\mathbb{R}^{(3 \times K_l) \times L}$ and b is in $\mathbb{R}^{(3 \times K_l)}$.

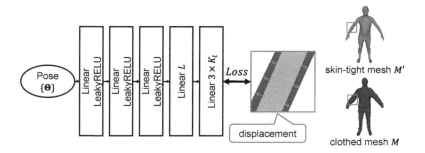

Fig. 2. Network architecture of BENN. When the target data are partially observed, we use visibility map not to calculate the gradient of unobserved body part.

In our case, both network (CRNN and BENN) are implemented in PyTorch [16]. We choose the mean squared error as loss function and Adam algorithm [10], which learning rate is set to 0.001 as optimizer. Examples of the reconstructed shapes are shown in Fig. 4. The results of estimating bases is better than only regress coefficient. Here, we do not perform eigen-deformation and regression for not clothed body part (*e.g.* face and hands) because such parts must not deform.

3.5 Handling Partially Observed Data

Our technique can efficiently handle partially observed data by training the BENN using a visibility map to mask the loss of invisible body parts. The visibility map represents whether each vertex of the mesh in the training dataset is visible or not. The map can be created by detecting collisions between the ray from each vertex to the principal point and each mesh. This allows us to back propagate only from the unit of the output layer corresponding to the visible body vertex. To utilize this mask based method, subjects have to show all body parts at least once.

4   Experiment

To evaluate our method, we used the public dataset [22] and compared the results obtained with our proposed method with the results obtained with previous methods [9,24] quantitatively and qualitatively. We also demonstrate the ability of our proposed method to cope with partially observed data, which we created from the public dataset [22]. We also captured a sequence of RGB-D images of a moving person with three depth cameras and compared qualitatively the results obtained with our proposed method with those obtained with the method proposed in [26].

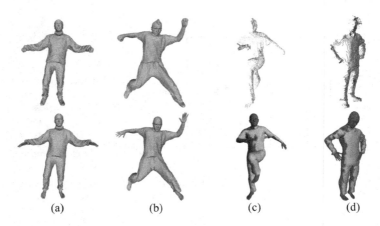

(a)   (b)   (c)   (d)

Fig. 3. The result of non-rigid registration (Sect. 3.2). Top row shows target scan data and bottom shows the result of non-rigid registration. (a) and (b) shows the result of full-body target data (For the visibility, the target scans are showed with mesh which is not used). (c) and (d) shows the result of partially observed data (dark gray means invisible body parts and light gray means visible body parts).

Table 1. Average RMSE of each vertex position in mm. Ours means the result of BENN. (The value of first row is cited from [24].)

Seq	Bounc.	Hand.	Crane	Jump.	Mar. 1	Mar. 2	Squ. 1	Squ. 2
Yang *et al.* [24]	10.27	–	**4.27**	–	3.93	–	4.31	–
Kimura *et al.* [9] (CRNN)	5.45	3.45	7.61	**9.24**	3.06	8.25	3.20	7.36
Ours (BENN)	**5.28**	**3.03**	7.70	9.52	**2.87**	**8.13**	**2.87**	**7.29**

4.1 Non-rigid Registration Using SMPL Model

We performed non-rigid registration as explained in Sect. 3.2, to the meshes publicly available from [22], which consists of people with loose clothes, and point clouds captured by Kinect V2. Results are shown in Fig. 3, where the top row is the target scan data and bottom row is the result of our non-rigid registration. From the results, we can confirm that most parts of our fully registered mesh (clothed mesh) are visually close to the original mesh. However, some differences are still observable (*e.g.* there are some gap around crotch in Fig. 3(c)). Although this problem occurs only about 2% of the entire sequence, it can interfere with the training of NN. Therefore, at this moment, problematic frames are manually adjusted. We will investigate how to solve this problem in our future work.

4.2 Inter-frame Interpolation

In this section, we compare the reconstruction results obtained with our proposed method with those obtained with the previous methods [9,24] using the publicly available dataset [22], which consists of human mesh with loose clothes. On one

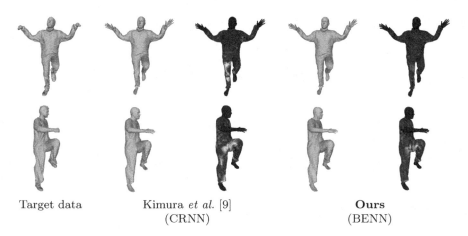

Target data	Kimura *et al.* [9]	**Ours**
	(CRNN)	(BENN)

Fig. 4. Qualitative comparison using the public dataset. The left most column shows target data, next two columns show the results of Kimura *et al.* [9] (CRNN) and last two column show the results of the our proposed method (BENN). The second column of each results shows error in color. (Blue = 0 mm and red >= 50 mm) (Color figure online)

Fig. 5. Each left column shows the target scan data of non-rigid registration and right shows the results of intra-frame interpolation. Even in the invisible body part the clothes deformations are reconstructed well.

hand, Kimura *et al.* [9] have the same strategy as our method, which means that they also firstly fit the model to the target scan data and regress clothes deformations. On the other hand, Yang *et al.* [24] calculate the displacements between models and target mesh without fitting strategy. Instead, they assume that the input scan data has mesh consistency.

Following Yang *et al.* [24], we also use 80% of each sequence for training and others for testing. Although Yang *et al.* used 40 bases for regression, we and Kimura *et al.* [9] (CRNN) use only 30 bases. The quantitative comparison result is shown in Table 1. In this table, **Ours** means the result of BENN. The table reports average of RMSE (root mean squared error) in *mm* of each vertex. Here, because the density of vertices is different between the target point clouds and our outputs, we could not simply calculate the error using one-to-one correspondence of points between them. Therefore, we calculate the error between clothed

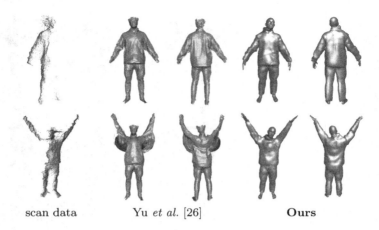

scan data   Yu *et al.* [26]   **Ours**

Fig. 6. Qualitative comparison with [26] using Kinect V2. Left column of each result shows front view and right shows back-side view. Our result represents pose-dependent deformation (*e.g.*clothes back). DoubleFusion has some artifacts (*e.g.*armpit), whereas no artifacts in ours.

meshes obtained at non-rigid registration stage (Sect. 3.2) and the results of our proposed method. It is reasonable to calculate the error in this way because we use clothed meshes as training data for BENN. Our method outperforms previous methods in most sequences while using less bases than Yang *et al.* and the same amount of bases as Kimura *et al.* The qualitative comparison is shown in Fig. 4. The first column shows the target data of non-rigid registration. Next two columns show the results obtained with the method of Kimura *et al.* (CRNN) and the right two columns show the results obtained with our proposed method. The first column of each set of two columns shows the results of regressed deformation and the second shows the error with pseudo-color (blue = 0 mm and red $>= 50$ mm). From these results, we can also confirm that our proposed BENN works well qualitatively.

4.3   Intra-frame Interpolation

Owing to our BENN implementation, we can ignore the invisible parts of the scanned data. This allows us to use partially observed data to train our network. In this section, we estimate clothes deformations of such an invisible body part using BENN trained with only the visible body part data. We performed intra-frame interpolation to the partially observed data that we generated from the public dataset [22]. We also captured a sequence of RGB-D images of human in motion using Kinect V2 and performed intra-frame interpolation to compare the results obtained with our proposed method with those obtained with DoubleFusion [26], which is a real-time system that can reconstruct not only the human inner body (optimized parameters of the SMPL model) but also the clothes that the subject is wearing, with using a single depth camera

(Kinect V2). The results are shown in Figs. 5 and 6. To obtain enough data for training, we used the data which is visible from the front view and the data which is visible from the back-side view as training data separately. Note that, we only use the displacements of visible body parts to train BENN. Invisible body parts are reconstructed through the regression step. These results show the effectiveness of our proposed method to handle partially observed data. In Fig. 6, the first column shows target data of non-rigid registration for our proposed method and input data for DoubleFusion. Next two columns show the results obtained by [26] and the right two columns show the results obtained by our proposed method. Here, to obtain enough data for training, we used three Kinect V2 cameras, which are placed in circle centered on the subject, to capture the sequence. Again, we use the data which is visible from each view as training data separately. In the case of DoubleFusion, the results were sometimes collapsed (*e.g.* head and armpit). This means that this method deforms the node-graph and cannot describe the pose-dependent deformations. Although the results obtained with DoubleFusion can represent fine details of the clothes, they cannot describe the pose-dependent deformations because this technique only deforms the node-graph. In contrast, the results obtained with our proposed method could represent the pose-dependent deformations (wrinkles around back side in Fig. 6). Again, we do not use the displacements of the occluded body parts from the front view at the network training step.

5   Conclusion

In this paper, we present a full-body human with loose clothes reconstruction method from point clouds measurements using neural network based regressors, even when the target data has largely occluded. Our fitting method and neural network based regression outperform previous methods, which is proved by numerical evaluations. Moreover, our BENN can also reconstruct full-body even if the training data have only partially observed data. We visually confirm that the regression ability is sufficient and better than previous method. We believe that this method have a impact to many applications, such as AR/VR, virtual try-on, avatar making, etc.

References

1. Anguelov, D., Srinivasan, P., Koller, D., Thrun, S., Rodgers, J., Davis, J.: SCAPE: shape completion and animation of people. In: ACM Transactions on Graphics (TOG), vol. 24, pp. 408–416. ACM (2005)
2. Bogo, F., Black, M.J., Loper, M., Romero, J.: Detailed full-body reconstructions of moving people from monocular RGB-D sequences. In: Proceedings of the IEEE International Conference on Computer Vision, pp. 2300–2308 (2015)
3. Bogo, F., Kanazawa, A., Lassner, C., Gehler, P., Romero, J., Black, M.J.: Keep it SMPL: automatic estimation of 3D human pose and shape from a single image. In: Leibe, B., Matas, J., Sebe, N., Welling, M. (eds.) ECCV 2016. LNCS, vol. 9909, pp. 561–578. Springer, Cham (2016). https://doi.org/10.1007/978-3-319-46454-1_34

4. Chen, Y., Liu, Z., Zhang, Z.: Tensor-based human body modeling. In: Proceedings of the IEEE Conference on Computer Vision and Pattern Recognition (CVPR), pp. 105–112 (2013)
5. Habermann, M., Xu, W., Zollhöfer, M., Pons-Moll, G., Theobalt, C.: Livecap: real-time human performance capture from monocular video. ACM Trans. Graph. (TOG) **38**(2), 14 (2019)
6. Innmann, M., Zollhöfer, M., Nießner, M., Theobalt, C., Stamminger, M.: VolumeDeform: real-time volumetric non-rigid reconstruction. In: Leibe, B., Matas, J., Sebe, N., Welling, M. (eds.) ECCV 2016. LNCS, vol. 9912, pp. 362–379. Springer, Cham (2016). https://doi.org/10.1007/978-3-319-46484-8_22
7. Joo, H., Simon, T., Sheikh, Y.: Total capture: a 3D deformation model for tracking faces, hands, and bodies. In: Proceedings of the IEEE Conference on Computer Vision and Pattern Recognition, pp. 8320–8329 (2018)
8. Kanazawa, A., Black, M.J., Jacobs, D.W., Malik, J.: End-to-end recovery of human shape and pose. In: Computer Vision and Pattern Regognition (CVPR) (2018)
9. Kimura, R., et al.: Representing a partially observed non-rigid 3D human using eigen-texture and eigen-deformation. In: 2018 24th International Conference on Pattern Recognition (ICPR), pp. 1043–1048. IEEE (2018)
10. Kingma, D.P., Ba, J.: Adam: a method for stochastic optimization. arXiv preprint arXiv:1412.6980 (2014)
11. Loper, M., Mahmood, N., Romero, J., Pons-Moll, G., Black, M.J.: SMPL: a skinned multi-person linear model. ACM Trans. Graph. (Proc. SIGGRAPH Asia) **34**(6), 248:1–248:16 (2015)
12. Malleson, C., Klaudiny, M., Hilton, A., Guillemaut, J.Y.: Single-view RGBD-based reconstruction of dynamic human geometry. In: IEEE International Conference on Computer Vision Workshops, pp. 307–314 (2013)
13. Nealen, A., Igarashi, T., Sorkine, O., Alexa, M.: Laplacian mesh optimization. In: Proceedings of the 4th International Conference on Computer Graphics and Interactive Techniques in Australasia and Southeast Asia, pp. 381–389. ACM (2006)
14. Newcombe, R.A., Fox, D., Seitz, S.M.: Dynamicfusion: reconstruction and tracking of non-rigid scenes in real-time. In: Proceedings of the IEEE Conference on Computer Vision and Pattern Recognition, pp. 343–352 (2015)
15. Omran, M., Lassner, C., Pons-Moll, G., Gehler, P.V., Schiele, B.: Neural body fitting: unifying deep learning and model-based human pose and shape estimation, Verona, Italy (2018)
16. Paszke, A., et al.: Automatic differentiation in pytorch (2017)
17. Pavlakos, G., et al.: Expressive body capture: 3D hands, face, and body from a single image. In: Proceedings IEEE Conference on Computer Vision and Pattern Recognition (CVPR) (2019)
18. Pons-Moll, G., Pujades, S., Hu, S., Black, M.: ClothCap: seamless 4D clothing capture and retargeting. ACM Trans. Graph. (Proc. SIGGRAPH) **36**(4), 73 (2017). https://doi.org/10.1145/3072959.3073711. Two first authors contributed equally
19. Sorkine, O., Cohen-Or, D., Lipman, Y., Alexa, M., Rössl, C., Seidel, H.P.: Laplacian surface editing. In: Proceedings of the 2004 Eurographics/ACM SIGGRAPH Symposium on Geometry Processing, pp. 175–184. ACM (2004)
20. Tan, V., Budvytis, I., Cipolla, R.: Indirect deep structured learning for 3D human body shape and pose prediction (2018)
21. Varol, G., et al.: BodyNet: volumetric inference of 3D human body shapes. In: Ferrari, V., Hebert, M., Sminchisescu, C., Weiss, Y. (eds.) ECCV 2018. LNCS, vol. 11211, pp. 20–38. Springer, Cham (2018). https://doi.org/10.1007/978-3-030-01234-2_2

22. Vlasic, D., Baran, I., Matusik, W., Popović, J.: Articulated mesh animation from multi-view silhouettes. ACM Trans. Graph. **27**(3), 97:1–97:9 (2008). https://doi.org/10.1145/1360612.1360696
23. Xiang, D., Joo, H., Sheikh, Y.: Monocular total capture: posing face, body, and hands in the wild (2018)
24. Yang, J., Franco, J.-S., Hétroy-Wheeler, F., Wuhrer, S.: Analyzing clothing layer deformation statistics of 3D human motions. In: Ferrari, V., Hebert, M., Sminchisescu, C., Weiss, Y. (eds.) ECCV 2018. LNCS, vol. 11211, pp. 245–261. Springer, Cham (2018). https://doi.org/10.1007/978-3-030-01234-2_15
25. Yu, T., et al.: Bodyfusion: real-time capture of human motion and surface geometry using a single depth camera. In: Proceedings of the IEEE International Conference on Computer Vision, pp. 910–919 (2017)
26. Yu, T., et al.: Doublefusion: real-time capture of human performances with inner body shapes from a single depth sensor. In: Proceedings of the IEEE Conference on Computer Vision and Pattern Recognition, pp. 7287–7296 (2018)

Improved Saliency-Enhanced Multi-cue Correlation-Filter-Based Visual Tracking

Syeda Fouzia[1(✉)], Mark Bell[2], and Reinhard Klette[1]

[1] Department of Electrical and Electronic Engineering,
School of Engineering, Computer and Mathematical Sciences,
Auckland University of Technology, Auckland, New Zealand
`syeda.fouzia@aut.ac.nz`
[2] Crown Lift Trucks Ltd., Auckland, New Zealand
`mark.bell@crown.com`

Abstract. A discrete correlation-filter-based multi-cue-analysis framework is constructed by fusing different feature types to form potential *candidate trackers* that track the target independently. The selection of corresponding cues and the exploitation of their individual or combined strengths is a less researched topic especially in the context of ensemble tracking. Every candidate tracker from the ensemble is chosen according to the degree of its robustness per frame. We argue that, if each of the candidate trackers is guided by higher-level semantic information (i.e. pixel-wise saliency maps in ensemble-based tracker), this will make tracking better to cope with appearance or view point changes. Recently, saliency prediction using deep architectures have made this process accurate and fast. The formation of multiple candidate trackers by saliency-guided features along with other different handcrafted and hierarchical feature types enhances the robustness score for that specific tracker. It improved multiple tracker-based DCF frameworks in efficiency and accuracy as reported in our experimental evaluation, compared to state-of-the-art ensemble trackers.

1 Introduction

Visual object tracking (VOT) is a challenging computer vision problem where the target of interest needs to be tracked in every frame. Challenges might include target deformation caused by frequent appearance changes, abrupt motion, background clutter, or partial or full occlusions. Two types of approaches exist to handle such problems, either *generative* [22,23] or *discriminative* methods [3,14].

Generative methods for visual tracking tackle the problem by searching for regions which seem to be most alike the target candidate model. The models can either be based on templates or subspaces.

The discriminative approach aims to differentiate the target from the background by considering tracking as a binary classification problem. It employs both the target object and background information to search for a decision boundary for differentiating the target object from the background region.

© Springer Nature Switzerland AG 2019
C. Lee et al. (Eds.): PSIVT 2019, LNCS 11854, pp. 240–254, 2019.
https://doi.org/10.1007/978-3-030-34879-3_19

Table 1. Candidate-trackers selection

Trackers	Feature type
Tracker I	Sal-feature and low (HOG)
Tracker II	Sal-feature and middle (conv3-4) of VGG-19
Tracker III	Sal-feature and high (conv5-4) of VGG-19
Tracker IV	Sal-feature and low, middle
Tracker V	Sal-feature and low, high
Tracker VI	Sal-feature and middle, high
Tracker VII	Sal-feature and low, middle, high

In *discrete correlation filter* (DCF) based tracking, an initial state of the object to be tracked is known, either by detecting the target automatically or by manually specifying its position in the initial frame. The correlation filters predict the maximum filter response by learning a least-squares classifier in the region of interest of the target where the maximum response map corresponds to the location of the target [6]. The key to these filter successes is exploiting all the negative training data by including all shifted versions of the training patches. Moreover, this kind of method mostly follows the tracking-by-detection paradigm where each frame of the target is regarded as a detection problem. The classifier is trained to distinguish the target object from its background.

For multi-cue tracking, an adaptive tracking switch mechanism is employed where the tracker adaptively transfers the tracking task to one of the ensemble candidate trackers [32]. The candidate, which results in precise target localisation and which is consistent in its results, is chosen to track in a given frame. Such tracking candidates might be constructed by fusing the handcrafted low-level features, such as HOG [8], colour names [30], or middle and higher level deep activation features using outputs from conv3-4, conv4-4, and conv5-4 layers from a VGG-19 pretrained model [28]. See Table 1 for an example of an ensemble. State-of-the-art results on visual recognition tasks are obtained by exploiting rich hierarchies in features in deep architectures and learning multi-layer correlation response maps. Response maps are analysed in a coarse to refined manner to include the features that are most appropriate for tracking tasks.

For deep *convolutional neural networks* (CNNs), features from the last convolution layers are more closely related to object category level semantic information. These feature maps though are robust to intra-class appearance variations but fail the objective to locate targets precisely. Earlier convolution layer outputs are more appropriate for target object fine-spatial appearance information, but not for the semantics [26].

We propose that *saliency is a discriminant feature* that aids in differentiating the target from background and can be useful and efficient way to attain robustness against target appearance changes at semantically higher level. We argue that incorporating a *saliency feature* as a complimentary high-level feature, and learning correlation filters for them separately, will aid the tracking quality for each tracker in an ensemble. A candidate tracker employing this semantic aware higher-level feature will benefit in track accuracy and precision and thus the final tracking robustness against appearance and viewpoint changes.

This can also be verified in a performance gain attained for the candidate trackers. The corresponding weight for the saliency response will be chosen adaptively according to the its consistency over time for the saliency feature in consecutive frames. We treat saliency and other features separately [2] for each tracker. This benefits the framework effectively, especially under occlusions and frequent scale variations of the target.

The structure of the paper is as follows. Section 2 reports about related work. Section 4 explains our chosen approach. Section 5 illustrates experimental settings, results and provides an analysis. Section 6 concludes.

2   Related Work

Bolme et al. proposed a correlation filter, a minimum output sum of square errors (MOSSE) for target appearance, based on a single luminance channel in visual tracking [6]. Ma et al. suggested that multiple correlation filters can be learned on hierarchical convolution layers [26]. Semantic and spatial information is captured by constructing multiple DCFs on low, middle and higher convolution layers.

By exploiting the circulant structure for training samples, Heriques et al. proposed to derive closed-form solutions for training and detection with several types of kernels, including the popular Gaussian and polynomial kernels [5]. Zhang et al. incorporate spatio-temporal contextual relationships between the target of interest and its local context in a Bayesian framework; this aids to model the statistical correlation between low-level features from the target and outside regions for visual tracking [36].

Spatially regularized discriminative correlation filters (SRDCFs) introduced spatially regularized components in learning by alleviating the unwanted boundary effects by penalizing correlation filter coefficients depending on the spatial location [9]. Qi et al. propose an algorithm to fuse several DCFs through an adaptive hedged method. Staple complimentary learners for real time tracking combine DCF and complimentary cues like colour histograms to achieve a real-time state-of-the-art tracking model. DCF *with channel and spatial reliability* (CSR-DCF) introduced a spatial reliability map in filter learning and the updating process. C-COT adopts a training of continuous-domain convolution filters in learning DCF and integration of multi-resolution deep feature maps, leading to a top performance on several tracking benchmarks [10]. The enhanced version of CCOT is ECO (efficient convolutional operators for tracking), which improves both speed and performance by introducing several efficient strategies.

ECO is a fast DCF implementation with factorized convolutional operators to reduce the number of parameters in the model [11]. For achieving tracker robustness, *ensemble* based feature fusion methods employing dynamic programming have been used [4]. Though dynamic programming-based tracking methods' computational efficiency is determined by the number of trackers in the ensemble; it is reduced if this number increases. Also, sparse representation-based methods suffer from low frame rates due to the fact that the overall speed being decided by the slowest tracker in the ensemble. For a *multi-expert entropy minimisation* (MEEM) algorithm, based on exploiting the relation between current tracking and historical samples using an entropy minimisation concept, see [34]. A discrete graph-based optimised framework is an extended version for MEEM [21].

Target state prediction is made based on a framework using a partition fusion method to group an ensemble of trackers [16]. In many of the fusion-based methods, the trajectory is calculated twice in forward and backward direction which makes the tracker run twice. Also, tracker results are not fed back to individual trackers that make a transient drift accumulate and build-up tracking errors.

The MCCT tracker employs a decision level fusion strategy and a robustness evaluation criterion for ranking tracking experts in order of their reliability. It employs a training-sample-sharing strategy and adaptive expert updates. The tracker output is a feedback to the individual experts to prevent expert corruption over time [32].

3   Saliency Feature

Saliency-based trackers show the usefulness for using saliency features over various other cues such as motion, texture, gradient or colour. An object is represented and tracked based on a human attentive mechanism using visual saliency maps. Such methods are more robust for occluded and cluttered scenes. Traditionally different visual cues, such as compactness or uniqueness, have been used to detect salient pixels in images [7].

Uniqueness-based methods can be further split into local and global contrast methods. Uniqueness-based methods typically use low-level features (i.e.

Fig. 1. Saliency detection example

color, direction, or intensity) to find contrast between image regions and their surrounding pixels.

Compactness-based methods are based on variance of spatial features. Salient image pixels tend to have a small spatial variance in the image space. The image background has a high spatial variance. Single visual cue-based methods have few limitations in detecting accurate salient pixels. Different cues can also be combined to form a composite framework [27].

A combination for features like colour-texture, colour-saliency, or colour-direction is explored [29]. To track non-rigid objects, spatio-temporal discriminative saliency maps were used. This gives accurate regions occupied by the targets as tracking results. A *tailored fully convolutional neural network* (TFCN) is developed. It is used to model the local saliency of regions of interest. Finally, these local saliency maps are fused with a weighted entropy method, resulting in a final discriminative saliency map [35].

In this work, *deep hierarchical saliency network prediction* (DHSnet) is employed to output the saliency map of an image using a deep CNN. It uses the whole image as a computational unit and feedforward the image for testing without any post processing. First a coarse saliency map is generated for global view for a rough estimation of salient objects. By incorporating local context in the image, a refined saliency map is obtained through a recurrent CNN. This refinement is done in many steps hierarchically and successively [24]. Refer to Fig. 1 for saliency detection examples.

4   Our Approach

A brief outline of our approach is as follows:

1. First, a discrete correlation filter is learned from the appearance of the object at a given frame. Features are extracted from chosen ROI where f_{sal} and $f_{HOG-CNN}$ denote the feature maps for saliency, and HOG and CNN.
2. Second, the previously learned correlation filters for saliency and other features denoted by g_{sal} and g_{feat}, respectively, are convolved with the extracted feature maps for them in order to obtain responses (scores) R_{sal} and R_{feat}.
3. Finally, the filter is updated according to the new appearance which is obtained from the location found in the second step according to the proposed adaptive update strategy.

These steps will become more clear with the explanations below.

The robustness of different trackers varies with regard to various feature models employed for them. One dynamic feature model will not suffice to deal with varying challenges faced by the visual trackers [26]. Low, middle and high-level features are combined into 7 candidate trackers (see Table 1), working independently in an ensemble where the low-level HOG feature is 31-dimensional. Settings are re-used as employed in hierarchical convolutional features (HCF) for different level response maps [26]. Tracking diversity is achieved by adaptively choosing the trackers according to it robustness for the current frame.

Trackers using just a single feature may not be sufficiently robust to an optimum extent, but the addition of a complimentary sal-feature improved the results. We tested the sal-feature-guided strategy for our 7 different trackers in the ensemble and found that the response for each candidate was improved. Tracker VII, based on three kinds of feature hierarchy performances, is also improved and more robust to appearance changes. Section 5 depicts detailed quantitative experimental results.

Saliency response and other feature response maps from each tracker is obtained separately and denoted as R_{sal} and R_{feat}, respectively. Refer to Fig. 2 for an overview. Every tracker is proposed to employ saliency as a high-level complimentary feature, though reliability of the saliency needs to be estimated for each incoming frame.

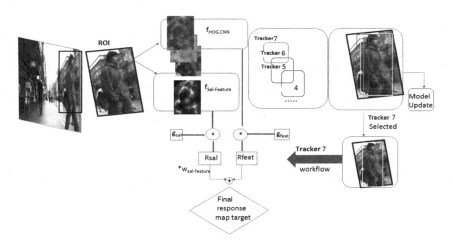

Fig. 2. Suggested update concept for feature and decision fusion

First we estimated the saliency based on DHSNet [24]. This saliency prediction network is based on a hierarchical end-to-end deep convolution neural network. This network learns global saliency cues like contrast, objectness, compactness with the added recurrent neural network to refine the saliency map details by adding local contextual details. This network is trained by employing a bulk of images and their corresponding saliency masks.

To estimate the similarity between the vectorized saliency maps Sal_t and Sal_{t+1} at frames t and $t+1$, *cosine similarity* is used which is described by

$$\mathcal{C}_{sim}\left(Sal_t, Sal_{t+1}\right) = \frac{Sal_t \cdot Sal_{t+1}}{||Sal_t||_2 \cdot ||Sal_{t+1}||_2} \qquad (1)$$

A maximum contribution of the saliency is selected adaptively based on the previous and current saliency response. The weight of the saliency for frame t is given by

$$w\left(t\right) = M\left[\left(1 - \lambda\right) w\left(t - 1\right) + \lambda \cdot C_{sim}\left(Sal_t, Sal_{t+1}\right)\right] \tag{2}$$

We choose M to be 0.5 that is the maximum suggested contribution assigned to the saliency feature. This value is adaptively chosen based on scene statistics. The learning rate λ is chosen to be 0.01 owing to the intention that the update of saliency is assumed to be gradual due to noise. The initial weight of saliency is chosen to be $w(t = 0) = 0.25$, i.e. half of the possible maximum contribution. We based our choices on settings employed by [2].

4.1   DCF Overview

An image patch $\mathbf{x}$ of size $M \times N$ has its centre on the target. Training samples are generated from circular shifts along M and N dimensions. Shifted samples of $\mathbf{x}$, denoted as $\mathbf{x}(m, n)$, are a subset of $\{0, 1, ..., M - 1\} \times \{0, 1, ..., N - 1\}$ and used as training samples, with a Gaussian function label of $\mathbf{y}(m, n)$. A correlation filter $\mathbf{w}$ of the same size as $\mathbf{x}$ is learned by minimising the regression problem

$$\min_{\mathbf{w}} ||\mathbf{Xw} - \mathbf{y}||_2^2 + \lambda ||\mathbf{w}||_2^2 \tag{3}$$

$\mathbf{X}$ is the data matrix obtained by concatenating all the circular shifts for the training patches. λ is the regularization parameter ($\lambda \geq 0$).

For $d \in \{1, ..., D\}$, the learned filter weight on the $d - th$ channel equals

$$\mathbf{w}_d^* = \frac{\hat{y} \odot \hat{\mathbf{x}}_d^*}{\sum_{i=1}^{D} \hat{\mathbf{x_i}}^* \odot \hat{\mathbf{x_i}} + \lambda} \tag{4}$$

where operator $\odot$ is the Hadamard or element-wise product. The hat symbol denotes the discrete Fourier transform (DFT) for the vector and $*$ symbol denotes the conjugate complex for that vector. Response map R for z is as follows:

$$\mathbf{R} = \mathcal{F}^{-1}\left(\sum_{i=1}^{D} \hat{\mathbf{w}_d} \odot \hat{\mathbf{z}_d}^*\right) \tag{5}$$

where $\mathbf{z}$ is a ROI patch with same size as $\mathbf{x}$, cropped in the next frame to track the target of interest. The target is localised where the response is maximized.

Numerator and denominator are updated online for the filter $\hat{\mathbf{w}_d}^*$ as follows:

$$\hat{\mathbf{A}}_d^t = (1 - \eta)\,\hat{\mathbf{A}}_{t-1}^d + \eta\hat{\mathbf{y}} \odot \hat{\mathbf{x}}_d^{*t} \tag{6}$$

$$\hat{\mathbf{B}}_d^t = (1 - \eta)\,\hat{\mathbf{B}}_{t-1}^d + \eta \sum_{i=1}^{D} \hat{\mathbf{x}}_i^{*t} \odot \hat{\mathbf{x}}_i^t \tag{7}$$

During the filter learning step, a Hann window is applied to avoid the boundary effect problem. The learning rate is adjusted by parameter η for the frame index t and the scale is selected based on the DSST tracker methodology [12]:

$$\hat{\mathbf{w}}_d^{*t} = \frac{\hat{\mathbf{A}}_d^t}{\hat{\mathbf{B}}_d^t + \lambda} \tag{8}$$

4.2 Tracker Robustness Measurement

Each tracker is employing the same region of interest and sharing similar training samples during filter learning and the tracking update process. By exploiting the refined feedback results from each tracker for target localisation, weak tracking outputs, especially during tracking drift scenarios and failures, are improved. This is the main reason for framework computational efficiency as well. The feature extraction is done only twice, rather than 14 times.

Peak to side lobe ratio (PSR) is commonly used in a standard DCF framework to estimate reliability of tracking outputs. Often this measure fails to quantify the reliability properly when un-reliable samples have same PSR as target of interest. Robustness score for the candidate trackers is computed from two measures. *tracker pairs evaluation* stands for the degree of consistency between pairs of trackers for each frame, and *tracker self-evaluation* stands for the trajectory smoothness of a candidate tracker hypothesis at every frame.

Let $\{T_1, T_2, T_3, ..., T_7\}$ denote the seven hypothesis trackers. In the t-th frame, Tracker i's bounding box is denoted by $B_{T_i}^t$, and Tracker j's bounding box accordingly by $B_{T_j}^t$.

The overlap ratio O_{T_i, T_j}^t is defined by

$$O_{T_i, T_j}^t = \frac{B_{T_i}^t \cap B_{T_j}^t}{B_{T_i}^t \cup B_{T_j}^t} \tag{9}$$

Tracker pair robustness score is given by

$$Score_{pair}^t (T_i) = \frac{M_{T_i}^t}{F_{T_i}^t + \eta} \tag{10}$$

where $M_{T_i}^t$ is the mean of the overlap ratios and $F_{T_i}^t$ is extent of fluctuation of overlap ratios for t frames computed as in [32].

Self evaluation measure for candidate tracker is measured by *Euclidean distance* shift between centres of the previous and current bounding boxes denoted by distance $d_{T_i}^t$, and is given by

$$\exp\left(\frac{-1}{2\sigma_{T_i}^2} \left(F_i^t\right)^2\right) \tag{11}$$

where σ_{E_i} is the average of the width and height of bounding box given by tracker i.

Tracker robustness degree is the linear sum of both pair-wise evaluation and self-evaluation. After evaluation of the overall reliability for each one, that tracker with the highest robustness score is selected and its tracking result is taken for the current frame:

$$R^t(T_i) = R^t_{pair}(T_i) + R^t_{self}(T_i) \qquad (12)$$

See Fig. 3.

5   Experimentation and Analysis

For experimentation, the DCF method is employed for forming candidate trackers [15]. MATLAB 2017a is used for tracker implementation. A GeForce GTX 1080 Titanium GPU with compute capability 6.1 and 12 GB memory is used for experimentation and testing. The MatConvNet toolbox is used for extraction of deep features from VGG-19 [31]. This framework runs at about 1 FPS on CPU. The GPU version of MCCT tracker runs at about 7 FPS.

The evaluation measure for tracking is chosen as the *area under success curve* (AUC). It is plotted between overlap threshold and success rate. Overlap between ground truth and tracking result is calculated as follows:

$$O(T, GT) = \frac{|T \cap GT|}{|T \cup GT|} \qquad (13)$$

If $O(T, GT)$ is greater than an overlap threshold, then tracking is a success. The success rate is the ratio of successfully tracked frames to the total number of frames in the sequence.

AUC is the average of all success rates at different overlap thresholds when these threshold values are evenly distributed [17].

In *one-pass evaluation* (OPE), a tracker is initialized in the first frame, so tracking is sensitive to frame number and bounding box spatial location for target. Average success is calculated.

Spatial robustness evaluation (SRE), tracking is done by starting it at various positions employing 4 spatial shifts around centre and corner and scale variations. Amount of this shift is 10% target with scale variations of 0.8, 0.9, 1.1, and 1.2. Average performance is reported with tracker evaluated 12 times.

For *temporal robustness evaluation* (TRE), the video is divided into 20 segments and tracking is performed for 20 segments with different initial frames each time. Average performance is calculated for all video segments.

We employed two datasets for evaluation. One is the $OTB-2015$ [33] dataset and the other one is $VOT2016$ [17,18]. Trackers are evaluated using an overlap threshold of 0.5. Overlap success plots using *one-pass evaluation* are generated as well for OTB-2015.

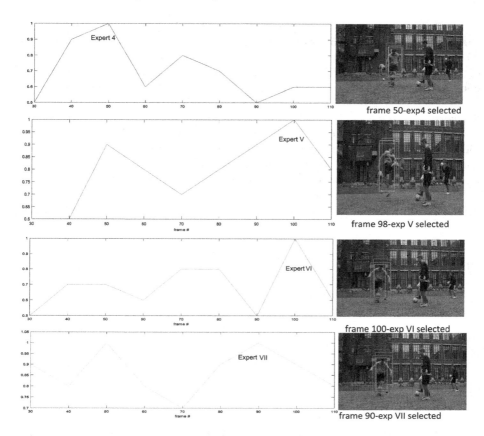

Fig. 3. *Left.* Tracker with peak robustness measure of 1 will be chosen for tracking for that frame. *Right.* Depicts bounding-box tracking outputs for all candidate trackers.

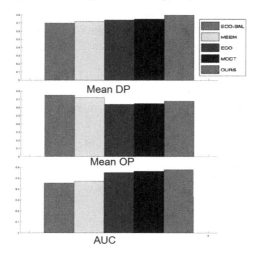

Fig. 4. Mean DP, OP and AUC results on OTB-2015 sequence

Refer to Fig. 4 for OPE comparative values for mean distance precision at a threshold of 20 pixels, mean overlap precision at 0.5 threshold and AUC for OTB-2015 dataset. Also under challenging attributes like low illumination, clutter, occlusion or motion blur, OPE is evaluated for the dataset for experimental comparison to other state of art trackers like MEEM [34], ECO [11], ECO-SAL [2], VTD [19], VTS [20], LSK [25], FRAG [1], CXT [13] and baseline MCCT trackers [32]. Refer to Fig. 5 for OPE results for those.

The visual object-tracking challenge 2016 (VOT2016) [17] benchmark provides an evaluation toolkit. It re-initializes the tracker to the correct position to continue tracking when tracking failure occurs. In VOT2016, the expected average overlap (EAO) is used for ranking trackers, which combine the raw values of per-frame accuracies and failures (tracker robustness). EAO is an estimation of the average overlap; it is expected for a tracker to attain on a number of smaller sequences [18]. See Fig. 6.

Table 2. Accuracy, robustness and EAO scores for various state-of-the-art trackers

Quantitative evaluation					
Metrics	MCCT [32]	ECO [11]	ECO-SAL [2]	MEEM [34]	Ours
Accuracy	0.56	0.51	0.59	0.55	0.58
Failure rate	0.74	0.72	0.91	0.85	0.71
EAO score	0.37	0.35	0.36	0.31	0.39

Table 2 details the quantitative comparison between the EAO scores, accuracy and failure rate for comparative study. Figure 5 provides an insight into trackers numbered in order of EAO scores.

OPE, SRE (spatial robustness evaluation) and TRE (temporal robustness evaluation) results for OTB2015, under various challenging attributes, are shown in Tables 3, 4 and 5, respectively. We denote the occlusion challenge by *OC*, low illumination as *LI*, scale variation challenge as *SV*, and background clutter as *BKC*.

It can be seen that under *low illumination* (LI) conditions, our framework results have not shown much improvement over MCCT framework. The reason is that saliency prediction is less discriminant in such scenes.

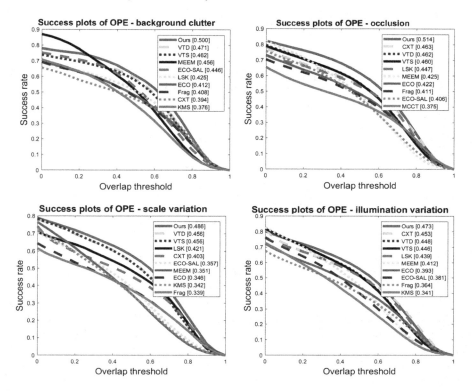

Fig. 5. One-pass evaluation OPE plot for various attributes.

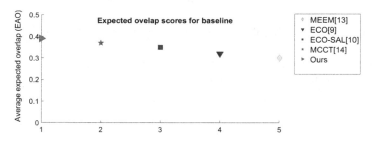

Fig. 6. EAO curve with trackers labelled in order of EAO values

Table 3. Comparison to the baseline: one pass evaluation (OPE)

One-pass evaluation-OTB2015				
	OC	LI	SV	BKC
MCCT	0.71	0.71	0.76	0.64
Ours	0.76	0.61	0.78	0.71

Table 4. Comparison to the baseline: spatial robustness evaluation (SRE)

Robustness analysis-OTB2015			
	OC	LI	SV	BKC
MCCT	0.61	0.69	0.66	0.64
Ours	0.66	0.61	0.68	0.71

Table 5. Comparison to the baseline: temporal robustness evaluation (TRE)

Robustness analysis-OTB2015			
	OC	LI	SV	BKC
MCCT	0.74	0.79	0.67	0.67
Ours	0.66	0.71	0.78	0.70

6   Conclusions and Discussion

In this paper, we proposed saliency-guided correlation tracking with 7 candidate trackers. Our experimental results demonstrate that employing the saliency feature as complimentary feature in multi-cue-based ensemble tracking is helpful for improving the tracking performance. We suggest that saliency map-based region semantic information has further potentials when used as a higher-level tracking feature.

Moreover, we have shown that ensemble tracking benefited from improved candidate tracker robustness. We assume that this feature can benefit many other baseline tracking paradigms as well. This scheme also helps to reduce the tracking model drift problem caused by occluders. It will prevent trackers corruption over time.

Finally, extensive experiments show that our tracker outperformed state-of-the-art methods on popular benchmark datasets.

References

1. Adam, A., Rivlin, E., Shimshoni, I.: Robust fragments-based tracking using the integral histogram. In: IEEE Conference on Computer Vision Pattern Recognition, vol. 1, pp. 798–805 (2011)
2. Aytekin, C., Cricri, F., Aksu, E.: Saliency-enhanced robust visual tracking. In: European Workshop Visual Information Processing arXiv:1802.02783 (2018)
3. Babenko, B., Yang, M.H., Belongie, S.: Robust object tracking with online multiple instance learning. IEEE Trans. Pattern Anal. Mach. Intell. **33**(8), 1619–1632 (2010)
4. Bailer, C., Pagani, A., Stricker, D.: A superior tracking approach: building a strong tracker through fusion. In: Fleet, D., Pajdla, T., Schiele, B., Tuytelaars, T. (eds.) ECCV 2014. LNCS, vol. 8695, pp. 170–185. Springer, Cham (2014). https://doi.org/10.1007/978-3-319-10584-0_12

5. Bertinetto, L., Valmadre, J., Henriques, J.F., Vedaldi, A., Torr, P.H.S.: Fully-convolutional siamese networks for object tracking. In: Hua, G., Jégou, H. (eds.) ECCV 2016. LNCS, vol. 9914, pp. 850–865. Springer, Cham (2016). https://doi.org/10.1007/978-3-319-48881-3_56

6. Bolme, D.S., Beveridge, J.R., Draper, B.A., Lui, Y.M.: Visual object tracking using adaptive correlation filters. In: Proceedings of the IEEE Conference on Computer Vision Pattern Recognition, pp. 2544–2550 (2010)

7. Cheng, M.M., Mitra, N.J., Huang, X., Torr, P.H., Hu, S.M.: Global contrast based salient region detection. IEEE Trans. Pattern Anal. Mach. Intell. **37**(3), 569–582 (2015)

8. Dalal, N., Triggs, B.: Histograms of oriented gradients for human detection. In: IEEE Conference on Computer Vision Pattern Recognition (2005)

9. Danelljan, M., Hager, G., Shahbaz Khan, F., Felsberg, M.: Learning spatially regularized correlation filters for visual tracking. In: Proceedings of the IEEE International Conference on Computer Vision, pp. 4310–4318 (2015)

10. Danelljan, M., Robinson, A., Khan, F.S., Felsberg, M.: Beyond correlation filters: learning continuous convolution operators for visual tracking. In: Leibe, B., Matas, J., Sebe, N., Welling, M. (eds.) ECCV 2016. LNCS, vol. 9909, pp. 472–488. Springer, Cham (2016). https://doi.org/10.1007/978-3-319-46454-1_29

11. Danelljan, M., Bhat, G., Shahbaz Khan, F., Felsberg, M.: Eco: efficient convolution operators for tracking. In: Proceedings of the IEEE Conference on Computer Vision Pattern Recognition, pp. 6638–6646 (2017)

12. Danelljan, M., Häger, G., Khan, F., Felsberg, M.: Accurate scale estimation for robust visual tracking. In: British Machine Vision Conference (2014)

13. Dinh, T.B., Vo, N., Medioni, G.: Context tracker: exploring supporters and distracters in unconstrained environments. In: IEEE Conference on Computer Vision Pattern Recognition, pp. 1177–1184 (2011)

14. Hare, S., et al.: Struck: structured output tracking with kernels. IEEE Trans. Pattern Anal. Mach. Intell. **38**(10), 2096–2109 (2015)

15. Henriques, J.F., Caseiro, R., Martins, P., Batista, J.: High-speed tracking with kernelized correlation filters. IEEE Trans. Pattern Anal. Mach. Intell. **37**(3), 583–596 (2014)

16. Khalid, O., SanMiguel, J.C., Cavallaro, A.: Multi-tracker partition fusion. IEEE Trans. Circ. Syst. Video Technol. **27**(7), 1527–1539 (2016)

17. Kristan, M., et al.: The visual object tracking VOT2016 challenge results. In: Proceedings of the European Conference on Computer Vision Workshops, pp. 777–823 (2016)

18. Kristan, M., et al.: The visual object tracking VOT2017 challenge results. In: Proceedings of the IEEE International Conference on Computer Vision Workshops, pp. 1949–1972 (2017)

19. Kwon, J., Lee, K.M.: Visual tracking decomposition. In: IEEE Conference on Computer Vision Pattern Recognition, pp. 1269–1276 (2010)

20. Kwon, J., Lee, K.M.: Tracking by sampling trackers. In: IEEE International Conference on Computer Vision, pp. 1195–1202 (2010)

21. Li, J., Deng, C., Da Xu, R.Y., Tao, D., Zhao, B.: Robust object tracking with discrete graph-based multiple experts. IEEE Trans. Image Process. **26**(6), 2736–2750 (2017)

22. Li, H., Shen, C., Shi, Q.: Real-time visual tracking using compressive sensing. In: Proceedings of the IEEE Conference on Computer Vision Pattern Recognition, pp. 1305–1312 (2011)

23. Lin, Z., Hua, G., Davis, L.S.: Multiple instance feature for robust part-based object detection. In: Proceedings of the IEEE Conference on Computer Vision Pattern Recognition, pp. 405–412 (2009)
24. Liu, N., Han, J.: DhsNet: deep hierarchical saliency network for salient object detection. In: Proceedings of the IEEE Conference on Computer Vision Pattern Recognition, pp. 678–686 (2016)
25. Liu, B., Huang, J., Yang, L., Kulikowsk, C.: Robust tracking using local sparse appearance model and k-selection. In: IEEE Conference on Computer Vision Pattern Recognition, pp. 1313–1320 (2011)
26. Ma, C., Huang, J.B., Yang, X., Yang, M.H.: Hierarchical convolutional features for visual tracking. In: Proceedings of the IEEE International Conference on Computer Vision, pp. 3074–3082 (2015)
27. Perazzi, F., Krahenbuhl, P., Pritch, Y., Hornung, A.: Saliency filters, contrast based filtering for salient region detection. In: Proceedings IEEE Conference on Computing Vision Pattern Recognition, pp. 733–740 (2012)
28. Simonyan, K., Zisserman, A.: Very deep convolutional networks for large-scale image recognition. arXiv preprint arXiv:1409.1556 (2014)
29. Tavakoli, H.R., Moin, M.S., Heikkila, J.: Local similarity number and its application to object tracking. Int. J. Adv. Robot. Syst. **10**(3), 184 (2013)
30. Van De Weijer, J., Schmid, C., Verbeek, J., Larlus, D.: Learning color names for real-world applications. IEEE Trans. Image Process. **18**(7), 1512–1523 (2009)
31. Vedaldi, A., Lenc, K.: MatConvNet: convolutional neural networks for Matlab. In: ACM International Conference on Multimedia, pp. 689–692 (2015)
32. Wang, N., Zhou, W., Tian, Q., Hong, R., Wang, M., Li, H.: Multi-cue correlation filters for robust visual tracking. In: Proceedings of the IEEE Conference on Computer Vision Pattern Recognition, pp. 4844–4853 (2018)
33. Wu, Y., Lim, J., Yang, M.H.: Object tracking benchmark. IEEE Trans. Pattern Anal. Mach. Intell. **37**(9), 1834–1848 (2015)
34. Zhang, J., Ma, S., Sclaroff, S.: MEEM: robust tracking via multiple experts using entropy minimization. In: Fleet, D., Pajdla, T., Schiele, B., Tuytelaars, T. (eds.) ECCV 2014. LNCS, vol. 8694, pp. 188–203. Springer, Cham (2014). https://doi.org/10.1007/978-3-319-10599-4_13
35. Zhang, P., Wang, D., Lu, H., Wang, H.: Non-rigid object tracking via deep multi-scale spatial-temporal discriminative saliency maps. arXiv preprint arXiv:1802.07957 (2018)
36. Zhang, K., Zhang, L., Liu, Q., Zhang, D., Yang, M.-H.: Fast visual tracking via dense spatio-temporal context learning. In: Fleet, D., Pajdla, T., Schiele, B., Tuytelaars, T. (eds.) ECCV 2014. LNCS, vol. 8693, pp. 127–141. Springer, Cham (2014). https://doi.org/10.1007/978-3-319-10602-1_9

Measuring Apple Size Distribution from a Near Top–Down Image

Luke Butters[1](✉), Zezhong Xu[2](✉), Khoa Le Trung[3](✉),
and Reinhard Klette[3](✉)

[1] Hectre - Orchard Management Software, Auckland 1021, New Zealand
luke.butters0@gmail.com
[2] Changzhou Institute of Technology, Changzhou 213031, China
xuzz_1999@263.net
[3] Department of Electrical and Electronic Engineering,
Auckland University of Technology, Auckland 1010, New Zealand
bxp3319@autuni.ac.nz, rklette@aut.ac.nz

Abstract. The paper presents a method for estimating size information of a bin of apples; we document the machine learning and computer vision techniques applied or developed for solving this task. The system was required to return a statistical distribution of diameter sizes based off visible fruit on the top layer of an apple bin image. A custom data–set was collected before training a *Mask R-CNN* object detector. Image transformations were used to recover real world dimensions. The presented research was undertaken for further integration into an app where apple growers have the ability to get fast estimations of apple size.

1 Introduction

Automation [14], to enhance human capabilities, has been developing strongly since the 1900s. More time and resource efficient systems allowed for higher production and in turn, higher wages.

Today *Industry 4.0* [10] describes a new wave of automation where data exchange is being utilised like never before. Such technologies are further improving the human potential. An important date in an apple growers calender is picking time. The farm can employ dozens or hundreds of workers to delicately fill bins of apples; see Fig. 1. Once the bins are filled they are sent to a pack–house for packing, often being a third party organisation. At the time of bin filling on the farm, there is no recorded data indicating fruit size. The following issues would be resolved by forecasting an estimation of fruit size before being sent for packing:

1. Pack–house managers could improve logistics by stationing workers at the optimal positions,
2. sales and marketing process improvement due to improved quality forecasting,

© Springer Nature Switzerland AG 2019
C. Lee et al. (Eds.): PSIVT 2019, LNCS 11854, pp. 255–268, 2019.
https://doi.org/10.1007/978-3-030-34879-3_20

Fig. 1. A full bin of apples taken at an orchard in the Nelson region of New Zealand.

3. provide an additional level of checking so growers can hold pack–houses accountable.

Currently pack–house managers are undergoing extra efforts in logistics stationing workers in the correct locations around the facility. When new fruit enters the sorting machine, repositioning of workers is common. Workers must adapt to a new batch of fruit which handles differently to the previous batch. By forecasting an estimation of the incoming fruit before entering the pack–house, these changes can be more efficiently handled.

Fruit growers often send their fruit to the pack–house without having any record of what the size of their fruit may be. They rely entirely on the packing company providing transparent information regarding the size of their fruit. By giving growers the freedom to estimate size themselves, an additional 'check & balance' provides more accountability.

A method was developed incorporating a mobile camera for data acquisition. This paper delivers the machine learning and computer vision [9] techniques designed or selected and used:

1. Forming a custom image data–set,
2. training a *Mask R-CNN* object detector [5,8],
3. applying geometric transforms,
4. producing statistical size distributions from object detection.

To train a custom object detector to locate individual apples in an image, a balanced data–set of $3,000$ apple bin images (similar to Fig. 1) were acquired.[1]

---

[1] Three apple orchards in the Nelson region of New Zealand agreed for us to photograph: Hoddys Fruit Company, Tyrella Orchards and McLean Orchard.

Training an object detection algorithm required the selection of sufficient training data. Utilising transfer learning from the open source COCO data–set, ten training images were selected from the data–set to form a training sub–set. 1,000 apples were individually labelled across the ten selected training images. *Mask R-CNN* was trained with the labelled test images to produce a model ready for inference.

With the object detection scheme returning bounding box and mask image pixel coordinates, a transformation processes was included to convert to real world coordinates. Due to the app users standing height in the orchard during image acquisition, it was impractical to achieve a direct top–down angle. It was important to present meaningful data to the user who understands millimetres or inches. The four apple bin corner coordinates were stored using a manual selection before a perspective transform [12] was applied to the image. With physical bin dimensions known, the apple bin top was transformed to simulate a top–down view of the bin where one edge pixel equalled 1.00 mm.

Considering apple shape distortions introduced by the perspective transformation, measurements of apple diameter were taken using two possible methods. Utilising detected individual apple bounding box dimensions, the box height was discarded while the box width was taken as apple diameter. An alternative approach discussed involved fitting ellipses over the individual apple masks before taking the ellipse minor diameter as the apple diameter.

An assumption was made where apples were considered to be round, any maximum distance measurement detected would be considered as apple width. This assumption naturally creates a limitation with the technology. In reality apples can vary in width and height, even within the same variety.

2   COCO Trained Model for Quick Inference

To run accurate and robust apple detections across images, it was apparent that a custom data–set of apple bin images was needed to be collected. Once sufficient data was acquired, a training sub–set could be selected for labelling and then re–training of an object detector model.

Prior to acquiring images, an 'off–the–shelf' *Mask R–CNN* object detection model, pre–trained with the COCO [4] data–set, was considered [6]. Running inference on such pre–trained models was seen as a fast way to determine how the results of a custom trained model may behave. It was also important to establish if it necessary to acquire huge quantities of data when open–source data was available.

Common Objects in Context (COCO) is a large open–source data–set sponsored by *Common Visual Data Foundation* (CVDF), *Microsoft*, *Facebook* and *Might AI*. It contains over 330k images with over 200k already labelled, making it ideal for object detection and segmentation. Over 80 object categories are present within the data–set including 'apple'.

Testing images were acquired to and detections were made. A near top–down image (Fig. 2) along with a close–up image (Fig. 3) were considered.

Fig. 2. Detection visualisation for an apple bin image using *Mask R-CNN* pre–trained with COCO data–set.

Fig. 3. Detection visualisation for an apple bin image using *Mask R-CNN* pre–trained with COCO data–set.

Objects labelled as 'apple' in the data–set were labelled for a range of apple appearances. Not only individual apples came under the category, but also groups and slices of apples. This caused poor false detections when tested. It was clear that the entire apple bin top had been classified as part of the 'apple' class. Positive detections proved to fit masks accurately through visual inspection, with a low confidence level.

Running testing images through the *Mask R-CNN* object detector pre–trained with COCO data–set proved that it was necessary to collect custom data to eliminate groups of apples being detected, and successfully detect more apples from the top–down view.

3   Custom Training Data and Labelling

Data–sets are a crucial element for the application of machine learning and computer vision. Unlike image classification, object detection requires not only large amounts of data, but also labelled data. This usually results in expensive and time consuming training development where each image in a data–set must be individually labelled to distinguish which objects within an image relate to those of the defined classes.

Given the opportunity to acquire custom data, a field trip was undertaken in the Nelson region of New Zealand. The region is well known for its apple orchards. Three apple orchards were visited over two days where 3, 000 full apple bin images were taken.

To ensure robust and accurate individual apple detection in varying environments, it was important to ensure the data–set include the correct data to form a balanced training sub–set. Given only a single class, the following were considered when forming the balanced set:

1. Camera angle including pitch and rotation,
2. image scale,
3. weather conditions including sunny, overcast and rainy.

By ensuring that each consideration was well represented in the training data, the detections produced could be generated accurately over a range of input image conditions. Given the practical application, apple growers needed to be able to take measurements in any of the proposed weather conditions. There was also no guarantee that they would take the image with perfect scale and angle, therefore the system was designed to provide such flexibility.

Ten images were hand picked from the data–set to form the training sub–set. *VGG Image Annotator* [13], a browser based tool used for labelling image data was used to label the ten training images with 1,000 total individual apples. A validation set was also selected and contained 150 individual apples across a single image.

Considering the custom data–set described, *Mask R-CNN* object detection scheme was utilised. To get the most out of a small custom data–set, transfer learning was applied where the training labels were used to retrain the model over the open source COCO [4] data–set. The training processed output a *.h5* Keras weight file used for model inference.

4   Perspective Transformation

With the Keras weight file ready for deployment, inference was possible with an apple bin input image. Given the project scope, the real world coordinates were

Fig. 4. Apple bin image after perspective transformation into real world coordinates from top–down view.

needed. Simply applying object detection and returning pixel coordinates was not sufficient. Given that physical apple bin dimensions were a known quantity, a perspective transformation [2] was applied as a step to recover real world coordinates. This re–shaped the image such that it appeared as a top–down image.

The OpenCV *warpPerspective*() function [11] was applied where *src* was the input image, *dst* was the output image and $\mathbf{M} = (M_{i,j})$ was the 3×3 transformation matrix:

$$dst(x,y) = src\left(\frac{M_{11}x + M_{12}y + M_{13}}{M_{31}x + M_{32}y + M_{33}}, \frac{M_{21}x + M_{22}y + M_{23}}{M_{31}x + M_{32}y + M_{33}}\right)$$

Input images to the proposed detection scheme could appear with varying angle, pitch or scale. Given that all four corners of the apple bin were visible within the input image, the corner coordinates were recorded within the image space. A perspective transform was applied to warp the image to a normalised $1,200 \times 1,155$ pixels. This corresponded to 1 pixel per 1.00 mm; see Fig. 4.

For app implementation, apple bin corner coordinates could be acquired by one of the following:

1. Manually select the corner positions using the touch screen, or
2. implement a light weight object detection scheme such as *SSD Mobilenet* [7] to automate.

5   Object Detection

Having the input image for inference in the top–down normalised view, *Mask R-CNN* object detection was applied [1]. The purpose to draw masks and bounding boxes around individual apples visible on the top layer of the apple bin. The perspective transform giving conversion from image coordinates to world coordinates, the pixel measurements obtained by the object detection were displayed in millimetres for the $1,200 \times 1,155$ input image.

Fig. 5. Apple bin image with fitted masks and bounding boxes after perspective transformation into real world coordinates from top–down view.

The following configuration parameters were chosen for object detection:

1. Maximum number of detections $= 300$,
2. non–maximum suppression $= 0.2$,
3. minimum confidence $= 0.5$.

Results of the proposed *Mask R-CNN* object detection scheme were accurate considering visual inspection with fitting masks and boxes around individual apples; see Fig. 5. A further improvement could be seen by retraining the model using labels of perspective warped apples as well as un–transformed apples.

6   Real World Coordinates

Data returned from the object detector describing the mask and bounding box information was used to determine the true physical diameters of the visible

Fig. 6. Apple bin image with fitted masks and bounding boxes after perspective transformation into real world coordinates from top–down view. Shape distortion seen in height and width direction due to poor input image angle and position.

apples. It was important to understand the apple diameters in millimetres or inches.

During the process of perspective transformation, apple shape distortion or stretching was seen to occur. The distortion itself was most radical when the input apple bin image was far away from the top–down angle and pitch; see Fig. 6. When the input image was closer to the top–down angle and pitch, the shape distortion was minimised; see Fig. 5.

To mitigate apple shape distortions seen at the output of the perspective transformed image, two methods were considered to recover the real world coordinates:

1. Fitting ellipses over the detected apple masks and measuring minor diameter, or
2. taking individual bounding box widths for controlled camera angles.

6.1 Ellipse Fitting and Minor Diameter Measurement

Apple shape distortion when referenced to individual apples occurred in one direction. By fitting ellipses over each apple in the perspective transformed image, the minor diameter remained undistorted where as the major diameter experienced the most change in shape.

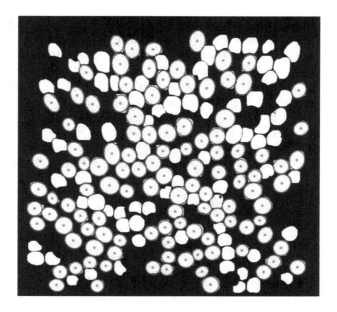

Fig. 7. Ellipses, calculated following [15], fitted over binary apple segments.

A method proposed by [3,15] was used to fit ellipses over a binary image of detected apple segments; see Fig. 7. The chosen ellipse fitting algorithm is a region-based (as opposed to contour-based) method and deals with clusters of apples well.

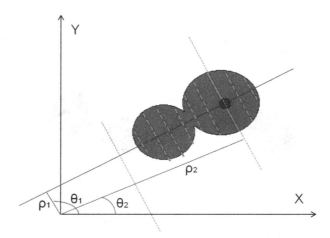

Fig. 8. Mathematical representation of two touching apple segments.

In our application of apple diameter detection regrading two touching apples, they are detected as one elliptic object with our method. The detected ellipse is denoted as $(x_0, y_0), a, b, \theta_1$, and the corresponding voting distance along voting angle θ_1 is denoted as ρ_1. The count of pixels in this segment is denoted as P. Figure 8 shows a mathematical representation of two touching apple shapes.

If $P > 2,500$ and $a/b > 1.5$, we assume a segment describes two touching apples. If $\theta_1 < 90$, let $\theta_2 = \theta_1 + 90$. Otherwise, let $\theta_2 = \theta_1 - 90$.

In the θ_2 column of the accumulator, the maximum voting value is searched, and denoted by M. The corresponding voting distance is denoted by ρ_2. Then a circular object is defined as the following. The radius R is $M/2$ and the center (x_0, y_0) is:

$$x_0 = \frac{\rho_2 \cdot \sin \theta_1 - \rho_1 \cdot \sin \theta_2}{\sin(\theta_1 - \theta_2)}$$

$$y_0 = \frac{\rho_1 \cdot \cos \theta_2 - \rho_2 \cdot \cos \theta_1}{\sin(\theta_1 - \theta_2)}$$

After a circular object is detected, the corresponding votes are removed in the accumulator. In column θ_i of the accumulator, this circular object votes for the limited amount of cells, which ranges from ρ_b to ρ_t, where

$$\rho_b = x_0 \cdot \cos \theta_i + y_0 \cdot \sin \theta_i - R$$
$$\rho_t = x_0 \cdot \cos \theta_i + y_0 \cdot \sin \theta_i + R$$

From ρ_b to ρ_t, the voting value $A(\rho, \theta_i)$ of a cell is reduced by

$$2 \cdot \sqrt{R^2 - (\rho - (x_0 \cdot \cos \theta_i + y_0 \cdot \sin \theta_i))^2}$$

Then the maximum voting value is re–searched, a circular object is defined similarly. Fig. 9 shows touching apple shapes with fitted ellipse before and after the proposed method.

Fig. 9. Touching apple shapes before and after applying the proposed method.

A histogram (see Fig. 10) was produced to visualise the distribution of the fitted ellipses minor diameters from Fig. 7.

The proposed ellipse method for recovering near true apple diameter was reliant on object detection with masks (instance segmentation). Bounding box fitting would not be possible with this option.

6.2   Box Width Measurement

An additional method for recovering the true apple diameter was proposed where the bounding box widths were taken as the near true apple diameter. When the input image was taken as close to top–down as possible from the position seen in Fig. 5, the shape distortion was reduced and most radical in the box height direction. The box widths were not affected to the same extent.

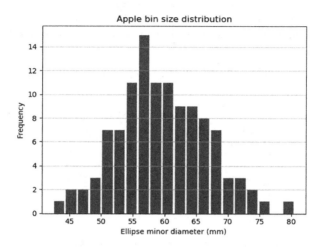

Fig. 10. Distribution function generated from a list of returned minor diameter size values in millimetres considering the detected apples from a processed input image Fig. 7.

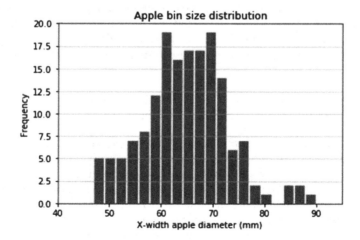

Fig. 11. Distribution function generated from a list of returned apple size values in millimetres considering the detected apples from a processed input image.

A size distribution plot was generated based on a list of detected apple bounding box widths; see Fig. 11. Key apple information including maximum size. minimum size, mean size, standard deviation and variance were all stored in reference to the input apple bin image.

6.3   Method Comparison

The two proposed methods for retrieving the apple size information were compared for the input image used to produce Fig. 5. Where the ellipse method used included 68.48% of the data points from the bounding box method.

Table 1. Return data comparison for the two proposed methods; ellipse and bounding box width.

Data	Ellipse result (mm)	Bounding box width results (mm)
Mean	59.7	64.8
Variance	49.2	65.6
Standard–deviation	7.0	8.1
Maximum	80.5	90.0
Minimum	42.4	47.0

A comparison was made between the two proposed methods; ellipse minor diameter measurements and bounding box width measurements seen in Table 1. With a reduced sample size of 68.48% when compared to the bounding box width method, the ellipse minor diameter method results varied. It was expected that the maximum and minimum values of the ellipse method would be less than those of the bounding box method due to the nature of the measurement. When taking the width of an apple segment that has been distorted mostly in the height (but also the width) direction, its fitted ellipse minor diameter will always remain smaller.

7   Conclusion

The proposed methods introduced throughout the paper formed the basis proof of concept for the future implementation of a vision system capable of detecting visible apples on the top layer of a full apple bin (see Fig. 12) and estimating their individual sizes. Apple growers adopting the technology will have the opportunity to estimate their product value at time of picking to streamline the sales and logistics process along with increase information transparency with pack–houses.

To train an object detector, a custom data–set was collected in the Nelson region of New Zealand across three apple orchards. Ten carefully selected images of the data–set were hand picked to form a training sub–set. The images represented various weather/illumination, camera angle, pitch and scale conditions. It

Fig. 12. Colour–splash visualisation of correctly detected apples over a grey apple bin image in the orchard setting.

was necessary to form a balanced training sub–set to allow the object detector to run inference accurately under a range of input conditions. Across the ten training images, 1,000 visible apples were individually labelled to retrain a *Mask R-CNN* object detection model over the COCO open source data–set.

For input images, a perspective transformation was applied to adjust the image to a top–down view of the apple bin. Creating an image to real world coordinate conversion. Given the physical apple bin dimensions were known, the adjusted bin image was scaled to 1 pixel per 1.00 mm.

Mask R-CNN object detection was applied to the top–down normalised view input images to fit masks and bounding boxes around visible images. To determine near true apple size in millimetres, two options were considered where one relied on fitted mask data and the other on bounding box data.

Using mask image data, ellipses were fit over a binary segmentation map of the detected apples. A list of minor ellipse diameters were returned to form a distribution of apple size estimation. The proposed option assumes that the minor diameter values were not affected by perspective transformation shape distortions, while the major diameter was affected.

Bounding box data was used as a second approach to estimate the apple sizes based off *Mask R-CNN* detections. For input images taken from the ideal position (see Fig. 5), bounding box widths were affected by shape distortions far less than bounding box heights. A list of bounding box widths were returned as near true apple sizes.

Acknowledgement. This research has been supported by Hectre - Orchard Management Software, New Zealand. Authors thank orchards in the Nelson region of New Zealand (Hoddys Fruit Company, Tyrella Orchards and McLean Orchard) for collaboration.

References

1. Analytics Vidya Guide: Building a Mask R-CNN Model for Detecting Car Damage. http://analyticsvidhya.com/blog/2018/07/building-mask-r-cnn-model-detecting-damage-cars-python/. Accessed 19 July 2019
2. Blinn, J.: A trip down the graphics pipeline: the homogeneous perspective transform. IEEE Comput. Graph. Appl. **13**(3), 75–80 (1993)
3. Butters, L., Xu, Z., Klette, R.: Using machine vision to command a 6-axis robot arm to act on a randomly placed zinc die cast product. In: Proceedings of the International Conference on Control Computer Vision, South Korea (2019, to appear)
4. Common Objects in Context. http://cocodataset.org/#home. Accessed 6 July 2019
5. Dhiman, A., Khan, W., Klette, R.: Pothole detection using deep learning. In: Proceedings of the t-TECH19, Christchurch (2019). http://itsnz.org/files-reports
6. GitHub repository: Matterport Mask R-CNN. http://github.com/matterport/Mask_RCNN. Accessed 19 July 2019
7. Howard, A., et al.: MobileNets: efficient convolutional neural networks for mobile vision applications. arXiv:1704.04861 (2017)
8. He, K., Gkioxari, G., Dollar, P., Girshick, R.: Mask R-CNN. In: IEEE International Conference on Computer Vision, pp. 2961–2969 (2017)
9. Klette, R.: Concise Computer Vision. Springer, London (2014). https://doi.org/10.1007/978-1-4471-6320-6
10. Lasi, H., Fettke, P., Kemper, H., Feld, T., Hoffman, M.: Industry 4.0. Bus. Inf. Syst. Eng. **6**(4), 239–242 (2014)
11. OpenCV Documentation on Geometric Transformations. http://docs.opencv.org/2.4/modules/imgproc/doc/geometric_transformations.html. Accessed 14 July 2019
12. Py Image Search: 4 Point OpenCV getPerspective Transform Example. http://pyimagesearch.com/2014/08/25/4-point-opencv-getperspective-transform-example/. Accessed 6 July 2019
13. VGG Image Annotator 1.0.6. http://robots.ox.ac.uk/~vgg/software/via/via-1.0.6.html. Accessed 6 July 2019
14. Wikipedia 20th Century Automation. https://en.wikipedia.org/wiki/Automation/#20th_century. Accessed 18 Jun 2019
15. Xu, Z., Xu, S., Qian, C., Klette, R.: Accurate ellipse extraction in low-quality images. In: Proceedings of the Machine Vision Applications, pp. 1–5 (2019)

Multi-temporal Registration of Environmental Imagery Using Affine Invariant Convolutional Features

Asim Khan[1(✉)], Anwaar Ulhaq[1,2(✉)], and Randall W. Robinson[1]

[1] Institute for Sustainable Industries Liveable Cities, Victoria University,
Melbourne, VIC, Australia
asim.khan@live.vu.edu.au
[2] Charles Sturt University, Dubbo, NSW, Australia
aulhaq@csu.edu.au

Abstract. Repeat photography is a practice of collecting multiple images of the same subject at the same location but at different times-tamps for comparative analysis. The visualisation of such imagery can provide a valuable insight for continuous monitoring and change detection. In Victoria, Australia, citizen science and environmental monitoring are integrated through the visitor-based repeat photography of national parks and coastal areas. Repeat photography, however, poses enormous challenges for automated data analysis and visualisation due to variations in viewpoints, scales, luminosity and camera attributes. To address these challenges brought by data variability, this paper introduces a robust multi-temporal image registration approach based on affine invariance and convolutional neural network architecture. Our experimental evaluation on a large repeat photography dataset validates the role of multi-temporal image registration for better visualisation of environmental monitoring imagery. Our research will establish a baseline for the broad area of multi-temporal analysis.

Keywords: Repeat photography · Image registration · Deep learning · Descriptors

1 Introduction

Australia is the 6th largest country in the world by land with 16% area covered by naive vegetation, forests and woodlands. There are more than 500 national parks with almost 4% land. Australian government is seriously taking every step to take care of the natural environment and keep this country green. Federal and state governments organise various projects to give fresh and healthy air to the people and play a vital role in the global warming reduction. Environmental monitoring is essential for all these natural resources especially to protect and conserve the green areas and national parks. This is being achieved with the help of land-care groups, environment groups, indigenous organisations and local

© Springer Nature Switzerland AG 2019
C. Lee et al. (Eds.): PSIVT 2019, LNCS 11854, pp. 269–280, 2019.
https://doi.org/10.1007/978-3-030-34879-3_21

councils by various means such as through drones/UAVs, satellite and remote sensing. However, such efforts and approaches have their pros and cons and require extensive resources for operation.

An alternative approach for environmental monitoring could be based on citizen science, which actually engages local communities and visitors to look after the natural resources. It is achievable by taking photos of visited areas through their smart phones and cameras and sharing with environmental scientists. Those photographs can be helpful for important observations and appropriate interventions could be designed if any significant change is found during manual inspection. One example of such projects is the "The Flucker Post Project" [1], which involves numerous points in more than 150 locations all over Australia. Visitors and local communities are encouraged to take photos and send them back to the main website. Such projects are based on the concept of repeat photography which is an approach for comparing photos of the same location taken at different timestamps [2]. To date, the project is successfully running and have collected valuable imaging data about vegetation, parks, catchments and waterways. One Example is shown in Fig. 1. This extensive image data is currently being monitored manually to suggest appropriate interventions by state organisations like Parks Victoria. This manual approach, however, is less effective due to the abundance of data and thus more automation is required to facilitate and speed up the data analysis. It is even more challenging in case of repeat photography data as manual image analysis is so cumbersome and inefficient.

However, direct automation of such large image collection is not suitable for any image analysis due to variations in imaging conditions such as variations in viewpoints, scales, luminosity and camera characteristics. In other words, this multi-temporal image data is not registered. Thus, robust multi-temporal image registration is urgently required. This paper proposes a robust multi-temporal image registration technique for environmental repeat photography data based on deep convolutional networks to facilitate automated environmental monitoring.

Multi-temporal image registration is a process of overlaying at least two or more images of the same subject but taken on different time, from different view points and sensors. Actually this process aligns geometrically two images known as sensed and reference images respectively. Over the years, various multi-temporal image registration approaches are proposed for applications such as remote sensing. It can be based on area (intensity values) or features (hand crafted feature like SIFT [3]). There is abundance of hand-crafted or shallow learning feature based techniques due to their robustness against different imaging variations. Most recently, few robust approaches are proposed based on deep features [4,5] that provide better accuracy and quality performance compared to hand crafted feature based techniques due to end-to-end feature learning. However, these approaches are not robust against affine transformations which is imperative feature of repeat photography. It is partially due to the fact that deep convolutional networks do not provide good generalisation for small image transformations [6]. A deformable image registration for medical images is introduced by De Vos et al. [7] but the scope is different from multi-temporal nature of environmental imagery. To address this gap in literature, this paper has introduced an affine invariant deep image registration techniques that can handle imaging variations well in repeat photography while maintaining the quality performance.

We attempt to answer the following research questions: (i) How deep learning and citizen science can be combined to achieve automated community based environmental monitoring? (ii) How multi-temporal image registration can simultaneously be made accurate with deep convolutional networks and robust against affine transformations? (iii) Can deepness of convolutional models increase the performance in image registration?

By addressing these research questions, this paper makes the following contributions: (i) We introduce a deep affine invariant network for non-rigid image registration of multi-temporal repeat photography; (ii) We integrate affine invariance and robust outlier detection for image point matching for robust multi-temporal image registration.

The rest of this paper is organized as follows: Sect. 1 reviews the related work. Section 3 provides a detailed description of our proposed network design and discusses how robust point matching is performed. Section 4 outlines our experimental set-up and interprets the results. Section 5 summarizes this paper.

Fig. 1. Illustrative repeat photography from Flucker Post community based image collection: Right image is reference post (coded as WEPS1) installed at Point Richie, Warrnambool, Victoria, Australia, left six photos were taken by different visitors at different times of the year. It can be observed that there is little control how visitors capture images from post or its surroundings. Variations in viewpoints, scales, lighting conditions and seasonal variations pose enormous challenges for automated multi-temporal image registration.

2   Prior Work

Community Based Monitoring (CBM): Community based monitoring (CBM) is defined by Whitelaw et al. [8] as "process where concerned citizens, government agencies, industry, academia, community groups, and local institutions collaborate to monitor, track and respond to issues of common community (environmental) concern". Over the last few years, a large number of CBM projects were initiated from around the world mostly located in the USA, Australia, Canada, and the Russian Federation. Lawrence and Pretty [9,10] have reported that since 1990s, up to 500,000 community based groups were established in varying environmental and social contexts only in the USA and Canada. Mobile services and technology for community based monitoring is covered [11]. Internet of things (IoT) and related CBM architecture for smart cities [12]. Notable reviews [11–16] provide valuable insight into community based monitoring projects. These projects collect abundant multi-model data for analysis.

Repeat Photography: Is used in CBM research studies due to availability of low cost cameras and smart phones. Different methods and applications of repeat photography is presented by Webb [17]. Various projects are available in literature. An analysis of vegetation change in the San Juan Mountains using repeat photography was given by Zier et al. [18] and in the Appalachian Mountains by Hendrick et al. [19]. Digital repeat photography for phenological research in forest ecosystems was conducted by Sonnentag et al. [2]. A tourist-based environmental monitoring system based on principals of repeat photography is introduced by Augar and Fluker [1] with the help of Flucker posts at various locations in Australia. School kids were involved to collect environmental imagery [20]. Repeat photography has rarely been used in Australia. Vegetation changes in Australia over a century using repeat photography was presented by Pickard et al. [21]. However, majority of all mentioned approaches involve cumbersome manual inspection work and lack automation. Recent advances in computer vision, image processing and deep learning enable us to automate analysis of repeat photography. Deep learning techniques especially convolutional neural networks have appeared as revolutionary development tool for automated recognition and image analysis [22].

Image Registration and Deep Learning: Repeat photography based environmental monitoring requires precessing of image collection captured over time. One of the most important steps is image registration; more specifically, in the context of the present study, it is multi-temporal image registration. Image registration seeks to remove the two-date images geometric position inconsistent, making the same image coordinates reflect the same objects. Notable surveys [23–26] cover various techniques for image registration. Image registration techniques can be classified based on area (e.g. raw intensity values) or features (e.g SIFT [3]). Success of deep learning has also effected registration process: Recently, deep approaches are proposed [4,5,27] that provide better accuracy and quality performance compared to hand crafted feature based techniques due to end-to-end feature learning. However, these approaches are not robust against affine transformations which is imperative feature of repeat photogra-phy. Although our work is related to the similar domain, we attempt to address shortcomings of the previous work in our proposed approach.

3   The Proposed Deep Image Registration Framework

In this section, we describe the architecture of the proposed deep image regis-tration framework for multi-temporal image registration of repeat photographic data.

Feature based image registration usually comprises the following stages: At first, a pair of images (sensed and reference) are submitted for feature detection and feature descriptors are calculated. Preliminary point-wise correspondence or point sets are then estimated according to distance based metrics as feature pre-matching step refined by inlier detection. It is then followed by optimal transformation parameters estimation that guides the re-sampling and image transformation of the sensed image.

The first goal is to find deep discriminative descriptors. For this purpose, we make use of deep convolutional network that comprises two parts. The first part spatially transforms input image by generating an affine transformation for each input sample. It then extracts local key points from feature maps of a convolutional neural network. The second part outputs local descriptors given patches cropped around the key points. We name these parts as affine-invariant deep feature extractor and deep feature descriptor.

Generation of Feature Maps: We first use ResNet [28] to generate a rich fea-ture map from an image I, which can be used to extract deep keypoint locations. The reason to select ResNet is its effectiveness to build deep networks without overfitting by injecting identity mappings or so-called shortcut connections. It also solves vanishing gradient problem, which refers to the situation that the gra-dients from where the loss function is calculated, when the network is too deep, would shrink to zero after several iterations of the chain rule. Such a problem causes the weights never updating their values and thus results in no learning. ResNet with three blocks, block of convolutional filters of 5×5 followed by batch normalization, ReLU activations, and another group of 5×5 convolutions. These convolutions are zero-padded to get the same output size as the input, with 16 output channels.

Affine-Invariant Deep Feature Extractor: After each block, we integrate spatial transformer module [29] into the network that introduces explicit spatial transformations on feature maps, without making any changes to CNN loss function. During spatial transformer implementation, we use 2D spatial affine transformations that help during affine invariant keypoint detection. Suppose that the output pixels are defined to lie on a regular grid $G = G_i$ of elements of a generic feature map, τ_θ is affine transformations, a_i^s, b_i^s as the source coordinates in the input feature map, and a_i^t, b_i^t as the target coordinates of the regular grid in the output feature map. We can write the transformation introduced by affine transformer as:

$$\begin{bmatrix} a_i^s \\ b_i^s \end{bmatrix} = \tau_\theta(G_i) = \tau_\theta \begin{bmatrix} a_i^t \\ b_i^t \\ 1 \end{bmatrix} = \begin{bmatrix} \theta_{11} & \theta_{12} & \theta_{13} \\ \theta_{21} & \theta_{22} & \theta_{23} \end{bmatrix} \begin{bmatrix} a_i^t \\ b_i^t \\ 1 \end{bmatrix} \tag{1}$$

The first part of spatial transformer is a localisation network that takes the feature map as an input, and outputs the parameters of the spatial transformation that should be applied to the feature map. In second part, the grid generator takes the predicted transformation parameters and use them to generate a sampling grid (a set of points where the input map should be sampled to produce the transformed output). At last, the sampler takes the feature map and the sampling grid are taken as inputs to the sampler, generating the output map sampled from the input at the grid points. For more implementation details of spatial transformer, please refer to previous work [29]. The transformed feature maps are robust to affine-transformations and we use them to extract affine-invariant deep discriminative features.

For capturing scale-space response, we resize each feature map n times, at uniform intervals between $1/t$ and t, where n = 3 and t = 2. The resulting maps are then convolved with n 5×5 filters, resulting in n score maps. It is then followed by non-maximum suppression by using a softmax operator over 15×15 windows in a convolutional manner, which results in n saliency maps. These saliency maps are again resized to original image size and score is unaffected due to their scale-invariant nature. All these saliency maps are then merged into one map M using another softmax function. Similarly, orientation map θ is calculated using the arctan function following an existing framework [30]. We choose the top K elements of M as keypoint and we have the information of the form $\{x, y, s, \theta\}$ about these keypoints. These keypoints are invariant to affine transformations and we call them affine-invariant deep discriminative features.

Deep Feature Descriptors: For this goal, we crop image patches around the selected key point locations. We crop and resize them to 32×32. Our descriptor network is an L2 Net [31]. It comprises convolutional layers followed by Local Response Normalization layer (LRN) as the output layer to produce unit descriptors. It results in 128 dimensional descriptor D for every patch.

Feature Pre-matching and Outlier Removal: For feature matching, we use Euclidean-distance d between the respective feature descriptors of feature points p and q as:

$$d(p, q) = d(D(p), D(q)) \tag{2}$$

These matches may have many outliers for multi-temporal image registration. In other words, we are interested in detecting among F nearest points in a given feature map, $(p_k)_{k=1,\dots,F}$ and their predicted corresponding matches $r(p_k)_{k=1,\dots,F}$ in the corresponding reference feature map, that is, the largest subset of key points that follow the same affine model. To achieve such outlier removal, we use an algorithm, namely the Affine Parameters Estimation by Random Sampling (APERS) [32], which detects the outliers in a given set of matched points.

Non-rigid Transformation Estimation: Finding point sets and their correspondences is the most crucial step. Point sets are represented by sensed set, $(x_i | x_i \in R^d, i = \{1, \ldots, N\})$ and target set $(t_i | t_i \in R^d, i = \{1, \ldots, M\})$, where the sensed set is faced with a transformation τ. Due to repeat photography, we assume that there exists a significant overlap between the sensed and reference point sets. If we know the feature descriptor D that can be used to get correspondence, following the approach described in [33], the point set registration can be formulated as follows:

$$E(\tau) = \lambda \phi(\tau) + \sum_{i=1}^{N} \sum_{j=1}^{M} exp\left(\frac{||t_j - x'_j||^2}{\sigma^2}\right.$$
$$\left. - \frac{(D(t_j) - D(x'_j))^T \sum^{-1} D(t_j) - D(x'_j)}{\xi^2}\right) \qquad (3)$$

where $x'_i = x_i = \tau$ is the transformed point, $\sum$ denotes the covariance matrix of the feature descriptors, $\sigma.\xi$ are scales, $\phi(.)$, the regularization, and λ is used to control the level of smoothness. We use spatially constrained Gaussian Fields (SCGF) for non-rigid transformation estimation [33].

Image Resampling and Transformation: The estimated transformation parameters finally guide the re-sampling and warping of the sensed image for getting registered image. Due to artefacts and simplicity of pixel level registration, the refinement of coarsely registered images to sub-pixel accuracy is performed. However, rather interpolating image grayscales, we uses functions of the graylevels like [34].

4   Experimental Results and Discussion

We conducted experimental studies based on publicly available image dataset. In this section, we will provide a brief description of the dataset (Flucker Post Vegetation Dataset), registration accuracy and other performance comparison with state-of-the-art techniques. Our network is based on keras (with TensorFlow backend) and NVIDIA P2000 Quadro GPU.

Flucker Post Vegetation Dataset: This image dataset is collected as a part of the "The Flucker Post Project" [1]. This project is based on citizen science and a part of the project is to place photo capturing posts in over 150 locations all over Australia. Visitors and local communities are encouraged to take photos and send them back to the main website. In each location, multiple images are taken from same point called as Flucker post. This project has now more than 2000 images, all of which are organized in different albums related to different locations across Australia. The web address of this project is http://www.flukerpost.com/. However, the problem is that all those photos are taken from different viewpoints and camera sensors. The image resolution also varies across the dataset. Photos are captured in different seasons as well as different timestamps of the day. All these make the work challenging. Therefore, it becomes very difficult to compare and extract some valuable information like vegetational change detection.

Subjective Comparison: We developed a baseline image registration based on SIFT hand-crafted features. For evaluation, we compare our convolutional feature with SIFT. For subjective comparison, we have displayed feature correspondences. Figure 2 displays a scenario of image registration and feature matching. We calculated the matching features and warped the images according to the matching. In Fig. 3, we also displayed checkerboard to show the parts of the images that suffered the transformational effects. Both images clearly show that our feature matching is dense and robust to different variations compared to SIFT.

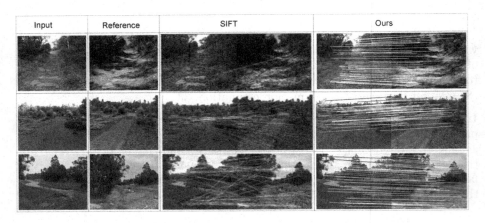

Fig. 2. Illustrative repeat photography image registration from Flucker Post community based image collection: First Column: All images are input images of different locations in Australia, Second Column, these images are reference images from relevant Flucker Post, third column shows the point correspondences after SIFT matching and the last Column shows the point correspondences obtained after automated deep multi-temporal image registration.

Table 1. Feature pre-matching precision test result for Flucker Post Vegetation Dataset. The used unit is percentage.

Index	SIFT	Ours
Average	70.75 %	96.35%
Minimum	35.41%	89.76%
Maximum	92.50%	99.6%

Input	Reference	Checkerboard

Fig. 3. Illustrative repeat photography image registration from Flucker Post community based image collection: First Column: All images are input images of different locations in Australia, Second Column, these images are reference images from relevant Flucker Post, last Column shows the registered image with varied sections shown by checkerboard after automated deep multi-temporal image registration.

Objective Comparison: For objective comparison, we used different metrics. In each corresponding image pair, we extract feature points using both methods and use the most reliable 95–105 pairs of matches and measure precision P as

$$P = \frac{TP}{TP + TF}$$

Table 1 shows the comparison of our approach vs SIFT. Additionally, we mark landmark in 15 points and record the locations of the landmarks for measuring error like root mean squared distance (RMSD), mean absolute distance (MAD), median of distance (MED) and the standard deviation of distance (STD).

Table 2 shows the performance of our algorithm compared to other approaches. It can be observed that our approach is more reliable than all other approaches.

Algorithm 1. Point Set registration Algorithm

input: p, q
output: p'
Initialize: $iterations = 30, \phi, \alpha = 0$
for $k = 0, k < iterations, k + +$ **do**
    Get descriptors $d(p), d(q)$
    Assign the correspondences weight C by Eq: 5,6,7 in [33]
    Construct the RBF kernel matrix $\mathcal{K}$
    Compute the transformation parameter α using Spatially Constrained Gaussian Fields (SCGF)[33]
        Update the model point set $p' = p + \mathcal{K}\alpha$
end for
Return p'

Table 2. Comparative analysis in terms of registration accuracy test result on Flucker Post Vegetation Dataset in terms of different error matrices

Method	RMSD	MAD	MED	STD
CPD [35]	12.67	15.38	5.67	8.75
GLMDTPS [36]	26.87	28.92	8.60	11.48
GL-CATE [37]	10.94	14.89	4.25	8.57
Deep features [4]	9.79	9.23	7.41	5.12
Ours	8.62	8.67	5.68	3.67

5   Conclusion

In this paper, we investigated the integration of citizen science and deep learning based image registration to facilitate automated image analytics for environmental monitoring. We proposed a novel deep affine invariant network for non-rigid image registration of multi-temporal repeat photography. We also integrated robust point matching and affine invariance into our framework for robust multi-temporal image registration. Extensive experimental studies have been conducted to evaluate the underlying design based on the public datasets. The experimental results indicated that the proposed approach delivered higher quality performance than the existing techniques. This work would open up new research direction to achieve fully automated environmental monitoring system.

References

1. Augar, N., Fluker, M.: Towards understanding user perceptions of a tourist-based environmental monitoring system: an exploratory case study. Asia Pac. J. Tourism Res. **20**(10), 1081–1093 (2015)
2. Sonnentag, O., et al.: Digital repeat photography for phenological research in forest ecosystems. Agric. For. Meteorol. **152**, 159–177 (2012)

3. Lowe, D.G., et al.: Object recognition from local scale-invariant features. In: ICCV, vol. 99, pp. 1150–1157 (1999)

4. Yang, Z., Dan, T., Yang, Y.: Multi-temporal remote sensing image registration using deep convolutional features. IEEE Access **6**, 38544–38555 (2018)

5. Cao, X., Yang, J., Wang, L., Xue, Z., Wang, Q., Shen, D.: Deep learning based inter-modality image registration supervised by intra-modality similarity. In: Shi, Y., Suk, H.-I., Liu, M. (eds.) MLMI 2018. LNCS, vol. 11046, pp. 55–63. Springer, Cham (2018). https://doi.org/10.1007/978-3-030-00919-9_7

6. Azulay, A., Weiss, Y.: Why do deep convolutional networks generalize so poorly to small image transformations? arXiv preprint arXiv:1805.12177

7. de Vos, B.D., Berendsen, F.F., Viergever, M.A., Sokooti, H., Staring, M., Išgum, I.: A deep learning framework for unsupervised affine and deformable image registration. Med. Image Anal. **52**, 128–143 (2019)

8. Whitelaw, G., Vaughan, H., Craig, B., Atkinson, D.: Establishing the canadian community monitoring network. Environ. Monit. Assess. **88**(1–3), 409–418 (2003)

9. Pretty, J.: Social capital and the collective management of resources. Science **302**(5652), 1912–1914 (2003)

10. Lawrence, A.: 'No personal motive?' volunteers, biodiversity, and the false dichotomies of participation. Ethics Place Environ. **9**(3), 279–298 (2006)

11. Castell, N., et al.: Mobile technologies and services for environmental monitoring: the citi-sense-mob approach. Urban Clim. **14**, 370–382 (2015)

12. Montori, F., Bedogni, L., Bononi, L.: A collaborative internet of things architecture for smart cities and environmental monitoring. IEEE Internet Things J. **5**(2), 592–605 (2018)

13. Conrad, C.C., Hilchey, K.G.: A review of citizen science and community-based environmental monitoring: issues and opportunities. Environ. Monit. Assess. **176**(1–4), 273–291 (2011)

14. Conrad, C.T., Daoust, T.: Community-based monitoring frameworks: Increasing the effectiveness of environmental stewardship. Environ. Manage. **41**(3), 358–366 (2008)

15. Israel, B.A., et al.: Community-Based Participatory Research, p. 272. Urban Health (2019)

16. Sharpe, A., Conrad, C.: Community based ecological monitoring in nova scotia: challenges and opportunities. Environ. Monit. Assess. **113**(1–3), 395–409 (2006)

17. Webb, R.H.: Repeat Photography: Methods and Applications in the Natural Sciences. Island Press, Washington (2010)

18. Zier, J.L., Baker, W.L.: A century of vegetation change in the san juan mountains, colorado: an analysis using repeat photography. For. Ecol. Manage. **228**(1–3), 251–262 (2006)

19. Hendrick, L.E., Copenheaver, C.A.: Using repeat landscape photography to assess vegetation changes in rural communities of the southern appalachian mountains in virginia, usa. Mt. Res. Dev. **29**(1), 21–30 (2009)

20. Lynch, J., Eilam, E., Fluker, M., Augar, N.: Community-based environmental monitoring goes to school: translations, detours and escapes. Environ. Educ. Res. **23**(5), 708–721 (2017)

21. Pickard, J.: Assessing vegetation change over a century using repeat photography. Aust. J. Bot. **50**(4), 409–414 (2002)

22. Gu, J., et al.: Recent advances in convolutional neural networks. Pattern Recogn. **77**, 354–377 (2018)

23. Brown, L.G.: A survey of image registration techniques. ACM Comput. Surv. (CSUR) **24**(4), 325–376 (1992)

24. Zitova, B., Flusser, J.: Image registration methods: a survey. Image Vis. Comput. **21**(11), 977–1000 (2003)
25. Guizar-Sicairos, M., Thurman, S.T., Fienup, J.R.: Efficient subpixel image registration algorithms. Opt. Lett. **33**(2), 156–158 (2008)
26. Erdt, M., Steger, S., Sakas, G.: Regmentation: a new view of image segmentation and registration. J. Radiat. Oncol. Inform. **4**(1), 1–23 (2017)
27. Fernandez-Beltran, R., Pla, F., Plaza, A.: Intersensor remote sensing image registration using multispectral semantic embeddings. IEEE Geosci. Remote Sensing Lett
28. He, K., Zhang, X., Ren, S., Sun, J.: Deep residual learning for image recognition, in: Proceedings of the IEEE Conference on Computer Vision and Pattern Recognition, pp. 770–778 (2016)
29. Jaderberg, M., Simonyan, K., Zisserman, A., et al.: Spatial transformer networks. In: Advances in Neural Information Processing Systems, pp. 2017–2025 (2015)
30. Ono, Y., Trulls, E., Fua, P., Yi, K.M.: LF-net: learning local features from images. In: Advances in Neural Information Processing Systems, pp. 6234–6244 (2018)
31. Tian, Y., Fan, B., Wu, F.: L2-net: deep learning of discriminative patch descriptor in Euclidean space. In: Proceedings of the IEEE Conference on Computer Vision and Pattern Recognition, pp. 661–669 (2017)
32. Beckouche, S., Leprince, S., Sabater, N., Ayoub, F.: Robust outliers detection in image point matching. In: 2011 IEEE International Conference on Computer Vision Workshops (ICCV Workshops), pp. 180–187. IEEE (2011)
33. Wang, G., Zhou, Q., Chen, Y.: Robust non-rigid point set registration using spatially constrained gaussian fields. IEEE Trans. Image Process. **26**(4), 1759–1769 (2017)
34. Thévenaz, P., Blu, T., Unser, M.: Interpolation revisited [medical images application]. IEEE Trans. Med. Imaging **19**(7), 739–758 (2000)
35. Myronenko, A., Song, X.: Point set registration: coherent point drift. IEEE Trans. Pattern Anal. Mach. Intell. **32**(12), 2262–2275 (2010)
36. Figgis, P.: Australia's National Parks and Protected Areas: Future Directions: A Disscussion Paper, Australian Committee for IUCN Incorporated (1999)
37. Zhang, S., Yang, Y., Yang, K., Luo, Y., Ong, S.-H.: Point set registration with global-local correspondence and transformation estimation. In: Proceedings of the IEEE International Conference on Computer Vision, pp. 2669–2677 (2017)

Multimodal 3D Facade Reconstruction Using 3D LiDAR and Images

Haotian Xu[✉], Chia-Yen Chen, Patrice Jean Delmas, Trevor Edwin Gee,
and Wannes van der Mark

The University of Auckland, Auckland 1010, New Zealand
hxu454@aucklanduni.ac.nz

Abstract. Reconstruction of 3D facades is an important problem in systems that reconstruct urban scenes. Facade reconstruction can be challenging due to the typically large featureless surfaces involved. In this work, we investigate the use of combining a commercially available LiDAR with a GoPro camera to serve as inputs for a system that generates accurate 3D facade reconstructions. A key challenge is that 3D point clouds from LiDARs tend to be sparse. We propose to overcome this by the use of semantic information extracted from RGB images, along with a state-of-the-art depth completion method. Our results demonstrate that the proposed approach is capable of producing highly accurate 3D reconstructions of building facades that rival the current state-of-the-art.

Keywords: 3D reconstruction · Depth completion · Facade segmentation

1 Introduction

Three-dimensional (3D) urban reconstruction is an active research area which is significant for many applications, such as virtual tours and urban planning [3]. 3D facade reconstruction is an essential task for urban reconstruction, since buildings are common in urban environments.

Accurate depth estimation is a crucial problem to overcome when performing 3D reconstruction. In urban environments, the advantage encountering many objects with simple geometric shapes and smooth surfaces, is often offset by the abundance of large featureless surfaces which cause depth estimation ambiguities in many approaches. There are two main strategies used for depth estimation, namely passive depth sensing (stereo matching) and active depth estimation (which involves projecting some sort of radiation into the scene, to see how it reacts to the environment). The passive approach, namely stereo matching, often struggles in urban environments, since many scene elements lack good tracking features [16]. Also, since urban buildings are typically large and tall, wide baselines are often required, which are notoriously difficult to work with. Active depth sensing on the other hand, does not entirely solve the problem either, with popular RGB-D cameras such as the Intel Realsense and Microsoft Kinect

© Springer Nature Switzerland AG 2019
C. Lee et al. (Eds.): PSIVT 2019, LNCS 11854, pp. 281–295, 2019.
https://doi.org/10.1007/978-3-030-34879-3_22

being unsuitable for outdoor conditions, since they limited depth range [29] and fail in sunlight. This in this work we look at laser systems, which operate well in outdoor environments and can capture large objects, albeit have problems of their own.

Existing 3D facade reconstruction research based on laser scanning techniques utilize either high-resolution laser scanners [1,8,21,27,28] or 3D Light Detection and Ranging (LiDAR) [11,12] to measure range data. High-resolution laser scanners can produce dense point clouds but are usually slow in acquiring even small volumes of data, whereas 3D real-time LiDAR devices can work fast with ease but generate relatively sparse point clouds [12]. Due to its speed and mobility, 3D LiDAR is more suitable for large-scale 3D urban reconstruction. In addition to LiDAR scans, images are another important data type for 3D facade reconstruction [19]. Some existing facade reconstruction studies also employ images to refine the 3D point clouds captured by high-resolution laser scanners [1,21,27] or 3D LiDAR [11,12].

In this paper, we propose a new 3D facade reconstruction method based on the fusion of 3D LiDAR and images. To handle the problem of the sparsity of LiDAR scans, we first employ instance segmentation to extract the rich semantic information in images and use it to estimate the missing depth data of the glass area of facade depth maps such as windows or glass doors. Then, we use a depth completion method based on convolutional neural networks (CNNs) to generate a dense depth map for 3D facade reconstruction. Our data collection process using 3D LiDAR and a synchronized camera is relatively fast, capturing the point cloud of a partial facade in just 0.1 s.

Our paper is organized as follows: in Sect. 2, the related works are introduced; in Sect. 3, our proposed reconstruction method is introduced; in Sect. 4, the evaluation of the proposed method is presented; in Sect. 5, an comparison experiment is presented; in Sect. 6, we present the conclusion of this paper and the potential future work.

2   Related Work

Studies on 3D facade reconstruction based on the fusion the laser scanning and images can be classified into two groups looking at how images are used in the reconstruction process. The first group uses images only for texturing the dense 3D point cloud of facades captured by high-resolution laser scanners. Some studies employ laser scanners and cameras whose relative position and orientation are fixed in the 2D and 3D data collection process [6,30], while the other studies use non-registered laser scanners and cameras [14,15,23,24].

Another group uses images for both texturing and refinement of the point clouds captured by laser scanning. Studies in this group usually consolidate the facade structure in 3D point clouds by utilizing the features extracted from images, such as linear features [20,27], planar features [12], or facade elements like window crossbars [2]. The fusion of images and LiDAR scans can also be used to determine the particular shape grammar of facades [11].

3   Multimodal 3D Facade Reconstruction

Given a sparse 3D point clouds generated by a 3D LiDAR and an associated image of a facade, our target is to produce an accurate 3D model of buildings. Using sparse LiDAR scans to reconstruct 3D facade models is challenging due to the large areas of missing depth estimates. Also, LiDAR systems cannot acquire active depth estimates of windows or other glass areas, since the laser beam emitted from LiDAR does not reflect off glass [4].

Recently, several CNN-based depth completion methods with relatively good performance have been proposed. Also, most of the urban building facades have a regular structure and can be parsed through images, which can then be used for predicting the relevant missing LiDAR depth data. In older buildings, the depth of windows and doors is often larger than that of its surrounding walls while windows and doors can be located by using image segmentation techniques, both very useful for estimating the depth of the glass areas in facades. Our main task is to leverage the rich semantic information in images and use depth completion method to estimate the missing depth data in the input sparse LiDAR data to produce more accurate 3D models of buildings.

There are three main steps in our proposed 3D facade reconstruction method:

1. **Data collection and pre-processing**
   (a) Using a LiDAR and a camera which are pre-calibrated and rigidly mounted on a board to collect the sparse 3D point cloud and the corresponding photograph of a target facade.
   (b) Undistorting the image and segmenting facade from the image; removing the useless data points from the point cloud.
2. **Dense RGB-D data generation**:
   (a) Converting the 3D sparse LiDAR point cloud to a corresponding sparse depth map by using LiDAR-camera calibration parameters and camera intrinsic parameters; locating all the glass areas (e.g., windows and glass doors) of the input facade image and generating the masks for these areas.
   (b) Estimating the depth data of all the glass areas in sparse depth maps by using the corresponding masks.
   (c) Using depth completion techniques to generate a dense depth map based on the input facade image and the corresponding processed sparse depth map.

Fig. 1. Our experimental mobile setup; Velodyne HDL-32E LiDAR (centre) and GoPro HERO5 camera (left).

3.1   Data Collection and Pre-processing

The first stage of our method is data collection and pre-processing. For testing purposes, we built a new dataset containing facade data from buildings at the University of Auckland. We used the Velodyne HDL-32E LiDAR[1] and a GoPro HERO 5 Black camera[2]. The two devices were registered using the approach in [7]. Both devices rigidly mounted on a trolley (Fig. 1).

The Velodyne HDL-32E is a 3D real-time LiDAR with 32 lasers, with a 40° vertical field of view (FOV) and a 360° horizontal FOV. The maximum range is 100 m and the scan rate is 10 Hz with 1.39 million depth points acquired per second. The GoPro Hero5 Black can capture 12 million pixels with a fish-eye lens allowing a full facade texture acquisition in a single image.

Overview of Facades. Our data-set features various facade styles and various types of materials. These include facades of building made of stone, brick or wood and range from historic old buildings to super modern recent constructions (Fig. 2).

(a) An example of the facade of the *traditional style*.

(b) An example of the facade of the *traditional style containing connected windows*.

Fig. 2. The examples of the two facade styles of our dataset.

Data Pre-processing. The first stage is to pre-process the input data. Firstly the building is segmented out from the background elements in both LiDAR data and the RGB data. Next, the GoPro Hero5 Black camera intrinsic parameters are estimated and used remove distortion from RGB images.

3.2   Dense RGB-D Data Generation

Original Sparse Depth Map Generation. The second stage is to estimate the missing depth information in the input LiDAR scans by using depth completion and the semantic information extracted from the input image. The pre-processed LiDAR point cloud can be easily projected onto the pre-processed image to produce the associated sparse depth map as follows:

---

[1] https://velodynelidar.com/hdl-32e.html.
[2] https://www.dxomark.com/Cameras/GoPro/HERO5-Black---Specifications.

1. Transforming data points from LiDAR space to camera space by using Eq. 1, where $\mathbf{p}_i = (X_i, Y_i, Z_i)^\mathsf{T}$ denotes a point in the camera coordinate system, $\mathbf{l}_i = (X'_i, Y'_i, Z'_i)^\mathsf{T}$ denotes a point in the LiDAR coordinate system, $\mathbf{R}, \mathbf{t}$ denote the rotation matrix and translation vector of the 3D rigid body transformation from LiDAR space to camera space.

$$\mathbf{p}_i = \mathbf{R}\mathbf{l}_i + \mathbf{t} \tag{1}$$

2. Computing the 2D image coordinates for every data point in the 3D camera space by using the following equations, where $(u_i, v_i)^\mathsf{T}$ denotes a 2D point in the image coordinate system which is corresponding to the 3D data point $(X_i, Y_i, Z_i)^\mathsf{T}$ in the camera coordinate system, Z_i denotes the depth, f_x and f_y denote the focal length of the camera in x axis and y axis respectively, (c_x, c_y) denotes the camera center of the camera. The depth value of each data point in the final depth map is equal to sZ_i where s denotes the resizing scale for LiDAR distance measurement and is typically equal to 1000 (if applicable).

$$u_i = \frac{X_i \cdot f_x}{Z_i} + c_x, \; v_i = \frac{Y_i \cdot f_y}{Z_i} + c_y \tag{2}$$

Locating All the Facade Elements Made of Glass in Images. Since glass does not reflect laser, the LiDAR does not produce distance measurements of glass elements [4]. Thus we aim to correct this. We apply the heuristic that depth of the plane of glass areas (e.g., windows and glass doors) is typically greater than the depth of the plane of their surrounding walls. Also, these areas are typically parallel to the corresponding walls. Thus, given the plane of the corresponding surrounding walls, the plane of these glass areas can be guessed.

Since images have high resolution and rich semantic information, we can locate the facade elements made of glass in the image by employing image segmentation techniques. As the camera intrinsic parameters are known, we can transform the coordinates of data points between 3D camera space and 2D image space by using Eq. 2. In other words, once we detect these facade elements in the image, we can locate them in both 2D and 3D space.

Image segmentation can be classified into two groups which are semantic segmentation and instance segmentation. Semantic segmentation is a fundamental computer vision task, which aims to produce the semantic label for every pixel in an image [5], while instance segmentation requires not only the semantic segmentation for an image but also the differentiation of individual instances [9]. In our proposed method, we employ instance segmentation techniques to locate facade elements made of glass because we need to estimate the depth data of each of them separately in the later process.

Mask R-CNN [9] is one of the SOTA instance segmentation methods. In this paper, we employ this method for segmenting all the facade elements made of glass in facade images. As windows and glass doors are the two most typical facade elements made of glass, we train a Mask R-CNN model to segment only windows and doors in this paper. The dataset that we use for training and testing the Mask R-CNN to segment windows and doors are combined from the CMP Facade Database [26], the ICG Graz50 dataset [22], and the Ecole Centrale Paris Facades Database [17]. The CMP Facade Database is composed of 606 facade images with semantic segmentation annotations, which were taken from many different sources. The ICG Graz50 dataset is comprised of 50 facade images taken from Graz, Austria with corresponding semantic segmentation labels. The Ecole Centrale Paris (ECP) Facades Database consists of 104 facade images taken from Ecole Centrale Paris with the corresponding semantic segmentation label.

The total number of images of our datasets is 760. We use 67% of the data for training, 29% of the data for validating, and 4% of the data for testing. Our training set is 511 facade images from the CMP Facade Database. Our validation set is 219 facade images which contain 95 images from the CMP Facade Database, 20 images from the ICG Graz50 dataset, and 104 images from the ECP Facades Database. Our testing set is 30 images from the ICG Graz50 dataset.

Furthermore, we also use a threshold of the confidence factor of generated window/door masks to filter out those less correct or incorrect window masks. This threshold value can be set manually and appropriately based on the facade segmentation results. This is to make sure that only correctly detected windows/doors will be refined in the subsequent steps.

We utilize ResNet-101 [10] as the network backbone of the Mask R-CNN model and pre-trained the model on the Microsoft COCO dataset [13]. The Mask R-CNN model was tested on the training set and the validation set with an NVIDIA Tesla K80 GPU for 40 epochs. We evaluated the trained Mask R-CNN model on our test set using the standard VOC-style mean average precision (mAP) at an intersection over union (IOU) threshold of 0.5. The mAP of the trained Mask R-CNN model is 0.893. An example of the facade segmentation result is shown in Fig. 3a.

Estimating the Depth Data of the Facade Elements Made of Glass. Once all the elements made of glass in a facade image are located, the sparse depth map can be refined by estimating the depth data of these elements:

1. **Removing the depth data of the facade elements made of glass in the sparse depth map**: As the depth data of the glass area captured by LiDAR is usually inaccurate, first the depth data in the glass area (such as windows and glass doors) should be removed. This is achieved by setting the depth of corresponding pixels to 0 in the depth map.

2. **Detecting all the different planes in the facade in the 3D camera space**: A facade is generally composed of different planes each of which is a single wall that may contain windows, doors, or nothing. As the depth of facade elements made of glass (e.g., windows and glass doors) usually is slightly larger than the depth of their surrounding walls and these elements are usually parallel to the corresponding walls, their plane models can be determined based on the plane model of the corresponding surrounding walls. The plane model of these elements can be subsequently used for computing

their exact depth values. To detect all the different planes in the facade in 3D camera space, the depth map without the depth data of the elements made of glass first should be converted to the corresponding point cloud in 3D camera space by using Eq. 2. Then, all the different planes can be detected in the point cloud by using the M-estimator SAmple Consensus (MSAC) algorithm [25].

3. **Estimating the plane model of every elements made of glass in the 3D camera space:** Once all the planes are detected, the model for each plane can be represented by Eq. 3.

$$ax + by + cz + d = 0 \tag{3}$$

Hence, the plane model for the windows or glass doors in the corresponding wall plane can be represented by using Eq. 4.

$$ax + by + cz + \hat{d} = 0 \tag{4}$$

The relation between plane of the wall and the plane of the window or door can be represented by Eq. 5, where r is the ratio used for translating the plane of the wall to the plane of the window or door and can be set properly according to different facades.

$$\hat{d} = d(1 + r) \tag{5}$$

4. **Computing the depth value of every facade elements made of glass in the 3D camera space:** After the plane model of every facade elements made of glass are determined, the exact depth value of each pixel in these areas can be computed by using Eq. 6 where $(u, v)^\intercal$ denotes the coordinates of each pixel of the located elements in the image coordinate system, f_x and f_y denote the focal length of the camera in x axis and y axis respectively, (c_x, c_y) denotes the camera center of the camera, a, b, c, and $\hat{d}$ denote the plane model parameters of the located elements in camera space. The depth value of each data point in the final depth map is equal to $Z_i \times s$ where s denotes the resizing scale for LiDAR distance measurement and is typically equal to 1000 (if applicable).

$$Z = \frac{-\hat{d} f_x f_y}{a f_y (u - c_x) + b f_x (v - c_y) + c f_x f_y} \tag{6}$$

Depth Completion. The last step of dense RGB-D data generation is depth completion. We used a CNN-based depth completion method proposed in [29] for its relatively good performance for depth completion. We used the associated pre-trained model provided in the GitHub repository[3]. Figure 3b shows an example of depth completion.

In order to visualize our reconstruction results, we converted the dense RGB-D data to 3D colored mesh models. First, the dense RGB-D data is converted to

---

[3] https://github.com/yindaz/DeepCompletionRelease/tree/master/pre_train_model.

the corresponding colored point cloud in 3D camera space by using Eq. 2. Next, the 3D colored point cloud is converted to a 3D colored mesh model using the meshing approach introduced in [18]. An example of the produced facade mesh model is shown in Fig. 3c.

4   Evaluations

In this section, we present the evaluation of our experimental results. As we do not have the ground truth of the building in our dataset, we evaluated our experimental results of different stages by using a qualitative way. Basically, the core problem that our 3D facade reconstruction pipeline aims to solve is how to estimate the missing depth data in input RGB-D data. Based on this idea, we use two modules to solve the depth completion problem.

(a) The segmentation result.   (b) The completed depth map.   (c) The mesh model.

Fig. 3. Examples of our 3D facade completion experimental results. Since the model is reconstructed from RGB-D data which are taken from a given angle, there may be some missing parts in the final 3D mesh model.

The first module is the estimation of the depth data of the facade elements made of glass. In this module, we use the semantic information extracted from RGB images and weak architectural constraints to re-estimate the exact depth values of the glass areas in facade depth maps. The semantic information is the extraction of glass-made facade elements (e.g., windows and glass doors), which is achieved by an instance segmentation model (Mask R-CNN). The semantic information is the fundamental data for this module, which means that the better the performance of the instance segmentation technique, the better the estimation of these glass areas in depth maps and vice versa. Thus, the evaluation of the results of instance segmentation is one of the targets of the evaluation.

The second module is the final depth completion algorithm which predicts all the remaining missing depth data in the refined depth map generated from the first module. Since in the first module of the proposed method only estimates the depth data of the glass-made facade elements and may omit some parts of these glass areas due to the imperfectness of the instance segmentation technique, there is still a large proportion of facade areas in depth maps which does not have depth data. Therefore, the final depth completion module is indispensable for the proposed pipeline. The result of this module is the final dense RGB-D data. Since dense RGB-D data are converted to mesh models for better visualization, we qualitatively evaluated the final mesh model of facades for evaluating the depth completion module.

Although we do not have the ground truth for the facades in our dataset, we can still evaluate the proposed method by evaluating the output data of different stages of the proposed pipeline. Also, we have classified the facade styles in our dataset into different categories. With this information, we can determine how effective are the two modules for different types of facade styles. As a result, we can make a relatively objective evaluation for the proposed 3D facade reconstruction method.

4.1 Evaluation of the Segmentation of the Facade Elements Made of Glass in Images

Traditional Style. Figure 4 shows the segmentation result for the images of the facade of the *traditional style*. It can be seen from these results that the trained Mask R-CNN model can relatively accurately extract the windows and doors from the images of this type of facade style. This may result from that our training set contains a lot of images of the facade of this style. Also, it can be seen from the segmentation results shown in Fig. 4 that the confidence of most of the detected windows and doors are very high. Therefore, the trained Mask R-CNN can perform well on the images of the facades of the *traditional style*.

(a) The Merchant House.   (b) The Old Choral Hall.

Fig. 4. The segmentation results of the images of the facade of the *traditional style*. The text in the images shows the predicted label and the confidence of the corresponding facade elements.

Traditional Style Containing Connected Windows. The segmentation results of the facades whose facade style is the *traditional style containing connected windows* are shown in Fig. 5. This kind of window style is basically not included in our training set. Windows in the same row are connected or have unclear boundaries, which increases the difficulty of window segmentation. Therefore, it can be seen from Fig. 5 that the window segmentation result is relatively poor. According to the segmentation results shown in Fig. 5, the confidence of the detected windows that are not connected to the other windows is relatively high, while the confidence of the windows that are connected to the other windows is relatively low. Besides, for this kind of facade style, windows occupy a large area of facade regions. Hence, the poor instance segmentation performance would have a negative effect on the final reconstruction result.

4.2 Evaluation of Facade Mesh Models

In this section, we show the colored facade mesh models generated by our proposed facade reconstruction method. As we do not have the ground truth for the facades reconstructed in our experimentation, we only qualitatively evaluated the results.

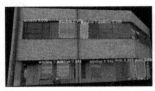

(a) The front of the CLL building.

(b) The back of the CLL building.

Fig. 5. The segmentation results of the images of the facade of the *traditional style containing connected windows*. The text in the images shows the predicted label and the confidence of the corresponding facade elements.

Traditional Style. Figure 6 shows the colored mesh models of the facades of the *traditional style*. As the window and door segmentation result of this kind of facade style is relatively good, most of the window and door areas of these facades are reconstructed well. Overall, the depth completion module in our facade reconstruction pipeline can work well for the facades of this type of facade style.

(a) The Merchant House.

(b) The Languages International.

Fig. 6. The colored mesh models of the facade of the *traditional style*.

Traditional Style Containing Connected Windows. Figure 7 shows the reconstruction results of the facades of the *traditional style containing connected windows*. It can be seen from Fig. 7 that our proposed approach can reconstruct the overall structure of these facades. However, the glass-made elements of these facades were not reconstructed well because of the poor facade segmentation results. All in all, the successful reconstruction of the overall structure of these facades can prove that the depth completion module of the proposed pipeline can handle this kind of facade style.

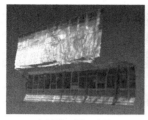 

(a) The Elam B.   (b) The back of the CLL building.

Fig. 7. The colored mesh models of the facades of the *traditional style containing connected windows.*

5   Comparison Study

We ran an experiment to investigate how the refinement process of the area of facade elements made of glass (e.g., windows) on original sparse depth maps may improve final reconstruction results. In this refinement process, the original depth data of these elements on original sparse depth maps are first removed, then the exact depth values of these elements are estimated based on instance segmentation results in 2D images and plane fitting results in 3D camera space. As glass areas generally cannot reflect laser beams properly, the depth values of glass areas captured by LiDAR are usually incorrect, which would misguide the subsequent depth completion process. Therefore, the original depth data of these areas should be removed. Also, as the depth completion module requires both RGB images and existing sparse depth data to guide the depth estimation process [29], the estimated depth data of glass areas would be problematic if there are no depth data in these areas of input sparse depth maps.

We first conducted a qualitative comparison between the model generated by our proposed refinement approach and the model generated using no refinement process. The experimental results of this comparison study showed that the refinement process can successfully reconstruct the facade elements made of glass. A 3D facade model was first reconstructed directly based on the original sparse depth map (see Fig. 8a). In the reconstruction process of this model, there was no refinement process for the area of facade elements made of glass on the input sparse depth map. Figure 8a illustrates a reconstructed facade model with very bumpy glass areas. Figure 8b illustrates a 3D facade reconstruction model generated with the refined sparse depth map proposed in this paper. It is evident that the window area of this facade model is relatively flatter than in the model shown in Fig. 8a.

We also conducted a quantitative comparison of our reconstructions. Due to a lack of LiDAR+camera ground truth data, we measured the "flatness" of the reconstructed window areas. Points in the windows masked areas were extracted, and a plane was fitted through them using the MSAC algorithm. The average of all the points absolute distances (or Mean Error) to this plane was considered a reliable indicator of the area flatness. The Mean Error values for

(a) An example of the reconstruction result with no refinement process.

(b) An example of the reconstruction result which is based on our proposed refinement approach.

(c) An example of the corresponding colored mesh model.

Fig. 8. Comparison between the reconstruction results with or without the refinement of glass areas in the depth maps. Missing data (holes) in the models are due to the RGB-D image viewpoint occlusions.

Table 1. The two Mean Error values for the facade of the *traditional style* (Fig. 6). Mean Error 1 denotes the Mean Error for the model generated based on no refinement process. Mean Error 2 denotes the Mean Error for the model generated based on the proposed refinement process.

Result	Mean Error 1 (mm)	Mean Error 2 (mm)
The Merchant House	1.5667	0.79102
The Languages International	2.1012	0.7035
The Old Choral Hall	1.9932	0.91136
The Clock Tower Easting Wing	2.3978	0.82754

the models generated with or without refinement process were introduced. As the segmentation results of the facade of the *traditional style* is the best, we only computed the Mean Error values for this kind of facade style. The two Mean Error values for the facade of the *traditional style* are shown in Table 1. The Mean Error of the model produced with our proposed refinement process is consistently lower than the Mean Error for the model without refinement process.

6 Conclusion

In this paper, we proposed a new method for 3D facade reconstruction using the fusion of sparse 3D LiDAR and images of the same facade. This method can be used for reconstructing the facade which mainly contains windows and doors. The main idea of the proposed pipeline is to use depth completion techniques and the combination of prior knowledge and image segmentation techniques to estimate the scale of missing depth data in LiDAR scans. There are two significant merits of our proposed method. The first one is the fast data collection speed, which makes this approach very useful for large-scale urban reconstruction. The second one is that this method can generate semantic labels for facade elements which can be further used for semantically labelling of 3D models. The comparison study shows that the refinement process for the facade elements made of glass (e.g., windows) in original depth maps can improve the accuracy of the reconstruction results.

We evaluated the proposed 3D facade reconstruction pipeline on the facade data of the two facade styles, respectively. We found that the proposed method can handle the facades of the *traditional style* but have some problems with the facades of the *traditional style containing connected windows*. Specifically, the segmentation module of the proposed pipeline cannot correctly extract the windows which are connected to adjacent windows or have unclear boundaries with adjacent windows in the images of the facades of the *traditional style containing connected windows*. This results from that this kind of window style is not included in the training set of the instance segmentation module.

The main limitation of our 3D facade reconstruction pipeline is that the quality of the reconstruction results heavily rely on the performance of the instance segmentation module and the depth completion module. Our future work will focus on how to employ more prior knowledge and more accurate instance segmentation models in the pipeline to estimate the depth data of other kinds of facade elements like balconies.

References

1. Becker, S., Haala, N.: Combined feature extraction for façade reconstruction. In: Proceedings of ISPRS Workshop Laser Scanning, pp. 241–247 (2007)
2. Becker, S., Haala, N.: Refinement of building facades by integrated processing of lidar and image data. Int. Arch. Photogram. Remote Sensing Spat. Inf. Sci. **36**, 7–12 (2007)
3. Biljecki, F., Stoter, J., Ledoux, H., Zlatanova, S., Çöltekin, A.: Applications of 3D city models: state of the art review. ISPRS Int. J. Geo Inf. **4**(4), 2842–2889 (2015). https://doi.org/10.3390/ijgi4042842
4. Chen, J., Chen, B.: Architectural modeling from sparsely scanned range data. Int. J. Comput. Vis. **78**(2), 223–236 (2008)
5. Chen, L.C., Zhu, Y., Papandreou, G., Schroff, F., Adam, H.: Encoder-decoder with atrous separable convolution for semantic image segmentation. In: The European Conference on Computer Vision, September 2018
6. Fruh, C., Zakhor, A.: 3D model generation for cities using aerial photographs and ground level laser scans. In: The IEEE Computer Society Conference on Computer Vision and Pattern Recognition, vol. 2, pp. II–II, December 2001. https://doi.org/10.1109/CVPR.2001.990921
7. Gee, T., James, J., Van Der Mark, W., Strozzi, A.G., Delmas, P., Gimel'farb, G.: Estimating extrinsic parameters between a stereo rig and a multi-layer lidar using plane matching and circle feature extraction. In: The Fifteenth IAPR International Conference on Machine Vision Applications, pp. 21–24, May 2017. https://doi.org/10.23919/MVA.2017.7986763
8. Hao, W., Wang, Y., Liang, W.: Slice-based building facade reconstruction from 3D point clouds. Int. J. Remote Sensing **39**(20), 6587–6606 (2018)

9. He, K., Gkioxari, G., Dollar, P., Girshick, R.: Mask R-CNN. In: The IEEE International Conference on Computer Vision, October 2017. https://doi.org/10.1109/ICCV.2017.322

10. He, K., Zhang, X., Ren, S., Sun, J.: Deep residual learning for image recognition. In: The IEEE Conference on Computer Vision and Pattern Recognition, June 2016. https://doi.org/10.1109/CVPR.2016.90

11. Hohmann, B., Krispel, U., Havemann, S., Fellner, D.: Cityfit-high-quality urban reconstructions by fitting shape grammars to images and derived textured point clouds. In: The 3rd ISPRS International Workshop 3D-ARCH, pp. 25–28 (2009)

12. Li, Y., Zheng, Q., Sharf, A., Cohen-Or, D., Chen, B., Mitra, N.J.: 2D–3D fusion for layer decomposition of urban facades. In: The IEEE International Conference on Computer Vision, pp. 882–889, November 2011. https://doi.org/10.1109/ICCV.2011.6126329

13. Lin, T., et al.: Microsoft COCO: common objects in context. CoRR (2014). http://arxiv.org/abs/1405.0312

14. Liu, L., Stamos, I.: Automatic 3D to 2D registration for the photorealistic rendering of urban scenes. In: The IEEE Computer Society Conference on Computer Vision and Pattern Recognition, vol. 2, pp. 137–143 (2005). https://doi.org/10.1109/CVPR.2005.80

15. Liu, L., Stamos, I.: A systematic approach for 2D-image to 3D-range registration in urban environments. In: The IEEE International Conference on Computer Vision, pp. 1–8, October 2007. https://doi.org/10.1109/ICCV.2007.4409215

16. Ma, F., Karaman, S.: Sparse-to-dense: depth prediction from sparse depth samples and a single image. In: IEEE International Conference on Robotics and Automation, May 2018

17. Martinović, A., Mathias, M., Weissenberg, J., Van Gool, L.: A three-layered approach to facade parsing. In: The European Conference on Computer Vision, pp. 416–429 (2012)

18. Marton, Z.C., Rusu, R.B., Beetz, M.: On fast surface reconstruction methods for large and noisy datasets. In: The IEEE International Conference on Robotics and Automation, May 2009. https://doi.org/10.1109/ROBOT.2009.5152628

19. Müller, P., Zeng, G., Wonka, P., Van Gool, L.: Image-based procedural modeling of facades. In: ACM SIGGRAPH 2007 Papers, SIGGRAPH 2007, ACM, New York (2007). https://doi.org/10.1145/1275808.1276484

20. Pu, S., Vosselman, G.: Building facade reconstruction by fusing terrestrial laser points and images. Sensors 9(6), 4525–4542 (2009)

21. Pu, S., Vosselman, G.: Refining building facade models with images. In: ISPRS Workshop, CMRT09-City Models, Roads and Traffic, vol. 38, pp. 3–4 (2009)

22. Riemenschneider, H., et al.: Irregular lattices for complex shape grammar facade parsing. In: The IEEE Conference on Computer Vision and Pattern Recognition, pp. 1640–1647, June 2012

23. Stamos, I., Allen, P.K.: 3-D model construction using range and image data. In: The IEEE Conference on Computer Vision and Pattern Recognition, p. 1531, June 2000. https://doi.org/10.1109/CVPR.2000.855865

24. Stamos, I., Allen, P.K.: Automatic registration of 2-D with 3-D imagery in urban environments. In: The IEEE International Conference on Computer Vision, vol. 2, pp. 731–736 (2001). https://doi.org/10.1109/ICCV.2001.937699

25. Torr, P.H., Zisserman, A.: MLESAC: a new robust estimator with application to estimating image geometry. Comput. Vis. Image Underst. 78(1), 138–156 (2000)

26. Tyleček, R., Šára, R.: Spatial pattern templates for recognition of objects with regular structure. In: GCPR: Pattern Recognition, pp. 364–374 (2013)

27. Yang, L., Sheng, Y., Wang, B.: 3D reconstruction of building facade with fused data of terrestrial lidar data and optical image. Optik Int. J. Light and Electron Opt. **127**(4), 2165–2168 (2016). https://doi.org/10.1016/j.ijleo.2015.11.147
28. Yu, Q., Helmholz, P., Belton, D.: Semantically enhanced 3D building model reconstruction from terrestrial laser-scanning data. J. Surveying Eng. **143**(4) (2017). https://doi.org/10.1061/(ASCE)SU.1943-5428.0000232
29. Zhang, Y., Funkhouser, T.A.: Deep depth completion of a single RGB-D image. CoRR abs/1803.09326 (2018)
30. Zhao, H., Shibasaki, R.: Reconstructing a textured cad model of an urban environment using vehicle-borne laser range scanners and line cameras. Mach. Vis. Appl. **14**(1), 35–41 (2003)

Multiview Dimension Reduction Based on Sparsity Preserving Projections

Haohao Li[1], Yu Cai[1], Guohui Zhao[1], Hu Lin[2], Zhixun Su[1(✉)], and Ximin Liu[1]

[1] School of Mathematical Sciences, Dalian University of Technology,
Dalian District of Ganjingzi City Road 2, Dalian 116024, China
`zxsu@dlut.edu.cn`
[2] Dalian Shipbuilding Industry Co., Dalian, China
`297001945@qq.com`

Abstract. In this paper, we focus on boosting the subspace learning by exploring the complimentary and compatible information from multi-view features. A novel multi-view dimension reduction method is proposed named Multiview Sparsity Preserving Projection (MSPP) for this task. MSPP aims to seek a set of linear transforms to project multi-view features into subspace where the sparse reconstructive weights of multi-view features are preserved as much as possible. And the Hilbert Schmidt Independence Criterion (HSIC) is utilized as a dependence term to explore the compatible and complementary information from multi-view features. An efficient alternative iterating optimization is presented to obtain the optimal solution of MSPP. Experiments on image datasets and multi-view textual datasets well demonstrate the excellent performance of MSPP.

Keywords: Dimension reduction · Multi-view learning · Co-regularization

1 Introduction

Nowadays, multi-view data is very common in many applications because many techniques have been developed to describe the same sample from multiple perspectives [19]. For example, one image can be presented by multi-view features, such as Scale Invariant Feature (SIFT) [16], Local Binary Patters (LBP) [19] and Edge Direction Histogram (EDH) [8]. However, these views features always contain incomplete information because different views are obtained by different feature extractors and reflect different properties of the sample. Therefore, how to integrate the complementary information from multi-view features is important for multi-view dimension reduction.

For some real-word application domains, such as text categorization [13], face recognition [22,30] and image classification [6,17,34], most features are extracted with high-dimension. However, the intrinsic dimension of the data might be lower. Therefore, manipulating these features directly is time consuming and computationally expensive. This leads researchers to develop a large

© Springer Nature Switzerland AG 2019
C. Lee et al. (Eds.): PSIVT 2019, LNCS 11854, pp. 296–309, 2019.
https://doi.org/10.1007/978-3-030-34879-3_23

number of dimension reduction methods [1,10,11,29,33] to find the intrinsic low-dimensional subspace preserving some properties of samples. Principal Component Analysis (PCA) [29] is a classical unsupervised linear dimension reduction method which constructs the subspace by projecting the data along the directions of maximal variance. Linear Discriminant Analysis (LDA) [1] is a supervised dimension reduction method which utilizes the label information to improve discriminative ability. LDA constructs the subspace by maximizing the ratio between the trace of between-scatter and within-class scatter. However, both PCA and LDA neglect the local correlations between samples. Locality Preserving Projections (LPP) [11] constructs the subspace by a linear transformation that preserves local neighborhood information in a certain sense. Neighborhood Preserving Embedding (NPE) [10] and Marginal Fisher Analysis(MFA) [33] are also local methods that construct the subspace based on different means. While above methods are all linear method, there are also many manifold learning methods [2,21] have been proposed for dimension reduction, such as Locally Linear Embedding (LLE) [21] and Laplacian Eigenmaps (LE) [2]. These manifold learning methods are more effective to deal with the high-dimensional features which lie on a submanifold of the original space. Sparse Subspace Learning (SSL)[3] is a family of dimension reduction methods which is based on the Sparse Representation (SR). Among these methods, Sparse Preserve Projection (SPP) [20] is a famous one. SPP constructs the subspace which aims to preserve the sparse reconstructive weights computed by sparse representation. And there are many other famous dimension reduction approaches, such as Locality Sensitive Discriminant Analysis (LSDA) [4] and Local Tangent Space Alignment (LTSA) [35]. Although many dimension reduction methods have been proposed, most of these methods always fail to exploit the complementary information from multi-view features to obtain the subspace.

In past decades, multi-view learning has been well generalized in various fields [5,7,14,15,18,23–28,31,32,36]. Many researchers focus on combining the multi-view setting with single view clustering. In [15], a multiview clustering method based on a co-regularized framework has been proposed. This approach utilizes a co-regularized term to limit the clusterings that are compatible across the graphs defined over each of the views. In [18], an auto-weighted method is proposed based on the relationship between multiview features clustering and semi-supervised classification. In [5], the smooth representation clustering (SMR) is extended into the multi-view domain, and Hilbert Schmidt Independence Criterion (HSIC) is utilized as a diversity term to jointly learning the representation from multi-view features. Some researchers focus on extending the traditional single view dimension reduction methods to multi-view dimension reduction model. In [14], the LDA is extended to Multiview Discriminant Analysis (MvDA) by jointly learning multiple view-specific linear transforms. Multiview Spectral Embedding (MSE) [31] combines the traditional spectral-embedding approach with multi-view data to construct the low-dimensional embedding of original multi-view data.

In this paper, we propose a novel multi-view dimension reduction method, which learns one common subspace to explore complementary information from multiple views. Toward this goal, we propose the MSPP based on SPP and HSIC [9]. On one hand, for each single view features we exploit SPP to seek the optimal subspace, where the sparse reconstructive weights are preserved best. On the other hand, we maximize the HSIC to ensure the dependence of different subspace, which aims to exploit the compatible and complementary information from multi-view features. An alternative iterating algorithm is utilized to obtain the optimal solution. The pipeline of this paper is shown in Fig. 1. The highlights of this paper are summarized as follows:

(i) We propose a novel multi-view dimension reduction approach, which is simple and effective.
(ii) Our algorithm simultaneously seeks one common optimal subspace based on SPP and explores complex correlation across multiple views in a unified framework based on HSIC.
(iii) Experimental results on the real-world datasets validate the effectiveness of our approach.

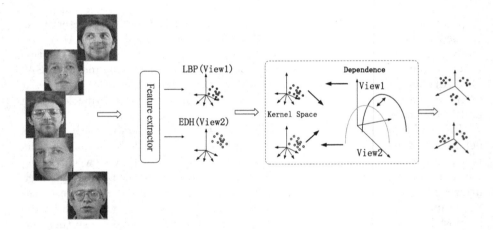

Fig. 1. The pipeline of this paper.

1.1 Organization

The rest of this paper is organized as follows: Sect. 2 provides a brief review of the single view dimension reduction algorithm SPP and a multi-view subspace clustering method. In Sect. 3, we describe details of the construction of MSPP and the optimization procedure. In Sect. 4, some experiments are conducted, which demonstrate the excellent performance of MSPP. In Sect. 5, we conclude this paper.

2   Related Work

In this section, we first introduce a traditional sparse subspace learning method SPP. Then we review a multi-view subspace clustering method, which illustrates some elements of multi-view learning.

2.1   Sparse Preserve Projection

Given a dataset that consists of N samples with m representations, the vth view features are expressed as: $\boldsymbol{X}^{(v)} = [\boldsymbol{x}_1^v, \boldsymbol{x}_2^v, ..., \boldsymbol{x}_N^v] \in \mathbb{R}^{d_v \times N}$. The dimension of vth features is d_v. SPP utilizes the sparse representation to compute a reconstructive weight matrix first. Then the projections are constructed to preserve the reconstructive weight matrix. For the given vth view features $\boldsymbol{X}^{(v)}$, the sparse reconstructive weights are constructed by:

$$\min_{\boldsymbol{z}_i^{(v)}} \quad ||\boldsymbol{z}_i^{(v)}||_1$$
$$s.t. \quad \boldsymbol{x}_i^{(v)} = \boldsymbol{X}^{(v)} \boldsymbol{z}_i^{(v)}, \quad 1 = \boldsymbol{1}^T \boldsymbol{z}_i, \tag{1}$$

where $\boldsymbol{z}_i^{(v)} = [z_{i,1}^{(v)}, ..., z_{i,i-1}^{(v)}, 0, z_{i,i+1}^{(v)}, ..., z_{i,N}^{(v)}]$ is an N-dimensional vector, in which the ith element is zero, and $\boldsymbol{1} \in \mathbb{R}^N$ is a vector of all ones. Each element $z_{ij}^{(v)}, i \neq j$ denotes the contribution of each $\boldsymbol{x}_j^{(v)}$ to reconstructing $\boldsymbol{x}_i^{(v)}$. After computing the weight vector $\boldsymbol{z}_i^{(v)}$ for each $\boldsymbol{x}_i^{(v)}$, the sparse reconstructive weight matrix $Z^{(v)}$ can be defined as:

$$\boldsymbol{Z}^{(v)} = [\boldsymbol{z}_1^{(v)}, \boldsymbol{z}_2^{(v)}, ..., \boldsymbol{z}_N^{(v)}]. \tag{2}$$

Then the objective function of the SPP can be formulated as follows:

$$\min_{\boldsymbol{w}^{(v)}} \sum_i^N ||(\boldsymbol{w}^{(v)})^T \boldsymbol{x}_i^{(v)} - (\boldsymbol{w}^{(v)})^T \boldsymbol{X}^{(v)} \boldsymbol{z}_i^{(v)}||^2. \tag{3}$$

where $\boldsymbol{w}^{(v)} \in \mathbb{R}^{d_v}$ is the projection direction. With simple algebraic operations, we can reformulate the Eq. (3) as:

$$\min_{\boldsymbol{w}^{(v)}} \sum_i^N ||(\boldsymbol{w}^{(v)})^T \boldsymbol{x}_i^{(v)} - (\boldsymbol{w}^{(v)})^T \boldsymbol{X}^{(v)} \boldsymbol{z}_i^{(v)}||^2$$
$$= (\boldsymbol{w}^{(v)})^T \boldsymbol{X}^{(v)} (\boldsymbol{I} - \boldsymbol{Z}^{(v)} - (\boldsymbol{Z}^{(v)})^T + (\boldsymbol{Z}^{(v)})^T \boldsymbol{Z}^{(v)}) (\boldsymbol{X}^{(v)})^T \boldsymbol{w}^{(v)}. \tag{4}$$

For the compactness of the formulation, we transform the Eq. (5) as:

$$\max_{\boldsymbol{w}^{(v)}} \quad (\boldsymbol{w}^{(v)})^T \boldsymbol{X}^{(v)} \boldsymbol{P}^{(v)} (\boldsymbol{X}^{(v)})^T \boldsymbol{w}^{(v)}$$
$$s.t. \quad (\boldsymbol{w}^{(v)})^T \boldsymbol{X}^{(v)} (\boldsymbol{X}^{(v)})^T \boldsymbol{w}^{(v)} = 1, \tag{5}$$

where $P^{(v)} = Z^{(v)} + (Z^{(v)})^T - (Z^{(v)})^T Z^{(v)}$, and the constraint $(w^{(v)})^T X^{(v)}$ $(X^{(v)})^T w^{(v)} = 1$ is to avoid degenerated solutions. The optimal projection matrix for Eq. (5) $W^{(v)} = [w_1^{(v)}, w_2^{(v)}, ..., w_d^{(v)}]$ consists of eigenvectors corresponding to the largest d eigenvalues of a generalized eigenvalue problem of Eq. (5).

2.2 Diversity-Induced Multi-view Subspace Clustering

Diversity-induced Multi-view Subspace Clustering (DiMSC) is a subspace clustering method which extends the Smooth Representation (SMR) clustering into the multi-view domain based on the complementary principle. The HSIC is utilized as the diversity term to explore the complementarity of multi-view features representations. The DiMSC encourages the new representations of different views to be of sufficient diversity, which can enforce the representations of each view to be novel to each other. The objective function of DiMSC is expressed as follows:

$$\min_{Z^{(1)}, Z^{(2)}, ..., Z^{(m)}} \sum_{v=1}^{m} (||X^{(v)} - X^{(v)} Z^{(v)}||_F^2 + \lambda_1 Tr(Z^{(v)} L^{(v)} (Z^{(v)})^T)) \\ + \sum_{v \neq w} \lambda_2 \mathrm{HSIC}(Z^{(v)}, Z^{(w)}), \tag{6}$$

where $L^{(v)}$ is a graph Laplace matrix for vth view features. The details of constructing $L^{(v)}$ is illustrated in [12]. $Tr(\cdot)$ is trace operator. The λ_1 and λ_2 are regularization parameters which control the trade-off between three terms of Eq.(6). The alternating minimizing optimization is adopted to solve the objective function.

3 Multiview Sparsity Preserving Projection

In this section, we first construct the formulation of the Multiview Sparsity Preserving Projection (MSPP) in Sect. 3.1, which can integrate the compatible and complementary information from multi-view features to construct sparse subspace for each view. In Sect. 3.2, we illustrate the optimization procedure of MSPP, which is solved by an iterative alternating strategy.

3.1 The Construction of MSPP

MSPP aims to find one common low-dimensional subspace for each view features. However, jointly analyzing the multiple features directly is challenging, because the features from different views are located in different dimensional spaces. Therefore, we utilize the kernel method to eliminate the problem. For the vth view features, $X^{(v)} = [x_1^{(v)}, x_2^{(v)}, ..., x_N^{(v)}]$, we define a nonlinear map ϕ which maps $x_i^{(v)}$ into the kernel space F as :

$$\phi : \mathbb{R}^{d_v} \to F, \quad x_i^{(v)} \to \phi(x_i^{(v)}). \tag{7}$$

Then for the vth view features, SPP can be reformulated as:

$$\max_{\hat{w}^{(v)}} \quad (\hat{w}_\phi^{(v)})^T X_\phi^{(v)} P^{(v)} (X_\phi^{(v)})^T \hat{w}_\phi^{(v)}$$
$$s.t. \quad (\hat{w}_\phi^{(v)})^T X_\phi^{(v)} (X_\phi^{(v)})^T \hat{w}_\phi^{(v)} = 1, \tag{8}$$

where $X_\phi^{(v)} = [\phi(x_1^{(v)}), \phi(x_2^{(v)}), ..., \phi(x_N^{(v)})]$ and $P^{(v)} = Z^{(v)} + (Z^{(v)})^T - (Z^{(v)})^T Z^{(v)}$ which is same as original SPP. We can learn from the Kernel PCA that $\hat{w}_\phi^{(v)}$ can be expressed as a linear combination of $\phi(x_1^{(v)}), \phi(x_2^{(v)}), ..., \phi(x_N^{(v)})$:

$$\hat{w}_\phi^{(v)} = \sum_{j=1}^{N} u_j^{(v)} \phi(x_j^{(v)}) = X_\phi^{(v)} w^{(v)}, \tag{9}$$

where $w^{(v)} = [u_1^{(v)}, u_2^{(v)}, ..., u_N^{(v)}]^T \in \mathbb{R}^N$. The we can reformulate Eq.(7) as follows:

$$\max_{w^{(v)}} \quad (w^{(v)})^T (X_\phi^{(v)})^T X_\phi^{(v)} P^{(v)} (X_\phi^{(v)})^T X_\phi^{(v)} w^{(v)}$$
$$= (w^{(v)})^T K^{(v)} P^{(v)} (K^{(v)})^T w^{(v)}, \tag{10}$$
$$s.t. \quad (w^{(v)})^T X^{(v)} (X^{(v)})^T w^{(v)} = 1.$$

Similar to SPP, in order to get the optimal low-dimensional subspace, we need to seek the optimal coefficients matrix $W^{(v)} = [w_1^{(v)}, w_2^{(v)}, ..., w_d^{(v)}]$ consisting of eigenvectors corresponding to the largest d eigenvalues of a generalized eigenvalue problem of Eq. (10). We formulate the objective function based on the coefficients matrix for all views as:

$$\max_{W^{(1)}, W^{(2)}, ..., W^{(m)}} \quad \sum_{v=1}^{m} Tr((W^{(v)})^T K^{(v)} P^{(v)} K^{(v)} W^{(v)}),$$
$$s.t. \quad (W^{(v)})^T K^{(v)} K^{(v)} W^{(v)} = I \quad v = 1, 2, ...m. \tag{11}$$

Benefitting from the kernel method, we can exploit the multi-view features from various dimensional spaces directly, which makes MSPP easily to find the optimal subspace for each views jointly. In order to utilize the compatible and complementary information of multi-view features, we make a hypothesis that low-dimensional representations of features from multiple views are similar across all the views. Therefore, we enforce features from each view to be more dependent and utilize the HSIC to measure the dependence between two views in our method. We can maximize the HSIC of two view features to enhance the dependence between them. Hence, we propose the following version of HSIC in our algorithm as a measurement of dependence between two views:

$$\text{HSIC}(Y^{(v)}, Y^{(w)}) = (N-1)^2 Tr(K_{Y^{(v)}} H K_{Y^{(w)}} H), \tag{12}$$

where $Y^{(v)}$ is the low-dimensional representation of $X^{(v)}$ and can be expressed as:

$$Y^{(v)} = (X_\phi^{(v)} W^{(v)})^T X_\phi^{(v)} = (W^{(v)})^T K^{(v)} \in \mathbb{R}^{d \times N}. \tag{13}$$

And $\boldsymbol{H} = (h_{ij}), h_{ij} = \delta_{ij} - \frac{1}{N}$. Maximizing Eq. (12) guarantees these features to be dependent, which can share compatible and complementary information to help MSPP to construct the subspace for multi-view features. For the kernel $\boldsymbol{K}_{\boldsymbol{Y}^{(v)}}$ we choose the inner product function, i.e., $\boldsymbol{K}_{\boldsymbol{Y}^{(v)}} = (\boldsymbol{Y}^{(v)})^T \boldsymbol{Y}^{(v)}$. Substituting this and the expression of $\boldsymbol{Y}^{(v)}$ into Eq. (12), we can get the following formulation:

$$\text{HSIC}(\boldsymbol{Y}^{(v)}, \boldsymbol{Y}^{(l)}) = (N-1)^2 Tr((\boldsymbol{W}^{(v)})^T \boldsymbol{K}^{(v)} \boldsymbol{G}^{(l)} (\boldsymbol{K}^{(v)})^T \boldsymbol{W}^{(v)}), \qquad (14)$$

where $\boldsymbol{G}^{(l)} = \boldsymbol{H}(\boldsymbol{K}^{(l)})^T \boldsymbol{W}^{(l)} (\boldsymbol{W}^{(l)})^T \boldsymbol{K}^{(l)} \boldsymbol{H}$.

The features from multiple views have different information to describe the sample. In order to well exploit the compatible and complementary information of different views, we impose on part optimization of different views independently by a set of nonnegative weights $\boldsymbol{\alpha} = [\alpha_1, \alpha_2, ..., \alpha_m]$. Then we can get the following maximization problem for MSPP:

$$\max_{\boldsymbol{W}^{(1)}, \boldsymbol{W}^{(2)}, ..., \boldsymbol{W}^{(m)}, \boldsymbol{\alpha}} \sum_{v=1}^{m} \alpha_v^r Tr((\boldsymbol{W}^{(v)})^T \boldsymbol{K}^{(v)} \boldsymbol{P}^{(v)} \boldsymbol{K}^{(v)} \boldsymbol{W}^{(v)})$$

$$+ \sum_{v \neq l} \beta HSIC(\boldsymbol{Y}^{(v)}, \boldsymbol{Y}^{(l)}), \qquad (15)$$

$$s.t. \quad (\boldsymbol{W}^{(v)})^T \boldsymbol{K}^{(v)} \boldsymbol{K}^{(v)} \boldsymbol{W}^{(v)} = I, \quad v = 1, 2, ...m \quad \text{and} \quad \sum_{v=1}^{m} \alpha_v = 1,$$

where $\beta > 0$ is the regularization parameter that controls the trade-off between two terms of Eq. (15). And we set $r > 1$ here to avoid that the optimal solution of $\boldsymbol{\alpha}$ is an one-hot vector [31]. The first term preserves the sparse reconstructive weights in the low-dimensional space and the second term ensure the dependence between any two views. We can obtain the low-dimensional subspace of vth view features as: $\boldsymbol{Y}^{(v)} = (\boldsymbol{X}_\phi^{(v)} \boldsymbol{W}^{(v)})^T \boldsymbol{X}_\phi^{(v)} = (\boldsymbol{W}^{(v)})^T \boldsymbol{K}^{(v)} \in \mathbb{R}^{d \times N}$.

We can find that the calculation of $\boldsymbol{W}(v)$ exploits all other $\boldsymbol{W}^{(l)}$ and the corresponding kernel ($v \neq l$). Therefore, maximizing the Eq. (15) constructs the subspace for each view features by integrating the compatible and complementary information from multi-view features and preserves the sparsity as much as possible.

3.2 Optimization of MSPP

In this section, we propose the optimization procedure of MSPP in detail. To the best of our knowledge, optimizing $\boldsymbol{\alpha}$ and $W^{(v)}$ directly is a tough task. Therefore, in this paper, we derive an alternating optimization strategy to obtain an local optimal solution.

First, we fix $W^{(v)}$ for all views to update $\boldsymbol{\alpha}$. By using a Lagrange multiplier λ to take the constraint $\sum_{v=1}^{m} \alpha_v = 1$ into consideration, we get the Lagrange function as:

$$\mathcal{L}(\boldsymbol{\alpha}, \lambda) = \sum_{v=1}^{m} \alpha_v^r Tr((\boldsymbol{W}^{(v)})^T \boldsymbol{K}^{(v)} \boldsymbol{P}^{(v)} \boldsymbol{K}^{(v)} \boldsymbol{W}^{(v)}) - \lambda(\sum_{i=1}^{m} \alpha_i - 1). \qquad (16)$$

By setting the derivative of L with respect to α_v and λ to 0, we can obtain:

$$\begin{cases} \dfrac{\partial \mathcal{L}(\boldsymbol{\alpha}, \lambda)}{\partial \alpha_v} = r\alpha_v^{r-1} Tr((\boldsymbol{W}^{(v)})^T \boldsymbol{K}^{(v)} \boldsymbol{P}^{(v)} \boldsymbol{K}^{(v)} \boldsymbol{W}^{(v)}) - \lambda = 0, \\ \dfrac{\partial \mathcal{L}(\boldsymbol{\alpha}, \lambda)}{\partial \lambda} = \displaystyle\sum_{i=1}^{m} \alpha_i - 1 = 0. \end{cases} \tag{17}$$

Therefore, α_v can be obtained as:

$$\alpha_v = \frac{(1/Tr((\boldsymbol{W}^{(v)})^T \boldsymbol{K}^{(v)} \boldsymbol{P}^{(v)} \boldsymbol{K}^{(v)} \boldsymbol{W}^{(v)}))^{1/(r-1)}}{\sum_{l=1}^{m} (1/Tr((\boldsymbol{W}^{(v)})^T \boldsymbol{K}^{(v)} \boldsymbol{P}^{(v)} \boldsymbol{K}^{(v)} \boldsymbol{W}^{(v)}))^{1/(r-1)}}. \tag{18}$$

Then, we fix $\boldsymbol{\alpha}$ to update $\boldsymbol{W}^{(v)}$ for all views. For vth view, we fix all $\boldsymbol{W}^{(l)}$ but $\boldsymbol{W}^{(v)}$. Equation (15) can be transformed as the following equation:

$$\begin{aligned} \max \omega(\boldsymbol{W}^{(v)}) &= \alpha_v^r Tr\{(\boldsymbol{W}^{(v)})^T \boldsymbol{K}^{(v)} \boldsymbol{P}^{(v)} \boldsymbol{K}^{(v)} \boldsymbol{W}^{(v)}\} \\ &+ \sum_{v \neq l} \beta(N-1)^2 tr\{(\boldsymbol{W}^{(v)})^T \boldsymbol{K}^{(v)} \boldsymbol{G}^{(l)} (\boldsymbol{K}^{(v)})^T \boldsymbol{W}^{(v)}\} \\ &= Tr\{(\boldsymbol{W}^{(v)})^T (\alpha_v^r \boldsymbol{K}^{(v)} \boldsymbol{P}^{(v)} \boldsymbol{K}^{(v)} + \sum_{v \neq l} (N-1)^2 \beta \boldsymbol{K}^{(v)} \boldsymbol{G}^{(l)} (\boldsymbol{K}^{(v)})) \boldsymbol{W}^{(v)}\}, \\ s.t. \quad & (\boldsymbol{W}^{(v)})^T \boldsymbol{K}^{(v)} \boldsymbol{K}^{(v)} \boldsymbol{W}^{(v)} = \boldsymbol{I}. \end{aligned}$$

$$(19)$$

Equation (19) is a generalized eigenvalue problem and the optimization of $\boldsymbol{W}^{(v)}$ can be solved by eigenvectors which corresponds to the smallest d eigenvalues. Other $\boldsymbol{W}^{(l)}$s can also be solved by similar procedure for updating themselves.

4 Experiment

In this section, we conduct some experiments to evaluate the performance of MSPP in comparison with some dimension reduction methods using 5 multi-view datasets.

4.1 Datasets

In our experiments, 5 datasets are utilized, including 3Sources, Yale, ORL and Caltech 101. The Yale, ORL and Caltech 101 are 3 benchmark image datasets. WebKB and 3Sources are textual datasets.

3Sources has been collected from 3 famous new sources: Reuters, Guardian and the BBC, and consists of 169 news in total. Each source is treated as on view. WebKB contains 4 subsets of samples with 6 labels. ORL and Yale are two face image datasets and some examples of them are shown in Figs. 3 and 4 respectively. We extract the local binary patterns (LBP), gray-scale intensity and edge direction histogram (EDH) as 3 view features. Caltech 101 Fig. 2 is a benchmark image dataset which contains 9144 images of 102 objects and features

Table 1. The classification average accuracies on 3Sources dataset.

3Sources	PCA	LPP	SPP	SPP_CON	MCCA	MvDA	MvSPP	MSPP
Dim = 30	63.23	56.21	51.23	50.19	64.18	76.72	80.10	**83.08**
Dim = 50	76.35	62.17	64.73	63.41	74.98	84.57	82.32	**88.67**

from 5 views are extracted using bag-of-words, locality-constrained linear coding (LLC), local binary patterns,edge direction histogram and gist.

In our experiments, the MSPP is evaluated by comparing some traditional dimension reduction methods and multi-viwe subspace learning methods, including: 1. PCA, 2. LPP, 3. SPP, 4. SPP with features concatenation (SPP_CON), 5. MCCA, 6. MvDA, 7. MvSPP.

4.2 Experiments on Datasets

This section conducts the experiments on 5 datasets to evalute the performance of MSPP. All the methods are used to obtain an optimal subspace and 1NN classifier is exploited to classify the testing samples. For traditional single view dimension reduction methods, we choose the best performance from all the single views. For our method, we utilize the Gaussian kernel with setting the width parameter $\delta = 1.5$. The parameter are set as $\lambda = 0.5$ and the $r = 2$.

Fig. 2. Some examples of Caltech 101.

For 3Sources dataset, we select 90 samples randomly as the training set. With the given training set, the 30 and 50 dimensional subspaces are learned by all methods respectively. Then, the test samples are transformed to the subspaces by the learned projection matrixes. In this experiment, 30 training/test splits are randomly generated and the average classification accuracies are shown in Table 1.

For WebKB dataset, we select 100 samples randomly as the training set. With the given training set, the 30 and 50 dimensional subspaces are learned by all methods respectively. Then, the test samples are transformed to the subspaces

Fig. 3. Some examples of ORL.

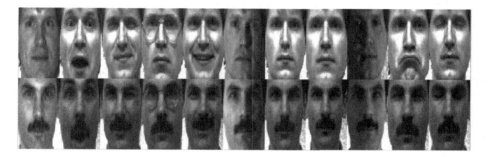

Fig. 4. Some examples of Yale.

Table 2. The classification average accuracies on WebKB dataset.

WebKB	PCA	LPP	SPP	SPP_CON	MCCA	MvDA	MvDA	MSPP
Dim = 30	68.95	66.21	74.32	70.94	73.22	75.39	73.39	**86.22**
Dim = 50	77.95	77.35	78.11	72.49	77.14	79.33	83.39	**89.28**

by the learned projection matrixes. In this experiment, 30 training/test splits are randomly generated and the average classification accuracies are shown in Table 2.

For ORL dataset, we select 180 samples and 300 samples randomly as the training set respectively. All dimension reduction methods are used to construct the 30 and 50 dimensional subspaces for all view features based on the training set. Then, the test samples are transformed to the subspaces by the learned projection matrixes. In this experiment, 20 training/test splits are randomly generated and the average classification accuracies are shown in Tables 3 and 4.

For Yale dataset, we select 75 samples and 105 samples randomly as the training set respectively. All dimension reduction methods are used to construct the 30 and 50 dimensional subspaces for all view features based on the training

Table 3. The classification average accuracies on image datasets.

Method	ORL		Yale		Caltech 101	
	Dim = 30	Dim = 50	Dim = 30	Dim = 50	Dim = 30	Dim = 50
PCA	71.24	75.12	69.01	75.37	63.52	64.85
LPP	72.21	78.33	70.23	73.26	63.36	65.92
SPP	73.21	77.16	70.11	70.20	65.79	67.70
SPP_CON	70.48	71.58	67.98	74.36	61.33	60.99
MCCA	73.49	78.47	71.07	77.32	64.75	69.35
MvDA	76.78	77.14	73.28	75.91	66.92	73.74
MvSPP	78.39	76.26	75.33	79.27	**70.02**	72.09
MSPP	**78.97**	**81.64**	**79.46**	**83.81**	69.78	**75.07**

Table 4. The classification average accuracies on image datasets.

Method	ORL		Yale		Caltech 101	
	Dim = 30	Dim = 50	Dim = 30	Dim = 50	Dim = 30	Dim = 50
PCA	72.35	78.27	72.23	79.82	66.63	68.47
LPP	74.56	78.33	73.14	74.26	64.53	67.26
SPP	75.48	81.16	73.22	76.20	68.22	70.01
SPP_CON	71.23	74.68	70.17	74.92	62.25	65.82
MCCA	74.85	79.25	74.60	78.21	66.23	67.18
MvDA	78.21	79.14	74.16	79.87	67.10	74.02
MvSPP	80.63	82.65	78.13	82.67	70.95	73.26
MSPP	**83.16**	**85.92**	**81.58**	**84.22**	**74.29**	**78.31**

set. Then, the test samples are transformed to the subspaces by the learned projection matrixes. In this experiment, 20 training/test splits are randomly generated and the average classification accuracies are shown in Tables 3 and 4.

For Caltech 101 dataset, we utilize 15 classes of Caltech 101 in our experiments. Then we randomly select 50% and 60% of the images per class as the training set respectively. With the given training set, the 30 and 50 dimensional subspaces are learned by all methods respectively. Then, the test samples are transformed to the subspaces by the learned projection matrixes. In this experiment, 30 training/test splits are randomly generated and the average classification accuracies are shown in Tables 3 and 4.

We can see from the results that MSPP outperforms other dimension reduction methods in most situations. The comparison with single view SPP_CON verifies that MSPP can fully integrate complementary information from multiview feature. In addition, the comparison with MvSPP verifies that the autoweighted trick and the co-regularization can improve the performance of the algorithm (Fig. 5).

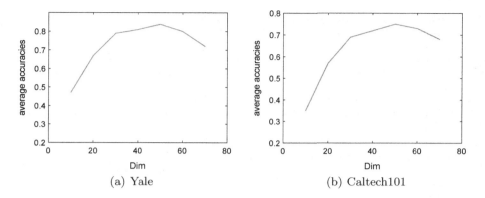

(a) Yale   (b) Caltech101

Fig. 5. Average accuracies with different dimensions in two image datasets.

5 Conclusion

In this paper, we propose a novel multi-view subspace learning method named Multiview Sparsity Preserving Projection (MSPP). MSPP aims to find the optimal subspace for each view, where the sparse reconstructive weights are preserved as much as possible. Meanwhile, the compatible and complementary information from multi-view features are utilized to construct the subspace by HSIC term. A plenty of experiments verify that MSPP is an effective multi-view dimension reduction method.

Acknowledgment. This work is supported by the Natural Science Foundation of China [No. 61572099]; Major National Science and Technology of China 2018ZX04011001-007, 2018ZX04016001-011.

References

1. Balakrishnama, S., Ganapathiraju, A.: Linear discriminant analysis-a brief tutorial. Inst. Signal Inf. Process. **18**, 1–8 (1998)
2. Belkin, M., Niyogi, P.: Laplacian eigenmaps for dimensionality reduction and data representation. Neural Comput. **15**(6), 1373–1396 (2003)
3. Cai, D., He, X., Han, J.: Spectral regression: a unified approach for sparse subspace learning. In: Seventh IEEE International Conference on Data Mining (ICDM 2007), pp. 73–82. IEEE (2007)
4. Cai, D., He, X., Zhou, K., Han, J., Bao, H.: Locality sensitive discriminant analysis. In: IJCAI, vol. 2007, pp. 1713–1726 (2007)
5. Cao, X., Zhang, C., Fu, H., Liu, S., Zhang, H.: Diversity-induced multi-view subspace clustering. In: Proceedings of the IEEE Conference on Computer Vision and Pattern Recognition, pp. 586–594 (2015)
6. Chapelle, O., Haffner, P., Vapnik, V.: Support vector machines for histogram-based image classification. IEEE Trans. Neural Networks **10**(5), 1055–1064 (1999)
7. Dhillon, P., Foster, D.P., Ungar, L.H.: Multi-view learning of word embeddings via CCA. In: Advances in Neural Information Processing Systems, pp. 199–207 (2011)

8. Gao, X., Xiao, B., Tao, D., Li, X.: Image categorization: graph edit direction histogram. Pattern Recogn. **41**(10), 3179–3191 (2008)
9. Gretton, A., Bousquet, O., Smola, A., Schölkopf, B.: Measuring statistical dependence with Hilbert-Schmidt norms. In: Jain, S., Simon, H.U., Tomita, E. (eds.) ALT 2005. LNCS (LNAI), vol. 3734, pp. 63–77. Springer, Heidelberg (2005). https://doi.org/10.1007/11564089_7
10. He, X., Cai, D., Yan, S., Zhang, H.J.: Neighborhood preserving embedding. In: Tenth IEEE International Conference on Computer Vision (ICCV 2005) Volume 1, vol. 2, pp. 1208–1213. IEEE (2005)
11. He, X., Niyogi, P.: Locality preserving projections. In: Advances in Neural Information Processing Systems, pp. 153–160 (2004)
12. Hu, H., Lin, Z., Feng, J., Zhou, J.: Smooth representation clustering. In: Proceedings of the IEEE Conference on Computer Vision and Pattern Recognition, pp. 3834–3841 (2014)
13. Joachims, T.: Transductive inference for text classification using support vector machines (1999)
14. Kan, M., Shan, S., Zhang, H., Lao, S., Chen, X.: Multi-view discriminant analysis. IEEE Trans. Pattern Anal. Mach. Intell. **38**(1), 188–194 (2015)
15. Kumar, A., Rai, P., Daume, H.: Co-regularized multi-view spectral clustering. In: Advances in Neural Information Processing Systems, pp. 1413–1421 (2011)
16. Lowe, D.G.: Distinctive image features from scale-invariant keypoints. Int. J. Comput. Vision **60**(2), 91–110 (2004)
17. Lu, D., Weng, Q.: A survey of image classification methods and techniques for improving classification performance. Int. J. Remote Sensing **28**(5), 823–870 (2007)
18. Nie, F., Cai, G., Li, J., Li, X.: Auto-weighted multi-view learning for image clustering and semi-supervised classification. IEEE Trans. Image Process. **27**(3), 1501–1511 (2017)
19. Ojala, T., Pietikainen, M., Maenpaa, T.: Multiresolution gray-scale and rotation invariant texture classification with local binary patterns. IEEE Trans. Pattern Anal. Mach. Intell. **24**(7), 971–987 (2002). https://doi.org/10.1109/TPAMI.2002.1017623
20. Qiao, L., Chen, S., Tan, X.: Sparsity preserving projections with applications to face recognition. Pattern Recogn. **43**(1), 331–341 (2010)
21. Roweis, S.T., Saul, L.K.: Nonlinear dimensionality reduction by locally linear embedding. Science **290**(5500), 2323–2326 (2000)
22. Tao, D., Jin, L.: Discriminative information preservation for face recognition. Neurocomputing **91**(2), 11–20 (2012)
23. Wang, H., Feng, L., Zhang, J., Liu, Y.: Semantic discriminative metric learning for image similarity measurement. IEEE Trans. Multimedia **18**(8), 1579–1589 (2016). https://doi.org/10.1109/TMM.2016.2569412
24. Wang, H., Feng, L., Yu, L., Zhang, J.: Multi-view sparsity preserving projection for dimension reduction. Neurocomputing **216**, 286–295 (2016)
25. Wang, H., Li, H., Fu, X.: Auto-weighted mutli-view sparse reconstructive embedding. Multimedia Tools Appl. 1–15 (2019)
26. Wang, H., Li, H., Peng, J., Fu, X.: Multi-feature distance metric learning for nonrigid 3D shape retrieval. Multimedia Tools Appl. 1–16 (2019)
27. Wang, H., Lin, F., Meng, X., Chen, Z., Yu, L., Zhang, H.: Multi-view metric learning based on KL-divergence for similarity measurement. Neurocomputing **238**(C), 269–276 (2017)
28. Wang, H., Peng, J., Fu, X.: Co-regularized multi-view sparse reconstruction embedding for dimension reduction. Neurocomputing **347**, 191–199 (2019)

29. Wold, S.: Principal component analysis. Chemometr. Intell. Lab. Syst. **2**(1), 37–52 (1987)
30. Wright, J., Yang, A.Y., Ganesh, A., Sastry, S.S., Ma, Y.: Robust face recognition via sparse representation. IEEE Trans. Pattern Anal. Mach. Intell. **31**(2), 210–227 (2008)
31. Xia, T., Tao, D., Mei, T., Zhang, Y.: Multiview spectral embedding. IEEE Trans. Syst. Man Cybern. Part B (Cybern.) **40**(6), 1438–1446 (2010)
32. Xu, C., Tao, D., Xu, C.: A survey on multi-view learning. arXiv preprint arXiv:1304.5634 (2013)
33. Xu, D., Yan, S., Tao, D., Lin, S., Zhang, H.J.: Marginal fisher analysis and its variants for human gait recognition and content-based image retrieval. IEEE Trans. Image Process. **16**(11), 2811–2821 (2007)
34. Yang, J., Kai, Y., Gong, Y., Huang, T.: Linear spatial pyramid matching using sparse coding for image classification. In: CVPR, pp. 1794–1801 (2009)
35. Zhang, Z., Zha, H.: Principal manifolds and nonlinear dimensionality reduction via tangent space alignment. SIAM J. Sci. Comput. **26**(1), 313–338 (2004)
36. Zhao, J., Xie, X., Xu, X., Sun, S.: Multi-view learning overview: recent progress and new challenges. Inf. Fusion **38**, 43–54 (2017)

RETRACTED CHAPTER: Non-peaked Discriminant Analysis for Image Representation

Xijian Fan[✉] and Qiaolin Ye

Nanjing Forestry University, Nanjing, China
{xijian.fan,qiaolin.ye}@njfu.edu.cn

Abstract. The L1-norm has been used as the distance metric in robust discriminant analysis. However, it is not sufficiently robust and thus we propose the use of cutting L1-norm. Since this norm is helpful for eliminating outliers in learning models, the proposed non-peaked discriminant analysis is better able to perform feature extraction tasks for image classification. We also show that cutting L1-norm can be equivalently computed using the difference of two special convex functions and present an efficient iterative algorithm for the optimization of proposed objective. The theoretical insights and effectiveness of the proposed algorithm are verified by experimental results on images from three datasets.

Keywords: Discriminant analysis · Cutting L1-norm distance · Image classification

1 Introduction

Data representation techniques are widely used in computer vision to discover the intrinsic structure of high-dimensional visual data using subspace learning (SL) and dimension reduction methods. Linear Discriminant Analysis (LDA) is one of the most representative SL methods. Traditional LDA suffers from being sensitive to outliers due to the use of squared L2-norm within- and between-class distances. To overcome this problem, Lai et al. [1] proposed rotational invariant LDA (RILDA), which measures the distance using L2,1-norm. However, the iterative algorithm for the formulation is not theoretically convergent. Motivated by the success of L1-norm related Principal Component Analysis (PCA) algorithms, Wang et al. [2] extended LDA to L1-norm LDA (LDA-L1) for robustness improvement, which replaces the squared L2-norm with L1-norm. LDA-L1 is advantageous to RILDA in terms of performance [2, 3]. In [4], Zheng et al. proposed L1-LDA under the framework of Bayes error bound. One disadvantage of L1-LDA is that a Bayes optimal solution is not guaranteed, its discriminant power is thus limited for image analysis and classification [4]. Chen et al. [5] and Ye et al. [6] optimized the LDA-L1 objective problem by employing a non-greedy gradient ascending algorithm. Compared to PCA, LDA has a more complex objective problem since it involves distance maximization and minimization terms.

The original version of this chapter was retracted: The retraction note to this chapter is available at https://doi.org/10.1007/978-3-030-34879-3_32

This has resulted in many extensions, such as [2, 3, 7, 8]. Due to its ability to eliminate outliers, L1-norm distance has been introduced for heteroscedastic discriminant analysis [4], k-plane clustering [6], distance metric learning [10], and discriminant local preserving projection [11, 12].

Although L1-norm related LDA algorithms have been shown to be effective in SL for image classification tasks, they are not sufficiently robust [13–15]. In this paper, we propose a novel formulation for discriminant analysis called Non-peaked Discriminant Analysis (NPLDA) with L1-norm as the distance metric. Since the cutting L1-norm distance metric is helpful for eliminating outliers whose distances to the total mean dominate the objective in the learning process, the proposed method is better able to perform feature extraction tasks. However, our formulation is a maximization-minimization problem and the cutting L1-norm distance measurement is not convex, thus it is challenging to solve it. To address this problem, we show that the cutting L1-norm distance can be equivalently computed using the difference of two special convex functions. Based on this finding, we propose a novel optimization algorithm to efficiently solve the proposed NPLDA problem. Also, we conduct rigorous theoretical proofs on the convergence of the algorithm. The theoretical insights and effectiveness of the proposed method are verified by image classification results on several real datasets.

2   Motivation and Proposed Objective Function

Assume that $\mathbf{X} = [\mathbf{x}_1, \mathbf{x}_2, \ldots, \mathbf{x}_n] \in \mathbf{R}^{d \times n}$ is a training set with n data samples belonging to c classes. Let $\mathbf{x}_j^i$ and n_i be the j-th sample and the number of the i-th class. Let $\mathrm{sgn}(\cdot)$ be a sign function with $\mathrm{sgn}(\cdot) = -1$ if $(\cdot)$ is a negative value and $\mathrm{sgn}(\cdot) = 1$ otherwise. Subspace learning maps each sample $\mathbf{x}_i$ in input space to a lower r-dimensional vector $\mathbf{z}_i$ by $\mathbf{z}_i = \mathbf{W}^T \mathbf{x}_i$, where $\mathbf{W} = [\mathbf{w}_1, \ldots, \mathbf{w}_r] \in \mathbf{R}^{d \times r}$ denotes the computed projection matrix.

The core idea of LDA-L2 is to find the projection matrix $\mathbf{W}$ maximizing the between-class scatter and simultaneously minimizing the within-class scatter by optimizing

$$\max_{\mathbf{W}} \frac{\sum_{i=1}^{c} n_i \|\mathbf{W}^T(\mathbf{m}_i - \mathbf{m})\|_2^2}{\sum_{i=1}^{c} \sum_{j=1}^{n_i} \|\mathbf{W}^T(\mathbf{x}_j^i - \mathbf{m}_i)\|_2^2}, \tag{1}$$

where $\mathbf{m}_i = 1/n_i \sum_{i=1}^{n_i} \mathbf{x}_i$ denotes the average vector of the i-th class and $\mathbf{m} = 1/n \sum_{i=1}^{n} \mathbf{x}_i$ denotes the total mean of training set. Problem (1) is a generalized eigenvalue problem. Theoretically, solving (1) is equivalent to solving the following problem

$$\max_{\mathbf{W}} \frac{\sum_{i=1}^{c} n_i \|\mathbf{W}^T(\mathbf{m}_i - \mathbf{m})\|_2^2}{\sum_{i=1}^{n} \|\mathbf{W}^T(\mathbf{x}_i - \mathbf{m})\|_2^2}. \tag{2}$$

When outliers are present, LDA-L2 usually achieves suboptimal projection vectors that drift from the desired directions due to the squared L2-norm. To improve the robustness, LDA-L1 [2, 4, 7, 8] replaces the squared L2-norm in (1) with L1-norm, i.e.,

$$\max_{\mathbf{W}, \mathbf{W}^T\mathbf{W}=\mathbf{I}} \frac{\sum_{i=1}^c n_i ||\mathbf{W}^T(\mathbf{m}_i - \mathbf{m})||_1}{\sum_{i=1}^c \sum_{j=1}^{n_i} ||\mathbf{W}^T(\mathbf{x}_j^i - \mathbf{m}_i)||_1}, \tag{3}$$

where $\mathbf{W}^T\mathbf{W} = \mathbf{I}$ emphasizes the orthogonality relationships between the projection vectors. The objective optimization in (3) is difficult, and this led to two common practices to handle this problem. The first is converting it into a series of $r - 1$ problems by a greedy procedure where each step produces only a projection vector [2–4, 12]. The second is applying a non-greedy algorithm [8].

Zheng et al. [9] derived the L1-norm discriminant criterion function by substituting L1-norm distance metric into (2)

$$\max_{\mathbf{W}, \mathbf{W}^T\mathbf{W}=\mathbf{I}} \frac{\sum_{i=1}^c n_i ||\mathbf{W}^T(\mathbf{m}_i - \mathbf{m})||_1}{\sum_{i=1}^n ||\mathbf{W}^T(\mathbf{x}_i - \mathbf{m})||_1}. \tag{4}$$

However, the obtained solution by (4) cannot guarantee the maximization of (3) that is formulated based on the true objective function of LDA-L2, due to the non-equivalence between (3) and (4) [3]. Furthermore, the Bayes error upper bound of (4) is looser than that of (3) [3].

From (3), for existing LDA-L1 methods, the distances between each data point and its class mean need to be computed. The optimal projection should minimize these distances, i.e., $\min \sum_{i=1}^c \sum_{j=1}^{n_i} ||\mathbf{W}^T(\mathbf{x}_j^i - \mathbf{m}_i)||_1$. Suppose that the first s points of the training set which belong to the first class are outliers, we rewrite the problem as

$$\min_{\mathbf{W}} \sum_{i=2}^c \sum_{j=1}^{n_i} ||\mathbf{W}^T(\mathbf{x}_j^i - \mathbf{m}_i)||_1 \\ + \sum_{j=1}^s ||\mathbf{W}^T(\mathbf{x}_j^1 - \mathbf{m}_1)||_1 + \sum_{j=s+1}^{n_1} ||\mathbf{W}^T(\mathbf{x}_j^1 - \mathbf{m}_1)||_1 \tag{5}$$

The outliers cause the projection direction to drift from the desired only when the last term of (3) dominates the objective. Assume that $\mathbf{W}_o$ is an ideal projection matrix that is not sensitive to the outliers. If we want to acquire such a projection, we must guarantee that

$$\sum_{j=1}^s ||\mathbf{W}_o^T(\mathbf{x}_j^1 - \mathbf{m}_1)||_1 \\ \leq \sum_{i=2}^c \sum_{j=1}^{n_i} ||\mathbf{W}_o^T(\mathbf{x}_j^i - \mathbf{m}_i)||_1 + \sum_{j=s+1}^{n_1} ||\mathbf{W}_o^T(\mathbf{x}_j^1 - \mathbf{m}_1)||_1 \tag{6}$$

i.e., the distances between each of the outliers and its class mean, after the projection on $\mathbf{W}_o$, cannot dominate the objective. We note that these distances are usually larger than those from each data point to its class mean. Thus, when the value of s is very small, (6) can be easily satisfied. However, the inequality may be violated if s is larger. In this case, despite the verified robustness in SL, LDA-L1 can only cope with small number of outliers. The same argument can be made on the maximization in (3), i.e., $\max \sum_{i=1}^{c} n_i \|\mathbf{W}^T(\mathbf{m}_i - \mathbf{m})\|_1$.

From the above analyses, we note that L1-norm may not help LDA-L1 to effectively extract the features of data in the presence of outliers, which usually have larger projected distances dominating the objective. To address this problem, we assign smaller values to these distances, such that their effects in the model are reduced. Thus, the use of cutting L1-norm as the distance metric. Specifically, in order to maximize the between-class dispersion, we treat h if the distance from the projected $\mathbf{m}_i$ to the projected total mean $\mathbf{m}$ is greater than h. This is implemented by

$$\max_{\mathbf{W}, \mathbf{W}^T\mathbf{W}=\mathbf{I}} \sum_{i=1}^{c} \min(h, n_i\|\mathbf{W}^T(\mathbf{m}_i - \mathbf{m})\|_1), \tag{7}$$

where $h > 0$. Also, we minimize the within-class dispersion and simultaneously constrain it to be s if it is greater than s. This is achieved by

$$\min_{\mathbf{W}, \mathbf{W}^T\mathbf{W}=\mathbf{I}} \sum_{i=1}^{c} \sum_{j=1}^{n_i} \min(s, \|\mathbf{W}^T(\mathbf{x}_j^i - \mathbf{m}_i)\|_1), \tag{8}$$

where $s > 0$. This final objective function, after combining (7) and (8), is

$$\max_{\mathbf{W}, \mathbf{W}^T\mathbf{W}=\mathbf{I}} \frac{\sum_{i=1}^{c} \min(h, n_i\|\mathbf{W}^T(\mathbf{m}_i - \mathbf{m})\|_1)}{\sum_{i=1}^{c} \sum_{j=1}^{n_i} \min(s, \|\mathbf{W}^T(\mathbf{x}_j^i - \mathbf{m}_i)\|_1)}. \tag{9}$$

Using the greedy strategy [2, 4, 7], (9) is simplified into a series of $r = 1$ problems. Let $\mathbf{p}_i = n_i(\mathbf{m}_i - \mathbf{m})$, $\mathbf{f}_j^i = \mathbf{x}_j^i - \mathbf{m}_i$, and $r = 1$, (9) becomes

$$\max \frac{\sum_{i=1}^{c} \min(h, |\mathbf{w}^T\mathbf{p}_i|)}{\sum_{i=1}^{c} \sum_{j=1}^{n_i} \min(s, |\mathbf{w}^T\mathbf{f}_j^i|)}. \tag{10}$$

We plot the distance curve w.r.t. $\min(s, |\mathbf{w}^T\mathbf{f}_j^i|)$ (see Fig. 1). When $s = inf$, the distance reverts to the L1-norm. In this case, after the projection onto $\mathbf{w}$, the distances from the outliers to the corresponding class mean usually locate the peak of the curve. When $s \neq inf$, we obtain a non-peaked distance curve. The cutting norm distance treat s if $|\mathbf{w}^T\mathbf{f}_j^i|$ is greater than s. This makes our objective more robust to outliers.

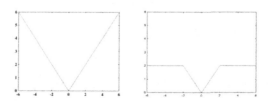

Fig. 1. The distance curve with respect to $\min(s, |\mathbf{w}^T\mathbf{f}_j^i|)$. The abscissa is the value of $\mathbf{w}^T\mathbf{f}_j^i$. Left:$s = inf$. Right:$s = 2$.

Our formulation is novel as follows: (1) We propose a technique that treats projected distances of outliers as smaller values, enabling strong suppression of outliers; (2) Although there are recent works on support vector machine and matrix recovery [13, 14], which successfully employ a cutting L1-norm loss function but their ideas have not been extended for SL for image classification, due to different goals and formulations; (3) Cutting L1-norm distance increases the difficulty in optimizing (10), e.g., there are the non-smoothness results from the definitions of both cutting norm and L1-norm in the distance measurement of cutting L1-norm. Thus, we propose an equivalent formulation to (10), and an effective iterative algorithm to solve this formulation, proving the convergence of the algorithm; and (4) Our method is a general supervised robust algorithm for SL.

3 Equivalent Formulation and Solution

3.1 An Equivalent Formulation

Solving (10) is difficult and thus we provide an equivalent formulation to (8) as follows.

Theorem 1: Define

$$r_i = 1, \ i \in [1, \dots, c],$$

$$r_i = -1, \ i \in [c+1, \dots, 2c], \ and \ \mathbf{w}^T \mathbf{p}_i = -\mathbf{w}^T \mathbf{p}_{i-c}, \ i \in [c+1, \dots, 2c].$$

Our optimization problem (10) is equivalent to the following formulation

$$\max_{\mathbf{w}} \ \frac{\sum_{i=1}^{c} |\mathbf{w}^T \mathbf{p}_i| - \sum_{i=1}^{2c} \max(0, r_i \mathbf{w}^T \mathbf{p}_i - h)}{\sum_{i=1}^{c} \sum_{j=1}^{n_i} \min(s, |\mathbf{w}^T \mathbf{f}_j^i|)}. \tag{11}$$

Proof: Noting that if the value of $\mathbf{w}^T \mathbf{p}_i$ is greater or equal to zero, then

$$\min(h, |\mathbf{w}^T \mathbf{p}_i|) = \min(h, \mathbf{w}^T \mathbf{p}_i). \tag{12}$$

Otherwise,

$$\min(h, |\mathbf{w}^T \mathbf{p}_i|) = \min(h, -\mathbf{w}^T \mathbf{p}_i). \tag{13}$$

This can be implemented with the following formulation

$$\min(h, |\mathbf{w}^T \mathbf{p}_i|) = \min(h, \max(0, \mathbf{w}^T \mathbf{p}_i)) + \min(h, \max(0, -\mathbf{w}^T \mathbf{p}_i)), \tag{14}$$

leading to

$$\sum_{i=1}^{c} \min(h, |\mathbf{w}^T \mathbf{p}_i|)$$
$$= \sum_{i=1}^{c} \min(h, \max(0, \mathbf{w}^T \mathbf{p}_i)) + \sum_{i=1}^{c} \min(h, \max(0, -\mathbf{w}^T \mathbf{p}_i)) \quad (15)$$

It is understandable that $\min(h, \max(0, \mathbf{w}^T \mathbf{p}_i))$ can be rewritten as

$$\min(h, \max(0, \mathbf{w}^T \mathbf{p}_i)) = \max(0, \mathbf{w}^T \mathbf{p}_i) - \max(0, \mathbf{w}^T \mathbf{p}_i - h)), \quad (16)$$

difference of two convex functions.

With the same argument, $\min(h, \max(0, -\mathbf{w}^T \mathbf{p}_i))$ can be written as

$$\min(h, \max(0, -\mathbf{w}^T \mathbf{p}_i))$$
$$= \max(0, -\mathbf{w}^T \mathbf{p}_i) - \max(0, -\mathbf{w}^T \mathbf{p}_i - h). \quad (17)$$

Thus, (15) can be rewritten as

$$\sum_{i=1}^{c} \min(h, |\mathbf{w}^T \mathbf{p}_i|)$$
$$= \sum_{i=1}^{c} \max(0, \mathbf{w}^T \mathbf{p}_i) + \max(0, -\mathbf{w}^T \mathbf{p}_i) \quad (18)$$
$$- (\sum_{i=1}^{c} \max(0, \mathbf{w}^T \mathbf{p}_i - h) + \max(0, -\mathbf{w}^T \mathbf{p}_i - h))$$

Since

$$\sum_{i=1}^{c} \max(0, \mathbf{w}^T \mathbf{p}_i) + \max(0, -\mathbf{w}^T \mathbf{p}_i) = \sum_{i=1}^{c} |\mathbf{w}^T \mathbf{p}_i| \quad (19)$$

and

$$\sum_{i=1}^{c} (\max(0, \mathbf{w}^T \mathbf{p}_i - h)) + \max(0, -\mathbf{w}^T \mathbf{p}_i - h)))$$
$$= \sum_{i=1}^{2c} \max(0, r_i \mathbf{w}^T \mathbf{p}_i - h), \quad (20)$$

we can rewrite (15) as

$$\sum_{i=1}^{c} \min(h, |\mathbf{w}^T \mathbf{p}_i|) = \sum_{i=1}^{c} |\mathbf{w}^T \mathbf{p}_i| - \sum_{i=1}^{2c} \max(0, r_i \mathbf{w}^T \mathbf{p}_i - h). \quad (21)$$

Replacing the numerator in (10) with (21), we obtain (11). Thus, Q.E.D.

3.2 Solution Algorithm

From the proof of Theorem 1, we note that the cutting L1-norm distance can be decomposed into the difference of two convex functions, and an equivalence between (10) and (11) exists. Suppose that

$$\lambda^{(t)} = \frac{\sum_{i=1}^{c} |\mathbf{w}^{(t)^T} \mathbf{p}_i| - \sum_{i=1}^{2c} \max(0, r_i \mathbf{w}^{(t)^T} \mathbf{p}_i - h)}{\sum_{i=1}^{c} \sum_{j=1}^{n_i} \min(s, |\mathbf{w}^{(t)^T} \mathbf{f}_j^i|)} \tag{22}$$

is the objective value of (11) after the t iteration, where $\mathbf{w}^{(t)}$ is the optimal discriminant vector solved at iteration t-th. We solve the following problem to obtain the solution of the $(t+1)$-th iteration

$$\mathbf{w}^{(t+1)} = \underset{\mathbf{w}}{\operatorname{argmax}} \sum_{i=1}^{c} |\mathbf{w}^T \mathbf{p}_i| - \sum_{i=1}^{2c} \max(0, r_i \mathbf{w}^T \mathbf{p}_i - h)$$
$$- \lambda^{(t)} \sum_{i=1}^{c} \sum_{j=1}^{n_i} \min(s, |\mathbf{w}^T \mathbf{f}_j^i|) \tag{23}$$

which is equivalent to

$$\mathbf{w}^{(t+1)} = \underset{\mathbf{w}, \pi}{\operatorname{argmax}} \sum_{i=1}^{c} |\mathbf{w}^T \mathbf{p}_i| - \sum_{i=1}^{2c} \pi_i - \lambda^{(t)} \sum_{i=1}^{c} \sum_{j=1}^{n_i} \min(s, |\mathbf{w}^T \mathbf{f}_j^i|),$$
$$\text{s.t.} \quad h + \pi_i \geq r_i \mathbf{w}^T \mathbf{p}_i, \pi_i \geq 0, i = 1, \dots, 2c. \tag{24}$$

The Lagrangian corresponding to the problem in (24) is provided by

$$\mathcal{L}(\mathbf{w}, \pi, \boldsymbol{\alpha}, \boldsymbol{\beta}) = \sum_{i=1}^{c} |\mathbf{w}^T \mathbf{p}_i| - \sum_{i=1}^{2c} \pi_i - \lambda^{(t)} \sum_{i=1}^{c} \sum_{j=1}^{n_i} \min(s, |\mathbf{w}^T \mathbf{f}_j^i|)$$
$$- \sum_{i=1}^{2c} \alpha_i (h + \pi_i - r_i \mathbf{w}^T \mathbf{p}_i) - \sum_{i=1}^{2c} \beta_i \pi_i \tag{25}$$

where $\alpha_i \geq 0$ and $\beta_i \geq 0$ are the values of Lagrange multipliers. Setting the gradient of (25) w.r.t. $\mathbf{w}$ as zero gives

$$\mathbf{w} = \frac{1}{2} (\lambda^{(t)} \sum_{i=1}^{c} \sum_{j=1}^{n_i} \rho_i \mathbf{f}_j^i (\mathbf{f}_j^i)^T)^{-1} (\sum_{i=1}^{c} \theta_i \mathbf{p}_i + \sum_{i=1}^{2c} \alpha_i r_i \mathbf{p}_i), \tag{26}$$

where $\theta_i = \operatorname{sgn}(\mathbf{w}^T \mathbf{p}_i)$ and

$$\rho_i = \begin{cases} 1/(2|\mathbf{w}^T \mathbf{f}_j^i|), & \text{if } |\mathbf{w}^T \mathbf{f}_j^i| < s, \\ 0, & \text{otherwise.} \end{cases} \tag{27}$$

Clearly if θ_i and ρ_i are given, (26) is solution to the following problem:

$$\mathbf{w}^{(t+1)} = \arg \max_{\mathbf{w}} \sum_{i=1}^{c} \theta_i \mathbf{w}^T \mathbf{p}_i - \sum_{i=1}^{2c} \max(0, r_i \mathbf{w}^T \mathbf{p}_i - h)$$
$$- \lambda^{(t)} \sum_{i=1}^{c} \sum_{j=1}^{n_i} \rho_i \mathbf{w}^T \mathbf{f}_j^i (\mathbf{f}_j^i)^T \mathbf{w} \tag{28}$$

which is a quadratic convex programming problem (QCPP) and whose solution is obtained by the corresponding Wolf dual formulation. This can be implemented by an iterative procedure as follows. For the updated $\mathbf{w}$, we first compute θ_i and ρ_i using the current $\mathbf{w}$ solved in last iteration. We complete the computation of (10) as in Algorithm 1.

Note that $\rho_i^{(t)}$ may not be well defined if $|\mathbf{w}^{(t)^T}\mathbf{f}_j^i|$ tends to zero. We address this problem by regularizing it as $|\mathbf{w}^{(t)^T}\mathbf{f}_j^i| + \varepsilon$, where ε is a small positive value. Also, at iteration $t+1$, the objective value of (10) remains invariant when $\mathbf{w}^{(t+1)}$, h, and s are scaled by the length of $\mathbf{w}^{(t+1)}$, due to the quotient form (i.e., only the direction of $\mathbf{w}^{(t+1)}$ is interesting). However, the normalization is helpful to guarantee orthogonalization of the projection vectors in extracting multiple features [2]. The objective is clearly a QCPP in step 3. The time complexity of solving the problem is at most $O(c^3)$.

Algorithm 1 An effective iterative algorithm to optimize the problem (8).

Input: Data matrix $\mathbf{X} = [\mathbf{x}_1, \mathbf{x}_2, ..., \mathbf{x}_n] \in \mathbf{R}^{d \times n}$.

Initialize $\mathbf{w}$ and set $t = 1$.

For each pair (i, j), compute $\mathbf{p}_i = n_i(\mathbf{m}_i - \mathbf{m})$ and $\mathbf{f}_j^i = \mathbf{x}_j^i - \mathbf{m}_i$, $i = 1, ..., c$, $j = 1, ...$.

While not converge do

1. Compute the objective value using (20).

2. For each i, compute the $i-th$ elements of $\theta^{(t)}$ and $\rho^{(t)}$ by $\theta_i^{(t)} = \text{sgn}(\mathbf{w}^{(t)^T}\mathbf{p}_i)$

and $\rho_i^{(t)} = \begin{cases} 1/(2|\mathbf{w}^{(t)^T}\mathbf{f}_j^i|), & \text{if } |\mathbf{w}^{(t)^T}\mathbf{f}_j^i| < s, \\ 0, & \text{otherwise.} \end{cases}$

3. Obtain the $(t+1)$-th $\mathbf{w}^{(t+1)}$ using

$$\mathbf{w}^{(t+1)} = \operatorname*{argmax}_{\mathbf{w}} \sum_{i=1}^{c} \theta_i^{(t)}\mathbf{w}^T\mathbf{p}_i - \sum_{i=1}^{2c} \max(0, r_i\mathbf{w}^T\mathbf{p}_i - h)$$
$$-\lambda^{(t)} \sum_{i=1}^{c}\sum_{j=1}^{n_i} \rho_i^{(t)}\mathbf{w}^T\mathbf{f}_j^i(\mathbf{f}_j^i)^T\mathbf{w}$$

4. Normalize $\mathbf{w}^{(t+1)}$, h, and s by the length of $\mathbf{w}^{(t+1)}$ and set $t = t+1$.

End while

Output: $\mathbf{w}$.

3.3   Proof of Convergence

Now, we are ready to analyze the convergence of the proposed iterative algorithm. We begin with the following Theorem 2.

Theorem 2: Let $\rho_i^{(t)} = \begin{cases} 1/(2|\mathbf{w}^{(t)^T}\mathbf{f}_j^i|), & \text{if } |\mathbf{w}^{(t)^T}\mathbf{f}_j^i| < s, \\ 0, & \text{otherwise.} \end{cases}$ For each pair (i, j), inequality

$$\min(s, |\mathbf{w}^{(t+1)^T}\mathbf{f}_j^i|) - \rho_i^{(t)}\mathbf{w}^{(t+1)^T}\mathbf{f}_j^i(\mathbf{f}_j^i)^T\mathbf{w}^{(t+1)}$$
$$\leq \min(s, |\mathbf{w}^{(t)^T}\mathbf{f}_j^i|) - \rho_i^{(t)}\mathbf{w}^{(t)^T}\mathbf{f}_j^i(\mathbf{f}_j^i)^T\mathbf{w}^{(t)}$$

(29)

holds.

Proof: In the case of $|\mathbf{w}^{(t)^T}\mathbf{f}_j^i| \geq s$, $\rho_i^{(t)} = 0$, then,

$$
\begin{aligned}
\min(s, |\mathbf{w}^{(t+1)^T}\mathbf{f}_j^i|) - \rho_i^{(t)}\mathbf{w}^{(t+1)^T}\mathbf{f}_j^i(\mathbf{f}_j^i)^T\mathbf{w}^{(t+1)} &= \min(s, |\mathbf{w}^{(t+1)^T}\mathbf{f}_j^i|) \\
\leq s &= \min(s, |\mathbf{w}^{(t)^T}\mathbf{f}_j^i|) - \rho_i^{(t)}\mathbf{w}^{(t)^T}\mathbf{f}_j^i(\mathbf{f}_j^i)^T\mathbf{w}^{(t)}
\end{aligned}
\tag{30}
$$

which indicates that (29) holds. We now consider the case of $|\mathbf{w}^{(t)^T}\mathbf{f}_j^i| < s$.

For any $\mathbf{w}^{(t+1)}$, the following inequality always holds:

$$
\begin{aligned}
&(|\mathbf{w}^{(t+1)^T}\mathbf{f}_j^i| - |\mathbf{w}^{(t)^T}\mathbf{f}_j^i|)^2 \geq 0 \\
\Rightarrow~ &|\mathbf{w}^{(t+1)^T}\mathbf{f}_j^i|^2 + |\mathbf{w}^{(t)^T}\mathbf{f}_j^i|^2 - 2|\mathbf{w}^{(t)^T}\mathbf{f}_j^i||(\mathbf{f}_j^i)^T\mathbf{w}^{(t)}| \geq 0 \\
\Rightarrow~ &\frac{\mathbf{w}^{(t+1)^T}\mathbf{f}_j^i(\mathbf{f}_j^i)^T\mathbf{w}^{(t+1)}}{2|(\mathbf{f}_j^i)^T\mathbf{w}^{(t)}|} + \frac{1}{2}|\mathbf{w}^{(t)^T}\mathbf{f}_j^i| - |\mathbf{w}^{(t+1)^T}\mathbf{f}_j^i| \geq 0 \\
\Rightarrow~ &|\mathbf{w}^{(t+1)^T}\mathbf{f}_j^i| - \rho_i^{(t)}\mathbf{w}^{(t+1)^T}\mathbf{f}_j^i(\mathbf{f}_j^i)^T\mathbf{w}^{(t+1)} \leq 1/2|\mathbf{w}^{(t)^T}\mathbf{f}_j^i|.
\end{aligned}
\tag{31}
$$

Suppose that $|\mathbf{w}^{(t+1)^T}\mathbf{f}_j^i| \geq s$, it is true that $\min(s, |\mathbf{w}^{(t+1)^T}\mathbf{f}_j^i|) = s$, the following always holds:

$$
\min(s, |\mathbf{w}^{(t+1)^T}\mathbf{f}_j^i|) - \rho_i^{(t)}\mathbf{w}^{(t+1)^T}\mathbf{f}_j^i(\mathbf{f}_j^i)^T\mathbf{w}^{(t+1)} \leq 1/2|\mathbf{w}^{(t)^T}\mathbf{f}_j^i|.
\tag{32}
$$

When $|\mathbf{w}^{(t+1)^T}\mathbf{f}_j^i| < s$, we have $\min(s, |\mathbf{w}^{(t+1)^T}\mathbf{f}_j^i|) = |\mathbf{w}^{(t+1)^T}\mathbf{f}_j^i|$. In this case, (32) holds. We note that when $\rho_i^{(t)} = 1/(2|\mathbf{w}^{(t)^T}\mathbf{f}_j^i|)$ and $|\mathbf{w}^{(t)^T}\mathbf{f}_j^i| < s$,

$$
\min(s, |\mathbf{w}^{(t)^T}\mathbf{f}_j^i|) - \rho_i^{(t)}\mathbf{w}^{(t)^T}\mathbf{f}_j^i(\mathbf{f}_j^i)^T\mathbf{w}^{(t)} = 1/2|\mathbf{w}^{(t)^T}\mathbf{f}_j^i|.
\tag{33}
$$

Thus, we have

$$
\begin{aligned}
&\min(s, |\mathbf{w}^{(t+1)^T}\mathbf{f}_j^i|) - \rho_i^{(t)}\mathbf{w}^{(t+1)^T}\mathbf{f}_j^i(\mathbf{f}_j^i)^T\mathbf{w}^{(t+1)} \\
&\leq \min(s, |\mathbf{w}^{(t)^T}\mathbf{f}_j^i|) - \rho_i^{(t)}\mathbf{w}^{(t)^T}\mathbf{f}_j^i(\mathbf{f}_j^i)^T\mathbf{w}^{(t)}
\end{aligned}
$$

which is (29). Thus, Q.E.D.

Theorem 3: *Algorithm 1 monotonically increases the objective of (10) in each iteration.*

Proof: According to step 3 of Algorithm 1, for each iteration we have

$$
\begin{aligned}
&\sum_{i=1}^{c} \theta_i^{(t)} \mathbf{w}^{(t+1)^T} \mathbf{p}_i - \sum_{i=1}^{2c} \max(0, r_i \mathbf{w}^{(t+1)^T} \mathbf{p}_i - h) \\
&- \lambda^{(t)} \sum_{i=1}^{c} \sum_{j=1}^{n_i} \rho_i^{(t)} \mathbf{w}^{(t+1)^T} \mathbf{f}_j^i (\mathbf{f}_j^i)^T \mathbf{w}^{(t+1)} \\
&\geq \sum_{i=1}^{c} \theta_i^{(t)} \mathbf{w}^{(t)^T} \mathbf{p}_i - \sum_{i=1}^{2c} \max(0, r_i \mathbf{w}^{(t)^T} \mathbf{p}_i - h) \\
&- \lambda^{(t)} \sum_{i=1}^{c} \sum_{j=1}^{n_i} \rho_i^{(t)} \mathbf{w}^{(t)^T} \mathbf{f}_j^i (\mathbf{f}_j^i)^T \mathbf{w}^{(t)}.
\end{aligned}
\tag{34}
$$

With the definition of $\theta_i^{(t)}$, (30) can be expressed by the following equivalent formulation

$$
\begin{aligned}
&\sum_{i=1}^{c} \operatorname{sgn}(\mathbf{w}^{(t)^T} \mathbf{p}_i) \mathbf{w}^{(t+1)^T} \mathbf{p}_i - \sum_{i=1}^{2c} \max(0, r_i \mathbf{w}^{(t+1)^T} \mathbf{p}_i - h) \\
&- \lambda^{(t)} \sum_{i=1}^{c} \sum_{j=1}^{n_i} \rho_i^{(t)} \mathbf{w}^{(t+1)^T} \mathbf{f}_j^i (\mathbf{f}_j^i)^T \mathbf{w}^{(t+1)} \\
&\geq \sum_{i=1}^{c} \left| \mathbf{w}^{(t)^T} \mathbf{p}_i \right| - \sum_{i=1}^{2c} \max(0, r_i \mathbf{w}^{(t)^T} \mathbf{p}_i - h) \\
&- \lambda^{(t)} \sum_{i=1}^{c} \sum_{j=1}^{n_i} \rho_i^{(t)} \mathbf{w}^{(t)^T} \mathbf{f}_j^i (\mathbf{f}_j^i)^T \mathbf{w}^{(t)}.
\end{aligned}
\tag{35}
$$

According to Theorem 1, for each pair (i,j), (2) holds. Thus,

$$
\begin{aligned}
&\lambda^{(t)} \sum_{i=1}^{c} \sum_{j=1}^{n_i} \rho_i^{(t)} \mathbf{w}^{(t+1)^T} \mathbf{f}_j^i (\mathbf{f}_j^i)^T \mathbf{w}^{(t+1)} - \min(s, |\mathbf{w}^{(t+1)^T} \mathbf{f}_j^i|) \\
&\geq \lambda^{(t)} \sum_{i=1}^{c} \sum_{j=1}^{n_i} \rho_i^{(t)} \mathbf{w}^{(t)^T} \mathbf{f}_j^i (\mathbf{f}_j^i)^T \mathbf{w}^{(t)} - \min(s, |\mathbf{w}^{(t)^T} \mathbf{f}_j^i|).
\end{aligned}
\tag{36}
$$

Since for each i,

$$
|\mathbf{w}^{(t+1)^T} \mathbf{p}_i| - \operatorname{sgn}(\mathbf{w}^{(t+1)^T} \mathbf{p}_i) \mathbf{w}^{(t+1)^T} \mathbf{p}_i \geq \operatorname{sgn}(\mathbf{w}^{(t)^T} \mathbf{p}_i) \mathbf{w}^{(t+1)^T} \mathbf{p}_i,
$$

then $|\mathbf{w}^{(t+1)^T} \mathbf{p}_i| - \operatorname{sgn}(\mathbf{w}^{(t)^T} \mathbf{p}_i) \mathbf{w}^{(t+1)^T} \mathbf{p}_i \geq 0$. Since $|\mathbf{w}^{(t)^T} \mathbf{p}_i| - \operatorname{sgn}(\mathbf{w}^{(t)^T} \mathbf{p}_i) \mathbf{w}^{(t)^T} \mathbf{p}_i = 0$, one gets

$$
\begin{aligned}
&|\mathbf{w}^{(t+1)^T} \mathbf{p}_i| - \operatorname{sgn}(\mathbf{w}^{(t)^T} \mathbf{p}_i) \mathbf{w}^{(t+1)^T} \mathbf{p}_i \\
&\geq |\mathbf{w}^{(t)^T} \mathbf{p}_i| - \operatorname{sgn}(\mathbf{w}^{(t)^T} \mathbf{p}_i) \mathbf{w}^{(t)^T} \mathbf{p}_i
\end{aligned}
\tag{37}
$$

For each i, (37) holds, thus,

$$
\begin{aligned}
&\sum_{i=1}^{c} |\mathbf{w}^{(t+1)^T} \mathbf{p}_i| - \operatorname{sgn}(\mathbf{w}^{(t)^T} \mathbf{p}_i) \mathbf{w}^{(t+1)^T} \mathbf{p}_i \\
&\geq \sum_{i=1}^{c} |\mathbf{w}^{(t)^T} \mathbf{p}_i| - \operatorname{sgn}(\mathbf{w}^{(t)^T} \mathbf{p}_i) \mathbf{w}^{(t)^T} \mathbf{p}_i
\end{aligned}
\tag{38}
$$

Summing over (29), (34) and (36) on two sides, we obtain

$$
\begin{aligned}
&\sum_{i=1}^{c}\left|\mathbf{w}^{(t+1)^{T}}\mathbf{p}_{i}\right| - \sum_{i=1}^{2c}\max(0, r_{i}\mathbf{w}^{(t+1)^{T}}\mathbf{p}_{i} - h) \\
&-\lambda^{(t)}\sum_{i=1}^{c}\sum_{j=1}^{n_{i}}\min(s, |\mathbf{w}^{(t+1)^{T}}\mathbf{f}_{j}^{i}|) \\
&\geq \sum_{i=1}^{c}\left|\mathbf{w}^{(t)^{T}}\mathbf{p}_{i}\right| - \sum_{i=1}^{2c}\max(0, r_{i}\mathbf{w}^{(t)^{T}}\mathbf{p}_{i} - h) \\
&-\lambda^{(t)}\sum_{i=1}^{c}\sum_{j=1}^{n_{i}}\min(s, |\mathbf{w}^{(t)^{T}}\mathbf{f}_{j}^{i}|)
\end{aligned}
\tag{39}
$$

Since $\lambda^{(t)} = \dfrac{\sum_{i=1}^{c}|\mathbf{w}^{(t)^{T}}\mathbf{p}_{i}| - \sum_{i=1}^{2c}\max(0, r_{i}\mathbf{w}^{(t)^{T}}\mathbf{p}_{i} - h)}{\sum_{i=1}^{c}\sum_{j=1}^{n_{i}}\min(s, |\mathbf{w}^{(t)^{T}}\mathbf{f}_{j}^{i}|)}$, then

$$
\begin{aligned}
&\sum_{i=1}^{c}\left|\mathbf{w}^{(t+1)^{T}}\mathbf{p}_{i}\right| - \sum_{i=1}^{2c}\max(0, r_{i}\mathbf{w}^{(t+1)^{T}}\mathbf{p}_{i} - h) \\
&-\lambda^{(t)}\sum_{i=1}^{c}\sum_{j=1}^{n_{i}}\min(s, \left|\mathbf{w}^{(t+1)^{T}}\mathbf{f}_{j}^{i}\right|) \geq 0,
\end{aligned}
$$

resulting in

$$
\begin{aligned}
&\frac{\sum_{i=1}^{c}|\mathbf{w}^{(t+1)^{T}}\mathbf{p}_{i}| - \sum_{i=1}^{2c}\max(0, r_{i}\mathbf{w}^{(t+1)^{T}}\mathbf{p}_{i} - h)}{\sum_{i=1}^{c}\sum_{j=1}^{n_{i}}\min(s, |\mathbf{w}^{(t+1)^{T}}\mathbf{f}_{j}^{i}|)} \\
&= \frac{\sum_{i=1}^{c}\min(h, n_{i}|\mathbf{w}^{(t+1)^{T}}\mathbf{p}_{i}|)}{\sum_{i=1}^{c}\sum_{j=1}^{n_{i}}\min(s, |\mathbf{w}^{(t+1)^{T}}\mathbf{f}_{j}^{i}|)} \\
&\geq \frac{\sum_{i=1}^{c}|\mathbf{w}^{(t)^{T}}\mathbf{p}_{i}| - \sum_{i=1}^{2c}\max(0, r_{i}\mathbf{w}^{(t)^{T}}\mathbf{p}_{i} - h)}{\sum_{i=1}^{c}\sum_{j=1}^{n_{i}}\min(s, |\mathbf{w}^{(t)^{T}}\mathbf{f}_{j}^{i}|)} \\
&= \frac{\sum_{i=1}^{c}\min(h, n_{i}|\mathbf{w}^{(t)^{T}}\mathbf{p}_{i}|)}{\sum_{i=1}^{c}\sum_{j=1}^{n_{i}}\min(s, |\mathbf{w}^{(t)^{T}}\mathbf{f}_{j}^{i}|)}
\end{aligned}
\tag{40}
$$

indicating the objective value of (10) monotonically increases in each iteration. Thus, Q.E.D.

The proof of the existence of the upper bound of the objective function is as follows.

Theorem The objective of (8) has an upper bound.

Proof Clearly, $\sum_{i=1}^{c}\min(h, n_{i}|\mathbf{w}^{T}\mathbf{p}_{i}|) \leq ch$. It is easy to check that $\sum_{i=1}^{c}\sum_{j=1}^{n_{i}}\min(s, |\mathbf{w}^{T}\mathbf{f}_{j}^{i}|)$ can be written as

$$
\sum_{i=1}^{c}\sum_{j=1}^{n_{i}}\min(s, |\mathbf{w}^{T}\mathbf{f}_{j}^{i}|) = \sum_{i=1}^{c}\sum_{j=1}^{q_{i}} s + \sum_{i=1}^{c}\sum_{j=q_{i}+1}^{n_{i}}|\mathbf{w}^{T}\mathbf{f}_{j}^{i}|,
$$

in which we suppose that for any class i, there are q_{i} points which satisfy $|\mathbf{w}^{T}\mathbf{f}_{j}^{i}| > s$. Let λ_{j}^{i} be the largest eigenvalue of $(\mathbf{f}_{j}^{i})^{T}\mathbf{f}_{j}^{i}$ and λ_{min} be the smallest value of all λ_{j}^{i}. For any pair (i, j), we have $|\mathbf{w}^{T}\mathbf{f}_{j}^{i}| = \sqrt{(\mathbf{w}^{T}\mathbf{f}_{j}^{i})^{2}} \geq \sqrt{\lambda_{j}^{i}} \geq \sqrt{\lambda_{min}}$. Thus,

$\sum_{i=1}^{c} \sum_{j=q_i+1}^{n_i} |\mathbf{w}^T \mathbf{f}_j^i| \geq \sqrt{\lambda_{min}}$. Finally, we have $\sum_{i=1}^{c} \sum_{j=1}^{n_i} \min(s, |\mathbf{w}^T \mathbf{f}_j^i|) \geq \sqrt{\lambda_{min}}$. Therefore, the objective of (10) is bounded by $ch/\sqrt{\lambda_{min}}$.

It follows from Theorems 3 and 4 that the iterative Algorithm 1 is convergent.

4 Experimental Results

To evaluate the discriminant power of our NPDA and verify the theoretical arguments made, we conducted image classification experiments on the ALOI [16], YALEB [17], and UCI [18] datasets. Each dataset is divided into training and testing sets. The proposed NPDA is compared with the following: LDA, OLDA, FDA-L1 [2], LDA-L1 [7], NLDA-L1 [8], L1-LDA [4], and RILDA [1]. LDA is the conventional discriminant analysis technique which takes squared L2-norm as the distance metric. The others use L1- or L2,1-norm distance metrics. The projection for each of the methods is learned on the training set, and used to evaluate on the testing set. Finally, nearest neighbour classifier is employed for image classification tasks. Six of the methods, i.e., FDA-L1, LDA-L1, NLDA-L1, L1-LDA, RILDA, and our NPDA, apply an iterative procedure for optimizing their objective. We set the maximum iterative number and the stopping criterion as 30 and the difference between the objective values of two successive iterations as less than 0.001. For their initializations, the solution of LDA is set as the initial discriminant vector, which has been widely used in more recent works and which makes the most of connections between these methods. For face recognition, LDA is well-known as Fisherfaces. The learning rate of LDA-L1 and NLDA-L1 are searched from the range $\{0.2^p | p = 1, \ldots, 10\}$. For our NPDA, there are two cutting parameters: h and s. Specifying their values are difficult. In the experiments, we empirically set the cutting parameters such that 5% of the training data with largest distances (i.e., the cutting rate) are seen as outliers which will be eliminated.

For ALOI dataset, we select the first $K = (5, 7, 9, 11)$ images per category for training and the remaining images for testing. The different methods are applied on the original and contaminated data to test their robustness against outliers or noisy data, and in the presence of a variation in illumination. The contaminated data is formed by inserting occlusion with black or white rectangle noise into a part of the training images at a random location with size of at least 20×20. A contamination level of 40% is used. The dimensions vary from 5 to 100 in step of 5. The lowest error rates of each method at the top dimension and the average error rates for various dimensions are reported in Table 1 and Fig. 2. From the table, we first see that NPDA performs best, i.e., NPDA effectively learns more robust discriminant vectors from images. NPDA is at least 40% lower error than the next best method when $K = 7, 9$, and 11. Also, although the introduction of contaminations in the images results in worse performances for each method, the contamination has very little effect on the performance of NPDA and NPDA still has lowest error rates and. In addition, the average error rates of NPDA with various number of extracted features are lower than those obtained by other methods. Specifically, in noisy scenarios, NPDA has at least 50% higher recognition rate than the best one of all the other methods in most cases. From the Fig. 2, we can see the top recognition rate of NPDA can be achieved at low dimension, showing the insensitiveness to the number of extracted features, which is not arisen in the other seven methods.

Table 1. Lowest error rate/average error rates of each method with various number of extracted features on ALOI. Key: Orig - Original data; Cont – Contaminated data.

Method		LDA	OLDA	FDA-L1	LDA-L1	NLDA-L1	L1-LDA	RILDA	NPDA
K = 5	Orig.	25.42/29.68	17.72/21.96	16.11/20.88	18.29/23.55	16.94/21.03	20.47/23.76	22.01/28.00	14.31/18.59
	Cont.	34.22/42.98	21.76/33.72	20.86/31.68	30.76/40.99	20.87/31.69	27.34/35.71	27.27/37.22	19.12/26.99
K = 7	Orig.	22.46/26.79	14.28/19.84	12.84/18.58	15.00/20.46	12.84/18.61	16.21/20.56	16.14/23.64	7.31/12.43
	Cont.	33.86/41.99	21.79/34.79	18.72/31.64	27.76/38.31	18.29/31.64	26.68/37.94	27.77/43.80	10.61/18.06
K = 9	Orig.	21.22/26.76	11.79/17.75	11.14/16.51	14.47/19.96	11.12/16.50	14.39/19.91	15.21/24.71	7.31/12.44
	Cont.	40.00/50.53	24.17/40.86	20.49/37.01	31.14/43.62	20.49/37.03	33.01/43.58	38.69/52.60	8.37/17.26
K = 11	Orig.	7.32/11.77	1.32/5.79	1.21/4.93	2.91/7.51	1.22/4.94	2.81/7.53	2.81/8.35	0.47/3.40
	Cont.	26.18/40.55	13.51/30.91	12.75/27.63	20.91/34.11	12.86/27.61	20.91/34.15	22.90/42.88	2.35/8.25

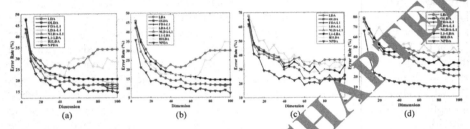

Fig. 2. Error rates of each method versus the variations of dimensions on the original and contaminated ALOI. (a) Original data in which K = 5, (b) original data in which K = 9, (c) contaminated data in which K = 5, and (d) contaminated data in which K = 9.

To further test the robustness of our method, we select K = 7 and 11 and consider different contamination levels from 0 to 50%. The lowest error and average error rates with various number of extracted features versus different contamination levels are illustrated in Fig. 3. From the figure, it is not difficult to find that some unarguable points consistent to those drawn from previous experiments. NDPA still outperforms the other methods. Also, for OLDA, FDA-L1, LDA-L1, NLDA-L1, and L1-LDA, the increase of contamination level greatly reduces the recognition rates, which, however, does not influence the results of NPDA too much. This again indicates the performance superiority of NPDA.

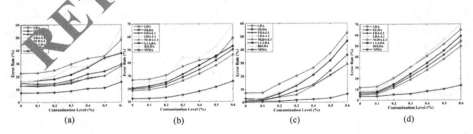

Fig. 3. Lowest error (a) and average error rates with various number of extracted features (b) versus different contamination levels on ALOI when K = 7. Lowest error (c) and average error rates of each method with various number of extracted features (d) versus different contamination level on ALOI when K = 11.

Table 2. Average error rates for various number of extracted features on extended YALEB

Method	LDA	OLDA	FDA-L1	LDA-L1	NLDA-L1	L1-LDA	RILDA	NPDA
K = 13	34.62 ± 2.78	33.24 ± 2.65	24.35 ± 1.86	26.08 ± 2.15	24.39 ± 1.88	26.07 ± 2.08	26.01 ± 2.01	22.16 ± 1.57
K = 16	33.05 ± 2.37	31.91 ± 2.47	22.57 ± 1.81	24.04 ± 1.88	22.60 ± 1.82	24.01 ± 1.88	24.60 ± 1.92	19.42 ± 1.45
K = 19	32.83 ± 1.45	31.37 ± 2.16	21.53 ± 1.47	23.05 ± 1.62	21.55 ± 0.47	22.99 ± 1.63	23.32 ± 1.81	17.49 ± 0.99

Table 3. Lowest error rates of various methods on UCI datasets.

Method	LDA	OLDA	FDA-L1	LDA-L1	NLDA-L1	L1-LDA	RILDA	NPDA
ARRHYTHMIA	48.27 ± 5.59	50.74 ± 4.61	44.02 ± 2.72	49.71 ± 3.59	44.67 ± 4.65	43.92 ± 4.68	48.31 ± 1.96	31.63 ± 2.62
ISOLET1	27.58 ± 4.22	19.19 ± 1.44	13.19 ± 1.19	15.55 ± 1.75	13.78 ± 1.21	18.71 ± 1.11	20.24 ± 2.86	9.55 ± 0.99
SOYBEAN	12.59 ± 2.72	10.00 ± 1.86	9.22 ± 1.46	10.07 ± 1.99	9.67 ± 2.32	13.31 ± 1.19	11.68 ± 1.75	8.3 ± 2.12
BREASTCC	37.07 ± 4.96	37.07 ± 4.96	32.75 ± 10.69	34.65 ± 5.03	36.20 ± 9.92	34.82 ± 5.91	33.11 ± 5.37	58 ± 3.39
PIMAID	38.88 ± 7.56	30.73 ± 1.78	30.10 ± 1.91	30.88 ± 1.85	30.72 ± 1.78	30.32 ± 1.92	31.6 ± 2.42	29.2 ± 1.96
TEACHINGA	46.05 ± 1.64	45.52 ± 5.75	45.78 ± 4.71	43.15 ± 4.22	47.63 ± 4.02	44.73 ± 4.61	18 79	3.42 ± 6.06
BUPALD	41.62 ± 4.61	41.62 ± 4.61	38.84 ± 3.23	40.05 ± 3.91	39.53 ± 3.63	40.92 ± 3.0	9.77 ± 3.	38.21 ± 3.88
SPORTAOA	47.28 ± 14.04	24.86 ± 1.29	24.12 ± 2.27	23.21 ± 1.14	24.86 ± 1.29	24.08 ± 1.1	9 ± 2.59	23.80 ± 2.77
ULTRFD	32.07 ± 5.58	27.28 ± 10.25	23.69 ± 8.87	23.37 ± 7.97	20.54 ± 6.21	18.2 ±	18.0 ± 4.29	15.00 ± 4.41
VOWEL	6.47 ± 1.51	5.00 ± 2.13	5.00 ± 1.71	17.65 ± 3.95	5.00 ± 1.71	5.45 07	5.64 ± 1.97	5.00 ± 1.71
IONOSPHERE	19.15 ± 3.12	19.15 ± 3.12	13.07 ± 2.87	11.81 ± 1.94	11.31 ± 1.35	14.72 ± 2.	13.19 ± 2.31	10.85 ± 1.92
BCANCER	4.56 ± 0.84	4.56 ± 0.84	3.62 ± 0.69	4.23 ± 1.04	3.65 ± 1.11	4. 0.74	4.21 ± 0.93	3.56 ± 1.11
DERMATOLOGY	4.23 ± 0.95	4.02 ± 1.15	5.32 ± 3.56	5.27 ± 1.83	3.3 09	5.05 ± 1.61	4.02 ± 1.47	3.21 ± 0.96
BALANCES	12.23 ± 1.13	12.17 ± 1.12	12.91 ± 2.21	12.97 ± 2.88	58 ±	11.31 ± 2.73	12.84 ± 1.84	12.17 ± 2.79
COIL20	9.17 ± 1.02	5.50 ± 1.05	3.34 ± 1.12	7.37 ± 1.1	4.9 1.19	8.17 ± 1.95	18.12 ± 2.42	2.61 ± 0.79

Table 2, the results on the extended YALEB dataset, shows that the average error rates of NPDA with various number of extracted features are the lowest, indicating it is least insensitive to dimensions as compared to other methods.

For each dataset of UCI, half of the samples were randomly taken for training, and the remaining samples for testing. We run the experiment ten times and obtained different training and testing sets for a fair evaluation of each method. The optimal dimension is searched twice as many as the number of classes. The average lowest error rates of other methods and NPDA across the ten tests are reported in Table 3. The results are consistent with those in the previous experiments. NPDA performs better than the others in most cases. Specially, on several higher-dimensional datasets, such as ARRHYTHMIA, ISOLET1, COIL20, and ULTRFD, the performance advantage of NPDA is more obvious.

5   Conclusion

This paper proposed NPDA, a novel robust SL technique. Instead of taking L1-norm as the distance metric, which is not sufficiently robust, NPDA uses cutting L1-norm as the distance metric. Such norm has the property of cutting some points with large distances in projection subspace, thus NPDA better eliminates numerous outliers in learning the model. The proposed method outperforms state-of-the-art methods in image classification.

References

1. Lai, Z., Xu, Y., Yang, J.: Rotational invariant dimensionality reduction algorithms. IEEE Trans. Cybern. **47**(11), 3733–3746 (2017)
2. Wang, H.X., Lu, X.S., Hu, Z.L., Zheng, W.M.: Fisher discriminant analysis with L1-norm. IEEE Trans. Cybern. **44**(6), 828–842 (2014)
3. Ye, Q.L., Yang, J., Liu, F., et al.: L1-norm distance linear discriminant analysis based on an effective iterative algorithm. IEEE Trans. Circuits Syst. Video Technol. **28**(1), 114–129 (2018)
4. Zheng, W., Lin, Z., Wang, H.: L1-norm kernel discriminant analysis via Bayes error bound optimization for robust feature extraction. IEEE Trans. Neural Netw. Learn. Syst. **25**(4), 793–805 (2014)
5. Chen, X., Yang, J., Jin, Z.: An improved linear discriminant analysis with L1-norm for robust feature extraction. In: Proceedings of International Conference on Pattern Recognition, pp. 1585–1590 (2014)
6. Ye, Q.L., Zhao, H.H., Fu, L.Y., et al.: Underlying connections between algorithms for nongreedy LDA-L1. IEEE Trans. Image Process. **27**(5), 2557–2559 (2018)
7. Zhong, F., Zhang, J.: Linear discriminant analysis based on L1-norm maximization. IEEE Trans. Image Process. **22**(8), 3018–3027 (2013)
8. Liu, Y., Gao, Q., Miao, S.: A non-greedy algorithm for L1-norm LDA. IEEE Trans. Image Process. **26**(2), 684–695 (2017)
9. Zheng, W., Lu, C., Lin, Z.C., et al.: L1-norm heteroscedastic discriminant analysis under mixture of gaussian distributions (2018). https://doi.org/10.1109/tnnls.2018.2863264
10. Wang, H., Nie, F., Huang, H.: Robust distance metric learning via simultaneous L1-norm minimization and maximization. In: Proceedings of International Conference on Machine Learning, pp. 1836–1844 (2014)
11. Wang, Q., Gao, Q., Xie, D., et al.: Robust DLPP with nongreedy L1-norm minimization and maximization. IEEE Trans. Neural Netw. Learn. Syst. **29**(3), 738–743 (2018)
12. Zhong, F., Zhang, J., Li, D.: Discriminant locality preserving projections based on L1-norm maximization. IEEE Trans. Neural Netw. Learn. Syst. **25**(11), 2065–2074 (2014)
13. Cevikalp, H.: Best fitting hyperplanes for classification. IEEE Trans. Pattern Anal. Mach. Intell. **39**(6), 1076–1088 (2017)
14. Nie, F.P., Huo, Z.Y., Huang, H.: Joint cutting norms minimization for robust matrix recovery. In: The 2017 International Joint Conference on Artificial Intelligence (IJCAI) (2017)
15. Gong, P., Ye, J., Zhang, C.: Multi-stage multi-task feature learning. J. Mach. Learn. Res. **14**(1), 2979–3010 (2013)
16. Geusebroek, J.M., Burghouts, G.J., Smeulders, A.: The Amsterdam library of object images. Int. J. Comput. Vis. **61**(1), 103–112 (2005)
17. Lee, K.C., Ho, J., Kriegman, D.: Acquiring linear subspaces for face recognition under variable lighting. IEEE Trans. Pattern Anal. Mach. Intell. **27**(5), 684–698 (2005)
18. Dua, D., Karra, E.T.: UCI Machine Learning Repository. University of California, School of Information and Computer Science, Irvine, CA (2017). Author, F.: Article title. Journal **2**(5), 99–110 (2016)

Prostate Cancer Classification Based on Best First Search and Taguchi Feature Selection Method

Md Akizur Rahman[1], Priyanka Singh[2], Ravie Chandren Muniyandi[1], Domingo Mery[3], and Mukesh Prasad[2(✉)]

[1] Research Center for Cyber Security, Faculty of Information Science and Technology, Universiti Kebangsaan Malaysia, 43600 UKM Bangi, Selangor, Malaysia
[2] School of Computer Science, FEIT, University of Technology Sydney, Ultimo, Sydney, Australia
mukesh.nctu@gmail.com
[3] Department of Computer Science, University of Chile, Santiago, Chile

Abstract. Prostate cancer is the second most common cancer occurring in men worldwide, about 1 in 41 men will die because of prostate cancer. Death rates of prostate cancer increases with age. Even though, it being a serious condition only about 1 man in 9 will be diagnosed with prostate cancer during his lifetime. Accurate and early diagnosis can help clinician to treat the cancer better and save lives. This paper proposes two phases feature selection method to enhance prostate cancer early diagnosis based on artificial neural network. In the first phase, Best First Search method is used to extract the relevant features from original dataset. In the second phase, Taguchi method is used to select the most important feature from the already extracted features from Best First Search method. A public available prostate cancer benchmark dataset is used for experiment, which contains two classes of data normal and abnormal. The proposed method outperforms other existing methods on prostate cancer benchmark dataset with classification accuracy of 98.6%. The proposed approach can help clinicians to reach at more accurate and early diagnosis of different stages of prostate cancer and so that they make most suitable treatment decision to save lives of patients and prevent death due to prostate cancer.

Keywords: Prostate cancer · Artificial neural network · Feature selection · Best First Search method · Taguchi method

1 Introduction

Prostate cancer is the second most common cancer occurring in men worldwide [1], about 1 in 41 men will die of prostate cancer. Death rates of prostate cancer increases with age, and almost 55% of all deaths occur after 65 years of age. Even though, it being a serious condition only about 1 in 9 men will be diagnosed with prostate cancer during his lifetime [2]. Clinicians treating prostate cancer face challenges in terms of early and accurate diagnosis of different stages of prostate cancer. An accurate and

© Springer Nature Switzerland AG 2019
C. Lee et al. (Eds.): PSIVT 2019, LNCS 11854, pp. 325–336, 2019.
https://doi.org/10.1007/978-3-030-34879-3_25

early diagnosis can help in deciding better treatment plan which can be more effective and increase the survival rate in patients suffering from prostate cancer.

Recently, Artificial Intelligence (AI) research has gained increased attention for early cancer diagnosis modelling including prostate cancer. AI encompasses intellectual mechanisms which reflect or mimic human ability to solve problems [3–5]. These intellectual mechanisms comprise of artificial neural network (ANN) and they offer several benefits such as learning capability, handling large amounts of data that are irrelevant from active and nonlinear methods, where nonlinearities and variable interactions have major importance. ANN is a powerful technique with capability of solving various real world problems in real time. Feature selection (FS) method is used to reduce dimensionality and redundancy of data. The applications of FS methods have become vital in AI, machine learning (ML) and data mining algorithms in order to be effective for classification of real-world problems [6]. FS selection method is mainly used to provide accurate classifier models for classification task.

Several studies have been carried out in past to enhance prostate cancer classification task. Aziz et al. [7] used fuzzy based feature selection method for machine learning classification of microarray data including prostate cancer dataset. This method used fuzzy backward feature elimination (FBFE) technique to improve Support Vector Machine (SVM) and Naïve Bayes (NB) classifier performance. This method selected 50 features from prostate cancer dataset and achieved the classification accuracy of 88.57%, 84.27% for SVM and NB classifier, respectively. Elyasigomari et al. [8] had developed a hybrid optimization algorithm to select gene for cancer classification, which used Cuckoo Optimization Algorithm (COA) and genetic algorithm (GA) for selecting valuable gene from microarray dataset including prostate cancer dataset. By using COA-GA method with SVM and Multilayer Perceptron (MLP) classifier, they achieved 96.6% and 94.2% of classification accuracy, respectively. Chen et al. [9] proposed Kernel-based culturing gene selection (KBCGS) method for selecting gene using different gene expression data including prostate cancer dataset. This method selected 10 gene by using proposed method and achieved 94.71% of classification accuracy. Nguyen et al. [10] proposed hidden Markov models (HMMs) for cancer classification, which achieved 92.01% lowest and 94.60% highest classification accuracy from prostate cancer dataset.

Gao et al. [11] used hybrid method based on information gain (IG) and SVM for feature selection in cancer classification. This method used IG for initial feature selection from prostate cancer dataset then SVM was used for final selection of features. For classification this method used 10-fold cross validation of LIBSVM classifier. Finally, 3 features are selected from prostate cancer and achieved 96.08% classification accuracy from IG-SVM. Dashtban et al. [12] used a novel evolutionary method based on genetic algorithm and artificial intelligence for selection of valuable features for cancer classification. This method used two filtering techniques namely, Fisher and Laplacian Score for feature selection. From Fisher Score technique, 5 valuable features are selected and achieved 92.6% of classification accuracy using K-nearest-neighbors (KNN) classifier. Ludwig et al. [13] used fuzzy decision tree (FDT) algorithm for classification of cancer data, which compared FDT result with the different classifier using prostate cancer dataset. They achieved 88.36% and 95.59% of classification accuracy for FDT and BN, respectively. Dashtban et al. [14] proposed a novel bio-inspired multi-objective approach for gene selection in microarray data classification including prostate cancer, which achieved 97.1% of classification accuracy by using Naïve Bayes (NB) classifier with 6 valuable selected features.

The above studies indicate that the classification accuracy of prostate cancer can be significantly improved by combination of different feature selection method. Therefore, this paper proposes two phases feature selection mechanism with two different feature selection method to enhance the prostate cancer classification accuracy. In the first phase, Best First Search method is used for feature extraction form the original dataset and then in the second phase Taguchi method is used to select the best valuable features extracted by Best First Search method. In summary, the contributions of this paper are as follows:

- Feature extraction is done by using Best First Search which has reduced the data in dimensionality and in specificity.
- Feature selection is done by using Taguchi method to select more valuable features. So, the results obtained have enhanced prostate cancer classification accuracy.
- Results obtained from this paper have been compared with the conventional studies to evaluate and compare the improved performance of the proposed method.

2   Research Materials and Methods

2.1   Prostate Cancer Data

This paper used a public available prostate cancer benchmark dataset [15], which includes 102 samples, containing 10509 features. The dataset contains two classes namely normal and abnormal. The collected prostate cancer dataset is pre-processed for making it usable for the proposed system. Best First Search method is used for extracting the irrelevant features and Taguchi Method is used to select the more valuable features.

2.2   Feature Selection

Feature selection is a process to reduce the number of attributes; it also involves the selection of subset of original features. The main goal of feature selection is to reduce the dimensionality of data and to provide better classifier model to improve classification accuracy. This paper uses Best First Search and Taguchi method for feature selection. Best First Search refers to the method of exploring the node with the best score and Taguchi method uses to analyze feature signal to noise ratio. This paper combined these two methods to select most valuable features which reduce the dimensionality of data and give accurate classifier model to achieve good classification accuracy. This section is illustrated in the feature selection model below, as shown in Fig. 1.

In the first step, Best First Search methods is used to extract the feature sets, which are generated using Weka by information gain. Through Weka, information gain calculates values of each feature and checks the rank. In accordance with the rank the

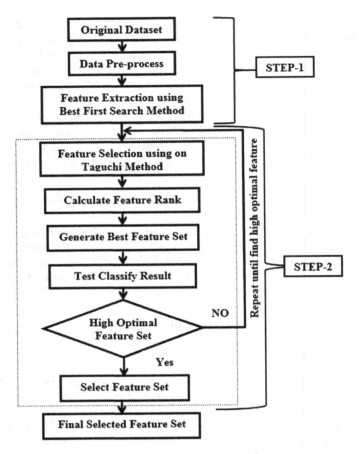

Fig. 1. Feature selection model

higher rank features are sorted. A total 114 features are extracted from 10509 original features of prostate cancer dataset. In the second step, Taguchi method is used to find high optimal feature set from the remaining extracted set of features by Best First Search method. Taguchi method is a robust experimental design which can be analyzed and improved by altering relative design factors. Taguchi method also named as statistical method, which has two mechanisms; orthogonal array and signal-to-noise ratio (SNR), for improvement and analysis. The details discussion about Taguchi methods can be found in [16]. After feature extraction, this paper followed Taguchi method, as mentioned earlier, it's an orthogonal array mechanism to select the features. The prostate cancer dataset has 114 features after extraction of features. Later, after applying final evaluation by Taguchi method, 87 most valuable features are selected for prostate cancer classification.

2.3   Prostate Cancer Classification

After the completion of feature selection, the selected feature passed through to the artificial neural network for the classification task. This paper used 15-neuron artificial neural network for prostate cancer classification. Figure 2 shows the architecture of 15-Neuron artificial neural network classifier.

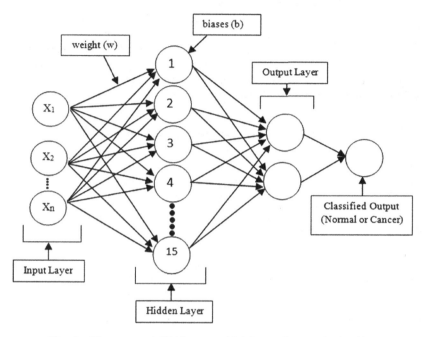

Fig. 2. The proposed 15-Neuron artificial neural network classifier

The proposed artificial neural network is implemented in MATLAB using the Neural Network Pattern Identification Tool. The standard network used for pattern recognition is a two-layer feed-forward neural network, in which a hidden layer contains the sigmoid and softmax transfer function in the output layer. For the proposed system, 15 hidden neurons are selected in the hidden layer; this is deemed acceptable. The output neurons are set to 2 as the same number of elements in the target vector. The proposed system uses prostate cancer dataset with total 102 samples and 87 valuable selected features, which is categorized as normal and abnormal samples. From the samples first two groups are randomly divided: 71 (70%) samples for training and 31 (30%) samples for testing. Further, 71 samples, are randomly divided into three groups: 49 (70%) samples for training and two other groups with 11 (15%) samples each for testing and validation. The performance of ANNs is evaluated on training, testing and validation dataset.

3   Result and Performance Comparisons

The experiment setup of the proposed method includes Core® i5-6400 Intel® CPU with 2.10 GHz processor; 8.00 GB memory; 64-bit Windows® 7 operating system and MATLAB (R2018b) environment. The performance of the proposed method is evaluated on prostate cancer benchmark dataset. The proposed method runs 30 times and achieved the average classification accuracy of 98.6% for both training and testing stage. The training performance of the proposed method is shown in Fig. 3. The proposed method, plot performance at the start of the training stage best validation performance achieved 0.1196 at epoch 8. At that point, the neural network halted the training for the improvement of generalization. Figure 4 shows the network training state performance plot. At the epoch 14 iteration, gradient is 0.003397. At that point the neural network halts the training for the improvement of generalization.

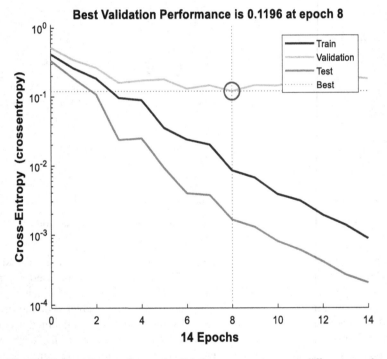

Fig. 3. The training, testing and validation cross entropy on different epochs

Figure 5 shows the error histogram performance. The error histogram plot represents the training, validation, and testing performance error which overlapped at the zero-error line. From the graphical illustration of the error histogram, it is found that the error for the proposed model is almost zero. Figure 6 shows the training confusion matrix performance. On the confusion matrix plot shown in Fig. 6, the rows of the predicted class (output class) and the columns reveal the true class (target class). The

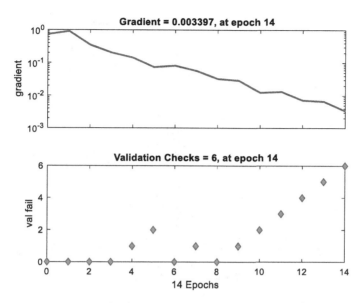

Fig. 4. The training state of the proposed method.

diagonal green cells represent the trained network correct classified percentages. The red diagonal cells represent the percentage of incorrectly classified samples. The column on the right side of the plot is an indicator of the accuracy for each predicted class while the row at the bottom of the plot is a representation of the accuracy for each true class. The blue cell of the plot represents the total accuracy. This confusion matrix plot shows that the overall classification accuracy with feature selection attaining 98.6% correct classification performance. The network gave the best classification performance for the proposed system at the training stage.

The neural network training performances with receiver operating characteristic (ROC) curves are shown in Fig. 7. The ROC curve is a graph illustrating the performance of the binary classification system with varying discrimination threshold. The curve was formed by plotting the true positive rate (TPR) against the false positive rate (FPR). From this ROC curve, the neural network increasing the performance responding to the number of iterations. The perfect classification result shown at the 14 iterations revealed that every class achieved the optimal classification accuracy. Iteration 14 is the optimal iterations for the proposed system where the neural network has given the maximum performance.

After completing the training session, this paper tested the network for accurate classification accuracy by using 30% test dataset for prostate cancer with feature selection. Figure 8 shows the test accuracy called classification accuracy. From the proposed system, the simulation result with test dataset of prostate cancer with feature selection shows that normal and abnormal are correctly classified and have achieved the highest accuracy value which is 100%, where the average value is 98.6%. Figure 9 shows the ROC curve using test dataset for Prostate cancer classification. The ROC

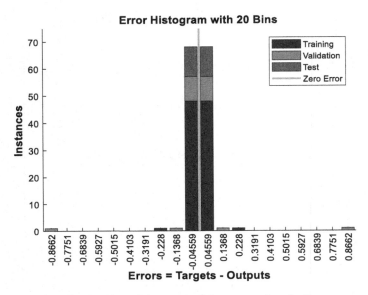

Fig. 5. The training error of the proposed method

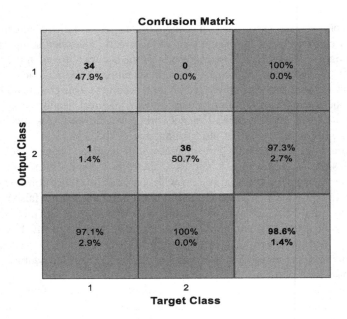

Fig. 6. Confusion matrix for training data of the proposed method (Color figure online)

curve shows the normal and abnormal classification reached the highest area under ROC curve (AUC). In addition, it indicates the highest faultless result for the test dataset of Prostate cancer.

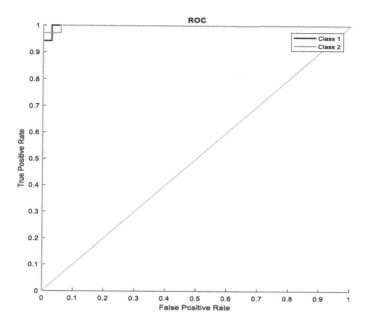

Fig. 7. ROC curve for training data of the proposed method

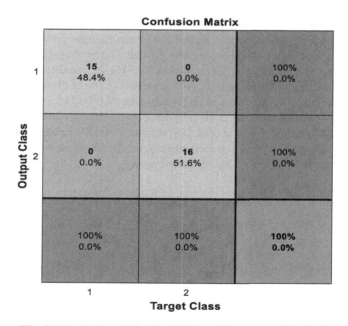

Fig. 8. Confusion matrix for test data of the proposed method

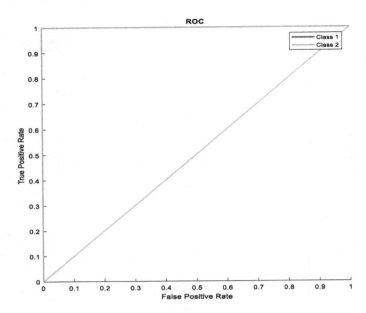

Fig. 9. ROC curve for test data of the proposed method

A comparison between the proposed method and other existing methods is carried out based on the prostate cancer dataset as shown in Table 1. This comparison result is based on the classification accuracy. Table 1 indicates that the proposed method outperforms the other existing method on given prostate cancer dataset. From Table 1, it can be observed that Chen et al. [9] achieves 94.71% of classification accuracy by using KBCGS method. Dashtban et al. [14] achieves 97.1% of classification accuracy by using NB method. Elyasigomari et al. [8] achieves 96.6% of classification accuracy by using COA-GA method. Gao et al. [11] achieves 96.1% of classification accuracy by using IG-SVM method. Ludwig et al. [13] achieves 95.6% of classification accuracy by using BN method. The proposed method achieves 98.6% of classification accuracy, which is superior that compared to other methods.

Table 1. The comparison of the proposed method with other methods

Method	Accuracy (%)
NB [14]	97.1
BN [13]	95.6
IG-SVM [11]	96.1
KBCGS [9]	94.71
COA-GA [8]	96.6
The proposed method	**98.6**

4 Conclusion

This paper presents two phases of feature selection mechanism with the artificial neural network to accurately classify the normal and abnormal class of the prostate cancer classification problem. The proposed method achieves an average of 98.6% classification accuracy on prostate cancer dataset. This is substantially good level of accuracy compared with other methods. Based on the proposed method performance, it can be concluded that the proposed feature selection method can enable clinicians to reach at accurate and early diagnosis of different stages of prostate cancer. Thus, the proposed method can be an important contribution in the field of cancer diagnosis and treatment that can save many lives and prevent suffering. As early and accurate diagnosis can help in planning appropriate and individualized treatment. Although this paper achieved the highest accuracy, however, it would be interesting to optimize the feature selection method for further reduced data dimensionality, which may increase the prostate cancer classification accuracy even more. Such an investigation can be taken as an extension to this paper.

References

1. Prostate Cancer Statistics. https://www.wcrf.org/dietandcancer/cancer-trends/prostate-cancer-statistics. Accessed 14 Jul 2019
2. Prostate Cancer Statistics. https://www.cancer.org/cancer/prostate-cancer/about/key-statistics.html
3. Ham, F.M., Kostanic, I.: Principles of Neurocomputing for Science and Engineering. McGraw Hill, New York (2001)
4. Chen, L.: Pattern classification by assembling small neural networks. In: Proceedings of 2005 IEEE International Joint Conference on Neural Networks, vol. 3, pp. 1947–1952 (2005)
5. Ibraheem, A.K.: An Application of Artificial Neural Network Classifier for Medical Diagnosis (2013)
6. Rahman, M.A., Muniyandi, R.C.: Feature selection from colon cancer dataset for cancer classification using artificial neural network. Int. J. Adv. Sci. Eng. Inf. Technol. 8(4–2), 1387 (2018)
7. Aziz, R., Verma, C.K., Srivastava, N.: A fuzzy based feature selection from independent component subspace for machine learning classification of microarray data. Genomics Data 8, 4–15 (2016)
8. Elyasigomari, V., Mirjafari, M.S., Screen, H.R.C., Shaheed, M.H.: Cancer classification using a novel gene selection approach by means of shuffling based on data clustering with optimization. Appl. Soft Comput. 35, 43–51 (2015)
9. Chen, H., Zhang, Y., Gutman, I.: A kernel-based clustering method for gene selection with gene expression data. J. Biomed. Inform. 62, 12–20 (2016)
10. Nguyen, T., Khosravi, A., Creighton, D., Nahavandi, S.: Hidden markov models for cancer classification using gene expression profiles. Inf. Sci. 316, 293–307 (2015)
11. Gao, L., Ye, M., Lu, X., Huang, D.: Hybrid method based on information gain and support vector machine for gene selection in cancer classification. Genomics Proteomics Bioinform. 15(6), 389–395 (2017)

12. Dashtban, M., Balafar, M.: Gene selection for microarray cancer classification using a new evolutionary method employing artificial intelligence concepts. Genomics **109**(2), 91–107 (2017)
13. Ludwig, S.A., Picek, S., Jakobovic, D.: Classification of cancer data: analyzing gene expression data using a fuzzy decision tree algorithm. In: Kahraman, C., Topcu, Y. (eds.) Operations Research Applications in Health Care Management. International Series in Operations Research & Management Science, vol. 262, pp. 327–347 (2018). Springer, Cham https://doi.org/10.1007/978-3-319-65455-3_13
14. Dashtban, M., Balafar, M., Suravajhala, P.: Gene selection for tumor classification using a novel bio-inspired multi-objective approach. Genomics **110**(1), 10–17 (2018)
15. gems-system.org. http://gems-system.org/. Accessed 21 May 2017
16. Wu, Y., Wu, A.: Taguchi Methods for Robust Design. ASME Press (2000)

Real-Time Retinal Vessel Segmentation on High-Resolution Fundus Images Using Laplacian Pyramids

Robert Dachsel[✉], Annika Jöster, and Michael Breuß

Brandenburg Technical University, Institute for Mathematics,
Platz der Deutschen Einheit 1, 03046 Cottbus, Germany
{dachsel,joester,breuss}@b-tu.de

Abstract. In ophthalmology, fundus images are commonly used to examine the human eye. The image data shows among others the capillary system of the retina. Recognising alternations in the retinal blood vessels is pivotal to diagnosing certain diseases. The visual inspection of those fundus images is a time-consuming process and a challenging task which has to be done by medical experts. Furthermore, rapid advances in medical imaging allow for generating fundus images of increased quality and resolution. Therefore, the support by computers for the analysis and evaluation of complex fundus image information is growing in importance and there is a corresponding need for fast and efficient algorithms.

In this paper, we present a well-engineered, robust real-time segmentation algorithm which is adapted to the recent and upcoming challenges of high resolution fundus images. Thereby we make use of the multiscale representation of the Laplacian pyramid which is fast to compute and useful for detecting coarse as well as finely branched blood vessels. It is possible to process images of size 3504×2336 pixels in 0.8 s on a standard desktop computer and 0.3 on a Nvidia Titan XP GPU. By a detailed evaluation at hand of an accessible high-resolution data set we demonstrate that our approach is competitive in quality to state of the art methods for segmenting blood vessels but much faster.

Keywords: Laplacian pyramids · Vessel segmentation · High-resolution fundus images · Real-time retinal imaging

1 Introduction

In ophthalmology, fundus images are commonly used to examine the human eye. During the examination a photo of the fundus of the eye, i.e. the eye ground is taken through the pupil by the use of a fundus camera. The photo shows among other aspects the capillary system of the retina. Recognizing alternations in the retinal blood vessels is crucial for diagnosing certain diseases such as retinopathy of prematurity [15] or arteriolar narrowing [13]. Due to rapid advances in medical imaging it is possible to generate images of increased quality and resolution. This

© Springer Nature Switzerland AG 2019
C. Lee et al. (Eds.): PSIVT 2019, LNCS 11854, pp. 337–350, 2019.
https://doi.org/10.1007/978-3-030-34879-3_26

allows for a more precise and conclusive examination and analysis of objects in medical images, such as vasculatures. Therefore physicians are faced with an increasing amount of high resolution image data. The visual inspection is a challenging task because, besides the capillary system of the retina, other components or background textures are also to be found in a fundus image impeding the analysis. Apart from that, blood vessels displayed in a fundus image vary in their size and end up in finely branched structures. Those finely branched vessels can hardly be detected with the human eye. Thus the need for support by computers for the analysis and evaluation of complex image information is growing, requiring fast and efficient methods and algorithms. In the context of this work an algorithm should segment blood vessels in fundus images of large and high resolution data sets as fast and precisely as possible. This is not only desirable in order to evaluate a huge database of fundus images that could accumulate in ophthalmologic practice: By real-time processing it also becomes possible to test the quality of a retinal image in interactive time, while the patient sits before the camera, and to take another image if necessary [16].

Over the last decade many retinal vessel segmentation algorithms have been presented [12]. Those algorithms are based on a large variety of methods, ranging from unsupervised approaches like matched filter methods [7,18,22], level set schemes [4,8] and morphology-based models [20,21] to supervised machine learning techniques and related trainable models [3,19], just to name a few of the approaches. For many of the existing unsupervised methods, a good segmentation performance often goes hand in hand with high computational needs, thus impeding real-time computation on high-resolution fundus images. Therefore it has been proposed for some unsupervised algorithms that they are accelerated using GPU hardware [16]. Machine learning techniques on the other hand, that may potentially lead to fast processing after training, often rely on the availability of a significant amount of annotated data, a source that is very sparse considering highly resolved imagery acquired by actual camera technology. Trainable models like in [3] that rely on filter optimization, often make use of a dedicated preprocessing and related choices for parameter estimation which does make these models easy to transfer to higher resolution or different camera technology.

Focusing on unsupervised techniques for high resolution images, multiscale approaches turn out to be remarkably useful for the detection of blood vessels which vary in size at multiple scales. With the use of multiscale approaches such information can be extracted. In [11], the authors proposed an approach that extracts local vessel features based on the eigenvalues of the Hessian matrix. The ratio of the eigenvalues is a good indicator of tubular vessel structures, based on the local principal directions of curvatures. The neighbourhood thereby is increased as long as it is larger than the expected thickest vessel.

On the other hand, multiscale representations in terms of image pyramids [2,6] are known as powerful tools in the computer vision and image processing community. The main idea is to sub-sample images by using a series of images at consecutively coarser length scales via Gaussian sampling with respect to the original image, called Gaussian pyramid. The conceptional advantage of this processing lies in its computational efficiency to analyse coarse vessel structures of a fundus image on a reduced resolution, whereas fine vessel-like structures require a high resolution. The method in [5] employs this technique improving the algorithm [11] by introducing an additional resolution hierarchy based on the Gaussian pyramid. Another example for the use of image pyramids in this context is a multiscale version of a line operator [10], computing a Gaussian pyramid of the fundus image. The line operator is applied to the image on each level of the pyramid separately, followed by a mapping from coarser scales to the finest level by using cubic splines.

Our Contribution. In this paper we propose the application of another type of the image pyramid representation called Laplacian pyramid [6]. In contrast to the Gaussian pyramid, the Laplacian pyramid serves as a bandpass filter, with the capacity to highlight the blood vessel system in a useful coarse-to-fine way. This representation is both computationally efficient, allowing real-time application, and is beneficial for detecting coarse and fine blood vessels. We demonstrate experimentally that our well-engineered multiscale segmentation method yields competitive results compared to other unsupervised state of the art techniques. Furthermore, we observe a substantially faster computational time.

2   Foundations of Our Approach

We briefly sketch the mechanism of image pyramids and their efficient implementation.

2.1   Gray Value Image and Convolution Filter

We start by defining a gray value or one-channel image by a mapping $I : \Omega \rightarrow [0,1]$ with $\Omega = \{1, \ldots, N\} \times \{1, \ldots, M\}$, where N and M denote the number of pixel columns and rows, respectively. The continuous range represents the intensity and is scaled such that a pixel at position (i,j) is black if $I(i,j) = 0$ and white if $I(i,j) = 1$.

Convolution filters are powerful tools in image processing with applications ranging from denoising and sharpening to edge detection. For a gray value image I we can view a filter operation as a discrete convolution

$$(h_\alpha * I)(i,j) = \sum_{u=-2}^{2} \sum_{v=-2}^{2} h_\alpha(3 + u, 3 + v) \cdot I(i - u, j - v), \tag{1}$$

where $h_\alpha \in \mathbb{R}^{5 \times 5}$ is a separable 2D filter kernel. Let us note that we fixed here the size of our filter kernel in accordance to the sampling procedure of the image pyramid and the most useful results obtained from experiments in our setting.

Reflecting boundary conditions are used to prevent the convolution operator from exceeding the boundary of the image. In this context, let us briefly recall two essential properties of convolution operations:

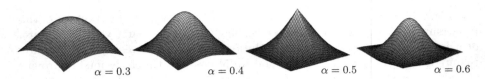

Fig. 1. The shape of the filter kernel h_a for different choices of α. For $\alpha \in [0.3, 0.5)$ the filter kernel acts as a low-pass filter (e.g. $\alpha = 0.4$ leads to the Gaussian filter).

Associativity: Assume h_1 and h_2 are filter kernels, then $(h_2 * h_1) * I = h_2 * (h_1 * I)$ holds.

Separability: For $h_\alpha \in \mathbb{R}^{5 \times 5}$ being separable, it can be decomposed into $h_\alpha = \tilde{h}_\alpha * \tilde{h}_\alpha^\top$ using a 1D filter kernel $\tilde{h}_\alpha \in \mathbb{R}^5$.

Using both properties, we express convolution as $h_\alpha * I = (\tilde{h}_\alpha * \tilde{h}_\alpha^\top) * I = \tilde{h}_\alpha * (\tilde{h}_\alpha^\top * I)$ with the $1D$ filter kernel

$$\tilde{h}_\alpha = \frac{1}{2} \left(\frac{1-2\alpha}{2} \quad \frac{1}{2} \quad 2\alpha \quad \frac{1}{2} \quad \frac{1-2\alpha}{2} \right)^\top, \tag{2}$$

where $\alpha \in [0.3, 0.6]$ is the filter parameter, as shown in Fig. 1. Due to the separability property of the kernel, the computational cost of operations per pixel is reduced from $5^2 = 25$ to $2 \cdot 5 = 10$.

For the detection of image structures of varying size, it is effective to examine images on different scales. Indeed it is more efficient to analyse coarse structure of an image on a reduced resolution, whereas fine structures do require a high resolution. In this work, the multiscale representation of an input image I consists of layers of successively decreasing resolution, expressed as a sequence $(K_0, K_1, \ldots, K_r)$. The first element $K_0 = I$ has the maximal resolution of the input image, whereas the last element K_r has the smallest resolution. Compared to the domain $\Omega_k = \{1, \ldots, N/2^k\} \times \{1, \ldots, M/2^k\}$ of the layer K_k, the domain of the following layer K_{k+1} was reduced by a factor of two in each direction, thus yielding $\Omega_{k+1} = \{1, \ldots, N/2^{k+1}\} \times \{1, \ldots, M/2^{k+1}\}$. In order to compare the layers, we need suitable operations for transferring one layer to another: Reducing an image at scale K_k to K_{k+1} and vice versa and expanding it from scale K_{k+1} to K_k.

Downsampling and Upsampling. The reduction of the resolution from K_k to K_{k+1} can be achieved by a combination of a removal of pixels and low pass filtering. Making use of (1), we define the *Reduce Operator* $\hat{\mathcal{R}}(K_k) = K_{k+1}$ as

$$\hat{\mathcal{R}}(K_k)(i, j) = \sum_{u=-2}^{2} \sum_{v=-2}^{2} h_a(u+3, v+3) \, K_k(2i+u, 2j+v), \tag{3}$$

where $i, j \in \Omega_{k+1}$.

The resolution of the layer K_{k+1} is expanded to layer K_k by an interpolation of missing pixels. Thus bilinear interpolation can be viewed as a convolution operation (1) which is used to define the *Expand Operator* $\tilde{K}_k(i,j) = \hat{\mathcal{E}}(K_{k+1})$ as

$$\hat{\mathcal{E}}(K_{k+1})(i,j) = 4 \cdot \sum_{u=-2}^{2} \sum_{v=-2}^{2} h_a(u+3, v+3)\, K_{k+1}\left(\frac{i+u}{2}, \frac{j+v}{2}\right), \quad (4)$$

where $i, j \in \Omega_k$. Only those terms for which $\frac{i+u}{2}$ and $\frac{j+v}{2}$ are integers contribute to the sum. For the case $\alpha = 0.5$ the kernel h_α performs a bilinear interpolation (see Fig. 1). Taking values $0.3 \leq \alpha < 0.5$ will lead to a combination of low-pass filtering and bilinear interpolation. Let us note explicitly that the smoothing property of bilinear interpolation which is in accordance with the convolutions that are employed along with its computational simplicity inspired us to employ this technique since both of these aspects are beneficial here.

Gaussian Pyramid. To generate the Gaussian pyramid, we apply the Reduce Operator (3) for $G_0 = I(i,j)$ recursively

$$G_{k+1} = \hat{\mathcal{R}}(G_k), \quad k = 1, \dots, r-1 \quad (5)$$

to obtain the layers of the pyramid, as shown in Fig. 2. By gradually applying the Reduce Operator, the effect of the filter increases and hence the image is successively smoothed.

Laplacian Pyramid. Using the definition of the Gaussian pyramid allows us to compute the Laplacian pyramid as follows

$$L_k = G_k - \hat{\mathcal{E}}(G_{k+1}), \quad k = 0, 1, \dots, r-1. \quad (6)$$

It corresponds to a pixelwise difference of two adjacent layers of the Gaussian pyramid, as shown in Fig. 3.

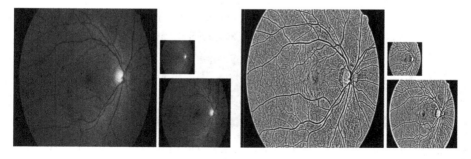

Fig. 2. First layers of the Gaussian pyramid (Left) and Laplacian pyramid (Right).

Since we subtracted two layers whose smoothness differ, the layers of the Laplacian pyramid constitute an efficiently computed bandpass filtered version of the input image. As shown in Fig. 2, the scales of the Laplacian pyramid highlight the blood vessel system in a useful way. With increasing layers, small structures of the blood vessel system disappear while thicker vessel components remain. This allows us to analyse and segment the blood vessel system on different scales, going from coarse to fine structures.

3   The Multiscale Segmentation Algorithm

The main goal of blood vessel segmentation is to simplify the representation of an input fundus image $I : \Omega \to [0,1]$ into something more meaningful for the detection of blood vessel structures S by separating them from the background B. More precisely, we seek a binary label matrix $S \in \{0,1\}^{N \times M}$ such that

$$S(i,j) = \begin{cases} 1, & \text{if } (i,j) \in \Omega \cap B \\ 0, & \text{if } (i,j) \in B \end{cases} \tag{7}$$

where pixels with the label 1 belong to the blood vessel system and those with label 0 form the background.

3.1   Our Approach

Creating the segmentation map S of the input fundus image includes the following three fundamental steps summarized in Figs. 4 and 5.

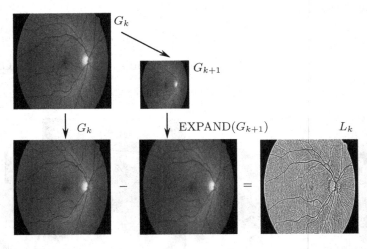

Fig. 3. The construction of kth Laplacian pyramid level using k^{th} and $(k+1)^{th}$ layer of the Gaussian pyramid.

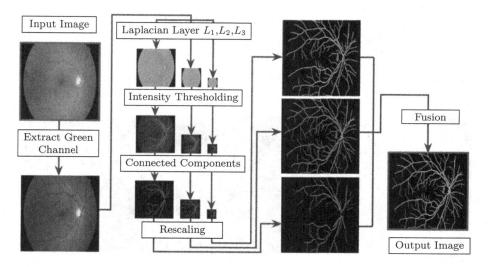

Fig. 4. Pipeline of the proposed segmentation algorithm.

Computing the Laplacian Pyramid. At first we extract the green channel from the input image since the green channel has the best contrast of the vasculature and the background, see also the related discussion in [3]. Afterwards, we compute the first four layers G_0 to G_3 of the Gaussian pyramid using Eq. (5). Those layers are the cornerstone for the construction of the three layers L_1 to L_3 of the Laplacian pyramid using Eq. (6). The first layer L_0 and layers beyond L_3 do not yield helpful information for the blood vessel segmentation within our algorithm. Finally, we stretched the intensity distribution of the layers using histogram equalisation with 512 quantisations steps such $L_k : \Omega_k \rightarrow \{z_1, \dots, z_{512}\}$.

Let us note that it is a standard proceeding not to construct the full image pyramid. The basic idea of the full pyramid would be to help in analysing all the scales of an image, whereas one has to focus on the relevant range of scales in an application as we do here.

Intensity Thresholding and Connected Components. As a first step we separate potential blood vessels from the background by using a global intensity threshold z^* such that the set of pixel positions $\Omega_k^* = \{(i,j) \in \Omega_k : L_k(i,j) \leq z^*\}$ are considered to be those of potential blood vessel pixels. In order to get a meaningful intensity threshold z^*, we make use of two observations: Blood vessel structures are darker than the background, thus are detectable at low intensity values and a small amount of the pixels (roughly 10%) correspond to blood vessel pixels. Taking this into account, we sort the intensity values of the image in ascending order and collect pixels in that order as long as the number of collected pixels does not exceed a threshold value β of the entire number of pixels of the pyramid layer. The largest intensity value among the collected pixels is the aforementioned global intensity threshold z^*. It can be written as

$$z^* = \max \{z_1, \ldots z_{512}\} \quad \text{s.t.} \quad \sum_{l=1}^{512} \sum_{i=1}^{N/2^k} \sum_{j=1}^{M/2^k} \delta_{z_l, L_k(i,j)} \leq \frac{\beta \cdot N \cdot M}{2^k}, \qquad (8)$$

where $\delta_{z_l, L_k(i,j)}$ is the Kronecker delta, being 1 for $z_l = L_k(i,j)$ and 0 else.

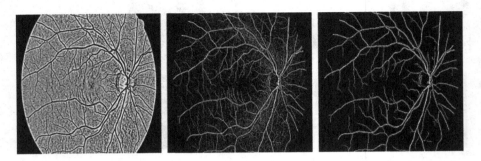

Fig. 5. Left: Laplacian pyramid L_k after histogram equalization. **Middle:** After Intensity thresholding, the pixel belonging to Ω_k^* are white. **Right:** After removing small connected components we obtain S_k.

Let us note that one may immediately think of a refinement of the method in terms of a local thresholding instead of a global thresholding as we propose here. However, in practical assessment of possible local thresholding algorithms for segmentation we did not observe a significant benefit in our application but obtained longer computational times.

In the next step of our method after intensity thresholding, we label all connected components in Ω_k^* using an algorithm which is outlined in [14]. For the pixel connectivity we use an 8-connected window, thus two pixels are connected if they share an edge or a corner. Two adjoint pixels are part of the same object if they are connected along the horizontal, vertical or diagonal direction. Based on the observation that the blood vessel system consists of connected components of greater size compared to connected objects that are part of the background, we can refine the segmentation by removing small objects of a certain size

$$\Gamma_k = \left\{ (i,j) \in \Omega_k^* : \text{size of connected object} \leq \frac{\gamma}{\sqrt{N \cdot M/2^k}} \right\} \qquad (9)$$

where γ is a relative threshold size of the connected object. The segmentation map of the kth layer then defined as

$$S_k(i,j) = \begin{cases} 1, & \text{for } (i,j) \in \Omega_k^* \setminus \Gamma_k \\ 0, & \text{else} \end{cases}. \qquad (10)$$

Rescaling and Fusion of Segmented Pyramid Layers. In the last step, we combine the segmented blood vessels from all layers via

$$S(i,j) = \begin{cases} 1, & \text{for } \hat{\mathcal{E}}(S_1)(i,j) = 1 \vee \hat{\mathcal{E}}^2(S_2)(i,j) = 1 \vee \hat{\mathcal{E}}^3(S_3)(i,j) = 1 \\ 0, & \text{else} \end{cases}. \quad (11)$$

The layers are expanded to the resolution of the input image using the Expand Operation.

Let us comment that by the fusion of connected components of several resolution layers we obtain a reasonable segmentation of blood vessels that are still connected in the total.

4   Experiments

Let us briefly comment on our experiments.

Dataset. As a first step the commonly used DRIVE [23] dataset is taken, containing 40 images with a resolution of 565×584 pixels.

Focusing on high resolution fundus images, we evaluated our methods on a high resolution images dataset, available in the public domain [5]. The database contains 45 images with a resolution of 3504×2336 pixels, subdivided into three categories (15 images per category): healthy, diabetic retinopathy and glaucomatous eyes.

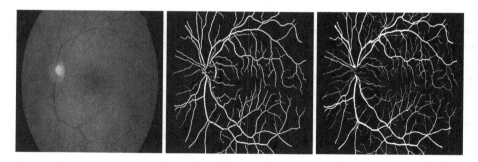

Fig. 6. Results on the High Resolution dataset. **Left:** Input fundus image. **Middle:** Segmented blood vessel system using our method. **Right:** Ground truth. The ratio of the images were changes to improve visualisation.

How to Evaluate. During the process of retinal vessel segmentation, each pixel is classified as blood vessel or background. Thereby, correct detections are expressed as True Positive (TP) and True Negative (TN). TP are correctly detected blood vessel pixel and TN represents the correctly detected background pixel. False segmented pixel are measured using False Negative (FN) and False

Positive (FP), where FP are falsely detected blood vessel pixels and FN represent false detected background pixels.

In order to evaluate the performance of the vessel segmentation algorithms, three commonly used metrics are applied [16, 17]:

$$\text{Se} = \frac{\text{TP}}{\text{TP} + \text{FN}}, \quad \text{Sp} = \frac{\text{TN}}{\text{TN} + \text{FP}} \quad \text{and} \quad \text{Acc} = \frac{\text{TP} + \text{TN}}{\text{TP} + \text{TN} + \text{FP} + \text{FN}}. \quad (12)$$

The *Sensitivity* Se reflects the algorithm's ability of correctly detecting blood vessel pixels. On the other hand, the *Specificity* Sp measures the algorithm's effectiveness in identifying background pixels. Finally, the *Accuracy* Acc is a global measure of classification performance combing both Se and Sp.

Implementation and Parameters. The algorithm is fully vectorised implemented using MATLAB, making it beneficial for GPU architecture. The parameters were set to $\alpha = 0.3$, $\beta = 0.1$ and $\gamma = 0.08$ for both, the DRIVE and High Resolution dataset. In order to get meaningful Laplace Pyramid layers on the low resolution DRIVE dataset, the input images where upscaled from 565×584 to 2048×2048.

4.1   Results

We will consider several aspects that combine into an useful assessment, namely qualitative performance, runtimes and robustness vs. parameter choices.

Performance. The performance is evaluated by taking the DRIVE and High Resolution dataset into account. In Fig. 6 the results of our method are shown exemplarily in comparison to the ground truth for one fundus image of the high resolution data set. On both datasets the choice of parameters was the same which demonstrates the high robustness of our approach. Let us remark that the other algorithms are reported to be highly parameter dependent. The results for the two datasets are displayed in Table 1. We observe that our method leads to very good results that are competitive to modern approaches from the literature.

Let us in addition comment that in previous literature, the performance of the human expert observer was estimated as Acc value 0.9473, TP as 0.7761, and FP as 0.0275 for the DRIVE database cf. [1]. Especially the Accuracy value (Acc) indicates that our method performs basically as good as the human observer.

As another comment, we would like to clarify that especially with machine learning and related supervised approaches, there are some results reported in the literature that may obtain in some tests somewhat better in quality than the ones reported here, see e.g. the already mentioned works [3, 19]. However, as already indicated, we do not rely on annotated data which is often a precious resource, especially when considering high-resolution data as in recent and upcoming developments in cameras for use, and we also do not consider here very special data preparation or calibration steps that have often been considered with these approaches.

Let us also remark in this context, that the measurable quality of results is given by comparison with ground truth data annotated by human experts, and (as noted again) assessment of human observers as documented via DRIVE gives about 95% accuracy based on that. We think that it appears reasonable to obtain an accuracy somewhere around this value, having in mind that also ground truth data often features some inaccuracies introduced by individual interpretation of the human expert (sometimes visible by annotating blood vessels in a disconnected way, or e.g. by fixing the end of a vessel at a point one may surely discuss upon).

Table 1. Performance of vessel segmentation using the DRIVE and the High Resolution dataset. The results for other techniques are taken from [5,9,16,20]. The run time (processing one single fundus image) was evaluated on a 2.3 GHz labtop with 4 GB RAM and CPU implementation of our approach was used.

Test datasets	DRIVE (565 × 584)			High Resolution (3504 × 2336)			
Method	Se	Sp	Acc	Se	Sp	Acc	Runtime
Our Approach	0.6534	0.9860	0.9572	0.694	0.981	0.955	1.81 s
Budai et al. [5]	0.644	0.987	0.9572	0.669	0.985	0.961	26.69 s
Fan et al. [9]	0.736	0.981	0.960	–	–	–	–
Frangi et al. [11]	0.660	0.985	0.9570	0.622	0.982	0.954	39.29 s
Krause et al. [16]	–	–	0.9468	–	–	–	–
Mendonça et al. [20]	–	–	0.9452	–	–	–	–
Odstrcilik et al. [22]	0.7060	0.9693	0.9340	0.774	0.966	0.949	18 min

Table 2. Performance of vessel segmentation using the High Resolution dataset for the three different categories.

Category	Healthy			Glaucomatous			Diabetic		
Method	Se	Sp	Acc	Se	Sp	Acc	Se	Sp	Acc
Our approach	0.700	0.988	0.956	0.710	0.979	0.956	0.674	0.978	0.952
Budai et al.	0.662	0.992	0.961	0.687	0.986	0.965	0.658	0.977	0.955
Frangi et al.	0.621	0.989	0.955	0.654	0.984	0.961	0.590	0.972	0.946
Odstrcilik et al.	0.786	0.975	0.953	0.791	0.964	0.949	0.746	0.961	0.944

Runtime. Considering the runtime, our approach outperforms easily all other methods on the High Resolution dataset, even when using the slower CPU implemented version. As shown in Fig. 7, our approach can even be more accelerated using a GPU implemented version. This version is enormously fast and beats other GPU based methods. The GPU runtime of the fast method Krause et al. [16] on a 4228 × 2848 pixel images takes 1.2 s, whereas our approach performs the computation only in 0.5 s. Furthermore our approach scales well when it comes to super high resolution input images. The computation on a 10000 × 10000 fundus images takes 4 s on a GPU and 11.5 s on a CPU.

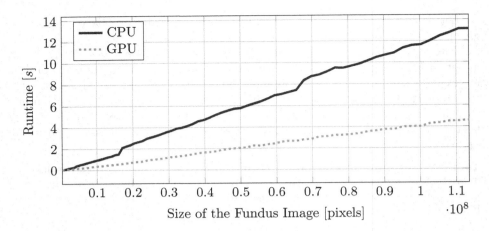

Fig. 7. Scalability of our approach using a CPU (Intel Xenon 3.7 GHz) and GPU (Nvidia Titan XP) implementation on a 8 GB RAM machine. Exemplary, operating on a 10000 × 10000 fundus images takes 4 s on a GPU and 11.5 s on a CPU.

Robustness. For the robustness of the parameter choice we investigate the segmentation performance of the three different categories of the High Resolution dataset, as it is shown in Table 2. In contrast to healthy fundus images, the diabetic retinopathy and glaucomatous fundus images contain additional background structure, making them more challenging for blood vessel segmentation. By comparing the results of the healthy and diabetic retinopathy fundus images, they gain similar segmentation results for all methods. The glaucomatous fundus images are more challenging due to green background spots. The performance, especially the sensitivity, is slightly decreasing for all considered methods.

Let us mention, that our method used the same choice of parameters for all categories, whereas the other methods need a tailored adjustment of those parameters. This can be seen as a significant practical advantage by making user-based readjustment of the parameters obsolete.

5   Summary and Conclusion

We introduced a well-engineered blood vessel segmentation algorithm for fundus images based on the multiscale representation of a Laplacian pyramid. Our method does not rely on a complex preprocessing and thus also not on some related, hidden parameter estimation step. Experimental results performed on the High Resolution and DRIVE data set illustrated the power of Laplacian pyramids and the usefulness of the approach for tackling the blood vessel segmentation problem. They confirm exemplarily that our novel segmentation approach may have a similar precision to other state of the art methods while being much faster in runtime and, perhaps even much more important, highly robust to parameter choices. By making use of our empirical parameter findings, our method can thus easily be defined effectively as a parameter-free scheme making it attractive for application.

In future work we aim to increase the quality of the developed algorithm without destroying its effectiveness. Let us note in this context that the results of the current method are already of comparable quality to the ones that could be given by a human observer, as evaluated via the DRIVE database, so we think that already its current version may be useful in practical application.

References

1. Drive database (2002). www.isi.uu.nl/Research/Databases/DRIVE/results.php
2. Adelson, E.H., Anderson, C.H., Bergen, J.R., Burt, P.J., Ogden, J.M.: Pyramid methods in image processing. RCA Eng. **29**, 33–41 (1984)
3. Azzopardi, G., Strisciuglio, N., Vento, M., Petkov, N.: Trainable COSFIRE filters for vessel delineation with application to retinal images. Med. Image Anal. **19**, 46–57 (2015)
4. Brieva, J., Gonzalez, E., Gonzalez, F., Bousse, A., Bellanger, J.J.: A level set method for vessel segmentation in coronary angiography. In: Proceedings of the 27th IEEE Annual International Conference of the Engineering in Medicine and Biology Society, pp. 6348–6351 (2006)
5. Budai, A., Bock, R., Maier, A., Hornegger, J., Michelson, G.: Robust vessel segmentation in fundus images. Int. J. Biomed. Imaging **2013**(6), 13 (2013)
6. Burt, P.J., Adelson, E.H.: The Laplacian pyramid as a compact image code. IEEE Trans. Commun. **31**, 532–540 (1983)
7. Chaudhuri, S., Chatterjee, S., Katz, N., Nelson, M., Goldbaum, M.: Detection of blood vessels in retinal images using two-dimensional matched filters. IEEE Trans. Med. Imaging **8**(3), 263–269 (1989)
8. Dizdaroglu, B., Ataer-Cansizoglu, E., Kalpathy-Cramer, J., Keck, M., Chiang, M.F., Erdogmus, D.: Level sets for retinal vasculature segmentation using seeds from ridges and edges from phase maps. In: Proceedings of the IEEE International Workshop on Machine Learning for Signal Processing (2012)
9. Fan, Z., Lu, J., Wei, C., Huang, H., Cai, X., Chen, X.: A hierarchical image matting model for blood vessel segmentation in fundus images. IEEE Trans. Image Process. **28**(5), 2367–2377 (2019)
10. Farnell, D.J.J., et al.: Enhancement of blood vessels in digital fundus photographs via the application of multiscale line operators. J. Franklin Inst. **345**, 748–765 (2008)
11. Frangi, A.F., Niessen, W.J., Vincken, K.L., Viergever, M.A.: Multiscale vessel enhancement filtering. In: Wells, W.M., Colchester, A., Delp, S. (eds.) MICCAI 1998. LNCS, vol. 1496, pp. 130–137. Springer, Heidelberg (1998). https://doi.org/10.1007/BFb0056195
12. Fraz, M., et al.: Blood vessel segmentation methodologies in retinal images - a survey. Comput. Methods Programs Biomed. **108**, 407–433 (2012)
13. Grisan, E., Ruggeri, A.: A divide et impera strategy for automatic classification of retinal vessels into arteries and veins. In: Proceedings of the 25th Annual International Conference of the IEEE, vol. 891, pp. 890–893 (2003)
14. Haralick, R.M., Shapiro, L.G.: Computer and Robot Vision, vol. 1, pp. 28–48. Addison-Wesley, Boston (1992)

15. Heneghan, C., Flynn, J., O'Keefe, M., Cahill, M.: Characterization of changes in blood vessel width and tortuosity in retinopathy of prematurity using image analysis. Med. Image Anal. **6**, 407–429 (2002)
16. Krause, M., Alles, R.M., Burgeth, B., Weickert, J.: Fast retinal vessel analysis. J. Real-Time Image Proc. **11**, 413–422 (2016)
17. Lee, C.C., Ku, S.C.: Blood vessel segmentation in retinal images based on the nonsubsampled contourlet transform. In: 2012 International Conference on Information Security and Intelligent Control, pp. 337–340. IEEE (2012)
18. Lowell, J., Hunter, A., Steel, D., Basu, A., Kennedy, R.L.: Measurement of retinal vessel widths from fundus images based on 2-D modeling. IEEE Trans. Med. Imaging **23**(10), 1196–1204 (2004)
19. Marin, D., Aquino, A., Emilio Gegundez-Arias, M., Manuel Bravo, J.: A new supervised method for blood vessel segmentation in retinal images by using gray-level and moment invariants-based features. IEEE Trans. Med. Imaging **30**, 146–158 (2011)
20. Mendonça, A.M., Campilho, A.: Segmentation of retinal blood vessels by combining the detection of centerlines and morphological reconstruction. IEEE Trans. Med. Imaging **25**, 1200–1213 (2006)
21. Miri, M.S., Mahloojifar, A.: Retinal image analysis using curvelet transform and multistructure elements morphology by reconstruction. IEEE Trans. Biomed. Eng. **58**, 1183–1192 (2011)
22. Odstrcilik, J., et al.: Retinal vessel segmentation by improved matched filtering: evaluation on a new high-resolution fundus image database. IET Image Process. **7**(4), 373–383 (2013)
23. Staal, J.J., Abramoff, M.D., Niemeijer, M., Viergever, M.A., Ginneken, V.B.: Ridge based vessel segmentation in color images of the retina. IEEE Trans. Med. Imaging **23**, 501–509 (2004)

RVNet: Deep Sensor Fusion of Monocular Camera and Radar for Image-Based Obstacle Detection in Challenging Environments

Vijay John$^{(\boxtimes)}$ and Seiichi Mita

Toyota Technological Institute, Nagoya, Japan
{vijayjohn,smita}@toyota-ti.ac.jp

Abstract. Camera and radar-based obstacle detection are important research topics in environment perception for autonomous driving. Camera-based obstacle detection reports state-of-the-art accuracy, but the performance is limited in challenging environments. In challenging environments, the camera features are noisy, limiting the detection accuracy. In comparison, the radar-based obstacle detection methods using the 77 GHZ long-range radar are not affected by these challenging environments. However, the radar features are sparse with no delineation of the obstacles. The camera and radar features are complementary, and their fusion results in robust obstacle detection in varied environments. Once calibrated, the radar features can be used for localization of the image obstacles, while the camera features can be used for the delineation of the localized obstacles. We propose a novel deep learning-based sensor fusion framework, termed as the "RVNet", for the effective fusion of the monocular camera and long-range radar for obstacle detection. The RVNet is a single shot object detection network with two input branches and two output branches. The RVNet input branches contain separate branches for the monocular camera and the radar features. The radar features are formulated using a novel feature descriptor, termed as the "sparse radar image". For the output branches, the proposed network contains separate branches for small obstacles and big obstacles, respectively. The validation of the proposed network with state-of-the-art baseline algorithm is performed on the Nuscenes public dataset. Additionally, a detailed parameter analysis is performed with several variants of the RVNet. The experimental results show that the proposed network is better than baseline algorithms in varying environmental conditions.

Keywords: Sensor fusion · Radar · Monocular camera

1 Introduction

Rapid development in autonomous driving has been witnessed in recent years [8, 9]. In this research area, obstacle detection is an important research task performed using sensors such as monocular camera, LIDAR, radar etc. Camera-based obstacle detection is popular owing to the low-cost of these sensors, and

© Springer Nature Switzerland AG 2019
C. Lee et al. (Eds.): PSIVT 2019, LNCS 11854, pp. 351–364, 2019.
https://doi.org/10.1007/978-3-030-34879-3_27

the rich appearance features obtained from them. Consequently, they report state-of-the-art in deep learning-based perception frameworks [11,16]. But the performance of the camera-based detection framework is limited in case of challenging environments such as low-illumination conditions, rainy weather and snowy weather. While the camera features are noisy in such environments, it is still possible to obtain the object boundaries to a certain degree (Fig. 1).

Fig. 1. An illustration of the camera-radar (left-right) features for varying scenes. Although, the vision-based appearance tends to be noisy in low-illuminated and rainy scenes, the object boundaries are still visible, to a certain degree, in the highlighted regions. The radar features, projected onto the image, are not affected by variations in the environment.

The radar-based obstacle detection are not affected by the varying environment. The 77 GHZ radar detects objects in low illumination and different weather conditions such as rain, snow and fog [13,14]. The milliwave radar can measure the object distance and velocity information at distances up to 250 m. However, the radar information is rather sparse. Moreover, it does not delineate the obstacles. The comparative analysis for the radar and monocular camera are provided in Table 1.

Table 1. Comparative study of the properties of the radar and monocular camera.

Sensor	Milliwave radar	Monocular camera
Weather	Not affected by adverse weather such as rain, snow and fog [14]	Susceptible to illumination variation and adverse weather [9]
Data density	Sparse with point-wise reflection	Dense with appearance information
Object boundary	No	Yes
Object speed	Yes	No
Multiclass classification	Discriminative for limited classes using radar features such as depth and velocity	Discriminative for higher number of classes [11]

Based on the comparative study of the two sensors, the main advantage of the radar is the identification of obstacles in varying environment. However, the radar is sparse and doesn't delineate the obstacles.

On the other hand, the camera provides dense appearance information in well-illuminated environment [9]. In case of the delineation, the monocular camera can generate the object boundaries in the image to a certain degree, even in adverse conditions.

The radar and camera features are complementary, and can be fused to enhance the robustness of obstacle detection in adverse weather conditions. We propose a deep sensor fusion framework termed as the RVNet for the effective fusion of the camera and radar sensors for 2D image-based obstacle detection. The RVNet is a binary single shot object detection network, based on the YOLO framework, and contains two feature extraction branches and two output branches. The two feature extraction branches contain separate branches for the camera-based images and the radar-based features. The radar features are formulated into a feature descriptor termed as the "sparse radar image". The features extracted by the input branches are then fed into the two output branches for detecting small obstacles and big obstacles using anchor boxes. The proposed end-to-end framework simultaneously performs effective feature-level radar and camera fusion, while detecting obstacles in the environment in real-time.

The RVNet is validated using the nuscenes public dataset [2] and a comparison is performed with the state-of-the-art baseline algorithms. A detailed parameter analysis is also performed with different variants of the RVNet. The experimental results show that the proposed framework effectively fuses the camera and radar features and performs better than the YOLO framework. To the best of our knowledge, the main contributions of the proposed framework are as follows:

- A novel deep learning-based obstacle detection framework termed as the RVNet is proposed for radar and camera fusion.
- Parametric analysis of several variants of the RVNet with different type of fusions, input features and classification.

The remainder of the paper is structured as follows. The literature is reviewed in Sect. 2 and the RVNet is presented in Sect. 3. The comparative and parametric analysis is presented in Sect. 4. Finally, the paper is concluded in Sect. 5.

2   Literature Review

Radar-vision fusion for obstacle detection is an important research topic, and can be primarily categorized into three, early-stage fusion [1,5,19], late-stage fusion methods [7,20,21] and feature-level fusion [3]. In the early-stage fusion, the radar features are used to localize the search area or identify candidate regions for vision-based perception. As a precursor to fusion, the radar and camera sensors are calibrated to the same reference system. Once calibrated, the radar features are transferred to the image plane, as candidate regions. These candidate regions are given as input to vision-based deep learning [6] and machine learning frameworks [10,15] for detection and classification. In the work by Bombini et al. [1], the radar features are transformed to the image reference system using perspective mapping transform, and used within the symmetry-based vehicle detection algorithm. Sugimoto et al. [19] use the radar features within a vision-based occupancy grid representation to detect the on-road obstacles. While early fusion provide accurate results, they are computationally expensive [18].

In late stage fusion, the outputs of the vision-based perception pipeline and the radar-based perception pipeline are combined in the final step before perception [7]. In the work by Garcia et al. [7], the output of the radar pipeline are used to validate the output of the optical flow-based vision pipeline. Similarly, Zhong et al. [21] perform a joint tracking in the final fusion step using the outputs of the radar and camera pipelines.

In feature level fusion, the radar features and vision features are fused for perception. Recently, Chadwick et al. [3], fuse the radar and vision features within a single shot object detector framework [12] to detect vehicles at distance. Compared to late fusion, in the feature-level fusion, a single radar-vision pipeline is used to detect the objects in a straightforward manner. Additionally, the radar pipeline's limitation of estimating the obstacle boundary is also addressed. Compared to early fusion, the single shot feature-level fusion is also computationally less expensive.

In our work, we also adopt a feature-level fusion approach in the novel RVNet, based on the YOLO framework [17], to detect obstacles in the environment. A detailed study of the proposed network and its variants are performed.

3   Algorithm

The RVNet is a novel deep learning framework which performs sensor fusion of camera and radar features for 2D image-based obstacle detection. The objects in the road environment, including vehicles, pedestrians, two-wheeled vehicles, movable objects and debris, are categorized as an obstacle. The RVNet architecture is a single shot object detection framework, similar to the SSD [12] and the

YOLO [17], where the need for candidate regions or proposals for CNN detection is avoided [18]. The single shot object detection frameworks utilize multi-scale features and anchor boxes to detect and classify the objects in the image in real-time.

The RVNet, based on the tiny YOLO network due to GPU memory considerations, performs binary 2D image-based obstacle detection by effectively fusing the radar and camera features. The RVNet contains two input branches for feature extraction and two output branches for the obstacle detection. The input branches are independent branches, which separately extract camera and radar features. These features are fused in the output branches, and the image obstacles of varying sizes are detected and classified. An overview of RVNet modules are shown in Fig. 2. As a precursor to describing the feature extraction branches in the architecture, we describe the data preprocessing step.

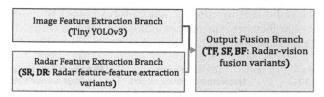

Fig. 2. An illustration of the branches of the RVNet. Variants of the radar feature extraction branch and the output fusion branch are also presented in this work.

3.1   Data Pre-processing

The RVNet was validated on the nuscenes dataset [2] using the front camera and the front radar, which are calibrated. The RVNet performs the 2D obstacle detection on the front camera images, after the fusion of the camera and radar features. Consequently, the fixed number of radar points (169) in the front radar's 3-D coordinate system λ_r, are transformed to the front camera's 3-D coordinate system λ_c. The number of radar points in the nuscenes dataset are fixed, and each point contains the depth, lateral velocity and longitudinal velocity information of objects. The velocity components are compensated by the velocity of the ego vehicle. An illustration of the coordinate transformation are given in Fig. 3.

3.2   Radar Feature Descriptor

Following the projection of the radar points onto the camera coordinate system λ_c, the radar points are further transformed onto the image coordinate system λ_i using the camera's intrinsic matrix $\mathbf{K}$, generating the "sparse radar image" (S). The "sparse radar image" is a 3-channel image of size (416×416), which directly corresponds to the image size (I). Each non-zero pixel in the S contains the depth and velocity radar features across the 3 channels. As the name implies, the radar image is highly sparse owing to the nature of the radar data. An illustration of the sparse radar image is given in Fig. 3. We next present the details of the architecture as shown in Fig. 4.

3.3 RVNet Architecture

Feature Extraction Branches. The RVNet has two input feature extraction branches which extract the features from the front camera image I and the "sparse radar image" S. By being independent, the two feature extraction branches extract image-specific and radar-specific features. The first input branch corresponding to the image feature extraction is designed to be similar to the feature extraction branch of the tiny Yolov3 model [17], in order to utilize the pre-trained weights of the tiny Yolov3 model trained on the Pascal VOC dataset [4].

The second input branch corresponding to the radar feature extraction branch is designed to extract features from S. In this regard, as S is highly sparse with pixel-wise radar features, the radar feature extraction branch contains 2D convolution filters with stride 1. By utilizing a single stride convolution operation, all the radar features are accounted for. In order to reduce the dimensionality of the radar features, the max-pooling operation is utilized. The detailed architecture of the feature extraction branches are given in Fig. 4.

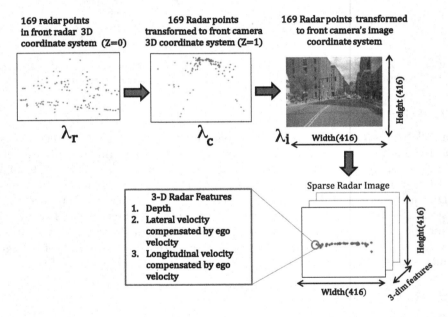

Fig. 3. An illustration of the coordinate transformation of the radar points to the image coordinate system, and the generation of the 3-D sparse radar feature.

Obstacle Detection. The fusion of the radar feature maps and image feature maps is performed across the two output branches. The first output branch detects small and medium obstacles, and the second output branch detects big obstacles. The fusion of the radar and image feature maps in the output branches are performed by concatenation. For both the output branches, the YOLOv3 loss function, is used within a binary classification framework. The YOLO output convolution and output reshape layers are similar to the YOLO output layer [17], where the 30 filters in the output convolution corresponds to the following breakdown: number-of-anchors (3) * (number-of-classes(2) +5). The details of the fusion are described in the architecture in Fig. 4.

Training. The RVNet is trained with the image, radar points and ground truth annotations from the nuscenes dataset, where the vehicles, motorcycles, cycles, pedestrians, movable objects and debris are considered as obstacles. To generate the background classes for the binary classification, bounding boxes of image regions without obstacles are utilized. As a precursor to the training, the pre-trained weights of the feature extraction layers of the tiny YOLOv3 network trained on the Pascal VOC dataset [4] are used to initialize the weights of the image feature extraction branch of the RVNet. The radar feature extraction branch and the output branches are trained from random weights without any fine-tuning, as these branches are either different (output) or not present (radar feature extraction) in the PASCAL tiny YOLOv3 network. The RVNet is trained with an Adam optimizer with learning rate of 0.001.

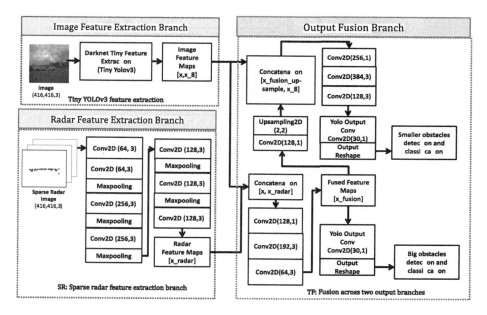

Fig. 4. The detailed architecture of the proposed RVNet with SR and TF branches as the feature extraction and output branches in Fig. 2. Conv2D(m,n) represents 2D convolution with m filters with size $n \times n$ and stride 1. Maxpooling 2D is performed with size (2,2).

3.4   RVNet Variants

We propose different variations of the proposed RVNet to perform a detailed study of the radar-vision fusion for perception.

Input Branch Variation. The input branch variation is represented by a different radar feature descriptor and feature extraction branch. Here, the "sparse radar image" is replaced by a "dense radar matrix", where the fixed number of radar points defined with respect to the image coordinate system (λ_i) are reshaped to a 5-D dense matrix form M. Each 5-dim entry in M corresponds to the radar point's depth, lateral ego-compensated velocity, longitudinal ego-compensated velocity, row pixel coordinate and column pixel coordinate. An illustration of the "dense radar matrix" is shown in Fig. 3 and the shallow feature extraction branch is shown in Fig. 5.

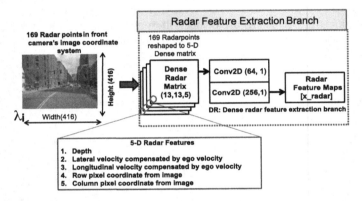

Fig. 5. The detailed architecture of the DR: dense radar matrix's feature extraction branch, which can be used as an input branch in Fig. 2. Conv2D(m,n) represents 2D convolution with m filters with size $n \times n$ and stride 1.

Output Branch Variation. The output branch variation is represented by two variants of the radar-vision fusion. In the first variant, the radar-vision fusion is utilized for the big obstacle output branch, while the vision features without fusion are utilized for the small obstacle output branch. This variant is termed as the "big" fusion. In the second variant, the radar-vision fusion is utilized for the small obstacle output branch, while the vision features without fusion are utilized for the bigger obstacles output branch. This variant is termed as the "small" fusion. The architectures for the big and small fusion are presented in Fig. 6.

Classification Variation The classification variation is represented by the reformulating the RVNet as a multiclass classifier. The original RVNet is designed as a binary classifier, detecting the obstacles in the environment, whereas the variant RVNet-based multiclass classifier, detects the types of

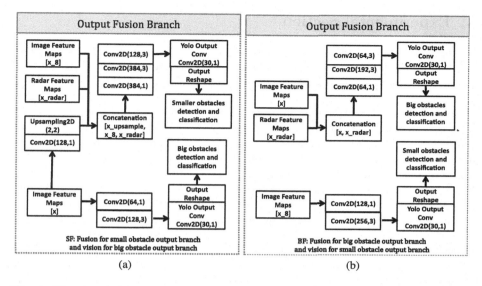

Fig. 6. The detailed architecture of the (a) SF: small fusion and (b) BF: big fusion output branch variations, which can be used as output branches in Fig. 2. Conv2D(m,n) represents 2D convolution with m filters with size $n \times n$ and stride 1. Maxpooling 2D is performed with size (2,2).

obstacles too. The multiclass classifier is formulated as 4-dim classifier with the following classes, namely, vehicles, pedestrians, two wheelers, and objects (movable objects and debris). The different RVNet variants are presented in Table 2.

Table 2. Different variations of the RVNet.

Network	Input branch	Output branch fusion
RVNet-proposed	Two individual branches with sparse radar image input for radar feature branch	Radar-vision fusion for both obstacle branches
RVNet-SR-BF	Two individual branches with sparse radar image input for radar feature branch	Radar-vision fusion for big obstacle branch Vision for small obstacle branch
RVNet-SR-SF	Two individual branches with sparse radar image input for radar feature branch	Radar-vision fusion for small obstacle branch Vision for big obstacle branch
RVNet-DR-TF	Two individual branches with dense radar image input for radar feature branch	Radar-vision fusion for both obstacle branches
RVNet-DR-BF	Two individual branches with dense radar image input for radar feature branch	Radar-vision fusion for big obstacle branch vision for small obstacle branch
RVNet-DR-SF	Two individual branches with dense radar image input for radar feature branch	Radar-vision fusion for small obstacle branch vision for big obstacle branch
Tiny Yolov3 (Image) [17]	One branch for vision	Vision for both obstacle branches
Tiny Yolov3 (Late fusion)	Vision pipeline: Tiny Yolov3 (Image) Radar pipeline: Rule-based classifier	Vision pipeline: Tiny Yolov3 (Image) Radar pipeline: Rule-based classifier

4   Experimental Section

Dataset: The different algorithms are validated on the nuscenes dataset with 3200 training and 1000 testing samples. The training data contain scenes from rainy weather and night-time. Example scenes from the dataset are shown in Fig. 1.

Baseline Algorithms: Multiple baseline algorithms based on the pre-trained tiny YOLOv3 network [17] are used for comparative analysis. In the first baseline, referred to as the Tiny Yolov3 (Image), the original multiclass tiny YOLOv3 is modified as a binary classifier. Consequently, the architecture of the Tiny Yolov3 (Image)'s output branch is modified, and trained from random initialization. On the other hand, the architecture of the input branch is not modified, and fine-tuned using the pre-trained weights of the original tiny YOLOv3.

In the second baseline, a late fusion approach, termed as the Tiny Yolov3 (Late Fusion), is adopted using the Tiny Yolov3 (Image). The late fusion approach is a conventional approach in radar-vision fusion, where the outputs of the separate vision and radar pipeline are fused in the final stage. In the Tiny Yolov3 (Late Fusion), the vision pipeline corresponds to the Tiny Yolov3 (Image). The radar pipeline is a naive rule-based obstacle classifier which uses the radar's velocity information to identify the spatial location of the obstacles. Since the radar pipeline does not have a bounding box prediction for the corresponding radar reflection points, a pre-defined bounding box is generated around radar points which are classified as obstacles.

Algorithm Parameters: The proposed algorithm and the baseline algorithms were trained with batch size 8 and epochs 20. The algorithms were implemented on Nvidia Geforce 1080 Ubuntu 18.04 machine using TensorFlow 2.0. The performance of the networks are reported using the Average Precision (AP) with IOU (intersection over threshold) of 0.5.

Results. The performance of the different algorithms tabulated in Table 3 show that the RVNet and its variants are better than the baseline. The computational time of all the algorithms are shown to be real-time.

Table 3. Comparative analysis of the RVNet (Binary classification) and its variants

Algo.	Average precision	Comp. Time (ms)
Tiny Yolov3 (Image) [17]	0.40	10
Tiny Yolov3 (Late Fusion)	0.40	14
RVNet (Proposed)	**0.56**	17
RVNet-SR-BF	0.50	17
RVNet-SR-SF	0.55	17
RVNet-DR-TF	0.44	12
RVNet-DR-BF	0.47	12
RVNet-DR-SF	0.54	12

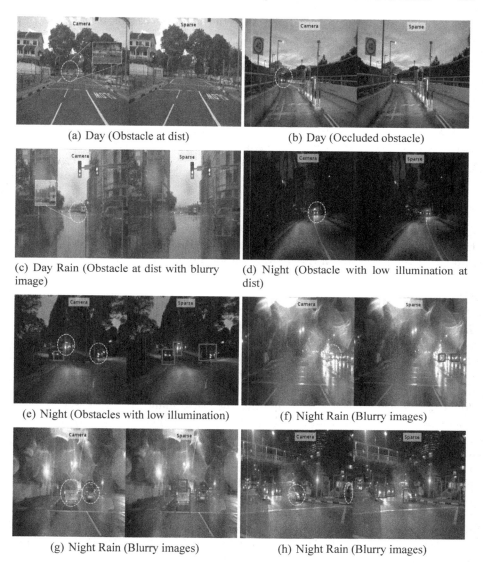

(a) Day (Obstacle at dist)

(b) Day (Occluded obstacle)

(c) Day Rain (Obstacle at dist with blurry image)

(d) Night (Obstacle with low illumination at dist)

(e) Night (Obstacles with low illumination)

(f) Night Rain (Blurry images)

(g) Night Rain (Blurry images)

(h) Night Rain (Blurry images)

Fig. 7. Detection result for the tiny YOLOv3 network and the RVNet for different scenarios. The red bounding boxes indicate the detected obstacles. The yellow circles indicate the objects missed by the $TinyYOLOv3(Image)$. (Color figure online)

Apart from the comparative analysis, we also validate the performance of all the networks with multiclass classification. As described earlier in Sect. 3.4, the multiclass classifier is formulated as 4-dim classifier with the following classes, namely, vehicles, pedestrians, two wheelers, and objects (movable objects and debris). For this experiment, the final output layer of all the binary classifiers are

Table 4. Comparative analysis of the multiclass classification

Algo.	Multiclass				
	AP (Cycle)	AP (Ped)	AP (Vehicle)	AP (Obs)	Mean AP
Tiny Yolov3 (Image) [17]	0.01	0.22	**0.59**	0.14	0.24
RVNet (Proposed)	0.02	0.14	**0.59**	0.26	0.25
RVNet-SR-BF	0.02	0.11	0.56	0.19	0.22
RVNet-SR-SF	0.03	0.19	0.56	0.31	**0.27**
RVNet-DR-TF	0.01	0.19	0.45	**0.35**	0.25
RVNet-DR-BF	**0.05**	**0.25**	0.51	0.10	0.23
RVNet-DR-SF	0	0.21	0.55	0.21	0.24

modified to a multiclass classifier. The results tabulated in Table 4, show that the vision-radar fusion does not significantly improve the detection accuracy, and the performance of all the networks are similar.

Discussion

RVNet: The results tabulated in Table 3 show that the RVNet and its variants report better detection and classification accuracy than the baseline algorithms. Thus validating the proposed framework and demonstrating the advantages of camera-radar fusion. Results of the sensor fusion are presented in (Fig. 7).

Radar-Based Classification: Comparing the performance of the baseline algorithms, the performance of the Tiny Yolov3 (Late Fusion) and Tiny Yolov3 (Image) are similar. This can be attributed to the error measure adopted for validation, (IOU-based average precision), which is not suitable for the radar pipeline of the late fusion. More specifically, the radar pipeline does identify the obstacle location in the image, but fails to delineate the obstacle correctly, resulting in lower IOU-based average precision.

To further substantiate this result, a fine-tuned tiny YOLOv3 with the sparse radar image as the input and binary classification was considered (Tiny Yolov3 (Sparse)) and validated. The experimental results showed us that the Tiny Yolov3 (Sparse) could not estimate the boundary or the bounding box of the obstacles, reporting a very low average precision.

The camera-radar fusion report good classification accuracy for 2D binary classification. This performance can be attributed to the following,

- Radar's ability to identify obstacles on the road even in adverse weather conditions.
- Camera's ability to delineate obstacles, to a certain degree, even in adverse weather conditions.

Binary and Multiclass Classification: Comparing the performance of the binary classifier (Table 3) and the multiclass classifier (Table 4), we can observe that the radar features utilized in this work (depth, lateral velocity and longitudinal velocity) are useful in detecting on-road obstacles in a binary classification framework. However, the same radar features are not useful in identifying the type of obstacles in a multiclass classification framework. This is observed in the last column (Table 4), where the performance of all the networks are similar. To enhance the accuracy of the camera-radar fusion for multiclass classification, additional discriminative radar features needs to be utilized.

Table 5. Analysis of the RVNet on the size of the obstacles its variants

Algo.	RVNet-SR-SF	RVNet-SR-BF	RVNet-DR-SF	RVNet-DR-BF
Avg Prec.	0.55	0.50	0.54	0.47

Fusion Strategies: Comparing the different fusion strategies across the two radar input features. The SF fusion strategy is better than the BF fusion strategy, where the advantages of the camera-radar fusion are more pronounced for smaller obstacles than bigger obstacles (Table 5).

5 Conclusion

A deep sensor fusion framework termed as the RVNet is proposed for the sensor fusion of the camera and radar for 2D image-based obstacle detection. The RVNet contains two feature extraction branches and two output branches. The feature extraction branches are independent and extract radar and camera specific features. These features are given to the output branches, where sensor fusion is performed and the obstacles are detected. We validate the proposed network on the nuscenes dataset and perform comparative analysis with baseline algorithms. The proposed algorithm reports better detection accuracy even in challenging environments in real-time. In our future work, we will consider incorporating other sensors such as LIDAR and thermal camera to further enhance the detection accuracy.

References

1. Bombini, L., Cerri, P., Medici, P., Aless, G.: Radar-vision fusion for vehicle detection. In: International Workshop on Intelligent Transportation, pp. 65–70 (2006)
2. Caesar, H., et al.: nuScenes: A multimodal dataset for autonomous driving. CoRR abs/1903.11027 (2019)
3. Chadwick, S., Maddern, W., Newman, P.: Distant vehicle detection using radar and vision. CoRR abs/1901.10951 (2019)
4. Everingham, M., Gool, L., Williams, C.K., Winn, J., Zisserman, A.: The Pascal visual object classes (VOC) challenge. Int. J. Comput. Vision **88**(2), 303–338 (2010)

5. Fang, Y., Masaki, I., Horn, B.: Depth-based target segmentation for intelligent vehicles: fusion of radar and binocular stereo. IEEE Trans. Intell. Transp. Syst. **3**(3), 196–202 (2002)

6. Gaisser, F., Jonker, P.P.: Road user detection with convolutional neural networks: an application to the autonomous shuttle WEpod. In: International Conference on Machine Vision Applications (MVA), pp. 101–104 (2017)

7. Garcia, F., Cerri, P., Broggi, A., de la Escalera, A., Armingol, J.M.: Data fusion for overtaking vehicle detection based on radar and optical flow. In: 2012 IEEE Intelligent Vehicles Symposium, pp. 494–499 (2012)

8. Jazayeri, A., Cai, H., Zheng, J.Y., Tuceryan, M.: Vehicle detection and tracking in car video based on motion model. IEEE Trans. Intell. Transp. Syst. **12**(2), 583–595 (2011)

9. John, V., Karunakaran, N.M., Guo, C., Kidono, K., Mita, S.: Free space, visible and missing lane marker estimation using the PsiNet and extra trees regression. In: 24th International Conference on Pattern Recognition, pp. 189–194 (2018)

10. Kato, T., Ninomiya, Y., Masaki, I.: An obstacle detection method by fusion of radar and motion stereo. IEEE Trans. Intell. Transp. Syst. **3**(3), 182–188 (2002)

11. Krizhevsky, A., Sutskever, I., Hinton, G.: Imagenet classification with deep convolutional neural networks. In: NIPS (2012)

12. Liu, W., et al.: SSD: single shot multibox detector. In: Leibe, B., Matas, J., Sebe, N., Welling, M. (eds.) ECCV 2016. LNCS, vol. 9905, pp. 21–37. Springer, Cham (2016). https://doi.org/10.1007/978-3-319-46448-0_2. CoRR abs/1512.02325

13. Macaveiu, A., Campeanu, A., Nafornita, I.: Kalman-based tracker for multiple radar targets. In: 2014 10th International Conference on Communications (COMM), pp. 1–4 (2014)

14. Manjunath, A., Liu, Y., Henriques, B., Engstle, A.: Radar based object detection and tracking for autonomous driving. In: 2018 IEEE MTT-S International Conference on Microwaves for Intelligent Mobility (ICMIM), pp. 1–4 (2018)

15. Milch, S., Behrens, M.: Pedestrian detection with radar and computer vision (2001)

16. Noh, H., Hong, S., Han, B.: Learning deconvolution network for semantic segmentation. CoRR abs/1505.04366 (2015)

17. Redmon, J., Farhadi, A.: YOLOv3: an incremental improvement (2018). http://arxiv.org/abs/1804.02767

18. Ren, S., He, K., Girshick, R., Sun, J.: Faster R-CNN: towards real-time object detection with region proposal networks. Adv. Neural Inf. Process. Syst. **28**, 91–99 (2015)

19. Sugimoto, S., Tateda, H., Takahashi, H., Okutomi, M.: Obstacle detection using millimeter-wave radar and its visualization on image sequence. In: Proceedings of the 17th International Conference on Pattern Recognition, ICPR 2004, vol. 3, pp. 342–345 (2004)

20. Wang, X., Xu, L., Sun, H., Xin, J., Zheng, N.: On-road vehicle detection and tracking using MMW radar and monovision fusion. IEEE Trans. Intell. Transp. Syst. **17**(7), 2075–2084 (2016)

21. Zhong, Z., Liu, S., Mathew, M., Dubey, A.: Camera radar fusion for increased reliability in ADAS applications. Electron. Imaging Auton. Veh. Mach. **1**(4), 258-1–258-4 (2018)

Semantic Segmentation of Grey-Scale Traffic Scenes

Trung Khoa Le$^{(\boxtimes)}$ and Reinhard Klette

School of Engineering, Computer and Mathematical Sciences,
Department of Electrical and Electronic Engineering,
Auckland University of Technology, Auckland, New Zealand
khoaletrung@gmail.com, rklette@aut.ac.nz

Abstract. In this paper we propose a novel architecture called KDNet that takes into account both spatial and temporal features for traffic scene labelling. One advantage of convolutional networks is the ability to yield hierarchical features that has been proved to bring high-quality result for scene labelling problem. We demonstrate that including temporal features has even better impact on segmenting the scene. We make use of convolutional long short-term memory cells in order to allow our model to take input at many different time steps. The backbone of our model is the well known fully convolutional network called FCN-8s. The model is built in an end-to-end manner, thus eliminating post-processing steps on its output. Our model outperforms FCN-8s at a significant margin on grey-scale video data.

Keywords: Semantic segmentation · Scene labelling · Per-pixel dense labelling · Grey-scale video data

1 Introduction

Semantic segmentation plays an important role in the field of computer vision. In general, image segmentation is the act of dividing an image into parts, called segments, which are essential for image analysis tasks [7]. Semantic segmentation describes the process of associating each pixel of an image with a class label, for example road, sky, or car. The created results are then leveraged in high-level tasks in order to understand the scene completely. Scene understanding is considered to be important as a core computer vision problem due to the fact that the number of applications developed by deducing the information from imagery is increasing. Some of the applications are driverless cars [3,4,6], augmented reality wearables, image search engines [8] and in medical image diagnostics, to name just a few.

In the past, traditional techniques have been used in order to solve such problems. For example, k-mean [2] and the *histogram of oriented gradients* (HOG) [1]. Although these methods mentioned are popular, the advent of deep learning has changed the situation. Deep learning architectures such as CNNs, are being used

© Springer Nature Switzerland AG 2019
C. Lee et al. (Eds.): PSIVT 2019, LNCS 11854, pp. 365–378, 2019.
https://doi.org/10.1007/978-3-030-34879-3_28

often in order to solve computer vision tasks [5, 9, 10]. Their performance is better than traditional techniques with regard to accuracy and efficiency.

The advanced features extracted by CNNs have been proved to be useful for semantic segmentation problem; they have been utilized in all almost previous approaches. It is unsurprising to say that temporal features can also be employed to segment images semantically. The related information between frames can enhance the performance of the segmentation network if the dataset is sequences of frames. The networks that consider temporal features, for example, are able to distinguish two objects - belonging to two different categories, having the same spatial features but occurring at different time steps.

A simple approach to construct a deep, fully convolutional network for pixel classification is to stack a number of convolutional layers (same padding applied to retain dimensions) on top of each other and outputting label results for all pixels at once. This learning procedure directly maps an input image to its corresponding segmentation using consecutive filters. The computational cost of this method is expensive due to the full image resolution preserved throughout the network.

In order to alleviate this computational burden, a network with encoder and decoder modules in the network has been suggested. The encoder part downsamples input spatial features and extracts important features specific for each class. The decoder part upsamples spatial feature representations to produce dense pixel-wise labelled outputs.

One of the first models of this type was introduced by Long *et al.* [11] in late 2014. Their study is the cornerstone of the whole semantic segmentation research that applies end-to-end deep convolutional networks. Many later state-of-the-art deep semantic segmentation models are built on the basis of that research.

In this paper, we propose a method, which makes use of temporal features, to segment our grey-level datasets. At the present, there is no research on semantic segmentation, which try to understand traffic scenes, carried on grey-level datasets. Therefore, we believe that our work is novel.

2   Related Work

The motivation for researchers to further explore the capacities of the classic networks [12–14] for semantic segmentation problems is due to their ability to learn proper hierarchical features for the problem at hand. Deep learning models solve the pixel-wise labelling problem in an end-to-end manner, thus getting rid of hand-engineering feature extraction tasks which are considered to be time-consuming and complicated.

The first research, which forms the basis for other successful end-to-end deep learning approaches for semantic segmentation, is fully convolutional network (FCN). The idea behind this work is that the authors transformed the classic networks, for example AlexNet [12], VGG-16 [13], and GoogLeNet [14], into fully convolutional networks by having the densely connected layers of those networks replaced by convolutional layers. After the transformation, the classic networks are now able to output spatial feature maps instead of classification scores. Those spatial feature maps are then upsampled using backward strided convolutions (also known as deconvolutions) to produce dense pixel-wise labelled results. This approach achieved impressive results as compared to traditional computer vision methods. The network can be fed in inputs of arbitrary sizes, and can be trained in an end-to-end manner. This method also has its own drawbacks that are time efficiency with high resolution inputs and no instance segmentation capacity.

A per-pixel labelling problem often requires information from different spatial scales to be integrated. In other words, there is a need for balance between local and global information. While local information or features ensure the achievement of pixel-level accuracy, global features help in clearing up local ambiguities. Vanilla CNNs usually struggle to achieve a balance between local and global information. This is because of pooling layers, which help the networks obtain several types of spatial invariance and hold the cost of computation at an accepted level, and thus eliminating the global features. Several methods have been proposed in order to help CNNs recognize the global context information, for example, conditional random fields (CRFs) [15, 16], dilated convolutions [17], multi-scale prediction [18] or using *recurrent neural networks* (RNNs) [19].

We have now reviewed the related methods that are commonly applied in semantic scene labelling. None of the above methods incorporate temporal features into the networks. Processing a single frame at a time is not feasible due to computational cost. Moreover, taking the temporal features into account might help improve the system's accuracy while reducing the execution time. In the next section, we discover the input data that we use in this paper.

3   Input Data

3.1   Data Collection

Several tens of thousands of images were acquired by a moving vehicle during the latter half of December 2018 in Binh Duong, Vietnam. We intend not to record in adverse weather conditions, in order to reduce the complexity of the semantic segmentation problem. At the time it was the rainy season in Vietnam, so we could not avoid getting poor quality images. The environment in which we collect images is mixed urban and residential.

The camera that we use does not indicate the modernity in the automotive industry. Frames are recorded using MYNT EYE S, a stereo camera developed and manufactured by MYNT EYE.[1] It is a monochrome stereo camera with a baseline of 120 mm and shutter speed of 17 ms. The stereo camera is mounted behind the windshield, and yields low dynamic-range (LDR) 8-bit grey-level images.

---

[1] www.mynteye.com/products/mynt-eye-stereo-camera.

3.2 Data Annotation

501 images are manually selected for pixel-wise annotating. We aim to cover objects that characterize the street scenes in Vietnam. Our 501 annotated images comprise layered polygons in much the same way as LabelMe [20]. We annotate the images coarsely, aiming to cover correctly as many pixels as possible. It takes us approximately six minutes to label an image completely. The only constraint that we follow is that one polygon solely contains pixels of a single object class.

We define 8 visual classes, including background. The object class names and their corresponding colours are shown in Table 1. We combine humans and motorbikes in our dataset, because the boundary between the human and the motorbike they sit on is not easily distinguished, and their sizes are tiny in our dataset.

Table 1. List of the object class names and their corresponding colours used for labelling.

Class name	Colour
Cars	
Road	
Vegetation	
Sky	
Sidewalk	
Motorbikes + humans	
Left kerb	
Background	

We split our dataset into training and test sets. 450 images go into the training set and 51 images go into the test set. We do not split the data aimlessly. The training and test sets are sequences of consecutive images. We further ensure the occurrence of the seven identified visual classes in both training and test sets.

3.3 Dataset Comparison

We compare our dataset with other datasets in order to reveal the challenges in our problem. The comparison criteria are (i) the size of dataset, (ii) the data distribution, and (iii) the resources involved.

For the first criterion, we compare our dataset with CamVid [21], DUS [22], and Cityscapes [3]. CamVid is 10-min video footage containing 701 annotated images. DUS is 5000-frame video sequence, of which 500 frames have been per-pixel labelled. Cityscapes has 5000 fine annotations and 20000 coarse annotations. Furthermore, Cityscapes has higher quality in annotation and greater diversity, as frames in Cityscapes are recorded from 50 different places. Our dataset has 501 annotated frames and is recorded in a single city only, which is similar to CamVid and DUS. We consider our dataset as a small dataset, as can be seen in Table 2.

Table 2. The number of annotated pixels. Table reproduced from [3]. Note that the number of annotated pixels of our dataset has been rounded.

	#annotated pixels $[10^9]$
Our dataset	**0.18**
Camvid	0.62
DUS	0.14
Cityscapes (fine)	9.43
Cityscapes (coarse)	26.0

Figures 1 and 2 show the data distribution of our dataset and the Cityscapes dataset respectively. Our dataset is unbalanced, and the background class has a substantial number of pixels.

Cityscapes [3] achieves the essential balance among classes. This achievement is due to the rich diversity of recording locations, substantially large area covered and scene labelled properly.

In terms of the resources involved, we compare our dataset with others based on sensors used, and the number of annotators taking part in. Our frames are collected using a camera that is not yet 1MP and worth about \$249. Cityscapes uses high-standard automotive sensors, $1/3$ in CMOS 2 MP sensors and CamVid uses three thousands' worth of digital camera. Only our dataset contains grey-level images. Labelling grey-level images is troublesome as grey-level images cause some confusion in determining boundaries at locations having similar pixel

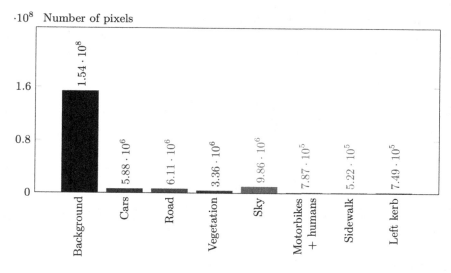

Fig. 1. Data distribution of our dataset. Note that these numbers presented here have been rounded for the ease of visualization.

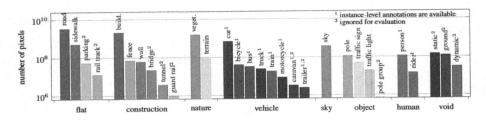

Fig. 2. Data distribution of Cityscapes dataset [3].

values. Regrading to the number of annotators, our project has only one person to label images while the other research projects have teams of annotators, for example, Camvid [21] hires 13 workers to annotate images. Altogether, our dataset is not as good as the others and harder to handle.

4 Proposed Network

4.1 Long Short-Term Memory

A *long short-term memory* (LSTM) network is considered to be a special type of RNN. Due to its stability, this type of network has been used in many previous works in order to model long-term dependencies [23–25]. The key to LSTM memory cell is c_t to which information can be added or removed. Accessing, writing and clearing the cell are carefully regulated by structures called gates. When a new input arrives, the input gate i_t decides whether to add that information to the cell or not. The forget gate f_t throws away the past cell status c_{t-1} if it is activated. The output gate o_t controls the propagation of the latest cell output c_t to the final state h_t. It is said that the gradient is kept in the cell, thus preventing vanishing too quickly [25]. The equations governing LSTM are as follows:

$$i_t = \sigma(W_{xi}x_t + W_{hi}h_{t-1} + W_{ci} \odot c_{t-1} + b_i) \tag{1}$$

$$f_t = \sigma(W_{xf}x_t + W_{hf}h_{t-1} + W_{cf} \odot c_{t-1} + b_f) \tag{2}$$

$$c_t = f_t \odot c_{t-1} + i_t \odot tanh(W_{xc}x_t + W_{hc}h_{t-1} + b_c) \tag{3}$$

$$o_t = \sigma(W_{xo}x_t + W_{ho}h_{t-1} + W_{co} \odot c_t + b_o) \tag{4}$$

$$h_t = o_t \odot tanh(c_t) \tag{5}$$

Symbol $\odot$ stands for element-wise product and the equations above have peephole connections added as in [23].

4.2 Convolutional LSTM

Because LSTM receives as an input one-dimensional data, it does not serve spatial data such as images and videos effectively. Thus, in this project we use an extension of LSTM proposed by Shi *et al.* [26]. This extended version convolutionalizes the input and the state of a cell. The equations governing convolutional LSTM (ConvLSTM) are as follows:

$$i_t = \sigma(W_{xi} * \mathcal{X}_t + W_{hi} * \mathcal{H}_{t-1} + W_{ci} \odot \mathcal{C}_{t-1} + b_i) \tag{6}$$

$$f_t = \sigma(W_{xf} * \mathcal{X}_t + W_{hf} * \mathcal{H}_{t-1} + W_{cf} \odot \mathcal{C}_{t-1} + b_f) \tag{7}$$

$$\mathcal{C}_t = f_t \odot \mathcal{C}_{t-1} + i_t \odot tanh(W_{xc} * \mathcal{X}_t + W_{hc} * \mathcal{H}_{t-1} + b_c) \tag{8}$$

$$o_t = \sigma(W_{xo} * \mathcal{X}_t + W_{ho} * \mathcal{H}_{t-1} + W_{co} \odot \mathcal{C}_t + b_o) \tag{9}$$

$$\mathcal{H}_t = o_t \odot tanh(\mathcal{C}_t) \tag{10}$$

Symbol $*$ denotes convolution operation and $\odot$ denotes element-wise product as before. All the inputs $\mathcal{X}_t$, the cell outputs $\mathcal{C}_{t-1}$ and gates i_t, f_t, o_t now become 3D tensors.

4.3   Fully Convolutional Network

Convnets learn patterns that are translation-invariant. Their basic building blocks are convolutions, pooling functions and activation functions, operating on local regions of the input and depending entirely on spatial axes. Let us call $\mathbf{x}_{ij}$ a vector of data at location (i, j) in one of the layers of a convnet, and $\mathbf{y}_{ij}$ a vector of data for the successive layer. $\mathbf{y}_{ij}$ can be determined by

$$\mathbf{y}_{ij} = f_{ks}(\{\mathbf{x}_{si+\delta i, sj+\delta j}\}_{0 \leq \delta i, \delta j \leq k}) \tag{11}$$

in which k is the filter size, s is the stride, and f_{ks} determines operation type of the layer which can be a matrix product for convolution, average pooling or max pooling for pooling layer, or element-wise nonlinear operation for activation function.

The transformation rule that kernel size and stride have to comply in order for that functional form holds true is by

$$f_{ks} \circ g_{k's'} = (f \circ g)_{k'+(k-1)s', ss'} \tag{12}$$

While an ordinary deep network creates a nonlinear function mapping input to output, a network containing only layers of this form creates a nonlinear filter [11], which is called *fully convolutional network*. A fully convolutional network accepts variably-sized inputs, and generates an output scaling in proportion to the input.

4.4   Spatial-Temporal Inference

Let us define $\mathbf{y}_{ij}^{[L]}$ as data vector at location (i, j) in layer L of FCN-8s, Ω_t as input features at time step t and $F_t^{(1..m)[L]}$ as a set of features with m different maps of the input features Ω_t in layer L.

When the input features Ω_t with dimensions $(h \times w \times d)$ are fed to the FCN-8s network [11], the FCN-8s downsamples the input features to dimensions $(h' \times w' \times d')$, where $h' \ll h$ and $w' \ll w$. At each layer we receive $F_t^{(1..m)[L]} = \{\mathbf{y}_{ij}^{[L]}\}$, with $1 \leq i \leq h'$, $1 \leq j \leq w'$ and $m = d'$. Figure 4 shows a features set at a particular layer in FCN-8s.

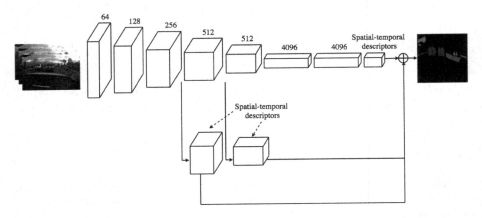

Fig. 3. By stacking long short-term memory units, spatial-temporal information is created. Predictions are made based on that information.

We put ConvLSTMs on top of the last convolutional layer *(conv7)*, the *pool4* layer and the *pool3* layer, as shown in Fig. 3. This defines a new features set for each of those layers at time step t as $FT_t^{(1..m)[L]}$ (L is equal to 3, 4, and 7) which is determined based on Eq. 10. The general update function is as follows:

$$FT_t^{(1..m)[L]} = o_t^{[L]} \odot tanh(\mathcal{C}_t^{[L]}) \tag{13}$$

We use information from current input features and previous inputs features in order to make dense predictions; this is an *one-to-many* problem. Figure 5 shows the overall scheme of our method.

5   Experimental Results

5.1   Performance Index

To evaluate the performance of our proposed method quantitatively, two metrics are used, mean intersection over union (mIoU) and pixel accuracy.

Intersection over Union. The intersection over union metric is often used to evaluate the percent overlap between the ground truth and the prediction of a model.

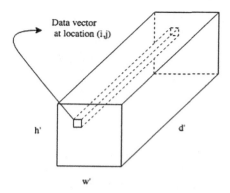

Fig. 4. A feature set $F_t^{(1..m)}$ at a particular layer in FCN-8s. The number of different maps in this case is $m = d'$.

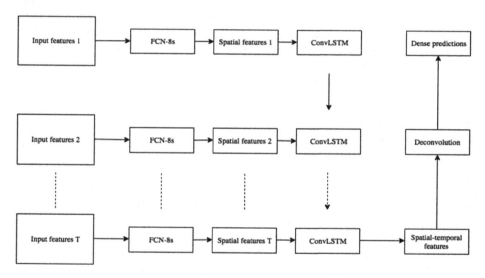

Fig. 5. The general principle of our method. A number of frames are fed into the network at the same time. Features learned from previous frames are fused with current frame that are then used to make predictions.

A *true positive* (TP) represents a pixel that is properly classified to belong to a given class (according to the ground truth), whereas a *true negative* (TN) describes a pixel that is correctly identified as not belonging to the given class. There are two types of error, which are type I error also known as a *false positive* (FP) which describes a pixel wrongly classified, and type II error also known as *false negative* (FN) which describes a missed case.

Quite simply, the IoU metric can be calculated as follows:

$$IoU = \frac{TP}{TP + FP + FN} \qquad (14)$$

The IoU score is calculated for each class individually. To achieve an overall result (mIoU) for semantic segmentation prediction, we need to average the IoU score of all classes.

Pixel Accuracy. Another way to evaluate the performance of a semantic segmentation model is to directly compute the percentage of pixels in the image that have been properly classified. We can use pixel accuracy to report for each individual class or for all classes. The pixel accuracy can be determined as follows:

$$ACC = \frac{TP + TN}{TP + TN + FP + FN} \qquad (15)$$

Sometimes when the class representation in the image is small, the pixel accuracy metric provides misleading information about the performance of semantic segmentation algorithm, because the metric is biased toward reporting the accuracy of identifying negative cases.

5.2   Implementation

We conduct all the experiments on HP Z440, a linux-based desktop workstation. This desktop has been equipped with GeForce GTX 1080 Ti with a memory size of 11 GB.

We define three scenarios in order to train the model. The first scenario is training without fine-tuning, in which all layers of VGG-16 are frozen. The second scenario is training with fine-tuning the last layer of VGG-16, which means we unfreeze the *conv5* and the *pool5* layers. In the final scenario, we train from scratch, all layers of VGG-16 are unfrozen.

The network is trained using the hyperparameters as follows: Adam optimization algorithm with momentum of 0.9, minibatch size of three images, learning rate of 10^{-4} and weight decay of 5^{-4}.

5.3   Results and Comparisons

We train the network for 200 epochs and evaluate on 20% of the training data. We then compare the results with FCN-8s.

Training Without Fine-Tuning. Our model outperforms FCN-8s by a significant margin in this scenario as shown in the Table 3. Our model does not overfit too much to the training data. All the validation values of our model are closer to the training values than those of FCN-8s.

Table 3. A comparison of our model and FCN-8s performing on our dataset. In this scenario, all layers of VGG-16 are frozen.

	Training pixel accuracy	Validation pixel accuracy	Training loss	Validation loss	mIoU
Our model	**92.03%**	**91.5%**	**0.2735**	**0.2842**	**26.3%**
FCN-8s	84.1%	82.92%	0.8328	0.8750	6.9%

Table 4. A comparison of our model and FCN-8s performing on our dataset. In this scenario, the *conv5* and the *pool5* layers of VGG-16 are unfrozen.

	Training pixel accuracy	Validation pixel accuracy	Training loss	Validation loss	mIoU
Our model	**91.69%**	**91.67%**	**0.2774**	**0.2783**	**25.6%**
FCN-8s	83.93%	83.56%	0.8417	0.8525	7%

Training with Fine-Tuning. In this scenario, we unfreeze the *conv5* and the *pool5* layers of VGG-16. Our model also surpasses FCN-8s. However, there is no significant improvement in terms of accuracy, loss and mIoU of the two models as compared with the first scenario. Table 4 shows the results of the two models.

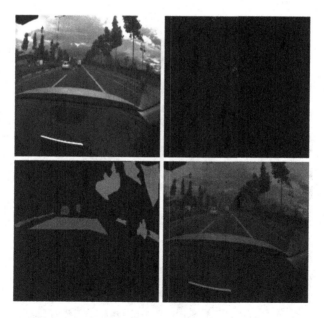

Fig. 6. Results produced by FCN-8s in the last scenario. *Top, left:* Input image. *Top, right:* Predicted classes. *Bottom, left:* True classes. *Bottom, right:* Overlaid image.

Table 5. A comparison of our model and FCN-8s performing on our dataset. In this scenario, all layers of VGG-16 are unfrozen.

	Training pixel accuracy	Validation pixel accuracy	Training loss	Validation loss	mIoU
Our model	**94.96%**	**94.07%**	**0.1574**	**0.1892**	**38.7%**
FCN-8s	84.13%	83.56%	0.6991	0.7237	7%

Table 6. The IoU of each individual class in three defined scenarios of our model.

	Background	Car	Road	Tree	Sky	Motorbike + human	Sidewalk	Left kerb
First scenario	90.8%	60%	60.8%	23.5%	65.2%	0%	0%	14.9%
Second scenario	91.1%	60.8%	59.8%	12.9%	65.8%	0%	0%	17.1%
Last scenario	**93.6%**	**76.3%**	**69%**	**53.1%**	**65.6%**	**50.5%**	**14.7%**	**41%**

Training from Scratch. In this scenario, all layers of VGG-16 are unfrozen. Our model produces astonishing results in this scenario. Table 5 shows the results of the two models. Our model achieves over 94% of accuracy in training time and validation time. The loss values reduce to under 0.2. Moreover, the mIoU reaches to nearly 40%.

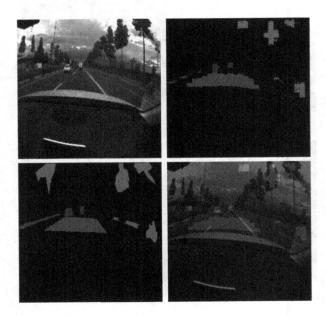

Fig. 7. Results produced by our model in the last scenario. *Top, left:* Input image. *Top, right:* Predicted classes. *Bottom, left:* True classes. *Bottom, right:* Overlaid image.

Overall Discussions. Our model surpasses FCN-8s in three defined scenarios. FCN-8s learns only spatial information and thus it is biased towards the majority class, given an unbalanced dataset. Our model is able to learn spatial and temporal information and therefore it still works well even the dataset is skewed negatively. The prediction results of the two models in the last scenario are shown in Figs. 6 and 7 respectively.

We realize that training our model from scratch yields better results than applying transfer learning. As can be seen in Fig. 7 the model is able to recognize the *motorbike + human* class, the *left kerb* class and the *sidewalk* class reasonably. We hypothesize that, as VGG-16 is pretrained on ImageNet, which contains hundreds of thousands RGB images, the features learned are not completely useful for our task, which uses grey-level images.

The figures in Table 6 affirms that our model produces the best results when it is trained from scratch.

6   Conclusions

In this paper, we proposed a new architecture that is able to learn spatial and temporal information for semantic segmentation. Our proposed model shows state-of-the-art performances on our own grey-level dataset as compared with FCN-8s. Our model can be trained end-to-end. There is no need to include post-processing modules, as can be seen in some other methods. We also revealed that the learned feature representations from the ImageNet dataset do not help in yielding a better result for our problem.

References

1. Bourdev, L., Maji, S., Brox, T., Malik, J.: Detecting people using mutually consistent poselet activations. In: Daniilidis, K., Maragos, P., Paragios, N. (eds.) ECCV 2010. LNCS, vol. 6316, pp. 168–181. Springer, Heidelberg (2010). https://doi.org/10.1007/978-3-642-15567-3_13
2. Chen, C.W., Luo, J., Parker, K.J.: Image segmentation via adaptive K-mean clustering and knowledge-based morphological operations with biomedical applications. IEEE Trans. Image Process. **7**, 1673–1683 (1998)
3. Cordts, M., et al.: The cityscapes dataset for semantic urban scene understanding. In: IEEE Conference on Computer Vision Pattern Recognition, pp. 3213–3223 (2016)
4. Ess, A., Mueller, T., Grabner, H., Van Gool, L.: Segmentation-based urban traffic scene understanding. In: British Machine Vision Conference (2009)
5. Feng, N., Delhomme, D., LeCun, Y., Piano, F., Bottou, L., Barbano, P.E.: Toward automatic phenotyping of developing embryos from videos. IEEE Trans. Image Process. **14**, 1360–1371 (2005)
6. Geiger, A., Lenz, P., Urtasun, R.: Are we ready for autonomous driving? The KITTI vision benchmark suite. In: IEEE Conference on Computer Vision and Pattern Recognition, pp. 3354–3361 (2012)
7. Klette, R.: Concise Computer Vision: An Introduction into Theory and Algorithms. UTCS. Springer, London (2014). https://doi.org/10.1007/978-1-4471-6320-6

8. Wan, J., et al.: Deep learning for content-based image retrieval: a comprehensive study. In: ACM International Conference on Multimedia, pp. 157–166 (2014)
9. Cireşan, D.C., Giusti, A., Gambardella, L.M., Schmidhuber, J.: Deep neural networks segment neuronal membranes in electron microscopy images. In: International Conference on Neural Information Processing Systems, pp. 2843–2851 (2012)
10. Farabet, C., Couprie, C., Najman, L., LeCun, Y.: Learning hierarchical features for scene labeling. IEEE Trans. Pattern Anal. Mach. Intell. **35**, 1915–1929 (2013)
11. Long, J., Shelhamer, E., Darrell, T.: Fully convolutional networks for semantic segmentation. In: IEEE Conference on Computer Vision Pattern Recognition, pp. 3431–3440 (2015)
12. Krizhevsky, A., Sutskever, I., Hinton, G.E.: ImageNet classification with deep convolutional neural networks. In: International Conference on Neural Information Processing Systems, pp. 1097–1105 (2012)
13. Simonyan, K., Zisserman, A.: Very deep convolutional networks for large-scale image recognition. arXiv preprint arXiv:1409.1556 (2014)
14. Szegedy, C., et al.: Going deeper with convolutions. In: IEEE Conference on Computer Vision Pattern Recognition, pp. 1–9 (2015)
15. Chen, L.C., Papandreou, G., Kokkinos, I., Murphy, K., Yuille, A.L.: Semantic image segmentation with deep convolutional nets and fully connected CRFs. arXiv preprint arXiv:1412.7062 (2014)
16. Chen, L.C., Papandreou, G., Kokkinos, I., Murphy, K., Yuille, A.L.: DeepLab: semantic image segmentation with deep convolutional nets, atrous convolution, and fully connected CRFs. IEEE Trans. Pattern Anal. Mach. Intell. **40**, 834–848 (2018)
17. Yu, F., Koltun, V.: Multi-scale context aggregation by dilated convolutions. arXiv preprint arXiv:1511.07122 (2015)
18. Roy, A., Todorovic, S.: A multi-scale CNN for affordance segmentation in RGB images. In: Leibe, B., Matas, J., Sebe, N., Welling, M. (eds.) ECCV 2016. LNCS, vol. 9908, pp. 186–201. Springer, Cham (2016). https://doi.org/10.1007/978-3-319-46493-0_12
19. Visin, F., et al.: ReSeg: a recurrent neural network-based model for semantic segmentation. In: IEEE Conference on Computer Vision Pattern Recognition Workshops, pp. 426–433 (2016)
20. Russell, B.C., Torralba, A., Murphy, K.P., Freeman, W.T.: LabelMe: a database and web-based tool for image annotation. Int. J. Comput. Vision **77**, 157–173 (2008)
21. Brostow, G.J., Fauqueur, J., Cipolla, R.: Semantic object classes in video: a high-definition ground truth database. Pattern Recogn. Lett. **30**, 88–97 (2009)
22. Scharwächter, T., Enzweiler, M., Franke, U., Roth, S.: Stixmantics: a medium-level model for real-time semantic scene understanding. In: Fleet, D., Pajdla, T., Schiele, B., Tuytelaars, T. (eds.) ECCV 2014. LNCS, vol. 8693, pp. 533–548. Springer, Cham (2014). https://doi.org/10.1007/978-3-319-10602-1_35
23. Alex, G.: Generating sequences with recurrent neural networks. CoRR (2013). http://arxiv.org/abs/1308.0850
24. Pascanu, R., Mikolov, T., Bengio, Y.: On the difficulty of training recurrent neural networks. In: International Conference on Machine Learning, pp. 1310–1318 (2013)
25. Hochreiter, S., Schmidhuber, J.: Long short-term memory. Neural Comput. **9**, 1735–1780 (1997)
26. Shi, X., Chen, Z., Wang, H., Yeung, D., Wong, W., Woo, W.: Convolutional LSTM network: a machine learning approach for precipitation nowcasting. CoRR (2015). http://arxiv.org/abs/1506.04214

Shoeprint Extraction via GAN

Junjie Cao[1]([✉]), RuYue Pan[1], LongKe Wang[1], Xu Xu[2], and Zhixu Su[1]

[1] School of Mathematical Sciences, Dalian University of Technology,
Dalian 116024, China
jjcao@dlut.edu.cn
[2] Dalian Everspry Sci & Tech Co., Ltd., Dalian 116024, China

Abstract. Shoeprints reflect some physiological characteristics of human beings, similar to fingerprints, which are important clues for criminal investigations. Extraction of shoeprints from images taken in crime scenes is a key preprocessing of the shoeprint image retrieval. It can be seen as a binary semantic image segmentation problem. Both traditional algorithms and existing deep learning approaches perform poorly for this problem, since shoeprint images contain various and strong background textures, are contaminated by serious noises and incomplete usually. This paper innovatively presents a framework with generative adversarial net (GAN) for the problem. Multiple generative networks, loses and adversarial networks are designed and compared within the framework. We also compared our method with the-state-of-the-art deep learning approaches on the professional shoeprint dataset with the evaluation criterion called MSS. The MSS of FCN, Deeplab-v3 and our method are 50.3%, 61.5%, and 75% on the dataset.

Keywords: Shoeprint · Semantic segmentation · Generative adversarial nets

1 Introduction

Similar to fingerprint, shoeprint is an important clue to criminal investigations. Shoeprint photos are from two sources: suspects in custody and crime scenes. Extracting shoeprints from photos is equivalent to binary semantic image segmentation problem. The patterns of target regions are very complex in geometry and topology, and are contaminated by serious noises, as shown in Fig. 1. The area of the target regions is usually small relative to the background, and the intensity or contrast of them is also unobvious compared with the colorful background with complex textures. These make the shoeprint segmentation a challenge for various traditional image segmentation methods and existing deep semantic segmentation approaches.

Traditional image segmentation methods are often based on the fact that the pixel intensities of the same region vary little. Then threshold-based methods [1] are presented to segment the images into foreground and background. These methods have low computational complexity, but poor results. Another approaches for image segmentation based on clustering methods [2], which are sensitive to hyper parameters. In addition, the algorithms [3] based on region growth select seed pixels as starting points and merge neighbor pixels similar with seed pixels repeatedly. The process is greatly

© Springer Nature Switzerland AG 2019
C. Lee et al. (Eds.): PSIVT 2019, LNCS 11854, pp. 379–389, 2019.
https://doi.org/10.1007/978-3-030-34879-3_29

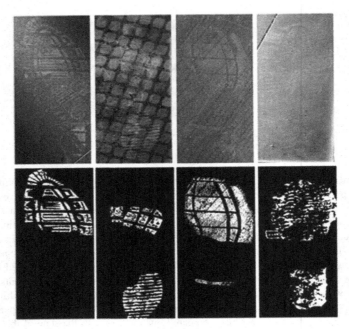

Fig. 1. Samples of the shoeprint dataset: the photos (top row) and the ground truth segmentations (bottom row).

affected by noise and texture. In general, the result of shoeprint segmentation of these traditional method is far lower than manual segmentations.

Recently deep learning has made great progress in image semantics segmentation. Fully convolutional neural network (FCN) [4] made a great breakthrough in this field. The network takes input images of any size for its fully convolutional structure. FCN proposes skip-connection that combines low resolution and high-resolution features to capture multi-scale semantic information. Unfortunately, its results may be too rough to lose the original fine structures of the object. Unet [7] further improves the skip-connection, and abstracts the image features step by step. The feature maps of the smallest resolution are up-sampled while the features of the same resolution in the coding path are fused to refined the results. Deeplab and its variants [6, 10, 11] contribute to semantic segmentation via hole convolution and CRF [10, 11]. Hole convolution expands the receptive fields and keeps the resolution of feature maps not too small, which is helpful for the restoration of fine details. CRF is used for the post-processing to make the boundaries of segmentation regions smoother. However, such post-processing operation is time consuming. Pspnet [5] introduces pyramidal pooling to improve the features extracted by residual network with different scales of pooling. To achieve the same objective, Deeplab-v3 [6] introduces a convolutional pyramid with holes and no longer requires CRF for post-processing. Although they can be trained on shoeprint dataset to improve traditional methods significantly. The results are still far inferior than our method.

To keep the fine structures in shoeprint photos and generate more faithful results, we present a binary semantic image segmentation framework based on generative adversarial networks. The main contributions of this paper are as follows:

(1) GAN is introduced for generating more faithful image segmentation.
(2) An improved U-net is presented to extract fine structures of the shoeprints.
(3) Our result is far precise than the previous end-to-end algorithms, such as FCN, Pspnet and Deeplab-v3.

2 Shoeprint Segmentation Framework via GAN

The segmentation framework proposed in this paper is based on the generative adversarial network. The structure of our framework is shown in Fig. 2. It contains a generative network (G) and an adversarial network (D). We wish that G extracts the segmentation probability, and D distinguishes whether the generated segmentation are true or false. The total loss L of our framework is consisting of loss functions of L_D and L_G, which will be described in the following sections respectively.

$$L = L_D + L_G \tag{1}$$

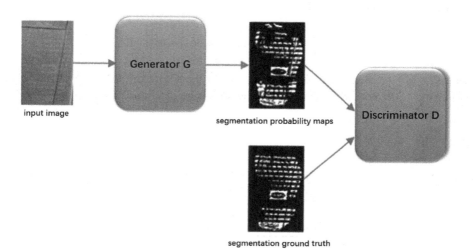

Fig. 2. Overview of our framework.

2.1 The Discriminative Network

The segmentation probabilities generated by the generator G is input to the discriminator D together with the corresponding ground truth data. G learns the probability distribution, while D gives the distribution difference between the generated samples and the real samples. Since binary segmentation involves only two categories, it is only necessary to predict the foreground (shoeprint) probability distribution.

The discriminative network is divided into three blocks, as shown in Table 1. We also use instance normalization [17] after each convolution layer except for the last one. The LeakyReLU [18] is used as the activation function, except for the last layer which uses a sigmoid function [19]. There are many variants of GAN. Vanilla GAN [8] and LSGAN [16] are compared in this paper. The loss function of the vanilla GAN is:

$$L_{GAN}(\omega, \theta) = \frac{1}{N} \sum_{i=1}^{N} \mathbb{E}_{\theta}[\log D(x)] + \mathbb{E}_{\omega}[\log(1 - D(G(x)))],$$

where N represents the batch size of each training, ω and θ are the parameters of G and D respectively. G and D are updated alternately. We find the performance can be further improved when LSGAN is applied and its objective functions are [16]:

$$V_{LSGAN}(\theta) = \frac{1}{2}\mathbb{E}_{y \sim p_{data}(x)}\left[(D(x|\Phi(y)) - 1)^2\right] + \frac{1}{2}\mathbb{E}_{z \sim p_z(z)}\left[(D(G(z)|\Phi(y)))^2\right]$$

$$V_{LSGAN}(\omega) = \frac{1}{2}\mathbb{E}_{z \sim p_z(z)}\left[\left(D(G(z)|\Phi(y)) - 1\right)^2\right]$$

The training process of GAN or LSGAN may be not very stable, so we introduce the feature matching loss [13]:

$$L_{fea}(\omega, \theta) = \frac{1}{N} \sum_{i=1}^{N} \left\| \phi_{\theta}^{l}(G_{\omega}(x_i)) - \phi_{\theta}^{l}(y_i)^2 \right\|,$$

where $\phi_{\theta}^{l}(y_i)$ represents the feature response to input x at the l-th layer of the discriminator. Therefore, the overall loss function of the discriminative network is:

$$L_D = \lambda_1 L_{GAN} + \lambda_2 L_{fea} \tag{2}$$

Table 1. Architecture of the discriminative network. "conv" denotes a convolutional layer.

	Block1		Block2	Tail	
Layer	Conv	Conv	Conv	Conv	Conv
Kernel number	64	128	256	512	1
Kernel size	4	4	4	4	4
Stride	2	2	2	1	1

2.2 The Generative Network

Figure 3 shows the structure of generative network G. The standard Unet is improved as G to predicts the probability of shoeprints. G is divided into encoding and decoding. When up-sampling the encoded low-resolution feature maps, the skip-connections are used and the features from the same level of coding path are connected with them. The connected features are inputted to the next layer, as shown in Fig. 3. Then the resolution of the feature maps gradually increases.

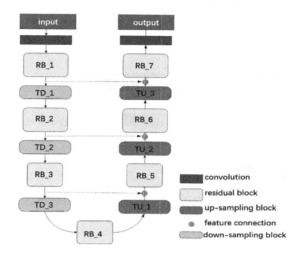

Fig. 3. Diagram of our generative network.

G consists of 7 residual blocks, each of them was a superposition of several residual layers. As shown in Fig. 4, the structure of each residual block is identical. The first three layers are bottleneck structure [9], which can reduce the amount of computation. The convolution in the middle is group convolution [12], which not only reduces parameters by a large margin, but also is a regulator. The next three layers called compression extracting block are used to extract the effective features. And for that, we first global pooling features to prevent spatial information from interfering with feature channels, and compress information through compressing channel dimension of the fully connection layer. A sigmoid function is activated by the fully connected layers which recovers the channel dimension and makes channel coefficient values between 0 and 1.

Cross entropy is often used in semantic segmentation [14], and binary cross entropy is required for binary segmentation, as shown in formula (3). However, by analysis of the datasets, we found that the ratio of image foreground to background pixel is about 1:7, and the unbalanced samples may lead to negative samples in network learning, that is, the pixel label is more likely to predict to be background [15]. To avoid this phenomenon, we used weighted binary cross entropy, as shown in formula (4). The weight p is the average of background and foreground ratio of each batch of samples, which is slightly different from [15], which takes the ratio of foreground and background prediction probability as p, our method is simpler and more reasonable.

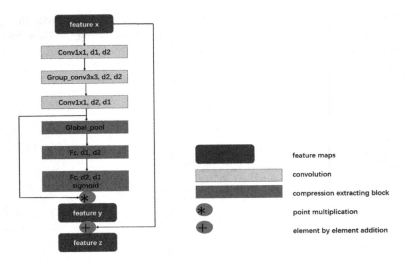

Fig. 4. Diagram of the residual blocks proposed.

$$L_{bc\tilde{e}}(\omega) = \sum_{i=1}^{N} y_i \log(\sigma(G_\omega(x_i))) + (1 - y_i) \log(1 - \sigma(G_\omega(x_i))) \qquad (3)$$

$$L_{bce}(\omega) = \sum_{i=1}^{N} p \cdot y_i \log(\sigma(G_\omega(x_i))) + (1 - y_i) \log(1 - \sigma(G_\omega(x_i))) \qquad (4)$$

$$p = \frac{1}{N} \sum_{i=1}^{N} \frac{\sum 1(y_i == 0)}{\sum 1(y_i == 1)}$$

In order to assist to learning of the generative network G, we also apply 1×1 convolution to fuse the feature maps of the residual blocks RB$_5$ and RB$_6$ into a probability map with channel size one, then calculate square loss between them and the ground truth:

$$L_{side}(\omega) = \frac{1}{N} \sum_{i=1}^{N} \sum_{j=RD_5}^{RD_6} \left\| \phi_\omega^j(x_i) - down^j(y_i) \right\|^2$$

where $down^j(y_i)$ down samples y_i to the size of the j-th layer feature maps Therefore, the overall loss function of the generative network is:

$$L_G = \lambda_3 L_{bce} + \lambda_4 L_{side} \qquad (5)$$

3 Experimental Results Datasets and Settings

The datasets we used was shoeprint images taken from the crime scene, and each image had its corresponding manually binary segmentation annotation, as shown in Fig. 1. The dataset has the following characteristics: (1) The background of shoeprint image is complex and changeable. (2) Background pixel information is generally much richer than shoeprint pixel information, which increases the difficulty of segmentation. (3) Poor image quality with large noise interference, incomplete, pattern discontinuity and uneven illumination. (4) Uneven distribution of data.

The shoeprint dataset is divided into training set, test set and cross validation set. There are 14,229 shoeprint images in the training set, 700 cross validation images, and 78 test images. The shoeprint is cut out from the original images and is interpolated into the size of 256 * 256.

Parameters are trained as follows: learning rate is 0.002, batch size is 4, and the number of residual layers in each residual block along the direction of encoding and decoding path is 3, 8, 36, 3, 36, 8, 3. In formula (1) of the total loss function, $\lambda_1 = \lambda_3 = 1, \lambda_2 = 0.01, \lambda_4 = 0.1$, during the training process. The model is evaluated each epoch, the model with the minimal loss is kept as the trained model, and the maximum epoch is no more than 40.

3.1 The Metric for Shoeprints Segmentation

We design a shoeprint segmentation evaluation metric, namely MSS. It is weighted sum of Mean Pixel Accuracy, Mean Intersection over Union, Cross correlation and Regularization term. They are briefly described as follows:

$$MSS = 0.2MPA + 0.2MIoU + 0.2Corr + 0.4Reg,$$

where the weights are derived from experimental experience.

Mean Pixel Accuracy (*MPA*). Calculate the proportion of the number of pixels which was correctly classified for each class, and then calculate the average of all classes. There are K + 1 classes and p_{ii} denotes the pixels which belong to class i, and the predicted results are also class i. It is defined as:

$$MPA = \frac{1}{k+1} \sum_{i=0}^{k} \frac{p_{ii}}{\sum_{j=0}^{k} p_{ij}}$$

Mean Intersection over Union (*MIoU*): Calculate the ratio of the intersection and union of the ground truth and the predicted segmentation. *IoU* is calculated on each class and then averaged. It is defined as:

$$MIoU = \frac{1}{k+1} \sum_{i=0}^{k} \frac{p_{ii}}{\sum_{j=0}^{k} p_{ij} + \sum_{j=0}^{k} p_{ji} - p_{ii}}$$

Cross correlation (*Corr*). The predicted mask and the corresponding groundtruth are used to calculate the cross correlation:

$$NCC(p,d) = \frac{\sum_{(x,y)\in W_p}\left(I_1(x,y) - \bar{I}_1(p_x,p_y)\right) \cdot \left(I_2(x+d,y) - \bar{I}_2(p_x+d,p_y)\right)}{\sqrt{\sum_{(x,y)\in W_p}\left(I_1(x,y) - \bar{I}_1(p_x,p_y)\right)^2 \cdot \sum_{(x,y)\in W_p}\left(I_2(x+d,y) - \bar{I}_2(p_x+d,p_y)\right)^2}}.$$

The value of $NCC(p,d)$ is between -1 and 1. W_p is the predicted mask. $I_1(x,y)$ denotes the pixel values of groundtruth located in (x,y). $\bar{I}_1(p_x,p_y)$ denotes the mean of pixel values of groundtruth. $I_2(x+d,y)$ denotes the mean of W_p. Set $I_2(x+d,y)$ as the pixel value of the groundtruth after the corresponding position in W_p Shifts d in the x axis. If $NCC = 1$, the correlation predicted results are significant correlated with groundtruth. On the contrary, $NCC = -1$ denotes predicted results are totally unrelated to groundtruth.

Regularization (Reg). The regularization is briefly described as follow:

$$Reg = dis^{cov}$$

dis is defined as:

$$dis = \frac{o_{dis}}{t_{dis}},$$

where o_{dis} and t_{dis} are the normalized average distance between the points on the contour and the center of the groundtruth and the predicted mask respectively. *cov* is defined as:

$$cov = \frac{o_{cov}}{t_{cov}},$$

where o_{cov} and t_{cov} are the normalized difference of the distance between the points on the contour and the center of the groundtruth and the center of the predicted mask, respectively.

3.2   Ablation Study

Generative Network. We have tried to use ResUnet, PspUnet and DenseUnet [20] as generative network of our framework. As shown in Table 2, the MSS of PspUnet is 0.705, which is a little lower than ResUnet. The MSS of DenseUnet is 0.715, which is 0.01 higher than ResUnet. But its memory consumption is too large. By default, we use the ResUnet, introduced in Sect. 2, as the generative network.

Table 2. MSS of different generative network structures using the vanilla GAN.

Generator	PspUnet	ResUnet	DenseUnet
MSS	0.705	0.714	0.715

GANs. As shown in Table 3, the MSS of LSGAN is 0.02 higher than vanilla GAN. By default, LSGAN is used. By using the model ensemble corresponding to the models saved at different time points, the final segmentation score can reach 0.750.

Table 3. MSS of using GAN and LSGAN.

GAN's variants	GAN	LSGAN
MSS	0.714	0.738

Feature Loss and weighted BCE. The effect of L_{fea} and weighted BCE are also compared. When cancelling L_{fea} or using standard BCE loss, the corresponding MSS are 0.731 and 0.699 respectively, as shown in Table 4. It shows that weighted binary cross entropy contributes more to the performance.

Table 4. MSS of canceling L_{fea}, using standard BCE, or weighted BCE

Variants	Canceling L_{fea}	Using standard BCE	Using weighted BCE
MSS	0.731	0.699	0.738

3.3 Comparisons with Other End-to-End Methods

The classical models of FCN-8 s, Deeplab-v3 and Pspnet were selected for comparison. The parameters almost followed the original setting. As shown in Fig. 5, the segmentation results of different methods are given. UGnet is the experimental result of our algorithm, and obviously FCN-8 s has the worst result which loses most of the structure of the shoeprint. Deeplab-v3 and Pspnet retain a rough outline of the shoeprint, but the results are too rough. However, the UGnet proposed in this paper can not only retain the outline of shoeprint, but also extract fine patterns, which is close to the manual annotation. The scores of the four methods on MSS are shown in Table 5. The scores of the four methods on MSS.

Table 5. The scores of the four methods on MSS.

Structure	FCN	Pspnet	Deeplab-v3	Ours
scores	0.503	0.605	0.615	**0.738**

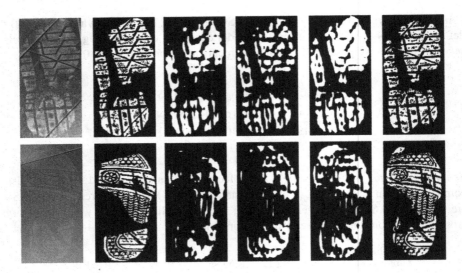

Fig. 5. Segmentations by different methods. From left to right are: input images, manually annotations, FCN-8 s, Deeplab-v3, PspNet and our method.

4   Conclusions

We present a binary semantic image segmentation framework based on generative adversarial networks for shoeprints extraction. An improved U-net is presented to keep the fine structures of the shoeprints. Our method is far precise than the previous end-to-end algorithms, such as FCN, PspNet and Deeplab-v3.

Acknowledgements. This work is supported by the Natural Science Foundation of China [grant numbers 61572099 and 61772104].

References

1. Sezgin, M., Sankur, B.: Survey over image thresholding techniques and quantitative performance evaluation. J. Electron. Imaging **13**(1), 146–166 (2004)
2. Venkatesan, R.: Cluster Analysis for Segmentation. In: Technical Note M-0748/Published March 22, University of Virginia. Darden Business Publishing, Charlottesville, VA (2007)
3. Fan, J., Zeng, G., Body, M. Hacid, M.S.: Seeded region growing: an extensive and comparative study. Pattern Recogn. Lett. **26**(8), 1139–1156 (2015)
4. Long, J., Shelhamer, E., Darrell, T.: Fully convolutional networks for semantic segmentation. In: Proceedings of the IEEE Conference on Computer Vision and Pattern Recognition, pp. 3431–3440 (2015)
5. Zhao, H., Shi, J., Qi, X., Wang, X., Jia, J.: Pyramid scene parsing network. In: Proceedings of the IEEE Conference on Computer Vision and Pattern Recognition, pp. 2881–2890 (2017)

6. Chen, L.C., Papandreou, G., Schroff, F.: Rethinking atrous convolution for semantic image segmentation. arXiv preprint arXiv:1706.05587 (2017)
7. Ronneberger, O., Fischer, P., Brox, T.: U-Net: convolutional networks for biomedical image segmentation. In: International Conference on Medical Image Computing and Computer-Assisted Intervention, pp. 234–241. Springer, Cham (2015)
8. Goodfellow, I.J., et al.: Generative adversarial nets. In: Advances in Neural Information Processing Systems, pp. 2672–2680 (2014)
9. He, K., Zhang, X., Ren, S., Sun, J.: Deep residual learning for image recognition. In: Proceedings of the IEEE Conference on Computer Vision and Pattern Recognition, pp. 770–778 (2016)
10. Chen, L.C., Papandreou, G., Kokkinos, I., Murphy, K., Yuille, A.L.: Semantic image segmentation with deep convolutional nets and fully connected CRFs. arXiv preprint arXiv:1412.7062 (2014)
11. Chen, L.C., Papandreou, G., Kokkinos, I., Murphy, K., Yuille, A.L.: DeepLab: semantic image segmentation with deep convolutional nets, atrous convolution, and fully connected CRFs. IEEE Trans. Pattern Anal. Mach. Intell. 40(4), 834–848 (2016)
12. Zhang, T., Qi, G.J., Xiao, B., Wang, J.: Interleaved group convolutions. In: Proceedings of the IEEE International Conference on Computer Vision, pp. 4373–4382 (2017)
13. Salimans, T., Goodfellow, I., Zaremba, W., Cheung, V., Radford, A., Chen, X.: Improved techniques for training gans. In: Advances in neural information processing systems, pp. 2234–2242 (2016)
14. Goodfellow, I., Bengio, Y., Courville, A.: Deep learning. Nature 521(7553), 436 (2015)
15. Sudre, C.H., Li, W., Vercauteren, T., Ourselin, S., Cardoso, M.J.: Generalised dice overlap as a deep learning loss function for highly unbalanced segmentations. In: Deep Learning in Medical Image Analysis and Multimodal Learning for Clinical Decision Support, pp. 240–248. Springer, Cham (2017)
16. Mao, X., Li, Q., Xie, H., Lau, R.Y., Wang, Z., Paul Smolley, S.: Least squares generative adversarial networks. In: Proceedings of the IEEE International Conference on Computer Vision, pp. 2794–2802 (2017)
17. Ulyanov, D., Vedaldi, A., Lempitsky, V.: Instance normalization: the missing ingredient for fast stylization. arXiv preprint arXiv:1607.08022 (2016)
18. Maas, A., Hannun, A., Ng, A.: Rectifier nonlinearities improve neural network acoustic models. In: Proceedings of ICML Workshop on Deep Learning for Audio, Speech and Language Processing (2013)
19. Radford, A., Metz, L., Chintala, S., et al.: Unsupervised representation learning with deep convolutional generative adversarial networks. arXiv preprint arXiv:1511.06434 (2015)
20. Jégou, S., Drozdzal, M., Vazquez, D., Romero, A., Bengio, Y.: The one hundred layers tiramisu: fully convolutional densenets for semantic segmentation. In: Proceedings of the IEEE Conference on Computer Vision and Pattern Recognition Workshops, pp. 11–19 (2017)

Turnstile Jumping Detection in Real-Time Video Surveillance

Huy Hoang Nguyen[✉] and Thi Nhung Ta

School of Electronics and Telecommunications, Hanoi University of Science and Technology, Hanoi, Vietnam
hoang.nguyenhuy@hust.edu.vn

Abstract. Turnstile jumping, a common action happening on a daily basis at high volume pedestrian areas, causes various problems for society. This study proposes a novel framework in detecting tunrstile jumping with no GPU necessary. The proposed model is a combination of a YOLO v2 based human detector, a Kernelized Correlation Filters (KCF) tracker and a Motion History Image (MHI)-based Convolutional Neural Network (CNN) classifier. Experimental results show that the developed model is not only capable of operating in real-time but can also detect suspicious human actions with an accuracy rate of 91.69%

Keywords: Abnormal human action · Object detection · CNN classification

1 Introduction

Turnstiles (or baffle gates) are access control systems permitting one individual to pass in one direction at a time. They not only maintain a smooth flow of pedestrian traffic but also ensure that the passage of pedestrians is limited to those who insert a coin, a ticket, a pass or another similar item. From a revenue viewpoint, baffle gates provide an accurate statistic in terms of the number of individuals entering a facility or a building. While from a security viewpoint, the electronic turnstile systems intergrating a card or biometric reader allow security guards to have a clear view of each passing turnstile user. Therefore, turnstiles have been widely utilised in various high volume pedestrian areas, such as sports venues, subways, amusement parks, office building lobbies, airports, ski resorts, music arenas, factories, casinos, and supermarkets.

A drawback of the turnstiles is that people can jump over it, usually called "turnstile jumping". In office buildings, a person jumping the turnstile can travel to floors without permission and perform unsafe actions, such as theft or vandalism. In supermarkets, this action usually pertains to shoplifters who leave the store without paying for items and cause losses for retailers. In train stations, this behaviour is a type of fare evasion. According to a report in 2018 by the New York City Transit Authority [1], the estimated revenue loss to ticket evasion was $215 million, and the uncollected revenue increased to $110 million compared

© Springer Nature Switzerland AG 2019
C. Lee et al. (Eds.): PSIVT 2019, LNCS 11854, pp. 390–403, 2019.
https://doi.org/10.1007/978-3-030-34879-3_30

to 2015. So while turnstile jumping is a simple action, it can lead to a range of serious problems.

In the past, security staff often based themselves at entrance and exit points to supervise pedestrian traffic and manually monitor CCTV cameras. This helped them to readily detect turnstile jumping but from a budgetary perspective, it increased the cost of labour. Additionally, monitoring multiple surveillance cameras for extended intervals had harmful health effects because many security guards experienced problems in terms of their eyesight. In recent years, intelligent video analysis has emerged as a promising approach to replace traditional and largely outmoded solutions. By combining Artificial Intelligence and image processing, this method treats turnstile jumping as an abnormal action and automatically analyses captured video frames to recognise suspicious events. If an abnormal action is detected, information (face, position, age, address, etc.) related to the individual who performed the action is extracted and then sent to a competent organisation to handle it.

With the intelligent surveillance system mentioned above, the unusual human action recognition algorithm plays an important role. Moreover, this algorithm must satisfy the requirement of real-time processing. Therefore, the goal of this study is to develop an algorithm which can detect turnstile jumping in real-time. The remainder of this paper is constructed as follows. Section 2 delivers a literature review related to our problem. Section 3 describes the details of the proposed method. Section 4 presents and discusses experimental results including environment setup, datasets, training and testing results and experiments. Finally, Sect. 5 concludes this study.

2   Literature Review

Jumping the turnstile is regarding as an abnormal human action at entrance/exit zones. In a study of Dhiman and Vishwakarma [2], researchers pointed out that state of the art techniques for abnormal human activity were devided into two groups including a group of deep features based techniques and a group of hand-crafted features based techniques. The first group is mainly based on feature learning by using a CNN model whereas the second group is based on understanding the characteristics of the abnormal human activity and adopting various algorithms to extract appropriate features [3].

2.1   Deep Features

In order to detect turnstile jumping, a popular approach utilised by developers is to first learn the normal patterns from the training videos, then to detect anomalies as events deviate from normal patterns [4]. Several works related to this approach are studies of Cong et al. [5], Li et al. [6], Lu et al. [7] and Zhao et al. [8]. Another approach adopted by Chong and Tay in their paper [4] is that when an abnormal event occurs, the most recent frames of video will be significantly different from the older frames. Despite the fact that these methods are successful in detecting abnormal events with a high degree of accuracy, they are not able to operate in real-time without a GPU due to their computational complexity.

2.2 Handcrafted Features

According to [9], many researchers have adopted a three-stage general framework consisting of object detection, feature extraction and abnormal action classification. In the first stage, regions indicating human movement are located in every frame. In the next stage, depending on each specific application, the different features (shape, posture or motion, etc.) of the object are extracted through various algorithms. In the last stage, the obtained feature information is treated as an input to the classifier. Then, an activity analysis is performed to compare the classifier's output with a threshold value to decide whether the action is suspicious.

As mentioned above, detecting the object is an initial and important phase of abnormal human action recognition. Over the last decade, Haar cascade [10] and Histogram of Oriented Gradients (HOG) [11] based approaches for human detection are two of the most popular methods. These methods provide good performance, robustness and, in some cases, real-time performance [12]. However, due to the diversity and complexity of human poses and light conditions, backgrounds, it is challenging to design an efficient manual feature extractor for human detection. In recent years, many modern approaches have been proposed, such as R-CNN [13], Fast R-CNN [14], Mask R-CNN [15], SSD [16], YOLO [17]. These modern detectors not only provide more accurate results but are capable of detecting various human postures. Nevertheless, their performance heavily depends on GPU acceleration. Therefore, these models may not be suitable for computationally limited platforms.

The next phase of suspicious human activity detection is to choose right features and extract the promising information from these features for classifying abnormal and normal actions. In the literature, shape, colour, posture and motion are the most common features used for abnormal human action recognition. Additionally, applications of abnormal human action recognition are mainly focuses on six different sectors including abandoned/removed object detection, theft detection, health monitoring, accidents/illegal parking detection on the road, violence activity detection, fire and smoke detection [9]. Surprisingly, none of the research related to the Motion History Image (MHI) [18] feature has been proposed to detect turnstile jumping at the entrance/exit zones.

In the last phase, a trained classifier performs a prediction to identify the type of action. Generally, popular machine learning algorithms used for developing the classifier contain k-Nearest Neighbor (k-NN), Support Vector Machine (SVM), Fuzzy and Neural Network (NN) [9]. Besides, many researchers have improved these approaches to enhance performance in several specific applications, such as applying the Fuzzy Self-Organising Neural Network to detect abnormal events in an open space [19], combining PCA and SVM to recognise criminal activities at ATM installations [20] or designing a Four-Layered MLP network with back propagation learning schema in fall detection [21].

3 Proposed Method

Based on the literature review, this paper aims to develop a novel algorithm which is capable of detecting turnstile jumping in real-time without GPU support. Theoretically, this method is a combination of a modern human detector, a tracker and a CNN classifier. Regions indicating human actions are detected by a frame-based human detector and a tracking algorithm. A position checker takes responsibility for determining whether the detected object has crossed the barrier. If there is an individual passing the turnstile, the CNN classifier is activated to classify human action. This classifier utilises the MHI region of the object as its input. The general framework of the proposed method is presented in Fig. 1.

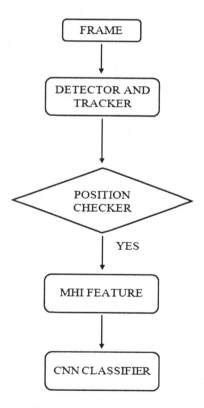

Fig. 1. The general framework of the proposed method.

3.1 Object Detection and Tracking

Real-Time Human Detector. In this study, the real-time human detector is based on the YOLOv2 [22] network. Several layers of the orginal YOLO v2 network are removed, then some other layers ard added to it. The number of filters in convolution layers of the first 17 layers is reduced twice compared to the original version. Batch nomalisation is also deleted to speed up the computation of the proposed model [23]. This modification allows the new obtained network to only detect human objects in real-time with no GPU necessary. The network structure of the proposed human detector is shown in Table 1.

Table 1. Proposed network structure

Layer	Filters	Size	Input	Output
0 conv	16	$3 \times 3/1$	$416 \times 416 \times 3$	$416 \times 416 \times 16$
1 max		$2 \times 2/2$	$416 \times 416 \times 16$	$208 \times 208 \times 16$
2 conv	32	$3 \times 3/1$	$208 \times 208 \times 16$	$208 \times 208 \times 32$
3 max		$2 \times 2/2$	$208 \times 208 \times 32$	$104 \times 104 \times 32$
4 conv	64	$3 \times 3/1$	$104 \times 104 \times 32$	$104 \times 104 \times 64$
5 conv	32	$1 \times 1/1$	$104 \times 104 \times 64$	$104 \times 104 \times 32$
6 conv	64	$3 \times 3/1$	$104 \times 104 \times 32$	$104 \times 104 \times 64$
7 max		$2 \times 2/2$	$104 \times 104 \times 64$	$52 \times 52 \times 64$
8 conv	128	$3 \times 3/1$	$52 \times 52 \times 64$	$52 \times 52 \times 128$
9 conv	64	$1 \times 1/1$	$52 \times 52 \times 128$	$52 \times 52 \times 64$
10 conv	128	$3 \times 3/1$	$52 \times 52 \times 64$	$52 \times 52 \times 128$
11 max		$2 \times 2/2$	$52 \times 52 \times 128$	$26 \times 26 \times 128$
12 conv	256	$3 \times 3/1$	$26 \times 26 \times 128$	$26 \times 26 \times 256$
13 conv	128	$1 \times 1/1$	$26 \times 26 \times 256$	$26 \times 26 \times 128$
14 conv	256	$3 \times 3/1$	$26 \times 26 \times 128$	$26 \times 26 \times 256$
15 conv	128	$1 \times 1/1$	$26 \times 26 \times 256$	$26 \times 26 \times 128$
16 conv	256	$3 \times 3/1$	$26 \times 26 \times 128$	$26 \times 26 \times 256$
17 max		$2 \times 2/2$	$26 \times 26 \times 256$	$13 \times 13 \times 256$
18 conv	256	$3 \times 3/1$	$13 \times 13 \times 256$	$13 \times 13 \times 256$
19 conv	256	$3 \times 3/1$	$13 \times 13 \times 256$	$13 \times 13 \times 256$
20 route 11				
21 conv	64	$1 \times 1/1$	$26 \times 26/128$	$26 \times 26/64$
22 reorg				
23 route 22 19				
24 conv	256	$3 \times 3/1$	$13 \times 13 \times 512$	$13 \times 13 \times 256$
25 conv	30	$1 \times 1/1$	$13 \times 13 \times 256$	$13 \times 13 \times 30$
26 detection				

In order to obtain an optimal human detector, the training process of the proposed model is implemented and based on the open-source neural network framework named Darknet [24]. The size of 416 × 416 pixels is chosen as the model's input, and the anchors' parameters are kept as they are in the orginal version. During the training, randomised input images are resized; therefore, the final model can effectively detect images with various sizes. The size of each batch case is 64 with 4 images in the sub-batch for the proposed model. The learning rate, momentum and decay values are set to 0.001, 0.9 and 0.0005, respectively. The number of iterations is 500200 in total.

KCF Tracker. In order to increase the capability of object detection, the proposed human detector and Kernelized Correlation Filters - KCF tracker [25] are used in combination. Due to the random appearance and disappearance of individuals in frames, three primary cases including "create a new track" , "update an existing track" and "remove a track" are defined in the data association problem. A new track is created and added into the tracking list when a new human object is detected. Then, a counter starts counting the number of frames that the track has been updated without detection. Consequently, if the detector does not detect the existing object in some frames, it can still be tracked by the tracker.

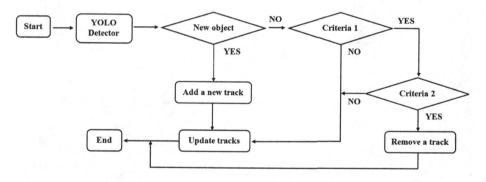

Fig. 2. Procedure for multiple detections and tracks

Two criteria are utilised to decide when a tracker is removed. The first criteria (Criteria 1) compares θ_t to a threshold ∂. In the Criteria 1, θ_t denotes an interval during which the tracker's output has not changed. The second criteria (Criteria 2) checks whether the detector detects an object whose location is matched with the tracker's calculation. If the interval θ_t is larger than the threshold ∂ in the Criteria 1 and no object satisfies the Criteria 2, the tracker is deleted. The procedure for solving multiple detection and tracks is displayed in Fig. 2.

3.2 Position Checking

After locating the human object, a position checker takes responsibility for estimating the position of the object's centroid against a pre-defined line. In order
to do this, a theory of signed distance from a point to a line is adopted and given
by an equation as follows:

$$d(M, \triangle) = \frac{\overrightarrow{AM} \times \overrightarrow{AB}}{||\overrightarrow{AB}||} \tag{1}$$

Where, point M denotes the centroid of the human object, A and B are two
points on the pre-defined line $\triangle$. The line $\triangle$ is created at the turnstile top. An
example of the pre-defined line is described in Fig. 3. After the signed distance
is calculated, it is normalised by Eq. (2):

$$d^*(M, \triangle) = \begin{cases} 1 & if\ d(M, \triangle) > 0 \\ -1 & if\ d(M, \triangle) < 0 \\ 0 & otherwise \end{cases} \tag{2}$$

Fig. 3. An example of the pre-defined line at the turnstile area

From the Eq. (2), when $d_t^* + d_{t-1}^* = 0$, this means that the human object
crossed the barrier and an abnormal action classifier is activated to classify the
human action at time t.

3.3   MHI-based Temporal Feature

In order to detect turnstile jumping, the MHI-based temporal feature is adopted as the input for the classifier. In a motion history image, the temporal motion information of the actor is stored in a single image where pixel intensity is a function of the motion history at that point and the pixel with the brighter value corresponds to a more recent motion. According to [26], MHI denoted as $h(x, y, t)$ is obtained by Eqs. (3–4):

$$d(x,y,t) = \begin{cases} 255 & if \ f(x,y,t) - f(x,y,t-1) > \xi_{thr} \\ 0 & otherwise \end{cases} \tag{3}$$

$$h(x,y,t) = \begin{cases} \tau & if \ (x,y,t) = 255 \\ max(0, h(x,y,t-1) - 1) & otherwise \end{cases} \tag{4}$$

Where, $f(x,y,t)$, $f(x,y,t-1)$, $d(x,y,t)$ are the current frame, the previous frame and a binary image of differences between two frames, respectively. τ is defined as the maximum duration that an action may take. τ and ξ_{thr} are experimentally chosen in this work.

3.4   CNN Abnormal Action Classification

The proposed CNN structure contains five sets of convolutional, average pooling and activation layers, followed by a flattening convolutional layer, then a fully-connected layer with 512 units and finally a softmax layer. All average pooling layers have the same filter size 2 × 2 and the same stride of 2. The activation function in all activation layers is Rectified Linear Unit (ReLU). Five convolutional layers (CLs) are designed as follows: CL–1 with 16 feature maps having size 3 × 3 and a stride of 1, CL–2 with 32 feature maps having size 3 × 3 and a stride of 1, CL–3 with 64 feature maps having size 3 × 3 and a stride of 1, CL–4 with 128 feature maps having size 3 × 3 and a stride of 1, CL–5 with 256 feature maps having size 3 × 3 and a stride of 1. The input size of the model is set to 40 × 40. The proposed structure of the classifier is shown in Table 2.

In order to obtain the optimal model, several parameters are configured before training the classifier. Adam is the main optimisation algorithm used in this work. Values of batch size, learning rate and epoch are 16, 0.001 and 40, respectively. Initial weights in each layer are randomly chosen by using a zero-mean Gaussian distribution with a standard deviation of 0.05.

4   Experiments

4.1   Experimental Environment

All experiments were performed on an Intel @ Xeon (R) CPU E5-2620 v4 @ 2.10 GHz × 16 with 64 GB RAM running 64 bit Ubuntu 16.04 operating system. A Quadro P4000 GPU was utilised to support the training of the proposed human detection model and the abnormal action classification model. To estimate the

Table 2. Proposed CNN classifier

Layer	Parameters
Convolutional 1	$3 \times 3 \times 16$ & stride $= 1$
Pooling	2×2 & stride $= 2$
Activation	ReLU
Convolutional 2	$3 \times 3 \times 32$ & stride $= 1$
Pooling	2×2 & stride $= 2$
Activation	ReLU
Convolutional 3	$3 \times 3 \times 64$ & stride $= 1$
Pooling	2×2 & stride $= 2$
Activation	ReLU
Convolutional 4	$3 \times 3 \times 128$ & stride $= 1$
Pooling	2×2 & stride $= 2$
Activation	ReLU
Convolutional 5	$3 \times 3 \times 256$ & stride $= 1$
Pooling	2×2 & stride $= 2$
Activation	ReLU
Flattening	
Fully connected	512
Softmax	

accuracy and efficiency of the trained models without GPU usage, these models were tested in Pycharm 2018 with Tensorflow package and OpenCV - DNN module. An experiment was implemented to verify the performance of the proposed abnormal human action detection algorithm in a real-life environment.

With the purpose of focusing on human detection, 66809 images indicating human objects were extracted from the Coco 2017 dataset [27] to create a new dataset named the Human Coco 2017 dataset. In this study, this dataset was adopted to train the proposed human detector with 64116 images for training and 2693 images for testing.

Since there was no MHI dataset related to the turnstile jumping, we created a new dataset to train the proposed CNN classifier. Cameras with a resolution of 1280 × 720 were mounted on three different positions around the turnstile area to capture MHI images of human motion. These cameras capture the abnormal and normal actions of 19 individuals at the barrier. A background subtraction technique was adopted to extract MHI regions describing human movement. Then, several data augmentation techniques (horizontal flip and crop) were implemented to make the dataset more complex. This dataset includes two classes: an abnormal class with 4612 images and a normal class with 4510 images. An 80/20 split was used to divide the dataset into training and testing sets. The abnormal class is related to the "jumping the turnstile" action while the normal class pertains to the "walking through the turnstile" action. Several images of this dataset are shown in Fig. 4.

4.2 Results and Discussion

In the first experiment, the proposed human detection model was trained with three different input sizes: 224×224, 416×416 and 608×608. Additionally, the original YOLO v2 based single object detection model was also trained on the Human Coco 2017 dataset. The average precision - AP [17] and the processing time per frame based measurement were utilised to evaluate the performance of the trained detectors. The goal of this experiment was to find a model so that it can run in real-time and its AP is slightly smaller than that of the original version. Results of the first experiment are shown in Table 3.

Table 3. Results on Human COCO 2017 dataset

Model	AP	Processing time
YOLO v2 (1 class) – 416×416	58.54%	141 ms
Proposed model – 608×608	59.23%	61 ms
Proposed model – 416×416	54.3 %	30 ms
Proposed model – 224×224	39.1 %	17 ms

From this table, the 608×608 proposed model achieves the highest AP value however its processing time is not suitable for a real-time application. Compared to the original YOLO v2 single object detector, the 416×416 proposed detector is less than about 4%, but it only takes 30 ms to process a frame. Despite the 224×224 detector operating faster than the 416×416 detector, its AP is lower. Therefore, the modified YOLO v2 based detector with an input size of 416×416 is suitable for the proposed framework.

The next experiment estimated the performance of the proposed classification model on the testing dataset. In this classification problem, the three metrics used for evaluation are True Positive Rate – TPR, False Positive Rate – FPR, and Accuracy [28]. During the training, different parameters were experimentally adjusted to find the optimal trained model. The goal of the second experiment is to find a classifier so that its TPR is larger than 90%, and FPR is lower than 10%. Table 4 reports the performance of the obtained optimal model on the testing dataset. It can be seen from Table 4 that the proposed model achieves the initial target.

The final experiment was implemented to verify the efficiency of the proposed turnstile jumping detection model in a real-life video with 25 FPS. The testing video was resized to 640×320. In this video, an individual performed two actions consisting of an abnormal action (jumping the turnstile) and a normal action

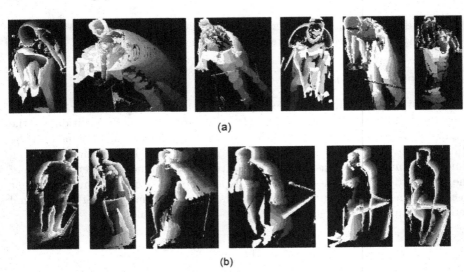

Fig. 4. MHI dataset: (a): Abnormal actions, (b): Normal actions

Table 4. Optimal trained model on the testing dataset

Model	True positive rate	False positive rate	Accuracy
Proposed model	91.75%	8.3%	91.69%

(walking through the turnstile). Two results of the video analysis are recorded. The first result shown in Table 5 is related to the average processing time of the proposed model. On the other hand, Fig. 5 reveals the second result.

Table 5. Average processing time of the proposed framework

Module	Detector	Tracker	MHI	CNN Classifier	Others	Total
Propossing time (ms)	29.2	2.5	2.35	2.05	5.5	41.6

Table 5 points out that the total processing time of the proposed approach is around 41.6 ms. Detailed results in this table also confirm the benefit of the KCF tracker and the MHI feature due to their low computation. This means that the proposed abnormal action detection model can be applied in real-time applications when combining the proposed detector, the KCF tracker and the MHI based CNN classifier. In Fig. 5, images (a) and (b) demonstrate a "walking through the turnstile" action. This action is classified as a normal action; therefore, no green bounding box covers the person. Images (c) and (d) demonstrate a "jumping the turnstile" action. This action is classified as an abnormal action, hence a green bounding box covers the individual.

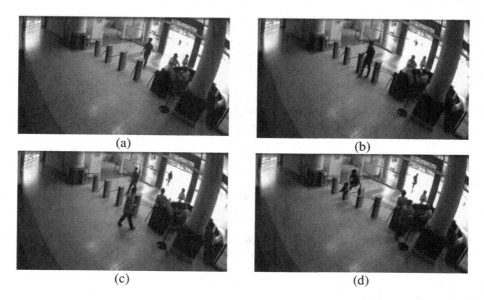

(a)   (b)

(c)   (d)

Fig. 5. Example frames show the abnormal action detected by our framework. (a), (b): a person jumped over the turnstile to get in, (c), (d): a person walked through the turn- stile

5   Conclusion and Future Work

This study presented a novel approach to detect turnstile jumping in video surveillance. This approach was a combination of a YOLOv2 based human detector, a KCF tracker and a MHI based CNN classifier. Experimental results verified that the goal of the proposed method was achieved. From a practical viewpoint, this method can be applied for video surveillance systems lacking GPU, and the modified YOLO v2 model in this paper can be utilised for other real-time human detection applications based on low computational platforms, such as elder monitoring, perimeter intrusion detection and pedestrian counting. However, the obtained MHI dataset does not cover the diversity and complexity of the jumping action and the experimental environments. In future work, we plan to further improve the MHI dataset and the proposed algorithm to achieve higher accuracy in various turnstile conditions. Additionally, a comparison between existing methods and our method will be reported to evaluate the efficiency of the proposed approach.

Acknowledgement. This research is funded by Ministry of Science and Technology of Vietnam (MOST) under grant number 10/2018/DTCTKC.01.14/16-20.

References

1. Fare evasion at NYCT. http://web.mta.info/mta/news/books/docs/special-finance-committee/Fare-evasion-board-doc_181130.pdf
2. Dhiman, C., Vishwakarma, D.K.: A review of state-of-the-art techniques for abnormal human activity recognition. Eng. Appl. Artif. Intell. **2**, 21–45 (2019)
3. Nanni, L., Ghidoni, S., Brahnam, S.: Handcrafted vs. non-handcrafted features for computer vision classification. Pattern Recognit. **71**, 158–172 (2017)
4. Chong, Y.S., Tay, Y.H.: Abnormal event detection in videos using spatiotemporal autoencoder. In: Cong, F., Leung, A., Wei, Q. (eds.) ISNN 2017. LNCS, vol. 10262, pp. 189–196. Springer, Cham (2017). https://doi.org/10.1007/978-3-319-59081-3_23
5. Cong, Y., Yuan, J., Liu, J.: Sparse reconstructioncost for abnormal event detection. In: Proceedings of the IEEE Computer Society Conference on Computer Vision and Pattern Recognition, pp. 3449–3456. IEEE (2011)
6. Li, C., Han, Z., Ye, Q., Jiao, J.: Abnormal behavior detection via sparse reconstruction analysis of trajectory. In: International Conference on Image and Graphics, pp. 807–810. IEEE (2011)
7. Lu, C., Shi, J., Jia, J.: Abnormal event detection at 150 FPS in MATLAB. In: International Conference on Computer Vision, pp. 2720–2727. IEEE (2013)
8. Zhao, B., Fei-Fei, L., Xing, E.P.: Online detection of unusual events in videos via dynamic sparse coding. In: Proceedings of the IEEE Computer Society Conference on Computer Vision and Pattern Recognition, pp. 3320–3323. IEEE (2011)
9. Tripathi, R.K., Jalal, A.S., Agrawal, S.C.: Suspicious human activity recognition: a review. Artif. Intell. Rev. **50**(2), 283–339 (2018)
10. Viola, P., Jones, M.: Rapid object detection using a boosted cascade of simple features. In: Proceedings of the IEEE Computer Society Conference on Computer Vision and Pattern Recognition, pp. 511–518. IEEE (2001)
11. Dalal, N., Triggs, B.: Histogram of oriented gradients for human detection. In: Proceedings of the IEEE Computer Society Conference on Computer Vision and Pattern Recognition, pp. 886–893. IEEE (2005)
12. Cruz, J.E.C., Shiguemori, E.H., Guimaraes, L.N.F.: A comparison of Haar-like, LBP and HOG approaches to concrete and asphalt runway detection in high resolution imagery. J. Comput. Interdisc. Sci. **6**(3), 121–136 (2016)
13. Girshick, R., Donahue, J., Darrell, T., Malik, J.: Rich feature hierachies for accurate object detection and semantic segmentation. In: Proceedings of the IEEE Computer Society Conference on Computer Vision and Pattern Recognition, pp. 580–587. IEEE (2014)
14. Girshick, R.: Fast R-CNN. In: International Conference on Computer Vision, pp. 1440–1448. IEEE (2015)
15. He, K., Gkioxari, G., Dollar, P., Girshick, R.: Mask R-CNN. In: International Conference on Computer Vision, pp. 2980–2988. IEEE (2017)
16. Liu, W., Anguelov, D., Erhan, D., Szegedy, C., Reed, S., Fu, C.-Y., Berg, A.C.: SSD: single shot multibox detector. In: Leibe, B., et al. (eds.) ECCV 2016. LNCS, vol. 9905, pp. 21–37. Springer, Cham (2016). https://doi.org/10.1007/978-3-319-46448-0_2
17. Redmon, J., Divvala, S., Girshick, R., Farhadi, A.: You only look once: unified, real-time object detection. In: Conference on Computer Vision and Pattern Recognition, pp. 779–788. IEEE (2016)

18. Bobick, A.F., Davis, J.W.: The recognition of human movement using temporal templates. IEEE Trans. Pattern Anal. Mach. Intell. **23**(3), 257–267 (2001)
19. Hsieh, C., Hsu, S.B., Han, C.C., Fan, K.C.: Abnormal event detection using trajectory features. J. Infer. Technol. Appl. **5**(1), 22–27 (2011)
20. Tripathi, V., Gangodkar, D., Vivek, L., Mittal, A.: Robust abnormal event recognition via motion and shape analysis at ATM installations. J. Electr. Comput. Eng. **2015**, 1–10 (2015)
21. Foroughi, H., Aski, B.S., Pourreza, H.: Intelligent video surveillance for monitoring fall detection of elderly in home environments. In: International Conference on Computer and Information Technology, pp. 219–224. IEEE (2008)
22. Redmon, J., Farhadi, A.: YOLO9000: better, faster, stronger. In: Conference on Computer Vision and Pattern Recognition, pp. 6517–6525. IEEE (2017)
23. Huan, R., Pedoeem, J., Chen, C.: YOLO-LITE: a real-time object detection algorithm optimized for non-GPU computers. In: Conference on Computer Vision and Pattern Recognition, pp. 2503–2510. IEEE (2018)
24. Darknet. https://pjreddie.com/darknet
25. João, F.H., Rui, C., Pedro, M., Jorge, B.: High-speed tracking with Kernelised correlation filters. IEEE Trans. Pattern Anal. Mach. Intell. **37**(3), 583–596 (2014)
26. Bobick, A.F., Davis, J.W.: Action recognition using temporal templates. In: Shah, M., Jain, R. (eds.) Motion-Based Recognition. Springer, Dordrecht (1997). https://doi.org/10.1007/978-94-015-8935-2_6
27. Caesar, H., Uijlings, J., Farrari, V.: COCO-stuff: thing and stuff classes in context. In: Conference on Computer Vision and Pattern Recognition, pp. 1209–1218. IEEE (2018)
28. Fawcett, T.: An introduction to ROC analysis. Pattern Recognit. Lett. **27**(8), 861–874 (2006)

Unsupervised Deep Features for Privacy Image Classification

Chiranjibi Sitaula[✉], Yong Xiang, Sunil Aryal, and Xuequan Lu

School of Information Technology, Deakin University, Geelong, Australia
{csitaul,yong.xiang,sunil.aryal,xuequan.lu}@deakin.edu.au

Abstract. Sharing images online poses security threats to a wide range of users due to the unawareness of privacy information. Deep features have been demonstrated to be a powerful representation for images. However, deep features usually suffer from the issues of a large size and requiring a huge amount of data for fine-tuning. In contrast to normal images (e.g., scene images), privacy images are often limited because of sensitive information. In this paper, we propose a novel approach that can work on limited data and generate deep features of smaller size. For training images, we first extract the initial deep features from the pre-trained model and then employ the K-means clustering algorithm to learn the centroids of these initial deep features. We use the learned centroids from training features to extract the final features for each testing image and encode our final features with the triangle encoding. To improve the discriminability of the features, we further perform the fusion of two proposed unsupervised deep features obtained from different layers. Experimental results show that the proposed features outperform state-of-the-art deep features, in terms of both classification accuracy and testing time.

Keywords: Privacy images · Unsupervised deep features · Image classification · ResNet-50 · Privacy and security

1 Introduction

Privacy image classification is becoming increasingly important nowadays, owing to the prevalent presence of social media on the web where people share personal and private images. The privacy image classification systems allow people to know if the images they share are private or public. Private images, such as images involving families, usually involve private information about the users. By contrast, public images generally involve scenes, objects, animals and so on, and do not include private information. The purpose of the privacy image classification is to make people alert while sharing images online. People sometimes may be unaware of whether they are doing right or wrong when sharing their images. In such cases, a system that is capable of classifying private and public images is very useful to users.

© Springer Nature Switzerland AG 2019
C. Lee et al. (Eds.): PSIVT 2019, LNCS 11854, pp. 404–415, 2019.
https://doi.org/10.1007/978-3-030-34879-3_31

For image classification, feature extraction from images is a fundamental step. Privacy images are challenging for classification, because they may contain high within-class dissimilarity. As shown in Fig. 1, we observe in both categories (private and public) that they have such patterns. Fortunately, there are only two categories in privacy images so that we do not need to consider such varying patterns as in other scene image classification which have far more than two categories [14].

Fig. 1. Images showing the private and public images from PicAlert [26] dataset.

In general, the existing feature extraction methods for privacy images comprise of traditional vision-based methods [26], deep learning-based methods [19–23,27], and semantic approaches [13,15]. While comparing traditional vision-based features against the deep learning-based features, we notice a significant improvement in classification accuracy with the aid of the latter features learned from the pre-trained deep learning models. By the help of the fine-tuned deep learning models, it can even achieve a higher classification accuracy which required a massive amount of data [23]. Nevertheless, in the task of privacy image classification, there is a very limited amount of data due to privacy issues. Simply extracting features from intermediate layers of those models makes the size of the features higher, thereby increasing computational burden during classification. To sum up, these existing methods on privacy images suffer from **two** problems: (1) the curse of dimensionality of features; and (2) requirements of massive data if we want to obtain a fine-tuned model or new deep learning model. As such, feature extraction methods favoring a low feature size and limited data are particularly needed for the task of privacy image classification.

In this paper, we propose a novel approach to extract the features of privacy images with the assistance of unsupervised feature learning, which not only works on a limited amount of privacy images but also yields a lower feature size. Inspired by the work in [20], where the authors claim the efficacy of the pre-trained models against the fine-tuned models over privacy images, we also choose a pre-trained model in this work. Specifically, among several pre-trained models, we choose the ResNet-50 [6] model, which has been found to have a lower error rate for the classification of different types of images than the state-of-the-art deep learning models such as VGG-Net [12] and GoogleNet [17]. Furthermore, the ResNet-50 also has a lower number of layers than its other versions (ResNet-101 and ResNet-152), thereby having a faster speed. To perform unsupervised feature learning, we perform the K-means clustering on the deep features extracted from the ResNet-50 [6] which has been pre-trained with a large dataset of labeled images (i.e., ImageNet [4]). Then, we encode the features using the triangle encoding [3] to achieve our unsupervised deep features. The K-means clustering can yield centroids of patterns (contexts) for privacy images. The features of the clustering method are (1) discriminable patterns of privacy images and (2) a lower feature size due to its dimension reduction capability. We tested our unsupervised deep features on PicAlert [25] and found that our features can produce better classification accuracies than deep learning features extracted by state-of-the-art models.

2   Related Works

Several studies have explored the privacy image classification problem with the use of different types of features such as SIFT (Scale Invariant Feature Transform) and RGB (Red Green Blue) [26], textual and deep learning based features [19–23,27], semantic features [15], and so on.

Zerr et al. [25] used various types of visual features such as quantized SIFT, color histogram, brightness and sharpness and the text features of the image. They have shown that the features designed by the fusion of textual and visual features are prominent than the visual features only. Similarly, the authors in [19,20,22] emphasized the usage of textual features such as deep tags (object tags and scene tags) and user tags (user annotated tags) based features for the classification of privacy images and claimed that the features designed based on tags outperform the state-of-the-art features such as SIFT, GIST (Generalized Search Tree) and fully connected features (FC-features of VGG-Net). Zhong et al. [27] chose FC-features of a deep learning model for the group-based personalized approach which further proved the applicability of high-level features such as FC-features for this domain. Similarly, Spyromitros et al. [15] explored the semantic features based on the output of a large array of classifiers. Their proposed semantic features outperform the generic traditional vision-based features such as SIFT, EDCH (Edge Direction Coherence) feature, etc.

More recently, Tonge et al. [21] explored textual features based on the pre-trained deep learning model, which yielded the scene information of the image, called scene tags. The authors unveiled that the combination of such scene tags with user tags and object tags outperforms features of individual tags. Likewise, Tran et al. [23] extracted hierarchical features by the concatenation of object features and convolutional features. For the experiments, the authors used two pipelined CNNs (Convolutional Neural Networks). The FC-features obtained after the fine-tuning operation over two deep learning models were concatenated to get the final hierarchical features of the image. Their method requires a massive amount of images for training. However, in the recent research by Tonge et al. [20] the features extracted from the pre-trained model (*FC*-features of AlexNet [8]) outperform the hierarchical features extracted from the fine-tuned deep learning models [23]. Thus, task-generic features which are extracted from the pre-trained models, became more prominent than task-specific features which are extracted from fine-tuned deep learning models, for privacy images. This opens a door to take advantage of the pre-trained models for the feature extraction of privacy images, given a limited amount of training images.

3   Unsupervised Features Extraction

To extract the unsupervised deep features, we chose the pre-trained ResNet-50 model. A pre-trained model is favorable owing to the following reasons: (1) fine-tuned models require massive data to overcome overfitting, and (2) there is a very limited amount of private images for the study. The overall approach, shown as a block diagram in Fig. 2, consists of three main steps to extract the unsupervised deep features, namely: initial deep features extraction (Sec. 3.1), K-means clustering on deep features (Sec. 3.2), and unsupervised deep features encoding (Sec. 3.3).

3.1   Initial Deep Features Extraction

We take the features from the top activation layers as the candidate deep features which can better represent images based on the objects' details in the images [14]. The original dimension of the deep features from the activation layers is $7 * 7 * 512$, which provides 512-D features (each feature map is $7 * 7$). To represent a feature map as a single value, we operate the global average pooling that exploits the properties of deep features with both high and low values. This results in a 512-D vector of an image where each component represents its corresponding feature map. Let H, W, and D denote the height, width , and depth of the candidate deep features of the top activation layers of the ResNet-50 model.

$$f(x_a) = \frac{1}{H * W} * \{ \sum_{i=1}^{H*W} x_{a1}^i, \sum_{i=1}^{H*W} x_{a2}^i, \sum_{i=1}^{H*W} x_{a3}^i, \ldots \sum_{i=1}^{H*W} x_{aD}^i \}, \tag{1}$$

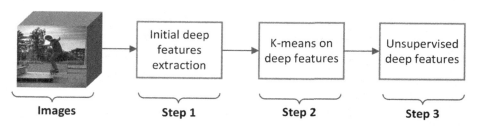

Fig. 2. Block diagram of the extraction of our proposed unsupervised deep features (UDF) encoding.

where $f(x_a)$ is the average pooled features of image x_a based on the feature maps $\{x_{a1}^i, x_{a2}^i, \cdots, x_{aD}^i\}_{i=1}^{H*W}$. Equation (1) computes the representative values of the corresponding feature maps.

The pooled features obtained from Eq. (1) are further processed by the two normalization strategies: power-normalization and L2-normalization. We first use the signed square root norm of the features for power-normalization and then perform L2-normalization, due to their higher performance [9,10].

$$f(x_a') = \sqrt{f(x_a)} \tag{2}$$

Equation (2) calculates the square root based power normalization ($f(x_a')$) of each element of the average pooled feature vector $f(x_a)$. Now, the features are normalized, as shown in the Eq. (3).

$$f(x_a'') = \frac{f(x_a')}{\|f(x_a')\|_2} \tag{3}$$

Similarly, Eq. (3) yields $f(x_a'')$, which is the L2-normalization of each element of the feature vector $f(x_a')$. The feature vectors of images extracted from Eq. (3) will be used to perform K-means clustering to learn the centroids (Sec. 3.2).

Table 1 lists detailed information about the layers used in this work. The first five activation layers are 512-D with a feature map size of 7 * 7. For the average pooling layer (avg_pool), the dimension is 2048-D in the ResNet-50 model with a feature map size of 1 * 1. We perform global averaged pooling of each feature map to get the aggregated value of the corresponding feature map.

3.2   K-Means Clustering over Deep Features

We perform K-means clustering to learn the centroids of the initial deep features for the training dataset. Firstly, we set k as an initial centroid number. Let c^k represent the kth cluster center. The k clusters and centroids are optimized based on the distances of data points to centroids. k is set to 250 (Sec. 4.3) which empirically produces a higher accuracy than others. While there are more delicately designed clustering algorithms, K-means is easy and simple to use, and we found it is effective in our context.

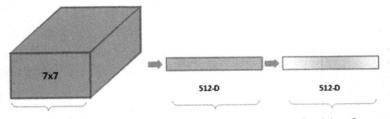

Feature map of 7x7x512   Average pooled feature map   Normalized deep feature

Fig. 3. The steps to extract the initial deep features of the selected activation layers (e.g., activation 48) from the pre-trained ResNet-50 model.

Table 1. Deep layers with sizes of feature maps and features from the pre-trained ResNet-50 model. The names in the bracket represent the activation layer name of the ResNet-50 model. We call these layers such as 42, 44, 45 and so on as methods because they output features.

Methods	Feat. map	Feat. size
ResNet-50(42)	$7 * 7$	512-D
ResNet-50(44)	$7 * 7$	512-D
ResNet-50(45)	$7 * 7$	512-D
ResNet-50(47)	$7 * 7$	512-D
ResNet-50(48)	$7 * 7$	512-D
ResNet-50(avg_pool)	$1 * 1$	2048-D

3.3 Unsupervised Deep Features Encoding

After the calculation of the learned centroids $\{c^k\}$, we calculate the strength of all the initial deep features using the triangle encoding technique [3] which has a higher performance than hard assignment coding schemes as described by Coates et al. [3].

$$f(\hat{x}_a) = max\{0, \mu - z_k\}, \tag{4}$$

where $z_k = d(f(x_a''), c^k)$ and μ is the average distance of all $f(x_a'')$ to all centriods and $f(\hat{x}_a)$ denotes the unsupervised deep features in Eq. (4).

$$d(f(x_a''), c^k) = \sqrt{(\sum (f(x_a'') - c^k)^2} \tag{5}$$

We calculate the Euclidean distances between any two points, shown in Eq. (5). After calculating the average distances from the corresponding initial features, we need to check if one distance is below or above its corresponding average distance. This is because the distances to all the centroids reveal the implicit relationship among centroids for the corresponding initial deep features. To do so, we set the distance to 0 if the distance is above the average distance. Otherwise we set it as the difference between the average distance and Euclidean distance of the corresponding point. Through this scheme, we are able to identify the importance of corresponding initial deep features to all centroids, which further facilitates the encoding of the features. In this work, the dimension of the resulting unsupervised deep features are k. Here, $k = 250$ resulting in a 250-D vector for each privacy image.

We assume that the initial deep features are represented by $f(x'')$ in Algorithm 1 for training. To extract the proposed features, we perform several steps. First of all, we perform K-means clustering over such deep features to obtain c_k cluster centroids and then perform the triangle encoding operation from lines 2 to 13. We repeat the lines from 2 to 13 for the extraction of proposed features of testing initial deep features, based on the centroids $\{c_k\}$ learned from training features.

Algorithm 1. Unsupervised deep features of training images

Input: $f(x'')$ ←training initial deep features, k ←number of cluster centroids
Output: $f(\hat{x})$ ←training unsupervised deep features,
 c^k ←cluster centroids of training features
1: Perform K-means clustering on $f(x'')$ and extract c^k centroids.
2: **for** $i = 0$ to n **do**
3: **for** $j = 0$ to k **do**
4:   $\sum = \sum_j d(f(x_i''), c^j)$
5: **end for**
6: **for** $l = 0$ to k **do**
7:   $\mu \leftarrow \sum /k$
8:   $z_l \leftarrow d(f(x_i''), c^l)$
9:   $\hat{x}_l \leftarrow max\{0, \mu - z_l\}$
10: **end for**
11: $f(\hat{x}_i) \leftarrow \hat{x}_l$
12: **end for**
13: **return** $f(\hat{x})$

---

4   Experimental Results

This section is divided into three sub-sections: Sect. 4.1 explains the dataset used; Sect. 4.2 explains our experimental setup; Sect. 4.3 discusses the analysis of different values of k in the experiment; and Sect. 4.4 discusses the results and testing time.

4.1   Dataset

We conduct experiments on the Flickr images sampled from the only available privacy image dataset, PicAlert [26], which was provided by Spyromitros et al. [15]. The dataset contains two categories of images: private and public. The number of private images in the dataset is lower than public images and we follow the similar configurations as suggested by Tonge et al. [22] for the train/test split in the experiment. The total number of images is 4700, in which, 3917 (83%) images are for training and 783 (17%) images are for testing. Similarly, the ratio of private/public images in each subset (training and testing) is 3 : 1.

4.2   Experimental Setup

The experiments have been performed on a laptop with NVIDIA 1050 GeForce GTX GPU and 16 GB RAM. We use the keras [2] package implemented in R [11], which is open source. Also, we test our proposed unsupervised deep features by utilizing the L2-regularized Logistic Regression (LR) classifier in Liblinear [5]. We fix bias as 1 and tune C, which is the main parameter to tune in L2-regularized Logistic Regression (LR) classifier. The grid search technique is used for C in the range of 1 and 50, to search the optimal value.

Table 2. Analysis of different k, number of clusters, using classification accuracy (%) while extracting unsupervised deep features (UDF) using ResNet-50(47) method.

k	100	150	200	250	300	350	400	450	500
Accuracy	84.54	84.92	85.05	**85.69**	85.18	85.18	85.05	85.18	85.56

4.3   Analysis of k

To select a best k, the number of clusters for our dataset, we perform an analysis using the features extracted from the ResNet-50(47) method in the experiment. The tested values for k are in the range of 100 and 500 as seen in Table 2. While observing in Table 2, we notice that the number of cluster $k = 250$ yielded a more prominent classification accuracy (**85.69%**) than other values. Thus, we empirically employed 250 as the number of clusters for K-means clustering to extract the proposed unsupervised deep features (UDF).

4.4   Analysis of Results

We discuss the results of classification accuracy and prediction timings in this section.

Classification Accuracy. We compare the proposed features with the state-of-the-art features (deep features extracted from various pre-trained deep learning models), in terms of classification accuracy. To examine what deep features are more effective, we evaluate the deep features from six different layers of ResNet-50 model. In Table 3, we see that our proposed unsupervised deep features extracted from each layer outperform the existing features of the corresponding layer. The highest accuracy is from the activation layer 48 (ResNet-50(48)), which is **85.95%**, among all unsupervised deep features. Similarly, the least accuracy is generated by the ResNet-50(42) which is 84.80%. We notice the interesting result from the ResNet-50(avg_pool) layer whose accuracy (85.56%) is same for both kinds of features. It is a top layer of the ResNet-50 model, which carries important information about objects in the images.

In spite of a lower size, the classification accuracies of the proposed features are consistently increased for each layer [6] except the top layer, compared to the corresponding original deep features. Furthermore, to improve the classification for privacy images, we fuse two unsupervised deep features. We tested the combination of two different deep features and empirically found that the combination of ResNet-50(47) and ResNet-50 (avg_pool) produces a higher separability. That is, the resulting features become more discriminable than other types of combinations. We use the serial feature fusion strategy [24] which produces 500-D features in total. The comparisons of our fused features with the state-of-the-art deep features are shown in Table 4. The compared deep features are extracted from various pre-trained deep learning models: VGG-Net

Table 3. Comparisons of the proposed unsupervised deep features (UDF) with the initial deep features (IDF) with regard to classification accuracy (%).

Methods	IDF	UDF
ResNet-50(42)	83.90	**84.80**
ResNet-50(44)	84.03	**85.05**
ResNet-50(45)	85.05	**85.82**
ResNet-50(47)	84.16	**85.69**
ResNet-50(48)	84.41	**85.95**
ResNet-50(avg_pool)	**85.56**	85.56

Table 4. Comparisons of the proposed features with the state-of-the-art deep features, which are extracted from different pre-trained deep learning models, in terms of classification accuracy (%) and testing time (seconds).

Methods	Feat. size	Acc.	Test. time
VGG-16(FC_1) [12]	4096-D	84.67	0.120
VGG-16(FC_2) [12]	4096-D	84.80	0.090
VGG-19(FC_1) [12]	4096-D	84.67	0.060
VGG-19(FC_2)[12]	4096-D	84.54	0.090
Inception-V3(avg_pool) [18]	2048-D	74.84	0.050
DenseNet-121(avg_pool) [7]	1024-D	79.56	0.025
DenseNet-169(avg_pool) [7]	1664-D	78.41	0.030
DenseNet-201(avg_pool) [7]	1920-D	79.05	0.020
Xception(avg_pool) [1]	2048-D	75.00	0.050
Inception-ResNet-v2(avg_pool) [16]	1536-D	74.96	0.020
Ours (Serial Fusion)	500-D	**86.33**	**0.015**

[12] (VGG-16 and VGG-19), ResNet-50 [6], DenseNet-121 [7], DenseNet-169 [7], DenseNet-201 [7], Inception-V3 [18], Xception [1], Inception-ResNet-v2 [16]. We observe that the lowest accuracy is 74.84% from Inception-ResNet-v2 [16]. VGG-Net [12] with VGG-16($FC2$) features yield an accuracy of 84.80% (which is the second highest accuracy on the dataset), which clearly benefits from a greater feature size. Our fused deep features produce an accuracy of **86.33**% which is 11.49% higher than the lowest accuracy [16]. The features from other pre-trained models except VGG-Net [12] and ResNet-50 [6] are not appropriate for the classification of privacy images because of their lower classification accuracies. We notice that our proposed features outperform the existing features in terms of classification accuracy.

Testing Time. We also analyze the efficiency of our proposed deep features, i.e., the testing time during classification. The testing time of the proposed unsu-

Table 5. Testing timings (in seconds) of the proposed unsupervised deep features (UDF) as well as the initial deep features (IDF).

Methods	IDF	UDF
ResNet-50(42)	0.017	**0.011**
ResNet-50(44)	0.009	**0.004**
ResNet-50(45)	0.015	**0.003**
ResNet-50(47)	0.011	**0.003**
ResNet-50(48)	0.009	**0.003**
ResNet-50(avg_pool)	0.160	**0.003**

Table 6. Sizes of the proposed unsupervised deep features (UDF) and the initial deep features (IDF).

Methods	IDF	UDF
ResNet-50(42)	512-D	250-D
ResNet-50(44)	512-D	250-D
ResNet-50(45)	512-D	250-D
ResNet-50(47)	512-D	250-D
ResNet-50(48)	512-D	250-D
ResNet-50(avg_pool)	2048-D	250-D

pervised features is compared with those of the state-of-the-art deep features (Table 4). The testing time is measured in seconds. Our fused features achieve **0.015** s and is the fastest among all. We also observe that the testing timings of the proposed features during classification are shorter compared to the corresponding deep features (Table 5). The minimum testing time reported is **0.003** s which is the least among all. This attributes to a lower size of the proposed features than the original deep features: a larger feature size often leads to a slower prediction speed. We list the feature sizes of original deep features and the proposed features in Table 6. Since we set 250 as the number of cluster centroids (k) during K-means clustering, the size of the proposed features is 250. Here, we notice that our proposed features outperform state-of-the-art deep features in terms of testing time as well.

5   Conclusion

In this paper, we have introduced the unsupervised deep features based on the deep features extracted from the ResNet-50 model. We first extract the deep features from top activation layers of the ResNet-50 model for each image, and then perform the K-means clustering over training set to learn the centroids. Finally, we encode the computed features to a feature vector for each image based on the learned centroids. The feature vector is taken as an input to our trained model which gives the prediction. Experiments show that our proposed features are more accurate in privacy image classification and produce shorter testing time than state-of-the-art deep features. In the future, we would like to investigate a more complicated classification of privacy images which involve more than two categories.

References

1. Chollet, F.: Xception: deep learning with depthwise separable convolutions. arXiv preprint, pp. 1610–02357 (2017)
2. Chollet, F., Allaire, J.: R interface to Keras. https://github.com/rstudio/keras
3. Coates, A., Ng, A., Lee, H.: An analysis of single-layer networks in unsupervised feature learning. In: AISTATS, pp. 215–223 (2011)
4. Deng, J., Dong, W., Socher, R., Li, L.J., Li, K., Fei-Fei, L.: ImageNet: a large-scale hierarchical image database. In: CVPR (2009)
5. Fan, R.E., Chang, K.W., Hsieh, C.J., Wang, X.R., Lin, C.J.: Liblinear: a library for large linear classification. J. Mach. Learn. Res. **9**, 1871–1874 (2008)
6. He, K., Zhang, X., Ren, S., Sun, J.: Deep residual learning for image recognition. In: CVPR, pp. 770–778 (2016)
7. Huang, G., Liu, Z., Van Der Maaten, L., Weinberger, K.: Densely connected convolutional networks. In: CVPR, vol. 1, p. 3 (2017)
8. Krizhevsky, A., Sutskever, I., Hinton, G.E.: Imagenet classification with deep convolutional neural networks. In: NIPS, pp. 1097–1105 (2012)
9. Lin, T.Y., RoyChowdhury, A., Maji, S.: Bilinear CNN models for fine-grained visual recognition. In: ICCV, pp. 1449–1457 (2015)
10. Lin, T.Y., RoyChowdhury, A., Maji, S.: Bilinear convolutional neural networks for fine-grained visual recognition. IEEE Trans. Pattern Anal. Mach. Intell. **40**(6), 1309–1322 (2017)
11. R Core Team: R: A Language and Environment for Statistical Computing. R Foundation for Statistical Computing, Vienna, Austria (2014)
12. Simonyan, K., Zisserman, A.: Very deep convolutional networks for large-scale image recognition. arXiv preprint arXiv:1409.1556 (2014)
13. Sitaula, C., Xiang, Y., Basnet, A., Aryal, S., Lu, X.: Tag-based semantic features for scene image classification. arXiv preprint arXiv:1909.09999 (2019)
14. Sitaula, C., Xiang, Y., Zhang, Y., Lu, X., Aryal, S.: Indoor image representation by high-level semantic features. IEEE Access **7**, 84967–84979 (2019)
15. Spyromitros-Xioufis, E., Papadopoulos, S., Popescu, A., Kompatsiaris, Y.: Personalized privacy-aware image classification. In: ICMR, pp. 71–78 (2016)
16. Szegedy, C., Ioffe, S., Vanhoucke, V., Alemi, A.A.: Inception-v4, inception-resnet and the impact of residual connections on learning. In: AAAI, vol. 4, p. 12 (2017)
17. Szegedy, C., et al.: Going deeper with convolutions. In: CVPR, pp. 1–9 (2015)
18. Szegedy, C., Vanhoucke, V., Ioffe, S., Shlens, J., Wojna, Z.: Rethinking the inception architecture for computer vision. In: CVPR, pp. 2818–2826 (2016)
19. Tonge, A., Caragea, C.: Privacy prediction of images shared on social media sites using deep features. arXiv preprint arXiv:1510.08583 (2015)
20. Tonge, A., Caragea, C.: On the use of deep features for online image sharing. In: Companion of the The Web Conference, pp. 1317–1321 (2018)

21. Tonge, A., Caragea, C., Squicciarini, A.C.: Uncovering scene context for predicting privacy of online shared images. In: AAAI, pp. 8167–8168 (2018)
22. Tonge, A.K., Caragea, C.: Image privacy prediction using deep features. In: AAAI, pp. 4266–4267 (2016)
23. Tran, L., Kong, D., Jin, H., Liu, J.: Privacy-CNH: a framework to detect photo privacy with convolutional neural network using hierarchical features. In: AAAI, pp. 1317–1323 (2016)
24. Yang, J., Yang, J., Zhang, D., Lu, J.F.: Feature fusion: parallel strategy vs. serial strategy. Pattern Recognit. **36**(6), 1369–1381 (2003)
25. Zerr, S., Siersdorfer, S., Hare, J.: Picalert!: a system for privacy-aware image classification and retrieval. In: CIKM, pp. 2710–2712. ACM (2012)
26. Zerr, S., Siersdorfer, S., Hare, J., Demidova, E.: Privacy-aware image classification and search. In: SIGIR, pp. 35–44 (2012)
27. Zhong, H., Squicciarini, A., Miller, D., Caragea, C.: A group-based personalized model for image privacy classification and labeling. In: IJCAI, pp. 3952–3958 (2017)

Retraction Note to: Non-peaked Discriminant Analysis for Image Representation

Xijian Fan and Qiaolin Ye

Retraction Note to:
Chapter "Non-peaked Discriminant Analysis for Image
Representation" in: C. Lee et al. (Eds.): *Image and Video*
Technology, **LNCS 11854,**
https://doi.org/10.1007/978-3-030-34879-3_24

The Editors have retracted this chapter [1] because it presents data without authorization for use and contains significant overlap with [2]. Both authors agree to this retraction but not to the wording of the retraction notice.

[1] Fan, X., Ye, Q.: Non-peaked discriminant analysis for image representation. In: Lee, C., Su, Z., Sugimoto, A. (eds.) PSIVT 2019. LNCS, vol. 11854. pp. 310–324. Springer, Cham (2019). https://doi.org/10.1007/978-3-030-34879-3_24

[2] Ye, Q., Li, Z., Fu, L., Zhang, Z., Yang, W., Yang, G.: Nonpeaked discriminant analysis for data representation. IEEE Trans. Neural Networks Learn. Syst. **30**(12), 3818–3832 (2019)

The retracted version of this chapter can be found at
https://doi.org/10.1007/978-3-030-34879-3_24

Author Index

Printed in the United States
By Bookmasters